The Prince (1532), The Leviathan (1651),
The Two Treatises of Government (1689), The Social Contract (1762),
The Constitution of Pennsylvania (1776)

The Original Texts from Machiavelli, Hobbes, Locke, Rousseau and
The Founding Fathers of the United States of America

Niccolo Machiavelli
William K. Marriott
Thomas Hobbes
John Locke
Jean Jaques Rousseau
G. D. H. Cole
Peter Kanzler

# Content

**The Prince from 1532**

by Niccolo Machiavelli

## CHAPTER I — HOW MANY KINDS OF PRINCIPALITIES THERE ARE, AND BY WHAT MEANS THEY ARE ACQUIRED

All states, all powers, that have held and hold rule over men have been and are either republics or principalities.

Principalities are either hereditary, in which the family has been long established; or they are new.

The new are either entirely new, as was Milan to Francesco Sforza, or they are, as it were, members annexed to the hereditary state of the prince who has acquired them, as was the kingdom of Naples to that of the King of Spain.

Such dominions thus acquired are either accustomed to live under a prince, or to live in freedom; and are acquired either by the arms of the prince himself, or of others, or else by fortune or by ability.

## CHAPTER II — CONCERNING HEREDITARY PRINCIPALITIES

I will leave out all discussion on republics, inasmuch as in another place I have written of them at length, and will address myself only to principalities. In doing so I will keep to the order indicated above, and discuss how such principalities are to be ruled and preserved.

I say at once there are fewer difficulties in holding hereditary states, and those long accustomed to the family of their prince, than new ones; for it is sufficient only not to transgress the customs of his ancestors, and to deal prudently with circumstances as they arise, for a prince of average powers to maintain himself in his state, unless he be deprived of it by some extraordinary and excessive force; and if he should be so deprived of it, whenever anything sinister happens to the usurper, he will regain it.

We have in Italy, for example, the Duke of Ferrara, who could not have withstood the attacks of the Venetians in '84, nor those of Pope Julius in '10, unless he had been long established in his dominions. For the hereditary prince has less cause and less necessity to offend; hence it happens that he will be more loved; and unless extraordinary vices cause him to be hated, it is reasonable to expect that his subjects will be naturally well disposed towards him; and in the antiquity and duration of his rule the memories and motives that make for change are lost, for one change always leaves the toothing for another.

## CHAPTER III — CONCERNING MIXED PRINCIPALITIES

But the difficulties occur in a new principality. And firstly, if it be not entirely new, but is, as it were, a member of a state which, taken collectively, may be called composite, the changes arise chiefly from an inherent difficulty which there is in all new principalities; for men change their rulers willingly, hoping to better themselves, and this hope induces them to take up arms against him who rules: wherein they are deceived, because they afterwards find by experience they have gone from bad to worse. This follows also on another natural and common necessity, which always causes a new prince to burden those who have submitted to him with his soldiery and with infinite other hardships which he must put upon his new acquisition.

In this way you have enemies in all those whom you have injured in seizing that principality, and you are not able to keep those friends who put you there because of your not being able to satisfy them in the way they expected, and you cannot take strong measures against them, feeling bound to them. For, although one may be very strong in armed forces, yet in entering a province one has always need of the goodwill of the natives.

For these reasons Louis the Twelfth, King of France, quickly occupied Milan, and as quickly lost it; and to turn him out the first time it only needed Lodovico's own forces; because those who had opened the gates to him, finding themselves deceived in their hopes of future benefit, would not endure the ill-treatment of the new prince. It is very true that, after acquiring rebellious provinces a second time, they are not so lightly lost afterwards, because the prince, with little reluctance, takes the opportunity of the rebellion to punish the delinquents, to clear out the suspects, and to strengthen himself in the weakest places. Thus to cause France to lose Milan the first time it was enough for the Duke Lodovico to raise insurrections on the borders; but to cause him to lose it a second time it was necessary to bring the whole world against him, and that his armies should be defeated and driven out of Italy; which followed from the causes above mentioned.

Nevertheless Milan was taken from France both the first and the second time. The general reasons for the first have been discussed; it remains to name those for the second, and to see what resources he had, and what any one in his situation would have had for maintaining himself more securely in his acquisition than did the King of France.

Now I say that those dominions which, when acquired, are added to an ancient state by him who acquires them, are either of the same country and language, or they are not. When they are, it is easier to hold them, especially when they have not been accustomed to self-government; and to hold them securely it is enough to have destroyed the family of the prince who was ruling them; because the two peoples, preserving in other things the old conditions, and not being unlike in customs, will live quietly together, as one has seen in Brittany, Burgundy, Gascony, and Normandy, which have been bound to France for so long a time: and, although there may be some difference in language, nevertheless the customs are alike, and the people will easily be able to get on amongst themselves. He who has annexed them, if he wishes to hold them, has only to bear in mind two considerations: the one, that the family of their former lord is extinguished; the other, that neither their laws nor their taxes are altered, so that in a very short time they will become entirely one body with the old principality.

But when states are acquired in a country differing in language, customs, or laws, there are difficulties, and good fortune and great energy are needed to hold them, and one of the greatest and most real helps would be that he who has acquired them should go and reside there. This would make his position more secure and durable, as it has made that of the Turk in Greece, who, notwithstanding all the other measures taken by him for holding that state, if he had not settled there, would not have been able to keep it. Because, if one is on the spot, disorders are seen as they spring up, and one can quickly remedy them; but if one is not at hand, they are heard of only when they are great, and then one can no longer remedy them. Besides this, the country is not pillaged by your officials; the subjects are satisfied by prompt recourse to the prince; thus, wishing to be good, they have more cause to love him, and wishing to be otherwise, to fear him. He who would attack that state from the outside must have the utmost caution; as long as the prince resides there it can only be wrested from him with the greatest difficulty.

The other and better course is to send colonies to one or two places, which may be as keys to that state, for it is necessary either to do this or else to keep there a great number of cavalry and infantry. A prince does not spend much on colonies, for with little or no expense he can send them out and keep them there, and he of-fends a minority only of the citizens from whom he takes lands and houses to give them to the new inhabi-tants; and those whom he offends, remaining poor and scattered, are never able to injure him; whilst the rest being uninjured are easily kept quiet, and at the same time are anxious not to err for fear it should happen to them as it has to those who have been despoiled. In conclusion, I say that these colonies are not costly, they are more faithful, they injure less, and the injured, as has been said, being poor and scattered, cannot hurt. Upon this, one has to remark that men ought either to be well treated or crushed, because they can avenge themselves of lighter injuries, of more serious ones they cannot; therefore the injury that is to be done to a man ought to be of such a kind that one does not stand in fear of revenge.

But in maintaining armed men there in place of colonies one spends much more, having to consume on the garrison all the income from the state, so that the acquisition turns into a loss, and many more are exasperated, because the whole state is injured; through the shifting of the garrison up and down all become acquainted with hardship, and all become hostile, and they are enemies who, whilst beaten on their own ground, are yet able to do hurt. For every reason, therefore, such guards are as useless as a colony is useful.

Again, the prince who holds a country differing in the above respects ought to make himself the head and defender of his less powerful neighbours, and to weaken the more powerful amongst them, taking care that no foreigner as powerful as himself shall, by any accident, get a footing there; for it will always happen that such a one will be introduced by those who are discontented, either through excess of ambition or through fear, as one has seen already. The Romans were brought into Greece by the Aetolians; and in every other country where they obtained a footing they were brought in by the inhabitants. And the usual course of affairs is that, as soon as a powerful foreigner enters a country, all the subject states are drawn to him, moved by the hatred which they feel against the ruling power. So that in respect to those subject states he has not to take any trou-ble to gain them over to himself, for the whole of them quickly rally to the state which he has acquired there. He has only to take care that they do not get hold of too much power and too much authority, and then with his own forces, and with their goodwill, he can easily keep down the more powerful of them, so as to remain entirely master in the country. And he who does not properly manage this business will soon lose what he has acquired, and whilst he does hold it he will have endless difficulties and troubles.

The Romans, in the countries which they annexed, observed closely these measures; they sent colonies and maintained friendly relations with the minor powers, without increasing their strength; they kept down the greater, and did not allow any strong foreign powers to gain authority. Greece appears to me sufficient for an example. The Achaeans and Aetolians were kept friendly by them, the kingdom of Macedonia was humbled, Antiochus was driven out; yet the merits of the Achaeans and Aetolians never secured for them permission to increase their power, nor did the persuasions of Philip ever induce the Romans to be his friends without first humbling him, nor did the influence of Antiochus make them agree that he should retain any lordship over the country. Because the Romans did in these instances what all prudent princes ought to do, who have to regard not only present troubles, but also future ones, for which they must prepare with every energy, because, when foreseen, it is easy to remedy them; but if you wait until they approach, the medicine is no longer in time be-cause the malady has become incurable; for it happens in this, as the physicians say it happens in hectic fever, that in the beginning of the malady it is easy to cure but difficult to detect, but in the course of time, not having been either detected or treated in the beginning, it becomes easy to detect but difficult to cure. Thus it happens in affairs of state, for when the evils that arise have been foreseen (which it is only given to a wise man to see), they can be quickly redressed, but when, through not having been foreseen, they have been permitted to grow in a way that every one can see them, there is no longer a remedy. Therefore, the Romans, foreseeing troubles, dealt with them at once, and, even to avoid a war, would not let them come to a head, for they knew that war is not to be avoided, but is only to be put off to the advantage of others; moreover they wished to fight with Philip and Antiochus in Greece so as not to have to do it in Italy; they could have avoided both, but this they did not wish; nor did that ever please them which is forever in the mouths of the wise ones of our time:—Let us enjoy the benefits of the time—but rather the benefits of their own valour and prudence, for time drives everything before it, and is able to bring with it good as well as evil, and evil as well as good.

But let us turn to France and inquire whether she has done any of the things mentioned. I will speak of Louis (and not of Charles) as the one whose conduct is the better to be observed, he having held possession of Italy for the longest period; and you will see that he has done the opposite to those things which ought to be done to retain a state composed of divers elements.

King Louis was brought into Italy by the ambition of the Venetians, who desired to obtain half the state of Lombardy by his intervention. I will not blame the course taken by the king, because, wishing to get a foothold in Italy, and having no friends there—seeing rather that every door was shut to him owing to the conduct of Charles—he was forced to accept those friendships which he could get, and he would have succeeded very quickly in his design if in other matters he had not made some mistakes. The king, however, having acquired Lombardy, regained at once the authority which Charles had lost: Genoa yielded; the Florentines became his friends; the Marquess of Mantua, the Duke of Ferrara, the Bentivogli, my lady of Forli, the Lords of Faenza, of Pesaro, of Rimini, of Camerino, of Piombino, the Lucchese, the Pisans, the Sienese—everybody made advances to him to become his friend. Then could the Venetians realize the rashness of the course taken by them, which, in order that they might secure two towns in Lombardy, had made the king master of two-thirds of Italy.

Let any one now consider with what little difficulty the king could have maintained his position in Italy had he observed the rules above laid down, and kept all his friends secure and protected; for although they were numerous they were both weak and timid, some afraid of the Church, some of the Venetians, and thus they would always have been forced to stand in with him, and by their means he could easily have made himself secure against those who remained powerful. But he was no sooner in Milan than he did the contrary by assisting Pope Alexander to occupy the Romagna. It never occurred to him that by this action he was weakening himself, depriving himself of friends and of those who had thrown themselves into his lap, whilst he aggrandized the Church by adding much temporal power to the spiritual, thus giving it greater authority. And having committed this prime error, he was obliged to follow it up, so much so that, to put an end to the ambition of Alexander, and to prevent his becoming the master of Tuscany, he was himself forced to come into Italy.

And as if it were not enough to have aggrandized the Church, and deprived himself of friends, he, wishing to have the kingdom of Naples, divided it with the King of Spain, and where he was the prime arbiter in Italy he takes an associate, so that the ambitious of that country and the malcontents of his own should have somewhere to shelter; and whereas he could have left in the kingdom his own pensioner as king, he drove him out, to put one there who was able to drive him, Louis, out in turn.

The wish to acquire is in truth very natural and common, and men always do so when they can, and for this they will be praised not blamed; but when they cannot do so, yet wish to do so by any means, then there is folly and blame. Therefore, if France could have attacked Naples with her own forces she ought to have done so; if she could not, then she ought not to have divided it. And if the partition which she made with the Venetians in Lombardy was justified by the excuse that by it she got a foothold in Italy, this other partition merited blame, for it had not the excuse of that necessity.

Therefore Louis made these five errors: he destroyed the minor powers, he increased the strength of one of the greater powers in Italy, he brought in a foreign power, he did not settle in the country, he did not send colonies. Which errors, had he lived, were not enough to injure him had he not made a sixth by taking away their dominions from the Venetians; because, had he not aggrandized the Church, nor brought Spain into Italy, it would have been very reasonable and necessary to humble them; but having first taken these steps, he ought never to have consented to their ruin, for they, being powerful, would always have kept off others from designs on Lombardy, to which the Venetians would never have consented except to become masters themselves there; also because the others would not wish to take Lombardy from France in order to give it to the Venetians, and to run counter to both they would not have had the courage.

And if any one should say: "King Louis yielded the Romagna to Alexander and the kingdom to Spain to avoid war," I answer for the reasons given above that a blunder ought never to be perpetrated to avoid war, because it is not to be avoided, but is only deferred to your disadvantage. And if another should allege the pledge which the king had given to the Pope that he would assist him in the enterprise, in exchange for the dissolution of his marriage and for the cap to Rouen, to that I reply what I shall write later on concerning the faith of princes, and how it ought to be kept.

Thus King Louis lost Lombardy by not having followed any of the conditions observed by those who have taken possession of countries and wished to retain them. Nor is there any miracle in this, but much that is reasonable and quite natural. And on these matters I spoke at Nantes with Rouen, when Valentino, as Cesare Borgia, the son of Pope Alexander, was usually called, occupied the Romagna, and on Cardinal Rouen observing to me that the Italians did not understand war, I replied to him that the French did not understand statecraft, meaning that otherwise they would not have allowed the Church to reach such greatness. And in fact it has been seen that the greatness of the Church and of Spain in Italy has been caused by France, and her ruin may be attributed to them. From this a general rule is drawn which never or rarely fails: that he who is the cause of another becoming powerful is ruined; because that predominancy has been brought about either by astuteness or else by force, and both are distrusted by him who has been raised to power.

## CHAPTER IV — WHY THE KINGDOM OF DARIUS, CONQUERED BY ALEXANDER, DID NOT REBEL AGAINST THE SUCCESSORS OF ALEXANDER AT HIS DEATH

Considering the difficulties which men have had to hold to a newly acquired state, some might wonder how, seeing that Alexander the Great became the master of Asia in a few years, and died whilst it was scarcely settled (whence it might appear reasonable that the whole empire would have rebelled), nevertheless his successors maintained themselves, and had to meet no other difficulty than that which arose among themselves from their own ambitions.

I answer that the principalities of which one has record are found to be governed in two different ways; either by a prince, with a body of servants, who assist him to govern the kingdom as ministers by his favour and permission; or by a prince and barons, who hold that dignity by antiquity of blood and not by the grace of the prince. Such barons have states and their own subjects, who recognize them as lords and hold them in natural affection. Those states that are governed by a prince and his servants hold their prince in more consideration, because in all the country there is no one who is recognized as superior to him, and if they yield obedience to another they do it as to a minister and official, and they do not bear him any particular affection.

The examples of these two governments in our time are the Turk and the King of France. The entire monarchy of the Turk is governed by one lord, the others are his servants; and, dividing his kingdom into sanjaks, he sends there different administrators, and shifts and changes them as he chooses. But the King of France is placed in the midst of an ancient body of lords, acknowledged by their own subjects, and beloved by them; they have their own prerogatives, nor can the king take these away except at his peril. Therefore, he who considers both of these states will recognize great difficulties in seizing the state of the Turk, but, once it is conquered, great ease in holding it. The causes of the difficulties in seizing the kingdom of the Turk are that the usurper cannot be called in by the princes of the kingdom, nor can he hope to be assisted in his designs by the revolt of those whom the lord has around him. This arises from the reasons given above; for his ministers, being all slaves and bondmen, can only be corrupted with great difficulty, and one can expect little advantage from them when they have been corrupted, as they cannot carry the people with them, for the reasons assigned. Hence, he who attacks the Turk must bear in mind that he will find him united, and he will have to rely more on his own strength than on the revolt of others; but, if once the Turk has been conquered, and routed in the field in such a way that he cannot replace his armies, there is nothing to fear but the family of this prince, and, this being exterminated, there remains no one to fear, the others having no credit with the people; and as the conqueror did not rely on them before his victory, so he ought not to fear them after it.

The contrary happens in kingdoms governed like that of France, because one can easily enter there by gaining over some baron of the kingdom, for one always finds malcontents and such as desire a change. Such men, for the reasons given, can open the way into the state and render the victory easy; but if you wish to hold it afterwards, you meet with infinite difficulties, both from those who have assisted you and from those you have crushed. Nor is it enough for you to have exterminated the family of the prince, because the lords that remain make themselves the heads of fresh movements against you, and as you are unable either to satisfy or exterminate them, that state is lost whenever time brings the opportunity.

Now if you will consider what was the nature of the government of Darius, you will find it similar to the kingdom of the Turk, and therefore it was only necessary for Alexander, first to overthrow him in the field, and then to take the country from him. After which victory, Darius being killed, the state remained secure to Alexander, for the above reasons. And if his successors had been united they would have enjoyed it securely and at their ease, for there were no tumults raised in the kingdom except those they provoked themselves.

But it is impossible to hold with such tranquillity states constituted like that of France. Hence arose those frequent rebellions against the Romans in Spain, France, and Greece, owing to the many principalities there were in these states, of which, as long as the memory of them endured, the Romans always held an insecure possession; but with the power and long continuance of the empire the memory of them passed away, and the Romans then became secure possessors. And when fighting afterwards amongst themselves, each one was able to attach to himself his own parts of the country, according to the authority he had assumed there; and the family of the former lord being exterminated, none other than the Romans were acknowledged.

When these things are remembered no one will marvel at the ease with which Alexander held the Empire of Asia, or at the difficulties which others have had to keep an acquisition, such as Pyrrhus and many more; this is not occasioned by the little or abundance of ability in the conqueror, but by the want of uniformity in the subject state.

## CHAPTER V — CONCERNING THE WAY TO GOVERN CITIES OR PRINCIPALITIES WHICH LIVED UNDER THEIR OWN LAWS BEFORE THEY WERE ANNEXED

Whenever those states which have been acquired as stated have been accustomed to live under their own laws and in freedom, there are three courses for those who wish to hold them: the first is to ruin them, the next is to reside there in person, the third is to permit them to live under their own laws, drawing a tribute, and establishing within it an oligarchy which will keep it friendly to you. Because such a government, being created by the prince, knows that it cannot stand without his friendship and interest, and does its utmost to support him; and therefore he who would keep a city accustomed to freedom will hold it more easily by the means of its own citizens than in any other way.

There are, for example, the Spartans and the Romans. The Spartans held Athens and Thebes, establishing there an oligarchy: nevertheless they lost them. The Romans, in order to hold Capua, Carthage, and Numantia, dismantled them, and did not lose them. They wished to hold Greece as the Spartans held it, making it free and permitting its laws, and did not succeed. So to hold it they were compelled to dismantle many cities in the country, for in truth there is no safe way to retain them otherwise than by ruining them. And he who becomes master of a city accustomed to freedom and does not destroy it, may expect to be destroyed by it, for in rebellion it has always the watchword of liberty and its ancient privileges as a rallying point, which neither time nor benefits will ever cause it to forget. And whatever you may do or provide against, they never forget that name or their privileges unless they are disunited or dispersed, but at every chance they immediately rally to them, as Pisa after the hundred years she had been held in bondage by the Florentines.

But when cities or countries are accustomed to live under a prince, and his family is exterminated, they, being on the one hand accustomed to obey and on the other hand not having the old prince, cannot agree in making one from amongst themselves, and they do not know how to govern themselves. For this reason they are very slow to take up arms, and a prince can gain them to himself and secure them much more easily. But in republics there is more vitality, greater hatred, and more desire for vengeance, which will never permit them to allow the memory of their former liberty to rest; so that the safest way is to destroy them or to reside there.

## CHAPTER VI — CONCERNING NEW PRINCIPALITIES WHICH ARE ACQUIRED BY ONE'S OWN ARMS AND ABILITY

Let no one be surprised if, in speaking of entirely new principalities as I shall do, I adduce the highest examples both of prince and of state; because men, walking almost always in paths beaten by others, and following by imitation their deeds, are yet unable to keep entirely to the ways of others or attain to the power of those they imitate. A wise man ought always to follow the paths beaten by great men, and to imitate those who have been supreme, so that if his ability does not equal theirs, at least it will savour of it. Let him act like the clever archers who, designing to hit the mark which yet appears too far distant, and knowing the limits to which the strength of their bow attains, take aim much higher than the mark, not to reach by their strength or arrow to so great a height, but to be able with the aid of so high an aim to hit the mark they wish to reach.

I say, therefore, that in entirely new principalities, where there is a new prince, more or less difficulty is found in keeping them, accordingly as there is more or less ability in him who has acquired the state. Now, as the fact of becoming a prince from a private station presupposes either ability or fortune, it is clear that one or other of these things will mitigate in some degree many difficulties. Nevertheless, he who has relied least on fortune is established the strongest. Further, it facilitates matters when the prince, having no other state, is compelled to reside there in person.

But to come to those who, by their own ability and not through fortune, have risen to be princes, I say that Moses, Cyrus, Romulus, Theseus, and such like are the most excellent examples. And although one may not discuss Moses, he having been a mere executor of the will of God, yet he ought to be admired, if only for that favour which made him worthy to speak with God. But in considering Cyrus and others who have acquired or founded kingdoms, all will be found admirable; and if their particular deeds and conduct shall be considered, they will not be found inferior to those of Moses, although he had so great a preceptor. And in examining their actions and lives one cannot see that they owed anything to fortune beyond opportunity, which brought them the material to mould into the form which seemed best to them. Without that opportunity their powers of mind would have been extinguished, and without those powers the opportunity would have come in vain.

It was necessary, therefore, to Moses that he should find the people of Israel in Egypt enslaved and oppressed by the Egyptians, in order that they should be disposed to follow him so as to be delivered out of bondage. It was necessary that Romulus should not remain in Alba, and that he should be abandoned at his birth, in order that he should become King of Rome and founder of the fatherland. It was necessary that Cyrus should find the Persians discontented with the government of the Medes, and the Medes soft and effeminate through their long peace. Theseus could not have shown his ability had he not found the Athenians dispersed. These opportunities, therefore, made those men fortunate, and their high ability enabled them to recognize the opportunity whereby their country was ennobled and made famous.

Those who by valorous ways become princes, like these men, acquire a principality with difficulty, but they keep it with ease. The difficulties they have in acquiring it rise in part from the new rules and methods which they are forced to introduce to establish their government and its security. And it ought to be remembered that there is nothing more difficult to take in hand, more perilous to conduct, or more uncertain in its success, than to take the lead in the introduction of a new order of things, because the innovator has for enemies all those who have done well under the old conditions, and lukewarm defenders in those who may do well under the new. This coolness arises partly from fear of the opponents, who have the laws on their side, and partly from the incredulity of men, who do not readily believe in new things until they have had a long experience of them. Thus it happens that whenever those who are hostile have the opportunity to attack they do it like partisans, whilst the others defend lukewarmly, in such wise that the prince is endangered along with them.

It is necessary, therefore, if we desire to discuss this matter thoroughly, to inquire whether these innovators can rely on themselves or have to depend on others: that is to say, whether, to consummate their enterprise, have they to use prayers or can they use force? In the first instance they always succeed badly, and never compass anything; but when they can rely on themselves and use force, then they are rarely endangered. Hence it is that all armed prophets have conquered, and the unarmed ones have been destroyed. Besides the reasons mentioned, the nature of the people is variable, and whilst it is easy to persuade them, it is difficult to fix them in that persuasion. And thus it is necessary to take such measures that, when they believe no longer, it may be possible to make them believe by force.

If Moses, Cyrus, Theseus, and Romulus had been unarmed they could not have enforced their constitutions for long—as happened in our time to Fra Girolamo Savonarola, who was ruined with his new order of things immediately the multitude believed in him no longer, and he had no means of keeping steadfast those who believed or of making the unbelievers to believe. Therefore such as these have great difficulties in consummating their enterprise, for all their dangers are in the ascent, yet with ability they will overcome them; but when these are overcome, and those who envied them their success are exterminated, they will begin to be respected, and they will continue afterwards powerful, secure, honoured, and happy.

To these great examples I wish to add a lesser one; still it bears some resemblance to them, and I wish it to suffice me for all of a like kind: it is Hiero the Syracusan. This man rose from a private station to be Prince of Syracuse, nor did he, either, owe anything to fortune but opportunity; for the Syracusans, being oppressed, chose him for their captain, afterwards he was rewarded by being made their prince. He was of so great ability, even as a private citizen, that one who writes of him says he wanted nothing but a kingdom to be a king. This man abolished the old soldiery, organized the new, gave up old alliances, made new ones; and as he had his own soldiers and allies, on such foundations he was able to build any edifice: thus, whilst he had endured much trouble in acquiring, he had but little in keeping.

## CHAPTER VII — CONCERNING NEW PRINCIPALITIES WHICH ARE ACQUIRED EITHER BY THE ARMS OF OTHERS OR BY GOOD FORTUNE

Those who solely by good fortune become princes from being private citizens have little trouble in rising, but much in keeping atop; they have not any difficulties on the way up, because they fly, but they have many when they reach the summit. Such are those to whom some state is given either for money or by the favour of him who bestows it; as happened to many in Greece, in the cities of Ionia and of the Hellespont, where princes were made by Darius, in order that they might hold the cities both for his security and his glory; as also were those emperors who, by the corruption of the soldiers, from being citizens came to empire. Such stand simply elevated upon the goodwill and the fortune of him who has elevated them—two most inconstant and unstable things. Neither have they the knowledge requisite for the position; because, unless they are men of great worth and ability, it is not reasonable to expect that they should know how to command, having always lived in a private condition; besides, they cannot hold it because they have not forces which they can keep friendly and faithful.

States that rise unexpectedly, then, like all other things in nature which are born and grow rapidly, cannot leave their foundations and correspondencies fixed in such a way that the first storm will not overthrow them; unless, as is said, those who unexpectedly become princes are men of so much ability that they know they have to be prepared at once to hold that which fortune has thrown into their laps, and that those foundations, which others have laid BEFORE they became princes, they must lay AFTERWARDS.

Concerning these two methods of rising to be a prince by ability or fortune, I wish to adduce two examples within our own recollection, and these are Francesco Sforza and Cesare Borgia. Francesco, by proper means and with great ability, from being a private person rose to be Duke of Milan, and that which he had acquired with a thousand anxieties he kept with little trouble. On the other hand, Cesare Borgia, called by the people Duke Valentino, acquired his state during the ascendancy of his father, and on its decline he lost it, notwithstanding that he had taken every measure and done all that ought to be done by a wise and able man to fix firmly his roots in the states which the arms and fortunes of others had bestowed on him.

Because, as is stated above, he who has not first laid his foundations may be able with great ability to lay them afterwards, but they will be laid with trouble to the architect and danger to the building. If, therefore, all the steps taken by the duke be considered, it will be seen that he laid solid foundations for his future power, and I do not consider it superfluous to discuss them, because I do not know what better precepts to give a new prince than the example of his actions; and if his dispositions were of no avail, that was not his fault, but the extraordinary and extreme malignity of fortune.

Alexander the Sixth, in wishing to aggrandize the duke, his son, had many immediate and prospective difficulties. Firstly, he did not see his way to make him master of any state that was not a state of the Church; and if he was willing to rob the Church he knew that the Duke of Milan and the Venetians would not consent, because Faenza and Rimini were already under the protection of the Venetians. Besides this, he saw the arms of Italy, especially those by which he might have been assisted, in hands that would fear the aggrandizement of the Pope, namely, the Orsini and the Colonnesi and their following. It behoved him, therefore, to upset this state of affairs and embroil the powers, so as to make himself securely master of part of their states. This was easy for him to do, because he found the Venetians, moved by other reasons, inclined to bring back the French into Italy; he would not only not oppose this, but he would render it more easy by dissolving the former marriage of King Louis. Therefore the king came into Italy with the assistance of the Venetians and the consent of Alexander. He was no sooner in Milan than the Pope had soldiers from him for the attempt on the Romagna, which yielded to him on the reputation of the king. The duke, therefore, having acquired the Romagna and beaten the Colonnesi, while wishing to hold that and to advance further, was hindered by two things: the one, his forces did not appear loyal to him, the other, the goodwill of France: that is to say, he feared that the forces of the Orsini, which he was using, would not stand to him, that not only might they hinder him from winning more, but might themselves seize what he had won, and that the king might also do the same. Of the Orsini he had a warning when, after taking Faenza and attacking Bologna, he saw them go very unwillingly to that attack. And as to the king, he learned his mind when he himself, after taking the Duchy of Urbino, attacked Tuscany, and the king made him desist from that undertaking; hence the duke decided to depend no more upon the arms and the luck of others.

For the first thing he weakened the Orsini and Colonnesi parties in Rome, by gaining to himself all their adherents who were gentlemen, making them his gentlemen, giving them good pay, and, according to their rank, honouring them with office and command in such a way that in a few months all attachment to the factions was destroyed and turned entirely to the duke. After this he awaited an opportunity to crush the Orsini, having scattered the adherents of the Colonna house. This came to him soon and he used it well; for the Orsini, perceiving at length that the aggrandizement of the duke and the Church was ruin to them, called a meeting of the Magione in Perugia. From this sprung the rebellion at Urbino and the tumults in the Romagna, with endless dangers to the duke, all of which he overcame with the help of the French. Having restored his authority, not to leave it at risk by trusting either to the French or other outside forces, he had recourse to his wiles, and he knew so well how to conceal his mind that, by the mediation of Signor Pagolo—whom the duke did not fail to secure with all kinds of attention, giving him money, apparel, and horses—the Orsini were reconciled, so that their simplicity brought them into his power at Sinigalia. Having exterminated the leaders, and turned their partisans into his friends, the duke laid sufficiently good foundations to his power, having all the Romagna and the Duchy of Urbino; and the people now beginning to appreciate their prosperity, he gained them all over to himself. And as this point is worthy of notice, and to be imitated by others, I am not willing to leave it out.

When the duke occupied the Romagna he found it under the rule of weak masters, who rather plundered their subjects than ruled them, and gave them more cause for disunion than for union, so that the country was full of robbery, quarrels, and every kind of violence; and so, wishing to bring back peace and obedience to authority, he considered it necessary to give it a good governor. Thereupon he promoted Messer Ramiro d'Orco, a swift and cruel man, to whom he gave the fullest power. This man in a short time restored peace and unity with the greatest success. Afterwards the duke considered that it was not advisable to confer such excessive authority, for he had no doubt but that he would become odious, so he set up a court of judgment in the country, under a most excellent president, wherein all cities had their advocates. And because he knew that the past severity had caused some hatred against himself, so, to clear himself in the minds of the people, and gain them entirely to himself, he desired to show that, if any cruelty had been practised, it had not originated with him, but in the natural sternness of the minister. Under this pretence he took Ramiro, and one morning caused him to be executed and left on the piazza at Cesena with the block and a bloody knife at his side. The barbarity of this spectacle caused the people to be at once satisfied and dismayed.

But let us return whence we started. I say that the duke, finding himself now sufficiently powerful and partly secured from immediate dangers by having armed himself in his own way, and having in a great measure crushed those forces in his vicinity that could injure him if he wished to proceed with his conquest, had next to consider France, for he knew that the king, who too late was aware of his mistake, would not support him. And from this time he began to seek new alliances and to temporize with France in the expedition which she was making towards the kingdom of Naples against the Spaniards who were besieging Gaeta. It was his intention to secure himself against them, and this he would have quickly accomplished had Alexander lived.

Such was his line of action as to present affairs. But as to the future he had to fear, in the first place, that a new successor to the Church might not be friendly to him and might seek to take from him that which Alexander had given him, so he decided to act in four ways. Firstly, by exterminating the families of those lords whom he had despoiled, so as to take away that pretext from the Pope. Secondly, by winning to himself all the gentlemen of Rome, so as to be able to curb the Pope with their aid, as has been observed. Thirdly, by converting the college more to himself. Fourthly, by acquiring so much power before the Pope should die that he could by his own measures resist the first shock. Of these four things, at the death of Alexander, he had accomplished three. For he had killed as many of the dispossessed lords as he could lay hands on, and few had escaped; he had won over the Roman gentlemen, and he had the most numerous party in the college. And as to any fresh acquisition, he intended to become master of Tuscany, for he already possessed Perugia and Piombino, and Pisa was under his protection. And as he had no longer to study France (for the French were already driven out of the kingdom of Naples by the Spaniards, and in this way both were compelled to buy his goodwill), he pounced down upon Pisa. After this, Lucca and Siena yielded at once, partly through hatred and partly through fear of the Florentines; and the Florentines would have had no remedy had he continued to prosper, as he was prospering the year that Alexander died, for he had acquired so much power and reputation that he would have stood by himself, and no longer have depended on the luck and the forces of others, but solely on his own power and ability.

But Alexander died five years after he had first drawn the sword. He left the duke with the state of Romagna alone consolidated, with the rest in the air, between two most powerful hostile armies, and sick unto death. Yet there were in the duke such boldness and ability, and he knew so well how men are to be won or lost, and so firm were the foundations which in so short a time he had laid, that if he had not had those armies on his back, or if he had been in good health, he would have overcome all difficulties. And it is seen that his foundations were good, for the Romagna awaited him for more than a month. In Rome, although but half alive, he remained secure; and whilst the Baglioni, the Vitelli, and the Orsini might come to Rome, they could not effect anything against him. If he could not have made Pope him whom he wished, at least the one whom he did not wish would not have been elected. But if he had been in sound health at the death of Alexander, everything would have been different to him. On the day that Julius the Second was elected, he told me that he had thought of everything that might occur at the death of his father, and had provided a remedy for all, except that he had never anticipated that, when the death did happen, he himself would be on the point to die.

When all the actions of the duke are recalled, I do not know how to blame him, but rather it appears to be, as I have said, that I ought to offer him for imitation to all those who, by the fortune or the arms of others, are raised to government. Because he, having a lofty spirit and far-reaching aims, could not have regulated his conduct otherwise, and only the shortness of the life of Alexander and his own sickness frustrated his designs. Therefore, he who considers it necessary to secure himself in his new principality, to win friends, to overcome either by force or fraud, to make himself beloved and feared by the people, to be followed and revered by the soldiers, to exterminate those who have power or reason to hurt him, to change the old order of things for new, to be severe and gracious, magnanimous and liberal, to destroy a disloyal soldiery and to create new, to maintain friendship with kings and princes in such a way that they must help him with zeal and offend with caution, cannot find a more lively example than the actions of this man.

Only can he be blamed for the election of Julius the Second, in whom he made a bad choice, because, as is said, not being able to elect a Pope to his own mind, he could have hindered any other from being elected Pope; and he ought never to have consented to the election of any cardinal whom he had injured or who had cause to fear him if they became pontiffs. For men injure either from fear or hatred. Those whom he had injured, amongst others, were San Pietro ad Vincula, Colonna, San Giorgio, and Ascanio. The rest, in becoming Pope, had to fear him, Rouen and the Spaniards excepted; the latter from their relationship and obligations, the former from his influence, the kingdom of France having relations with him. Therefore, above everything, the duke ought to have created a Spaniard Pope, and, failing him, he ought to have consented to Rouen and not San Pietro ad Vincula. He who believes that new benefits will cause great personages to forget old injuries is deceived. Therefore, the duke erred in his choice, and it was the cause of his ultimate ruin.

## CHAPTER VIII — CONCERNING THOSE WHO HAVE OBTAINED A PRINCIPALITY BY WICKEDNESS

Although a prince may rise from a private station in two ways, neither of which can be entirely attributed to fortune or genius, yet it is manifest to me that I must not be silent on them, although one could be more copiously treated when I discuss republics. These methods are when, either by some wicked or nefarious ways, one ascends to the principality, or when by the favour of his fellow-citizens a private person becomes the prince of his country. And speaking of the first method, it will be illustrated by two examples—one ancient, the other modern—and without entering further into the subject, I consider these two examples will suffice those who may be compelled to follow them.

Agathocles, the Sicilian, became King of Syracuse not only from a private but from a low and abject position. This man, the son of a potter, through all the changes in his fortunes always led an infamous life. Nevertheless, he accompanied his infamies with so much ability of mind and body that, having devoted himself to the military profession, he rose through its ranks to be Praetor of Syracuse. Being established in that position, and having deliberately resolved to make himself prince and to seize by violence, without obligation to others, that which had been conceded to him by assent, he came to an understanding for this purpose with Amilcar, the Carthaginian, who, with his army, was fighting in Sicily. One morning he assembled the people and the senate of Syracuse, as if he had to discuss with them things relating to the Republic, and at a given signal the soldiers killed all the senators and the richest of the people; these dead, he seized and held the princedom of that city without any civil commotion. And although he was twice routed by the Carthaginians, and ultimately besieged, yet not only was he able to defend his city, but leaving part of his men for its defence, with the others he attacked Africa, and in a short time raised the siege of Syracuse. The Carthaginians, reduced to extreme necessity, were compelled to come to terms with Agathocles, and, leaving Sicily to him, had to be content with the possession of Africa.

Therefore, he who considers the actions and the genius of this man will see nothing, or little, which can be attributed to fortune, inasmuch as he attained pre-eminence, as is shown above, not by the favour of any one, but step by step in the military profession, which steps were gained with a thousand troubles and perils, and were afterwards boldly held by him with many hazardous dangers. Yet it cannot be called talent to slay fellow-citizens, to deceive friends, to be without faith, without mercy, without religion; such methods may gain empire, but not glory. Still, if the courage of Agathocles in entering into and extricating himself from dangers be considered, together with his greatness of mind in enduring and overcoming hardships, it cannot be seen why he should be esteemed less than the most notable captain. Nevertheless, his barbarous cruelty and inhumanity with infinite wickedness do not permit him to be celebrated among the most excellent men. What he achieved cannot be attributed either to fortune or genius.

In our times, during the rule of Alexander the Sixth, Oliverotto da Fermo, having been left an orphan many years before, was brought up by his maternal uncle, Giovanni Fogliani, and in the early days of his youth sent to fight under Pagolo Vitelli, that, being trained under his discipline, he might attain some high position in the military profession. After Pagolo died, he fought under his brother Vitellozzo, and in a very short time, being endowed with wit and a vigorous body and mind, he became the first man in his profession. But it appearing a paltry thing to serve under others, he resolved, with the aid of some citizens of Fermo, to whom the slavery of their country was dearer than its liberty, and with the help of the Vitelleschi, to seize Fermo. So he wrote to Giovanni Fogliani that, having been away from home for many years, he wished to visit him and his city, and in some measure to look upon his patrimony; and although he had not laboured to acquire anything except honour, yet, in order that the citizens should see he had not spent his time in vain, he desired to come honourably, so would be accompanied by one hundred horsemen, his friends and retainers; and he entreated Giovanni to arrange that he should be received honourably by the Fermians, all of which would be not only to his honour, but also to that of Giovanni himself, who had brought him up.

Giovanni, therefore, did not fail in any attentions due to his nephew, and he caused him to be honourably received by the Fermians, and he lodged him in his own house, where, having passed some days, and having arranged what was necessary for his wicked designs, Oliverotto gave a solemn banquet to which he invited Giovanni Fogliani and the chiefs of Fermo. When the viands and all the other entertainments that are usual in such banquets were finished, Oliverotto artfully began certain grave discourses, speaking of the greatness of Pope Alexander and his son Cesare, and of their enterprises, to which discourse Giovanni and others answered; but he rose at once, saying that such matters ought to be discussed in a more private place, and he betook himself to a chamber, whither Giovanni and the rest of the citizens went in after him. No sooner were they seated than soldiers issued from secret places and slaughtered Giovanni and the rest. After these murders Oliverotto, mounted on horseback, rode up and down the town and besieged the chief magistrate in the palace, so that in fear the people were forced to obey him, and to form a government, of which he made himself the prince. He killed all the malcontents who were able to injure him, and strengthened himself with new civil and military ordinances, in such a way that, in the year during which he held the principality, not only was he secure in the city of Fermo, but he had become formidable to all his neighbours. And his destruction would have been as difficult as that of Agathocles if he had not allowed himself to be overreached by Cesare Borgia, who took him with the Orsini and Vitelli at Sinigalia, as was stated above. Thus one year after he had committed this parricide, he was strangled, together with Vitellozzo, whom he had made his leader in valour and wickedness.

Some may wonder how it can happen that Agathocles, and his like, after infinite treacheries and cruelties, should live for long secure in his country, and defend himself from external enemies, and never be conspired against by his own citizens; seeing that many others, by means of cruelty, have never been able even in peaceful times to hold the state, still less in the doubtful times of war. I believe that this follows from severities being badly or properly used. Those may be called properly used, if of evil it is possible to speak well, that are applied at one blow and are necessary to one's security, and that are not persisted in afterwards unless they can be turned to the advantage of the subjects. The badly employed are those which, notwithstanding they may be few in the commencement, multiply with time rather than decrease. Those who practise the first system are able, by aid of God or man, to mitigate in some degree their rule, as Agathocles did. It is impossible for those who follow the other to maintain themselves.

Hence it is to be remarked that, in seizing a state, the usurper ought to examine closely into all those injuries which it is necessary for him to inflict, and to do them all at one stroke so as not to have to repeat them daily; and thus by not unsettling men he will be able to reassure them, and win them to himself by benefits. He who does otherwise, either from timidity or evil advice, is always compelled to keep the knife in his hand; neither can he rely on his subjects, nor can they attach themselves to him, owing to their continued and repeated wrongs. For injuries ought to be done all at one time, so that, being tasted less, they offend less; benefits ought to be given little by little, so that the flavour of them may last longer.

And above all things, a prince ought to live amongst his people in such a way that no unexpected circumstances, whether of good or evil, shall make him change; because if the necessity for this comes in troubled times, you are too late for harsh measures; and mild ones will not help you, for they will be considered as forced from you, and no one will be under any obligation to you for them.

## CHAPTER IX — CONCERNING A CIVIL PRINCIPALITY

But coming to the other point—where a leading citizen becomes the prince of his country, not by wickedness or any intolerable violence, but by the favour of his fellow citizens—this may be called a civil principality: nor is genius or fortune altogether necessary to attain to it, but rather a happy shrewdness. I say then that such a principality is obtained either by the favour of the people or by the favour of the nobles. Because in all cities these two distinct parties are found, and from this it arises that the people do not wish to be ruled nor oppressed by the nobles, and the nobles wish to rule and oppress the people; and from these two opposite desires there arises in cities one of three results, either a principality, self-government, or anarchy.

A principality is created either by the people or by the nobles, accordingly as one or other of them has the opportunity; for the nobles, seeing they cannot withstand the people, begin to cry up the reputation of one of themselves, and they make him a prince, so that under his shadow they can give vent to their ambitions. The people, finding they cannot resist the nobles, also cry up the reputation of one of themselves, and make him a prince so as to be defended by his authority. He who obtains sovereignty by the assistance of the nobles maintains himself with more difficulty than he who comes to it by the aid of the people, because the former finds himself with many around him who consider themselves his equals, and because of this he can neither rule nor manage them to his liking. But he who reaches sovereignty by popular favour finds himself alone, and has none around him, or few, who are not prepared to obey him.

Besides this, one cannot by fair dealing, and without injury to others, satisfy the nobles, but you can satisfy the people, for their object is more righteous than that of the nobles, the latter wishing to oppress, while the former only desire not to be oppressed. It is to be added also that a prince can never secure himself against a hostile people, because of there being too many, whilst from the nobles he can secure himself, as they are few in number. The worst that a prince may expect from a hostile people is to be abandoned by them; but from hostile nobles he has not only to fear abandonment, but also that they will rise against him; for they, being in these affairs more far-seeing and astute, always come forward in time to save themselves, and to obtain favours from him whom they expect to prevail. Further, the prince is compelled to live always with the same people, but he can do well without the same nobles, being able to make and unmake them daily, and to give or take away authority when it pleases him.

Therefore, to make this point clearer, I say that the nobles ought to be looked at mainly in two ways: that is to say, they either shape their course in such a way as binds them entirely to your fortune, or they do not. Those who so bind themselves, and are not rapacious, ought to be honoured and loved; those who do not bind themselves may be dealt with in two ways; they may fail to do this through pusillanimity and a natural want of courage, in which case you ought to make use of them, especially of those who are of good counsel; and thus, whilst in prosperity you honour them, in adversity you do not have to fear them. But when for their own ambitious ends they shun binding themselves, it is a token that they are giving more thought to themselves than to you, and a prince ought to guard against such, and to fear them as if they were open enemies, because in adversity they always help to ruin him.

Therefore, one who becomes a prince through the favour of the people ought to keep them friendly, and this he can easily do seeing they only ask not to be oppressed by him. But one who, in opposition to the people, becomes a prince by the favour of the nobles, ought, above everything, to seek to win the people over to himself, and this he may easily do if he takes them under his protection. Because men, when they receive good from him of whom they were expecting evil, are bound more closely to their benefactor; thus the people quickly become more devoted to him than if he had been raised to the principality by their favours; and the prince can win their affections in many ways, but as these vary according to the circumstances one cannot give fixed rules, so I omit them; but, I repeat, it is necessary for a prince to have the people friendly, otherwise he has no security in adversity.

Nabis, Prince of the Spartans, sustained the attack of all Greece, and of a victorious Roman army, and against them he defended his country and his government; and for the overcoming of this peril it was only necessary for him to make himself secure against a few, but this would not have been sufficient had the people been hostile. And do not let any one impugn this statement with the trite proverb that "He who builds on the people, builds on the mud," for this is true when a private citizen makes a foundation there, and persuades himself that the people will free him when he is oppressed by his enemies or by the magistrates; wherein he would find himself very often deceived, as happened to the Gracchi in Rome and to Messer Giorgio Scali in Florence. But granted a prince who has established himself as above, who can command, and is a man of courage, undismayed in adversity, who does not fail in other qualifications, and who, by his resolution and energy, keeps the whole people encouraged—such a one will never find himself deceived in them, and it will be shown that he has laid his foundations well.

These principalities are liable to danger when they are passing from the civil to the absolute order of government, for such princes either rule personally or through magistrates. In the latter case their government is weaker and more insecure, because it rests entirely on the goodwill of those citizens who are raised to the magistracy, and who, especially in troubled times, can destroy the government with great ease, either by intrigue or open defiance; and the prince has not the chance amid tumults to exercise absolute authority, because the citizens and subjects, accustomed to receive orders from magistrates, are not of a mind to obey him amid these confusions, and there will always be in doubtful times a scarcity of men whom he can trust. For such a prince cannot rely upon what he observes in quiet times, when citizens have need of the state, because then every one agrees with him; they all promise, and when death is far distant they all wish to die for him; but in troubled times, when the state has need of its citizens, then he finds but few. And so much the more is this experiment dangerous, inasmuch as it can only be tried once. Therefore a wise prince ought to adopt such a course that his citizens will always in every sort and kind of circumstance have need of the state and of him, and then he will always find them faithful.

## CHAPTER X — CONCERNING THE WAY IN WHICH THE STRENGTH OF ALL PRINCIPALITIES OUGHT TO BE MEASURED

It is necessary to consider another point in examining the character of these principalities: that is, whether a prince has such power that, in case of need, he can support himself with his own resources, or whether he has always need of the assistance of others. And to make this quite clear I say that I consider those who are able to support themselves by their own resources who can, either by abundance of men or money, raise a sufficient army to join battle against any one who comes to attack them; and I consider those always to have need of others who cannot show themselves against the enemy in the field, but are forced to defend themselves by sheltering behind walls. The first case has been discussed, but we will speak of it again should it recur. In the second case one can say nothing except to encourage such princes to provision and fortify their towns, and not on any account to defend the country. And whoever shall fortify his town well, and shall have managed the other concerns of his subjects in the way stated above, and to be often repeated, will never be attacked without great caution, for men are always adverse to enterprises where difficulties can be seen, and it will be seen not to be an easy thing to attack one who has his town well fortified, and is not hated by his people.

The cities of Germany are absolutely free, they own but little country around them, and they yield obedience to the emperor when it suits them, nor do they fear this or any other power they may have near them, because they are fortified in such a way that every one thinks the taking of them by assault would be tedious and difficult, seeing they have proper ditches and walls, they have sufficient artillery, and they always keep in public depots enough for one year's eating, drinking, and firing. And beyond this, to keep the people quiet and without loss to the state, they always have the means of giving work to the community in those labours that are the life and strength of the city, and on the pursuit of which the people are supported; they also hold military exercises in repute, and moreover have many ordinances to uphold them.

Therefore, a prince who has a strong city, and had not made himself odious, will not be attacked, or if any one should attack he will only be driven off with disgrace; again, because that the affairs of this world are so changeable, it is almost impossible to keep an army a whole year in the field without being interfered with. And whoever should reply: If the people have property outside the city, and see it burnt, they will not remain patient, and the long siege and self-interest will make them forget their prince; to this I answer that a powerful and courageous prince will overcome all such difficulties by giving at one time hope to his subjects that the evil will not be for long, at another time fear of the cruelty of the enemy, then preserving himself adroitly from those subjects who seem to him to be too bold.

Further, the enemy would naturally on his arrival at once burn and ruin the country at the time when the spirits of the people are still hot and ready for the defence; and, therefore, so much the less ought the prince to hesitate; because after a time, when spirits have cooled, the damage is already done, the ills are incurred, and there is no longer any remedy; and therefore they are so much the more ready to unite with their prince, he appearing to be under obligations to them now that their houses have been burnt and their possessions ruined in his defence. For it is the nature of men to be bound by the benefits they confer as much as by those they receive. Therefore, if everything is well considered, it will not be difficult for a wise prince to keep the minds of his citizens steadfast from first to last, when he does not fail to support and defend them.

## CHAPTER XI — CONCERNING ECCLESIASTICAL PRINCIPALITIES

It only remains now to speak of ecclesiastical principalities, touching which all difficulties are prior to getting possession, because they are acquired either by capacity or good fortune, and they can be held without either; for they are sustained by the ancient ordinances of religion, which are so all-powerful, and of such a character that the principalities may be held no matter how their princes behave and live. These princes alone have states and do not defend them; and they have subjects and do not rule them; and the states, although unguarded, are not taken from them, and the subjects, although not ruled, do not care, and they have neither the desire nor the ability to alienate themselves. Such principalities only are secure and happy. But being upheld by powers, to which the human mind cannot reach, I shall speak no more of them, because, being exalted and maintained by God, it would be the act of a presumptuous and rash man to discuss them.

Nevertheless, if any one should ask of me how comes it that the Church has attained such greatness in temporal power, seeing that from Alexander backwards the Italian potentates (not only those who have been called potentates, but every baron and lord, though the smallest) have valued the temporal power very slightly —yet now a king of France trembles before it, and it has been able to drive him from Italy, and to ruin the Venetians—although this may be very manifest, it does not appear to me superfluous to recall it in some measure to memory.

Before Charles, King of France, passed into Italy, this country was under the dominion of the Pope, the Venetians, the King of Naples, the Duke of Milan, and the Florentines. These potentates had two principal anxieties: the one, that no foreigner should enter Italy under arms; the other, that none of themselves should seize more territory. Those about whom there was the most anxiety were the Pope and the Venetians. To restrain the Venetians the union of all the others was necessary, as it was for the defence of Ferrara; and to keep down the Pope they made use of the barons of Rome, who, being divided into two factions, Orsini and Colonnesi, had always a pretext for disorder, and, standing with arms in their hands under the eyes of the Pontiff, kept the pontificate weak and powerless. And although there might arise sometimes a courageous pope, such as Sixtus, yet neither fortune nor wisdom could rid him of these annoyances. And the short life of a pope is also a cause of weakness; for in the ten years, which is the average life of a pope, he can with difficulty lower one of the factions; and if, so to speak, one people should almost destroy the Colonnesi, another would arise hostile to the Orsini, who would support their opponents, and yet would not have time to ruin the Orsini. This was the reason why the temporal powers of the pope were little esteemed in Italy.

Alexander the Sixth arose afterwards, who of all the pontiffs that have ever been showed how a pope with both money and arms was able to prevail; and through the instrumentality of the Duke Valentino, and by reason of the entry of the French, he brought about all those things which I have discussed above in the actions of the duke. And although his intention was not to aggrandize the Church, but the duke, nevertheless, what he did contributed to the greatness of the Church, which, after his death and the ruin of the duke, became the heir to all his labours.

Pope Julius came afterwards and found the Church strong, possessing all the Romagna, the barons of Rome reduced to impotence, and, through the chastisements of Alexander, the factions wiped out; he also found the way open to accumulate money in a manner such as had never been practised before Alexander's time. Such things Julius not only followed, but improved upon, and he intended to gain Bologna, to ruin the Venetians, and to drive the French out of Italy. All of these enterprises prospered with him, and so much the more to his credit, inasmuch as he did everything to strengthen the Church and not any private person. He kept also the Orsini and Colonnesi factions within the bounds in which he found them; and although there was among them some mind to make disturbance, nevertheless he held two things firm: the one, the greatness of the Church, with which he terrified them; and the other, not allowing them to have their own cardinals, who caused the disorders among them. For whenever these factions have their cardinals they do not remain quiet for long, because cardinals foster the factions in Rome and out of it, and the barons are compelled to support them, and thus from the ambitions of prelates arise disorders and tumults among the barons. For these reasons his Holiness Pope Leo found the pontificate most powerful, and it is to be hoped that, if others made it great in arms, he will make it still greater and more venerated by his goodness and infinite other virtues.

## CHAPTER XII — HOW MANY KINDS OF SOLDIERY THERE ARE, AND CONCERNING MERCENARIES

Having discoursed particularly on the characteristics of such principalities as in the beginning I proposed to discuss, and having considered in some degree the causes of there being good or bad, and having shown the methods by which many have sought to acquire them and to hold them, it now remains for me to discuss generally the means of offence and defence which belong to each of them.

We have seen above how necessary it is for a prince to have his foundations well laid, otherwise it follows of necessity he will go to ruin. The chief foundations of all states, new as well as old or composite, are good laws and good arms; and as there cannot be good laws where the state is not well armed, it follows that where they are well armed they have good laws. I shall leave the laws out of the discussion and shall speak of the arms.

I say, therefore, that the arms with which a prince defends his state are either his own, or they are mercenaries, auxiliaries, or mixed. Mercenaries and auxiliaries are useless and dangerous; and if one holds his state based on these arms, he will stand neither firm nor safe; for they are disunited, ambitious, and without discipline, unfaithful, valiant before friends, cowardly before enemies; they have neither the fear of God nor fidelity to men, and destruction is deferred only so long as the attack is; for in peace one is robbed by them, and in war by the enemy. The fact is, they have no other attraction or reason for keeping the field than a trifle of stipend, which is not sufficient to make them willing to die for you. They are ready enough to be your soldiers whilst you do not make war, but if war comes they take themselves off or run from the foe; which I should have little trouble to prove, for the ruin of Italy has been caused by nothing else than by resting all her hopes for many years on mercenaries, and although they formerly made some display and appeared valiant amongst themselves, yet when the foreigners came they showed what they were. Thus it was that Charles, King of France, was allowed to seize Italy with chalk in hand; and he who told us that our sins were the cause of it told the truth, but they were not the sins he imagined, but those which I have related. And as they were the sins of princes, it is the princes who have also suffered the penalty.

I wish to demonstrate further the infelicity of these arms. The mercenary captains are either capable men or they are not; if they are, you cannot trust them, because they always aspire to their own greatness, either by oppressing you, who are their master, or others contrary to your intentions; but if the captain is not skilful, you are ruined in the usual way.

And if it be urged that whoever is armed will act in the same way, whether mercenary or not, I reply that when arms have to be resorted to, either by a prince or a republic, then the prince ought to go in person and perform the duty of a captain; the republic has to send its citizens, and when one is sent who does not turn out satisfactorily, it ought to recall him, and when one is worthy, to hold him by the laws so that he does not leave the command. And experience has shown princes and republics, single-handed, making the greatest progress, and mercenaries doing nothing except damage; and it is more difficult to bring a republic, armed with its own arms, under the sway of one of its citizens than it is to bring one armed with foreign arms. Rome and Sparta stood for many ages armed and free. The Switzers are completely armed and quite free.

Of ancient mercenaries, for example, there are the Carthaginians, who were oppressed by their mercenary soldiers after the first war with the Romans, although the Carthaginians had their own citizens for captains. After the death of Epaminondas, Philip of Macedon was made captain of their soldiers by the Thebans, and after victory he took away their liberty.

Duke Filippo being dead, the Milanese enlisted Francesco Sforza against the Venetians, and he, having overcome the enemy at Caravaggio, allied himself with them to crush the Milanese, his masters. His father, Sforza, having been engaged by Queen Johanna of Naples, left her unprotected, so that she was forced to throw herself into the arms of the King of Aragon, in order to save her kingdom. And if the Venetians and Florentines formerly extended their dominions by these arms, and yet their captains did not make themselves princes, but have defended them, I reply that the Florentines in this case have been favoured by chance, for of the able captains, of whom they might have stood in fear, some have not conquered, some have been opposed, and others have turned their ambitions elsewhere. One who did not conquer was Giovanni Acuto, and since he did not conquer his fidelity cannot be proved; but every one will acknowledge that, had he conquered, the Florentines would have stood at his discretion. Sforza had the Bracceschi always against him, so they watched each other. Francesco turned his ambition to Lombardy; Braccio against the Church and the kingdom of Naples. But let us come to that which happened a short while ago. The Florentines appointed as their captain Pagolo Vitelli, a most prudent man, who from a private position had risen to the greatest renown. If this man had taken Pisa, nobody can deny that it would have been proper for the Florentines to keep in with him, for if he became the soldier of their enemies they had no means of resisting, and if they held to him they must obey him. The Venetians, if their achievements are considered, will be seen to have acted safely and gloriously so long as they sent to war their own men, when with armed gentlemen and plebians they did valiantly. This was before they turned to enterprises on land, but when they began to fight on land they forsook this virtue and followed the custom of Italy. And in the beginning of their expansion on land, through not having much territory, and because of their great reputation, they had not much to fear from their captains; but when they expanded, as under Carmignuola, they had a taste of this mistake; for, having found him a most valiant man (they beat the Duke of Milan under his leadership), and, on the other hand, knowing how lukewarm he was in the war, they feared they would no longer conquer under him, and for this reason they were not willing, nor were they able, to let him go; and so, not to lose again that which they had acquired, they were compelled, in order to secure themselves, to murder him. They had afterwards for their captains Bartolomeo da Bergamo, Roberto da San Severino, the count of Pitigliano, and the like, under whom they had to dread loss and not gain, as happened afterwards at Vaila, where in one battle they lost that which in eight hundred years they had acquired with so much trouble. Because from such arms conquests come but slowly, long delayed and inconsiderable, but the losses sudden and portentous.

And as with these examples I have reached Italy, which has been ruled for many years by mercenaries, I wish to discuss them more seriously, in order that, having seen their rise and progress, one may be better prepared to counteract them. You must understand that the empire has recently come to be repudiated in Italy, that the Pope has acquired more temporal power, and that Italy has been divided up into more states, for the reason that many of the great cities took up arms against their nobles, who, formerly favoured by the emperor, were oppressing them, whilst the Church was favouring them so as to gain authority in temporal power: in many others their citizens became princes. From this it came to pass that Italy fell partly into the hands of the

Church and of republics, and, the Church consisting of priests and the republic of citizens unaccustomed to arms, both commenced to enlist foreigners.

The first who gave renown to this soldiery was Alberigo da Conio, the Romagnian. From the school of this man sprang, among others, Braccio and Sforza, who in their time were the arbiters of Italy. After these came all the other captains who till now have directed the arms of Italy; and the end of all their valour has been, that she has been overrun by Charles, robbed by Louis, ravaged by Ferdinand, and insulted by the Switzers. The principle that has guided them has been, first, to lower the credit of infantry so that they might increase their own. They did this because, subsisting on their pay and without territory, they were unable to support many soldiers, and a few infantry did not give them any authority; so they were led to employ cavalry, with a moderate force of which they were maintained and honoured; and affairs were brought to such a pass that, in an army of twenty thousand soldiers, there were not to be found two thousand foot soldiers. They had, besides this, used every art to lessen fatigue and danger to themselves and their soldiers, not killing in the fray, but taking prisoners and liberating without ransom. They did not attack towns at night, nor did the garrisons of the towns attack encampments at night; they did not surround the camp either with stockade or ditch, nor did they campaign in the winter. All these things were permitted by their military rules, and devised by them to avoid, as I have said, both fatigue and dangers; thus they have brought Italy to slavery and contempt.

## CHAPTER XIII — CONCERNING AUXILIARIES, MIXED SOLDIERY, AND ONE'S OWN

Auxiliaries, which are the other useless arm, are employed when a prince is called in with his forces to aid and defend, as was done by Pope Julius in the most recent times; for he, having, in the enterprise against Ferrara, had poor proof of his mercenaries, turned to auxiliaries, and stipulated with Ferdinand, King of Spain, for his assistance with men and arms. These arms may be useful and good in themselves, but for him who calls them in they are always disadvantageous; for losing, one is undone, and winning, one is their captive.

And although ancient histories may be full of examples, I do not wish to leave this recent one of Pope Julius the Second, the peril of which cannot fail to be perceived; for he, wishing to get Ferrara, threw himself entirely into the hands of the foreigner. But his good fortune brought about a third event, so that he did not reap the fruit of his rash choice; because, having his auxiliaries routed at Ravenna, and the Switzers having risen and driven out the conquerors (against all expectation, both his and others), it so came to pass that he did not become prisoner to his enemies, they having fled, nor to his auxiliaries, he having conquered by other arms than theirs.

The Florentines, being entirely without arms, sent ten thousand Frenchmen to take Pisa, whereby they ran more danger than at any other time of their troubles.

The Emperor of Constantinople, to oppose his neighbours, sent ten thousand Turks into Greece, who, on the war being finished, were not willing to quit; this was the beginning of the servitude of Greece to the infidels.

Therefore, let him who has no desire to conquer make use of these arms, for they are much more hazardous than mercenaries, because with them the ruin is ready made; they are all united, all yield obedience to others; but with mercenaries, when they have conquered, more time and better opportunities are needed to injure you; they are not all of one community, they are found and paid by you, and a third party, which you have made their head, is not able all at once to assume enough authority to injure you. In conclusion, in mercenaries dastardy is most dangerous; in auxiliaries, valour. The wise prince, therefore, has always avoided these arms and turned to his own; and has been willing rather to lose with them than to conquer with the others, not deeming that a real victory which is gained with the arms of others.

I shall never hesitate to cite Cesare Borgia and his actions. This duke entered the Romagna with auxiliaries, taking there only French soldiers, and with them he captured Imola and Forli; but afterwards, such forces not appearing to him reliable, he turned to mercenaries, discerning less danger in them, and enlisted the Orsini and Vitelli; whom presently, on handling and finding them doubtful, unfaithful, and dangerous, he destroyed and turned to his own men. And the difference between one and the other of these forces can easily be seen when one considers the difference there was in the reputation of the duke, when he had the French, when he had the Orsini and Vitelli, and when he relied on his own soldiers, on whose fidelity he could always count and found it ever increasing; he was never esteemed more highly than when every one saw that he was complete master of his own forces.

I was not intending to go beyond Italian and recent examples, but I am unwilling to leave out Hiero, the Syracusan, he being one of those I have named above. This man, as I have said, made head of the army by the Syracusans, soon found out that a mercenary soldiery, constituted like our Italian condottieri, was of no use; and it appearing to him that he could neither keep them not let them go, he had them all cut to pieces, and afterwards made war with his own forces and not with aliens.

I wish also to recall to memory an instance from the Old Testament applicable to this subject. David offered himself to Saul to fight with Goliath, the Philistine champion, and, to give him courage, Saul armed him with his own weapons; which David rejected as soon as he had them on his back, saying he could make no use of them, and that he wished to meet the enemy with his sling and his knife. In conclusion, the arms of others either fall from your back, or they weigh you down, or they bind you fast.

Charles the Seventh, the father of King Louis the Eleventh, having by good fortune and valour liberated France from the English, recognized the necessity of being armed with forces of his own, and he established in his kingdom ordinances concerning men-at-arms and infantry. Afterwards his son, King Louis, abolished the infantry and began to enlist the Switzers, which mistake, followed by others, is, as is now seen, a source of peril to that kingdom; because, having raised the reputation of the Switzers, he has entirely diminished the value of his own arms, for he has destroyed the infantry altogether; and his men-at-arms he has subordinated to others, for, being as they are so accustomed to fight along with Switzers, it does not appear that they can now conquer without them. Hence it arises that the French cannot stand against the Switzers, and without the Switzers they do not come off well against others. The armies of the French have thus become mixed, partly mercenary and partly national, both of which arms together are much better than mercenaries alone or auxiliaries alone, but much inferior to one's own forces. And this example proves it, for the kingdom of France would be unconquerable if the ordinance of Charles had been enlarged or maintained.

But the scanty wisdom of man, on entering into an affair which looks well at first, cannot discern the poison that is hidden in it, as I have said above of hectic fevers. Therefore, if he who rules a principality cannot recognize evils until they are upon him, he is not truly wise; and this insight is given to few. And if the first disaster to the Roman Empire should be examined, it will be found to have commenced only with the enlisting of the Goths; because from that time the vigour of the Roman Empire began to decline, and all that valour which had raised it passed away to others.

I conclude, therefore, that no principality is secure without having its own forces; on the contrary, it is entirely dependent on good fortune, not having the valour which in adversity would defend it. And it has always been the opinion and judgment of wise men that nothing can be so uncertain or unstable as fame or power not founded on its own strength. And one's own forces are those which are composed either of subjects, citizens, or dependents; all others are mercenaries or auxiliaries. And the way to make ready one's own forces will be easily found if the rules suggested by me shall be reflected upon, and if one will consider how Philip, the father of Alexander the Great, and many republics and princes have armed and organized themselves, to which rules I entirely commit myself.

## CHAPTER XIV — THAT WHICH CONCERNS A PRINCE ON THE SUBJECT OF THE ART OF WAR

A prince ought to have no other aim or thought, nor select anything else for his study, than war and its rules and discipline; for this is the sole art that belongs to him who rules, and it is of such force that it not only upholds those who are born princes, but it often enables men to rise from a private station to that rank. And, on the contrary, it is seen that when princes have thought more of ease than of arms they have lost their states. And the first cause of your losing it is to neglect this art; and what enables you to acquire a state is to be master of the art. Francesco Sforza, through being martial, from a private person became Duke of Milan; and the sons, through avoiding the hardships and troubles of arms, from dukes became private persons. For among other evils which being unarmed brings you, it causes you to be despised, and this is one of those ignominies against which a prince ought to guard himself, as is shown later on. Because there is nothing proportionate between the armed and the unarmed; and it is not reasonable that he who is armed should yield obedience willingly to him who is unarmed, or that the unarmed man should be secure among armed servants. Because, there being in the one disdain and in the other suspicion, it is not possible for them to work well together. And therefore a prince who does not understand the art of war, over and above the other misfortunes already mentioned, cannot be respected by his soldiers, nor can he rely on them. He ought never, therefore, to have out of his thoughts this subject of war, and in peace he should addict himself more to its exercise than in war; this he can do in two ways, the one by action, the other by study.

As regards action, he ought above all things to keep his men well organized and drilled, to follow incessantly the chase, by which he accustoms his body to hardships, and learns something of the nature of localities, and gets to find out how the mountains rise, how the valleys open out, how the plains lie, and to understand the nature of rivers and marshes, and in all this to take the greatest care. Which knowledge is useful in two ways. Firstly, he learns to know his country, and is better able to undertake its defence; afterwards, by means of the knowledge and observation of that locality, he understands with ease any other which it may be necessary for him to study hereafter; because the hills, valleys, and plains, and rivers and marshes that are, for instance, in Tuscany, have a certain resemblance to those of other countries, so that with a knowledge of the aspect of one country one can easily arrive at a knowledge of others. And the prince that lacks this skill lacks the essential which it is desirable that a captain should possess, for it teaches him to surprise his enemy, to select quarters, to lead armies, to array the battle, to besiege towns to advantage.

Philopoemen, Prince of the Achaeans, among other praises which writers have bestowed on him, is commended because in time of peace he never had anything in his mind but the rules of war; and when he was in the country with friends, he often stopped and reasoned with them: "If the enemy should be upon that hill, and we should find ourselves here with our army, with whom would be the advantage? How should one best advance to meet him, keeping the ranks? If we should wish to retreat, how ought we to pursue?" And he would set forth to them, as he went, all the chances that could befall an army; he would listen to their opinion and state his, confirming it with reasons, so that by these continual discussions there could never arise, in time of war, any unexpected circumstances that he could not deal with.

But to exercise the intellect the prince should read histories, and study there the actions of illustrious men, to see how they have borne themselves in war, to examine the causes of their victories and defeat, so as to avoid the latter and imitate the former; and above all do as an illustrious man did, who took as an exemplar one who had been praised and famous before him, and whose achievements and deeds he always kept in his mind, as it is said Alexander the Great imitated Achilles, Caesar Alexander, Scipio Cyrus. And whoever reads the life of Cyrus, written by Xenophon, will recognize afterwards in the life of Scipio how that imitation was his glory, and how in chastity, affability, humanity, and liberality Scipio conformed to those things which have been written of Cyrus by Xenophon. A wise prince ought to observe some such rules, and never in peaceful times stand idle, but increase his resources with industry in such a way that they may be available to him in adversity, so that if fortune chances it may find him prepared to resist her blows.

## CHAPTER XV — CONCERNING THINGS FOR WHICH MEN, AND ESPECIALLY PRINCES, ARE PRAISED OR BLAMED

It remains now to see what ought to be the rules of conduct for a prince towards subject and friends. And as I know that many have written on this point, I expect I shall be considered presumptuous in mentioning it again, especially as in discussing it I shall depart from the methods of other people. But, it being my intention to write a thing which shall be useful to him who apprehends it, it appears to me more appropriate to follow up the real truth of the matter than the imagination of it; for many have pictured republics and principalities which in fact have never been known or seen, because how one lives is so far distant from how one ought to live, that he who neglects what is done for what ought to be done, sooner effects his ruin than his preservation; for a man who wishes to act entirely up to his professions of virtue soon meets with what destroys him among so much that is evil.

Hence it is necessary for a prince wishing to hold his own to know how to do wrong, and to make use of it or not according to necessity. Therefore, putting on one side imaginary things concerning a prince, and discussing those which are real, I say that all men when they are spoken of, and chiefly princes for being more highly placed, are remarkable for some of those qualities which bring them either blame or praise; and thus it is that one is reputed liberal, another miserly, using a Tuscan term (because an avaricious person in our language is still he who desires to possess by robbery, whilst we call one miserly who deprives himself too much of the use of his own); one is reputed generous, one rapacious; one cruel, one compassionate; one faithless, another faithful; one effeminate and cowardly, another bold and brave; one affable, another haughty; one lascivious, another chaste; one sincere, another cunning; one hard, another easy; one grave, another frivolous; one religious, another unbelieving, and the like. And I know that every one will confess that it would be most praiseworthy in a prince to exhibit all the above qualities that are considered good; but because they can neither be entirely possessed nor observed, for human conditions do not permit it, it is necessary for him to be sufficiently prudent that he may know how to avoid the reproach of those vices which would lose him his state; and also to keep himself, if it be possible, from those which would not lose him it; but this not being possible, he may with less hesitation abandon himself to them. And again, he need not make himself uneasy at incurring a reproach for those vices without which the state can only be saved with difficulty, for if everything is considered carefully, it will be found that something which looks like virtue, if followed, would be his ruin; whilst something else, which looks like vice, yet followed brings him security and prosperity.

## CHAPTER XVI — CONCERNING LIBERALITY AND MEANNESS

Commencing then with the first of the above-named characteristics, I say that it would be well to be reputed liberal. Nevertheless, liberality exercised in a way that does not bring you the reputation for it, injures you; for if one exercises it honestly and as it should be exercised, it may not become known, and you will not avoid the reproach of its opposite. Therefore, any one wishing to maintain among men the name of liberal is obliged to avoid no attribute of magnificence; so that a prince thus inclined will consume in such acts all his property, and will be compelled in the end, if he wish to maintain the name of liberal, to unduly weigh down his people, and tax them, and do everything he can to get money. This will soon make him odious to his subjects, and becoming poor he will be little valued by any one; thus, with his liberality, having offended many and rewarded few, he is affected by the very first trouble and imperilled by whatever may be the first danger; recognizing this himself, and wishing to draw back from it, he runs at once into the reproach of being miserly.

Therefore, a prince, not being able to exercise this virtue of liberality in such a way that it is recognized, except to his cost, if he is wise he ought not to fear the reputation of being mean, for in time he will come to be more considered than if liberal, seeing that with his economy his revenues are enough, that he can defend himself against all attacks, and is able to engage in enterprises without burdening his people; thus it comes to pass that he exercises liberality towards all from whom he does not take, who are numberless, and meanness towards those to whom he does not give, who are few.

We have not seen great things done in our time except by those who have been considered mean; the rest have failed. Pope Julius the Second was assisted in reaching the papacy by a reputation for liberality, yet he did not strive afterwards to keep it up, when he made war on the King of France; and he made many wars without imposing any extraordinary tax on his subjects, for he supplied his additional expenses out of his long thriftiness. The present King of Spain would not have undertaken or conquered in so many enterprises if he had been reputed liberal. A prince, therefore, provided that he has not to rob his subjects, that he can defend himself, that he does not become poor and abject, that he is not forced to become rapacious, ought to hold of little account a reputation for being mean, for it is one of those vices which will enable him to govern.

And if any one should say: Caesar obtained empire by liberality, and many others have reached the highest positions by having been liberal, and by being considered so, I answer: Either you are a prince in fact, or in a way to become one. In the first case this liberality is dangerous, in the second it is very necessary to be considered liberal; and Caesar was one of those who wished to become pre-eminent in Rome; but if he had survived after becoming so, and had not moderated his expenses, he would have destroyed his government. And if any one should reply: Many have been princes, and have done great things with armies, who have been considered very liberal, I reply: Either a prince spends that which is his own or his subjects' or else that of others. In the first case he ought to be sparing, in the second he ought not to neglect any opportunity for liberality. And to the prince who goes forth with his army, supporting it by pillage, sack, and extortion, handling that which belongs to others, this liberality is necessary, otherwise he would not be followed by soldiers. And of that which is neither yours nor your subjects' you can be a ready giver, as were Cyrus, Caesar, and Alexander; because it does not take away your reputation if you squander that of others, but adds to it; it is only squandering your own that injures you.

And there is nothing wastes so rapidly as liberality, for even whilst you exercise it you lose the power to do so, and so become either poor or despised, or else, in avoiding poverty, rapacious and hated. And a prince should guard himself, above all things, against being despised and hated; and liberality leads you to both. Therefore it is wiser to have a reputation for meanness which brings reproach without hatred, than to be compelled through seeking a reputation for liberality to incur a name for rapacity which begets reproach with hatred.

## CHAPTER XVII — CONCERNING CRUELTY AND CLEMENCY, AND WHETHER IT IS BETTER TO BE LOVED THAN FEARED

Coming now to the other qualities mentioned above, I say that every prince ought to desire to be considered clement and not cruel. Nevertheless he ought to take care not to misuse this clemency. Cesare Borgia was considered cruel; notwithstanding, his cruelty reconciled the Romagna, unified it, and restored it to peace and loyalty. And if this be rightly considered, he will be seen to have been much more merciful than the Florentine people, who, to avoid a reputation for cruelty, permitted Pistoia to be destroyed. Therefore a prince, so long as he keeps his subjects united and loyal, ought not to mind the reproach of cruelty; because with a few examples he will be more merciful than those who, through too much mercy, allow disorders to arise, from which follow murders or robberies; for these are wont to injure the whole people, whilst those executions which originate with a prince offend the individual only.

And of all princes, it is impossible for the new prince to avoid the imputation of cruelty, owing to new states being full of dangers. Hence Virgil, through the mouth of Dido, excuses the inhumanity of her reign owing to its being new, saying:

Nevertheless he ought to be slow to believe and to act, nor should he himself show fear, but proceed in a temperate manner with prudence and humanity, so that too much confidence may not make him incautious and too much distrust render him intolerable.

Upon this a question arises: whether it be better to be loved than feared or feared than loved? It may be answered that one should wish to be both, but, because it is difficult to unite them in one person, it is much safer to be feared than loved, when, of the two, either must be dispensed with. Because this is to be asserted in general of men, that they are ungrateful, fickle, false, cowardly, covetous, and as long as you succeed they are yours entirely; they will offer you their blood, property, life, and children, as is said above, when the need is far distant; but when it approaches they turn against you. And that prince who, relying entirely on their promises, has neglected other precautions, is ruined; because friendships that are obtained by payments, and not by greatness or nobility of mind, may indeed be earned, but they are not secured, and in time of need cannot be relied upon; and men have less scruple in offending one who is beloved than one who is feared, for love is preserved by the link of obligation which, owing to the baseness of men, is broken at every opportunity for their advantage; but fear preserves you by a dread of punishment which never fails.

Nevertheless a prince ought to inspire fear in such a way that, if he does not win love, he avoids hatred; because he can endure very well being feared whilst he is not hated, which will always be as long as he abstains from the property of his citizens and subjects and from their women. But when it is necessary for him to proceed against the life of someone, he must do it on proper justification and for manifest cause, but above all things he must keep his hands off the property of others, because men more quickly forget the death of their father than the loss of their patrimony. Besides, pretexts for taking away the property are never wanting; for he who has once begun to live by robbery will always find pretexts for seizing what belongs to others; but reasons for taking life, on the contrary, are more difficult to find and sooner lapse. But when a prince is with his army, and has under control a multitude of soldiers, then it is quite necessary for him to disregard the reputation of cruelty, for without it he would never hold his army united or disposed to its duties.

Among the wonderful deeds of Hannibal this one is enumerated: that having led an enormous army, composed of many various races of men, to fight in foreign lands, no dissensions arose either among them or against the prince, whether in his bad or in his good fortune. This arose from nothing else than his inhuman cruelty, which, with his boundless valour, made him revered and terrible in the sight of his soldiers, but without that cruelty, his other virtues were not sufficient to produce this effect. And short-sighted writers admire his deeds from one point of view and from another condemn the principal cause of them. That it is true his other virtues would not have been sufficient for him may be proved by the case of Scipio, that most excellent man, not only of his own times but within the memory of man, against whom, nevertheless, his army rebelled in Spain; this arose from nothing but his too great forbearance, which gave his soldiers more license than is consistent with military discipline. For this he was upbraided in the Senate by Fabius Maximus, and called the corrupter of the Roman soldiery. The Locrians were laid waste by a legate of Scipio, yet they were not avenged by him, nor was the insolence of the legate punished, owing entirely to his easy nature. Insomuch that someone in the Senate, wishing to excuse him, said there were many men who knew much better how not to err than to correct the errors of others. This disposition, if he had been continued in the command, would have destroyed in time the fame and glory of Scipio; but, he being under the control of the Senate, this injurious characteristic not only concealed itself, but contributed to his glory.

Returning to the question of being feared or loved, I come to the conclusion that, men loving according to their own will and fearing according to that of the prince, a wise prince should establish himself on that which is in his own control and not in that of others; he must endeavour only to avoid hatred, as is noted.

## CHAPTER XVIII — CONCERNING THE WAY IN WHICH PRINCES SHOULD KEEP FAITH

Every one admits how praiseworthy it is in a prince to keep faith, and to live with integrity and not with craft. Nevertheless our experience has been that those princes who have done great things have held good faith of little account, and have known how to circumvent the intellect of men by craft, and in the end have overcome those who have relied on their word. You must know there are two ways of contesting, the one by the law, the other by force; the first method is proper to men, the second to beasts; but because the first is frequently not sufficient, it is necessary to have recourse to the second. Therefore it is necessary for a prince to understand how to avail himself of the beast and the man. This has been figuratively taught to princes by ancient writers, who describe how Achilles and many other princes of old were given to the Centaur Chiron to nurse, who brought them up in his discipline; which means solely that, as they had for a teacher one who was half beast and half man, so it is necessary for a prince to know how to make use of both natures, and that one without the other is not durable. A prince, therefore, being compelled knowingly to adopt the beast, ought to choose the fox and the lion; because the lion cannot defend himself against snares and the fox cannot defend himself against wolves. Therefore, it is necessary to be a fox to discover the snares and a lion to terrify the wolves. Those who rely simply on the lion do not understand what they are about. Therefore a wise lord cannot, nor ought he to, keep faith when such observance may be turned against him, and when the reasons that caused him to pledge it exist no longer. If men were entirely good this precept would not hold, but because they are bad, and will not keep faith with you, you too are not bound to observe it with them. Nor will there ever be wanting to a prince legitimate reasons to excuse this non-observance. Of this endless modern examples could be given, showing how many treaties and engagements have been made void and of no effect through the faithlessness of princes; and he who has known best how to employ the fox has succeeded best.

But it is necessary to know well how to disguise this characteristic, and to be a great pretender and dissembler; and men are so simple, and so subject to present necessities, that he who seeks to deceive will always find someone who will allow himself to be deceived. One recent example I cannot pass over in silence. Alexander the Sixth did nothing else but deceive men, nor ever thought of doing otherwise, and he always found victims; for there never was a man who had greater power in asserting, or who with greater oaths would affirm a thing, yet would observe it less; nevertheless his deceits always succeeded according to his wishes, because he well understood this side of mankind.

Therefore it is unnecessary for a prince to have all the good qualities I have enumerated, but it is very necessary to appear to have them. And I shall dare to say this also, that to have them and always to observe them is injurious, and that to appear to have them is useful; to appear merciful, faithful, humane, religious, upright, and to be so, but with a mind so framed that should you require not to be so, you may be able and know how to change to the opposite.

And you have to understand this, that a prince, especially a new one, cannot observe all those things for which men are esteemed, being often forced, in order to maintain the state, to act contrary to fidelity, friendship, humanity, and religion. Therefore it is necessary for him to have a mind ready to turn itself accordingly as the winds and variations of fortune force it, yet, as I have said above, not to diverge from the good if he can avoid doing so, but, if compelled, then to know how to set about it.

For this reason a prince ought to take care that he never lets anything slip from his lips that is not replete with the above-named five qualities, that he may appear to him who sees and hears him altogether merciful, faithful, humane, upright, and religious. There is nothing more necessary to appear to have than this last quality, inasmuch as men judge generally more by the eye than by the hand, because it belongs to everybody to see you, to few to come in touch with you. Every one sees what you appear to be, few really know what you are, and those few dare not oppose themselves to the opinion of the many, who have the majesty of the state to defend them; and in the actions of all men, and especially of princes, which it is not prudent to challenge, one judges by the result.

For that reason, let a prince have the credit of conquering and holding his state, the means will always be considered honest, and he will be praised by everybody; because the vulgar are always taken by what a thing seems to be and by what comes of it; and in the world there are only the vulgar, for the few find a place there only when the many have no ground to rest on.

One prince of the present time, whom it is not well to name, never preaches anything else but peace and good faith, and to both he is most hostile, and either, if he had kept it, would have deprived him of reputation and kingdom many a time.


## CHAPTER XIX — THAT ONE SHOULD AVOID BEING DESPISED AND HATED

Now, concerning the characteristics of which mention is made above, I have spoken of the more important ones, the others I wish to discuss briefly under this generality, that the prince must consider, as has been in part said before, how to avoid those things which will make him hated or contemptible; and as often as he shall have succeeded he will have fulfilled his part, and he need not fear any danger in other reproaches.

It makes him hated above all things, as I have said, to be rapacious, and to be a violator of the property and women of his subjects, from both of which he must abstain. And when neither their property nor their honor is touched, the majority of men live content, and he has only to contend with the ambition of a few, whom he can curb with ease in many ways.

It makes him contemptible to be considered fickle, frivolous, effeminate, mean-spirited, irresolute, from all of which a prince should guard himself as from a rock; and he should endeavour to show in his actions greatness, courage, gravity, and fortitude; and in his private dealings with his subjects let him show that his judgments are irrevocable, and maintain himself in such reputation that no one can hope either to deceive him or to get round him.

That prince is highly esteemed who conveys this impression of himself, and he who is highly esteemed is not easily conspired against; for, provided it is well known that he is an excellent man and revered by his people, he can only be attacked with difficulty. For this reason a prince ought to have two fears, one from within, on account of his subjects, the other from without, on account of external powers. From the latter he is defended by being well armed and having good allies, and if he is well armed he will have good friends, and affairs will always remain quiet within when they are quiet without, unless they should have been already disturbed by conspiracy; and even should affairs outside be disturbed, if he has carried out his preparations and has lived as I have said, as long as he does not despair, he will resist every attack, as I said Nabis the Spartan did.

But concerning his subjects, when affairs outside are disturbed he has only to fear that they will conspire secretly, from which a prince can easily secure himself by avoiding being hated and despised, and by keeping the people satisfied with him, which it is most necessary for him to accomplish, as I said above at length. And one of the most efficacious remedies that a prince can have against conspiracies is not to be hated and despised by the people, for he who conspires against a prince always expects to please them by his removal; but when the conspirator can only look forward to offending them, he will not have the courage to take such a course, for the difficulties that confront a conspirator are infinite. And as experience shows, many have been the conspiracies, but few have been successful; because he who conspires cannot act alone, nor can he take a companion except from those whom he believes to be malcontents, and as soon as you have opened your mind to a malcontent you have given him the material with which to content himself, for by denouncing you he can look for every advantage; so that, seeing the gain from this course to be assured, and seeing the other to be doubtful and full of dangers, he must be a very rare friend, or a thoroughly obstinate enemy of the prince, to keep faith with you.

And, to reduce the matter into a small compass, I say that, on the side of the conspirator, there is nothing but fear, jealousy, prospect of punishment to terrify him; but on the side of the prince there is the majesty of the principality, the laws, the protection of friends and the state to defend him; so that, adding to all these things the popular goodwill, it is impossible that any one should be so rash as to conspire. For whereas in general the conspirator has to fear before the execution of his plot, in this case he has also to fear the sequel to the crime; because on account of it he has the people for an enemy, and thus cannot hope for any escape.

Endless examples could be given on this subject, but I will be content with one, brought to pass within the memory of our fathers. Messer Annibale Bentivogli, who was prince in Bologna (grandfather of the present Annibale), having been murdered by the Canneschi, who had conspired against him, not one of his family survived but Messer Giovanni, who was in childhood: immediately after his assassination the people rose and murdered all the Canneschi. This sprung from the popular goodwill which the house of Bentivogli enjoyed in those days in Bologna; which was so great that, although none remained there after the death of Annibale who was able to rule the state, the Bolognese, having information that there was one of the Bentivogli family in Florence, who up to that time had been considered the son of a blacksmith, sent to Florence for him and gave him the government of their city, and it was ruled by him until Messer Giovanni came in due course to the government.

For this reason I consider that a prince ought to reckon conspiracies of little account when his people hold him in esteem; but when it is hostile to him, and bears hatred towards him, he ought to fear everything and everybody. And well-ordered states and wise princes have taken every care not to drive the nobles to desperation, and to keep the people satisfied and contented, for this is one of the most important objects a prince can have.

Among the best ordered and governed kingdoms of our times is France, and in it are found many good institutions on which depend the liberty and security of the king; of these the first is the parliament and its authority, because he who founded the kingdom, knowing the ambition of the nobility and their boldness, considered that a bit to their mouths would be necessary to hold them in; and, on the other side, knowing the hatred of the people, founded in fear, against the nobles, he wished to protect them, yet he was not anxious for this to be the particular care of the king; therefore, to take away the reproach which he would be liable to from the nobles for favouring the people, and from the people for favouring the nobles, he set up an arbiter, who should be one who could beat down the great and favour the lesser without reproach to the king. Neither could you have a better or a more prudent arrangement, or a greater source of security to the king and kingdom. From this one can draw another important conclusion, that princes ought to leave affairs of reproach to the management of others, and keep those of grace in their own hands. And further, I consider that a prince ought to cherish the nobles, but not so as to make himself hated by the people.

It may appear, perhaps, to some who have examined the lives and deaths of the Roman emperors that many of them would be an example contrary to my opinion, seeing that some of them lived nobly and showed great qualities of soul, nevertheless they have lost their empire or have been killed by subjects who have conspired against them. Wishing, therefore, to answer these objections, I will recall the characters of some of the emperors, and will show that the causes of their ruin were not different to those alleged by me; at the same time I will only submit for consideration those things that are noteworthy to him who studies the affairs of those times.

It seems to me sufficient to take all those emperors who succeeded to the empire from Marcus the philosopher down to Maximinus; they were Marcus and his son Commodus, Pertinax, Julian, Severus and his son Antoninus Caracalla, Macrinus, Heliogabalus, Alexander, and Maximinus.

There is first to note that, whereas in other principalities the ambition of the nobles and the insolence of the people only have to be contended with, the Roman emperors had a third difficulty in having to put up with the cruelty and avarice of their soldiers, a matter so beset with difficulties that it was the ruin of many; for it was a hard thing to give satisfaction both to soldiers and people; because the people loved peace, and for this reason they loved the unaspiring prince, whilst the soldiers loved the warlike prince who was bold, cruel, and rapacious, which qualities they were quite willing he should exercise upon the people, so that they could get double pay and give vent to their own greed and cruelty. Hence it arose that those emperors were always overthrown who, either by birth or training, had no great authority, and most of them, especially those who came new to the principality, recognizing the difficulty of these two opposing humours, were inclined to give satisfaction to the soldiers, caring little about injuring the people. Which course was necessary, because, as princes cannot help being hated by someone, they ought, in the first place, to avoid being hated by every one, and when they cannot compass this, they ought to endeavour with the utmost diligence to avoid the hatred of the most powerful. Therefore, those emperors who through inexperience had need of special favour adhered more readily to the soldiers than to the people; a course which turned out advantageous to them or not, accordingly as the prince knew how to maintain authority over them.

From these causes it arose that Marcus, Pertinax, and Alexander, being all men of modest life, lovers of justice, enemies to cruelty, humane, and benignant, came to a sad end except Marcus; he alone lived and died honoured, because he had succeeded to the throne by hereditary title, and owed nothing either to the soldiers or the people; and afterwards, being possessed of many virtues which made him respected, he always kept both orders in their places whilst he lived, and was neither hated nor despised.

But Pertinax was created emperor against the wishes of the soldiers, who, being accustomed to live licentiously under Commodus, could not endure the honest life to which Pertinax wished to reduce them; thus, having given cause for hatred, to which hatred there was added contempt for his old age, he was overthrown at the very beginning of his administration. And here it should be noted that hatred is acquired as much by good works as by bad ones, therefore, as I said before, a prince wishing to keep his state is very often forced to do evil; for when that body is corrupt whom you think you have need of to maintain yourself—it may be either the people or the soldiers or the nobles—you have to submit to its humours and to gratify them, and then good works will do you harm.

But let us come to Alexander, who was a man of such great goodness, that among the other praises which are accorded him is this, that in the fourteen years he held the empire no one was ever put to death by him unjudged; nevertheless, being considered effeminate and a man who allowed himself to be governed by his mother, he became despised, the army conspired against him, and murdered him.

Turning now to the opposite characters of Commodus, Severus, Antoninus Caracalla, and Maximinus, you will find them all cruel and rapacious-men who, to satisfy their soldiers, did not hesitate to commit every kind of iniquity against the people; and all, except Severus, came to a bad end; but in Severus there was so much valour that, keeping the soldiers friendly, although the people were oppressed by him, he reigned successfully; for his valour made him so much admired in the sight of the soldiers and people that the latter were kept in a way astonished and awed and the former respectful and satisfied. And because the actions of this man, as a new prince, were great, I wish to show briefly that he knew well how to counterfeit the fox and the lion, which natures, as I said above, it is necessary for a prince to imitate.

Knowing the sloth of the Emperor Julian, he persuaded the army in Sclavonia, of which he was captain, that it would be right to go to Rome and avenge the death of Pertinax, who had been killed by the praetorian soldiers; and under this pretext, without appearing to aspire to the throne, he moved the army on Rome, and reached Italy before it was known that he had started. On his arrival at Rome, the Senate, through fear, elected him emperor and killed Julian. After this there remained for Severus, who wished to make himself master of the whole empire, two difficulties; one in Asia, where Niger, head of the Asiatic army, had caused himself to be proclaimed emperor; the other in the west where Albinus was, who also aspired to the throne. And as he considered it dangerous to declare himself hostile to both, he decided to attack Niger and to deceive Albinus. To the latter he wrote that, being elected emperor by the Senate, he was willing to share that dignity with him and sent him the title of Caesar; and, moreover, that the Senate had made Albinus his colleague; which things were accepted by Albinus as true. But after Severus had conquered and killed Niger, and settled oriental affairs, he returned to Rome and complained to the Senate that Albinus, little recognizing the benefits that he had received from him, had by treachery sought to murder him, and for this ingratitude he was compelled to punish him. Afterwards he sought him out in France, and took from him his government and life. He who will, therefore, carefully examine the actions of this man will find him a most valiant lion and a most cunning fox; he will find him feared and respected by every one, and not hated by the army; and it need not be wondered at that he, a new man, was able to hold the empire so well, because his supreme renown always protected him from that hatred which the people might have conceived against him for his violence.

But his son Antoninus was a most eminent man, and had very excellent qualities, which made him admirable in the sight of the people and acceptable to the soldiers, for he was a warlike man, most enduring of fatigue, a despiser of all delicate food and other luxuries, which caused him to be beloved by the armies. Nevertheless, his ferocity and cruelties were so great and so unheard of that, after endless single murders, he killed a large number of the people of Rome and all those of Alexandria. He became hated by the whole world, and also feared by those he had around him, to such an extent that he was murdered in the midst of his army by a centurion. And here it must be noted that such-like deaths, which are deliberately inflicted with a resolved and desperate courage, cannot be avoided by princes, because any one who does not fear to die can inflict them; but a prince may fear them the less because they are very rare; he has only to be careful not to do any grave injury to those whom he employs or has around him in the service of the state. Antoninus had not taken this care, but had contumeliously killed a brother of that centurion, whom also he daily threatened, yet retained in his bodyguard; which, as it turned out, was a rash thing to do, and proved the emperor's ruin.

But let us come to Commodus, to whom it should have been very easy to hold the empire, for, being the son of Marcus, he had inherited it, and he had only to follow in the footsteps of his father to please his people and soldiers; but, being by nature cruel and brutal, he gave himself up to amusing the soldiers and corrupting them, so that he might indulge his rapacity upon the people; on the other hand, not maintaining his dignity, often descending to the theatre to compete with gladiators, and doing other vile things, little worthy of the imperial majesty, he fell into contempt with the soldiers, and being hated by one party and despised by the other, he was conspired against and was killed.

It remains to discuss the character of Maximinus. He was a very warlike man, and the armies, being disgusted with the effeminacy of Alexander, of whom I have already spoken, killed him and elected Maximinus to the throne. This he did not possess for long, for two things made him hated and despised; the one, his having kept sheep in Thrace, which brought him into contempt (it being well known to all, and considered a great indignity by every one), and the other, his having at the accession to his dominions deferred going to Rome and taking possession of the imperial seat; he had also gained a reputation for the utmost ferocity by having, through his prefects in Rome and elsewhere in the empire, practised many cruelties, so that the whole world was moved to anger at the meanness of his birth and to fear at his barbarity. First Africa rebelled, then the Senate with all the people of Rome, and all Italy conspired against him, to which may be added his own army; this latter, besieging Aquileia and meeting with difficulties in taking it, were disgusted with his cruelties, and fearing him less when they found so many against him, murdered him.

I do not wish to discuss Heliogabalus, Macrinus, or Julian, who, being thoroughly contemptible, were quickly wiped out; but I will bring this discourse to a conclusion by saying that princes in our times have this difficulty of giving inordinate satisfaction to their soldiers in a far less degree, because, notwithstanding one has to give them some indulgence, that is soon done; none of these princes have armies that are veterans in the governance and administration of provinces, as were the armies of the Roman Empire; and whereas it was then more necessary to give satisfaction to the soldiers than to the people, it is now more necessary to all princes, except the Turk and the Soldan, to satisfy the people rather the soldiers, because the people are the more powerful.

From the above I have excepted the Turk, who always keeps round him twelve thousand infantry and fifteen thousand cavalry on which depend the security and strength of the kingdom, and it is necessary that, putting aside every consideration for the people, he should keep them his friends. The kingdom of the Soldan is similar; being entirely in the hands of soldiers, it follows again that, without regard to the people, he must keep them his friends. But you must note that the state of the Soldan is unlike all other principalities, for the reason that it is like the Christian pontificate, which cannot be called either an hereditary or a newly formed principality; because the sons of the old prince are not the heirs, but he who is elected to that position by those who have authority, and the sons remain only noblemen. And this being an ancient custom, it cannot be called a new principality, because there are none of those difficulties in it that are met with in new ones; for although the prince is new, the constitution of the state is old, and it is framed so as to receive him as if he were its hereditary lord.

But returning to the subject of our discourse, I say that whoever will consider it will acknowledge that either hatred or contempt has been fatal to the above-named emperors, and it will be recognized also how it happened that, a number of them acting in one way and a number in another, only one in each way came to a happy end and the rest to unhappy ones. Because it would have been useless and dangerous for Pertinax and Alexander, being new princes, to imitate Marcus, who was heir to the principality; and likewise it would have been utterly destructive to Caracalla, Commodus, and Maximinus to have imitated Severus, they not having sufficient valour to enable them to tread in his footsteps. Therefore a prince, new to the principality, cannot imitate the actions of Marcus, nor, again, is it necessary to follow those of Severus, but he ought to take from Severus those parts which are necessary to found his state, and from Marcus those which are proper and glorious to keep a state that may already be stable and firm.

## CHAPTER XX — ARE FORTRESSES, AND MANY OTHER THINGS TO WHICH PRINCES OFTEN RESORT, ADVANTAGEOUS OR HURTFUL?

1. Some princes, so as to hold securely the state, have disarmed their subjects; others have kept their subject towns distracted by factions; others have fostered enmities against themselves; others have laid themselves out to gain over those whom they distrusted in the beginning of their governments; some have built fortresses; some have overthrown and destroyed them. And although one cannot give a final judgment on all of these things unless one possesses the particulars of those states in which a decision has to be made, nevertheless I will speak as comprehensively as the matter of itself will admit.

2. There never was a new prince who has disarmed his subjects; rather when he has found them disarmed he has always armed them, because, by arming them, those arms become yours, those men who were distrusted become faithful, and those who were faithful are kept so, and your subjects become your adherents. And whereas all subjects cannot be armed, yet when those whom you do arm are benefited, the others can be handled more freely, and this difference in their treatment, which they quite understand, makes the former your dependents, and the latter, considering it to be necessary that those who have the most danger and service should have the most reward, excuse you. But when you disarm them, you at once offend them by showing that you distrust them, either for cowardice or for want of loyalty, and either of these opinions breeds hatred against you. And because you cannot remain unarmed, it follows that you turn to mercenaries, which are of the character already shown; even if they should be good they would not be sufficient to defend you against powerful enemies and distrusted subjects. Therefore, as I have said, a new prince in a new principality has always distributed arms. Histories are full of examples. But when a prince acquires a new state, which he adds as a province to his old one, then it is necessary to disarm the men of that state, except those who have been his adherents in acquiring it; and these again, with time and opportunity, should be rendered soft and effeminate; and matters should be managed in such a way that all the armed men in the state shall be your own soldiers who in your old state were living near you.

3. Our forefathers, and those who were reckoned wise, were accustomed to say that it was necessary to hold Pistoia by factions and Pisa by fortresses; and with this idea they fostered quarrels in some of their tributary towns so as to keep possession of them the more easily. This may have been well enough in those times when Italy was in a way balanced, but I do not believe that it can be accepted as a precept for to-day, because I do not believe that factions can ever be of use; rather it is certain that when the enemy comes upon you in divided cities you are quickly lost, because the weakest party will always assist the outside forces and the other will not be able to resist. The Venetians, moved, as I believe, by the above reasons, fostered the Guelph and Ghibelline factions in their tributary cities; and although they never allowed them to come to bloodshed, yet they nursed these disputes amongst them, so that the citizens, distracted by their differences, should not unite against them. Which, as we saw, did not afterwards turn out as expected, because, after the rout at Vaila, one party at once took courage and seized the state. Such methods argue, therefore, weakness in the prince, because these factions will never be permitted in a vigorous principality; such methods for enabling one the more easily to manage subjects are only useful in times of peace, but if war comes this policy proves fallacious.

4. Without doubt princes become great when they overcome the difficulties and obstacles by which they are confronted, and therefore fortune, especially when she desires to make a new prince great, who has a greater necessity to earn renown than an hereditary one, causes enemies to arise and form designs against him, in order that he may have the opportunity of overcoming them, and by them to mount higher, as by a ladder which his enemies have raised. For this reason many consider that a wise prince, when he has the opportunity, ought with craft to foster some animosity against himself, so that, having crushed it, his renown may rise higher.

5. Princes, especially new ones, have found more fidelity and assistance in those men who in the beginning of their rule were distrusted than among those who in the beginning were trusted. Pandolfo Petrucci, Prince of Siena, ruled his state more by those who had been distrusted than by others. But on this question one cannot speak generally, for it varies so much with the individual; I will only say this, that those men who at the commencement of a princedom have been hostile, if they are of a description to need assistance to support themselves, can always be gained over with the greatest ease, and they will be tightly held to serve the prince with fidelity, inasmuch as they know it to be very necessary for them to cancel by deeds the bad impression which he had formed of them; and thus the prince always extracts more profit from them than from those who, serv-

ing him in too much security, may neglect his affairs. And since the matter demands it, I must not fail to warn a prince, who by means of secret favours has acquired a new state, that he must well consider the reasons which induced those to favour him who did so; and if it be not a natural affection towards him, but only discontent with their government, then he will only keep them friendly with great trouble and difficulty, for it will be impossible to satisfy them. And weighing well the reasons for this in those examples which can be taken from ancient and modern affairs, we shall find that it is easier for the prince to make friends of those men who were contented under the former government, and are therefore his enemies, than of those who, being discontented with it, were favourable to him and encouraged him to seize it.

6. It has been a custom with princes, in order to hold their states more securely, to build fortresses that may serve as a bridle and bit to those who might design to work against them, and as a place of refuge from a first attack. I praise this system because it has been made use of formerly. Notwithstanding that, Messer Nicolo Vitelli in our times has been seen to demolish two fortresses in Citta di Castello so that he might keep that state; Guido Ubaldo, Duke of Urbino, on returning to his dominion, whence he had been driven by Cesare Borgia, razed to the foundations all the fortresses in that province, and considered that without them it would be more difficult to lose it; the Bentivogli returning to Bologna came to a similar decision. Fortresses, therefore, are useful or not according to circumstances; if they do you good in one way they injure you in another. And this question can be reasoned thus: the prince who has more to fear from the people than from foreigners ought to build fortresses, but he who has more to fear from foreigners than from the people ought to leave them alone. The castle of Milan, built by Francesco Sforza, has made, and will make, more trouble for the house of Sforza than any other disorder in the state. For this reason the best possible fortress is—not to be hated by the people, because, although you may hold the fortresses, yet they will not save you if the people hate you, for there will never be wanting foreigners to assist a people who have taken arms against you. It has not been seen in our times that such fortresses have been of use to any prince, unless to the Countess of Forli, when the Count Girolamo, her consort, was killed; for by that means she was able to withstand the popular attack and wait for assistance from Milan, and thus recover her state; and the posture of affairs was such at that time that the foreigners could not assist the people. But fortresses were of little value to her afterwards when Cesare Borgia attacked her, and when the people, her enemy, were allied with foreigners. Therefore, it would have been safer for her, both then and before, not to have been hated by the people than to have had the fortresses. All these things considered then, I shall praise him who builds fortresses as well as him who does not, and I shall blame whoever, trusting in them, cares little about being hated by the people.

## CHAPTER XXI — HOW A PRINCE SHOULD CONDUCT HIMSELF SO AS TO GAIN RENOWN

Nothing makes a prince so much esteemed as great enterprises and setting a fine example. We have in our time Ferdinand of Aragon, the present King of Spain. He can almost be called a new prince, because he has risen, by fame and glory, from being an insignificant king to be the foremost king in Christendom; and if you will consider his deeds you will find them all great and some of them extraordinary. In the beginning of his reign he attacked Granada, and this enterprise was the foundation of his dominions. He did this quietly at first and without any fear of hindrance, for he held the minds of the barons of Castile occupied in thinking of the war and not anticipating any innovations; thus they did not perceive that by these means he was acquiring power and authority over them. He was able with the money of the Church and of the people to sustain his armies, and by that long war to lay the foundation for the military skill which has since distinguished him. Further, always using religion as a plea, so as to undertake greater schemes, he devoted himself with pious cruelty to driving out and clearing his kingdom of the Moors; nor could there be a more admirable example, nor one more rare. Under this same cloak he assailed Africa, he came down on Italy, he has finally attacked France; and thus his achievements and designs have always been great, and have kept the minds of his people in suspense and admiration and occupied with the issue of them. And his actions have arisen in such a way, one out of the other, that men have never been given time to work steadily against him.

Again, it much assists a prince to set unusual examples in internal affairs, similar to those which are related of Messer Bernabo da Milano, who, when he had the opportunity, by any one in civil life doing some extraordinary thing, either good or bad, would take some method of rewarding or punishing him, which would be much spoken about. And a prince ought, above all things, always endeavour in every action to gain for himself the reputation of being a great and remarkable man.

A prince is also respected when he is either a true friend or a downright enemy, that is to say, when, without any reservation, he declares himself in favour of one party against the other; which course will always be more advantageous than standing neutral; because if two of your powerful neighbours come to blows, they are of such a character that, if one of them conquers, you have either to fear him or not. In either case it will always be more advantageous for you to declare yourself and to make war strenuously; because, in the first case, if you do not declare yourself, you will invariably fall a prey to the conqueror, to the pleasure and satisfaction of him who has been conquered, and you will have no reasons to offer, nor anything to protect or to shelter you. Because he who conquers does not want doubtful friends who will not aid him in the time of trial; and he who loses will not harbour you because you did not willingly, sword in hand, court his fate.

Antiochus went into Greece, being sent for by the Aetolians to drive out the Romans. He sent envoys to the Achaeans, who were friends of the Romans, exhorting them to remain neutral; and on the other hand the Romans urged them to take up arms. This question came to be discussed in the council of the Achaeans, where the legate of Antiochus urged them to stand neutral. To this the Roman legate answered: "As for that which has been said, that it is better and more advantageous for your state not to interfere in our war, nothing can be more erroneous; because by not interfering you will be left, without favour or consideration, the guerdon of the conqueror." Thus it will always happen that he who is not your friend will demand your neutrality, whilst he who is your friend will entreat you to declare yourself with arms. And irresolute princes, to avoid present dangers, generally follow the neutral path, and are generally ruined. But when a prince declares himself gallantly in favour of one side, if the party with whom he allies himself conquers, although the victor may be powerful and may have him at his mercy, yet he is indebted to him, and there is established a bond of amity; and men are never so shameless as to become a monument of ingratitude by oppressing you. Victories after all are never so complete that the victor must not show some regard, especially to justice. But if he with whom you ally yourself loses, you may be sheltered by him, and whilst he is able he may aid you, and you become companions on a fortune that may rise again.

In the second case, when those who fight are of such a character that you have no anxiety as to who may conquer, so much the more is it greater prudence to be allied, because you assist at the destruction of one by the aid of another who, if he had been wise, would have saved him; and conquering, as it is impossible that he should not do with your assistance, he remains at your discretion. And here it is to be noted that a prince ought to take care never to make an alliance with one more powerful than himself for the purposes of attacking others, unless necessity compels him, as is said above; because if he conquers you are at his discretion, and princes ought to avoid as much as possible being at the discretion of any one. The Venetians joined with France against the Duke of Milan, and this alliance, which caused their ruin, could have been avoided. But when it cannot be avoided, as happened to the Florentines when the Pope and Spain sent armies to attack Lombardy, then in such a case, for the above reasons, the prince ought to favour one of the parties.

Never let any Government imagine that it can choose perfectly safe courses; rather let it expect to have to take very doubtful ones, because it is found in ordinary affairs that one never seeks to avoid one trouble without running into another; but prudence consists in knowing how to distinguish the character of troubles, and for choice to take the lesser evil.

A prince ought also to show himself a patron of ability, and to honour the proficient in every art. At the same time he should encourage his citizens to practise their callings peaceably, both in commerce and agriculture, and in every other following, so that the one should not be deterred from improving his possessions for fear lest they be taken away from him or another from opening up trade for fear of taxes; but the prince ought to offer rewards to whoever wishes to do these things and designs in any way to honour his city or state.

Further, he ought to entertain the people with festivals and spectacles at convenient seasons of the year; and as every city is divided into guilds or into societies, he ought to hold such bodies in esteem, and associate with them sometimes, and show himself an example of courtesy and liberality; nevertheless, always maintaining the majesty of his rank, for this he must never consent to abate in anything.

## CHAPTER XXII — CONCERNING THE SECRETARIES OF PRINCES

The choice of servants is of no little importance to a prince, and they are good or not according to the discrimination of the prince. And the first opinion which one forms of a prince, and of his understanding, is by observing the men he has around him; and when they are capable and faithful he may always be considered wise, because he has known how to recognize the capable and to keep them faithful. But when they are otherwise one cannot form a good opinion of him, for the prime error which he made was in choosing them.

There were none who knew Messer Antonio da Venafro as the servant of Pandolfo Petrucci, Prince of Siena, who would not consider Pandolfo to be a very clever man in having Venafro for his servant. Because there are three classes of intellects: one which comprehends by itself; another which appreciates what others comprehended; and a third which neither comprehends by itself nor by the showing of others; the first is the most excellent, the second is good, the third is useless. Therefore, it follows necessarily that, if Pandolfo was not in the first rank, he was in the second, for whenever one has judgment to know good and bad when it is said and done, although he himself may not have the initiative, yet he can recognize the good and the bad in his servant, and the one he can praise and the other correct; thus the servant cannot hope to deceive him, and is kept honest.

But to enable a prince to form an opinion of his servant there is one test which never fails; when you see the servant thinking more of his own interests than of yours, and seeking inwardly his own profit in everything, such a man will never make a good servant, nor will you ever be able to trust him; because he who has the state of another in his hands ought never to think of himself, but always of his prince, and never pay any attention to matters in which the prince is not concerned.

On the other hand, to keep his servant honest the prince ought to study him, honouring him, enriching him, doing him kindnesses, sharing with him the honours and cares; and at the same time let him see that he cannot stand alone, so that many honours may not make him desire more, many riches make him wish for more, and that many cares may make him dread chances. When, therefore, servants, and princes towards servants, are thus disposed, they can trust each other, but when it is otherwise, the end will always be disastrous for either one or the other.

## CHAPTER XXIII — HOW FLATTERERS SHOULD BE AVOIDED

I do not wish to leave out an important branch of this subject, for it is a danger from which princes are with difficulty preserved, unless they are very careful and discriminating. It is that of flatterers, of whom courts are full, because men are so self-complacent in their own affairs, and in a way so deceived in them, that they are preserved with difficulty from this pest, and if they wish to defend themselves they run the danger of falling into contempt. Because there is no other way of guarding oneself from flatterers except letting men understand that to tell you the truth does not offend you; but when every one may tell you the truth, respect for you abates.

Therefore a wise prince ought to hold a third course by choosing the wise men in his state, and giving to them only the liberty of speaking the truth to him, and then only of those things of which he inquires, and of none others; but he ought to question them upon everything, and listen to their opinions, and afterwards form his own conclusions. With these councillors, separately and collectively, he ought to carry himself in such a way that each of them should know that, the more freely he shall speak, the more he shall be preferred; outside of these, he should listen to no one, pursue the thing resolved on, and be steadfast in his resolutions. He who does otherwise is either overthrown by flatterers, or is so often changed by varying opinions that he falls into contempt.

I wish on this subject to adduce a modern example. Fra Luca, the man of affairs to Maximilian, the present emperor, speaking of his majesty, said: He consulted with no one, yet never got his own way in anything. This arose because of his following a practice the opposite to the above; for the emperor is a secretive man—he does not communicate his designs to any one, nor does he receive opinions on them. But as in carrying them into effect they become revealed and known, they are at once obstructed by those men whom he has around him, and he, being pliant, is diverted from them. Hence it follows that those things he does one day he undoes the next, and no one ever understands what he wishes or intends to do, and no one can rely on his resolutions.

A prince, therefore, ought always to take counsel, but only when he wishes and not when others wish; he ought rather to discourage every one from offering advice unless he asks it; but, however, he ought to be a constant inquirer, and afterwards a patient listener concerning the things of which he inquired; also, on learning that any one, on any consideration, has not told him the truth, he should let his anger be felt.

And if there are some who think that a prince who conveys an impression of his wisdom is not so through his own ability, but through the good advisers that he has around him, beyond doubt they are deceived, because this is an axiom which never fails: that a prince who is not wise himself will never take good advice, unless by chance he has yielded his affairs entirely to one person who happens to be a very prudent man. In this case indeed he may be well governed, but it would not be for long, because such a governor would in a short time take away his state from him.

But if a prince who is not inexperienced should take counsel from more than one he will never get united counsels, nor will he know how to unite them. Each of the counsellors will think of his own interests, and the prince will not know how to control them or to see through them. And they are not to be found otherwise, because men will always prove untrue to you unless they are kept honest by constraint. Therefore it must be inferred that good counsels, whencesoever they come, are born of the wisdom of the prince, and not the wisdom of the prince from good counsels.

## CHAPTER XXIV — WHY THE PRINCES OF ITALY HAVE LOST THEIR STATES

The previous suggestions, carefully observed, will enable a new prince to appear well established, and render him at once more secure and fixed in the state than if he had been long seated there. For the actions of a new prince are more narrowly observed than those of an hereditary one, and when they are seen to be able they gain more men and bind far tighter than ancient blood; because men are attracted more by the present than by the past, and when they find the present good they enjoy it and seek no further; they will also make the utmost defence of a prince if he fails them not in other things. Thus it will be a double glory for him to have established a new principality, and adorned and strengthened it with good laws, good arms, good allies, and with a good example; so will it be a double disgrace to him who, born a prince, shall lose his state by want of wisdom.

And if those seigniors are considered who have lost their states in Italy in our times, such as the King of Naples, the Duke of Milan, and others, there will be found in them, firstly, one common defect in regard to arms from the causes which have been discussed at length; in the next place, some one of them will be seen, either to have had the people hostile, or if he has had the people friendly, he has not known how to secure the nobles. In the absence of these defects states that have power enough to keep an army in the field cannot be lost.

Philip of Macedon, not the father of Alexander the Great, but he who was conquered by Titus Quintius, had not much territory compared to the greatness of the Romans and of Greece who attacked him, yet being a warlike man who knew how to attract the people and secure the nobles, he sustained the war against his enemies for many years, and if in the end he lost the dominion of some cities, nevertheless he retained the kingdom.

Therefore, do not let our princes accuse fortune for the loss of their principalities after so many years' possession, but rather their own sloth, because in quiet times they never thought there could be a change (it is a common defect in man not to make any provision in the calm against the tempest), and when afterwards the bad times came they thought of flight and not of defending themselves, and they hoped that the people, disgusted with the insolence of the conquerors, would recall them. This course, when others fail, may be good, but it is very bad to have neglected all other expedients for that, since you would never wish to fall because you trusted to be able to find someone later on to restore you. This again either does not happen, or, if it does, it will not be for your security, because that deliverance is of no avail which does not depend upon yourself; those only are reliable, certain, and durable that depend on yourself and your valour.

## CHAPTER XXV — WHAT FORTUNE CAN EFFECT IN HUMAN AFFAIRS AND HOW TO WITHSTAND HER

It is not unknown to me how many men have had, and still have, the opinion that the affairs of the world are in such wise governed by fortune and by God that men with their wisdom cannot direct them and that no one can even help them; and because of this they would have us believe that it is not necessary to labour much in affairs, but to let chance govern them. This opinion has been more credited in our times because of the great changes in affairs which have been seen, and may still be seen, every day, beyond all human conjecture. Sometimes pondering over this, I am in some degree inclined to their opinion. Nevertheless, not to extinguish our free will, I hold it to be true that Fortune is the arbiter of one-half of our actions,(*) but that she still leaves us to direct the other half, or perhaps a little less.

I compare her to one of those raging rivers, which when in flood overflows the plains, sweeping away trees and buildings, bearing away the soil from place to place; everything flies before it, all yield to its violence, without being able in any way to withstand it; and yet, though its nature be such, it does not follow therefore that men, when the weather becomes fair, shall not make provision, both with defences and barriers, in such a manner that, rising again, the waters may pass away by canal, and their force be neither so unrestrained nor so dangerous. So it happens with fortune, who shows her power where valour has not prepared to resist her, and thither she turns her forces where she knows that barriers and defences have not been raised to constrain her.

And if you will consider Italy, which is the seat of these changes, and which has given to them their impulse, you will see it to be an open country without barriers and without any defence. For if it had been defended by proper valour, as are Germany, Spain, and France, either this invasion would not have made the great changes it has made or it would not have come at all. And this I consider enough to say concerning resistance to fortune in general.

But confining myself more to the particular, I say that a prince may be seen happy to-day and ruined to-morrow without having shown any change of disposition or character. This, I believe, arises firstly from causes that have already been discussed at length, namely, that the prince who relies entirely on fortune is lost when it changes. I believe also that he will be successful who directs his actions according to the spirit of the times, and that he whose actions do not accord with the times will not be successful. Because men are seen, in affairs that lead to the end which every man has before him, namely, glory and riches, to get there by various methods; one with caution, another with haste; one by force, another by skill; one by patience, another by its opposite; and each one succeeds in reaching the goal by a different method. One can also see of two cautious men the one attain his end, the other fail; and similarly, two men by different observances are equally successful, the one being cautious, the other impetuous; all this arises from nothing else than whether or not they conform in their methods to the spirit of the times. This follows from what I have said, that two men working differently bring about the same effect, and of two working similarly, one attains his object and the other does not.

Changes in estate also issue from this, for if, to one who governs himself with caution and patience, times and affairs converge in such a way that his administration is successful, his fortune is made; but if times and affairs change, he is ruined if he does not change his course of action. But a man is not often found sufficiently circumspect to know how to accommodate himself to the change, both because he cannot deviate from what nature inclines him to do, and also because, having always prospered by acting in one way, he cannot be persuaded that it is well to leave it; and, therefore, the cautious man, when it is time to turn adventurous, does not know how to do it, hence he is ruined; but had he changed his conduct with the times fortune would not have changed.

Pope Julius the Second went to work impetuously in all his affairs, and found the times and circumstances conform so well to that line of action that he always met with success. Consider his first enterprise against Bologna, Messer Giovanni Bentivogli being still alive. The Venetians were not agreeable to it, nor was the King of Spain, and he had the enterprise still under discussion with the King of France; nevertheless he personally entered upon the expedition with his accustomed boldness and energy, a move which made Spain and the Venetians stand irresolute and passive, the latter from fear, the former from desire to recover the kingdom of Naples; on the other hand, he drew after him the King of France, because that king, having observed the movement, and desiring to make the Pope his friend so as to humble the Venetians, found it impossible to refuse him. Therefore Julius with his impetuous action accomplished what no other pontiff with simple human wisdom could have done; for if he had waited in Rome until he could get away, with his plans arranged and everything fixed, as any other pontiff would have done, he would never have succeeded. Because the King of France would have made a thousand excuses, and the others would have raised a thousand fears.

I will leave his other actions alone, as they were all alike, and they all succeeded, for the shortness of his life did not let him experience the contrary; but if circumstances had arisen which required him to go cautiously, his ruin would have followed, because he would never have deviated from those ways to which nature inclined him.

I conclude, therefore that, fortune being changeful and mankind steadfast in their ways, so long as the two are in agreement men are successful, but unsuccessful when they fall out. For my part I consider that it is better to be adventurous than cautious, because fortune is a woman, and if you wish to keep her under it is necessary to beat and ill-use her; and it is seen that she allows herself to be mastered by the adventurous rather than by those who go to work more coldly. She is, therefore, always, woman-like, a lover of young men, because they are less cautious, more violent, and with more audacity command her.

## CHAPTER XXVI — AN EXHORTATION TO LIBERATE ITALY FROM THE BARBARIANS

Having carefully considered the subject of the above discourses, and wondering within myself whether the present times were propitious to a new prince, and whether there were elements that would give an opportunity to a wise and virtuous one to introduce a new order of things which would do honour to him and good to the people of this country, it appears to me that so many things concur to favour a new prince that I never knew a time more fit than the present.

And if, as I said, it was necessary that the people of Israel should be captive so as to make manifest the ability of Moses; that the Persians should be oppressed by the Medes so as to discover the greatness of the soul of Cyrus; and that the Athenians should be dispersed to illustrate the capabilities of Theseus: then at the present time, in order to discover the virtue of an Italian spirit, it was necessary that Italy should be reduced to the extremity that she is now in, that she should be more enslaved than the Hebrews, more oppressed than the Persians, more scattered than the Athenians; without head, without order, beaten, despoiled, torn, overrun; and to have endured every kind of desolation.

Although lately some spark may have been shown by one, which made us think he was ordained by God for our redemption, nevertheless it was afterwards seen, in the height of his career, that fortune rejected him; so that Italy, left as without life, waits for him who shall yet heal her wounds and put an end to the ravaging and plundering of Lombardy, to the swindling and taxing of the kingdom and of Tuscany, and cleanse those sores that for long have festered. It is seen how she entreats God to send someone who shall deliver her from these wrongs and barbarous insolencies. It is seen also that she is ready and willing to follow a banner if only someone will raise it.

Nor is there to be seen at present one in whom she can place more hope than in your illustrious house,(*) with its valour and fortune, favoured by God and by the Church of which it is now the chief, and which could be made the head of this redemption. This will not be difficult if you will recall to yourself the actions and lives of the men I have named. And although they were great and wonderful men, yet they were men, and each one of them had no more opportunity than the present offers, for their enterprises were neither more just nor easier than this, nor was God more their friend than He is yours.

With us there is great justice, because that war is just which is necessary, and arms are hallowed when there is no other hope but in them. Here there is the greatest willingness, and where the willingness is great the difficulties cannot be great if you will only follow those men to whom I have directed your attention. Further than this, how extraordinarily the ways of God have been manifested beyond example: the sea is divided, a cloud has led the way, the rock has poured forth water, it has rained manna, everything has contributed to your greatness; you ought to do the rest. God is not willing to do everything, and thus take away our free will and that share of glory which belongs to us.

And it is not to be wondered at if none of the above-named Italians have been able to accomplish all that is expected from your illustrious house; and if in so many revolutions in Italy, and in so many campaigns, it has always appeared as if military virtue were exhausted, this has happened because the old order of things was not good, and none of us have known how to find a new one. And nothing honours a man more than to establish new laws and new ordinances when he himself was newly risen. Such things when they are well founded and dignified will make him revered and admired, and in Italy there are not wanting opportunities to bring such into use in every form.

Here there is great valour in the limbs whilst it fails in the head. Look attentively at the duels and the hand-to-hand combats, how superior the Italians are in strength, dexterity, and subtlety. But when it comes to armies they do not bear comparison, and this springs entirely from the insufficiency of the leaders, since those who are capable are not obedient, and each one seems to himself to know, there having never been any one so distinguished above the rest, either by valour or fortune, that others would yield to him. Hence it is that for so long a time, and during so much fighting in the past twenty years, whenever there has been an army wholly Italian, it has always given a poor account of itself; the first witness to this is Il Taro, afterwards Allesandria, Capua, Genoa, Vaila, Bologna, Mestri.

If, therefore, your illustrious house wishes to follow these remarkable men who have redeemed their country, it is necessary before all things, as a true foundation for every enterprise, to be provided with your own forces, because there can be no more faithful, truer, or better soldiers. And although singly they are good, altogether they will be much better when they find themselves commanded by their prince, honoured by him, and maintained at his expense. Therefore it is necessary to be prepared with such arms, so that you can be defended against foreigners by Italian valour.

And although Swiss and Spanish infantry may be considered very formidable, nevertheless there is a defect in both, by reason of which a third order would not only be able to oppose them, but might be relied upon to overthrow them. For the Spaniards cannot resist cavalry, and the Switzers are afraid of infantry whenever they encounter them in close combat. Owing to this, as has been and may again be seen, the Spaniards are unable to resist French cavalry, and the Switzers are overthrown by Spanish infantry. And although a complete proof of this latter cannot be shown, nevertheless there was some evidence of it at the battle of Ravenna, when the Spanish infantry were confronted by German battalions, who follow the same tactics as the Swiss; when the Spaniards, by agility of body and with the aid of their shields, got in under the pikes of the Germans and stood out of danger, able to attack, while the Germans stood helpless, and, if the cavalry had not dashed up, all would have been over with them. It is possible, therefore, knowing the defects of both these infantries, to invent a new one, which will resist cavalry and not be afraid of infantry; this need not create a new order of arms, but a variation upon the old. And these are the kind of improvements which confer reputation and power upon a new prince.

This opportunity, therefore, ought not to be allowed to pass for letting Italy at last see her liberator appear. Nor can one express the love with which he would be received in all those provinces which have suffered so much from these foreign scourings, with what thirst for revenge, with what stubborn faith, with what devotion, with what tears. What door would be closed to him? Who would refuse obedience to him? What envy would hinder him? What Italian would refuse him homage? To all of us this barbarous dominion stinks. Let, therefore, your illustrious house take up this charge with that courage and hope with which all just enterprises are undertaken, so that under its standard our native country may be ennobled, and under its auspices may be verified that saying of Petrarch:

*Virtu contro al Furore*

*Prendera l'arme, e fia il combatter corto:*
*Che l'antico valore*
*Negli italici cuor non e ancor morto.*

**The Leviathan from 1651**

by Thomas Hobbes

## INTRODUCTION

NATURE (the art whereby God hath made and governs the world) is by the art of man, as in many other things, so in this also imitated, that it can make an artificial animal. For seeing life is but a motion of limbs, the beginning whereof is in some principal part within, why may we not say that all automata (engines that move themselves by springs and wheels as doth a watch) have an artificial life? For what is the heart, but a spring; and the nerves, but so many strings; and the joints, but so many wheels, giving motion to the whole body, such as was intended by the Artificer? Art goes yet further, imitating that rational and most excellent work of Nature, man. For by art is created that great LEVIATHAN called a COMMONWEALTH, or STATE (in Latin, CIVITAS), which is but an artificial man, though of greater stature and strength than the natural, for whose protection and defence it was intended; and in which the sovereignty is an artificial soul, as giving life and motion to the whole body; the magistrates and other officers of judicature and execution, artificial joints; reward and punishment (by which fastened to the seat of the sovereignty, every joint and member is moved to perform his duty) are the nerves, that do the same in the body natural; the wealth and riches of all the particular members are the strength; salus populi (the people's safety) its business; counsellors, by whom all things needful for it to know are suggested unto it, are the memory; equity and laws, an artificial reason and will; concord, health; sedition, sickness; and civil war, death. Lastly, the pacts and covenants, by which the parts of this body politic were at first made, set together, and united, resemble that fiat, or the Let us make man, pronounced by God in the Creation. To describe the nature of this artificial man, I will consider * First, the matter thereof, and the artificer; both which is man. * Secondly, how, and by what covenants it is made; what are the rights and just power or authority of a sovereign; and what it is that preserveth and dissolveth it. * Thirdly, what is a Christian Commonwealth. * Lastly, what is the Kingdom of Darkness. Concerning the first, there is a saying much usurped of late, that wisdom is acquired, not by reading of books, but of men. Consequently whereunto, those persons, that for the most part can give no other proof of being wise, take great delight to show what they think they have read in men, by uncharitable censures of one another behind their backs. But there is another saying not of late understood, by which they might learn truly to read one another, if they would take the pains; and that is, Nosce teipsum, Read thyself: which was not meant, as it is now used, to countenance either the barbarous state of men in power towards their inferiors, or to encourage men of low degree to a saucy behaviour towards their betters; but to teach us that for the similitude of the thoughts and passions of one man, to the thoughts and passions of another, whosoever looketh into himself and considereth what he doth when he does think, opine, reason, hope, fear, etc., and upon what grounds; he shall thereby read and know what are the thoughts and passions of all other men upon the like occasions. I say the similitude of passions, which are the same in all men,- desire, fear, hope, etc.; not the similitude of the objects of the passions, which are the things desired, feared, hoped, etc.: for these the constitution individual, and particular education, do so vary, and they are so easy to be kept from our knowledge, that the characters of man's heart, blotted and confounded as they are with dissembling, lying, counterfeiting, and erroneous doctrines, are legible only to him that searcheth hearts. And though by men's actions we do discover their design sometimes; yet to do it without comparing them with our own, and distinguishing all circumstances by which the case may come to be altered, is to decipher without a key, and be for the most part deceived, by too much trust or by too much diffidence, as he that reads is himself a good or evil man. But let one man read another by his actions never so perfectly, it serves him only with his acquaintance, which are but few. He that is to govern a whole nation must read in himself, not this, or that particular man; but mankind: which though it be hard to do, harder than to learn any language or science; yet, when I shall have set down my own reading orderly and perspicuously, the pains left another will be only to consider if he also find not the same in himself. For this kind of doctrine admitteth no other demonstration.

# THE FIRST PART OF MAN

## CHAPTER I, OF SENSE

CONCERNING the thoughts of man, I will consider them first singly, and afterwards in train or dependence upon one another. Singly, they are every one a representation or appearance of some quality, or other accident of a body without us, which is commonly called an object. Which object worketh on the eyes, ears, and other parts of man's body, and by diversity of working produceth diversity of appearances. The original of them all is that which we call sense, (for there is no conception in a man's mind which hath not at first, totally or by parts, been begotten upon the organs of sense). The rest are derived from that original. To know the natural cause of sense is not very necessary to the business now in hand; and I have elsewhere written of the same at large. Nevertheless, to fill each part of my present method, I will briefly deliver the same in this place. The cause of sense is the external body, or object, which presseth the organ proper to each sense, either immediately, as in the taste and touch; or mediately, as in seeing, hearing, and smelling: which pressure, by the mediation of nerves and other strings and membranes of the body, continued inwards to the brain and heart, causeth there a resistance, or counter-pressure, or endeavour of the heart to deliver itself: which endeavour, because outward, seemeth to be some matter without. And this seeming, or fancy, is that which men call sense; and consisteth, as to the eye, in a light, or colour figured; to the ear, in a sound; to the nostril, in an odour; to the tongue and palate, in a savour; and to the rest of the body, in heat, cold, hardness, softness, and such other qualities as we discern by feeling. All which qualities called sensible are in the object that causeth them but so many several motions of the matter, by which it presseth our organs diversely. Neither in us that are pressed are they anything else but diverse motions (for motion produceth nothing but motion). But their appearance to us is fancy, the same waking that dreaming. And as pressing, rubbing, or striking the eye makes us fancy a light, and pressing the ear produceth a din; so do the bodies also we see, or hear, produce the same by their strong, though unobserved action. For if those colours and sounds were in the bodies or objects that cause them, they could not be severed from them, as by glasses and in echoes by reflection we see they are: where we know the thing we see is in one place; the appearance, in another. And though at some certain distance the real and very object seem invested with the fancy it begets in us; yet still the object is one thing, the image or fancy is another. So that sense in all cases is nothing else but original fancy caused (as I have said) by the pressure that is, by the motion of external things upon our eyes, ears, and other organs, thereunto ordained. But the philosophy schools, through all the universities of Christendom, grounded upon certain texts of Aristotle, teach another doctrine; and say, for the cause of vision, that the thing seen sendeth forth on every side a visible species, (in English) a visible show, apparition, or aspect, or a being seen; the receiving whereof into the eye is seeing. And for the cause of hearing, that the thing heard sendeth forth an audible species, that is, an audible aspect, or audible being seen; which, entering at the ear, maketh hearing. Nay, for the cause of understanding also, they say the thing understood sendeth forth an intelligible species, that is, an intelligible being seen; which, coming into the understanding, makes us understand. I say not this, as disapproving the use of universities: but because I am to speak hereafter of their office in a Commonwealth, I must let you see on all occasions by the way what things would be amended in them; amongst which the frequency of insignificant speech is one.

## CHAPTER II, OF IMAGINATION

THAT when a thing lies still, unless somewhat else stir it, it will lie still for ever, is a truth that no man doubts of. But that when a thing is in motion, it will eternally be in motion, unless somewhat else stay it, though the reason be the same (namely, that nothing can change itself), is not so easily assented to. For men measure, not only other men, but all other things, by themselves: and because they find themselves subject after motion to pain and lassitude, think everything else grows weary of motion, and seeks repose of its own accord; little considering whether it be not some other motion wherein that desire of rest they find in themselves consisteth. From hence it is that the schools say, heavy bodies fall downwards out of an appetite to rest, and to conserve their nature in that place which is most proper for them; ascribing appetite, and knowledge of what is good for their conservation (which is more than man has), to things inanimate, absurdly. When a body is once in motion, it moveth (unless something else hinder it) eternally; and whatsoever hindreth it, cannot in an instant, but in time, and by degrees, quite extinguish it: and as we see in the water, though the wind cease, the waves give not over rolling for a long time after; so also it happeneth in that motion which is made in the internal parts of a man, then, when he sees, dreams, etc. For after the object is removed, or the eye shut, we still retain an image of the thing seen, though more obscure than when we see it. And this is it the Latins call imagination, from the image made in seeing, and apply the same, though improperly, to all the other senses. But the Greeks call it fancy, which signifies appearance, and is as proper to one sense as to another. Imagination, therefore, is nothing but decaying sense; and is found in men and many other living creatures, as well sleeping as waking. The decay of sense in men waking is not the decay of the motion made in sense, but an obscuring of it, in such manner as the light of the sun obscureth the light of the stars; which stars do no less exercise their virtue by which they are visible in the day than in the night. But because amongst many strokes which our eyes, ears, and other organs receive from external bodies, the predominant only is sensible; therefore the light of the sun being predominant, we are not affected with the action of the stars. And any object being removed from our eyes, though the impression it made in us remain, yet other objects more present succeeding, and working on us, the imagination of the past is obscured and made weak, as the voice of a man is in the noise of the day. From whence it followeth that the longer the time is, after the sight or sense of any object, the weaker is the imagination. For the continual change of man's body destroys in time the parts which in sense were moved: so that distance of time, and of place, hath one and the same effect in us. For as at a great distance of place that which we look at appears dim, and without distinction of the smaller parts, and as voices grow weak and inarticulate: so also after great distance of time our imagination of the past is weak; and we lose, for example, of cities we have seen, many particular streets; and of actions, many particular circumstances. This decaying sense, when we would express the thing itself (I mean fancy itself), we call imagination, as I said before. But when we would express the decay, and signify that the sense is fading, old, and past, it is called memory. So that imagination and memory are but one thing, which for diverse considerations hath diverse names. Much memory, or memory of many things, is called experience. Again, imagination being only of those things which have been formerly perceived by sense, either all at once, or by parts at several times; the former (which is the imagining the whole object, as it was presented to the sense) is simple imagination, as when one imagineth a man, or horse, which he hath seen before. The other is compounded, when from the sight of a man at one time, and of a horse at another, we conceive in our mind a centaur. So when a man compoundeth the image of his own person with the image of the actions of another man, as when a man imagines himself a Hercules or an Alexander (which happeneth often to them that are much taken with reading of romances), it is a compound imagination, and properly but a fiction of the mind. There be also other imaginations that rise in men, though waking, from the great impression made in sense: as from gazing upon the sun, the impression leaves an image of the sun before our eyes a long time after; and from being long and vehemently attent upon geometrical figures, a man shall in the dark, though awake, have the images of lines and angles before his eyes; which kind of fancy hath no particular name, as being a thing that doth not commonly fall into men's discourse. The imaginations of them that sleep are those we call dreams. And these also (as all other imaginations) have been before, either totally or by parcels, in the sense. And because in sense, the brain and nerves, which are the necessary organs of sense, are so benumbed in sleep as not easily to be moved by the action of external objects, there can happen in sleep no imagination, and therefore no dream, but what proceeds from the agitation of the inward parts of man's body; which inward parts, for the connexion they have with the brain and other organs, when they be distempered do keep the same in motion; whereby the imaginations there formerly made, appear as if a man were waking; saving that the organs of sense being now benumbed, so as there is no new object which can master and obscure them with a more vigorous impression, a dream must needs be more clear, in this silence of sense, than are our waking thoughts. And hence it cometh to pass that it is a hard matter, and by many thought impossible, to distinguish exactly between sense and dreaming. For my part, when I consider that in dreams I do not often nor constantly think of the same persons, places, objects, and actions that I do waking, nor remember so long a train of coherent thoughts dreaming as at other times; and because waking I often observe the absurdity of dreams, but never dream of the absurdities of my waking thoughts, I am well satisfied that, being awake, I know I dream not; though when I dream, I think myself awake. And seeing dreams are caused by the distemper of some of the inward parts of the body, diverse distempers must needs cause different dreams. And hence it is that lying cold breedeth dreams of fear, and raiseth the thought and image of some fearful object, the motion from the brain to the inner parts, and from the inner parts to the brain being reciprocal; and that as anger causeth heat in some parts of the body when we are awake, so when we sleep the overheating of the same parts causeth anger, and raiseth up in the brain the imagination of an enemy. In the same manner, as natural kindness when we are awake causeth desire, and desire makes heat in certain other parts of the body; so also too much heat in those parts, while we sleep, raiseth in the brain an imagination of some kindness shown. In sum, our dreams are the reverse of our waking imaginations; the motion when we are awake beginning at one end, and when we dream, at another. The most difficult discerning of a man's dream from his waking thoughts is, then, when by some accident we observe not that we have slept: which is easy to happen to a man full of fearful thoughts; and whose conscience is much troubled; and that sleepeth without the circumstances of going to bed, or putting off his clothes, as one that noddeth in a chair. For he that taketh pains, and industriously lays himself to sleep, in case any uncouth and exorbitant fancy come unto him, cannot easily think it other than a dream. We read of Marcus Brutus (one that had his life given him by Julius Caesar, and was also his favorite, and notwithstanding murdered him), how at Philippi, the night before he gave battle to Augustus Caesar, he saw a fearful apparition, which is commonly related by historians as a vision, but, considering the circumstances, one may easily judge to have been but a short dream. For sitting in his tent, pensive and troubled with the horror of his rash act, it was not hard for him, slumbering in the cold, to dream of that which most affrighted him; which fear, as by degrees it made him wake, so also it must needs make the apparition by degrees to vanish: and having no assurance that he slept, he could have no cause to think it a dream, or anything but a vision. And this is no very rare accident: for even they that be perfectly awake, if they be timorous and superstitious, possessed with fearful tales, and alone in the dark, are subject to the like fancies, and believe they see spirits and dead men's ghosts walking in churchyards; whereas it is either their fancy only, or else the knavery of such persons as make use of such superstitious fear to pass disguised in the night to places they would not be known to haunt. From this ignorance of how to distinguish dreams, and other strong fancies, from vision and sense, did arise the greatest part of the religion of the Gentiles in time past, that worshipped satyrs, fauns, nymphs, and the like; and nowadays the opinion that rude people have of fairies, ghosts, and goblins, and of the power of witches. For, as for witches, I think not that their witchcraft is any real power, but yet that they are justly punished for the false belief they have that they can do such mischief, joined with their purpose to do it if they can, their trade being nearer to a new religion than to a craft or science. And for fairies, and walking ghosts, the opinion of them has, I think, been on purpose either taught, or not confuted, to keep in credit the use of exorcism, of crosses, of holy water, and other such inventions of ghostly men. Nevertheless, there is no doubt but God can make unnatural apparitions: but that He does it so often as men need to fear such things more than they fear the stay, or change, of the course of Nature, which he also can stay, and change, is no point of Christian faith. But evil men, under pretext that God can do anything, are so bold as to say anything when it serves their turn, though they think it untrue; it is the part of a wise man to believe them no further than right reason makes that which they say appear credible. If this superstitious fear of spirits were taken away, and with it prognostics from dreams, false prophecies, and many other things depending thereon, by which crafty ambitious persons abuse the simple people, men would be would be much more fitted than they are for civil obedience. And this ought to be the work of the schools, but they rather nourish such doctrine. For (not knowing what imagination, or the senses are) what they receive, they teach: some saying that imaginations rise of themselves, and have no cause; others that they rise most commonly from the will; and that good thoughts are blown (inspired) into a man by God, and evil thoughts, by the Devil; or that good thoughts are poured (infused) into a man by God, and evil ones by the Devil. Some say the senses receive the species of things, and deliver them to the common sense; and the common sense delivers them over to the fancy, and the fancy to the memory, and the memory to the judgement, like handing of things from one to another, with many words making nothing understood. The imagination that is raised in man (or any other creature endued with the faculty of imagining) by words, or other voluntary signs, is that we generally call understanding, and is common to man and beast. For a dog by custom will understand the call or the rating of his master; and so will many other beasts. That understanding which is peculiar to man is the understanding not only his will, but his conceptions and thoughts, by the sequel and contexture of the names of things into affirmations, negations, and other forms of speech: and of this kind of understanding I shall speak hereafter.

# CHAPTER III, OF THE CONSEQUENCE OR TRAIN OF IMAGINATIONS

BY CONSEQUENCE, or train of thoughts, I understand that succession of one thought to another which is called, to distinguish it from discourse in words, mental discourse. When a man thinketh on anything whatsoever, his next thought after is not altogether so casual as it seems to be. Not every thought to every thought succeeds indifferently. But as we have no imagination, whereof we have not formerly had sense, in whole or in parts; so we have no transition from one imagination to another, whereof we never had the like before in our senses. The reason whereof is this. All fancies are motions within us, relics of those made in the sense; and those motions that immediately succeeded one another in the sense continue also together after sense: in so much as the former coming again to take place and be predominant, the latter followeth, by coherence of the matter moved, in such manner as water upon a plain table is drawn which way any one part of it is guided by the finger. But because in sense, to one and the same thing perceived, sometimes one thing, sometimes another, succeedeth, it comes to pass in time that in the imagining of anything, there is no certainty what we shall imagine next; only this is certain, it shall be something that succeeded the same before, at one time or another. This train of thoughts, or mental discourse, is of two sorts. The first is unguided, without design, and inconstant; wherein there is no passionate thought to govern and direct those that follow to itself as the end and scope of some desire, or other passion; in which case the thoughts are said to wander, and seem impertinent one to another, as in a dream. Such are commonly the thoughts of men that are not only without company, but also without care of anything; though even then their thoughts are as busy as at other times, but without harmony; as the sound which a lute out of tune would yield to any man; or in tune, to one that could not play. And yet in this wild ranging of the mind, a man may oft-times perceive the way of it, and the dependence of one thought upon another. For in a discourse of our present civil war, what could seem more impertinent than to ask, as one did, what was the value of a Roman penny? Yet the coherence to me was manifest enough. For the thought of the war introduced the thought of the delivering up the King to his enemies; the thought of that brought in the thought of the delivering up of Christ; and that again the thought of the 30 pence, which was the price of that treason: and thence easily followed that malicious question; and all this in a moment of time, for thought is quick. The second is more constant, as being regulated by some desire and design. For the impression made by such things as we desire, or fear, is strong and permanent, or (if it cease for a time) of quick return: so strong it is sometimes as to hinder and break our sleep. From desire ariseth the thought of some means we have seen produce the like of that which we aim at; and from the thought of that, the thought of means to that mean; and so continually, till we come to some beginning within our own power. And because the end, by the greatness of the impression, comes often to mind, in case our thoughts begin to wander they are quickly again reduced into the way: which, observed by one of the seven wise men, made him give men this precept, which is now worn out: respice finem; that is to say, in all your actions, look often upon what you would have, as the thing that directs all your thoughts in the way to attain it. The train of regulated thoughts is of two kinds: one, when of an effect imagined we seek the causes or means that produce it; and this is common to man and beast. The other is, when imagining anything whatsoever, we seek all the possible effects that can by it be produced; that is to say, we imagine what we can do with it when we have it. Of which I have not at any time seen any sign, but in man only; for this is a curiosity hardly incident to the nature of any living creature that has no other passion but sensual, such as are hunger, thirst, lust, and anger. In sum, the discourse of the mind, when it is governed by design, is nothing but seeking, or the faculty of invention, which the Latins call sagacitas, and solertia; a hunting out of the causes of some effect, present or past; or of the effects of some present or past cause. Sometimes a man seeks what he hath lost; and from that place, and time, wherein he misses it, his mind runs back, from place to place, and time to time, to find where and when he had it; that is to say, to find some certain and limited time and place in which to begin a method of seeking. Again, from thence, his thoughts run over the same places and times to find what action or other occasion might make him lose it. This we call remembrance, or calling to mind: the Latins call it reminiscentia, as it were a re-conning of our former actions. Sometimes a man knows a place determinate, within the compass whereof he is to seek; and then his thoughts run over all the parts thereof in the same manner as one would sweep a room to find a jewel; or as a spaniel ranges the field till he find a scent; or as a man should run over the alphabet to start a rhyme. Sometimes a man desires to know the event of an action; and then he thinketh of some like action past, and the events thereof one after another, supposing like events will follow like actions. As he that foresees what will become of a criminal re-cons what he has seen follow on the like crime before, having this order of thoughts; the crime, the officer, the prison, the judge, and the gallows. Which kind of thoughts is called foresight, and prudence, or providence, and sometimes wisdom; though such conjecture, through the difficulty of observing all circumstances, be very fallacious. But this is certain: by how much one man has more experience of things past than another; by so much also he is more prudent, and his expectations the seldomer fail him. The present only has a being in nature; things past have a being in the memory only; but things to come have no being at all, the future being but a fiction of the mind, applying the sequels of actions past to the actions that are present; which with most certainty is done by him that has most experience, but not with certainty enough. And though it be called prudence when the event answereth our expectation; yet in its own nature it is but presumption. For the foresight of things to come, which is providence, belongs only to him by whose will they are to come. From him only, and supernaturally, proceeds prophecy. The best prophet naturally is the best guesser; and the best guesser, he that is most versed and studied in the matters he guesses at, for he hath most signs to guess by. A sign is the event antecedent of the consequent; and contrarily, the consequent of the antecedent, when the like consequences have been observed before: and the oftener they have been observed, the less uncertain is the sign. And therefore he that has most experience in any kind of business has most signs whereby to guess at the future time, and consequently is the most prudent: and so much more prudent than he that is new in that kind of business, as not to be equalled by any advantage of natural and extemporary wit, though perhaps many young men think the contrary. Nevertheless, it is not prudence that distinguisheth man from beast. There be beasts that at a year old observe more and pursue that which is for their good more prudently than a child can do at ten. As prudence is a presumption of the future, contracted from the experience of time past: so there is a presumption of things past taken from other things, not future, but past also. For he that hath seen by what courses and degrees a flourishing state hath first come into civil war, and then to ruin; upon the sight of the ruins of any other state will guess the like war and the like courses have been there also. But this conjecture has the same uncertainty almost with the conjecture of the future, both being grounded only upon experience. There is no other act of man's mind, that I can remember, naturally planted in him, so as to need no other thing to the exercise of it but to be born a man, and live with the use of his five senses. Those other faculties, of which I shall speak by and by, and which seem proper to man only, are acquired and increased by study and industry, and of most men learned by instruction and discipline, and proceed all from the invention of words and speech. For besides sense, and thoughts, and the train of thoughts, the mind of man has no other motion; though by the help of speech, and method, the same faculties may be improved to such a height as to distinguish men from all other living creatures. Whatsoever we imagine is finite. Therefore there is no idea or conception of anything we call infinite. No man can have in his mind an image of infinite magnitude; nor conceive infinite swiftness, infinite time, or infinite force, or infinite power. When we say anything is infinite, we signify only that we are not able to conceive the ends and bounds of the thing named, having no conception of the thing, but of our own inability. And therefore the name of God is used, not to make us conceive Him (for He is incomprehensible, and His greatness and power are unconceivable), but that we may honour Him. Also because whatsoever, as I said before, we conceive has been perceived first by sense, either all at once, or by parts, a man can have no thought representing anything not subject to sense. No man therefore can conceive anything, but he must conceive it in some place; and endued with some determinate magnitude; and which may be divided into parts; nor that anything is all in this place, and all in another place at the same time; nor that two or more things can be in one and the same place at once: for none of these things ever have or can be incident to sense, but are absurd speeches, taken upon credit, without any signification at all, from deceived philosophers and deceived, or deceiving, Schoolmen.

## CHAPTER IV, OF SPEECH

THE INVENTIONof printing, though ingenious, compared with the invention of letters is no great matter. But who was the first that found the use of letters is not known. He that first brought them into Greece, men say, was Cadmus, the son of Agenor, King of Phoenicia. A profitable invention for continuing the memory of time past, and the conjunction of mankind dispersed into so many and distant regions of the earth; and withal difficult, as proceeding from a watchful observation of the diverse motions of the tongue, palate, lips, and other organs of speech; whereby to make as many differences of characters to remember them. But the most noble and profitable invention of all other was that of speech, consisting of names or appellations, and their connexion; whereby men register their thoughts, recall them when they are past, and also declare them one to another for mutual utility and conversation; without which there had been amongst men neither Commonwealth, nor society, nor contract, nor peace, no more than amongst lions, bears, and wolves. The first author of speech was God himself, that instructed Adam how to name such creatures as He presented to his sight; for the Scripture goeth no further in this matter. But this was sufficient to direct him to add more names, as the experience and use of the creatures should give him occasion; and to join them in such manner by degrees as to make himself understood; and so by succession of time, so much language might be gotten as he had found use for, though not so copious as an orator or philosopher has need of. For I do not find anything in the Scripture out of which, directly or by consequence, can be gathered that Adam was taught the names of all figures, numbers, measures, colours, sounds, fancies, relations; much less the names of words and speech, as general, special, affirmative, negative, interrogative, optative, infinitive, all which are useful; and least of all, of entity, intentionality, quiddity, and other insignificant words of the school. But all this language gotten, and augmented by Adam and his posterity, was again lost at the tower of Babel, when by the hand of God every man was stricken for his rebellion with an oblivion of his former language. And being hereby forced to disperse themselves into several parts of the world, it must needs be that the diversity of tongues that now is, proceeded by degrees from them in such manner as need, the mother of all inventions, taught them, and in tract of time grew everywhere more copious. The general use of speech is to transfer our mental discourse into verbal, or the train of our thoughts into a train of words, and that for two commodities; whereof one is the registering of the consequences of our thoughts, which being apt to slip out of our memory and put us to a new labour, may again be recalled by such words as they were marked by. So that the first use of names is to serve for marks or notes of remembrance. Another is when many use the same words to signify, by their connexion and order one to another, what they conceive or think of each matter; and also what they desire, fear, or have any other passion for. And for this use they are called signs. Special uses of speech are these: first, to register what by cogitation we find to be the cause of anything, present or past; and what we find things present or past may produce, or effect; which, in sum, is acquiring of arts. Secondly, to show to others that knowledge which we have attained; which is to counsel and teach one another. Thirdly, to make known to others our wills and purposes that we may have the mutual help of one another. Fourthly, to please and delight ourselves, and others, by playing with our words, for pleasure or ornament, innocently. To these uses, there are also four correspondent abuses. First, when men register their thoughts wrong by the inconstancy of the signification of their words; by which they register for their conceptions that which they never conceived, and so deceive themselves. Secondly, when they use words metaphorically; that is, in other sense than that they are ordained for, and thereby deceive others. Thirdly, when by words they declare that to be their will which is not. Fourthly, when they use them to grieve one another: for seeing nature hath armed living creatures, some with teeth, some with horns, and some with hands, to grieve an enemy, it is but an abuse of speech to grieve him with the tongue, unless it be one whom we are obliged to govern; and then it is not to grieve, but to correct and amend. The manner how speech serveth to the remembrance of the consequence of causes and effects consisteth in the imposing of names, and the connexion of them. Of names, some are proper, and singular to one only thing; as Peter, John, this man, this tree: and some are common to many things; as man, horse, tree; every of which, though but one name, is nevertheless the name of diverse particular things; in respect of all which together, it is called a universal, there being nothing in the world universal but names; for the things named are every one of them individual and singular. One universal name is imposed on many things for their similitude in some quality, or other accident: and whereas a proper name bringeth to mind one thing only, universals recall any one of those many. And of names universal, some are of more and some of less extent, the larger comprehending the less large; and some again of equal extent, comprehending each other reciprocally. As for example, the name body is of larger signification than the word man, and comprehendeth it; and the names man and rational are of equal extent, comprehending mutually one another. But here we must take notice that by a name is not always understood, as in grammar, one only word, but sometimes by circumlocution many words together. For all these words, He that in his actions observeth the laws of his country, make but one name, equivalent to this one word, just. By this imposition of names, some of larger, some of stricter signification, we turn the reckoning of the consequences of things imagined in the mind into a reckoning of the consequences of appellations. For example, a man that hath no use of speech at all, (such as is born and remains perfectly deaf and dumb), if he set before his eyes a triangle, and by it two right angles (such as are the corners of a square figure), he may by meditation compare and find that the three angles of that triangle are equal to those two right angles that stand by it. But if another triangle be shown him different in shape from the former, he cannot know without a new labour whether the three angles of that also be equal to the same. But he that hath the use of words, when he observes that such equality was consequent, not to the length of the sides, nor to any other particular thing in his triangle; but only to this, that the sides were straight, and the angles three, and that that was all, for which he named it a triangle; will boldly conclude universally that such equality of angles is in all triangles whatsoever, and register his invention in these general terms: Every triangle hath its three angles equal to two right angles. And thus the consequence found in one particular comes to be registered and remembered as a universal rule; and discharges our mental reckoning of time and place, and delivers us from all labour of the mind, saving the first; and makes that which was found true here, and now, to be true in all times and places. But the use of words in registering our thoughts is in nothing so evident as in numbering. A natural fool that could never learn by heart the order of numeral words, as one, two, and three, may observe every stroke of the clock, and nod to it, or say one, one, one, but can never know what hour it strikes. And it seems there was a time when those names of number were not in use; and men were fain to apply their fingers of one or both hands to those things they desired to keep account of; and that thence it proceeded that now our numeral words are but ten, in any nation, and in some but five, and then they begin again. And he that can tell ten, if he recite them out of order, will lose himself, and not know when he has done: much less will he be able to add, and subtract, and perform all other operations of arithmetic. So that without words there is no possibility of reckoning of numbers; much less of magnitudes, of swiftness, of force, and other things, the reckonings whereof are necessary to the being or well-being of mankind. When two names are joined together into a consequence, or affirmation, as thus, A man is a living creature; or thus, If he be a man, he is a living creature; if the latter name living creature signify all that the former name man signifieth, then the affirmation, or consequence, is true; otherwise false. For true and false are attributes of speech, not of things. And where speech is not, there is neither truth nor falsehood. Error there may be, as when we expect that which shall not be, or suspect what has not been; but in neither case can a man be charged with untruth. Seeing then that truth consisteth in the right ordering of names in our affirmations, a man that seeketh precise truth had need to remember what every name he uses stands for, and to place it accordingly; or else he will find himself entangled in words, as a bird in lime twigs; the more he struggles, the more belimed. And therefore in geometry (which is the only science that it hath pleased God hitherto to bestow on mankind), men begin at settling the significations of their words; which settling of significations, they call definitions, and place them in the beginning of their reckoning. By this it appears how necessary it is for any man that aspires to true knowledge to examine the definitions of former authors; and either to correct them, where they are negligently set down, or to make them himself. For the errors of definitions multiply themselves, according as the reckoning proceeds, and lead men into absurdities, which at last they see, but cannot avoid, without reckoning anew from the beginning; in which lies the foundation of their errors. From whence it happens that they which trust to books do as they that cast up many little sums into a greater, without considering whether those little sums were rightly cast up or not; and at last finding the error visible, and not mistrusting their first grounds, know not which way to clear themselves, spend time in fluttering over their books; as birds that entering by the chimney, and finding themselves enclosed in a chamber, flutter at the false light of a glass window, for want of wit to consider which way they came in. So that in the right definition of names lies the first use of speech; which is the acquisition of science: and in wrong, or no definitions, lies the first abuse; from which proceed all false and senseless tenets; which make those men that take their instruction from the authority of books, and not from their own meditation, to be as much below the condition of ignorant men as men endued with true science are above it. For between true science and erroneous doctrines, ignorance is in the middle. Natural sense and imagination are not subject to absurdity. Nature itself cannot err: and as men abound in copiousness of language; so they become more wise, or more mad, than ordinary. Nor is it possible without letters for any man to become either excellently wise or (unless his memory be hurt by disease, or ill constitution of organs) excellently foolish. For words are wise men's counters; they do but reckon by them: but they are the money of fools, that value them by the authority of an Aristotle, a Cicero, or a Thomas, or any other doctor whatsoever, if but a man. Subject to names is whatsoever can enter into or be considered in an account, and be added one to another to make a sum, or subtracted one from another and leave a remainder. The Latins called accounts of money rationes, and accounting, ratiocinatio: and that which we in bills or books of account call items, they called nomina; that is, names: and thence it seems to proceed that they extended the word ratio to the faculty of reckoning in all other things. The Greeks have but one word, logos, for both speech and reason; not that they thought there was no speech without reason, but no reasoning without speech; and the act of reasoning they called syllogism; which signifieth summing up of the consequences of one saying to another. And because the same things may enter into account for diverse accidents, their names are (to show that diversity) diversely wrested and diversified. This diversity of names may be reduced to four general heads. First, a thing may enter into account for matter, or body; as living, sensible, rational, hot, cold, moved, quiet; with all which names the word matter, or body, is understood; all such being names of matter. Secondly, it may enter into account, or be considered, for some accident or quality which we conceive to be in it; as for being moved, for being so long, for being hot, etc.; and then, of the name of the thing itself, by a little change or wresting, we make a name for that accident which we consider; and for living put into the account life; for moved, motion; for hot, heat; for long, length, and the like: and all such names are the names of the accidents and properties by which one matter and body is distinguished from another. These are called names abstract, because severed, not from matter, but from the account of matter. Thirdly, we bring into account the properties of our own bodies, whereby we make such distinction: as when anything is seen by us, we reckon not the thing itself, but the sight, the colour, the idea of it in the fancy; and when anything is heard, we reckon it not, but the hearing or sound only, which is our fancy or conception of it by the ear: and such are names of fancies. Fourthly, we bring into account, consider, and give names, to names themselves, and to speeches: for, general, universal, special, equivocal, are names of names. And affirmation, interrogation, commandment, narration, syllogism, sermon, oration, and many other such are names of speeches. And this is all the variety of names positive; which are put to mark somewhat which is in nature, or may be feigned by the mind of man, as bodies that are, or may be conceived to be; or of bodies, the properties that are, or may be feigned to be; or words and speech. There be also other names, called negative; which are notes to signify that a word is not the name of the thing in question; as these words: nothing, no man, infinite, indocible, three want four, and the like; which are nevertheless of use in reckoning, or in correcting of reckoning, and call to mind our past cogitations, though they be not names of anything; because they make us refuse to admit of names not rightly used. All other names are but insignificant sounds; and those of two sorts. One, when they are new, and yet their meaning not explained by definition; whereof there have been abundance coined by Schoolmen and puzzled philosophers. Another, when men make a name of two names, whose significations are contradictory and inconsistent; as this name, an incorporeal body, or, which is all one, an incorporeal substance, and a great number more. For whensoever any affirmation is false, the two names of which it is composed, put together and made one, signify nothing at all. For example, if it be a false affirmation to say a quadrangle is round, the word round quadrangle signifies nothing, but is a mere sound. So likewise if it be false to say that virtue can be poured, or blown up and down, the words inpoured virtue, inblown virtue, are as absurd and insignificant as a round quadrangle. And therefore you shall hardly meet with a senseless and insignificant word that is not made up of some Latin or Greek names. Frenchman seldom hears our Saviour called by the name of Parole, but by the name of Verbe often; yet Verbe and Parole differ no more but that one is Latin, the other French. When a man, upon the hearing of any speech, hath those thoughts which the words of that speech, and their connexion, were ordained and constituted to signify, then he is said to understand it: understanding being nothing else but conception caused by speech. And therefore if speech be peculiar to man, as for ought I know it is, then is understanding peculiar to him also. And therefore of absurd and false affirmations, in case they be universal, there can be no understanding; though many think they understand then, when they do but repeat the words softly, or con them in their mind. What kinds of speeches signify the appetites, aversions, and passions of man's mind, and of their use and abuse, I shall speak when I have spoken of the passions. The names of such things as affect us, that is, which please and displease us, because all men be not alike affected with the same thing, nor the same man at all times, are in the common discourses of men of inconstant signification. For seeing all names are imposed to signify our conceptions, and all our affections are but conceptions; when we conceive the same things differently, we can hardly avoid different naming of them. For though the nature of that we conceive be the same; yet the diversity of our reception of it, in respect of different constitutions of body and prejudices of opinion, gives everything a tincture of our different passions. And therefore in reasoning, a man must take heed of words; which, besides the signification of what we imagine of their nature, have a signification also of the nature, disposition, and interest of the speaker; such as are the names of virtues and vices: for one man calleth wisdom what another calleth fear; and one cruelty what another justice; one prodigality what another magnanimity; and one gravity what another stupidity, etc. And therefore such names can never be true grounds of any ratiocination. No more can metaphors and tropes of speech: but these are less dangerous because they profess their inconstancy, which the other do not.


## CHAPTER V, OF REASON AND SCIENCE

WHEN man reasoneth, he does nothing else but conceive a sum total, from addition of parcels; or conceive a remainder, from subtraction of one sum from another: which, if it be done by words, is conceiving of the consequence of the names of all the parts, to the name of the whole; or from the names of the whole and one part, to the name of the other part. And though in some things, as in numbers, besides adding and subtracting, men name other operations, as multiplying and dividing; yet they are the same: for multiplication is but adding together of things equal; and division, but subtracting of one thing, as often as we can. These operations are not incident to numbers only, but to all manner of things that can be added together, and taken one out of another. For as arithmeticians teach to add and subtract in numbers, so the geometricians teach the same in lines, figures (solid and superficial), angles, proportions, times, degrees of swiftness, force, power, and the like; the logicians teach the same in consequences of words, adding together two names to make an affirmation, and two affirmations to make a syllogism, and many syllogisms to make a demonstration; and from the sum, or conclusion of a syllogism, they subtract one proposition to find the other. Writers of politics add together pactions to find men's duties; and lawyers, laws and facts to find what is right and wrong in the actions of private men. In sum, in what matter soever there is place for addition and subtraction, there also is place for reason; and where these have no place, there reason has nothing at all to do. Out of all which we may define (that is to say determine) what that is which is meant by this word reason when we reckon it amongst the faculties of the mind. For reason, in this sense, is nothing but reckoning (that is, adding and subtracting) of the consequences of general names agreed upon for the marking and signifying of our thoughts; I say marking them, when we reckon by ourselves; and signifying, when we demonstrate or approve our reckonings to other men. And as in arithmetic unpractised men must, and professors themselves may often, err, and cast up false; so also in any other subject of reasoning, the ablest, most attentive, and most practised men may deceive themselves, and infer false conclusions; not but that reason itself is always right reason, as well as arithmetic is a certain and infallible art: but no one man's reason, nor the reason of any one number of men, makes the certainty; no more than an account is therefore well cast up because a great many men have unanimously approved it. And therefore, as when there is a controversy in an account, the parties must by their own accord set up for right reason the reason of some arbitrator, or judge, to whose sentence they will both stand, or their controversy must either come to blows, or be undecided, for want of a right reason constituted by Nature; so is it also in all debates of what kind soever: and when men that think themselves wiser than all others clamour and demand right reason for judge, yet seek no more but that things should be determined by no other men's reason but their own, it is as intolerable in the society of men, as it is in play after trump is turned to use for trump on every occasion that suit whereof they have most in their hand. For they do nothing else, that will have every of their passions, as it comes to bear sway in them, to be taken for right reason, and that in their own controversies: bewraying their want of right reason by the claim they lay to it. The use and end of reason is not the finding of the sum and truth of one, or a few consequences, remote from the first definitions and settled significations of names; but to begin at these, and proceed from one consequence to another. For there can be no certainty of the last conclusion without a certainty of all those affirmations and negations on which it was grounded and inferred. As when a master of a family, in taking an account, casteth up the sums of all the bills of expense into one sum; and not regarding how each bill is summed up, by those that give them in account, nor what it is he pays for, he advantages himself no more than if he allowed the account in gross, trusting to every of the accountant's skill and honesty: so also in reasoning of all other things, he that takes up conclusions on the trust of authors, and doth not fetch them from the first items in every reckoning (which are the significations of names settled by definitions), loses his labour, and does not know anything, but only believeth. When a man reckons without the use of words, which may be done in particular things, as when upon the sight of any one thing, we conjecture what was likely to have preceded, or is likely to follow upon it; if that which he thought likely to follow follows not, or that which he thought likely to have preceded it hath not preceded it, this is called error; to which even the most prudent men are subject. But when we reason in words of general signification, and fall upon a general inference which is false; though it be commonly called error, it is indeed an absurdity, or senseless speech. For error is but a deception, in presuming that somewhat is past, or to come; of which, though it were not past, or not to come, yet there was no impossibility discoverable. But when we make a general assertion, unless it be a true one, the possibility of it is inconceivable. And words whereby we conceive nothing but the sound are those we call absurd, insignificant, and nonsense. And therefore if a man should talk to me of a round quadrangle; or accidents of bread in cheese; or immaterial substances; or of a free subject; a free will; or any free but free from being hindered by opposition; I should not say he were in an error, but that his words were without meaning; that is to say, absurd. I have said before, in the second chapter, that a man did excel all other animals in this faculty, that when he conceived anything whatsoever, he was apt to enquire the consequences of it, and what effects he could do with it. And now I add this other degree of the same excellence, that he can by words reduce the consequences he finds to general rules, called theorems, or aphorisms; that is, he can reason, or reckon, not only in number, but in all other things whereof one may be added unto or subtracted from another. But this privilege is allayed by another; and that is by the privilege of absurdity, to which no living creature is subject, but men only. And of men, those are of all most subject to it that profess philosophy. For it is most true that Cicero saith of them some-where; that there can be nothing so absurd but may be found in the books of philosophers. And the reason is manifest. For there is not one of them that begins his ratiocination from the definitions or explications of the names they are to use; which is a method that hath been used only in geometry, whose conclusions have there-by been made indisputable. 1. The first cause of absurd conclusions I ascribe to the want of method; in that they begin not their ratiocination from definitions; that is, from settled significations of their words: as if they could cast account without knowing the value of the numeral words, one, two, and three. 2. And whereas all bodies enter into account upon diverse considerations, which I have mentioned in the precedent chapter, these considerations being diversely named, diverse absurdities proceed from the confusion and unfit connexion of their names into assertions. And therefore, 3. The second cause of absurd assertions, I ascribe to the giving of names of bodies to accidents; or of accidents to bodies; as they do that say, faith is infused, or inspired; when nothing can be poured, or breathed into anything, but body; and that extension is body; that phantasms are spirits, etc. 4. The third I ascribe to the giving of the names of the accidents of bodies without us to the acci-dents of our own bodies; as they do that say, the colour is in the body; the sound is in the air, etc. 5. The fourth, to the giving of the names of bodies to names, or speeches; as they do that say that there be things uni-versal; that a living creature is genus, or a general thing, etc. 6. The fifth, to the giving of the names of acci-dents to names and speeches; as they do that say, the nature of a thing is its definition; a man's command is his will; and the like. 7. The sixth, to the use of metaphors, tropes, and other rhetorical figures, instead of words proper. For though it be lawful to say, for example, in common speech, the way goeth, or leadeth hither, or thither; the proverb says this or that (whereas ways cannot go, nor proverbs speak); yet in reckoning, and seeking of truth, such speeches are not to be admitted. 8. The seventh, to names that signify nothing, but are taken up and learned by rote from the Schools, as hypostatical, transubstantiate, consubstantiate, eternal-now, and the like canting of Schoolmen. To him that can avoid these things, it is not easy to fall into any absurdity, unless it be by the length of an account; wherein he may perhaps forget what went before. For all men by na-ture reason alike, and well, when they have good principles. For who is so stupid as both to mistake in geome-try, and also to persist in it, when another detects his error to him? By this it appears that reason is not, as sense and memory, born with us; nor gotten by experience only, as prudence is; but attained by industry: first in apt imposing of names; and secondly by getting a good and orderly method in proceeding from the ele-ments, which are names, to assertions made by connexion of one of them to another; and so to syllogisms, which are the connexions of one assertion to another, till we come to a knowledge of all the consequences of names appertaining to the subject in hand; and that is it, men call science. And whereas sense and memory are but knowledge of fact, which is a thing past and irrevocable, science is the knowledge of consequences, and dependence of one fact upon another; by which, out of that we can presently do, we know how to do some-thing else when we will, or the like, another time: because when we see how anything comes about, upon what causes, and by what manner; when the like causes come into our power, we see how to make it produce the like effects. Children therefore are not endued with reason at all, till they have attained the use of speech, but are called reasonable creatures for the possibility apparent of having the use of reason in time to come. And the most part of men, though they have the use of reasoning a little way, as in numbering to some degree; yet it serves them to little use in common life, in which they govern themselves, some better, some worse, ac-cording to their differences of experience, quickness of memory, and inclinations to several ends; but special-ly according to good or evil fortune, and the errors of one another. For as for science, or certain rules of their actions, they are so far from it that they know not what it is. Geometry they have thought conjuring: but for other sciences, they who have not been taught the beginnings, and some progress in them, that they may see how they be acquired and generated, are in this point like children that, having no thought of generation, are made believe by the women that their brothers and sisters are not born, but found in the garden. But yet they that have no science are in better and nobler condition with their natural prudence than men that, by misrea-soning, or by trusting them that reason wrong, fall upon false and absurd general rules. For ignorance of caus-es, and of rules, does not set men so far out of their way as relying on false rules, and taking for causes of what they aspire to, those that are not so, but rather causes of the contrary. To conclude, the light of humane minds is perspicuous words, but by exact definitions first snuffed, and purged from ambiguity; reason is the pace; increase of science, the way; and the benefit of mankind, the end. And, on the contrary, metaphors, and senseless and ambiguous words are like ignes fatui; and reasoning upon them is wandering amongst innumerable absurdities; and their end, contention and sedition, or contempt. As much experience is prudence, so is much science sapience. For though we usually have one name of wisdom for them both; yet the Latins did always distinguish between prudentia and sapientia; ascribing the former to experience, the latter to science. But to make their difference appear more clearly, let us suppose one man endued with an excellent natural use and dexterity in handling his arms; and another to have added to that dexterity an acquired science of where he can offend, or be offended by his adversary, in every possible posture or guard: the ability of the former would be to the ability of the latter, as prudence to sapience; both useful, but the latter infallible. But they that, trusting only to the authority of books, follow the blind blindly, are like him that, trusting to the false rules of a master of fence, ventures presumptuously upon an adversary that either kills or disgraces him. The signs of science are some certain and infallible; some, uncertain. Certain, when he that pretendeth the science of anything can teach the same; that is to say, demonstrate the truth thereof perspicuously to another: uncertain, when only some particular events answer to his pretence, and upon many occasions prove so as he says they must. Signs of prudence are all uncertain; because to observe by experience, and remember all circumstances that may alter the success, is impossible. But in any business, whereof a man has not infallible science to proceed by, to forsake his own natural judgment, and be guided by general sentences read in authors, and subject to many exceptions, is a sign of folly, and generally scorned by the name of pedantry. And even of those men themselves that in councils of the Commonwealth love to show their reading of politics and history, very few do it in their domestic affairs where their particular interest is concerned, having prudence enough for their private affairs; but in public they study more the reputation of their own wit than the success of another's business.

## CHAPTER VI, OF THE INTERIOR BEGINNINGS OF VOLUNTARY MOTIONS, COMMONLY CALLED THE PASSIONS; AND THE SPEECHES BY WHICH THEY ARE EXPRESSED

THERE be in animals two sorts of motions peculiar to them: One called vital, begun in generation, and continued without interruption through their whole life; such as are the course of the blood, the pulse, the breathing, the concoction, nutrition, excretion, etc.; to which motions there needs no help of imagination: the other is animal motion, otherwise called voluntary motion; as to go, to speak, to move any of our limbs, in such manner as is first fancied in our minds. That sense is motion in the organs and interior parts of man's body, caused by the action of the things we see, hear, etc., and that fancy is but the relics of the same motion, remaining after sense, has been already said in the first and second chapters. And because going, speaking, and the like voluntary motions depend always upon a precedent thought of whither, which way, and what, it is evident that the imagination is the first internal beginning of all voluntary motion. And although unstudied men do not conceive any motion at all to be there, where the thing moved is invisible, or the space it is moved in is, for the shortness of it, insensible; yet that doth not hinder but that such motions are. For let a space be never so little, that which is moved over a greater space, whereof that little one is part, must first be moved over that. These small beginnings of motion within the body of man, before they appear in walking, speaking, striking, and other visible actions, are commonly called endeavour. This endeavour, when it is toward something which causes it, is called appetite, or desire, the latter being the general name, and the other oftentimes restrained to signify the desire of food, namely hun
er and thirst. And when the endeavour is from ward something, it is generally called aversion. These words appetite and aversion we have from the Latins; and they both of them signify the motions, one of approaching, the other of retiring. So also do the Greek words for the same, which are orme and aphorme. For Nature itself does often press upon men those truths which afterwards, when they look for somewhat beyond Nature, they stumble at. For the Schools find in mere appetite to go, or move, no actual motion at all; but because some motion they must acknowledge, they call it metaphorical motion, which is but an absurd speech; for though words may be called metaphorical, bodies and motions cannot. That which men desire they are said to love, and to hate those things for which they have aversion. So that desire and love are the same thing; save that by desire, we signify the absence of the object; by love, most commonly the presence of the same. So also by aversion, we signify the absence; and by hate, the presence of the object. Of appetites and aversions, some are born with men; as appetite of food, appetite of excretion, and exoneration (which may also and more

properly be called aversions, from somewhat they feel in their bodies), and some other appetites, not many. The rest, which are appetites of particular things, proceed from experience and trial of their effects upon themselves or other men. For of things we know not at all, or believe not to be, we can have no further desire than to taste and try. But aversion we have for things, not only which we know have hurt us, but also that we do not know whether they will hurt us, or not. Those things which we neither desire nor hate, we are said to contemn: contempt being nothing else but an immobility or contumacy of the heart in resisting the action of certain things; and proceeding from that the heart is already moved otherwise, by other more potent objects, or from want of experience of them. And because the constitution of a man's body is in continual mutation, it is impossible that all the same things should always cause in him the same appetites and aversions: much less can all men consent in the desire of almost any one and the same object. But whatsoever is the object of any man's appetite or desire, that is it which he for his part calleth good; and the object of his hate and aversion, evil; and of his contempt, vile and inconsiderable. For these words of good, evil, and contemptible are ever used with relation to the person that useth them: there being nothing simply and absolutely so; nor any common rule of good and evil to be taken from the nature of the objects themselves; but from the person of the man, where there is no Commonwealth; or, in a Commonwealth, from the person that representeth it; or from an arbitrator or judge, whom men disagreeing shall by consent set up and make his sentence the rule thereof. The Latin tongue has two words whose significations approach to those of good and evil, but are not precisely the same; and those are pulchrum and turpe. Whereof the former signifies that which by some apparent signs promiseth good; and the latter, that which promiseth evil. But in our tongue we have not so general names to express them by. But for pulchrum we say in some things, fair; in others, beautiful, or handsome, or gallant, or honourable, or comely, or amiable: and for turpe; foul, deformed, ugly, base, nauseous, and the like, as the subject shall require; all which words, in their proper places, signify nothing else but the mien, or countenance, that promiseth good and evil. So that of good there be three kinds: good in the promise, that is pulchrum; good in effect, as the end desired, which is called jucundum, delightful; and good as the means, which is called utile, profitable; and as many of evil: for evil in promise is that they call turpe; evil in effect and end is molestum, unpleasant, troublesome; and evil in the means, inutile, unprofitable, hurtful. As in sense that which is really within us is, as I have said before, only motion, caused by the action of external objects but in appearance; to the sight, light and colour; to the ear, sound; to the nostril, odour, etc.: so, when the action of the same object is continued from the eyes, ears, and other organs to the heart, the real effect there is nothing but motion, or endeavour; which consisteth in appetite or aversion to or from the object moving. But the appearance or sense of that motion is that we either call delight or trouble of mind. This motion, which is called appetite, and for the appearance of it delight and pleasure, seemeth to be a corroboration of vital motion, and a help thereunto; and therefore such things as caused delight were not improperly called jucunda (a juvando), from helping or fortifying; and the contrary, molesta, offensive, from hindering and troubling the motion vital. Pleasure therefore, or delight, is the appearance or sense of good; and molestation or displeasure, the appearance or sense of evil. And consequently all appetite, desire, and love is accompanied with some delight more or less; and all hatred and aversion with more or less displeasure and offence. Of pleasures, or delights, some arise from the sense of an object present; and those may be called pleasures of sense (the word sensual, as it is used by those only that condemn them, having no place till there be laws). Of this kind are all onerations and exonerations of the body; as also all that is pleasant, in the sight, hearing, smell, taste, or touch. Others arise from the expectation that proceeds from foresight of the end or consequence of things, whether those things in the sense please or displease: and these are pleasures of the mind of him that draweth in those consequences, and are generally called joy. In the like manner, displeasures are some in the sense, and called pain; others, in the expectation of consequences, and are called grief. These simple passions called appetite, desire, love, aversion, hate, joy, and grief have their names for diverse considerations diversified. At first, when they one succeed another, they are diversely called from the opinion men have of the likelihood of attaining what they desire. Secondly, from the object loved or hated. Thirdly, from the consideration of many of them together. Fourthly, from the alteration or succession itself. For appetite with an opinion of attaining is called hope. The same, without such opinion, despair. Aversion, with opinion of hurt from the object, fear. The same, with hope of avoiding that hurt by resistence, courage. Sudden courage, anger. Constant hope, confidence of ourselves. Constant despair, diffidence of ourselves. Anger for great hurt done to another, when we conceive the same to be done by injury, indignation. Desire of good to another, benevolence, good will, charity. If to man generally, good nature. Desire of riches, covetousness: a name used always in signification of blame, because men contending for them are displeased with one another's attaining them; though the desire in itself be to be blamed, or allowed, according to the means by which those riches are sought. Desire of office, or precedence, ambition: a name used also in the worse sense, for the reason before mentioned. Desire of things that conduce but a little to our ends, and fear of things that are but of little hindrance, pusillanimity. Contempt of little helps, and hindrances, magnanimity. Magnanimity in danger of death, or wounds, valour, fortitude. Magnanimity in the use of riches, liberality. Pusillanimity in the same, wretchedness, miserableness, or parsimony, as it is liked, or disliked. Love of persons for society, kindness. Love of persons for pleasing the sense only, natural lust. Love of the same acquired from rumination, that is, imagination of pleasure past, luxury. Love of one singularly, with desire to be singularly beloved, the passion of love. The same, with fear that the love is not mutual, jealousy. Desire by doing hurt to another to make him condemn some fact of his own, revengefulness. Desire to know why, and how, curiosity; such as is in no living creature but man: so that man is distinguished, not only by his reason, but also by this singular passion from other animals; in whom the appetite of food, and other pleasures of sense, by predominance, take away the care of knowing causes; which is a lust of the mind, that by a perseverance of delight in the continual and indefatigable generation of knowledge, exceedeth the short vehemence of any carnal pleasure. Fear of power invisible, feigned by the mind, or imagined from tales publicly allowed, religion; not allowed, superstition. And when the power imagined is truly such as we imagine, true religion. Fear without the apprehension of why, or what, panic terror; called so from the fables that make Pan the author of them; whereas in truth there is always in him that so feareth, first, some apprehension of the cause, though the rest run away by example; every one supposing his fellow to know why. And therefore this passion happens to none but in a throng, or multitude of people. Joy from apprehension of novelty, admiration; proper to man, because it excites the appetite of knowing the cause. Joy arising from imagination of a man's own power and ability is that exultation of the mind which is called glorying: which, if grounded upon the experience of his own former actions, is the same with confidence: but if grounded on the flattery of others, or only supposed by himself, for delight in the consequences of it, is called vainglory: which name is properly given; because a well-grounded confidence begetteth attempt; whereas the supposing of power does not, and is therefore rightly called vain. Grief, from opinion of want of power, is called dejection of mind. The vainglory which consisteth in the feigning or supposing of abilities in ourselves, which we know are not, is most incident to young men, and nourished by the histories or fictions of gallant persons; and is corrected oftentimes by age and employment. Sudden glory is the passion which maketh those grimaces called laughter; and is caused either by some sudden act of their own that pleaseth them; or by the apprehension of some deformed thing in another, by comparison whereof they suddenly applaud themselves. And it is incident most to them that are conscious of the fewest abilities in themselves; who are forced to keep themselves in their own favour by observing the imperfections of other men. And therefore much laughter at the defects of others is a sign of pusillanimity. For of great minds one of the proper works is to help and free others from scorn, and compare themselves only with the most able. On the contrary, sudden dejection is the passion that causeth weeping; and is caused by such accidents as suddenly take away some vehement hope, or some prop of their power: and they are most subject to it that rely principally on helps external, such as are women and children. Therefore, some weep for the loss of friends; others for their unkindness; others for the sudden stop made to their thoughts of revenge, by reconciliation. But in all cases, both laughter and weeping are sudden motions, custom taking them both away. For no man laughs at old jests, or weeps for an old calamity. Grief for the discovery of some defect of ability is shame, or the passion that discovereth itself in blushing, and consisteth in the apprehension of something dishonourable; and in young men is a sign of the love of good reputation, and commendable: in old men it is a sign of the same; but because it comes too late, not commendable. The contempt of good reputation is called impudence. Grief for the calamity of another is pity; and ariseth from the imagination that the like calamity may befall himself; and therefore is called also compassion, and in the phrase of this present time a fellow-feeling: and therefore for calamity arriving from great wickedness, the best men have the least pity; and for the same calamity, those have least pity that think themselves least obnoxious to the same. Contempt, or little sense of the calamity of others, is that which men call cruelty; proceeding from security of their own fortune. For, that any man should take pleasure in other men's great harms, without other end of his own, I do not conceive it possible. Grief for the success of a competitor in wealth, honour, or other good, if it be joined with endeavour to enforce our own abilities to equal or exceed him, is called emulation: but joined with endeavour to supplant or hinder a competitor, envy. When in the mind of man appetites and aversions, hopes and fears, concerning one and the same thing, arise alternately; and diverse good and evil consequences of the doing or omitting the thing propounded come successively into our thoughts; so that sometimes we have an appetite to it, sometimes an aversion from it; sometimes hope to be able to do it, sometimes despair, or fear to attempt it; the whole sum of desires, aversions, hopes and fears, continued till the thing be either done, or thought impossible, is that we call deliberation. Therefore of things past there is no deliberation, because manifestly impossible to be changed; nor of things known to be impossible, or thought so; because men know or think such deliberation vain. But of things impossible, which we think possible, we may deliberate, not knowing it is in vain. And it is called deliberation; because it is a putting an end to the liberty we had of doing, or omitting, according to our own appetite, or aversion. This alternate succession of appetites, aversions, hopes and fears is no less in other living creatures than in man; and therefore beasts also deliberate. Every deliberation is then said to end when that whereof they deliberate is either done or thought impossible; because till then we retain the liberty of doing, or omitting, according to our appetite, or aversion. In deliberation, the last appetite, or aversion, immediately adhering to the action, or to the omission thereof, is that we call the will; the act, not the faculty, of willing. And beasts that have deliberation must necessarily also have will. The definition of the will, given commonly by the Schools, that it is a rational appetite, is not good. For if it were, then could there be no voluntary act against reason. For a voluntary act is that which proceedeth from the will, and no other. But if instead of a rational appetite, we shall say an appetite resulting from a precedent deliberation, then the definition is the same that I have given here. Will, therefore, is the last appetite in deliberating. And though we say in common discourse, a man had a will once to do a thing, that nevertheless he forbore to do; yet that is properly but an inclination, which makes no action voluntary; because the action depends not of it, but of the last inclination, or appetite. For if the intervenient appetites make any action voluntary, then by the same reason all intervenient aversions should make the same action involuntary; and so one and the same action should be both voluntary and involuntary. By this it is manifest that, not only actions that have their beginning from covetousness, ambition, lust, or other appetites to the thing propounded, but also those that have their beginning from aversion, or fear of those consequences that follow the omission, are voluntary actions. The forms of speech by which the passions are expressed are partly the same and partly different from those by which we express our thoughts. And first generally all passions may be expressed indicatively; as, I love, I fear, I joy, I deliberate, I will, I command: but some of them have particular expressions by themselves, which nevertheless are not affirmations, unless it be when they serve to make other inferences besides that of the passion they proceed from. Deliberation is expressed subjunctively; which is a speech proper to signify suppositions, with their consequences; as, If this be done, then this will follow; and differs not from the language of reasoning, save that reasoning is in general words, but deliberation for the most part is of particulars. The language of desire, and aversion, is imperative; as, Do this, forbear that; which when the party is obliged to do, or forbear, is command; otherwise prayer; or else counsel. The language of vainglory, of indignation, pity and revengefulness, optative: but of the desire to know, there is a peculiar expression called interrogative; as, What is it, when shall it, how is it done, and why so? Other language of the passions I find none: for cursing, swearing, reviling, and the like do not signify as speech, but as the actions of a tongue accustomed. These forms of speech, I say, are expressions or voluntary significations of our passions: but certain signs they be not; because they may be used arbitrarily, whether they that use them have such passions or not. The best signs of passions present are either in the countenance, motions of the body, actions, and ends, or aims, which we otherwise know the man to have. And because in deliberation the appetites and aversions are raised by foresight of the good and evil consequences, and sequels of the action whereof we deliberate, the good or evil effect thereof dependeth on the foresight of a long chain of consequences, of which very seldom any man is able to see to the end. But for so far as a man seeth, if the good in those consequences be greater than the evil, the whole chain is that which writers call apparent or seeming good. And contrarily, when the evil exceedeth the good, the whole is apparent or seeming evil: so that he who hath by experience, or reason, the greatest and surest prospect of consequences, deliberates best himself; and is able, when he will, to give the best counsel unto others. Continual success in obtaining those things which a man from time to time desireth, that is to say, continual prospering, is that men call felicity; I mean the felicity of this life. For there is no such thing as perpetual tranquillity of mind, while we live here; because life itself is but motion, and can never be without desire, nor without fear, no more than without sense. What kind of felicity God hath ordained to them that devoutly honour him, a man shall no sooner know than enjoy; being joys that now are as incomprehensible as the word of Schoolmen, beatifical vision, is unintelligible. The form of speech whereby men signify their opinion of the goodness of anything is praise. That whereby they signify the power and greatness of anything is magnifying. And that whereby they signify the opinion they have of a man's felicity is by the Greeks called makarismos, for which we have no name in our tongue. And thus much is sufficient for the present purpose to have been said of the passions.

## CHAPTER VII, OF THE ENDS OR RESOLUTIONS OF DISCOURSE

OF ALL discourse governed by desire of knowledge, there is at last an end, either by attaining or by giving over. And in the chain of discourse, wheresoever it be interrupted, there is an end for that time. If the discourse be merely mental, it consisteth of thoughts that the thing will be, and will not be; or that it has been, and has not been, alternately. So that wheresoever you break off the chain of a man's discourse, you leave him in a presumption of it will be, or, it will not be; or it has been, or, has not been. All which is opinion. And that which is alternate appetite, in deliberating concerning good and evil, the same is alternate opinion in the enquiry of the truth of past and future. And as the last appetite in deliberation is called the will, so the last opinion in search of the truth of past and future is called the judgement, or resolute and final sentence of him that discourseth. And as the whole chain of appetites alternate in the question of good or bad is called deliberation; so the whole chain of opinions alternate in the question of true or false is called doubt. No discourse whatsoever can end in absolute knowledge of fact, past or to come. For, as for the knowledge of fact, it is originally sense, and ever after memory. And for the knowledge of consequence, which I have said before is called science, it is not absolute, but conditional. No man can know by discourse that this, or that, is, has been, or will be; which is to know absolutely: but only that if this be, that is; if this has been, that has been; if this shall be, that shall be; which is to know conditionally: and that not the consequence of one thing to another, but of one name of a thing to another name of the same thing. And therefore, when the discourse is put into speech, and begins with the definitions of words, and proceeds by connexion of the same into general affirmations, and of these again into syllogisms, the end or last sum is called the conclusion; and the thought of the mind by it signified is that conditional knowledge, or knowledge of the consequence of words, which is commonly called science. But if the first ground of such discourse be not definitions, or if the definitions be not rightly joined together into syllogisms, then the end or conclusion is again opinion, namely of the truth of somewhat said, though sometimes in absurd and senseless words, without possibility of being understood. When two or more men know of one and the same fact, they are said to be conscious of it one to another; which is as much as to know it together. And because such are fittest witnesses of the facts of one another, or of a third, it was and ever will be reputed a very evil act for any man to speak against his conscience; or to corrupt or force another so to do: insomuch that the plea of conscience has been always hearkened unto very diligently in all times. Afterwards, men made use of the same word metaphorically for the knowledge of their own secret facts and secret thoughts; and therefore it is rhetorically said that the conscience is a thousand witnesses. And last of all, men, vehemently in love with their own new opinions, though never so absurd, and obstinately bent to maintain them, gave those their opinions also that reverenced name of conscience, as if they would have it seem unlawful to change or speak against them; and so pretend to know they are true, when they know at most but that they think so. When a man's discourse beginneth not at definitions, it beginneth either at some other contemplation of his own, and then it is still called opinion, or it beginneth at some saying of another, of whose ability to know the truth, and of whose honesty in not deceiving, he doubteth not; and then the discourse is not so much concerning the thing, as the person; and the resolution is called belief, and faith: faith, in the man; belief, both of the man, and of the truth of what he says. So that in belief are two opinions; one of the saying of the man, the other of his virtue. To have faith in, or trust to, or believe a man, signify the same thing; namely, an opinion of the veracity of the man: but to believe what is said signifieth only an opinion of the truth of the saying. But we are to observe that this phrase, I believe in; as also the Latin, credo in; and the Greek, piseno eis, are never used but in the writings of divines. Instead of them, in other writings are put: I believe him; I trust him; I have faith in him; I rely on him; and in Latin, credo illi; fido illi; and in Greek, piseno anto; and that this singularity of the ecclesiastic use of the word hath raised many disputes about the right object of the Christian faith. But by believing in, as it is in the Creed, is meant, not trust in the person, but confession and acknowledgement of the doctrine. For not only Christians, but all manner of men do so believe in God as to hold all for truth they hear Him say, whether they understand it or not, which is all the faith and trust can possibly be had in any person whatsoever; but they do not all believe the doctrine of the Creed. From whence we may infer that when we believe any saying, whatsoever it be, to be true, from arguments taken, not from the thing itself, or from the principles of natural reason, but from the authority and good opinion we have of him that hath said it; then is the speaker, or person we believe in, or trust in, and whose word we take, the object of our faith; and the honour done in believing is done to him only. And consequently, when we believe that the Scriptures are the word of God, having no immediate revelation from God Himself, our belief, faith, and trust is in the Church; whose word we take, and acquiesce therein. And they that believe that which a prophet relates unto them in the name of God take the word of the prophet, do honour to him, and in him trust and believe, touching the truth of what he relateth, whether he be a true or a false prophet. And so it is also with all other history. For if I should not believe all that is written by historians of the glorious acts of Alexander or Caesar, I do not think the ghost of Alexander or Caesar had any just cause to be offended, or anybody else but the historian. If Livy say the gods made once a cow speak, and we believe it not, we distrust not God therein, but Livy. So that it is evident that whatsoever we believe, upon no other reason than what is drawn from authority of men only, and their writings, whether they be sent from God or not, is faith in men only.

## CHAPTER VIII, OF THE VIRTUES COMMONLY CALLED INTELLECTUAL; AND THEIR CONTRARY DEFECTS

VIRTUE generally, in all sorts of subjects, is somewhat that is valued for eminence; and consisteth in comparison. For if all things were equally in all men, nothing would be prized. And by virtues intellectual are always understood such abilities of the mind as men praise, value, and desire should be in themselves; and go commonly under the name of a good wit; though the same word, wit, be used also to distinguish one certain ability from the rest. These virtues are of two sorts; natural and acquired. By natural, I mean not that which a man hath from his birth: for that is nothing else but sense; wherein men differ so little one from another, and from brute beasts, as it is not to be reckoned amongst virtues. But I mean that wit which is gotten by use only, and experience, without method, culture, or instruction. This natural wit consisteth principally in two things: celerity of imagining (that is, swift succession of one thought to another); and steady direction to some approved end. On the contrary, a slow imagination maketh that defect or fault of the mind which is commonly called dullness, stupidity, and sometimes by other names that signify slowness of motion, or difficulty to be moved. And this difference of quickness is caused by the difference of men's passions; that love and dislike, some one thing, some another: and therefore some men's thoughts run one way, some another, and are held to, observe differently the things that pass through their imagination. And whereas in this succession of men's thoughts there is nothing to observe in the things they think on, but either in what they be like one another, or in what they be unlike, or what they serve for, or how they serve to such a purpose; those that observe their similitudes, in case they be such as are but rarely observed by others, are said to have a good wit; by which, in this occasion, is meant a good fancy. But they that observe their differences, and dissimilitudes, which is called distinguishing, and discerning, and judging between thing and thing, in case such discerning be not easy, are said to have a good judgement: and particularly in matter of conversation and business, wherein times, places, and persons are to be discerned, this virtue is called discretion. The former, that is, fancy, without the help of judgement, is not commended as a virtue; but the latter which is judgement, and discretion, is commended for itself, without the help of fancy. Besides the discretion of times, places, and persons, necessary to a good fancy, there is required also an often application of his thoughts to their end; that is to say, to some use to be made of them. This done, he that hath this virtue will be easily fitted with similitudes that will please, not only by illustration of his discourse, and adorning it with new and apt metaphors, but also, by the rarity of their invention. But without steadiness, and direction to some end, great fancy is one kind of madness; such as they have that, entering into any discourse, are snatched from their purpose by everything that comes in their thought, into so many and so long digressions and parentheses, that they utterly lose themselves: which kind of folly I know no particular name for: but the cause of it is sometimes want of experience; whereby that seemeth to a man new and rare which doth not so to others: sometimes pusillanimity; by which that seems great to him which other men think a trifle: and whatsoever is new, or great, and therefore thought fit to be told, withdraws a man by degrees from the intended way of his discourse. In a good poem, whether it be epic or dramatic, as also in sonnets, epigrams, and other pieces, both judgement and fancy are required: but the fancy must be more eminent; because they please for the extravagancy, but ought not to displease by indiscretion. In a good history, the judgement must be eminent; because the goodness consisteth in the choice of the method, in the truth, and in the choice of the actions that are most profitable to be known. Fancy has no place, but only in adorning the style. In orations of praise, and in invectives, the fancy is predominant; because the design is not truth, but to honour or dishonour; which is done by noble or by vile comparisons. The judgement does but suggest what circumstances make an action laudable or culpable. In hortatives and pleadings, as truth or disguise serveth best to the design in hand, so is the judgement or the fancy most required. In demonstration, in council, and all rigorous search of truth, sometimes does all; except sometimes the understanding have need to be opened by some apt similitude, and then there is so much use of fancy. But for metaphors, they are in this case utterly excluded. For seeing they openly profess deceit, to admit them into council, or reasoning, were manifest folly. And in any discourse whatsoever, if the defect of discretion be apparent, how extravagant soever the fancy be, the whole discourse will be taken for a sign of want of wit; and so will it never when the discretion is manifest, though the fancy be never so ordinary. The secret thoughts of a man run over all things holy, prophane, clean, obscene, grave, and light, without shame, or blame; which verbal discourse cannot do, farther than the judgement shall approve of the time, place, and persons. An anatomist or physician may speak or write his judgement of unclean things; because it is not to please, but profit: but for another man to write his extravagant and pleasant fancies of the same is as if a man, from being tumbled into the dirt, should come and present himself before good company. And it is the want of discretion that makes the difference. Again, in professed remissness of mind, and familiar company, a man may play with the sounds and equivocal significations of words, and that many times with encounters of extraordinary fancy; but in a sermon, or in public, or before persons unknown, or whom we ought to reverence, there is no jingling of words that will not be accounted folly: and the difference is only in the want of discretion. So that where wit is wanting, it is not fancy that is wanting, but discretion. Judgement, therefore, without fancy is wit, but fancy without judgement, not. When the thoughts of a man that has a design in hand, running over a multitude of things, observes how they conduce to that design, or what design they may conduce unto; if his observations be such as are not easy, or usual, this wit of his is called prudence, and dependeth on much experience, and memory of the like things and their consequences heretofore. In which there is not so much difference of men as there is in their fancies and judgements; because the experience of men equal in age is not much unequal as to the quantity, but lies in different occasions, every one having his private designs. To govern well a family and a kingdom are not different degrees of prudence, but different sorts of business; no more than to draw a picture in little, or as great or greater than the life, are different degrees of art. A plain husbandman is more prudent in affairs of his own house than a Privy Counsellor in the affairs of another man. To prudence, if you add the use of unjust or dishonest means, such as usually are prompted to men by fear or want, you have that crooked wisdom which is called craft; which is a sign of pusillanimity. For magnanimity is contempt of unjust or dishonest helps. And that which the Latins call versutia (translated into English, shifting), and is a putting off of a present danger or incommodity by engaging into a greater, as when a man robs one to pay another, is but a shorter-sighted craft; called versutia, from versura, which signifies taking money at usury for the present payment of interest. As for acquired wit (I mean acquired by method and instruction), there is none but reason; which is grounded on the right use of speech, and produceth the sciences. But of reason and science, I have already spoken in the fifth and sixth chapters. The causes of this difference of wits are in the passions, and the difference of passions proceedeth partly from the different constitution of the body, and partly from different education. For if the difference proceeded from the temper of the brain, and the organs of sense, either exterior or interior, there would be no less difference of men in their sight, hearing, or other senses than in their fancies and discretions. It proceeds, therefore, from the passions; which are different, not only from the difference of men's complexions, but also from their difference of customs and education. The passions that most of all cause the differences of wit are principally the more or less desire of power, of riches, of knowledge, and of honour. All which may be reduced to the first, that is, desire of power. For riches, knowledge and honour are but several sorts of power. And therefore, a man who has no great passion for any of these things, but is as men term it indifferent; though he may be so far a good man as to be free from giving offence, yet he cannot possibly have either a great fancy or much judgement. For the thoughts are to the desires as scouts and spies to range abroad and find the way to the things desired, all steadiness of the mind's motion, and all quickness of the same, proceeding from thence. For as to have no desire is to be dead; so to have weak passions is dullness; and to have passions indifferently for everything, giddiness and distraction; and to have stronger and more vehement passions for anything than is ordinarily seen in others is that which men call madness. Whereof there be almost as may kinds as of the passions themselves. Sometimes the extraordinary and extravagant passion proceedeth from the evil constitution of the organs of the body, or harm done them; and sometimes the hurt, and indisposition of the organs, is caused by the vehemence or long continuance of the passion. But in both cases the madness is of one and the same nature. The passion whose violence or continuance maketh madness is either great vainglory, which is commonly called pride and self-conceit, or great dejection of mind. Pride subjecteth a man to anger, the excess whereof is the madness called rage, and fury. And thus it comes to pass that excessive desire of revenge, when it becomes habitual, hurteth the organs, and becomes rage: that excessive love, with jealousy, becomes also rage: excessive opinion of a man's own self, for divine inspiration, for wisdom, learning, form, and the like, becomes distraction and giddiness: the same, joined with envy, rage: vehement opinion of the truth of anything, contradicted by others, rage. Dejection subjects a man to causeless fears, which is a madness commonly called melancholy apparent also in diverse manners: as in haunting of solitudes and graves; in superstitious behaviour; and in fearing some one, some another, particular thing. In sum, all passions that produce strange and unusual behaviour are called by the general name of madness. But of the several kinds of madness, he that would take the pains might enrol a legion. And if the excesses be madness, there is no doubt but the passions themselves, when they tend to evil, are degrees of the same. For example, though the effect of folly, in them that are possessed of an opinion of being inspired, be not visible always in one man by any very extravagant action that proceedeth from such passion, yet when many of them conspire together, the rage of the whole multitude is visible enough. For what argument of madness can there be greater than to clamour, strike, and throw stones at our best friends? Yet this is somewhat less than such a multitude will do. For they will clamour, fight against, and destroy those by whom all their lifetime before they have been protected and secured from injury. And if this be madness in the multitude, it is the same in every particular man. For as in the midst of the sea, though a man perceive no sound of that part of the water next him, yet he is well assured that part contributes as much to the roaring of the sea as any other part of the same quantity: so also, though we perceive no great unquietness in one or two men, yet we may be well assured that their singular passions are parts of the seditious roaring of a troubled nation. And if there were nothing else that bewrayed their madness, yet that very arrogating such inspiration to themselves is argument enough. If some man in Bedlam should entertain you with sober discourse, and you desire in taking leave to know what he were that you might another time requite his civility, and he should tell you he were God the Father; I think you need expect no extravagant action for argument of his madness. This opinion of inspiration, called commonly, private spirit, begins very often from some lucky finding of an error generally held by others; and not knowing, or not remembering, by what conduct of reason they came to so singular a truth, as they think it, though it be many times an untruth they light on, they presently admire themselves as being in the special grace of God Almighty, who hath revealed the same to them supernaturally by his Spirit. Again, that madness is nothing else but too much appearing passion may be gathered out of the effects of wine, which are the same with those of the evil disposition of the organs. For the variety of behaviour in men that have drunk too much is the same with that of madmen: some of them raging, others loving, others laughing, all extravagantly, but according to their several domineering passions: for the effect of the wine does but remove dissimulation, and take from them the sight of the deformity of their passions. For, I believe, the most sober men, when they walk alone without care and employment of the mind, would be unwilling the vanity and extravagance of their thoughts at that time should be publicly seen, which is a confession that passions unguided are for the most part mere madness. The opinions of the world, both in ancient and later ages, concerning the cause of madness have been two. Some, deriving them from the passions; some, from demons or spirits, either good or bad, which they thought might enter into a man, possess him, and move his organs in such strange and uncouth manner as madmen use to do. The former sort, therefore, called such men, madmen: but the latter called them sometimes demoniacs (that is, possessed with spirits); sometimes energumeni (that is, agitated or moved with spirits); and now in Italy they are called not only pazzi, madmen; but also spiritati, men possessed. There was once a great conflux of people in Abdera, a city of the Greeks, at the acting of the tragedy of Andromeda, upon an extreme hot day: whereupon a great many of the spectators, falling into fevers, had this accident from the heat and from the tragedy together, that they did nothing but pronounce iambics, with the names of Perseus and Andromeda; which, together with the fever, was cured by the coming on of winter: and this madness was thought to proceed from the passion imprinted by the tragedy. Likewise there reigned a fit of madness in another Grecian city which seized only the young maidens, and caused many of them to hang themselves. This was by most then thought an act of the devil. But one that suspected that contempt of life in them might proceed from some passion of the mind, and supposing they did not contemn also their honour, gave counsel to the magistrates to strip such as so hanged themselves, and let them hang out naked. This, the story says, cured that madness. But on the other side, the same Grecians did often ascribe madness to the operation of the Eumenides, or Furies; and sometimes of Ceres, Phoebus, and other gods: so much did men attribute to phantasms as to think them aerial living bodies, and generally to call them spirits. And as the Romans in this held the same opinion with the Greeks, so also did the Jews; for they called madmen prophets, or, according as they thought the spirits good or bad, demoniacs; and some of them called both prophets and demoniacs madmen; and some called the same man both demoniac and madman. But for the Gentiles, it is no wonder; because diseases and health, vices and virtues, and many natural accidents were with them termed and worshipped as demons. So that a man was to understand by demon as well sometimes an ague as a devil. But for the Jews to have such opinion is somewhat strange.

For neither Moses nor Abraham pretended to prophesy by possession of a spirit, but from the voice of God, or by a vision or dream: nor is there anything in his law, moral or ceremonial, by which they were taught there was any such enthusiasm, or any possession. When God is said to take from the spirit that was in Moses, and give to the seventy elders, the spirit of God, taking it for the substance of God, is not divided. [Numbers, 11. 25] The Scriptures by the Spirit of God in man mean a man's spirit, inclined to godliness. And where it is said, "Whom I have filled with the spirit of wisdom to make garments for Aaron," [Exodus, 28. 3] is not meant a spirit put into them, that can make garments, but the wisdom of their own spirits in that kind of work. In the like sense, the spirit of man, when it produceth unclean actions, is ordinarily called an unclean spirit; and so other spirits, though not always, yet as often as the virtue or vice, so styled, is extraordinary and eminent. Neither did the other prophets of the Old Testament pretend enthusiasm, or that God spoke in them, but to them, by voice, vision, or dream; and the "burden of the Lord" was not possession, but command. How then could the Jews fall into this opinion of possession? I can imagine no reason but that which is common to all men; namely, the want of curiosity to search natural causes; and their placing felicity in the acquisition of the gross pleasures of the senses, and the things that most immediately conduce thereto. For they that see any strange and unusual ability or defect in a man's mind, unless they see withal from what cause it may probably proceed, can hardly think it natural; and if not natural, they must needs think it supernatural; and then what can it be, but that either God or the Devil is in him? And hence it came to pass, when our Saviour was compassed about with the multitude, those of the house doubted he was mad, and went out to hold him: but the Scribes said he had Beelzebub, and that was it, by which he cast out devils; as if the greater madman had awed the lesser. [Mark, 3. 21] And that some said, "He hath a devil, and is mad"; whereas others, holding him for a prophet, said, "These are not the words of one that hath a devil." [John, 10. 20] So in the Old Testament he that came to anoint Jehu was a Prophet; but some of the company asked Jehu, "What came that madman for?" [II Kings, 9. 11] So that, in sum, it is manifest that whosoever behaved himself in extraordinary manner was thought by the Jews to be possessed either with a good or evil spirit; except by the Sadducees, who erred so far on the other hand as not to believe there were at all any spirits, which is very near to direct atheism; and thereby perhaps the more provoked others to term such men demoniacs rather than madmen. But why then does our Saviour proceed in the curing of them, as if they were possessed, and not as it they were mad? To which I can give no other kind of answer but that which is given to those that urge the Scripture in like manner against the opinion of the motion of the earth. The Scripture was written to show unto men the kingdom of God, and to prepare their minds to become His obedient subjects, leaving the world, and the philosophy thereof, to the disputation of men for the exercising of their natural reason. Whether the earth's or sun's motion make the day and night, or whether the exorbitant actions of men proceed from passion or from the Devil, so we worship him not, it is all one, as to our obedience and subjection to God Almighty; which is the thing for which the Scripture was written. As for that our Saviour speaketh to the disease as to a person, it is the usual phrase of all that cure by words only, as Christ did, and enchanters pretend to do, whether they speak to a devil or not. For is not Christ also said to have rebuked the winds? [Matthew, 8. 26] Is not he said also to rebuke a fever? [Luke, 4. 39] Yet this does not argue that a fever is a devil. And whereas many of those devils are said to confess Christ, it is not necessary to interpret those places otherwise than that those madmen confessed Him. And whereas our Saviour speaketh of an unclean spirit that, having gone out of a man, wandereth through dry places, seeking rest, and finding none, and returning into the same man with seven other spirits worse than himself; [Matthew, 12. 43] it is manifestly a parable, alluding to a man that, after a little endeavour to quit his lusts, is vanquished by the strength of them, and becomes seven times worse than he was. So that I see nothing at all in the Scripture that requireth a belief that demoniacs were any other thing but madmen. There is yet another fault in the discourses of some men, which may also be numbered amongst the sorts of madness; namely, that abuse of words, whereof I have spoken before in the fifth chapter by the name of absurdity. And that is when men speak such words as, put together, have in them no signification at all, but are fallen upon, by some, through misunderstanding of the words they have received and repeat by rote; by others, from intention to deceive by obscurity. And this is incident to none but those that converse in questions of matters incomprehensible, as the Schoolmen; or in questions of abstruse philosophy. The common sort of men seldom speak insignificantly, and are therefore, by those other egregious persons, counted idiots. But to be assured their words are without anything correspondent to them in the mind, there would need some examples; which if any man require, let him take a Schoolman into his hands and see if he can translate any one chapter concerning any difficult point; as the Trinity, the Deity, the nature of Christ, transubstantiation, free will, etc., into any of the modern tongues, so as to make the same intelligible; or into any tolerable Latin, such as they were acquainted withal that lived when the Latin tongue was vulgar. What is the meaning of these words:

"The first cause does not necessarily inflow anything into the second, by force of the essential subordination of the second causes, by which it may help it to work?" They are the translation of the title of the sixth chapter of Suarez's first book, Of the Concourse, Motion, and Help of God. When men write whole volumes of such stuff, are they not mad, or intend to make others so? And particularly, in the question of transubstantiation; where after certain words spoken they that say, the whiteness, roundness, magnitude, quality, corruptibility, all which are incorporeal, etc., go out of the wafer into the body of our blessed Saviour, do they not make those nesses, tudes, and ties to be so many spirits possessing his body? For by spirits they mean always things that, being incorporeal, are nevertheless movable from one place to another. So that this kind of absurdity may rightly be numbered amongst the many sorts of madness; and all the time that, guided by clear thoughts of their worldly lust, they forbear disputing or writing thus, but lucid intervals. And thus much of the virtues and defects intellectual.

## CHAPTER IX, OF THE SEVERAL SUBJECT OF KNOWLEDGE

THERE are of are of knowledge two kinds, whereof one is knowledge of fact; the other, knowledge of the consequence of one affirmation to another. The former is nothing else but sense and memory, and is absolute knowledge; as when we see a fact doing, or remember it done; and this is the knowledge required in a witness. The latter is called science, and is conditional; as when we know that: if the figure shown be a circle, then any straight line through the center shall divide it into two equal parts. And this is the knowledge required in a philosopher; that is to say, of him that pretends to reasoning. The register of knowledge of fact is called history, whereof there be two sorts: one called natural history; which is the history of such facts, or effects of Nature, as have no dependence on man's will; such as are the histories of metals, plants, animals, regions, and the like. The other is civil history, which is the history of the voluntary actions of men in Commonwealths. The registers of science are such books as contain the demonstrations of consequences of one affirmation to another; and are commonly called books of philosophy; whereof the sorts are many, according to the diversity of the matter; and may be divided in such manner as I have divided them in the following table.

1. SCIENCE, that is, knowledge of consequences; which is called also PHILOSOPHY
    1. Consequences from accidents of bodies natural; which is called
        NATURAL PHILOSOPHY
        1. Consequences from accidents common to all bodies natural; which are quantity, and motion.
            1. Consequences from quantity, and motion indeterminate; which, being the principles or first foundation of philosophy, is called philosophia prima
                PHILOSOPHIA PRIMA
            2. Consequences from motion, and quantity determined
                1. Consequences from quantity, and motion determined By figure, By number Mathematics, + GEOMETRY + ARITHMETIC
                2. Consequences from motion, and quantity of bodies in special
                    1. Consequences from motion, and quantity of the great parts of the world, as the earth and stars, Cosmography + ASTRONOMY + GEOGRAPHY
                    2. Consequences from motion of special kinds, and figures of body, Mechanics, doctrine of weight + Science of ENGINEERS + ARCHITECTURE + NAVIGATION
        2. PHYSICS, or consequences from qualities
            1. Consequences from qualities of bodies transient, such as sometimes appear, sometimes vanish METEOROLOGY
            2. Consequences from qualities of bodies permanent
                1. Consequences from qualities of stars
                    1. Consequences from the light of the stars. Out of this, and the motion of the sun, is made the science of SCIOGRAPHY
                    2. Consequences from the influence of the stars, ASTROLOGY
                2. Consequences of qualities from liquid bodies that fill the space between the stars; such as are the air, or substance etherial
                3. Consequences from qualities of bodies terrestrial
                    1. Consequences from parts of the earth that are without sense,
                        1. Consequences from qualities of minerals, as stones, metals, etc.
                        2. Consequences from the qualities of vegetables
                    2. Consequences from qualities of animals
                      1. Consequences from qualities of animals in general
                          1. Consequences from vision, OPTICS
                          2. Consequences from sounds, MUSIC
                          3. Consequences from the rest of the senses
                      2. Consequences from qualities of men in special
                        1. Consequences from passions of men, ETHICS
                        2. Consequences from speech,
                          1. In magnifying, vilifying, etc. POETRY
                          2. In persuading, RHETORIC
                          3. In reasoning, LOGIC
                          4. In contracting, The Science of JUST and UNJUST
    2. Consequences from accidents of politic bodies; which is called
    POLITICS, AND CIVIL PHILOSOPHY
        1. Of consequences from the institution of COMMONWEALTHS, to the rights, and duties of the body politic, or sovereign
        2. Of consequences from the same, to the duty and right of the subjects

# CHAPTER X, OF POWER, WORTH, DIGNITY, HONOUR AND WORTHINESS

THE POWER of a man, to take it universally, is his present means to obtain some future apparent good, and is either original or instrumental. Natural power is the eminence of the faculties of body, or mind; as extraordinary strength, form, prudence, arts, eloquence, liberality, nobility. Instrumental are those powers which, acquired by these, or by fortune, are means and instruments to acquire more; as riches, reputation, friends, and the secret working of God, which men call good luck. For the nature of power is, in this point, like to fame, increasing as it proceeds; or like the motion of heavy bodies, which, the further they go, make still the more haste. The greatest of human powers is that which is compounded of the powers of most men, united by consent, in one person, natural or civil, that has the use of all their powers depending on his will; such as is the power of a Commonwealth: or depending on the wills of each particular; such as is the power of a faction, or of diverse. factions leagued. Therefore to have servants is power; to have friends is power: for they are strengths united. Also, riches joined with liberality is power; because it procureth friends and servants: without liberality, not so; because in this case they defend not, but expose men to envy, as a prey. Reputation of power is power; because it draweth with it the adherence of those that need protection. So is reputation of love of a man's country, called popularity, for the same reason. Also, what quality soever maketh a man beloved or feared of many, or the reputation of such quality, is power; because it is a means to have the assistance and service of many. Good success is power; because it maketh reputation of wisdom or good fortune, which makes men either fear him or rely on him. Affability of men already in power is increase of power; because it gaineth love. Reputation of prudence in the conduct of peace or war is power; because to prudent men we commit the government of ourselves more willingly than to others. Nobility is power, not in all places, but only in those Commonwealths where it has privileges; for in such privileges consisteth their power. Eloquence is power; because it is seeming prudence. Form is power; because being a promise of good, it recommendeth men to the favour of women and strangers. The sciences are small powers; because not eminent, and therefore, not acknowledged in any man; nor are at all, but in a few, and in them, but of a few things. For science is of that nature, as none can understand it to be, but such as in a good measure have attained it. Arts of public use, as fortification, making of engines, and other instruments of war, because they confer to defence and victory, are power; and though the true mother of them be science, namely, the mathematics yet, because they are brought into the light by the hand of the artificer, they be esteemed (the midwife passing with the vulgar for the mother) as his issue. The value or worth of a man is, as of all other things, his price; that is to say, so much as would be given for the use of his power, and therefore is not absolute, but a thing dependent on the need and judgement of another. An able conductor of soldiers is of great price in time of war present or imminent, but in peace not so. A learned and uncorrupt judge is much worth in time of peace, but not so much in war. And as in other things, so in men, not the seller, but the buyer determines the price. For let a man, as most men do, rate themselves at the highest value they can, yet their true value is no more than it is esteemed by others. The manifestation of the value we set on one another is that which is commonly called honouring and dishonouring. To value a man at a high rate is to honour him; at a low rate is to dishonour him. But high and low, in this case, is to be understood by comparison to the rate that each man setteth on himself. The public worth of a man, which is the value set on him by the Commonwealth, is that which men commonly call dignity. And this value of him by the Commonwealth is understood by offices of command, judicature, public employment; or by names and titles introduced for distinction of such value. To pray to another for aid of any kind is to honour; because a sign we have an opinion he has power to help; and the more difficult the aid is, the more is the honour. To obey s to honour; because no man obeys them who they think have no power to help or hurt them. And consequently to disobey is to dishonour. To give great gifts to a man is to honour him; because it is buying of protection, and acknowledging of power. To give little gifts is to dishonour; because it is but alms, and signifies an opinion of the need of small helps. To be sedulous in promoting another's good, also to flatter, is to honour; as a sign we seek his protection or aid. To neglect is to dishonour. To give way or place to another, in any commodity, is to honour; being a confession of greater power. To arrogate is to dishonour. To show any sign of love or fear of another is honour; for both to love and to fear is to value. To contemn, or less to love or fear than he expects, is to dishonour; for it is undervaluing. To praise, magnify, or call happy is to honour; because nothing but goodness, power, and felicity is valued. To revile, mock, or pity is to dishonour. To speak to another with consideration, to appear before him with decency and humility, is to honour him; as signs of fear to offend. To speak to him rashly, to do anything before him obscenely, slovenly, impudently is to dishonour. To believe, to trust, to rely on another, is to honour him; sign of opinion of his virtue and power. To distrust, or not believe, is to dishonour. To hearken to a man's counsel, or discourse of what kind soever, is to honour; as a sign we think him wise, or eloquent, or witty. To sleep, or go forth, or talk the while, is to dishonour. To do those things to another which he takes for signs of honour, or which the law or custom makes so, is to honour; because in approving the honour done by others, he acknowledgeth the power which others acknowledge. To refuse to do them is to dishonour. To agree with in opinion is to honour; as being a sign of approving his judgement and wisdom. To dissent is dishonour, and an upbraiding of error, and, if the dissent be in many things, of folly. To imitate is to honour; for it is vehemently to approve. To imitate one's enemy is to dishonour. To honour those another honours is to honour him; as a sign of approbation of his judgement. To honour his enemies is to dishonour him. To employ in counsel, or in actions of difficulty, is to honour; as a sign of opinion of his wisdom or other power. To deny employment in the same cases to those that seek it is to dishonour. All these ways of honouring are natural, and as well within, as without Commonwealths. But in Commonwealths where he or they that have the supreme authority can make whatsoever they please to stand for signs of honour, there be other honours. A sovereign doth honour a subject with whatsoever title, or office, or employment, or action that he himself will have taken for a sign of his will to honour him. The king of Persia honoured Mordecai when he appointed he should be conducted through the streets in the king's garment, upon one of the king's horses, with a crown on his head, and a prince before him, proclaiming, "Thus shall it be done to him that the king will honour." And yet another king of Persia, or the same another time, to one that demanded for some great service to wear one of the king's robes, gave him leave so to do; but with this addition, that he should wear it as the king's fool; and then it was dishonour. So that of civil honour, the fountain is in the person of the Commonwealth, and dependeth on the will of the sovereign, and is therefore temporary and called civil honour; such as are magistracy, offices, titles, and in some places coats and scutcheons painted: and men honour such as have them, as having so many signs of favour in the Commonwealth, which favour is power. Honourable is whatsoever possession, action, or quality is an argument and sign of power. And therefore to be honoured, loved, or feared of many is honourable, as arguments of power. To be honoured of few or none, dishonourable. Dominion and victory is honourable because acquired by power; and servitude, for need or fear, is dishonourable. Good fortune, if lasting, honourable; as a sign of the favour of God. Ill and losses, dishonourable. Riches are honourable, for they are power. Poverty, dishonourable. Magnanimity, liberality, hope, courage, confidence, are honourable; for they proceed from the conscience of power. Pusillanimity, parsimony, fear, diffidence, are dishonourable. Timely resolution, or determination of what a man is to do, is honourable, as being the contempt of small difficulties and dangers. And irresolution, dishonourable, as a sign of too much valuing of little impediments and little advantages: for when a man has weighed things as long as the time permits, and resolves not, the difference of weight is but little; and therefore if he resolve not, he overvalues little things, which is pusillanimity. All actions and speeches that proceed, or seem to proceed, from much experience, science, discretion, or wit are honourable; for all these are powers. Actions or words that proceed from error, ignorance, or folly, dishonourable. Gravity, as far forth as it seems to proceed from a mind employed on something else, is honourable; because employment is a sign of power. But if it seem to proceed from a purpose to appear grave, it is dishonourable. For the gravity of the former is like the steadiness of a ship laden with merchandise; but of the like the steadiness of a ship ballasted with sand and other trash. To be conspicuous, that is to say, to be known, for wealth, office, great actions, or any eminent good is honourable; as a sign of the power for which he is conspicuous. On the contrary, obscurity is dishonourable. To be descended from conspicuous parents is honourable; because they the more easily attain the aids and friends of their ancestors. On the contrary, to be descended from obscure parentage is dishonourable. Actions proceeding from equity, joined with loss, are honourable; as signs of magnanimity: for magnanimity is a sign of power. On the contrary, craft, shifting, neglect of equity, is dishonourable. Covetousness of great riches, and ambition of great honours, are honourable; as signs of power to obtain them. Covetousness, and ambition of little gains, or preferments, is dishonourable. Nor does it alter the case of honour whether an action (so it be great and difficult, and consequently a sign of much power) be just or unjust: for honour consisteth only in the opinion of power. Therefore, the ancient heathen did not think they dishonoured, but greatly honoured the gods, when they introduced them in their poems committing rapes, thefts, and other great, but unjust or unclean acts; in so much as nothing is so much celebrated in Jupiter as his adulteries; nor in Mercury as his frauds and thefts; of whose praises, in a hymn of Homer, the greatest is this, that being born in the morning, he had invented music at noon, and before night stolen away the cattle of Apollo from his herdsmen. Also amongst men, till there were constituted great Commonwealths, it was thought no dishonour to be a pirate, or a highway thief; but rather a lawful trade, not only amongst the Greeks, but also amongst all other nations; as is manifest by the of ancient time. And at this day, in this part of the world, private duels are, and always will be, honourable, though unlawful, till such time as there shall be honour ordained for them that refuse, and ignominy for them that make the challenge. For duels also are many times effects of courage, and the ground of courage is always strength or skill, which are power; though for the most part they be effects of rash speaking, and of the fear of dishonour, in one or both the combatants; who, engaged by rashness, are driven into the lists to avoid disgrace. Scutcheons and coats of arms hereditary, where they have any their a

y eminent privileges, are honourable; otherwise not for their power consisteth either in such privileges, or in riches, or some such thing as is equally honoured in other men. This kind of honour, commonly called gentry, has been derived from the ancient Germans. For there never was any such thing known where the German customs were unknown. Nor is it now anywhere in use where the Germans have not inhabited. The ancient Greek commanders, when they went to war, had their shields painted with such devices as they pleased; insomuch as an unpainted buckler was a sign of poverty, and of a common soldier; but they transmitted not the inheritance of them. The Romans transmitted the marks of their families; but they were the images, not the devices of their ancestors. Amongst the people of Asia, Africa, and America, there is not, nor was ever, any such thing. Germans only had that custom; from whom it has been derived into England, France, Spain and Italy, when in great numbers they either aided the Romans or made their own conquests in these western parts of the world. For Germany, being anciently, as all other countries in their beginnings, divided amongst an infinite number of little lords, or masters of families, that continually had wars one with another, those masters, or lords, principally to the end they might, when they were covered with arms, be known by their followers, and partly for ornament, both painted their armor, or their scutcheon, or coat, with the picture of some beast, or other thing, and also put some eminent and visible mark upon the crest of their helmets. And this ornament both of the arms and crest descended by inheritance to their children; to the eldest pure, and to the rest with some note of diversity, such as the old master, that is to say in Dutch, the Here-alt, thought fit. But when many such families, joined together, made a greater monarchy, this duty of the herald to distinguish scutcheons was made a private office apart. And the issue of these lords is the great and ancient gentry; which for the most part bear living creatures noted for courage and rapine; or castles, battlements, belts, weapons, bars, palisades, and other notes of war; nothing being then in honour, but virtue military. Afterwards, not only kings, but popular Commonwealths, gave diverse manners of scutcheons to such as went forth to the war, or returned from it, for encouragement or recompense to their service. All which, by an observing reader, may be found in such ancient histories, Greek and Latin, as make mention of the German nation and manners in their times. Titles of honour, such as are duke, count, marquis, and baron, are honourable; as signifying the value set upon them by the sovereign power of the Commonwealth: which titles were in old time titles of office and command derived some from the Romans, some from the Germans and French. Dukes, in Latin, duces, being generals in war; counts, comites, such as bore the general company out of friendship, and were left to govern and defend places conquered and pacified; marquises, marchioness, were counts that governed the marches, or bounds of the Empire. Which titles of duke, count, and marquis came into the Empire about the time of Constantine the Great, from the customs of the German militia. But baron seems to have been a title of the Gauls, and signifies a great man; such as were the kings' or princes' men whom they employed in war about their persons; and seems to be derived from vir, to ber, and bar, that signified the same in the language of the Gauls, that vir in Latin; and thence to bero and baro: so that such men were called berones, and after barones; and (in Spanish) varones. But he that would know more, particularly the original of titles of honour, may find it, as I have done this, in Mr. Selden's most excellent treatise of that subject. In process of time these offices of honour, by occasion of trouble, and for reasons of good and peaceable government, were turned into mere titles, serving, for the most part, to distinguish the precedence, place, and order of subjects in the Commonwealth: and men were made dukes, counts, marquises, and barons of places, wherein they had neither possession nor command, and other titles also were devised to the same end. Worthiness is a thing different from the worth or value of a man, and also from his merit or desert, and consisteth in a particular power or ability for that whereof he is said to be worthy; which particular ability is usually named fitness, or aptitude. For he is worthiest to be a commander, to be a judge, or to have any other charge, that is best fitted with the qualities required to the well discharging of it; and worthiest of riches, that has the qualities most requisite for the well using of them: any of which qualities being absent, one may nevertheless be a worthy man, and valuable for something else. Again, a man may be worthy of riches, office, and employment that nevertheless can plead no right to have it before another, and therefore cannot be said to merit or deserve it. For merit presupposeth a right, and that the thing deserved is due by promise, of which I shall say more hereafter when I shall speak of contracts.

## CHAPTER XI, OF THE DIFFERENCE OF MANNERS

BY MANNERS, I mean not here decency of behaviour; as how one man should salute another, or how a man should wash his mouth, or pick his teeth before company, and such other points of the small morals; but those qualities of mankind that concern their living together in peace and unity. To which end we are to consider that the felicity of this life consisteth not in the repose of a mind satisfied. For there is no such finis ultimus (utmost aim) nor summum bonum (greatest good) as is spoken of in the books of the old moral philosophers. Nor can a man any more live whose desires are at an end than he whose senses and imaginations are at a stand. Felicity is a continual progress of the desire from one object to another, the attaining of the former being still but the way to the latter. The cause whereof is that the object of man's desire is not to enjoy once only, and for one instant of time, but to assure forever the way of his future desire. And therefore the voluntary actions and inclinations of all men tend not only to the procuring, but also to the assuring of a contented life, and differ only in the way, which ariseth partly from the diversity of passions in diverse men, and partly from the difference of the knowledge or opinion each one has of the causes which produce the effect desired. So that in the first place, I put for a general inclination of all mankind a perpetual and restless desire of power after power, that ceaseth only in death. And the cause of this is not always that a man hopes for a more intensive delight than he has already attained to, or that he cannot be content with a moderate power, but because he cannot assure the power and means to live well, which he hath present, without the acquisition of more. And from hence it is that kings, whose power is greatest, turn their endeavours to the assuring it at home by laws, or abroad by wars: and when that is done, there succeedeth a new desire; in some, of fame from new conquest; in others, of ease and sensual pleasure; in others, of admiration, or being flattered for excellence in some art or other ability of the mind. Competition of riches, honour, command, or other power inclineth to contention, enmity, and war, because the way of one competitor to the attaining of his desire is to kill, subdue, supplant, or repel the other. Particularly, competition of praise inclineth to a reverence of antiquity. For men contend with the living, not with the dead; to these ascribing more than due, that they may obscure the glory of the other. Desire of ease, and sensual delight, disposeth men to obey a common power: because by such desires a man doth abandon the protection that might be hoped for from his own industry and labour. Fear of death and wounds disposeth to the same, and for the same reason. On the contrary, needy men and hardy, not contented with their present condition, as also all men that are ambitious of military command, are inclined to continue the causes of war and to stir up trouble and sedition: for there is no honour military but by war; nor any such hope to mend an ill game as by causing a new shuffle. Desire of knowledge, and arts of peace, inclineth men to obey a common power: for such desire containeth a desire of leisure, and consequently protection from some other power than their own. Desire of praise disposeth to laudable actions, such as please them whose judgement they value; for of those men whom we contemn, we contemn also the praises. Desire of fame after death does the same. And though after death there be no sense of the praise given us on earth, as being joys that are either swallowed up in the unspeakable joys of heaven or extinguished in the extreme torments of hell: yet is not such fame vain; because men have a present delight therein, from the foresight of it, and of the benefit that may redound thereby to their posterity: which though they now see not, yet they imagine; and anything that is pleasure in the sense, the same also is pleasure in the imagination. To have received from one, to whom we think ourselves equal, greater benefits than there is hope to requite, disposeth to counterfeit love, but really secret hatred, and puts a man into the estate of a desperate debtor that, in declining the sight of his creditor, tacitly wishes him there where he might never see him more. For benefits oblige; and obligation is thraldom; and unrequitable obligation, perpetual thraldom; which is to one's equal, hateful. But to have received benefits from one whom we acknowledge for superior inclines to love; because the obligation is no new depression: and cheerful acceptation (which men call gratitude) is such an honour done to the obliger as is taken generally for retribution. Also to receive benefits, though from an equal, or inferior, as long as there is hope of requital, disposeth to love: for in the intention of the receiver, the obligation is of aid and service mutual; from whence proceedeth an emulation of who shall exceed in benefiting; the most noble and profitable contention possible, wherein the victor is pleased with his victory, and the other revenged by confessing it. To have done more hurt to a man than he can or is willing to expiate inclineth the doer to hate the sufferer. For he must expect revenge or forgiveness; both which are hateful. Fear of oppression disposeth a man to anticipate or to seek aid by society: for there is no other way by which a man can secure his life and liberty. Men that distrust their own subtlety are in tumult and sedition better disposed for victory than they that suppose themselves wise or crafty. For these love to consult; the other, fearing to be circumvented to strike first. And in sedition, men being always in the precincts of battle, to hold together and use all advantages of force is a better stratagem than any that can proceed from subtlety of wit. Vainglorious men, such as without being conscious to themselves of great sufficiency, delight in supposing themselves gallant men, are inclined only to ostentation, but not to attempt; because when danger or difficulty appears, they look for nothing but to have their insufficiency discovered. Vain, glorious men, such as estimate their sufficiency by the flattery of other men, or the fortune of some precedent action, without assured ground of hope from the true knowledge of themselves, are inclined to rash engaging; and in the approach of danger, or difficulty, to retire if they can: because not seeing the way of safety they will rather hazard their honour, which may be salved with an excuse, than their lives, for which no salve is sufficient. Men that have a strong opinion of their own wisdom in matter of government are disposed to ambition. Because without public employment in counsel or magistracy, the honour of their wisdom is lost. And therefore eloquent speakers are inclined to ambition; for eloquence seemeth wisdom, both to themselves and others. Pusillanimity disposeth men to irresolution, and consequently to lose the occasions and fittest opportunities of action. For after men have been in deliberation till the time of action approach, if it be not then manifest what is best to be done, it is a sign the difference of motives the one way and the other are not great: therefore not to resolve then is to lose the occasion by weighing of trifles, which is pusillanimity. Frugality, though in poor men a virtue, maketh a man unapt to achieve such actions as require the strength of many men at once: for it weakeneth their endeavour, which to be nourished and kept in vigour by reward. Eloquence, with flattery, disposeth men to confide in them that have it; because the former is seeming wisdom, the latter seeming kindness. Add to them military reputation and it disposeth men to adhere and subject themselves to those men that have them. The two former, having given them caution against danger from him, the latter gives them caution against danger from others. Want of science, that is, ignorance of causes, disposeth or rather constraineth a man to rely on the advice and authority of others. For all men whom the truth concerns, if they rely not on their own, must rely on the opinion of some other whom they think wiser than themselves, and see not why he should deceive them. Ignorance of the signification of words, is want of understanding, disposeth men to take on trust, not only the truth they know not, but also the errors; and which is more, the nonsense of them they trust: for neither error nor nonsense can, without a perfect understanding of words, be detected. From the same it proceedeth that men give different names to one and the same thing from the difference of their own passions: as they that approve a private opinion call it opinion; but they that mislike it, heresy: and yet heresy signifies no more than private opinion; but has only a greater tincture of choler. From the same also it proceedeth that men cannot distinguish, without study and great understanding between one action of many men and many actions of one multitude; as for example, between the one action of all the senators of Rome in killing Catiline, and the many actions of a number of senators in killing Caesar; and therefore are disposed to take for the action of the people that which is a multitude of actions done by a multitude of men, led perhaps by the persuasion of one. Ignorance of the causes, and original constitution of right, equity, law, and justice, disposeth a man to make custom and example the rule of his actions; in such manner as to think that unjust which it hath been the custom to punish; and that just, of the impunity and approbation whereof they can produce an example or (as the lawyers which only use this false measure of justice barbarously call it) a precedent; like little children that have no other rule of good and evil manners but the correction they receive from their parents and masters; save that children are constant to their rule, whereas men are not so; because grown strong and stubborn, they appeal from custom to reason, and from reason to custom, as it serves their turn, receding from custom when their interest requires it, and setting themselves against reason as oft as reason is against them: which is the cause that the doctrine of right and wrong is perpetually disputed, both by the pen and the sword: whereas the doctrine of lines and figures is not so; because men care not, in that subject, what be truth, as a thing that crosses no man's ambition, profit, or lust. For I doubt not, but if it had been a thing contrary to any man's right of dominion, or to the interest of men that have dominion, that the three angles of a triangle should be equal to two angles of a square, that doctrine should have been, if not disputed, yet by the burning of all books of geometry suppressed, as far as he whom it concerned was able. Ignorance of remote causes disposeth men to attribute all events to the causes immediate and instrumental: for these are all the causes they perceive. And hence it comes to pass that in all places men that are grieved with payments to the public discharge their anger upon the publicans, that is to say, farmers, collectors, and other officers of the public revenue, and adhere to such as find fault with the public government; and thereby, when they have engaged themselves beyond hope of justification, fall also upon the supreme authority, for fear of punishment, or shame of receiving pardon. Ignorance of natural causes disposeth a man to credulity, so as to believe many times impassibilities: for such know nothing to the contrary, but that they may be true, being unable to detect the impossibility. And credulity, because men love to be hearkened unto in company, disposeth them to lying: so that ignorance itself, without malice, is able to make a man both to believe lies and tell them, and sometimes also to invent them. Anxiety for the future time disposeth men to inquire into the causes of things: because the knowledge of them maketh men the better able to order the present to their best advantage. Curiosity, or love of the knowledge of causes, draws a man from consideration of the effect to seek the cause; and again, the cause of that cause; till of necessity he must come to this thought at last, that there is some cause whereof there is no former cause, but is eternal; which is it men call God. So that it is impossible to make any profound inquiry into natural causes without being inclined thereby to believe there is one God eternal; though they cannot have any idea of Him in their mind answerable to His nature. For as a man that is born blind, hearing men talk of warming themselves by the fire, and being brought to warm himself by the same, may easily conceive, and assure himself, there is somewhat there which men call fire and is the cause of the heat he feels, but cannot imagine what it is like, nor have an idea of it in his mind such as they have that see it: so also, by the visible things of this world, and their admirable order, a man may conceive there is a cause of them, which men call God, and yet not have an idea or image of Him in his mind. And they that make little or no inquiry into the natural causes of things, yet from the fear that proceeds from the ignorance itself of what it is that hath the power to do them much good or harm are inclined to suppose, and feign unto themselves, several kinds of powers invisible, and to stand in awe of their own imaginations, and in time of distress to invoke them; as also in the time of an expected good success, to give them thanks, making the creatures of their own fancy their gods. By which means it hath come to pass that from the innumerable variety of fancy, men have created in the world innumerable sorts of gods. And this fear of things invisible is the natural seed of that which every one in himself calleth religion; and in them that worship or fear that power otherwise than they do, superstition. And this seed of religion, having been observed by many, some of those that have observed it have been inclined thereby to nourish, dress, and form it into laws; and to add to it, of their own invention, any opinion of the causes of future events by which they thought they should best be able to govern others and make unto themselves the greatest use of their powers.

**CHAPTER XII, OF RELIGION**

SEEING there are no signs nor fruit of religion but in man only, there is no cause to doubt but that the seed of religion is also only in man; and consisteth in some peculiar quality, or at least in some eminent degree thereof, not to be found in other living creatures. And first, it is peculiar to the nature of man to be inquisitive into the causes of the events they see, some more, some less, but all men so much as to be curious in the search of the causes of their own good and evil fortune. Secondly, upon the sight of anything that hath a beginning, to think also it had a cause which determined the same to begin then when it did, rather than sooner or later. Thirdly, whereas there is no other felicity of beasts but the enjoying of their quotidian food, ease, and lusts; as having little or no foresight of the time to come for want of observation and memory of the order, consequence, and dependence of the things they see; man observeth how one event hath been produced by another, and remembereth in them antecedence and consequence; and when he cannot assure himself of the true causes of things (for the causes of good and evil fortune for the most part are invisible), he supposes causes of them, either such as his own fancy suggesteth, or trusteth to the authority of other men such as he thinks to be his friends and wiser than himself. The two first make anxiety. For being assured that there be causes of all things that have arrived hitherto, or shall arrive hereafter, it is impossible for a man, who continually endeavoureth to secure himself against the evil he fears, and procure the good he desireth, not to be in a perpetual solicitude of the time to come; so that every man, especially those that are over-provident, are in an estate like to that of Prometheus. For as Prometheus (which, interpreted, is the prudent man) was bound to the hill Caucasus, a place of large prospect, where an eagle, feeding on his liver, devoured in the day as much as was repaired in the night: so that man, which looks too far before him in the care of future time, hath his heart all the day long gnawed on by fear of death, poverty, or other calamity; and has no repose, nor pause of his anxiety, but in sleep. This perpetual fear, always accompanying mankind in the ignorance of causes, as it were in the dark, must needs have for object something. And therefore when there is nothing to be seen, there is nothing to accuse either of their good or evil fortune but some power or agent invisible: in which sense perhaps it was that some of the old poets said that the gods were at first created by human fear: which, spoken of the gods (that is to say, of the many gods of the Gentiles), is very true. But the acknowledging of one God eternal, infinite, and omnipotent may more easily be derived from the desire men have to know the causes of natural bodies, and their several virtues and operations, than from the fear of what was to befall them in time to come. For he that, from any effect he seeth come to pass, should reason to the next and immediate cause thereof, and from thence to the cause of that cause, and plunge himself profoundly in the pursuit of causes, shall at last come to this, that there must be (as even the heathen philosophers confessed) one First Mover; that is, a first and an eternal cause of all things; which is that which men mean by the name of God: and all this without thought of their fortune, the solicitude whereof both inclines to fear and hinders them from the search of the causes of other things; and thereby gives occasion of feigning of as many gods as there be men that feign them. And for the matter, or substance, of the invisible agents, so fancied, they could not by natural cogitation fall upon any other concept but that it was the same with that of the soul of man; and that the soul of man was of the same substance with that which appeareth in a dream to one that sleepeth; or in a looking-glass to one that is awake; which, men not knowing that such apparitions are nothing else but creatures of the fancy, think to be real and external substances, and therefore call them ghosts; as the Latins called them imagines and umbrae and thought them spirits (that is, thin aerial bodies), and those invisible agents, which they feared, to be like them, save that they appear and vanish when they please. But the opinion that such spirits were incorporeal, or immaterial, could never enter into the mind of any man by nature; because, though men may put together words of contradictory signification, as spirit and incorporeal, yet they can never have the imagination of anything answering to them: and therefore, men that by their own meditation arrive to the acknowledgement of one infinite, omnipotent, and eternal God choose rather to confess He is incomprehensible and above their understanding than to define His nature by spirit incorporeal, and then confess their definition to be unintelligible: or if they give him such a title, it is not dogmatically, with intention to make the Divine Nature understood, but piously, to honour Him with attributes of significations as remote as they can from the grossness of bodies visible. Then, for the way by which they think these invisible agents wrought their effects; that is to say, what immediate causes they used in bringing things to pass, men that know not what it is that we call causing (that is, almost all men) have no other rule to guess by but by observing and remembering what they have seen to precede the like effect at some other time, or times before, without seeing between the antecedent and subsequent event any dependence or connexion at all: and therefore from the like things past, they expect the like things to come; and hope for good or evil luck, superstitiously, from things that have no part at all in the causing of it: as the Athenians did for their war at Lepanto demand another Phormio; the Pompeian faction for their war in Africa, another Scipio; and others have done in diverse other occasions since. In like manner they attribute their fortune to a stander by, to a lucky or unlucky place, to words spoken, especially if the name of God be amongst them, as charming, and conjuring (the liturgy of witches); insomuch as to believe they have power to turn a stone into bread, bread into a man, or anything into anything. Thirdly, for the worship which naturally men exhibit to powers invisible, it can be no other but such expressions of their reverence as they would use towards men; gifts, petitions, thanks, submission of body, considerate addresses, sober behaviour, premeditated words, swearing (that is, assuring one another of their promises), by invoking them. Beyond that, reason suggesteth nothing, but leaves them either to rest there, or for further ceremonies to rely on those they believe to be wiser than themselves. Lastly, concerning how these invisible powers declare to men the things which shall hereafter come to pass, especially concerning their good or evil fortune in general, or good or ill success in any particular undertaking, men are naturally at a stand; save that using to conjecture of the time to come by the time past, they are very apt, not only to take casual things, after one or two encounters, for prognostics of the like encounter ever after, but also to believe the like prognostics from other men of whom they have once conceived a good opinion. And in these four things, opinion of ghosts, ignorance of second causes, devotion towards what men fear, and taking of things casual for prognostics, consisteth the natural seed of religion; which, by reason of the different fancies, judgements, and passions of several men, hath grown up into ceremonies so different that those which are used by one man are for the most part ridiculous to another. For these seeds have received culture from two sorts of men. One sort have been they that have nourished and ordered them, according to their own invention. The other have done it by God's commandment and direction. But both sorts have done it with a purpose to make those men that relied on them the more apt to obedience, laws, peace, charity, and civil society. So that the religion of the former sort is a part of human politics; and teacheth part of the duty which earthly kings require of their subjects. And the religion of the latter sort is divine politics; and containeth precepts to those that have yielded themselves subjects in the kingdom of God. Of the former sort were all the founders of Commonwealths, and the lawgivers of the Gentiles: of the latter sort were Abraham, Moses, and our blessed Saviour, by whom have been derived unto us the laws of the kingdom of God. And for that part of religion which consisteth in opinions concerning the nature of powers invisible, there is almost nothing that has a name that has not been esteemed amongst the Gentiles, in one place or another, a god or devil; or by their poets feigned to be animated, inhabited, or possessed by some spirit or other. The unformed matter of the world was a god by the name of Chaos. The heaven, the ocean, the planets, the fire, the earth, the winds, were so many gods. Men, women, a bird, a crocodile, a calf, a dog, a snake, an onion, a leek, were deified. Besides that, they filled almost all places with spirits called demons: the plains, with Pan and Panises, or Satyrs; the woods, with Fauns and Nymphs; the sea, with Tritons and other Nymphs; every river and fountain, with a ghost of his name and with Nymphs; every house, with its Lares, or familiars; every man, with his Genius; Hell, with ghosts and spiritual officers, as Charon, Cerberus, and the Furies; and in the night time, all places with larvae, lemures, ghosts of men deceased, and a whole kingdom of fairies and bugbears. They have also ascribed divinity, and built temples, to mere accidents and qualities; such as are time, night, day, peace, concord, love, contention, virtue, honour, health, rust, fever, and the like; which when they prayed for, or against, they prayed to as if there were ghosts of those names hanging over their heads, and letting fall or withholding that good, or evil, for or against which they prayed. They invoked also their own wit, by the name of Muses; their own ignorance, by the name of Fortune; their own lust, by the name of Cupid; their own rage, by the name Furies; their own privy members by the name of Priapus; and attributed their pollutions to incubi and succubae: insomuch as there was nothing which a poet could introduce as a person in his poem which they did not make either a god or a devil. The same authors of the religion of the Gentiles, observing the second ground for religion, which is men's ignorance of causes, and thereby their aptness to attribute their fortune to causes on which there was no dependence at all apparent, took occasion to obtrude on their ignorance, instead of second causes, a kind of second and ministerial gods; ascribing the cause of fecundity to Venus, the cause of arts to Apollo, of subtlety and craft to Mercury, of tempests and storms to Aeolus, and of other effects to other gods; insomuch as there was amongst the heathen almost as great variety of gods as of business. And to the worship which naturally men conceived fit to be used towards their gods, namely, oblations, prayers, thanks, and the rest formerly named, the same legislators of the Gentiles have added their images, both in picture and sculpture, that the more ignorant sort (that is to say, the most part or generality of the people), thinking the gods for whose representation they were made were really included and as it were housed within them, might so much the more stand in fear of them: and endowed them with lands, and houses, and officers, and revenues, set apart from all other human uses; that is, consecrated, made holy to those their idols; as caverns, groves, woods, mountains, and whole islands; and have attributed to them, not only the shapes, some of men, some of beasts, some of monsters, but also the faculties and passions of men and beasts; as sense, speech, sex, lust, generation, and this not only by mixing one with another to propagate the kind of gods, but also by mixing with men and women to beget mongrel gods, and but inmates of heaven, as Bacchus, Hercules, and others; besides, anger, revenge, and other passions of living creatures, and the actions proceeding from them, as fraud, theft, adultery, sodomy, and any vice that may be taken for an effect of power or a cause of pleasure; and all such vices as amongst men are taken to be against law rather than against honour. Lastly, to the prognostics of time to come, which are naturally but conjectures upon the experience of time past, and supernaturally, divine revelation, the same authors of the religion of the Gentiles, partly upon pretended experience, partly upon pretended revelation, have added innumerable other superstitious ways of divination, and made men believe they should find their fortunes, sometimes in the ambiguous or senseless answers of the priests at Delphi, Delos, Ammon, and other famous oracles; which answers were made ambiguous by design, to own the event both ways; or absurd, by the intoxicating vapour of the place, which is very frequent in sulphurous caverns: sometimes in the leaves of the Sibyls, of whose prophecies, like those perhaps of Nostradamus (for the fragments now extant seem to be the invention of later times), there were some books in reputation in the time of the Roman republic: sometimes in the insignificant speeches of madmen, supposed to be possessed with a divine spirit, which possession they called enthusiasm; and these kinds of foretelling events were accounted theomancy, or prophecy: sometimes in the aspect of the stars at their nativity, which was called horoscopy, and esteemed a part of judiciary astrology: sometimes in their own hopes and fears, called and fears, called thumomancy, or presage: sometimes in the prediction of witches that pretended conference with the dead, which is called necromancy, conjuring, and witchcraft, and is but juggling and confederate knavery: sometimes in the casual flight or feeding of birds, called augury: sometimes in the entrails of a sacrificed beast, which was haruspicy: sometimes in dreams: sometimes in croaking of ravens, or chattering of birds: sometimes in the lineaments of the face, which was called metoposcopy; or by palmistry in the lines of the hand, in casual words called omina: sometimes in monsters or unusual accidents; as eclipses, comets, rare meteors, earthquakes, inundations, uncouth births, and the like, which they called portenta, and ostenta, because they thought them to portend or foreshow some great calamity to come: sometimes in mere lottery, as cross and pile; counting holes in a sieve; dipping of verses in Homer and Virgil; and innumerable other such vain conceits. So easy are men to be drawn to believe anything from such men as have gotten credit with them; and can with gentleness, and dexterity, take hold of their fear and ignorance. And therefore the first founders and legislators of Commonwealths amongst the Gentiles, whose ends were only to keep the people in obedience and peace, have in all places taken care: first, to imprint their minds a belief that those precepts which they gave concerning religion might not be thought to proceed from their own device, but from the dictates of some god or other spirit; or else that they themselves were of a higher nature than mere mortals, that their laws might the more easily be received; so Numa Pompilius pretended to receive the ceremonies he instituted amongst the Romans from the nymph Egeria and the first king and founder of the kingdom of Peru pretended himself and his wife to be the children of the sun; and Mahomet, to set up his new religion, pretended to have conferences with the Holy Ghost in form of a dove. Secondly, they have had a care to make it believed that the same things were displeasing to the gods which were forbidden by the laws. Thirdly, to prescribe ceremonies, supplications, sacrifices, and festivals by which they were to believe the anger of the gods might be appeased; and that ill success in war, great contagions of sickness, earthquakes, and each man's private misery came from the anger of the gods; and their anger from the neglect of their worship, or the forgetting or mistaking some point of the ceremonies required. And though amongst the ancient Romans men were not forbidden to deny that which in the poets is written of the pains and pleasures after this life, which divers of great authority and gravity in that state have in their harangues openly derided, yet that belief was always more cherished, than the contrary. And by these, and such other institutions, they obtained in order to their end, which was the peace of the Commonwealth, that the common people in their misfortunes, laying the fault on neglect, or error in their ceremonies, or on their own disobedience to the laws, were the less apt to mutiny against their governors. And being entertained with the pomp and pastime of festivals and public games made in honour of the gods, needed nothing else but bread to keep them from discontent, murmuring, and commotion against the state. And therefore the Romans, that had conquered the greatest part of the then known world, made no scruple of tolerating any religion whatsoever in the city of Rome itself, unless it had something in it that could not consist with their civil government; nor do we read that any religion was there forbidden but that of the Jews, who (being the peculiar kingdom of God) thought it unlawful to acknowledge subjection to any mortal king or state whatsoever. And thus you see how the religion of the Gentiles was a part of their policy. But where God himself by supernatural revelation planted religion, there he also made to himself a peculiar kingdom, and gave laws, not only of behaviour towards himself, but also towards one another; and thereby in the kingdom of God, the policy and laws civil are a part of religion; and therefore the distinction of temporal and spiritual domination hath there no place. It is true that God is king of all the earth; yet may He be king of a peculiar and chosen nation. For there is no more incongruity therein than that he that hath the general command of the whole army should have withal a peculiar regiment or company of his own. God is king of all the earth by His power, but of His chosen people, He is king by covenant. But to speak more largely of the kingdom of God, both by nature and covenant, I have in the following discourse assigned another place. From the propagation of religion, it is not hard to understand the causes of the resolution of the same into its first seeds or principles; which are only an opinion of a deity, and powers invisible and supernatural; that can never be so abolished out of human nature, but that new religions may again be made to spring out of them by the culture of such men as for such purpose are in reputation. For seeing all formed religion is founded at first upon the faith which a multitude hath in some one person, whom they believe not only to be a wise man and to labour to procure their happiness, but also to be a holy man to whom God Himself vouchsafeth to declare His will supernaturally, it followeth necessarily when they that have the government of religion shall come to have either the wisdom of those men, their sincerity, or their love suspected, or that they shall be unable to show any probable token of divine revelation, that the religion which they desire to uphold must be suspected likewise and (without the fear of the civil sword) contradicted and rejected. That which taketh away the reputation of wisdom in him that formeth a religion, or addeth to it when it is already formed, is the enjoining of a belief of contradictories: for both parts of a contradiction cannot possibly be true, and therefore to enjoin the belief of them is an argument of ignorance, which detects the author in that, and discredits him in all things else he shall propound as from revelation supernatural: which revelation a man may indeed have of many things above, but of nothing against natural reason. That which taketh away the reputation of sincerity is the doing or saying of such things as appear to be signs that what they require other men to believe is not believed by themselves; all which doings or sayings are therefore called scandalous because they be stumbling-blocks that make men to fall in the way of religion: as injustice, cruelty, profaneness, avarice, and luxury. For who can believe that he that doth ordinarily such actions, as proceed from any of these roots, believeth there is any such invisible power to be feared as he affrighteth other men withal for lesser faults? That which taketh away the reputation of love is the being detected of private ends: as when the belief they require of others conduceth, or seemeth to conduce, to the acquiring of dominion, riches, dignity, or secure pleasure to themselves only or specially. For that which men reap benefit by to themselves they are thought to do for their own sakes, and not for love of others. Lastly, the testimony that men can render of divine calling can be no other than the operation of miracles, or true prophecy (which also is a miracle), or extraordinary felicity. And therefore, to those points of religion which have been received from them that did such miracles, those that are added by such as approve not their calling by some miracle obtain no greater belief than what the custom and laws of the places in which they be educated have wrought into them. For as in natural things men of judgement require natural signs and arguments, so in supernatural things they require signs supernatural (which are miracles) before they consent inwardly and from their hearts. All which causes of the weakening of men's faith do manifestly appear in the examples following. First, we have the example of the children of Israel, who, when Moses that had approved his calling to them by miracles, and by the happy conduct of them out of Egypt, was absent but forty days, revolted from the worship of the true God recommended to them by him, and, setting up[Exodus, 32. 1, 2] a golden calf for their god, relapsed into the idolatry of the Egyptians from whom they had been so lately delivered. And again, after Moses, Aaron, Joshua, and that generation which had seen the great works of God in Israel were dead, another generation arose and served Baal. [Judges, 2. 11] So that Miracles failing, faith also failed. Again, when the sons of Samuel, being constituted by their father judges in Beersheba, received bribes and judged unjustly, the people of Israel refused any more to have God to be their king in other manner than He was king of other people, and therefore cried out to Samuel to choose them a king after the manner of the nations. I Samuel, 8. 3] So that justice failing, faith also failed, insomuch as they deposed their God from reigning over them. And whereas in the planting of Christian religion the oracles ceased in all parts of the Roman Empire, and the number of Christians increased wonderfully every day and in every place by the preaching of the Apostles and Evangelists, a great part of that success may reasonably be attributed to the contempt into which the priests of the Gentiles of that time had brought themselves by their uncleanness, avarice, and juggling between princes. Also the religion of the Church of Rome was partly for the same cause abolished in England and many other parts of Christendom, insomuch as the failing of virtue in the pastors maketh faith fail in the people, and partly from bringing of the philosophy and doctrine of Aristotle into religion by the Schoolmen; from whence there arose so many contradictions and absurdities as brought the clergy into a reputation both of ignorance and of fraudulent intention, and inclined people to revolt from them, either against the will of their own princes as in France and Holland, or with their will as in England. Lastly, amongst the points by the Church of Rome declared necessary for salvation, there be so many manifestly to the advantage of the Pope so many of his spiritual subjects residing in the territories of other Christian princes that, were it not for the mutual emulation of those princes, they might without war or trouble exclude all foreign authority, as easily as it has been excluded in England. For who is there that does not see to whose benefit it conduceth to have it believed that a king hath not his authority from Christ unless a bishop crown him? That a king, if he be a priest, cannot marry? That whether a prince be born in lawful marriage, or not, must be judged by authority from Rome? That subjects may be freed from their allegiance if by the court of Rome the king be judged a heretic? That a king, as Childeric of France, may be deposed by a Pope, as Pope Zachary, for no cause, and his kingdom given to one of his subjects? That the clergy, and regulars, in what country soever, shall be exempt from the jurisdiction of their king in cases criminal? Or who does not see to whose profit redound the fees of private Masses, and vales of purgatory, with other signs of private interest enough to mortify the most lively faith, if, as I said, the civil magistrate and custom did not more sustain it than any opinion they have of the sanctity, wisdom, or probity of their teachers? So that I may attribute all the changes of religion in the world to one and the same cause, and that is unpleasing priests; and those not only amongst catholics, but even in that Church that hath presumed most of reformation.

## CHAPTER XIII, OF THE NATURAL CONDITION OF MANKIND AS CONCERNING THEIR FELICITY AND MISERY

NATURE hath made men so equal in the faculties of body and mind as that, though there be found one man sometimes manifestly stronger in body or of quicker mind than another, yet when all is reckoned together the difference between man and man is not so considerable as that one man can thereupon claim to himself any benefit to which another may not pretend as well as he. For as to the strength of body, the weakest has strength enough to kill the strongest, either by secret machination or by confederacy with others that are in the same danger with himself. And as to the faculties of the mind, setting aside the arts grounded upon words, and especially that skill of proceeding upon general and infallible rules, called science, which very few have and but in few things, as being not a native faculty born with us, nor attained, as prudence, while we look after somewhat else, I find yet a greater equality amongst men than that of strength. For prudence is but experience, which equal time equally bestows on all men in those things they equally apply themselves unto. That which may perhaps make such equality incredible is but a vain conceit of one's own wisdom, which almost all men think they have in a greater degree than the vulgar; that is, than all men but themselves, and a few others, whom by fame, or for concurring with themselves, they approve. For such is the nature of men that howsoever they may acknowledge many others to be more witty, or more eloquent or more learned, yet they will hardly believe there be many so wise as themselves; for they see their own wit at hand, and other men's at a distance. But this proveth rather that men are in that point equal, than unequal. For there is not ordinarily a greater sign of the equal distribution of anything than that every man is contented with his share. From this equality of ability ariseth equality of hope in the attaining of our ends. And therefore if any two men desire the same thing, which nevertheless they cannot both enjoy, they become enemies; and in the way to their end (which is principally their own conservation, and sometimes their delectation only) endeavour to destroy or subdue one another. And from hence it comes to pass that where an invader hath no more to fear than another man's single power, if one plant, sow, build, or possess a convenient seat, others may probably be expected to come prepared with forces united to dispossess and deprive him, not only of the fruit of his labour, but also of his life or liberty. And the invader again is in the like danger of another. And from this diffidence of one another, there is no way for any man to secure himself so reasonable as anticipation; that is, by force, or wiles, to master the persons of all men he can so long till he see no other power great enough to endanger him: and this is no more than his own conservation requireth, and is generally allowed. Also, because there be some that, taking pleasure in contemplating their own power in the acts of conquest, which they pursue farther than their security requires, if others, that otherwise would be glad to be at ease within modest bounds, should not by invasion increase their power, they would not be able, long time, by standing only on their defence, to subsist. And by consequence, such augmentation of dominion over men being necessary to a man's conservation, it ought to be allowed him. Again, men have no pleasure (but on the contrary a great deal of grief) in keeping company where there is no power able to overawe them all. For every man looketh that his companion should value him at the same rate he sets upon himself, and upon all signs of contempt or undervaluing naturally endeavours, as far as he dares (which amongst them that have no common power to keep them in quiet is far enough to make them destroy each other), to extort a greater value from his contemners, by damage; and from others, by the example. So that in the nature of man, we find three principal causes of quarrel. First, competition; secondly, diffidence; thirdly, glory. The first maketh men invade for gain; the second, for safety; and the third, for reputation. The first use violence, to make themselves masters of other men's persons, wives, children, and cattle; the second, to defend them; the third, for trifles, as a word, a smile, a different opinion, and any other sign of undervalue, either direct in their persons or by reflection in their kindred, their friends, their nation, their profession, or their name. Hereby it is manifest that during the time men live without a common power to keep them all in awe, they are in that condition which is called war; and such a war as is of every man against every man. For war consisteth not in battle only, or the act of fighting, but in a tract of time, wherein the will to contend by battle is sufficiently known: and therefore the notion of time is to be considered in the nature of war, as it is in the nature of weather. For as the nature of foul weather lieth not in a shower or two of rain, but in an inclination thereto of many days together: so the nature of war consisteth not in actual fighting, but in the known disposition thereto during all the time there is no assurance to the contrary. All other time is peace. Whatsoever therefore is consequent to a time of war, where every man is enemy to every man, the same consequent to the time wherein men live without other security than what their own strength and their own invention shall furnish them withal. In such condition there is no place for industry, because the fruit thereof is uncertain: and consequently no culture of the earth; no navigation, nor use of the commodities that may be imported by sea; no commodious building; no instruments of moving and removing such things as require much force; no knowledge of the face of the earth; no account of time; no arts; no letters; no society; and which is worst of all, continual fear, and danger of violent death; and the life of man, solitary, poor, nasty, brutish, and short. It may seem strange to some man that has not well weighed these things that Nature should thus dissociate and render men apt to invade and destroy one another: and he may therefore, not trusting to this inference, made from the passions, desire perhaps to have the same confirmed by experience. Let him therefore consider with himself: when taking a journey, he arms himself and seeks to go well accompanied; when going to sleep, he locks his doors; when even in his house he locks his chests; and this when he knows there be laws and public officers, armed, to revenge all injuries shall be done him; what opinion he has of his fellow subjects, when he rides armed; of his fellow citizens, when he locks his doors; and of his children, and servants, when he locks his chests. Does he not there as much accuse mankind by his actions as I do by my words? But neither of us accuse man's nature in it. The desires, and other passions of man, are in themselves no sin. No more are the actions that proceed from those passions till they know a law that forbids them; which till laws be made they cannot know, nor can any law be made till they have agreed upon the person that shall make it. It may peradventure be thought there was never such a time nor condition of war as this; and I believe it was never generally so, over all the world: but there are many places where they live so now. For the savage people in many places of America, except the government of small families, the concord whereof dependeth on natural lust, have no government at all, and live at this day in that brutish manner, as I said before. Howsoever, it may be perceived what manner of life there would be, where there were no common power to fear, by the manner of life which men that have formerly lived under a peaceful government use to degenerate into a civil war. But though there had never been any time wherein particular men were in a condition of war one against another, yet in all times kings and persons of sovereign authority, because of their independency, are in continual jealousies, and in the state and posture of gladiators, having their weapons pointing, and their eyes fixed on one another; that is, their forts, garrisons, and guns upon the frontiers of their kingdoms, and continual spies upon their neighbours, which is a posture of war. But because they uphold thereby the industry of their subjects, there does not follow from it that misery which accompanies the liberty of particular men. To this war of every man against every man, this also is consequent; that nothing can be unjust. The notions of right and wrong, justice and injustice, have there no place. Where there is no common power, there is no law; where no law, no injustice. Force and fraud are in war the two cardinal virtues. Justice and injustice are none of the faculties neither of the body nor mind. If they were, they might be in a man that were alone in the world, as well as his senses and passions. They are qualities that relate to men in society, not in solitude. It is consequent also to the same condition that there be no propriety, no dominion, no mine and thine distinct; but only that to be every man's that he can get, and for so long as he can keep it. And thus much for the ill condition which man by mere nature is actually placed in; though with a possibility to come out of it, consisting partly in the passions, partly in his reason. The passions that incline men to peace are: fear of death; desire of such things as are necessary to commodious living; and a hope by their industry to obtain them. And reason suggesteth convenient articles of peace upon which men may be drawn to agreement. These articles are they which otherwise are called the laws of nature, whereof I shall speak more particularly in the two following chapters.

## CHAPTER XIV, OF THE FIRST AND SECOND NATURAL LAWS, AND OF CONTRACTS

THE right of nature, which writers commonly call jus naturale, is the liberty each man hath to use his own power as he will himself for the preservation of his own nature; that is to say, of his own life; and consequently, of doing anything which, in his own judgement and reason, he shall conceive to be the aptest means thereunto. By liberty is understood, according to the proper signification of the word, the absence of external impediments; which impediments may oft take away part of a man's power to do what he would, but cannot hinder him from using the power left him according as his judgement and reason shall dictate to him. A law of nature, lex naturalis, is a precept, or general rule, found out by reason, by which a man is forbidden to do that which is destructive of his life, or taketh away the means of preserving the same, and to omit that by which he thinketh it may be best preserved. For though they that speak of this subject use to confound jus and lex, right and law, yet they ought to be distinguished, because right consisteth in liberty to do, or to forbear; whereas law determineth and bindeth to one of them: so that law and right differ as much as obligation and liberty, which in one and the same matter are inconsistent. And because the condition of man (as hath been declared in the precedent chapter) is a condition of war of every one against every one, in which case every one is governed by his own reason, and there is nothing he can make use of that may not be a help unto him in preserving his life against his enemies; it followeth that in such a condition every man has a right to every thing, even to one another's body. And therefore, as long as this natural right of every man to every thing endureth, there can be no security to any man, how strong or wise soever he be, of living out the time which nature ordinarily alloweth men to live. And consequently it is a precept, or general rule of reason: that every man ought to endeavour peace, as far as he has hope of obtaining it; and when he cannot obtain it, that he may seek and use all helps and advantages of war. The first branch of which rule containeth the first and fundamental law of nature, which is: to seek peace and follow it. The second, the sum of the right of nature, which is: by all means we can to defend ourselves. From this fundamental law of nature, by which men are commanded to endeavour peace, is derived this second law: that a man be willing, when others are so too, as far forth as for peace and defence of himself he shall think it necessary, to lay down this right to all things; and be contented with so much liberty against other men as he would allow other men against himself. For as long as every man holdeth this right, of doing anything he liketh; so long are all men in the condition of war. But if other men will not lay down their right, as well as he, then there is no reason for anyone to divest himself of his: for that were to expose himself to prey, which no man is bound to, rather than to dispose himself to peace. This is that law of the gospel: Whatsoever you require that others should do to you, that do ye to them. And that law of all men, quod tibi fieri non vis, alteri ne feceris. To lay down a man's right to anything is to divest himself of the liberty of hindering another of the benefit of his own right to the same. For he that renounceth or passeth away his right giveth not to any other man a right which he had not before, because there is nothing to which every man had not right by nature, but only standeth out of his way that he may enjoy his own original right without hindrance from him, not without hindrance from another. So that the effect which redoundeth to one man by another man's defect of right is but so much diminution of impediments to the use of his own right original. Right is laid aside, either by simply renouncing it, or by transferring it to another. By simply renouncing, when he cares not to whom the benefit thereof redoundeth. By transferring, when he intendeth the benefit thereof to some certain person or persons. And when a man hath in either manner abandoned or granted away his right, then is he said to be obliged, or bound, not to hinder those to whom such right is granted, or abandoned, from the benefit of it: and that he ought, and it is duty, not to make void that voluntary act of his own: and that such hindrance is injustice, and injury, as being sine jure; the right being before renounced or transferred. So that injury or injustice, in the controversies of the world, is somewhat like to that which in the disputations of scholars is called absurdity. For as it is there called an absurdity to contradict what one maintained in the beginning; so in the world it is called injustice, and injury voluntarily to undo that which from the beginning he had voluntarily done. The way by which a man either simply renounceth or transferreth his right is a declaration, or signification, by some voluntary and sufficient sign, or signs, that he doth so renounce or transfer, or hath so renounced or transferred the same, to him that accepteth it. And these signs are either words only, or actions only; or, as it happeneth most often, both words and actions. And the same are the bonds, by which men are bound and obliged: bonds that have their strength, not from their own nature (for nothing is more easily broken than a man's word), but from fear of some evil consequence upon the rupture. Whensoever a man transferreth his right, or renounceth it, it is either in consideration of some right reciprocally transferred to himself, or for some other good he hopeth for thereby. For it is a voluntary act: and of the voluntary acts of every man, the object is some good to himself. And therefore there be some rights which no man can be understood by any words, or other signs, to have abandoned or transferred. As first a man cannot lay down the right of resisting them that assault him by force to take away his life, because he cannot be understood to aim thereby at any good to himself. The same may be said of wounds, and chains, and imprisonment, both because there is no benefit consequent to such patience, as there is to the patience of suffering another to be wounded or imprisoned, as also because a man cannot tell when he seeth men proceed against him by violence whether they intend his death or not. And lastly the motive and end for which this renouncing and transferring of right is introduced is nothing else but the security of a man's person, in his life, and in the means of so preserving life as not to be weary of it. And therefore if a man by words, or other signs, seem to despoil himself of the end for which those signs were intended, he is not to be understood as if he meant it, or that it was his will, but that he was ignorant of how such words and actions were to be interpreted. The mutual transferring of right is that which men call contract. There is difference between transferring of right to the thing, the thing, and transferring or tradition, that is, delivery of the thing itself. For the thing may be delivered together with the translation of the right, as in buying and selling with ready money, or exchange of goods or lands, and it may be delivered some time after. Again, one of the contractors may deliver the thing contracted for on his part, and leave the other to perform his part at some determinate time after, and in the meantime be trusted; and then the contract on his part is called pact, or covenant: or both parts may contract now to perform hereafter, in which cases he that is to perform in time to come, being trusted, his performance is called keeping of promise, or faith, and the failing of performance, if it be voluntary, violation of faith. When the transferring of right is not mutual, but one of the parties transferreth in hope to gain thereby friendship or service from another, or from his friends; or in hope to gain the reputation of charity, or magnanimity; or to deliver his mind from the pain of compassion; or in hope of reward in heaven; this is not contract, but gift, free gift, grace: which words signify one and the same thing. Signs of contract are either express or by inference. Express are words spoken with understanding of what they signify: and such words are either of the time present or past; as, I give, I grant, I have given, I have granted, I will that this be yours: or of the future; as, I will give, I will grant, which words of the future are called promise. Signs by inference are sometimes the consequence of words; sometimes the consequence of silence; sometimes the consequence of actions; sometimes the consequence of forbearing an action: and generally a sign by inference, of any contract, is whatsoever sufficiently argues the will of the contractor. Words alone, if they be of the time to come, and contain a bare promise, are an insufficient sign of a free gift and therefore not obligatory. For if they be of the time to come, as, tomorrow I will give, they are a sign I have not given yet, and consequently that my right is not transferred, but remaineth till I transfer it by some other act. But if the words be of the time present, or past, as, I have given, or do give to be delivered tomorrow, then is my tomorrow's right given away today; and that by the virtue of the words, though there were no other argument of my will. And there is a great difference in the signification of these words, volo hoc tuum esse cras, and cras dabo; that is, between I will that this be thine tomorrow, and, I will give it thee tomorrow: for the word I will, in the former manner of speech, signifies an act of the will present; but in the latter, it signifies a promise of an act of the will to come: and therefore the former words, being of the present, transfer a future right; the latter, that be of the future, transfer nothing. But if there be other si

ns of the will to transfer a right besides words; then, though the gift be free, yet may the right be understood to pass by words of the future: as if a man propound a prize to him that comes first to the end of a race, the gift is free; and though the words be of the future, yet the right passeth: for if he would not have his words so be understood, he should not have let them run. In contracts the right passeth, not only where the words are of the time present or past, but also where they are of the future, because all contract is mutual translation, or change of right; and therefore he that promiseth only, because he hath already received the benefit for which he promiseth, is to be understood as if he intended the right should pass: for unless he had been content to have his words so understood, the other would not have performed his part first. And for that cause, in buying, and selling, and other acts of contract, a promise is equivalent to a covenant, and therefore obligatory. He that performeth first in the case of a contract is said to merit that which he is to receive by the performance of the other, and he hath it as due. Also when a prize is propounded to many, which is to be given to him only that winneth, or money is thrown amongst many to be enjoyed by them that catch it; though this be a free gift, yet so to win, or so to catch, is to merit, and to have it as due. For the right is transferred in the propounding of the prize, and in throwing down the money, though it be not determined to whom, but by the event of the contention. But there is between these two sorts of merit this difference, that in contract I merit by virtue of my own power and the contractor's need, but in this case of free gift I am enabled to merit only by the benignity of the giver: in contract I merit at the contractor's hand that he should depart with his right; in this case of gift, I merit not that the giver should part with his right, but that when he has parted with it, it should be mine rather than another's. And this I think to be the meaning of that distinction of the Schools between meritum congrui and meritum condigni. For God Almighty, having promised paradise to those men, hoodwinked with carnal desires, that can walk through this world according to the precepts and limits prescribed by him, they say he that shall so walk shall merit paradise ex congruo. But because no man can demand a right to it by his own righteousness, or any other power in himself, but by the free grace of God only, they say no man can merit paradise ex condigno. This, I say, I think is the meaning of that distinction; but because disputers do not agree upon the signification of their own terms of art longer than it serves their turn, I will not affirm anything of their meaning: only this I say; when a gift is given indefinitely, as a prize to be contended for, he that winneth meriteth, and may claim the prize as due. If a covenant be made wherein neither of the parties perform presently, but trust one another, in the condition of mere nature (which is a condition of war of every man against every man) upon any reasonable suspicion, it is void: but if there be a common power set over them both, with right and force sufficient to compel performance, it is not void. For he that performeth first has no assurance the other will perform after, because the bonds of words are too weak to bridle men's ambition, avarice, anger, and other passions, without the fear of some coercive power; which in the condition of mere nature, where all men are equal, and judges of the justness of their own fears, cannot possibly be supposed.

And therefore he which performeth first does but betray himself to his enemy, contrary to the right he can never abandon of defending his life and means of living. But in a civil estate, where there a power set up to constrain those that would otherwise violate their faith, that fear is no more reasonable; and for that cause, he which by the covenant is to perform first is obliged so to do. The cause of fear, which maketh such a covenant invalid, must be always something arising after the covenant made, as some new fact or other sign of the will not to perform, else it cannot make the covenant void. For that which could not hinder a man from promising ought not to be admitted as a hindrance of performing. He that transferreth any right transferreth the means of enjoying it, as far as lieth in his power. As he that selleth land is understood to transfer the herbage and whatsoever grows upon it; nor can he that sells a mill turn away the stream that drives it. And they that give to a man the right of government in sovereignty are understood to give him the right of levying money to maintain soldiers, and of appointing magistrates for the administration of justice. To make covenants with brute beasts is impossible, because not understanding our speech, they understand not, nor accept of any translation of right, nor can translate any right to another: and without mutual acceptation, there is no covenant. To make covenant with God is impossible but by mediation of such as God speaketh to, either by revelation supernatural or by His lieutenants that govern under Him and in His name: for otherwise we know not whether our covenants be accepted or not. And therefore they that vow anything contrary to any law of nature, vow in vain, as being a thing unjust to pay such vow. And if it be a thing commanded by the law of nature, it is not the vow, but the law that binds them. The matter or subject of a covenant is always something that falleth under deliberation, for to covenant is an act of the will; that is to say, an act, and the last act, of deliberation; and is therefore always understood to be something to come, and which judged possible for him that covenanteth to perform. And therefore, to promise that which is known to be impossible is no covenant. But if that prove impossible afterwards, which before was thought possible, the covenant is valid and bindeth, though not to the thing itself, yet to the value; or, if that also be impossible, to the unfeigned endeavour of performing as much as is possible, for to more no man can be obliged. Men are freed of their covenants two ways; by performing, or by being forgiven. For performance is the natural end of obligation, and forgiveness the restitution of liberty, as being a retransferring of that right in which the obligation consisted. Covenants entered into by fear, in the condition of mere nature, are obligatory. For example, if I covenant to pay a ransom, or service for my life, to an enemy, I am bound by it. For it is a contract, wherein one receiveth the benefit of life; the other is to receive money, or service for it, and consequently, where no other law (as in the condition of mere nature) forbiddeth the performance, the covenant is valid. Therefore prisoners of war, if trusted with the payment of their ransom, are obliged to pay it: and if a weaker prince make a disadvantageous peace with a stronger, for fear, he is bound to keep it; unless (as hath been said before) there ariseth some new and just cause of fear to renew the war. And even in Commonwealths, if I be forced to redeem myself from a thief by promising him money, I am bound to pay it, till the civil law discharge me. For whatsoever I may lawfully do without obligation, the same I may lawfully covenant to do through fear: and what I lawfully covenant, I cannot lawfully break. A former covenant makes void a later. For a man that hath passed away his right to one man today hath it not to pass tomorrow to another: and therefore the later promise passeth no right, but is null. A covenant not to defend myself from force, by force, is always void. For (as I have shown before) no man can transfer or lay down his right to save himself from death, wounds, and imprisonment, the avoiding whereof is the only end of laying down any right; and therefore the promise of not resisting force, in no covenant transferreth any right, nor is obliging. For though a man may covenant thus, unless I do so, or so, kill me; he cannot covenant thus, unless I do so, or so, I will not resist you when you come to kill me. For man by nature chooseth the lesser evil, which is danger of death in resisting, rather than the greater, which is certain and present death in not resisting. And this is granted to be true by all men, in that they lead criminals to execution, and prison, with armed men, notwithstanding that such criminals have consented to the law by which they are condemned. A covenant to accuse oneself, without assurance of pardon, is likewise invalid. For in the condition of nature where every man is judge, there is no place for accusation: and in the civil state the accusation is followed with punishment, which, being force, a man is not obliged not to resist. The same is also true of the accusation of those by whose condemnation a man falls into misery; as of a father, wife, or benefactor. For the testimony of such an accuser, if it be not willingly given, is presumed to be corrupted by nature, and therefore not to be received: and where a man's testimony is not to be credited, he is not bound to give it. Also accusations upon torture are not to be reputed as testimonies. For torture is to be used but as means of conjecture, and light, in the further examination and search of truth: and what is in that case confessed tendeth to the ease of him that is tortured, not to the informing of the torturers, and therefore ought not to have the credit of a sufficient testimony: for whether he deliver himself by true or false accusation, he does it by the right of preserving his own life. The force of words being (as I have formerly noted) too weak to hold men to the performance of their covenants, there are in man's nature but two imaginable helps to strengthen it. And those are either a fear of the consequence of breaking their word, or a glory or pride in appearing not to need to break it. This latter is a generosity too rarely found to be presumed on, especially in the pursuers of wealth, command, or sensual pleasure, which are the greatest part of mankind. The passion to be reckoned upon is fear; whereof there be two very general objects: one, the power of spirits invisible; the other, the power of those men they shall therein offend. Of these two, though the former be the greater power, yet the fear of the latter is commonly the greater fear. The fear of the former is in every man his own religion, which hath place in the nature of man before civil society. The latter hath not so; at least not place enough to keep men to their promises, because in the condition of mere nature, the inequality of power is not discerned, but by the event of battle. So that before the time of civil society, or in the interruption thereof by war, there is nothing can strengthen a covenant of peace agreed on against the temptations of avarice, ambition, lust, or other strong desire, but the fear of that invisible power which they every one worship as God, and fear as a revenger of their perfidy. All therefore that can be done between two men not subject to civil power is to put one another to swear by the God he feareth: which swearing, or oath, is a form of speech, added to a promise, by which he that promiseth signifieth that unless he perform he renounceth the mercy of his God, or calleth to him for vengeance on himself. Such was the heathen form, Let Jupiter kill me else, as I kill this beast. So is our form, I shall do thus, and thus, so help me God. And this, with the rites and ceremonies which every one useth in his own religion, that the fear of breaking faith might be the greater. By this it appears that an oath taken according to any other form, or rite, than his that sweareth is in vain and no oath, and that there is no swearing by anything which the swearer thinks not God. For though men have sometimes used to swear by their kings, for fear, or flattery; yet they would have it thereby understood they attributed to them divine honour. And that swearing unnecessarily by God is but profaning of his name: and swearing by other things, as men do in common discourse, is not swearing, but an impious custom, gotten by too much vehemence of talking. It appears also that the oath adds nothing to the obligation. For a covenant, if lawful, binds in the sight of God, without the oath, as much as with it; if unlawful, bindeth not at all, though it be confirmed with an oath.

## CHAPTER XV, OF OTHER LAWS OF NATURE

FROM that law of nature by which we are obliged to transfer to another such rights as, being retained, hinder the peace of mankind, there followeth a third; which is this: that men perform their covenants made; without which covenants are in vain, and but empty words; and the right of all men to all things remaining, we are still in the condition of war. And in this law of nature consisteth the fountain and original of justice. For where no covenant hath preceded, there hath no right been transferred, and every man has right to everything and consequently, no action can be unjust. But when a covenant is made, then to break it is unjust and the definition of injustice is no other than the not performance of covenant. And whatsoever is not unjust is just. But because covenants of mutual trust, where there is a fear of not performance on either part (as hath been said in the former chapter), are invalid, though the original of justice be the making of covenants, yet injustice actually there can be none till the cause of such fear be taken away; which, while men are in the natural condition of war, cannot be done. Therefore before the names of just and unjust can have place, there must be some coercive power to compel men equally to the performance of their covenants, by the terror of some punishment greater than the benefit they expect by the breach of their covenant, and to make good that propriety which by mutual contract men acquire in recompense of the universal right they abandon: and such power there is none before the erection of a Commonwealth. And this is also to be gathered out of the ordinary definition of justice in the Schools, for they say that justice is the constant will of giving to every man his own. And therefore where there is no own, that is, no propriety, there is no injustice; and where there is no coercive power erected, that is, where there is no Commonwealth, there is no propriety, all men having right to all things: therefore where there is no Commonwealth, there nothing is unjust. So that the nature of justice consisteth in keeping of valid covenants, but the validity of covenants begins not but with the constitution of a civil power sufficient to compel men to keep them: and then it is also that propriety begins. The fool hath said in his heart, there is no such thing as justice, and sometimes also with his tongue, seriously alleging that every man's conservation and contentment being committed to his own care, there could be no reason why every man might not do what he thought conduced thereunto: and therefore also to make, or not make; keep, or not keep, covenants was not against reason when it conduced to one's benefit. He does not therein deny that there be covenants; and that they are sometimes broken, sometimes kept; and that such breach of them may be called injustice, and the observance of them justice: but he questioneth whether injustice, taking away the fear of God (for the same fool hath said in his heart there is no God), not sometimes stand with that reason which dictateth to every man his own good; and particularly then, when it conduceth to such a benefit as shall put a man in a condition to neglect not only the dispraise and revilings, but also the power of other men. The kingdom of God is gotten by violence: but what if it could be gotten by unjust violence? Were it against reason so to get it, when it is impossible to receive hurt by it? And if it be not against reason, it is not against justice: or else justice is not to be approved for good. From such reasoning as this, successful wickedness hath obtained the name of virtue: and some that in all other things have disallowed the violation of faith, yet have allowed it when it is for the getting of a kingdom. And the heathen that believed that Saturn was deposed by his son Jupiter believed nevertheless the same Jupiter to be the avenger of injustice, somewhat like to a piece of law in Coke's Commentaries on Littleton; where he says if the right heir of the crown be attainted of treason, yet the crown shall descend to him, and eo instante the attainder be void: from which instances a man will be very prone to infer that when the heir apparent of a kingdom shall kill him that is in possession, though his father, you may call it injustice, or by what other name you will; yet it can never be against reason, seeing all the voluntary actions of men tend to the benefit of themselves; and those actions are most reasonable that conduce most to their ends. This specious reasoning is nevertheless false. For the question is not of promises mutual, where there is no security of performance on either side, as when there is no civil power erected over the parties promising; for such promises are no covenants: but either where one of the parties has performed already, or where there is a power to make him perform, there is the question whether it be against reason; that is, against the benefit of the other to perform, or not. And I say it is not against reason. For the manifestation whereof we are to consider; first, that when a man doth a thing, which notwithstanding anything can be foreseen and reckoned on tendeth to his own destruction, howsoever some accident, which he could not expect, arriving may turn it to his benefit; yet such events do not make it reasonably or wisely done. Secondly, that in a condition of war, wherein every man to every man, for want of a common power to keep them all in awe, is an enemy, there is no man can hope by his own strength, or wit, to himself from destruction without the help of confederates; where every one expects the same defence by the confederation that any one else does: and therefore he which declares he thinks it reason to deceive those that help him can in reason expect no other means of safety than what can be had from his own single power. He, therefore, that breaketh his covenant, and consequently declareth that he thinks he may with reason do so, cannot be received into any society that unite themselves for peace and defence but by the error of them that receive him; nor when he is received be retained in it without seeing the danger of their error; which errors a man cannot reasonably reckon upon as the means of his security: and therefore if he be left, or cast out of society, he perisheth; and if he live in society, it is by the errors of other men, which he could not foresee nor reckon upon, and consequently against the reason of his preservation; and so, as all men that contribute not to his destruction forbear him only out of ignorance of what is good for themselves. As for the instance of gaining the secure and perpetual felicity of heaven by any way, it is frivolous; there being but one way imaginable, and that is not breaking, but keeping of covenant. And for the other instance of attaining sovereignty by rebellion; it is manifest that, though the event follow, yet because it cannot reasonably be expected, but rather the contrary, and because by gaining it so, others are taught to gain the same in like manner, the attempt thereof is against reason. Justice therefore, that is to say, keeping of covenant, is a rule of reason by which we are forbidden to do anything destructive to our life, and consequently a law of nature. There be some that proceed further and will not have the law of nature to be those rules which conduce to the preservation of man's life on earth, but to the attaining of an eternal felicity after death; to which they think the breach of covenant may conduce, and consequently be just and reasonable; such are they that think it a work of merit to kill, or depose, or rebel against the sovereign power constituted over them by their own consent. But because there is no natural knowledge of man's estate after death, much less of the reward that is then to be given to breach of faith, but only a belief grounded upon other men's saying that they know it supernaturally or that they know those that knew them that knew others that knew it supernaturally, breach of faith cannot be called a precept of reason or nature. Others, that allow for a law of nature the keeping of faith, do nevertheless make exception of certain persons; as heretics, and such as use not to perform their covenant to others; and this also is against reason. For if any fault of a man be sufficient to discharge our covenant made, the same ought in reason to have been sufficient to have hindered the making of it. The names of just and unjust when they are attributed to men, signify one thing, and when they are attributed to actions, another. When they are attributed to men, they signify conformity, or inconformity of manners, to reason. But when they are attributed to action they signify the conformity, or inconformity to reason, not of manners, or manner of life, but of particular actions. A just man therefore is he that taketh all the care he can that his actions may be all just; and an unjust man is he that neglecteth it. And such men are more often in our language styled by the names of righteous and unrighteous than just and unjust though the meaning be the same. Therefore a righteous man does not lose that title by one or a few unjust actions that proceed from sudden passion, or mistake of things or persons, nor does an unrighteous man lose his character for such actions as he does, or forbears to do, for fear: because his will is not framed by the justice, but by the apparent benefit of what he is to do. That which gives to human actions the relish of justice is a certain nobleness or gallantness of courage, rarely found, by which a man scorns to be beholding for the contentment of his life to fraud, or breach of promise. This justice of the manners is that which is meant where justice is called a virtue; and injustice, a vice. But the justice of actions denominates men, not just, but guiltless: and the injustice of the same (which is also called injury) gives them but the name of guilty. Again, the injustice of manners is the disposition or aptitude to do injury, and is injustice before it proceed to act, and without supposing any individual person injured. But the injustice of an action (that is to say, injury) supposeth an individual person injured; namely him to whom the covenant was made: and therefore many times the injury is received by one man when the damage redoundeth to another. As when the master commandeth his servant to give money to stranger; if it be not done, the injury is done to the master, whom he had before covenanted to obey; but the damage redoundeth to the stranger, to whom he had no obligation, and therefore could not injure him. And so also in Commonwealths private men may remit to one another their debts, but not robberies or other violences, whereby they are endamaged; because the detaining of debt is an injury to themselves, but robbery and violence are injuries to the person of the Commonwealth. Whatsoever is done to a man, conformable to his own will signified to the doer, is not injury to him. For if he that doeth it hath not passed away his original right to do what he please by some antecedent covenant, there is no breach of covenant, and therefore no injury done him. And if he have, then his will to have it done, being signified, is a release of that covenant, and so again there is no injury done him. Justice of actions is by writers divided into commutative and distributive: and the former they say consisteth in proportion arithmetical; the latter in proportion geometrical. Commutative, therefore, they place in the equality of value of the things contracted for; and distributive, in the distribution of equal benefit to men of equal merit. As if it were injustice to sell dearer than we buy, or to give more to a man than he merits. The value of all things contracted for is measured by the appetite of the contractors, and therefore the just value is that which they be contented to give. And merit (besides that which is by covenant, where the performance on one part meriteth the performance of the other part, and falls under justice commutative, not distributive) is not due by justice, but is rewarded of grace only. And therefore this distinction, in the sense wherein it useth to be expounded, is not right. To speak properly, commutative justice is the justice of a contractor; that is, a performance of covenant in buying and selling, hiring and letting to hire, lending and borrowing, exchanging, bartering, and other acts of contract. And distributive justice, the justice of an arbitrator; that is to say, the act of defining what is just. Wherein, being trusted by them that make him arbitrator, if he perform his trust, he is said to distribute to every man his own: and this is indeed just distribution, and may be called, though improperly, distributive justice, but more properly equity, which also is a law of nature, as shall be shown in due place. As justice dependeth on antecedent covenant; so does gratitude depend on antecedent grace; that is to say, antecedent free gift; and is the fourth law of nature, which may be conceived in this form: that a man which receiveth benefit from another of mere grace endeavour that he which giveth it have no reasonable cause to repent him of his good will. For no man giveth but with intention of good to himself, because gift is voluntary; and of all voluntary acts, the object is to every man his own good; of which if men see they shall be frustrated, there will be no beginning of benevolence or trust, nor consequently of mutual help, nor of reconciliation of one man to another; and therefore they are to remain still in the condition of war, which is contrary to the first and fundamental law of nature which commandeth men to seek peace. The breach of this law is called ingratitude, and hath the same relation to grace that injustice hath to obligation by covenant. A fifth law of nature is complaisance; that is to say, that every man strive to accommodate himself to the rest. For the understanding whereof we may consider that there is in men's aptness to society a diversity of nature, rising from their diversity of affections, not unlike to that we see in stones brought together for building of an edifice. For as that stone which by the asperity and irregularity of figure takes more room from others than itself fills, and for hardness cannot be easily made plain, and thereby hindereth the building, is by the builders cast away as unprofitable and troublesome: so also, a man that by asperity of nature will strive to retain those things which to himself are superfluous, and to others necessary, and for the stubbornness of his passions cannot be corrected, is to be left or cast out of society as cumbersome thereunto. For seeing every man, not only by right, but also by necessity of nature, is supposed to endeavour all he can to obtain that which is necessary for his conservation, he that shall oppose himself against it for things superfluous is guilty of the war that thereupon is to follow, and therefore doth that which is contrary to the fundamental law of nature, which commandeth to seek peace. The observers of this law may be called sociable, (the Latins call them commodi); the contrary, stubborn, insociable, forward, intractable. A sixth law of nature is this: that upon caution of the future time, a man ought to pardon the offences past of them that, repenting, desire it. For pardon is nothing but granting of peace; which though granted to them that persevere in their hostility, be not peace, but fear; yet not granted to them that give caution of the future time is sign of an aversion to peace, and therefore contrary to the law of nature. A seventh is: that in revenges (that is, retribution of evil for evil), men look not at the greatness of the evil past, but the greatness of the good to follow. Whereby we are forbidden to inflict punishment with any other design than for correction of the offender, or direction of others. For this law is consequent to the next before it, that commandeth pardon upon security of the future time. Besides, revenge without respect to the example and profit to come is a triumph, or glorying in the hurt of another, tending to no end (for the end is always somewhat to come); and glorying to no end is vain-glory, and contrary to reason; and to hurt without reason tendeth to the introduction of war, which is against the law of nature, and is commonly styled by the name of cruelty. And because all signs of hatred, or contempt, provoke to fight; insomuch as most men choose rather to hazard their life than not to be revenged, we may in the eighth place, for a law of nature, set down this precept: that no man by deed, word, countenance, or gesture, declare hatred or contempt of another. The breach of which law is commonly called contumely. The question who is the better man has no place in the condition of mere nature, where (as has been shown before) all men are equal. The inequality that now is has been introduced by the laws civil. I know that Aristotle in the first book of his Politics, for a foundation of his doctrine, maketh men by nature, some more worthy to command, meaning the wiser sort, such as he thought himself to be for his philosophy; others to serve, meaning those that had strong bodies, but were not philosophers as he; as master and servant were not introduced by consent of men, but by difference of wit: which is not only against reason, but also against experience. For there are very few so foolish that had not rather govern themselves than be governed by others: nor when the wise, in their own conceit, contend by force with them who distrust their own wisdom, do they always, or often, or almost at any time, get the victory. If nature therefore have made men equal, that equality is to be acknowledged: or if nature have made men unequal, yet because men that think themselves equal will not enter into conditions of peace, but upon equal terms, such equality must be admitted. And therefore for the ninth law of nature, I put this: that every man acknowledge another for his equal by nature. The breach of this precept is pride. On this law dependeth another: that at the entrance into conditions of peace, no man require to reserve to himself any right which he is not content should he reserved to every one of the rest. As it is necessary for all men that seek peace to lay down certain rights of nature; that is to say, not to have liberty to do all they list, so is it necessary for man's life to retain some: as right to govern their own bodies; enjoy air, water, motion, ways to go from place to place; and all things else without which a man cannot live, or not live well. If in this case, at the making of peace, men require for themselves that which they would not have to be granted to others, they do contrary to the precedent law that commandeth the acknowledgement of natural equality, and therefore also against the law of nature. The observers of this law are those we call modest, and the breakers arrogant men. The Greeks call the violation of this law pleonexia; that is, a desire of more than their share. Also, if a man he trusted to judge between man and man, it is a precept of the law of nature that he deal equally between them. For without that, the controversies of men cannot be determined but by war. He therefore that is partial in judgement, doth what in him lies to deter men from the use of judges and arbitrators, and consequently, against the fundamental law of nature, is the cause of war. The observance of this law, from the equal distribution to each man of that which in reason belonged to him, is called equity, and (as I have said before) distributive justice: the violation, acception of persons, prosopolepsia. And from this followeth another law: that such things as cannot he divided be enjoyed in common, if it can be; and if the quantity of the thing permit, without stint; otherwise proportionably to the number of them that have right. For otherwise the distribution is unequal, and contrary to equity. But some things there be that can neither be divided nor enjoyed in common. Then, the law of nature which prescribeth equity requireth: that the entire right, or else (making the use alternate) the first possession, be determined by lot. For equal distribution is of the law of nature; and other means of equal distribution cannot be imagined. Of lots there be two sorts, arbitrary and natural. Arbitrary is that which is agreed on by the competitors; natural is either primogeniture (which the Greek calls kleronomia, which signifies, given by lot), or first seizure. And therefore those things which cannot be enjoyed in common, nor divided, ought to be adjudged to the first possessor; and in some cases to the first born, as acquired by lot. It is also a law of nature: that all men that mediate peace he allowed safe conduct. For the law that commandeth peace, as the end, commandeth intercession, as the means; and to intercession the means is safe conduct. And because, though men be never so willing to observe these laws, there may nevertheless arise questions concerning a man's action; first, whether it were done, or not done; secondly, if done, whether against the law, or not against the law; the former whereof is called a question of fact, the latter a question of right; therefore unless the parties to the question covenant mutually to stand to the sentence of another, they are as far from peace as ever. This other, to whose sentence they submit, is called an arbitrator. And therefore it is of the law of nature that they that are at controversy submit their right to the judgement of an arbitrator. And seeing every man is presumed to do all things in order to his own benefit, no man is a fit arbitrator in his own cause: and if he were never so fit, yet equity allowing to each party equal benefit, if one be admitted to be judge, the other is to be admitted also; and so the controversy, that is, the cause of war, remains, against the law of nature. For the same reason no man in any cause ought to be received for arbitrator to whom greater profit, or honour, or pleasure apparently ariseth out of the victory of one party than of the other: for he hath taken, though an unavoidable bribe, yet a bribe; and no man can be obliged to trust him. And thus also the controversy and the condition of war remaineth, contrary to the law of nature. And in a controversy of fact, the judge being to give no more credit to one than to the other, if there be no other arguments, must give credit to a third; or to a third and fourth; or more: for else the question is undecided, and left to force, contrary to the law of nature. These are the laws of nature, dictating peace, for a means of the conservation of men in multitudes; and which only concern the doctrine of civil society. There be other things tending to the destruction of particular men; as drunkenness, and all other parts of intemperance, which may therefore also be reckoned amongst those things which the law of nature hath forbidden, but are not necessary to be mentioned, nor are pertinent enough to this place. And though this may seem too subtle a deduction of the laws of nature to be taken notice of by all men, whereof the most part are too busy in getting food, and the rest too negligent to understand; yet to leave all men inexcusable, they have been contracted into one easy sum, intelligible even to the meanest capacity; and that is: Do not that to another which thou wouldest not have done to thyself, which showeth him that he has no more to do in learning the laws of nature but, when weighing the actions of other men with his own they seem too heavy, to put them into the other part of the balance, and his own into their place, that his own passions and self-love may add nothing to the weight; and then there is none of these laws of nature that will not appear unto him very reasonable. The laws of nature oblige in foro interno; that is to say, they bind to a desire they should take place: but in foro externo; that is, to the putting them in act, not always. For he that should be modest and tractable, and perform all he promises in such time and place where no man else should do so, should but make himself a prey to others, and procure his own certain ruin, contrary to the ground of all laws of nature which tend to nature's preservation. And again, he that having sufficient security that others shall observe the same laws towards him, observes them not himself, seeketh not peace, but war, and consequently the destruction of his nature by violence. And whatsoever laws bind in foro interno may be broken, not only by a fact contrary to the law, but also by a fact according to it, in case a man think it contrary. For though his action in this case be according to the law, yet his purpose was against the law; which, where the obligation is in foro interno, is a breach. The laws of nature are immutable and eternal; for injustice, ingratitude, arrogance, pride, iniquity, acception of persons, and the rest can never be made lawful. For it can never be that war shall preserve life, and peace destroy it. The same laws, because they oblige only to a desire and endeavour, mean an unfeigned and constant endeavour, are easy to be observed. For in that they require nothing but endeavour, he that endeavoureth their performance fulfilleth them; and he that fulfilleth the law is just. And the science of them is the true and only moral philosophy. For moral philosophy is nothing else but the science of what is good and evil in the conversation and society of mankind. Good and evil are names that signify our appetites and aversions, which in different tempers, customs, and doctrines of men are different: and diverse men differ not only in their judgement on the senses of what is pleasant and unpleasant to the taste, smell, hearing, touch, and sight; but also of what is conformable or disagreeable to reason in the actions of common life. Nay, the same man, in diverse times, differs from himself; and one time praiseth, that is, calleth good, what another time he dispraiseth, and calleth evil: from whence arise disputes, controversies, and at last war. And therefore so long as a man is in the condition of mere nature, which is a condition of war, private appetite is the measure of good and evil: and consequently all men agree on this, that peace is good, and therefore also the way or means of peace, which (as I have shown before) are justice, gratitude, modesty, equity, mercy, and the rest of the laws of nature, are good; that is to say, moral virtues; and their contrary vices, evil. Now the science of virtue and vice is moral philosophy; and therefore the true doctrine of the laws of nature is the true moral philosophy. But the writers of moral philosophy, though they acknowledge the same virtues and vices; yet, not seeing wherein consisted their goodness, nor that they come to be praised as the means of peaceable, sociable, and comfortable living, place them in a mediocrity of passions: as if not the cause, but the degree of daring, made fortitude; or not the cause, but the quantity of a gift, made liberality. These dictates of reason men used to call by the name of laws, but improperly: for they are but conclusions or theorems concerning what conduceth to the conservation and defence of themselves; whereas law, properly, is the word of him that by right hath command over others. But yet if we consider the same theorems as delivered in the word of God that by right commandeth all things, then are they properly called laws.

## CHAPTER XVI, OF PERSONS, AUTHORS, AND THINGS PERSONATED

A PERSON is he whose words or actions are considered, either as his own, or as representing the words or actions of another man, or of any other thing to whom they are attributed, whether truly or by fiction. When they are considered as his own, then is he called a natural person: and when they are considered as representing the words and actions of another, then is he a feigned or artificial person. The word person is Latin, instead whereof the Greeks have prosopon, which signifies the face, as persona in Latin signifies the disguise, or outward appearance of a man, counterfeited on the stage; and sometimes more particularly that part of it which disguiseth the face, as a mask or vizard: and from the stage hath been translated to any representer of speech and action, as well in tribunals as theatres. So that a person is the same that an actor is, both on the stage and in common conversation; and to personate is to act or represent himself or another; and he that acteth another is said to bear his person, or act in his name (in which sense Cicero useth it where he says, Unus sustineo tres personas; mei, adversarii, et judicis- I bear three persons; my own, my adversary's, and the judge's), and is called in diverse occasions, diversely; as a representer, or representative, a lieutenant, a vicar, an attorney, a deputy, a procurator, an actor, and the like. Of persons artificial, some have their words and actions owned by those whom they represent. And then the person is the actor, and he that owneth his words and actions is the author, in which case the actor acteth by authority. For that which in speaking of goods and possessions is called an owner, and in Latin dominus in Greek kurios; speaking of actions, is called author. And as the right of possession is called dominion so the right of doing any action is called authority. So that by authority is always understood a right of doing any act; and done by authority, done by commission or license from him whose right it is. From hence it followeth that when the actor maketh a covenant by authority, he bindeth thereby the author no less than if he had made it himself; and no less subjecteth him to all the consequences of the same. And therefore all that hath been said formerly (Chapter XIV) of the nature of covenants between man and man in their natural capacity is true also when they are made by their actors, representers, or procurators, that have authority from them, so far forth as is in their commission, but no further. And therefore he that maketh a covenant with the actor, or representer, not knowing the authority he hath, doth it at his own peril. For no man is obliged by a covenant whereof he is not author, nor consequently by a covenant made against or beside the authority he gave. When the actor doth anything against the law of nature by command of the author, if he be obliged by former covenant to obey him, not he, but the author breaketh the law of nature: for though the action be against the law of nature, yet it is not his; but, contrarily, to refuse to do it is against the law of nature that forbiddeth breach of covenant. And he that maketh a covenant with the author, by mediation of the actor, not knowing what authority he hath, but only takes his word; in case such authority be not made manifest unto him upon demand, is no longer obliged: for the covenant made with the author is not valid without his counterassurance. But if he that so covenanteth knew beforehand he was to expect no other assurance than the actor's word, then is the covenant valid, because the actor in this case maketh himself the author. And therefore, as when the authority is evident, the covenant obligeth the author, not the actor; so when the authority is feigned, it obligeth the actor only, there being no author but himself. There are few things that are incapable of being represented by fiction. Inanimate things, as a church, a hospital, a bridge, may be personated by a rector, master, or overseer. But things inanimate cannot be authors, nor therefore give authority to their actors: yet the actors may have authority to procure their maintenance, given them by those that are owners or governors of those things. And therefore such things cannot be personated before there be some state of civil government. Likewise children, fools, and madmen that have no use of reason may be personated by guardians, or curators, but can be no authors during that time of any action done by them, longer than (when they shall recover the use of reason) they shall judge the same reasonable. Yet during the folly he that hath right of governing them may give authority to the guardian. But this again has no place but in a state civil, because before such estate there is no dominion of persons. An idol, or mere figment of the brain, may be personated, as were the gods of the heathen, which, by such officers as the state appointed, were personated, and held possessions, and other goods, and rights, which men from time to time dedicated and consecrated unto them. But idols cannot be authors: for an idol is nothing. The authority proceeded from the state, and therefore before introduction of civil government the gods of the heathen could not be personated. The true God may be personated. As He was: first, Moses, who governed the Israelites, that were that were not his, but God's people; not in his own name, with hoc dicit Moses, but in God's name, with hoc dicit Dominus. Secondly, by the Son of Man, His own Son, our blessed Saviour Jesus Christ, that came to reduce the Jews and induce all nations into the kingdom of his Father; not as of himself, but as sent from his Father. And thirdly, by the Holy Ghost, or Comforter, speaking and working in the Apostles; which Holy Ghost was a Comforter that came not of himself, but was sent and proceeded from them both. A multitude of men are made one person when they are by one man, or one person, represented; so that it be done with the consent of every one of that multitude in particular. For it is the unity of the representer, not the unity of the represented, that maketh the person one. And it is the representer that beareth the person, and but one person: and unity cannot otherwise be understood in multitude. And because the multitude naturally is not one, but many, they cannot be understood for one, but in any authors, of everything their representative saith or doth in their name; every man giving their common representer authority from himself in particular, and owning all the actions the representer doth, in case they give him authority without stint: otherwise, when they limit him in what and how far he shall represent them, none of them owneth more than they gave him commission to act. And if the representative consist of many men, the voice of the greater number must be considered as the voice of them all. For if the lesser number pronounce, for example, in the affirmative, and the greater in the negative, there will be negatives more than enough to destroy the affirmatives, and thereby the excess of negatives, standing uncontradicted, are the only voice the representative hath. And a representative of even number, especially when the number is not great, whereby the contradictory voices are oftentimes equal, is therefore oftentimes mute and incapable of action. Yet in some cases contradictory voices equal in number may determine a question; as in condemning, or absolving, equality of votes, even in that they condemn not, do absolve; but not on the contrary condemn, in that they absolve not. For when a cause is heard, not to condemn is to absolve; but on the contrary to say that not absolving is condemning is not true. The like it is in deliberation of executing presently, or deferring till another time: for when the voices are equal, the not decreeing execution is a decree of dilation. Or if the number be odd, as three, or more, men or assemblies, whereof every one has, by a negative voice, authority to take away the effect of all the affirmative voices of the rest, this number is no representative; by the diversity of opinions and interests of men, it becomes oftentimes, and in cases of the greatest consequence, a mute person and unapt, as for many things else, so for the government of a multitude, especially in time of war. Of authors there be two sorts. The first simply so called, which I have before defined to be him that owneth the action of another simply. The second is he that owneth an action or covenant of another conditionally; that is to say, he undertaketh to do it, if the other doth it not, at or before a certain time. And these authors conditional are generally called sureties, in Latin, fidejussores and sponsores; and particularly for debt, praedes and for appearance before a judge or magistrate, vades.

## THE SECOND PART, OF COMMONWEALTH

## CHAPTER XVII, OF THE CAUSES, GENERATION, AND DEFINITION OF A COMMONWEALTH

THE final cause, end, or design of men (who naturally love liberty, and dominion over others) in the introduction of that restraint upon themselves, in which we see them live in Commonwealths, is the foresight of their own preservation, and of a more contented life thereby; that is to say, of getting themselves out from that miserable condition of war which is necessarily consequent, as hath been shown, to the natural passions of men when there is no visible power to keep them in awe, and tie them by fear of punishment to the performance of their covenants, and observation of those laws of nature set down in the fourteenth and fifteenth chapters. For the laws of nature, as justice, equity, modesty, mercy, and, in sum, doing to others as we would be done to, of themselves, without the terror of some power to cause them to be observed, are contrary to our natural passions, that carry us to partiality, pride, revenge, and the like. And covenants, without the sword, are but words and of no strength to secure a man at all. Therefore, notwithstanding the laws of nature (which every one hath then kept, when he has the will to keep them, when he can do it safely), if there be no power erected, or not great enough for our security, every man will and may lawfully rely on his own strength and art for caution against all other men. And in all places, where men have lived by small families, to rob and spoil one another has been a trade, and so far from being reputed against the law of nature that the greater spoils they gained, the greater was their honour; and men observed no other laws therein but the laws of honour; that is, to abstain from cruelty, leaving to men their lives and instruments of husbandry. And as small families did then; so now do cities and kingdoms, which are but greater families (for their own security), enlarge their dominions upon all pretences of danger, and fear of invasion, or assistance that may be given to invaders; endeavour as much as they can to subdue or weaken their neighbours by open force, and secret arts, for want of other caution, justly; and are remembered for it in after ages with honour. Nor is it the joining together of a small number of men that gives them this security; because in small numbers, small additions on the one side or the other make the advantage of strength so great as is sufficient to carry the victory, and therefore gives encouragement to an invasion. The multitude sufficient to confide in for our security is not determined by any certain number, but by comparison with the enemy we fear; and is then sufficient when the odds of the enemy is not of so visible and conspicuous moment to determine the event of war, as to move him to attempt. And be there never so great a multitude; yet if their actions be directed according to their particular judgements, and particular appetites, they can expect thereby no defence, nor protection, neither against a common enemy, nor against the injuries of one another. For being distracted in opinions concerning the best use and application of their strength, they do not help, but hinder one another, and reduce their strength by mutual opposition to nothing: whereby they are easily, not only subdued by a very few that agree together, but also, when there is no common enemy, they make war upon each other for their particular interests. For if we could suppose a great multitude of men to consent in the observation of justice, and other laws of nature, without a common power to keep them all in awe, we might as well suppose all mankind to do the same; and then there neither would be, nor need to be, any civil government or Commonwealth at all, because there would be peace without subjection. Nor is it enough for the security, which men desire should last all the time of their life, that they be governed and directed by one judgement for a limited time; as in one battle, or one war. For though they obtain a victory by their unanimous endeavour against a foreign enemy, yet afterwards, when either they have no common enemy, or he that by one part is held for an enemy is by another part held for a friend, they must needs by the difference of their interests dissolve, and fall again into a war amongst themselves. It is true that certain living creatures, as bees and ants, live sociably one with another (which are therefore by Aristotle numbered amongst political creatures), and yet have no other direction than their particular judgements and appetites; nor speech, whereby one of them can signify to another what he thinks expedient for the common benefit: and therefore some man may perhaps desire to know why mankind cannot do the same. To which I answer, First, that men are continually in competition for honour and dignity, which these creatures are not; and consequently amongst men there ariseth on that ground, envy, and hatred, and finally war; but amongst these not so. Secondly, that amongst these creatures the common good differeth not from the private; and being by nature inclined to their private, they procure thereby the common benefit. But man, whose joy consisteth in comparing himself with other men, can relish nothing but what is eminent. Thirdly, that these creatures, having not, as man, the use of reason, do not see, nor think they see, any fault in the administration of their common business: whereas amongst men there are very many that think themselves wiser and abler to govern the public better than the rest, and these strive to reform and innovate, one this way, another that way; and thereby bring it into distraction and civil war. Fourthly, that these creatures, though they have some use of voice in making known to one another their desires and other affections, yet they want that art of words by which some men can represent to others that which is good in the likeness of evil; and evil, in the likeness of good; and augment or diminish the apparent greatness of good and evil, discontenting men and troubling their peace at their pleasure. Fifthly, irrational creatures cannot distinguish between injury and damage; and therefore as long as they be at ease, they are not offended with their fellows: whereas man is then most troublesome when he is most at ease; for then it is that he loves to show his wisdom, and control the actions of them that govern the Commonwealth. Lastly, the agreement of these creatures is natural; that of men is by covenant only, which is artificial: and therefore it is no wonder if there be somewhat else required, besides covenant, to make their agreement constant and lasting; which is a common power to keep them in awe and to direct their actions to the common benefit. The only way to erect such a common power, as may be able to defend them from the invasion of foreigners, and the injuries of one another, and thereby to secure them in such sort as that by their own industry and by the fruits of the earth they may nourish themselves and live contentedly, is to confer all their power and strength upon one man, or upon one assembly of men, that may reduce all their wills, by plurality of voices, unto one will: which is as much as to say, to appoint one man, or assembly of men, to bear their person; and every one to own and acknowledge himself to be author of whatsoever he that so beareth their person shall act, or cause to be acted, in those things which concern the common peace and safety; and therein to submit their wills, every one to his will, and their judgements to his judgement. This is more than consent, or concord; it is a real unity of them all in one and the same person, made by covenant of every man with every man, in such manner as if every man should say to every man: I authorise and give up my right of governing myself to this man, or to this assembly of men, on this condition; that thou give up, thy right to him, and authorise all his actions in like manner. This done, the multitude so united in one person is called a COMMONWEALTH; in Latin, CIVITAS. This is the generation of that great LEVIATHAN, or rather, to speak more reverently, of that mortal god to which we owe, under the immortal God, our peace and defence. For by this authority, given him by every particular man in the Commonwealth, he hath the use of so much power and strength conferred on him that, by terror thereof, he is enabled to form the wills of them all, to peace at home, and mutual aid against their enemies abroad. And in him consisteth the essence of the Commonwealth; which, to define it, is: one person, of whose acts a great multitude, by mutual covenants one with another, have made themselves every one the author, to the end he may use the strength and means of them all as he shall think expedient for their peace and common defence. And he that carryeth this person is called sovereign, and said to have sovereign power; and every one besides, his subject. The attaining to this sovereign power is by two ways. One, by natural force: as when a man maketh his children to submit themselves, and their children, to his government, as being able to destroy them if they refuse; or by war subdueth his enemies to his will, giving them their lives on that condition. The other, is when men agree amongst themselves to submit to some man, or assembly of men, voluntarily, on confidence to be protected by him against all others. This latter may be called a political Commonwealth, or Commonwealth by Institution; and the former, a Commonwealth by acquisition. And first, I shall speak of a Commonwealth by institution.

## CHAPTER XVIII OF THE RIGHTS OF SOVEREIGNS BY INSTITUTION

A COMMONWEALTH is said to be instituted when a multitude of men do agree, and covenant, every one with every one, that to whatsoever man, or assembly of men, shall be given by the major part the right to present the person of them all, that is to say, to be their representative; every one, as well he that voted for it as he that voted against it, shall authorize all the actions and judgements of that man, or assembly of men, in the same manner as if they were his own, to the end to live peaceably amongst themselves, and be protected against other men. From this institution of a Commonwealth are derived all the rights and faculties of him, or them, on whom the sovereign power is conferred by the consent of the people assembled. First, because they covenant, it is to be understood they are not obliged by former covenant to anything repugnant hereunto. And consequently they that have already instituted a Commonwealth, being thereby bound by covenant to own the actions and judgements of one, cannot lawfully make a new covenant amongst themselves to be obedient to any other, in anything whatsoever, without his permission. And therefore, they that are subjects to a monarch cannot without his leave cast off monarchy and return to the confusion of a disunited multitude; nor transfer their person from him that beareth it to another man, other assembly of men: for they are bound, every man to every man, to own and be reputed author of all that already is their sovereign shall do and judge fit to be done; so that any one man dissenting, all the rest should break their covenant made to that man, which is injustice: and they have also every man given the sovereignty to him that beareth their person; and therefore if they depose him, they take from him that which is his own, and so again it is injustice. Besides, if he that attempteth to depose his sovereign be killed or punished by him for such attempt, he is author of his own punishment, as being, by the institution, author of all his sovereign shall do; and because it is injustice for a man to do anything for which he may be punished by his own authority, he is also upon that title unjust. And whereas some men have pretended for their disobedience to their sovereign a new covenant, made, not with men but with God, this also is unjust: for there is no covenant with God but by mediation of somebody that representeth God's person, which none doth but God's lieutenant who hath the sovereignty under God. But this pretence of covenant with God is so evident a lie, even in the pretenders' own consciences, that it is not

only an act of an unjust, but also of a vile and unmanly disposition. Secondly, because the right of bearing the person of them all is given to him they make sovereign, by covenant only of one to another, and not of him to any of them, there can happen no breach of covenant on the part of the sovereign; and consequently none of his subjects, by any pretence of forfeiture, can be freed from his subjection. That he which is made sovereign maketh no covenant with his subjects before hand is manifest; because either he must make it with the whole multitude, as one party to the covenant, or he must make a several covenant with every man. With the whole, as one party, it is impossible, because as they are not one person: and if he make so many several covenants as there be men, those covenants after he hath the sovereignty are void; because what act soever can be pretended by any one of them for breach thereof is the act both of himself, and of all the rest, because done in the person, and by the right of every one of them in particular. Besides, if any one or more of them pretend a breach of the covenant made by the sovereign at his institution, and others or one other of his subjects, or himself alone, pretend there was no such breach, there is in this case no judge to decide the controversy: it returns therefore to the sword again; and every man recovereth the right of protecting himself by his own strength, contrary to the design they had in the institution. It is therefore in vain to grant sovereignty by way of precedent covenant. The opinion that any monarch receiveth his power by covenant, that is to say, on condition, proceedeth from want of understanding this easy truth: that covenants being but words, and breath, have no force to oblige, contain, constrain, or protect any man, but what it has from the public sword; that is, from the untied hands of that man, or assembly of men, that hath the sovereignty, and whose actions are avouched by them all, and performed by the strength of them all, in him united. But when an assembly of men is made sovereign, then no man imagineth any such covenant to have passed in the institution: for no man is so dull as to say, for example, the people of Rome made a covenant with the Romans to hold the sovereignty on such or such conditions; which not performed, the Romans might lawfully depose the Roman people. That men see not the reason to be alike in a monarchy and in a popular government proceedeth from the ambition of some that are kinder to the government of an assembly, whereof they may hope to participate, than of monarchy, which they despair to enjoy. Thirdly, because the major part hath by consenting voices declared a sovereign, he that dissented must now consent with the rest; that is, be contented to avow all the actions he shall do, or else justly be destroyed by the rest. For if he voluntarily entered into the congregation of them that were assembled, he sufficiently declared thereby his will, and therefore tacitly covenanted, to stand to what the major part should ordain: and therefore if he refuse to stand thereto, or make protestation against any of their decrees, he does contrary to his covenant, and therefore unjustly. And whether he be of the congregation or not, and whether his consent be asked or not, he must either submit to their decrees or be left in the condition of war he was in before; wherein he might without injustice be destroyed by any man whatsoever. Fourthly, because every subject is by this institution author of all the actions and judgements of the sovereign instituted, it follows that whatsoever he doth, can be no injury to any of his subjects; nor ought he to be by any of them accused of injustice. For he that doth anything by authority from another doth therein no injury to him by whose authority he acteth: but by this institution of a Commonwealth every particular man is author of all the sovereign doth; and consequently he that complaineth of injury from his sovereig
complaineth of that whereof he himself is author, and therefore ought not to accuse any man but himself; no, nor himself of injury, because to do injury to oneself is impossible. It is true that they that have sovereign power may commit iniquity, but not injustice or injury in the proper signification. Fifthly, and consequently to that which was said last, no man that hath sovereign power can justly be put to death, or otherwise in any manner by his subjects punished. For seeing every subject is author of the actions of his sovereign, he punisheth another for the actions committed by himself. And because the end of this institution is the peace and defence of them all, and whosoever has right to the end has right to the means, it belonged of right to whatsoever man or assembly that hath the sovereignty to be judge both of the means of peace and defence, and also of the hindrances and disturbances of the same; and to do whatsoever he shall think necessary to be done, both beforehand, for the preserving of peace and security, by prevention of discord at home, and hostility from abroad; and when peace and security are lost, for the recovery of the same. And therefore, Sixthly, it is annexed to the sovereignty to be judge of what opinions and doctrines are averse, and what conducing to peace; and consequently, on what occasions, how far, and what men are to be trusted withal in speaking to multitudes of people; and who shall examine the doctrines of all books before they be published. For the actions of men proceed from their opinions, and in the well governing of opinions consisteth the well governing of men's actions in order to their peace and concord. And though in matter of doctrine nothing to be regarded but the truth, yet this is not repugnant to regulating of the same by peace. For doctrine repugnant to peace can no more be true, than peace and concord can be against the law of nature. It is true that in a Commonwealth,

where by the negligence or unskillfulness of governors and teachers false doctrines are by time generally received, the contrary truths may be generally offensive: yet the most sudden and rough bustling in of a new truth that can be does never break the peace, but only sometimes awake the war. For those men that are so remissly governed that they dare take up arms to defend or introduce an opinion are still in war; and their condition, not peace, but only a cessation of arms for fear of one another; and they live, as it were, in the procincts of battle continually. It belonged therefore to him that hath the sovereign power to be judge, or constitute all judges of opinions and doctrines, as a thing necessary to peace; thereby to prevent discord and civil war. Seventhly, is annexed to the sovereignty the whole power of prescribing the rules whereby every man may know what goods he may enjoy, and what actions he may do, without being molested by any of his fellow subjects: and this is it men call propriety. For before constitution of sovereign power, as hath already been shown, all men had right to all things, which necessarily causeth war: and therefore this propriety, being necessary to peace, and depending on sovereign power, is the act of that power, in order to the public peace. These rules of propriety (or meum and tuum) and of good, evil, lawful, and unlawful in the actions of subjects are the civil laws; that is to say, the laws of each Commonwealth in particular; though the name of civil law be now restrained to the ancient civil laws of the city of Rome; which being the head of a great part of the world, her laws at that time were in these parts the civil law. Eighthly, is annexed to the sovereignty the right of judicature; that is to say, of hearing and deciding all controversies which may arise concerning law, either civil or natural, or concerning fact. For without the decision of controversies, there is no protection of one subject against the injuries of another; the laws concerning meum and tuum are in vain, and to every man remaineth, from the natural and necessary appetite of his own conservation, the right of protecting himself by his private strength, which is the condition of war, and contrary to the end for which every Commonwealth is instituted. Ninthly, is annexed to the sovereignty the right of making war and peace with other nations and Commonwealths; that is to say, of judging when it is for the public good, and how great forces are to be assembled, armed, and paid for that end, and to levy money upon the subjects to defray the expenses thereof. For the power by which the people are to be defended consisteth in their armies, and the strength of an army in the union of their strength under one command; which command the sovereign instituted, therefore hath, because the command of the militia, without other institution, maketh him that hath it sovereign. And therefore, whosoever is made general of an army, he that hath the sovereign power is always generalissimo. Tenthly, is annexed to the sovereignty the choosing of all counsellors, ministers, magistrates, and officers, both in peace and war. For seeing the sovereign is charged with the end, which is the common peace and defence, he is understood to have power to use such means as he shall think most fit for his discharge. Eleventhly, to the sovereign is committed the power of rewarding with riches or honour; and of punishing with corporal or pecuniary punishment, or with ignominy, every subject according to the law he hath formerly made; or if there be no law made, according as he shall judge most to conduce to the encouraging of men to serve the Commonwealth, or deterring of them from doing disservice to the same. Lastly, considering what values men are naturally apt to set upon themselves, what respect they look for from others, and how little they value other men; from whence continually arise amongst them, emulation, quarrels, factions, and at last war, to the destroying of one another, and diminution of their strength against a common enemy; it is necessary that there be laws of honour, and a public rate of the worth of such men as have deserved or are able to deserve well of the Commonwealth, and that there be force in the hands of some or other to put those laws in execution. But it hath already been shown that not only the whole militia, or forces of the Commonwealth, but also the judicature of all controversies, is annexed to the sovereignty. To the sovereign therefore it belonged also to give titles of honour, and to appoint what order of place and dignity each man shall hold, and what signs of respect in public or private meetings they shall give to one another. These are the rights which make the essence of sovereignty, and which are the marks whereby a man may discern in what man, or assembly of men, the sovereign power is placed and resideth. For these are incommunicable and inseparable. The power to coin money, to dispose of the estate and persons of infant heirs, to have pre-emption in markets, and all other statute prerogatives may be transferred by the sovereign, and yet the power to protect his subjects be retained. But if he transfer the militia, he retains the judicature in vain, for want of execution of the laws; or if he grant away the power of raising money, the militia is in vain; or if he give away the government of doctrines, men will be frighted into rebellion with the fear of spirits. And so if we consider any one of the said rights, we shall presently see that the holding of all the rest will produce no effect in the conservation of peace and justice, the end for which all Commonwealths are instituted. And this division is it whereof it is said, a kingdom divided in itself cannot stand: for unless this division precede, division into opposite armies can never happen. If there had not first been an opinion received of the greatest part of England that these powers were divided between the King and the Lords and the House of Commons, the people had never been divided and fallen into this Civil War; first between those that disagreed in politics, and after between the dissenters about the liberty of religion, which have so instructed men in this point of sovereign right that there be few now in England that do not see that these rights are inseparable, and will be so generally acknowledged at the next return of peace; and so continue, till their miseries are forgotten, and no longer, except the vulgar be better taught than they have hitherto been. And because they are essential and inseparable rights, it follows necessarily that in whatsoever words any of them seem to be granted away, yet if the sovereign power itself be not in direct terms renounced and the name of sovereign no more given by the grantees to him that grants them, the grant is void: for when he has granted all he can, if we grant back the sovereignty, all is restored, as inseparably annexed thereunto. This great authority being indivisible, and inseparably annexed to the sovereignty, there is little ground for the opinion of them that say of sovereign kings, though they be singulis majores, of greater power than every one of their subjects, yet they be universis minores, of less power than them all together. For if by all together, they mean not the collective body as one person, then all together and every one signify the same; and the speech is absurd. But if by all together, they understand them as one person (which person the sovereign bears), then the power of all together is the same with the sovereign's power; and so again the speech is absurd: which absurdity they see well enough when the sovereignty is in an assembly of the people; but in a monarch they see it not; and yet the power of sovereignty is the same in whomsoever it be placed. And as the power, so also the honour of the sovereign, ought to be greater than that of any or all the subjects. For in the sovereignty is the fountain of honour. The dignities of lord, earl, duke, and prince are his creatures. As in the presence of the master, the servants are equal, and without any honour at all; so are the subjects, in the presence of the sovereign. And though they shine some more, some less, when they are out of his sight; yet in his presence, they shine no more than the stars in presence of the sun. But a man may here object that the condition of subjects is very miserable, as being obnoxious to the lusts and other irregular passions of him or them that have so unlimited a power in their hands. And commonly they that live under a monarch think it the fault of monarchy; and they that live under the government of democracy, or other sovereign assembly, attribute all the inconvenience to that form of Commonwealth; whereas the power in all forms, if they be perfect enough to protect them, is the same: not considering that the estate of man can never be without some incommodity or other; and that the greatest that in any form of government can possibly happen to the people in general is scarce sensible, in respect of the miseries and horrible calamities that accompany a civil war, or that dissolute condition of masterless men without subjection to laws and a coercive power to tie their hands from rapine and revenge: nor considering that the greatest pressure of sovereign governors proceedeth, not from any delight or profit they can expect in the damage weakening of their subjects, in whose vigour consisteth their own strength and glory, but in the restiveness of themselves that, unwillingly contributing to their own defence, make it necessary for their governors to draw from them what they can in time of peace that they may have means on any emergent occasion, or sudden need, to resist or take advantage on their enemies. For all men are by nature provided of notable multiplying glasses (that is their passions and self-love) through which every little payment appeareth a great grievance, but are destitute of those prospective glasses (namely moral and civil science) to see afar off the miseries that hang over them and cannot without such payments be avoided.

## CHAPTER XIX, OF THE SEVERAL KINDS OF COMMONWEALTH BY INSTITUTION, AND OF SUCCESSION TO THE SOVEREIGN POWER

THE difference of Commonwealths consisteth in the difference of the sovereign, or the person representative of all and every one of the multitude. And because the sovereignty is either in one man, or in an assembly of more than one; and into that assembly either every man hath right to enter, or not every one, but certain men distinguished from the rest; it is manifest there can be but three kinds of Commonwealth. For the representative must needs be one man, or more; and if more, then it is the assembly of all, or but of a part. When the representative is one man, then is the Commonwealth a monarchy; when an assembly of all that will come together, then it is a democracy, or popular Commonwealth; when an assembly of a part only, then it is called an aristocracy. Other kind of Commonwealth there can be none: for either one, or more, or all, must have the sovereign power (which I have shown to be indivisible) entire. There be other names of government in the histories and books of policy; as tyranny and oligarchy; but they are not the names of other forms of government, but of the same forms misliked. For they that are discontented under monarchy call it tyranny; and they that are displeased with aristocracy call it oligarchy: so also, they which find themselves grieved under a democracy call it anarchy, which signifies want of government; and yet I think no man believes that want of government is any new kind of government: nor by the same reason ought they to believe that the government is of one kind when they like it, and another when they mislike it or are oppressed by the governors. It is manifest that men who are in absolute liberty may, if they please, give authority to one man to represent them every one, as well as give such authority to any assembly of men whatsoever; and consequently may subject themselves, if they think good, to a monarch as absolutely as to other representative. Therefore, where there is already erected a sovereign power, there can be no other representative of the same people, but only to certain particular ends, by the sovereign limited. For that were to erect two sovereigns; and every man to have his person represented by two actors that, by opposing one another, must needs divide that power, which (if men will live in peace) is indivisible; and thereby reduce the multitude into the condition of war, contrary to the end for which all sovereignty is instituted. And therefore as it is absurd to think that a sovereign assembly, inviting the people of their dominion to send up their deputies with power to make known their advice or desires should therefore hold such deputies, rather than themselves, for the absolute representative of the people; so it is absurd also to think the same in a monarchy. And I know not how this so manifest a truth should of late be so little observed: that in a monarchy he that had the sovereignty from a descent of six hundred years was alone called sovereign, had the title of Majesty from every one of his subjects, and was unquestionably taken by them for their king, was notwithstanding never considered as their representative; that name without contradiction passing for the title of those men which at his command were sent up by the people to carry their petitions and give him, if he permitted it, their advice. Which may serve as an admonition for those that are the true and absolute representative of a people, to instruct men in the nature of that office, and to take heed how they admit of any other general representation upon any occasion whatsoever, if they mean to discharge the trust committed to them. The difference between these three kinds of Commonwealth consisteth, not in the difference of power, but in the difference of convenience or aptitude to produce the peace and security of the people; for which end they were instituted. And to compare monarchy with the other two, we may observe: first, that whosoever beareth the person of the people, or is one of that assembly that bears it, beareth also his own natural person. And though he be careful in his politic person to procure the common interest, yet he is more, or no less, careful to procure the private good of himself, his family, kindred and friends; and for the most part, if the public interest chance to cross the private, he prefers the private: for the passions of men are commonly more potent than their reason. From whence it follows that where the public and private interest are most closely united, there is the public most advanced. Now in monarchy the private interest is the same with the public. The riches, power, and honour of a monarch arise only from the riches, strength, and reputation of his subjects. For no king can be rich, nor glorious, nor secure, whose subjects are either poor, or contemptible, or too weak through want, or dissension, to maintain a war against their enemies; whereas in a democracy, or aristocracy, the public prosperity confers not so much to the private fortune of one that is corrupt, or ambitious, as doth many times a perfidious advice, a treacherous action, or a civil war. Secondly, that a monarch receiveth counsel of whom, when, and where he pleaseth; and consequently may hear the opinion of men versed in the matter about which he deliberates, of what rank or quality soever, and as long before the time of action and with as much secrecy as he will. But when a sovereign assembly has need of counsel, none are admitted but such as have a right thereto from the beginning; which for the most part are of those who have been versed more in the acquisition of wealth than of knowledge, and are to give their advice in long discourses which may, and do commonly, excite men to action, but not govern them in it. For the understanding is by the flame of the passions never enlightened, but dazzled: nor is there any place or time wherein an assembly can receive counsel secrecy, because of their own multitude. Thirdly, that the resolutions of a monarch are subject to no other inconstancy than that of human nature; but in assemblies, besides that of nature, there ariseth an inconstancy from the number. For the absence of a few that would have the resolution, once taken, continue firm (which may happen by security, negligence, or private impediments), or the diligent appearance of a few of the contrary opinion, undoes today all that was concluded yesterday. Fourthly, that a monarch cannot disagree with himself, out of envy or interest; but an assembly may; and that to such a height as may produce a civil war. Fifthly, that in monarchy there is this inconvenience; that any subject, by the power of one man, for the enriching of a favourite or flatterer, may be deprived of all he possesseth; which I confess is a great an inevitable inconvenience. But the same may as well happen where the sovereign power is in an assembly: for their power is the same; and they are as subject to evil counsel, and to be seduced by orators, as a monarch by flatterers; and becoming one another's flatterers, serve one another's covetousness and ambition by turns. And whereas the favourites of monarchs are few, and they have none else to advance but their own kindred; the favourites of an assembly are many, and the kindred much more numerous than of any monarch. Besides, there is no favourite of a monarch which cannot as well succour his friends as hurt his enemies: but orators, that is to say, favourites of sovereign assemblies, though they have great power to hurt, have little to save. For to accuse requires less eloquence (such is man's nature) than to excuse; and condemnation, than absolution, more resembles justice. Sixthly, that it is an inconvenience in monarchy that the sovereignty may descend upon an infant, or one that cannot discern between good and evil: and consisteth in this, that the use of his power must be in the hand of another man, or of some assembly of men, which are to govern by his right and in his name as curators and protectors of his person and authority. But to say there is inconvenience in putting the use of the sovereign power into the hand of a man, or an assembly of men, is to say that all government is more inconvenient than confusion and civil war. And therefore all the danger that can be pretended must arise from the contention of those that, for an office of so great honour and profit, may become competitors. To make it appear that this inconvenience proceedeth not from that form of government we call monarchy, we are to consider that the precedent monarch hath appointed who shall have the tuition of his infant successor, either expressly by testament, or tacitly by not controlling the custom in that case received: and then such inconvenience, if it happen, is to be attributed, not to the monarchy, but to the ambition and injustice of the subjects, which in all kinds of government, where the people are not well instructed in their duty and the rights of sovereignty, is the same. Or else the precedent monarch hath not at all taken order for such tuition; and then the law of nature hath provided this sufficient rule, that the tuition shall be in him that hath by nature most interest in the preservation of the authority of the infant, and to whom least benefit can accrue by his death or diminution. For seeing every man by nature seeketh his own benefit and promotion, to put an infant into the power of those that can promote themselves by his destruction or damage is not tuition, but treachery. So that sufficient provision being taken against all just quarrel about the government under a child, if any contention arise to the disturbance of the public peace, it is not to be attributed to the form of monarchy, but to the ambition of subjects and ignorance of their duty. On the other side, there is no great Commonwealth, the sovereignty whereof is in a great assembly, which is not, as to consultations of peace, and war, and making of laws, in the same condition as if the government were in a child. For as a child wants the judgement to dissent from counsel given him, and is thereby necessitated to take the advice of them, or him, to whom he is committed; so an assembly wanteth the liberty to dissent from the counsel of the major part, be it good or bad. And as a child has need of a tutor, or protector, to preserve his person and authority; so also in great Commonwealths the sovereign assembly, in all great dangers and troubles, have need of custodes libertatis; that is, of dictators, or protectors of their authority; which are as much as temporary monarchs to whom for a time they may commit the entire exercise of their power; and have, at the end of that time, been oftener deprived thereof than infant kings by their protectors, regents, or any other tutors. Though the kinds of sovereignty be, as I have now shown, but three; that is to say, monarchy, where one man has it; or democracy, where the general assembly of subjects hath it; or aristocracy, where it is in an assembly of certain persons nominated, or otherwise distinguished from the rest: yet he that shall consider the particular Commonwealths that have been and are in the world will not perhaps easily reduce them to three, and may thereby be inclined to think there be other forms arising from these mingled together. As for example, elective kingdoms; where kings have the sovereign power put into their hands for a time; or kingdoms wherein the king hath a power limited: which governments are nevertheless by most writers called monarchy. Likewise if a popular or aristocratical Commonwealth subdue an enemy's country, and govern the same by a president, procurator, or other magistrate, this may seem perhaps, at first sight, to be a democratical or aristocratical government. But it is not so. For elective kings are not sovereigns, but ministers of the sovereign; nor limited kings sovereigns, but ministers of them that have the sovereign power; nor are those provinces which are in subjection to a democracy or aristocracy of another Commonwealth democratically or aristocratically governed, but monarchically. And first, concerning an elective king, whose power is limited to his life, as it is in many places of Christendom at this day; or to certain years or months, as the dictator's power amongst the Romans; if he have right to appoint his successor, he is no more elective but hereditary. But if he have no power to elect his successor, then there is some other man, or assembly known, which after his decease may elect a new; or else the Commonwealth dieth, and dissolveth with him, and returneth to the condition of war. If it be known who have the power to give the sovereignty after his death, it is known also that the sovereignty was in them before: for none have right to give that which they have not right to possess, and keep to themselves, if they think good. But if there be none that can give the sovereignty after the decease of him that was first elected, then has he power, nay he is obliged by the law of nature, to provide, by establishing his successor, to keep to those that had trusted him with the government from relapsing into the miserable condition of civil war. And consequently he was, when elected, a sovereign absolute. Secondly, that king whose power is limited is not superior to him, or them, that have the power to limit it; and he that is not superior is not supreme; that is to say, not sovereign. The sovereignty therefore was always in that assembly which had the right to limit him, and by consequence the government not monarchy, but either democracy or aristocracy; as of old time in Sparta, where the kings had a privilege to lead their armies, but the sovereignty was in the Ephori. Thirdly, whereas heretofore the Roman people governed the land of Judea, for example, by a president; yet was not Judea therefore a democracy, because they were not governed by any assembly into which any of them had right to enter; nor by an aristocracy, because they were not governed by any assembly into which any man could enter by their election: but they were governed by one person, which though as to the people of Rome was an assembly of the people, or democracy; yet as to the people of Judea, which had no right at all of participating in the government, was a monarch. For though where the people are governed by an assembly, chosen by themselves out of their own number, the government is called a democracy, or aristocracy; yet when they are governed by an assembly not of their own choosing, it is a monarchy; not of one man over another man, but of one people over another people. Of all these forms of government, the matter being mortal, so that not only monarchs, but also whole assemblies die, it is necessary for the conservation of the peace of men that as there was order taken for an artificial man, so there be order also taken for an artificial eternity of life; without which men that are governed by an assembly should return into the condition of war in every age; and they that are governed by one man, as soon as their governor dieth. This artificial eternity is that which men call the right of succession. There is no perfect form of government, where the disposing of the succession is not in the present sovereign. For if it be in any other particular man, or private assembly, it is in a person subject, and may be assumed by the sovereign at his pleasure; and consequently the right is in himself. And if it be in no particular man, but left to a new choice; then is the Commonwealth dissolved, and the right is in him that can get it, contrary to the intention of them that did institute the Commonwealth for their perpetual, and not temporary, security. In a democracy, the whole assembly cannot fail unless the multitude that are to be governed fail. And therefore questions of the right of succession have in that form of government no place at all. In an aristocracy, when any of the assembly dieth, the election of another into his room belonged to the assembly, as the sovereign, to whom belonged the choosing of all counsellors and officers. For that which the representative doth, as actor, every one of the subjects doth, as author. And though the sovereign assembly may give power to others to elect new men, for supply of their court, yet it is still by their authority that the election is made; and by the same it may, when the public shall require it, be recalled. The greatest difficulty about the right of succession is in monarchy: and the difficulty ariseth from this, that at first sight, it is not manifest who is to appoint the successor; nor many times who it is whom he hath appointed. For in both these cases, there is required a more exact ratiocination than every man is accustomed to use. As to the question who shall appoint the successor of a monarch that hath the sovereign authority; that is to say, who shall determine of the right of inheritance (for elective kings and princes have not the sovereign power in propriety, but in use only), we are to consider that either he that is in possession has right to dispose of the succession, or else that right is again in the dissolved multitude. For the death of him that hath the sovereign power in property leaves the multitude without any sovereign at all; that is, without any representative in whom they should be united, and be capable of doing any one action at all: and therefore they are incapable of election of any new monarch, every man having equal right to submit himself to such as he thinks best able to protect him; or, if he can, protect himself by his own sword; which is a return to confusion and to the condition of a war of every man against every man, contrary to the end for which monarchy had its first institution. Therefore it is manifest that by the institution of monarchy, the disposing of the successor is always left to the judgement and will of the present possessor. And for the question which may arise sometimes, who it is that the monarch in possession hath designed to the succession and inheritance of his power, it is determined by his express words and testament; or by other tacit signs sufficient. By express words, or testament, when it is declared by him in his lifetime, viva voce, or by writing; as the first emperors of Rome declared who should be their heirs. For the word heir does not of itself imply the children or nearest kindred of a man; but whomsoever a man shall any way declare he would have to succeed him in his estate. If therefore a monarch declare expressly that such a man shall be his heir, either by word or writing, then is that man immediately after the decease of his predecessor invested in the right of being monarch. But where testament and express words are wanting, other natural signs of the will are to be followed: whereof the one is custom. And therefore where the custom is that the next of kindred absolutely succeedeth, there also the next of kindred hath right to the succession; for that, if the will of him that was in possession had been otherwise, he might easily have declared the same in his lifetime. And likewise where the custom is that the next of the male kindred succeedeth, there also the right of succession is in the next of the kindred male, for the same reason. And so it is if the custom were to advance the female. For whatsoever custom a man may by a word control, and does not, it is a natural sign he would have that custom stand. But where neither custom nor testament hath preceded, there it is to he understood; first, that a monarch's will is that the government remain monarchical, because he hath approved that government in himself. Secondly, that a child of his own, male or female, be preferred before any other, because men are presumed to be more inclined by nature to advance their own children than the children of other men; and of their own, rather a male than a female, because men are naturally fitter than women for actions of labour and danger. Thirdly, where his own issue faileth, rather a brother than a stranger, and so still the nearer in blood rather than the more remote, because it is always presumed that the nearer of kin is the nearer in affection; and it is evident that a man receives always, by reflection, the most honour from the greatness of his nearest kindred. But if it be lawful for a monarch to dispose of the succession by words of contract, or testament, men may perhaps object a great inconvenience: for he may sell or give his right of governing to a stranger; which, because strangers (that is, men not used to live under the same government, nor speaking the same language) do commonly undervalue one another, may turn to the oppression of his subjects, which is indeed a great inconvenience: but it proceedeth not necessarily from the subjection to a stranger's government, but from the unskillfulness of the governors, ignorant of the true rules of politics. And therefore the Romans, when they had subdued many nations, to make their government digestible were wont to take away that grievance as much as they thought necessary by giving sometimes to whole nations, and sometimes to principal men of every nation they conquered, not only the privileges, but also the name of Romans; and took many of them into the Senate, and offices of charge, even in the Roman city. And this was it our most wise king, King James, aimed at in endeavouring the union of his two realms of England and Scotland. Which, if he could have obtained, had in all likelihood prevented the civil wars which both those kingdoms, at this present, miserable. It is not therefore any injury to the people for a monarch to dispose of the succession by will; though by the fault of many princes, it hath been sometimes found inconvenient. Of the lawfulness of it, this also is an argument; that whatsoever inconvenience can arrive by giving a kingdom to a stranger, may arrive also by so marrying with strangers, as the right of succession may descend upon them: yet this by all men is accounted lawful.

## CHAPTER XX, OF DOMINION PATERNAL AND DESPOTICAL

A COMMONWEALTH by acquisition is that where the sovereign power is acquired by force; and it is acquired by force when men singly, or many together by plurality of voices, for fear of death, or bonds, do authorise all the actions of that man, or assembly, that hath their lives and liberty in his power. And this kind of dominion, or sovereignty, differeth from sovereignty by institution only in this, that men who choose their sovereign do it for fear of one another, and not of him whom they institute: but in this case, they subject themselves to him they are afraid of. In both cases they do it for fear: which is to be noted by them that hold all such covenants, as proceed from fear of death or violence, void: which, if it were true, no man in any kind of Commonwealth could be obliged to obedience. It is true that in a Commonwealth once instituted, or acquired, promises proceeding from fear of death or violence are no covenants, nor obliging, when the thing promised is contrary to the laws; but the reason is not because it was made upon fear, but because he that promiseth hath no right in the thing promised. Also, when he may lawfully perform, and doth not, it is not the invalidity of the covenant that absolveth him, but the sentence of the sovereign. Otherwise, whensoever a man lawfully promiseth, he unlawfully breaketh: but when the sovereign, who is the actor, acquitteth him, then he is acquitted by him that extorted the promise, as by the author of such absolution. But the rights and consequences of sovereignty are the same in both. His power cannot, without his consent, be transferred to another: he cannot forfeit it: he cannot be accused by any of his subjects of injury: he cannot be punished by them: he is judge of what is necessary for peace, and judge of doctrines: he is sole legislator, and supreme judge of controversies, and of the times and occasions of war and peace: to him it belonged to choose magistrates, counsellors, commanders, and all other officers and ministers; and to determine of rewards and punishments, honour and order. The reasons whereof are the same which are alleged in the precedent chapter for the same rights and consequences of sovereignty by institution. Dominion is acquired two ways: by generation and by conquest. The right of dominion by generation is that which the parent hath over his children, and is called paternal. And is not so derived from the generation, as if therefore the parent had dominion over his child because he begat him, but from the child's consent, either express or by other sufficient arguments declared. For as to the generation, God hath ordained to man a helper, and there be always two that are equally parents: the dominion therefore over the child should belong equally to both, and he be equally subject to both, which is impossible; for no man can obey two masters. And whereas some have attributed the dominion to the man only, as being of the more excellent sex, they misreckon in it. For there is not always that difference of strength or prudence between the man and the woman as that the right can be determined without war. In Commonwealths this controversy is decided by the civil law: and for the most part, but not always, the sentence is in favour of the father, because for the most part Commonwealths have been erected by the fathers, not by the mothers of families. But the question lieth now in the state of mere nature where there are supposed no laws of matrimony, no laws for the education of children, but the law of nature and the natural inclination of the sexes, one to another, and to their children. In this condition of mere nature, either the parents between themselves dispose of the dominion over the child by contract, or do not dispose thereof at all. If they dispose thereof, the right passeth according to the contract. We find in history that the Amazons contracted with the men of the neighbouring countries, to whom they had recourse for issue, that the issue male should be sent back, but the female remain with themselves: so that the dominion of the females was in the mother. If there be no contract, the dominion is in the mother. For in the condition of mere nature, where there are no matrimonial laws, it cannot be known who is the father unless it be declared by the mother; and therefore the right of dominion over the child dependeth on her will, and is consequently hers. Again, seeing the infant is first in the power of the mother, so as she may either nourish or expose it; if she nourish it, it oweth its life to the mother, and is therefore obliged to obey her rather than any other; and by consequence the dominion over it is hers. But if she expose it, and another find and nourish it, dominion is in him that nourisheth it. For it ought to obey him by whom it is preserved, because preservation of life being the end for which one man becomes subject to another, every man is supposed to promise obedience to him in whose power it is to save or destroy him. If the mother be the father's subject, the child is in the father's power; and if the father be the mother's subject (as when a sovereign queen marrieth one of her subjects), the child is subject to the mother, because the father also is her subject. If a man and a woman, monarchs of two several kingdoms, have a child, and contract concerning who shall have the dominion of him, the right of the dominion passeth by the contract. If they contract not, the dominion followeth the dominion of the place of his residence. For the sovereign of each country hath dominion over all that reside therein. He that hath the dominion over the child hath dominion also over the children of the child, and over their children's children. For he that hath dominion over the person of a man hath dominion over all that is his, without which dominion were but a title without the effect. The right of succession to paternal dominion proceedeth in the same manner as doth the right of succession to monarchy, of which I have already sufficiently spoken in the precedent chapter. Dominion acquired by conquest, or victory in war, is that which some writers call despotical from Despotes, which signifieth a lord or master, and is the dominion of the master over his servant. And this dominion is then acquired to the victor when the vanquished, to avoid the present stroke of death, covenanteth, either in express words or by other sufficient signs of the will, that so long as his life and the liberty of his body is allowed him, the victor shall have the use thereof at his pleasure. And after such covenant made, the vanquished is a servant, and not before: for by the word servant (whether it be derived from servire, to serve, or from servare, to save, which I leave to grammarians to dispute) is not meant a captive, which is kept in prison, or bonds, till the owner of him that took him, or bought him of one that did, shall consider what to do with him: for such men, commonly called slaves, have no obligation at all; but may break their bonds, or the prison; and kill, or carry away captive their master, justly: but one that, being taken, hath corporal liberty allowed him; and upon promise not to run away, nor to do violence to his master, is trusted by him. It is not therefore the victory that giveth the right of dominion over the vanquished, but his own covenant. Nor is he obliged because he is conquered; that is to say, beaten, and taken, or put to flight; but because he cometh in and submitteth to the victor; nor is the victor obliged by an enemy's rendering himself, without promise of life, to spare him for this his yielding to discretion; which obliges not the victor longer than in his own discretion he shall think fit. And that which men do when they demand, as it is now called, quarter (which the Greeks called Zogria, taking alive) is to evade the present fury of the victor by submission, and to compound for their life with ransom or service: and therefore he that hath quarter hath not his life given, but deferred till further deliberation; for it is not a yielding on condition of life, but to discretion. And then only is his life in security, and his service due, when the victor hath trusted him with his corporal liberty. For slaves that work in prisons, or fetters, do it not of duty, but to avoid the cruelty of their taskmasters. The master of the servant is master also of all he hath, and may exact the use thereof; that is to say, of his goods, of his labour, of his servants, and of his children, as often as he shall think fit. For he holdeth his life of his master by the covenant of obedience; that is, of owning and authorising whatsoever the master shall do. And in case the master, if he refuse, kill him, or cast him into bonds, or otherwise punish him for his disobedience, he is himself the author of the same, and cannot accuse him of injury. In sum, the rights and consequences of both paternal and despotical dominion are the very same with those of a sovereign by institution; and for the same reasons: which reasons are set down in the precedent chapter. So that for a man that is monarch of diverse nations, he hath in one the sovereignty by institution of the people assembled, and in another by conquest; that is by the submission of each particular, to avoid death or bonds; to demand of one nation more than of the other, from the title of conquest, as being a conquered nation, is an act of ignorance of the rights of sovereignty. For the sovereign is absolute over both alike; or else there is no sovereignty at all, and so every man may lawfully protect himself, if he can, with his own sword, which is the condition of war. By this it appears that a great family, if it be not part of some Commonwealth, is of itself, as to the rights of sovereignty, a little monarchy; whether that family consist of a man and his children, or of a man and his servants, or of a man and his children and servants together; wherein the father or master is the sovereign. But yet a family is not properly a Commonwealth, unless it be of that power by its own number, or by other opportunities, as not to be subdued without the hazard of war. For where a number of men are manifestly too weak to defend themselves united, every one may use his own reason in time of danger to save his own life, either by flight, or by submission to the enemy, as he shall think best; in the same manner as a very small company of soldiers, surprised by an army, may cast down their arms and demand quarter, or run away rather than be put to the sword. And thus much shall suffice concerning what I find by speculation, and deduction, of sovereign rights, from the nature, need, and designs of men in erecting of Commonwealths, and putting themselves under monarchs or assemblies entrusted with power enough for their protection. Let us now consider what the Scripture teacheth in the same point. To Moses the children of Israel say thus: "Speak thou to us, and we will hear thee; but let not God speak to us, lest we die." [Exodus, 20. 19] This is absolute obedience to Moses. Concerning the right of kings, God Himself, by the mouth of Samuel, saith, "This shall be the right of the king you will have to reign over you. He shall take your sons, and set them to drive his chariots, and to be his horsemen, and to run before his chariots, and gather in his harvest; and to make his engines of war, and instruments of his chariots; and shall take your daughters to make perfumes, to be his cooks, and bakers. He shall take your fields, your vineyards, and your olive-yards, and give them to his servants. He shall take the tithe of your corn and wine, and give it to the men of his chamber, and to his other servants. He shall take your man-servants, and your maidservants, and the choice of your youth, and employ them in his business. He shall take the tithe of your flocks; and you shall be his servants." [I Samuel, 8. 11-17] This is absolute power, and summed up in the last words, you shall be his servants. Again, when the people heard what power their king was to have, yet they consented thereto, and say thus, "We will be as all other nations, and our king shall judge our causes, and go before us, to conduct our wars." [Ibid., 8. 19, 20] Here is confirmed the right that sovereigns have, both to the militia and to all judicature; in which is contained as absolute power as one man can possibly transfer to another. Again, the prayer of King Solomon to God was this: "Give to thy servant understanding, to judge thy people, and to discern between good and evil." [I Kings, 3. 9] It belonged therefore to the sovereign to be judge, and to prescribe the rules of discerning good and evil: which rules are laws; and therefore in him is the legislative power. Saul sought the life of David; yet when it was in his power to slay Saul, and his servants would have done it, David forbade them, saying, "God forbid I should do such an act against my Lord, the anointed of God." [I Samuel, 24. 6] For obedience of servants St. Paul saith, "Servants obey your masters in all things";[Colossians, 3. 22] and, "Children obey your parents in all things." )[ Ibid., 3. 20] There is simple obedience in those that are subject to paternal or despotical dominion. Again, "The scribes and Pharisees sit in Moses' chair, and therefore all that they shall bid you observe, that observe and do." [Matthew, 23. 2, 3] There again is simple obedience. And St. Paul, "Warn them that they subject themselves to princes, and to those that are in authority, and obey them." [Titus, 3. 1] This obedience is also simple. Lastly, our Saviour Himself acknowledges that men ought to pay such taxes as are by kings imposed, where He says, "Give to Caesar that which is Caesar's"; and paid such taxes Himself. And that the king's word is sufficient to take anything from any subject, when there is need; and that the king is judge of that need: for He Himself, as king of the Jews, commanded his Disciples to take the ass and ass's colt to carry him into Jerusalem, saying, "Go into the village over against you, and you shall find a she ass tied, and her colt with her; untie them, and bring them to me. And if any man ask you, what you mean by it, say the Lord hath need of them: and they will let them go." [Matthew, 21. 2, 3] They will not ask whether his necessity be a sufficient title; nor whether he be judge of that necessity; but acquiesce in the will of the Lord. To these places may be added also that of Genesis, "You shall be as gods, knowing good and evil." [Genesis, 3. 5] And, "Who told thee that thou wast naked? Hast thou eaten of the tree, of which I commanded thee thou shouldest not eat?" [Ibid., 3. 11] For the cognizance or judicature of good and evil, being forbidden by the name of the fruit of the tree of knowledge, as a trial of Adam's obedience, the devil to inflame the ambition of the woman, to whom that fruit already seemed beautiful, told her that by tasting it they should be as gods, knowing good and evil. Whereupon having both eaten, they did indeed take upon them God's office, which is judicature of good and evil, but acquired no new ability to distinguish between them aright. And whereas it is said that, having eaten, they saw they were naked; no man hath so interpreted that place as if they had been formerly blind, and saw not their own skins: the meaning is plain that it was then they first judged their nakedness (wherein it was God's will to create them) to be uncomely; and by being ashamed did tacitly censure God Himself. And thereupon God saith, "Hast thou eaten," etc., as if He should say, doest thou that owest me obedience take upon thee to judge of my commandments? Whereby it is clearly, though allegorically, signified that the commands of them that have the right to command are not by their subjects to be censured nor disputed. So that it appeareth plainly, to my understanding, both from reason and Scripture, that the sovereign power, whether placed in one man, as in monarchy, or in one assembly of men, as in popular and aristocratical Commonwealths, is as great as possibly men can be imagined to make it. And though of so unlimited a power, men may fancy many evil consequences, yet the consequences of the want of it, which is perpetual war of every man against his neighbour, are much worse. The condition of man in this life shall never be without inconveniences; but there happeneth in no Commonwealth any great inconvenience but what proceeds from the subjects' disobedience and breach of those covenants from which the Commonwealth hath its being. And whosoever, thinking sovereign power too great, will seek to make it less, must subject himself to the power that can limit it; that is to say, to a greater. The greatest objection is that of the practice; when men ask where and when such power has by subjects been acknowledged. But one may ask them again, when or where has there been a kingdom long free from sedition and civil war? In those nations whose Commonwealths have been long-lived, and not been destroyed but by foreign war, the subjects never did dispute of the sovereign power. But howsoever, an argument from the practice of men that have not sifted to the bottom, and with exact reason weighed the causes and nature of Commonwealths, and suffer daily those miseries that proceed from the ignorance thereof, is invalid. For though in all places of the world men should lay the foundation of their houses on the sand, it could not thence be inferred that so it ought to be. The skill of making and maintaining Commonwealths consisteth in certain rules, as doth arithmetic and geometry; not, as tennis play, on practice only: which rules neither poor men have the leisure, nor men that have had the leisure have hitherto had the curiosity or the method, to find out.

## CHAPTER XXI, OF THE LIBERTY OF SUBJECTS

LIBERTY, or freedom, signifieth properly the absence of opposition (by opposition, I mean external impediments of motion); and may be applied no less to irrational and inanimate creatures than to rational. For whatsoever is so tied, or environed, as it cannot move but within a certain space, which space is determined by the opposition of some external body, we say it hath not liberty to go further. And so of all living creatures, whilst they are imprisoned, or restrained with walls or chains; and of the water whilst it is kept in by banks or vessels that otherwise would spread itself into a larger space; we use to say they are not at liberty to move in such manner as without those external impediments they would. But when the impediment of motion is in the constitution of the thing itself, we use not to say it wants the liberty, but the power, to move; as when a stone lieth still, or a man is fastened to his bed by sickness. And according to this proper and generally received meaning of the word, a freeman is he that, in those things which by his strength and wit he is able to do, is not hindered to do what he has a will to. But when the words free and liberty are applied to anything but bodies, they are abused; for that which is not subject to motion is not to subject to impediment: and therefore, when it is said, for example, the way is free, no liberty of the way is signified, but of those that walk in it without stop. And when we say a gift is free, there is not meant any liberty of the gift, but of the giver, that was not bound by any law or covenant to give it. So when we speak freely, it is not the liberty of voice, or pronunciation, but of the man, whom no law hath obliged to speak otherwise than he did. Lastly, from the use of the words free will, no liberty can be inferred of the will, desire, or inclination, but the liberty of the man; which consisteth in this, that he finds no stop in doing what he has the will, desire, or inclination to do. Fear and liberty are consistent: as when a man throweth his goods into the sea for fear the ship should sink, he doth it nevertheless very willingly, and may refuse to do it if he will; it is therefore the action of one that was free: so a man some-times pays his debt, only for fear of imprisonment, which, because no body hindered him from detaining, was the action of a man at liberty. And generally all actions which men do in Commonwealths, for fear of the law, are actions which the doers had liberty to omit. Liberty and necessity are consistent: as in the water that hath not only liberty, but a necessity of descending by the channel; so, likewise in the actions which men voluntari-ly do, which, because they proceed their will, proceed from liberty, and yet because every act of man's will and every desire and inclination proceedeth from some cause, and that from another cause, in a continual chain (whose first link is in the hand of God, the first of all causes), proceed from necessity. So that to him that could see the connexion of those causes, the necessity of all men's voluntary actions would appear mani-fest. And therefore God, that seeth and disposeth all things, seeth also that the liberty of man in doing what he will is accompanied with the necessity of doing that which God will and no more, nor less. For though men may do many things which God does not command, nor is therefore author of them; yet they can have no pas-sion, nor appetite to anything, of which appetite God's will is not the cause. And did not His will assure the necessity of man's will, and consequently of all that on man's will dependeth, the liberty of men would be a contradiction and impediment to the omnipotence and liberty of God. And this shall suffice, as to the matter in hand, of that natural liberty, which only is properly called liberty. But as men, for the attaining of peace and conservation of themselves thereby, have made an artificial man, which we call a Commonwealth; so also have they made artificial chains, called civil laws, which they themselves, by mutual covenants, have fastened at one end to the lips of that man, or assembly, to whom they have given the sovereign power, and at the other to their own ears. These bonds, in their own nature but weak, may nevertheless be made to hold, by the dan-ger, though not by the difficulty of breaking them. In relation to these bonds only it is that I am to speak now of the liberty of subjects. For seeing there is no Commonwealth in the world wherein there be rules enough set down for the regulating of all the actions and words of men (as being a thing impossible): it followeth nec-essarily that in all kinds of actions, by the laws pretermitted, men have the liberty of doing what their own reasons shall suggest for the most profitable to themselves. For if we take liberty in the proper sense, for cor-poral liberty; that is to say, freedom from chains and prison, it were very absurd for men to clamour as they do for the liberty they so manifestly enjoy. Again, if we take liberty for an exemption from laws, it is no less ab-surd for men to demand as they do that liberty by which all other men may be masters of their lives. And yet as absurd as it is, this is it they demand, not knowing that the laws are of no power to protect them without a sword in the hands of a man, or men, to cause those laws to be put in execution. The liberty of a subject lieth therefore only in those things which, in regulating their actions, the sovereign hath pretermitted: such as is the liberty to buy, and sell, and otherwise contract with one another; to choose their own abode, their own diet, their own trade of life, and institute their children as they themselves think fit; and the like. Nevertheless we are not to understand that by such liberty the sovereign power of life and death is either abolished or limited. For it has been already shown that nothing the sovereign representative can do to a subject, on what pretence soever, can properly be called injustice or injury; because every subject is author of every act the sovereign doth, so that he never wanteth right to any thing, otherwise than as he himself is the subject of God, and bound thereby to observe the laws of nature. And therefore it may and doth often happen in Commonwealths that a subject may be put to death by the command of the sovereign power, and yet neither do the other wrong; as when Jephthah caused his daughter to be sacrificed: in which, and the like cases, he that so dieth had liberty to do the action, for which he is nevertheless, without injury, put to death. And the same holdeth also in a sovereign prince that putteth to death an innocent subject. For though the action be against the law of nature, as being contrary to equity (as was the killing of Uriah by David); yet it was not an injury to Uriah, but to God. Not to Uriah, because the right to do what he pleased was given him by Uriah himself; and yet to God, because David was God's subject and prohibited all iniquity by the law of nature. Which distinction, David himself, when he repented the fact, evidently confirmed, saying, "To thee only have I sinned." In the same manner, the people of Athens, when they banished the most potent of their Commonwealth for ten years, thought they committed no injustice; and yet they never questioned what crime he had done, but what hurt he would do: nay, they commanded the banishment of they knew not whom; and every citizen bringing his oyster shell into the market place, written with the name of him he desired should be banished, without ac-tually accusing him sometimes banished an Aristides, for his reputation of justice; and sometimes a scurrilous jester, as Hyperbolus, to make a jest of it. And yet a man cannot say the sovereign people of Athens wanted right to banish them; or an Athenian the liberty to jest, or to be just. The liberty whereof there is so frequent and honourable mention in the histories and philosophy of the ancient Greeks and Romans, and in the writ-ings and discourse of those that from them have received all their learning in the politics, is not the liberty of particular men, but the liberty of the Commonwealth: which is the same with that which every man then should have, if there were no civil laws nor Commonwealth at all. And the effects of it also be the same. For as amongst masterless men, there is perpetual war of every man against his neighbour; no inheritance to transmit to the son, nor to expect from the father; no propriety of goods or lands; no security; but a full and absolute liberty in every particular man: so in states and Commonwealths not dependent on one another, every Commonwealth, not every man, has an absolute liberty to do what it shall judge, that is to say, what that man or assembly that representeth it shall judge, most conducing to their benefit. But withal, they live in the condition of a perpetual war, and upon the confines of battle, with their frontiers armed, and cannons planted against their neighbours round about. The Athenians and Romans were free; that is, free Commonwealths: not that any particular men had the liberty to resist their own representative, but that their representative had the liberty to resist, or invade, other people. There is written on the turrets of the city of Luca in great characters at this day, the word LIBERTAS; yet no man can thence infer that a particular man has more liberty or immunity from the service of the Commonwealth there than in Constantinople. Whether a Commonwealth be monarchical or popular, the freedom is still the same. But it is an easy thing for men to be deceived by the specious name of liberty; and, for want of judgement to distinguish, mistake that for their private inheritance and birthright which is the right of the public only. And when the same error is confirmed by the authority of men in reputation for their writings on this subject, it is no wonder if it produce sedition and change of government. In these western parts of the world we are made to receive our opinions concerning the institution and rights of Commonwealths from Aristotle, Cicero, and other men, Greeks and Romans, that, living under popular states, derived those rights, not from the principles of nature, but transcribed them into their books out of the practice of their own Commonwealths, which were popular; as the grammarians describe the rules of language out of the practice of the time; or the rules of poetry out of the poems of Homer and Virgil. And because the Athenians were taught (to keep them from desire of changing their government) that they were freemen, and all that lived under monarchy were slaves; therefore Aristotle puts it down in his Politics "In democracy, liberty is to be supposed: for it is commonly held that no man is free in any other government." [Aristotle, Politics, Bk VI] And as Aristotle, so Cicero and other writers have grounded their civil doctrine on the opinions of the Romans, who were taught to hate monarchy: at first, by them that, having deposed their sovereign, shared amongst them the sovereignty of Rome; and afterwards by their successors. And by reading of these Greek and Latin authors, men from their childhood have gotten a habit, under a false show of liberty, of favouring tumults, and of licentious controlling the actions of their sovereigns; and again of controlling those controllers; with the effusion of so much blood, as I think I may truly say there was never anything so dearly bought as these western parts have bought the learning of the Greek and Latin tongues. To come now to the particulars of the true liberty of a subject; that is to say, what are the things which, though commanded by the sovereign, he may nevertheless without injustice refuse to do; we are to consider what rights we pass away when we make a Commonwealth; or, which is all one, what liberty we deny ourselves by owning all the actions, without exception, of the man or assembly we make our sovereign. For in the act of our submission consisteth both our obligation and our liberty; which must therefore be inferred by arguments taken from thence; there being no obligation on any man which ariseth not from some act of his own; for all men equally are by nature free. And because such arguments must either be drawn from the express words, "I authorise all his actions," or from the intention of him that submitteth himself to his power (which intention is to be understood by the end for which he so submitteth), the obligation and liberty of the subject is to be derived either from those words, or others equivalent, or else from the end of the institution of sovereignty; namely, the peace of the subjects within themselves, and their defence against a common enemy. First therefore, seeing sovereignty by institution is by covenant of every one to every one; and sovereignty by acquisition, by covenants of the vanquished to the victor, or child to the parent; it is manifest that every subject has liberty in all those things the right whereof cannot by covenant be transferred. I have shown before, in the fourteenth Chapter, that covenants not to defend a man's own body are void. Therefore, If the sove

eign command a man, though justly condemned, to kill, wound, or maim himself; or not to resist those that assault him; or to abstain from the use of food, air, medicine, or any other thing without which he cannot live; yet hath that man the liberty to disobey. If a man be interrogated by the sovereign, or his authority, concerning a crime done by himself, he is not bound (without assurance of pardon) to confess it; because no man, as I have shown in the same chapter, can be obliged by covenant to accuse himself. Again, the consent of a subject to sovereign power is contained in these words, "I authorise, or take upon me, all his actions"; in which there is no restriction at all of his own former natural liberty: for by allowing him to kill me, I am not bound to kill myself when he commands me. It is one thing to say, "Kill me, or my fellow, if you please"; another thing to say, "I will kill myself, or my fellow." It followeth, therefore, that No man is bound by the words themselves, either to kill himself or any other man; and consequently, that the obligation a man may sometimes have, upon the command of the sovereign, to execute any dangerous or dishonourable office, dependeth not on the words of our submission, but on the intention; which is to be understood by the end thereof. When therefore our refusal to obey frustrates the end for which the sovereignty was ordained, then there is no liberty to refuse; otherwise, there is. Upon this ground a man that is commanded as a soldier to fight against the enemy, though his sovereign have right enough to punish his refusal with death, may nevertheless in many cases refuse, without injustice; as when he substituteth a sufficient soldier in his place: for in this case he deserteth not the service of the Commonwealth. And there is allowance to be made for natural timorousness, not only to women (of whom no such dangerous duty is expected), but also to men of feminine courage. When armies fight, there is on one side, or both, a running away; yet when they do it not out of treachery, but fear, they are not esteemed to do it unjustly, but dishonourably. For the same reason, to avoid battle is not injustice, but cowardice. But he that enrolleth himself a soldier, or taketh impressed money, taketh away the excuse of a timorous nature, and is obliged, not only to go to the battle, but also not to run from it without his captain's leave. And when the defence of the Commonwealth requireth at once the help of all that are able to bear arms, every one is obliged; because otherwise the institution of the Commonwealth, which they have not the purpose or courage to preserve, was in vain. To resist the sword of the Commonwealth in defence of another man, guilty or innocent, no man hath liberty; because such liberty takes away from the sovereign the means of protecting us, and is therefore destructive of the very essence of government. But in case a great many men together have already resisted the sovereign power unjustly, or committed some capital crime for which every one of them expecteth death, whether have they not the liberty then to join together, and assist, and defend one another? Certainly they have: for they but defend their lives, which the guilty man may as well do as the innocent. There was indeed injustice in the first breach of their duty: their bearing of arms subsequent to it, though it be to maintain what they have done, is no new unjust act. And if it be only to defend their persons, it is not unjust at all. But the offer of pardon taketh from them to whom it is offered the plea of self-defence, and maketh their perseverance in assisting or defending the rest unlawful. As for other liberties, they depend on the silence of the law. In cases where the sovereign has prescribed no rule, there the subject hath the liberty to do, or forbear, according to his own discretion. And therefore such liberty is in some places more, and in some less; and in some times more, in other times less, according as they that have the sovereignty shall think most convenient. As for example, there was a time when in England a man might enter into his own land, and dispossess such as wrongfully possessed it, by force. But in after times that liberty of forcible entry was taken away by a statute made by the king in Parliament. And in some places of the world men have the liberty of many wives: in other places, such liberty is not allowed. If a subject have a controversy with his sovereign of debt, or of right of possession of lands or goods, or concerning any service required at his hands, or concerning any penalty, corporal or pecuniary, grounded on a precedent law, he hath the same liberty to sue for his right as if it were against a subject, and before such judges as are appointed by the sovereign. For seeing the sovereign demandeth by force of a former law, and not by virtue of his power, he declareth thereby that he requireth no more than shall appear to be due by that law. The suit therefore is not contrary to the will of the sovereign, and consequently the subject hath the liberty to demand the hearing of his cause, and sentence according to that law. But if he demand or take anything by pretence of his power, there lieth, in that case, no action of law: for all that is done by him in virtue of his power is done by the authority of every subject, and consequently, he that brings an action against the sovereign brings it against himself. If a monarch, or sovereign assembly, grant a liberty to all or any of his subjects, which grant standing, he is disabled to provide for their safety; the grant is void, unless he directly renounce or transfer the sovereignty to another. For in that he might openly (if it had been his will), and in plain terms, have renounced or transferred it and did not, it is to be understood it was not his will, but that the grant proceeded from ignorance of the repugnancy between such a liberty and the sovereign power: and therefore the sovereignty is still retained, and consequently all those powers which are necessary to the exercising thereof; such as are the power of war and peace, of judicature, of appointing officers and counsellors, of levying money, and the rest named in the eighteenth Chapter. The obligation of subjects to the sovereign is understood to last as long, and no longer, than the power lasteth by which he is able to protect them. For the right men have by nature to protect themselves, when none else can protect them, can by no covenant be relinquished. The sovereignty is the soul of the Commonwealth; which, once departed from the body, the members do no more receive their motion from it. The end of obedience is protection; which, wheresoever a man seeth it, either in his own or in another's sword, nature applieth his obedience to it, and his endeavour to maintain it. And though sovereignty, in the intention of them that make it, be immortal; yet is it in its own nature, not only subject to violent death by foreign war, but also through the ignorance and passions of men it hath in it, from the very institution, many seeds of a natural mortality, by intestine discord. If a subject be taken prisoner in war, or his person or his means of life be within the guards of the enemy, and hath his life and corporal liberty given him on condition to be subject to the victor, he hath liberty to accept the condition; and, having accepted it, is the subject of him that took him; because he had no other way to preserve himself. The case is the same if he be detained on the same terms in a foreign country. But if a man be held in prison, or bonds, or is not trusted with the liberty of his body, he cannot be understood to be bound by covenant to subjection, and therefore may, if he can, make his escape by any means whatsoever. If a monarch shall relinquish the sovereignty, both for himself and his heirs, his subjects return to the absolute liberty of nature; because, though nature may declare who are his sons, and who are the nearest of his kin, yet it dependeth on his own will, as hath been said in the precedent chapter, who shall be his heir. If therefore he will have no heir, there is no sovereignty, nor subjection. The case is the same if he die without known kindred, and without declaration of his heir. For then there can no heir be known, and consequently no subjection be due. If the sovereign banish his subject, during the banishment he is not subject. But he that is sent on a message, or hath leave to travel, is still subject; but it is by contract between sovereigns, not by virtue of the covenant of subjection. For whosoever entereth into another's dominion is subject to all the laws thereof, unless he have a privilege by the amity of the sovereigns, or by special license. If a monarch subdued by war render himself subject to the victor, his subjects are delivered from their former obligation, and become obliged to the victor. But if he be held prisoner, or have not the liberty of his own body, he is not understood to have given away the right of sovereignty; and therefore his subjects are obliged to yield obedience to the magistrates formerly placed, governing not in their own name, but in his. For, his right remaining, the question is only of the administration; that is to say, of the magistrates and officers; which if he have not means to name, he is supposed to approve those which he himself had formerly appointed.

## CHAPTER XXII, OF SYSTEMS SUBJECT POLITICAL AND PRIVATE

HAVING spoken of the generation, form, and power of a Commonwealth, I am in order to speak next of the parts thereof. And first of systems, which resemble the similar parts or muscles of a body natural. By systems, I understand any numbers of men joined in one interest or one business. Of which some are regular, and some irregular. Regular are those where one man, or assembly of men, is constituted representative of the whole number. All other are irregular. Of regular, some are absolute and independent, subject to none but their own representative: such are only Commonwealths, of which I have spoken already in the five last precedent chapters. Others are dependent; that is to say, subordinate to some sovereign power, to which every one, as also their representative, is subject. Of systems subordinate, some are political, and some private. Political (otherwise called bodies politic and persons in law) are those which are made by authority from the sovereign power of the Commonwealth. Private are those which are constituted by subjects amongst themselves, or by authority from a stranger. For no authority derived from foreign power, within the dominion of another, is public there, but private. And of private systems, some are lawful; some unlawful: lawful are those which are allowed by the Commonwealth; all other are unlawful. Irregular systems are those which, having no representative, consist only in concourse of people; which if not forbidden by the Commonwealth, nor made on evil design (such as are conflux of people to markets, or shows, or any other harmless end), are lawful. But when the intention is evil, or (if the number be considerable) unknown, they are unlawful. In bodies politic the power of the representative is always limited: and that which prescribeth the limits thereof is the power sovereign. For power unlimited is absolute sovereignty. And the sovereign, in every Commonwealth, is the absolute representative of all the subjects; and therefore no other can be representative of any part of them, but so far forth as he shall give leave: and to give leave to a body politic of subjects to have an absolute representative, to all intents and purposes, were to abandon the government of so much of the Commonwealth, and to divide the dominion, contrary to their peace and defence, which the sovereign cannot be understood to do, by any grant that does not plainly and directly discharge them of their subjection. For consequences of words are not the signs of his will, when other consequences are signs of the contrary; but rather signs of error and misreckoning, to which all mankind is too prone. The bounds of that power which is given to the representative of a body politic are to be taken notice of from two things. One is their writ, or letters from the sovereign: the other is the law of the Commonwealth. For though in the institution or acquisition of a Commonwealth, which is independent, there needs no writing, because the power of the representative has there no other bounds but such as are set out by the unwritten law of nature; yet in subordinate bodies, there are such diversities of limitation necessary, concerning their businesses, times, and places, as can neither be remembered without letters, nor taken notice of, unless such letters be patent, that they may be read to them, and withal sealed, or testified, with the seals or other permanent signs of the authority sovereign. And because such limitation is not always easy or perhaps possible to be described in writing, the ordinary laws, common to all subjects, must determine what the representative may lawfully do in all cases where the letters themselves are silent. And therefore In a body politic, if the representative be one man, whatsoever he does in the person of the body which is not warranted in his letters, nor by the laws, is his own act, and not the act of the body, nor of any other member thereof besides himself: because further than his letters or the laws limit, he representeth no man's person, but his own. But what he does according to these is the act of every one: for of the act of the sovereign every one is author, because he is their representative unlimited; and the act of him that recedes not from the letters of the sovereign is the act of the sovereign, and therefore every member of the body is author of it. But if the representative be an assembly, whatsoever that assembly shall decree, not warranted by their letters or the laws, is the act of the assembly, or body politic, and the act of every one by whose vote the decree was made; but not the act of any man that being present voted to the contrary; nor of any man absent, unless he voted it by procreation. It is the act of the assembly because voted by the major part; and if it be a crime, the assembly may be punished, as far forth as it is capable, as by dissolution, or forfeiture of their letters (which is to such artificial and fictitious bodies, capital) or, if the assembly have a common stock, wherein none of the innocent members have propriety, by pecuniary mulct. For from corporal penalties nature hath bodies politic. But they that gave not their vote are therefore innocent, because the assembly cannot represent any man in things unwarranted by their letters, and consequently are not involved in their votes. If the person of the body politic, being in one man, borrow money of a stranger, that is, of one that is not of the same body (for no letters need limit borrowing, seeing it is left to men's own inclinations to limit lending), the debt is the representative's. For if he should have authority from his letters to make the members pay what he borroweth, he should have by consequence the sovereignty of them; and therefore the grant were either void, as proceeding from error, commonly incident to human nature, and an insufficient sign of the will of the granter; or if it be avowed by him, then is the representer sovereign, and falleth not under the present question, which is only of bodies subordinate. No member therefore is obliged to pay the debt so borrowed, but the representative himself: because he that lendeth it, being a stranger to the letters, and to the qualification of the body, understandeth those only for his debtors that are engaged; and seeing the representer can engage himself, and none else, has him only debtor, who must therefore pay him, out of the common stock, if there be any, or, if there be none, out of his own estate. If he come into debt by contract, or mulct, the case is the same. But when the representative is an assembly, and the debt to a stranger; all they, and only they, are responsible for the debt that gave their votes to the borrowing of it, or to the contract that made it due, or to the fact for which the mulct was imposed; because every one of those in voting did engage himself for the payment: for he that is author of the borrowing is obliged to the payment, even of the whole debt, though when paid by any one, he be discharged. But if the debt be to one of the assembly, the assembly only is obliged to the payment, out of their common stock, if they have any: for having liberty of vote, if he vote the money shall be borrowed, he votes it shall be paid; if he vote it shall not be borrowed, or be absent, yet because in lending he voteth the borrowing, he contradicteth his former vote, and is obliged by the latter, and becomes both borrower and lender, and consequently cannot demand payment from any particular man, but from the common treasury only; which failing, he hath no remedy, nor complaint but against himself, that being privy to the acts of the assembly, and to their means to pay, and not being enforced, did nevertheless through his own folly lend his money. It is manifest by this that in bodies politic subordinate, and subject to a sovereign power, it is sometimes not only lawful, but expedient, for a particular man to make open protestation against the decrees of the representative assembly, and cause their dissent to be registered, or to take witness of it; because otherwise they may be obliged to pay debts contracted, and be responsible for crimes committed by other men. But in a sovereign assembly that liberty is taken away, both because he that protesteth there denies their sovereignty, and also because whatsoever is commanded by the sovereign power is as to the subject (though not so always in the sight of God) justified by the command: for of such command every subject is the author. The variety of bodies is almost infinite: for they are not only distinguished by the several affairs for which they are constituted, wherein there is an unspeakable diversity; but also by the times, places, and numbers, subject to many limitations. And as to their affairs, some are ordained for government; as first, the government of a province may be committed to an assembly of men, wherein all resolutions shall depend on the votes of the major part; and then this assembly is a body politic, and their power limited by commission. This word province signifies a charge or care of business, which he whose it is committeth to another man to be administered for and under him; and therefore when in one Commonwealth there be diverse countries that have their laws distinct one from another, or are far distant in place, the administration of the government being committed to diverse persons, those countries where the sovereign is not resident, but governs by commission, are called provinces. But of the government of a province, by an assembly residing in the province itself, there be few examples. The Romans, who had the sovereignty of many provinces, yet governed them always by presidents and praetors; and not by assemblies, as they governed the city of Rome and territories adjacent. In like manner, when there were colonies sent from England to plant Virginia, and Summer Islands, though the government of them here were committed to assemblies in London, yet did those assemblies never commit the government under them to any assembly there, but did to each plantation send one governor: for though every man, where he can be present by nature, desires to participate of government; yet where they cannot be present, they are by nature also inclined to commit the government of their common interest rather to a monarchical, than a popular, form of government: which is also evident in those men that have great private estates; who, when they are unwilling to take the pains of administering the business that belongs to them, choose rather to trust one servant than an assembly either of their friends or servants. But howsoever it be in fact, yet we may suppose the government of a province or colony committed to an assembly: and when it is, that which in this place I have to say is this: that whatsoever debt is by that assembly contracted, or whatsoever unlawful act is decreed, is the act only of those that assented, and not of any that dissented, or were absent, for the reasons before alleged. Also that an assembly residing out of the bounds of that colony whereof they have the government cannot execute any power over the persons or goods of any of the colony, to seize on them for debt, or other duty, in any place without the colony itself, as having no jurisdiction nor authority elsewhere, but are left to the remedy which the law of the place alloweth them. And though the assembly have right to impose mulct upon any of their members that shall break the laws they make; yet out of the colony itself, they have no right to execute the same. And that which is said here of the rights of an assembly for the government of a province, or a colony, is applicable also to an assembly for the government of a town, a university, or a college, or a church, or for any other government over the persons of men. And generally, in all bodies politic, if any if any particular member conceive himself injured by the body itself, the cognizance of his cause belonged to the sovereign, and those the sovereign hath ordained for judges in such causes, or shall ordain for that particular cause; and not to the body itself. For the whole body is in this case his fellow subject, which, in a sovereign assembly, is otherwise: for there, if the sovereign be not judge, though in his own cause, there can be no judge at all. In a body politic, for the well ordering of foreign traffic, the most commodious representative is an assembly of all the members; that is to say, such a one as every one that adventureth his money may be present at all the deliberations and resolutions of the body, if they will themselves. For proof whereof we are to consider the end for which men that are merchants, and may buy and sell, export and import their merchandise, according to their own discretions, do nevertheless bind themselves up in one corporation. It is true, there be few merchants that with the merchandise they buy at home can freight a ship to export it; or with that they buy abroad, to bring it home; and have therefore need to join together in one society, where every man may either participate of the gain, according to the proportion of his adventure, or take his own, and sell what he transports, or imports, at such prices as he thinks fit. But this is no body politic, there being no common representative to oblige them to any other law than that which is common to all other subjects. The end of their incorporating is to make their gain the greater; which is done two ways: by sole buying, and sole selling, both at home and abroad. So that to grant to a company of merchants to be a corporation, or body politic, is to grant them a double monopoly, whereof one is to be sole buyers; another to be sole sellers. For when there is a company incorporate for any particular foreign country, they only export the commodities vendible in that country; which is sole buying at home, and sole selling abroad. For at home there is but one buyer, and abroad but one that selleth; both which is gainful to the merchant, because thereby they buy at home at lower, and sell abroad at higher, rates: and abroad there is but one buyer of foreign merchandise, and but one that sells them at home, both which again are gainful to the adventurers. Of this double monopoly one part is disadvantageous to the people at home, the other to foreigners. For at home by their sole exportation they set what price they please on the husbandry and handiworks of the people, and by the sole importation, what price they please on all foreign commodities the people have need of, both which are ill for the people. On the contrary, by the sole selling of the native commodities abroad, and sole buying the foreign commodities upon the place, they raise the price of those, and abate the price of these, to the disadvantage of the foreigner: for where but one selleth, the merchandise is the dearer; and where but one buyeth, the cheaper: such corporations therefore are no other than monopolies, though they would be very profitable for a Commonwealth, if, being bound up into one body in foreign markets, they were at liberty at home, every man to buy and sell at what price he could. The end then of these bodies of merchants, being not a common benefit to the whole body (which have in this case no common stock, but what is deducted out of the particular adventures, for building, buying, victualling and manning of ships), but the particular gain of every adventurer, it is reason that every one be acquainted with the employment of his own; that is, that every one be of the assembly that shall have the power to order the same; and be acquainted with their accounts. And therefore the representative of such a body must be an assembly, where every member of the body may be present at the consultations, if he will. If a body politic of merchants contract a debt to a stranger by the act of their representative assembly, every member is liable by himself for the whole. For a stranger can take no notice of their private laws, but considereth them as so many particular men, obliged every one to the whole payment, till payment made by one dischargeth all the rest: but if the debt be to one of the company, the creditor is debtor for the whole to himself, and cannot therefore demand his debt, but only from the common stock, if there be any. If the Commonwealth impose a tax upon the body, it is understood to be laid upon every member proportionably to his particular adventure in the company. For there is in this case no other common stock, but what is made of their particular adventures. If a mulct be laid upon the body for some unlawful act, they only are liable by whose votes the act was decreed, or by whose assistance it was executed; for in none of the rest is there any other crime but being of the body; which, if a crime, because the body was ordained by the authority of the Commonwealth, is not his. If one of the members be indebted to the body, he may be sued by the body, but his goods cannot be taken, nor his person imprisoned by the authority of the body; but only by authority of the Commonwealth: for they can do it by their own authority, they can by their own authority give judgement that the debt is due; which is as much as to be judge in their own cause. These bodies made for the government of men, or of traffic, be either perpetual, or for a time prescribed by writing. But there be bodies also whose times are limited, and that only by the nature of their business. For example, if a sovereign monarch, or a sovereign assembly, shall think fit to give command to the towns and other several parts of their territory to send to him their deputies to inform him of the condition and necessities of the subjects, or to advise with him for the making of good laws, or for any other cause, as with one person representing the whole country, such deputies, having a place and time of meeting assigned them, are there, and at that time, a body politic, representing every subject of that dominion; but it is only for such matters as shall be propounded unto them by that man, or assembly, that by the sovereign authority sent for them; and when it shall be declared that nothing more shall be propounded, nor debated by them, the body is dissolved. For if they were the absolute representative of the people, then were it the sovereign assembly; and so there would be two sovereign assemblies, or two sovereigns, over the same people; which cannot consist with their peace. And therefore where there is once a sovereignty, there can be no absolute representation of the people, but by it. And for the limits of how far such a body shall represent the whole people, they are set forth in the writing by which they were sent for. For the people cannot choose their deputies to other intent than is in the writing directed to them from their sovereign expressed. Private bodies regular and lawful are those that are constituted without letters, or other written authority, saving the laws common to all other subjects. And because they be united in one person representative, they are held for regular; such as are all families, in which the father or master ordereth the whole family. For he obligeth his children, and servants, as far as the law permitteth, though not further, because none of them are bound to obedience in those actions which the law hath forbidden to be done. In all other actions, during the time they are under domestic government, they are subject to their fathers and masters, as to their immediate sovereigns. For the father and master being before the institution of Commonwealth absolute sovereigns in their own families, they lose afterward no more of their authority than the law of the Commonwealth taketh from them. Private bodies regular, but unlawful, are those that unite themselves into one person representative, without any public authority at all; such as are the corporations of beggars, thieves and gipsies, the better to order their trade of begging and stealing; and the corporations of men that by authority from any foreign person themselves in another's dominion, for the easier propagation of doctrines, and for making a party against the power of the Commonwealth. Irregular systems, in their nature but leagues, or sometimes mere concourse of people without union to any particular design, not by obligation of one to another, but proceeding only from a similitude of wills and inclinations, become lawful, or unlawful, according to the lawfulness, or unlawfulness, of every particular man's design therein: and his design is to be understood by the occasion. The leagues of subjects, because leagues are commonly made for mutual defence, are in a Commonwealth (which is no more than a league of all the subjects together) for the most part unnecessary, and savour of unlawful design; and are for that cause unlawful, and go commonly by the name of factions, or conspiracies. For a league being a connexion of men by covenants,

103

if there be no power given to any one man or assembly (as in the condition of mere nature) to compel them to performance, is so long only valid as there ariseth no just cause of distrust: and therefore leagues between Commonwealths, over whom there is no human power established to keep them all in awe, are not only lawful, but also profitable for the time they last. But leagues of the subjects of one and the same Commonwealth, where every one may obtain his right by means of the sovereign power, are unnecessary to the maintaining of peace and justice, and, in case the design of them be evil or unknown to the Commonwealth, unlawful. For all uniting of strength by private men is, if for evil intent, unjust; if for intent unknown, dangerous to the public, and unjustly concealed. If the sovereign power be in a great assembly, and a number of men, part of the assembly, without authority consult a part to contrive the guidance of the rest, this is a faction, or conspiracy unlawful, as being a fraudulent seducing of the assembly for their particular interest. But if he whose private interest is to be debated and judged in the assembly make as many friends as he can, in him it is no injustice, because in this case he is no part of the assembly. And though he hire such friends with money, unless there be an express law against it, yet it is not injustice. For sometimes, as men's manners are, justice cannot be had without money, and every man may think his own cause just till it be heard and judged. In all Commonwealths, if a private man entertain more servants than the government of his estate and lawful employment he has for them requires, it is faction, and unlawful. For having the protection of the Commonwealth, he needeth not the defence of private force. And whereas in nations not thoroughly civilized, several numerous families have lived in continual hostility and invaded one another with private force, yet it is evident enough that they have done unjustly, or else that they had no Commonwealth. And as factions for kindred, so also factions for government of religion, as of Papists, Protestants, etc., or of state, as patricians and plebeians of old time in Rome, and of aristocraticals and democraticals of old time in Greece, are unjust, as being contrary to the peace and safety of the people, and a taking of the sword out of the hand of the sovereign. Concourse of people is an irregular system, the lawfulness or unlawfulness whereof dependeth on the occasion, and on the number of them that are assembled. If the occasion be lawful, and manifest, the concourse is lawful; as the usual meeting of men at church, or at a public show, in usual numbers: for if the numbers be extraordinarily great, the occasion is not evident; and consequently he that cannot render a particular and good account of his being amongst them is to be judged conscious of an unlawful and tumultuous design. It may be lawful for a thousand men to join in a petition to be delivered to a judge or magistrate; yet if a thousand men come to present it, it is a tumultuous assembly, because there needs but one or two for that purpose. But in such cases as these, it is not a set number that makes the assembly unlawful, but such a number as the present officers are not able to suppress and bring to justice. When an unusual number of men assemble against a man whom they accuse, the assembly is an unlawful tumult; because they may deliver their accusation to the magistrate by a few, or by one man. Such was the case of St. Paul at Ephesus; where Demetrius, and a great number of other men, brought two of Paul's companions before the magistrate, saying with one voice, "Great is Diana of the Ephesians"; which was their way of demanding justice against them for teaching the people such doctrine as was against their religion and trade. The occasion here, considering the laws of that people, was just; yet was their assembly judged unlawful, and the magistrate reprehended them for it, in these words, "If Demetrius and the other workmen can accuse any man of any thing, there be pleas, and deputies; let them accuse one another. And if you have any other thing to demand, your case may be judged in an assembly lawfully called. For we are in danger to be accused for this day's sedition, because there is no cause by which any man can render any reason of this concourse of people." [Acts, 19. 40] Where he calleth an assembly whereof men can give no just account, a sedition, and such as they could not answer for. And this is all I shall say concerning systems, and assemblies of people, which may be compared, as I said, to the similar parts of man's body: such as be lawful, to the muscles; such as are unlawful, to wens, biles, and apostems, engendered by the unnatural conflux of evil humours.

## CHAPTER XXIII, OF THE PUBLIC MINISTERS OF SOVEREIGN POWER

IN THE last chapter I have spoken of the similar parts of a Commonwealth: in this I shall speak of the parts organical, which are public ministers. A public minister is he that by the sovereign, whether a monarch or an assembly, is employed in any affairs, with authority to represent in that employment the person of the Commonwealth. And whereas every man or assembly that hath sovereignty representeth two persons, or, as the more common phrase is, has two capacities, one natural and another politic; as a monarch hath the person not only of the Commonwealth, but also of a man, and a sovereign assembly hath the person not only of the Commonwealth, but also of the assembly: they that be servants to them in their natural capacity are not public ministers; but those only that serve them in the administration of the public business. And therefore neither ushers, nor sergeants, nor other officers that wait on the assembly for no other purpose but for the commodity of the men assembled, in an aristocracy or democracy; nor stewards, chamberlains, cofferers, or any other officers of the household of a monarch, are public ministers in a monarchy. Of public ministers, some have charge committed to them of a general administration, either of the whole dominion or of a part thereof. Of the whole, as to a protector, or regent, may be committed by the predecessor of an infant king, during his minority, the whole administration of his kingdom. In which case, every subject is so far obliged to obedience as the ordinances he shall make, and the commands he shall give, be in the king's name, and not inconsistent with his sovereign power. Of a part, or province; as when either a monarch or a sovereign assembly shall give the general charge thereof to a governor, lieutenant, prefect or viceroy: and in this case also, every one of that province is obliged to all he shall do in the name of the sovereign, and that not incompatible with the sovereign's right. For such protectors, viceroys, and governors have no other right but what depends on the sovereigns will; and no commission that can be given them can be interpreted for a declaration of the will to transfer the sovereignty, without express and perspicuous words to that purpose. And this kind of public ministers resembleth the nerves and tendons that move the several limbs of a body natural. Others have special administration; that is to say, charges of some special business, either at home or abroad: as at home, first, for the economy of a Commonwealth, they that have authority concerning the treasury, as tributes, impositions, rents, fines, or whatsoever public revenue, to collect, receive, issue, or take the accounts thereof, are public ministers: ministers, because they serve the person representative, and can do nothing against his command, nor without his authority; public, because they serve him in his political capacity. Secondly, they that have authority concerning the militia; to have the custody of arms, forts, ports; to levy, pay, or conduct soldiers; or to provide for any necessary thing for the use of war, either by land or sea, are public ministers. But a soldier without command, though he fight for the Commonwealth, does not therefore represent the person of it; because there is none to represent it to. For every one that hath command represents it to them only whom he commandeth. They also that have authority to teach, or to enable others to teach the people their duty to the sovereign power, and instruct them in the knowledge of what is just and unjust, thereby to render them more apt to live in godliness and in peace amongst themselves, and resist the public enemy, are public ministers: ministers, in that they do it not by their own authority, but by another's; and public, because they do it, or should do it, by no authority but that of the sovereign. The monarch or the sovereign assembly only hath immediate authority from God to teach and instruct the people; and no man but the sovereign receiveth his power Dei gratia simply; that is to say, from the favour of none but God: all other receive theirs from the favour and providence of God and their sovereigns; as in a monarchy Dei gratia et regis; or Dei providentia et voluntate regis. They also to whom jurisdiction is given are public ministers. For in their seats of justice they represent the person of the sovereign; and their sentence is his sentence; for, as hath been before declared, all judicature is essentially annexed to the sovereignty; and therefore all other judges are but ministers of him or them that have the sovereign power. And as controversies are of two sorts, namely of fact and of law; so are judgements, some of fact, some of law: and consequently in the same controversy, there may be two judges, one of fact, another of law. And in both these controversies, there may arise a controversy between the party judged and the judge; which, because they be both subjects to the sovereign, ought in equity to be judged by men agreed on by consent of both; for no man can be judge in his own cause. But the sovereign is already agreed on for judged by them both, and is therefore either to hear the cause, and determine it himself, or appoint for judge such as they shall both agree on. And this agreement is then understood to be made between them diverse ways; as first, if the defendant be allowed to except against such of his judges whose interest maketh him suspect them (for as to the complainant, he hath already chosen his own judge); those which he excepteth not against are judges he himself agrees on. Secondly, if he appeal to any other judge, he can appeal no further; for his appeal is his choice. Thirdly, if he appeal to the sovereign himself, and he by himself, or by delegates which the parties shall agree on, give sentence; that sentence is final: for the defendant is judged by his own judges, that is to say, by himself. These properties of just and rational judicature considered, I cannot forbear to observe the excellent constitution of the courts of justice established both for common and also for public pleas in England. By common pleas, I mean those where both the complainant and defendant are subjects: and by public (which are also called pleas of the crown) those where the complainant is the sovereign. For whereas there were two orders of men, whereof one was lords, the other commons, the lords had this privilege, to have for judges in all capital crimes none but lords; and of them, as many as would be present; which being ever acknowledged as a privilege of favour, their judges were none but such as they had themselves desired. And in all controversies, every subject (as also in civil controversies the lords) had for judges men of the country where the matter in controversy lay; against which he might make his exceptions, till at last twelve men without exception being agreed on, they were judged by those twelve. So that having his own judges, there could be nothing alleged by the party why the sentence should not be final. These public persons, with authority from the sovereign power, either to instruct or judge the people, are such members of the Commonwealth as may fitly be compared to the organs of voice in a body natural. Public ministers are also all those that have authority from the sovereign to procure the execution of judgements given; to publish the sovereigns commands; to suppress tumults; to apprehend and imprison malefactors; and other acts tending to the conservation of the peace. For every act they do by such authority is the act of the Commonwealth; and their service answerable to that of the hands in a body natural. Public ministers abroad are those that represent the person of their own sovereign to foreign states. Such are ambassadors, messengers, agents, and heralds, sent by public authority, and on public business. But such as are sent by authority only of some private party of a troubled state, though they be received, are neither public nor private ministers of the Commonwealth, because none of their actions have the Commonwealth for author. Likewise, an ambassador sent from a prince to congratulate, condole, or to assist at a solemnity; though the authority be public, yet because the business is private, and belonging to him in his natural capacity, is a private person. Also if a man be sent into another country, secretly to explore their counsels and strength; though both the authority and the business be public, yet because there is none to take notice of any person in him, but his own, he is but a private minister; but yet a minister of the Commonwealth; and may be compared to an eye in the body natural. And those that are appointed to receive the petitions or other informations of the people, and are, as it were, the public ear, are public ministers and represent their sovereign in that office. Neither a counsellor, nor a council of state, if we consider with no authority judicature or command, but only of giving advice to the sovereign when it is required, or of offering it when it is not required, is a public person. For the advice is addressed to the sovereign only, whose person cannot in his own presence be represented to him by another. But a body of counsellors are never without some other authority, either of judicature or of immediate administration: as in a monarchy, they represent the monarch in delivering his commands to the public ministers: in a democracy, the council or senate propounds the result of their deliberations to the people, as a council; but when they appoint judges, or hear causes, or give audience to ambassadors, it is in the quality of a minister of the people: and in an aristocracy the council of state is the sovereign assembly itself, and gives counsel to none but themselves.

## CHAPTER XXIV, OF THE NUTRITION AND PROCREATION OF A COMMONWEALTH

THE NUTRITION of a Commonwealth consisteth in the plenty and distribution of materials conducing to life: in concoction or preparation, and, when concocted, in the conveyance of it by convenient conduits to the public use. As for the plenty of matter, it is a thing limited by nature to those commodities which, from the two breasts of our common mother, land and sea, God usually either freely giveth or for labour selleth to mankind. For the matter of this nutriment consisting in animals, vegetables, and minerals, God hath freely laid them before us, in or near to the face of the earth, so as there needeth no more but the labour and industry of receiving them. Insomuch as plenty dependeth, next to God's favour, merely on the labour and industry of men. This matter, commonly called commodities, is partly native and partly foreign: native, that which is to be had within the territory of the Commonwealth; foreign, that which is imported from without. And because there is no territory under the dominion of one Commonwealth, except it be of very vast extent, that produceth all things needful for the maintenance and motion of the whole body; and few that produce not something more than necessary; the superfluous commodities to be had within become no more superfluous, but supply these wants at home, by importation of that which may be had abroad, either by exchange, or by just war, or by labour: for a man's labour also is a commodity exchangeable for benefit, as well as any other thing: and there have been Commonwealths that, having no more territory than hath served them for habitation, have nevertheless not only maintained, but also increased their power, partly by the labour of trading from one place to another, and partly by selling the manufactures, whereof the materials were brought in from other places. The distribution of the materials of this nourishment is the constitution of mine, and thine, and his; that is to say, in one word, propriety; and belonged in all kinds of Commonwealth to the sovereign power. For where there is no Commonwealth, there is, as hath been already shown, a perpetual war of every man against his neighbour; and therefore everything is his that getteth it and keepeth it by force; which is neither propriety nor community, but uncertainty. Which is so evident that even Cicero, a passionate defender of liberty, in a public pleading attributeth all propriety to the law civil: "Let the civil law," saith he, "be once abandoned, or but negligently guarded, not to say oppressed, and there is nothing that any man can be sure to receive from his ancestor, or leave to his children." And again: "Take away the civil law, and no man knows what is his own, and what another man's." Seeing therefore the introduction of propriety is an effect of Commonwealth, which can do nothing but by the person that represents it, it is the act only of the sovereign; and consisteth in the laws, which none can make that have not the sovereign power. And this they well knew of old, who called that Nomos (that is to say, distribution), which we call law; and defined justice by distributing to every man his own. In this distribution, the first law is for division of the land itself: wherein the sovereign assigneth to every man a portion, according as he, and not according as any subject, or any number of them, shall judge agreeable to equity and the common good. The children of Israel were a Commonwealth in the wilderness; but wanted the commodities of the earth till they were masters of the Land of Promise; which afterward was divided amongst them, not by their own discretion, but by the discretion of Eleazar the priest, and Joshua their general: who when there were twelve tribes, making them thirteen by subdivision of the tribe of Joseph, made nevertheless but twelve portions of the land, and ordained for the tribe of Levi no land, but assigned them the tenth part of the whole fruits; which division was therefore arbitrary. And though a people coming into possession of a land by war do not always exterminate the ancient inhabitants, as did the Jews, but leave to many, or most, or all of them their estates; yet it is manifest they hold them afterwards, as of the victor's distribution; as the people of England held all theirs of William the Conqueror. From whence we may collect that the propriety which a subject hath in his lands consisteth in a right to exclude all other subjects from the use of them; and not to exclude their sovereign, be it an assembly or a monarch. For seeing the sovereign, that is to say, the Commonwealth (whose person he representeth), is understood to do nothing but in order to the common peace and security, this distribution of lands is to be understood as done in order to the same: and consequently, whatsoever distribution he shall make in prejudice thereof is contrary to the will of every subject that committed his peace and safety to his discretion and conscience, and therefore by the will of every one of them is to be reputed void. It is true that a sovereign monarch, or the greater part of a sovereign assembly, may ordain the doing of many things in pursuit of their passions, contrary to their own consciences, which is a breach of trust and of the law of nature; but this is not enough to authorize any subject, either to make war upon, or so much as to accuse of injustice, or any way to speak evil of their sovereign; because they have authorized all his actions, and, in bestowing the sovereign power, made them their own. But in what cases the commands of sovereigns are contrary to equity and the law of nature is to be considered hereafter in another place. In the distribution of land, the Commonwealth itself may be conceived to have a portion, and possess and improve the same by their representative; and that such portion may be made sufficient to sustain the whole expense to the common peace and defence necessarily required: which were very true, if there could be any representative conceived free from human passions and infirmities. But the nature of men being as it is, the setting forth of public land, or of any certain revenue for the Commonwealth, is in vain, and tendeth to the dissolution of government, to the condition of mere nature, and war, as soon as ever the sovereign power falleth into the hands of a monarch, or of an assembly, that are either too negligent of money or too hazardous in engaging the public stock into long or costly war. Commonwealths can endure no diet: for seeing their expense is not limited by their own appetite but by external accidents, and the appetites of their neighbours, the public riches cannot be limited by other limits than those which the emergent occasions shall require. And whereas in England, there were by the Conqueror diverse lands reserved to his own use (besides forests and chases, either for his recreation or for preservation of woods), and diverse services reserved on the land he gave his subjects; yet it seems they were not reserved for his maintenance in his public, but in his natural capacity: for he and his successors did, for all that, lay arbitrary taxes on all subjects' land when they judged it necessary. Or if those public lands and services were ordained as a sufficient maintenance of the Commonwealth, it was contrary to the scope of the institution, being (as it appeared by those ensuing taxes) insufficient and (as it appears by the late small revenue of the Crown) subject to alienation and diminution. It is therefore in vain to assign a portion to the Commonwealth, which may sell or give it away, and does sell and give it away when it is done by their representative. As the distribution of lands at home, so also to assign in what places, and for what commodities, the subject shall traffic abroad belonged to the sovereign. For if it did belong to private persons to use their own discretion therein, some of them would be drawn for gain, both to furnish the enemy with means to hurt the Commonwealth, and hurt it themselves by importing such things as, pleasing men's appetites, be nevertheless noxious, or at least unprofitable to them. And therefore it belonged to the Commonwealth (that is, to the sovereign only) to approve or disapprove both of the places and matter of foreign traffic. Further, seeing it is not enough to the sustentation of a Commonwealth that every man have a propriety in a portion of land, or in some few commodities, or a natural property in some useful art, and there is no art in the world but is necessary either for the being or well-being almost of every particular man; it is necessary that men distribute that which they can spare, and transfer their propriety therein mutually one to another by exchange and mutual contract. And therefore it belonged to the Commonwealth (that is to say, to the sovereign) to appoint in what manner all kinds of contract between subjects (as buying, selling, exchanging, borrowing, lending, letting, and taking to hire) are to be made, and by what words and words and sign they shall be understood for valid. And for the matter and distribution of the nourishment to the several members of the Commonwealth, thus much, considering the model of the whole work, is sufficient. By concoction, I understand the reducing of all commodities which are not presently consumed, but reserved for nourishment in time to come, to something of equal value, and withal so portable as not to hinder the motion of men from place to place; to the end a man may have in what place soever such nourishment as the place affordeth. And this is nothing else but gold, and silver, and money. For gold and silver, being, as it happens, almost in all countries of the world highly valued, is a commodious measure of the value of all things else between nations; and money, of what matter soever coined by the sovereign of a Commonwealth, is a sufficient measure of the value of all things else between the subjects of that Commonwealth. By the means of which measures all commodities, movable and immovable, are made to accompany a man to all places of his resort, within and without the place of his ordinary residence; and the same passeth from man to man within the Commonwealth, and goes round about, nourishing, as it passeth, every part thereof; in so much as this concoction is, as it were, the sanguification of the Commonwealth: for natural blood is in like manner made of the fruits of the earth; and, circulating, nourisheth by the way every member of the body of man. And because silver and gold have their value from the matter itself, they have first this privilege; that the value of them cannot be altered by the power of one nor of a few Commonwealths; as being a common measure of the commodities of all places. But base money may easily be enhanced or abased. Secondly, they have the privilege to make Commonwealths move and stretch out their arms, when need is, into foreign countries; and supply, not only private subjects that travel, but also whole armies with provision. But that coin, which is not considerable for the matter, but for the stamp of the place, being unable to endure change of air, hath its effect at home only; where also it is subject to the change of laws, and thereby to have the value diminished, to the prejudice many times of those that have it. The conduits and ways by which it is conveyed to the public use are of two sorts: one, that conveyeth it to the public coffers; the other, that issueth the same out again for public payments. Of the first sort are collectors, receivers, and treasurers; of the second are the treasurers again, and the officers appointed for payment of several public or private ministers. And in this also the artificial man maintains his resemblance with the natural; whose veins, receiving the blood from the several parts of the body, carry it to the heart; where, being made vital, the heart by the arteries sends it out again, to enliven and enable for motion all the members of the same. The procreation or children of a Commonwealth are those we call plantations, or colonies; which are numbers of men sent out from the Commonwealth, under a conductor or governor, to inhabit a foreign country, either formerly void of inhabitants, or made void then by war. And when a colony is settled, they are either a Commonwealth of themselves, discharged of their subjection to their sovereign that sent them (as hath been done by many Commonwealths of ancient time), in which case the Commonwealth from which they went was called their metropolis, or mother, and requires no more of them than fathers require of the children whom they emancipate and make free from their domestic government, which is honour and friendship; or else they remain united to their metropolis, as were the colonies of the people of Rome; and then they are no Commonwealths themselves, but provinces, and parts of the Commonwealth that sent them. So that the right of colonies, saving honour and league with their metropolis, dependeth wholly on their license, or letters, by which their sovereign authorized them to plant.


## CHAPTER XXV, OF COUNSEL


HOW fallacious it is to judge of the nature of things by the ordinary and inconstant use of words appeareth in nothing more than in the confusion of counsels and commands, arising from the imperative manner of speaking in them both, and in many other occasions besides. For the words do this are the words not only of him that commandeth; but also of him that giveth counsel; and of him that exhorteth; and yet there are but few that see not that these are very different things; or that cannot distinguish between when they when they perceive who it is that speaketh, and to whom the speech is directed, and upon what occasion. But finding those phrases in men's writings, and being not able or not willing to enter into a consideration of the circumstances, they mistake sometimes the precepts of counsellors for the precepts of them that command; and sometimes the contrary; according as it best agreeth with the conclusions they would infer, or the actions they approve. To avoid which mistakes and render to those terms of commanding, counselling, and exhorting, their proper and distinct significations, I define them thus. Command is where a man saith, "Do this," or "Do not this," without expecting other reason than the will of him that says it. From this it followeth manifestly that he that commandeth pretendeth thereby his own benefit: for the reason of his command is his own will only, and the proper object of every man's will is some good to himself. Counsel is where a man saith, "Do," or "Do not this," and deduceth his reasons from the benefit that arriveth by it to him to whom he saith it. And from this it is evident that he that giveth counsel pretendeth only (whatsoever he intendeth) the good of him to whom he giveth it. Therefore between counsel and command, one great difference is that command is directed to a man's own benefit, and counsel to the benefit of another man. And from this ariseth another difference, that a man may be obliged to do what he is commanded; as when he hath covenanted to obey: but he cannot be obliged to do as he is counselled, because the hurt of not following it is his own; or if he should covenant to follow it, then is the counsel turned into the nature of a command. A third difference between them is that no man can pretend a right to be of another man's counsel; because he is not to pretend benefit by it to himself: but to demand right to counsel another argues a will to know his designs, or to gain some other good to himself; which, as I said before, is of every man's will the proper object. This also is incident to the nature of counsel; that whatsoever it be, he that asketh it cannot in equity accuse or punish it: for to ask counsel of another is to permit him to give such counsel as he shall think best; and consequently, he that giveth counsel to his sovereign (whether a monarch or an assembly) when he asketh it, cannot in equity be punished for it, whether the same be conformable to the opinion of the most, or not, so it be to the proposition in debate. For if the sense of the assembly can be taken notice of, before the debate be ended, they should neither ask nor take any further counsel; for sense of the assembly is the resolution of the debate and end of all deliberation. And generally he that demandeth counsel is author of it, and therefore cannot punish it; and what the sovereign cannot, no man else can. But if one subject giveth counsel to another to do anything contrary to the laws, whether that counsel proceed from evil intention or from ignorance only, it is punishable by the Commonwealth; because ignorance of the law is no good excuse, where every man is bound to take notice of the laws to which he is subject. Exhortation, and dehortation is counsel, accompanied with signs in him that giveth it of vehement desire to have it followed; or, to say it more briefly, counsel vehemently pressed. For he that exhorteth doth not deduce the consequences of what he adviseth to be done, and tie himself therein to the rigor of true reasoning, but encourages him he counselleth to action: as he that dehorteth deterreth him from it. And therefore they have in their speeches a regard to the common passions and opinions of men, in deducing their reasons; and make use of similitudes, metaphors, examples, and other tools of oratory, to persuade their hearers of the utility, honour, or justice of following their advice. From whence may be inferred, first, that exhortation and dehortation is directed to the good of him that giveth the counsel, not of him that asketh it, which is contrary to the duty of a counsellor; who, by the definition of counsel, ought to regard, not his own benefit, but his whom he adviseth. And that he directeth his counsel to his own benefit is manifest enough by the long and vehement urging, or by the artificial giving thereof; which being not required of him, and consequently proceeding from his own occasions, is directed principally to his own benefit, and but accidentally to the good of him that is counselled, or not at all. Secondly, that the use of exhortation and dehortation lieth only where a man is to speak to a multitude, because when the speech is addressed to one, he may interrupt him and examine his reasons more rigorously than can be done in a multitude; which are too many to enter into dispute and dialogue with him that speaketh indifferently to them all at once. Thirdly, that they that exhort and dehort, where they are required to give counsel, are corrupt counsellors and, as it were, bribed by their own interest. For though the counsel they give be never so good, yet he that gives it is no more a good counsellor than he that giveth a just sentence for a reward is a just judge. But where a man may lawfully command, as a father in his family, or a leader in an army, his exhortations and dehortations are not only lawful, but also necessary and laudable: but when they are no more counsels, but commands; which when they are for execution of sour labour, sometimes necessity, and always humanity, requireth to be sweetened in the delivery by encouragement, and in the tune and phrase of counsel rather than in harsher language of command. Examples of the difference between command and counsel we may take from the forms of speech that express them in Holy Scripture. "Have no other Gods but me"; "Make to thyself no graven image"; "Take not God's name in vain"; "Sanctify the Sab-

bath"; "Honour thy parents"; "Kill not"; "Steal not," etc. are commands, because the reason for which we are to obey them is drawn from the will of God our King, whom we are obliged to obey. But these words, "Sell all thou hast; give it to the poor; and follow me," are counsel, because the reason for which we are to do so is drawn from our own benefit, which is this; that we shall have "treasure in Heaven." These words, "Go into the village over against you, and you shall find an ass tied, and her colt; loose her, and bring her to me," are a command; for the reason of their f
ct is drawn from the will of their master: but these words, "Repent, and be baptized in the name of Jesus," are counsel; because the reason why we should so do tendeth not to any benefit of God Almighty, who shall still be King in what manner soever we rebel, but of ourselves, who have no other means of avoiding the punishment hanging over us for our sins. As the difference of counsel from command hath been now deduced from the nature of counsel, consisting in a deducing of the benefit or hurt that may arise to him that is to be to be counselled, by the necessary or probable consequences of the action he propoundeth; so may also the differences between apt and inept counsellors be derived from the same. For experience, being but memory of the consequences of like actions formerly observed, and counsel but the speech whereby that experience is made known to another, the virtues and defects of counsel are the same with the virtues and defects intellectual: and to the person of a Commonwealth, his counsellors serve him in the place of memory and mental discourse. But with this resemblance of the Commonwealth to a natural man, there is one dissimilitude joined, of great importance; which is that a natural man receiveth his experience from the natural objects of sense, which work upon him without passion or interest of their own; whereas they that give counsel to the representative person of a Commonwealth may have, and have often, their particular ends and passions that render their counsels always suspected, and many times unfaithful. And therefore we may set down for the first condition of a good counsellor: that his ends and interest be not inconsistent with the ends and interest of him he counselleth. Secondly, because the office of a counsellor, when an action comes into deliberation, is to make manifest the consequences of it in such manner as he that is counselled may be truly and evidently informed, he ought to propound his advice in such form of speech as may make the truth most evidently appear; that is to say, with as firm ratiocination, as significant and proper language, and as briefly, as the evidence will permit. And therefore rash and unevident inferences, such as are fetched only from examples, or authority of books, and are not arguments of what is good or evil, but witnesses of fact or of opinion; obscure, confused, and ambiguous expressions; also all metaphorical speeches tending to the stirring up of passion (because such reasoning and such expressions are useful only to deceive or to lead him we counsel towards other ends than his own), are repugnant to the office of a counsellor. Thirdly, because the ability of counselling proceedeth from experience and long study, and no man is presumed to have experience in all those things that to the administration of a great Commonwealth are necessary to be known, no man is presumed to be a good counsellor but in such business as he hath not only been much versed in, but hath also much meditated on and considered. For seeing the business of a Commonwealth is this; to preserve the people in peace at home, and defend them against foreign invasion; we shall find it requires great knowledge of the disposition of mankind, of the rights of government, and of the nature of equity, law, justice, and honour, not to be attained without study; and of the strength, commodities, places, both of their own country and their neighbours'; as also of the inclinations and designs of all nations that may any way annoy them. And this is not attained to without much experience. Of which things, not only the whole sum, but every one of the particulars requires the age and observation of a man in years, and of more than ordinary study. The wit required for counsel, as I have said before (Chapter VIII), is judgement. And the differences of men in that point come from different education; of some, to one kind of study or business, and of others, to another. When for the doing of anything there be infallible rules (as in engines and edifices, the rules of geometry), all the experience of the world cannot equal his counsel that has learned or found out the rule. And when there is no such rule, he that hath most experience in that particular kind of business has therein the best judgement, and is the best counsellor. Fourthly, to be able to give counsel to a Commonwealth, in a business that hath reference to another Commonwealth, it is necessary to be acquainted with the intelligences and letters that come from thence, and with all the records of treaties and other transactions of state between them; which none can do but such as the representative shall think fit. By which we may see that they who are not called to counsel can have no good counsel in such cases to obtrude. Fifthly, supposing the number of counsellors equal, a man is better counselled by hearing them apart than in an assembly; and that for many causes. First, in hearing them apart, you have the advice of every man; but in an assembly many of them deliver their advice with aye or no, or with their hands or feet, not moved by their own sense, but by the eloquence of another, or for fear of displeasing some that have spoken, or the whole by contradiction, or for fear of appearing duller in apprehension than those that have applauded the

contrary opinion. Secondly, in an assembly of many there cannot choose but be some interests are contrary to that of the public; and these their interests make passionate, and passion eloquent, and eloquence draws others into the same advice. For the passions of men, which asunder are moderate, as the heat of one brand; in assembly are like many brands that inflame one another (especially when they blow one another with orations) to the setting of the Commonwealth on fire, under pretence of counselling it. Thirdly, in hearing every man apart, one may examine, when there is need, the truth or probability of his reasons, and of the grounds of the advice he gives, by frequent interruptions and objections; which cannot be done in an assembly, where in every difficult question a man is rather astonied and dazzled with the variety of discourse upon it, than informed of the course he ought to take. Besides, there cannot be an assembly of many, called together for advice, wherein there be not some that have the ambition the ambition to be thought eloquent, and also learned in the politics; and give not their advice with care of the business propounded, but of the applause of their motley orations, made of the diverse colored threads or shreds of thread or shreds of authors; which is an impertinence, at least, that takes away the time of serious consultation, and in the secret way of counselling apart is easily avoided. Fourthly, in deliberations that ought to be kept secret, whereof there be many occasions in public business, the counsels of many, and especially in assemblies, are dangerous; and therefore great assemblies are necessitated to commit such affairs to lesser numbers, and of such persons as are most versed, and in whose fidelity they have most confidence. To conclude, who is there that so far approves far approves the taking of counsel from a great assembly of counsellors, that wisheth for, or would accept of their pains, when there is a question of marrying his children, disposing of his lands, governing his household, or managing his private estate, especially if there be amongst them such as wish not his prosperity? A man that doth his business by the help of many prudent counsellors, with every one consulting apart in his proper element, does it best; as he that useth able seconds at tennis play, placed in their proper stations. He does next best that useth his own judgement only; as he that has no second at all. But he that is carried up and down to his business in a framed counsel, which cannot move but by the plurality of consenting opinions, the execution whereof is commonly, out of envy or interest, retarded by the part dissenting, does it worst of all, and like one that is carried to the ball, though by good players, yet in a wheelbarrow, or other frame, heavy of itself, and retarded by the also by the inconcurrent judgements and endeavours of them that drive it; and so much the more, as they be more that set their hands to it; and most of all, when there is one or more amongst them that desire to have him lose. And though it be true that many eyes see more than one, yet it is not to be understood of many counsellors, but then only when the final resolution is in one in one man. Otherwise, because many eyes see the same thing in diverse lines, and are apt to look asquint towards their private benefit; they that desire not to miss their mark, though they look about with two eyes, yet they never aim but with one: and therefore no great popular Commonwealth was ever kept up, but either by a foreign enemy that united them; or by the reputation of some one eminent man amongst them; or by the secret counsel of a few; or by the mutual fear of equal factions; and not by the open consultations of the assembly. And as for very little Commonwealths, be they popular or monarchical, there is no human wisdom can uphold them longer than the jealousy lasteth of their potent neighbours.

**CHAPTER XXVI, OF CIVIL LAWS**

BY civil laws, I understand the laws that men are therefore bound to observe, because they are members, not of this or that Commonwealth in particular, but of a Commonwealth. For the knowledge of particular laws belongeth to them that profess the study of the laws of their several countries; but the knowledge of civil law in general, to any man. The ancient law of Rome was called their civil law, from the word civitas, which signifies a Commonwealth: and those countries which, having been under the Roman Empire and governed by that law, retain still such part thereof as they think fit, call that part the civil law to distinguish it from the rest of their own civil laws. But that is not it I intend to speak of here; my design being not to show what is law here and there, but what is law; as Plato, Aristotle, Cicero, and diverse others have done, without taking upon them the profession of the study of the law. And first it is manifest that law in general is not counsel, but command; nor a command of any man to any man, but only of him whose command is addressed to one formerly obliged to obey him. And as for civil law, it addeth only the name of the person commanding, which is persona civitatis, the person of the Commonwealth. Which considered, I define civil law in this manner. Civil law is to every subject those rules which the Commonwealth hath commanded him, by word, writing, or other sufficient sign of the will, to make use of for the distinction of right and wrong; that is to say, of that is contrary and what is not contrary to the rule. In which definition there is nothing that is that is not at first sight evident. For every man seeth that some laws are addressed to all the subjects in general; some to particular provinces; some to particular vocations; and some to particular men; and are therefore laws to every of those to whom the command is directed, and to none else. As also, that laws are the rules of just and unjust, nothing being reputed unjust that is not contrary to some law. Likewise, that none can make laws but the Commonwealth, because our subjection is to the Commonwealth only; and that commands are to be signified by sufficient signs, because a man knows not otherwise how to obey them. And therefore, whatsoever can from this definition by necessary consequence be deduced, ought to be acknowledged for truth. Now I deduce from it this that followeth. 1. The legislator in all Commonwealths is only the sovereign, be he one man, as in a monarchy, or one assembly of men, as in a democracy or aristocracy. For the legislator is he that maketh the law. And the Commonwealth only prescribes and commandeth the observation of those rules which we call law: therefore the Commonwealth is the legislator. But the Commonwealth is no person, nor has capacity to do anything but by the representative, that is, the sovereign; and therefore the sovereign is the sole legislator. For the same reason, none can abrogate a law made, but the sovereign, because a law is not abrogated but by another law that forbiddeth it to be put in execution. 2. The sovereign of a Commonwealth, be it an assembly or one man, is not subject to the civil laws. For having power to make and repeal laws, he may, when he pleaseth, free himself from that subjection by repealing those laws that trouble him, and making of new; and consequently he was free before. For he is free that can be free when he will: nor is it possible for any person to be bound to himself, because he that can bind can release; and therefore he that is bound to himself only is not bound. 3. When long use obtaineth the authority of a law, it is not the length of time that maketh the authority, but the will of the sovereign signified by his silence (for silence is sometimes an signified by his silence (for silence is sometimes an argument of consent); and it is no longer law, than the sovereign shall be silent therein. And therefore if the sovereign shall have a question of right grounded, not upon his present will, but upon the laws formerly made, the length of time shall bring no prejudice to his right: but the question shall be judged by equity. For many unjust actions and unjust sentences go uncontrolled a longer time than any man can remember. And our lawyers account no customs law but such as reasonable, and that evil customs are to be abolished: but the judgement of what is reasonable, and of what is to be abolished, belonged to him that maketh the law, which is the sovereign assembly or monarch. 4. The law of nature and the civil law contain each other and are of equal extent. For the laws of nature, which consist in equity, justice, gratitude, and other moral virtues on these depending, in the condition of mere nature (as I have said before in the end of the fifteenth Chapter), are not properly laws, but qualities that dispose men to peace and to obedience. When a Commonwealth is once settled, then are they actually laws, and not before; as being then the commands of the Commonwealth; and therefore also civil laws: for it is the sovereign power that obliges men to obey them. For the differences of private men, to declare what is equity, what is justice, and is moral virtue, and to make them binding, there is need of the ordinances of sovereign power, and punishments to be ordained for such as shall break them; which ordinances are therefore part of the civil law. The law of nature therefore is a part of the civil law in all Commonwealths of the world. Reciprocally also, the civil law is a part of the dictates of nature. For justice, that is to say, performance of covenant, and giving to every man his own, is a dictate of the law of nature. But every subject in a Commonwealth hath covenanted to obey the civil law; either one with another, as when they assemble to make a common representative, or with the representative itself one by one when, subdued by the sword, they promise obedience that they may receive life; and therefore obedience to the civil law is part also of the law of nature. Civil and natural law are not different kinds, but different parts of law; whereof one part, being written, is called civil the other unwritten, natural. But the right of nature, that is, the natural liberty of man, may by the civil law be abridged and restrained: nay, the end of making laws is no other but such restraint, without which there cannot possibly be any peace. And law was brought into the world for nothing else but to limit the natural liberty of particular men in such manner as they might not hurt, but assist one another, and join together against a common enemy. 5. If the sovereign of one Commonwealth subdue a people that have lived under other written laws, and afterwards govern them by the same laws by which they were governed before, yet those laws are the civil laws of the victor, and not of the vanquished Commonwealth. For the legislator is he, not by whose authority the laws were first made, but by whose authority they now continue to be laws. And therefore where there be diverse provinces within the dominion of a Commonwealth, and in those provinces diversity of laws, which commonly are called the customs of each several province, we are not to understand that such customs have their force only from length of time; but that they were anciently laws written, or otherwise made known, for the constitutions and statutes of their sovereigns; and are now laws, not by virtue of the prescription of time, but by the constitutions of their present sovereigns. But if an unwritten law, in all the provinces of a dominion, shall be generally observed, and no iniquity appear in the use thereof, that law can be no other but a law of nature, equally obliging all mankind. 6. Seeing then all laws, written and unwritten, have their authority and force from the will of the Commonwealth; that is to say, from the will of the representative, which in a monarchy is the monarch, and in other Commonwealths the sovereign assembly; a man may wonder from whence proceed such opinions as are found in the books of lawyers of eminence in several Commonwealths, directly or by consequence making the legislative power depend on private men or subordinate judges. As for example, that the common law hath no controller but the Parliament; which is true only where a parliament has the sovereign power, and cannot be assembled nor dissolved, but by their own discretion. For if there be a right in any else to dissolve them, there is a right also to control them, and consequently to control their controllings. And if there be no such right, then the controller of laws is not parlamentum, but rex in parlamento. And where a parliament is sovereign, if it should assemble never so many or so wise men from the countries subject to them, for whatsoever cause, yet there is no man will believe that such an assembly hath thereby acquired to themselves a legislative power. Item, that the two arms of a Commonwealth are force and justice; the first whereof is in the king, the other deposited in the hands of the Parliament. As if a Commonwealth could consist where the force were in any hand which justice had not the authority to command and govern. 7. That law can never be against reason, our lawyers are agreed: and that not the letter (that is, every construction of it), but that which is according to the intention of the legislator, is the law. And it is true: but the doubt is of whose reason it is that shall be received for law. It is not meant of any private reason; for then there would be as much contradiction in the laws as there is in the Schools; nor yet, as Sir Edward Coke makes it, an "Artificial perfection of reason, gotten by long study, observation, and experience," as his was. For it is possible long study may increase and confirm erroneous sentences: and where men build on false grounds, the more they build, the greater is the ruin: and of those that study and observe with equal time and diligence, the reasons and resolutions are, and must remain, discordant: and therefore it is not that juris prudentia, or wisdom of subordinate judges, but the reason of this our artificial man the Commonwealth, and his command, that maketh law: and the Commonwealth being in their representative but one person, there cannot easily arise any contradiction in the laws; and when there doth, the same reason is able, by interpretation or alteration, to take it away. In all courts of justice, the sovereign (which is the person of the Commonwealth) is he that judgeth: the subordinate judge ought to have regard to the reason which moved his sovereign to make such law, that his sentence may be according thereunto, which then is his sovereigns sentence; otherwise it is his own, and an unjust one. 8. From this, that the law is a command, and a command consisteth in declaration or manifestation of the will of him that commandeth, by voice, writing, or some other sufficient argument of the same, we may understand that the command of the Commonwealth is law only to those that have means to take notice of it. Over natural fools, children, or madmen there is no law, no more than over brute beasts; nor are they capable of the title of just or unjust, because they had never power to make any covenant or to understand the consequences thereof, and consequently never took upon them to authorize the actions of any sovereign, as they must do that make to themselves a Commonwealth. And as those from whom nature or accident hath taken away the notice of all laws in general; so also every man, from whom any accident not proceeding from his own default, hath taken away the means to take notice of any particular law, is excused if he observe it not; and to speak properly, that law is no law to him. It is therefore necessary to consider in this place what arguments and signs be sufficient for the knowledge of what is the law; that is to say, what is the will of the sovereign, as well in monarchies as in other forms of government. And first, if it be a law that obliges all the subjects without exception, and is not written, nor otherwise published in such places as they may take notice thereof, it is a law of nature. For whatever men are to take knowledge of for law, not upon other men's words, but every one from his own reason, must be such as is agreeable to the reason of all men; which no law can be, but the law of nature. The laws of nature therefore need not any publishing nor proclamation; as being contained in this one sentence, approved by all the world, Do not that to another which thou thinkest unreasonable to be done by another to thyself. Secondly, if it be a law that obliges only some condition of men, or one particular man, and be not written, nor published by word, then also it is a law of nature, and known by the same arguments and signs that distinguish those in such a condition from other subjects. For whatsoever law is not written, or some way published by him that makes it law, can be known no way but by the reason of him that is to obey it; and is therefore also a law not only civil, but natural. For example, if the sovereign employ a public minister, without written instructions what to do, he is obliged to take for instructions the dictates of reason: as if he make a judge, the judge is to take notice that his sentence ought to be according to the reason of his sovereign, which being always understood to be equity, he is bound to it by the law of nature: or if an ambassador, he is, in all things not contained in his written instructions, to take for instruction that which reason dictates to be most conducing to his sovereign's interest; and so of all other ministers of the sovereignty, public and private. All which instructions of natural reason may be comprehended under one name of fidelity, which is a branch of natural justice. The law of nature excepted, it belonged to the essence of all other laws to be made known to every man that shall be obliged to obey them, either by word, or writing, or some other act known to proceed from the sovereign authority. For the will of another cannot be understood but by his own word, or act, or by conjecture taken from his scope and purpose; which in the person of the Commonwealth is to be supposed always consonant to equity and reason. And in ancient time, before letters were in common use, the laws were many times put into verse; that the rude people, taking pleasure in singing or reciting them, might the more easily retain them in memory. And for the same reason Solomon adviseth a man to bind the Ten Commandments upon his ten fingers. [Proverbs, 7. 3] And for the Law which Moses gave to the people of Israel at the renewing of the Covenant, he biddeth them to teach it their children, by discoursing of it both at home and upon the way, at going to bed and at rising from bed; and to write it upon the posts and doors of their houses; [Deuteronomy, 11. 19] and to assemble the people, man, woman, and child, to hear it read. [Ibid., 31. 12] Nor is it enough the law be written and published, but also that there be manifest signs that it proceedeth from the will of the sovereign. For private men, when they have, or think they have, force enough to secure their unjust designs, and convoy them safely to their ambitious ends, may publish for laws what they please, without or against the legislative authority. There is therefore requisite, not only a declaration of the law, but also sufficient signs of the author and authority. The author or legislator is supposed in every Commonwealth to be evident, because he is the sovereign, who, having been constituted by the consent of every one, is supposed by every one to be sufficiently known. And though the ignorance and security of men be such, for the most part, as that when the memory of the first constitution of their Commonwealth is worn out, they do not consider by whose power they use to be defended against their enemies, and to have their industry protected, and to be righted when injury is done them; yet because no man that considers can make question of it, no excuse can be derived from the ignorance of where the sovereignty is placed. And it is a dictate of natural reason, and consequently an evident law of nature, that no man ought to weaken that power the protection whereof he hath himself demanded or wittingly received against others. Therefore of who is sovereign, no man, but by his own fault (whatsoever evil men suggest), can make any doubt. The difficulty cocsisteth in the evidence of the authority derived from him; the removing whereof dependeth on the knowledge of the public registers, public counsels, public ministers, and public seals; by which all laws are sufficiently verified; verified, I say, not authorized: for the verification is but the testimony and record; not the authority of the law, which consisteth in the command of the sovereign only. If therefore a man have a question of injury, depending on the law of nature; that is to say, on common equity; the sentence of the judge, that by commission hath authority to take cognizance of such causes, is a sufficient verification of the law of nature in that individual case. For though the advice of one that professeth the study of the law be useful for the avoiding of contention, yet it is but advice: it is the judge must tell men what is law, upon the hearing of the controversy. But when the question is of injury, or crime, upon a written law, every man by recourse to the registers by himself or others may, if he will, be sufficiently informed, before he do such injury, or commit the crime, whether it be an injury or not; nay, he ought to do so: for when a man doubts whether the act he goeth about be just or unjust, and may inform himself if he will, the doing is unlawful. In like manner, he that supposeth himself injured, in a case determined by the written law, which he may by himself or others see and consider; if he complain before he consults with the law, he does unjustly, and bewrayeth a disposition rather to vex other men than to demand his own right. If the question be of obedience to a public officer, to have seen his commission with the public seal, and heard it read, or to have had the means to be informed of it, if a man would, is a sufficient verification of his authority. For every man is obliged to do his best endeavour to inform himself of all written laws that may concern his own future actions. The legislator known, and the laws either by writing or by the light of nature sufficiently published, there wanteth yet another very material circumstance to make them obligatory. For it is not the letter, but the intendment, or meaning; that is to say, the authentic interpretation of the law (which is the sense of the legislator), in which the nature of the law consisteth; and therefore the interpretation of all laws dependeth on the authority sovereign; and the interpreters can be none but those which the sovereign, to whom only the subject oweth obedience, shall appoint. For else, by the craft of an interpreter, the law may be made to bear a sense contrary to that of the sovereign, by which means the interpreter becomes the legislator. All laws, written and unwritten, have need of interpretation. The unwritten law of nature, though it be easy to such as without partiality and passion make use of their natural reason, and therefore leaves the violators thereof without excuse; yet considering there be very few, perhaps none, that in some cases are not blinded by self-love, or some other passion, it is now become of all laws the most obscure, and has consequently the greatest need of able interpreters. The written laws, if laws, if they be short, are easily misinterpreted, for the diverse significations of a word or two; if long, they be more obscure by the diverse significations of many words: in so much as no written law, delivered in few or many words, can be well understood without a perfect understanding of the final causes for which the law was made; the knowledge of which final causes is in the legislator. To him therefore there cannot be any knot in the law insoluble, either by finding out the ends to undo it by, or else by making what ends he will (as Alexander did with his sword in the Gordian knot) by the legislative power; which no other interpreter can do. The interpretation of the laws of nature in a Commonwealth dependeth not on the books of moral philosophy. The authority of writers, without the authority of the Commonwealth, maketh not their opinions law, be they never so true. That which I have written in this treatise concerning the moral virtues, and of their necessity for the procuring and maintaining peace, though it be evident truth, is not therefore presently law, but because in all Commonwealths in the world it is part of the civil law. For though it be naturally reasonable, yet it is by the sovereign power that it is law: otherwise, it were a great error to call the laws of nature unwritten law; whereof we see so many volumes published, and in them so many contradictions of one another and of themselves. The interpretation of the law of nature is the sentence of the judge constituted by the sovereign authority to hear and determine such controversies as depend thereon, and consisteth in the application of the law to the present case. For in the act of judicature the judge doth no more but consider whether the demand of the party be consonant to natural reason and equity; and the sentence he giveth is therefore the interpretation of the law of nature; which interpretation is authentic, not because it is his private sentence, but because he giveth it by authority of the sovereign, whereby it becomes the sovereign's sentence; which is law for that time to the parties pleading. But because there is no judge subordinate, nor sovereign, but may err in a judgement equity; if afterward in another like case he find it more consonant to equity to give a contrary sentence, he is obliged to do it. No man's error becomes his own law, nor obliges him to persist in it. Neither, for the same reason, becomes it a law to other judges, though sworn to follow it. For though a wrong sentence given by authority of the sovereign, if he know and allow it, in such laws as are mutable, be a constitution of a new law in cases in which every little circumstance is the same; yet in laws immutable, such as are the laws of nature, they are no laws to the same or other judges in the like cases for ever after. Princes succeed one another; and one judge passeth, another cometh; nay, heaven and earth shall pass; but not one tittle of the law of nature shall pass; for it is the eternal law of God. Therefore all the sentences of precedent judges that have ever been cannot all together make a law contrary to natural equity. Nor any examples of former judges can warrant an unreasonable sentence, or discharge the present judge of the trouble of studying what is equity (in the case he is to judge) from the principles of his own natural reason. For example sake, it is against the law of nature to punish the innocent; and innocent is he that acquitteth himself judicially and is acknowledged for innocent by the judge. Put the case now that a man is accused of a capital crime, and seeing the power and malice of some enemy, and the frequent corruption and partiality of judges, runneth away for fear of the event, and afterwards is taken and brought to a legal trial, and maketh it sufficiently appear he was not guilty of the crime, and being thereof acquitted is nevertheless condemned to lose his goods; this is a manifest condemnation of the innocent. I say therefore that there is no place in the world where this can be an interpretation of a law of nature, or be made a law by the sentences of precedent judges that had done the same. For he that judged it first judged unjustly; and no injustice can be a pattern of judgement to succeeding judges. A written law may forbid innocent men to fly, and they may be punished for flying: but that flying for fear of injury should be taken for presumption of guilt, after a man is already absolved of the crime judicially, is contrary to the nature of a presumption, which hath no place after judgement given. Yet this is set down by a great lawyer for the common law of England: "If a man," saith he, "that is innocent be accused of felony, and for fear flyeth for the same; albeit he judicially acquitteth himself of the felony; yet if it be found that he fled for the felony, he shall, notwithstanding his innocency, forfeit all his goods, chattels, debts, and duties. For as to the forfeiture of them, the law will admit no proof against the presumption in law, grounded upon his flight." Here you see an innocent man, judicially acquitted, notwithstanding his innocency (when no written law forbade him to fly) after his acquittal, upon a presumption in law, condemned to lose all the goods he hath. If the law ground upon his flight a presumption of the fact, which was capital, the sentence ought to have been capital: the presumption were not of the fact, for what then ought he to lose his goods? This therefore is no law of England; nor is the condemnation grounded upon a presumption of law, but upon the presumption of the judges. It is also against law to say that no proof shall be admitted against a presumption of law. For all judges, sovereign and subordinate, if they refuse to hear proof, refuse to do justice: for though the sentence be just, yet the judges that condemn, without hearing the proofs offered, are unjust judges; and their presumption is but prejudice; which no man ought to bring with him to the seat of justice whatsoever precedent judgements or examples he shall pretend to follow. There be other things of this nature, wherein men's judgements have been perverted by trusting to precedents: but this is enough to show that though the sentence of the judge be a law to the party pleading, yet it is no law any judge that shall succeed him in that office. In like manner, when question is of the meaning of written laws, he is not the interpreter of them that writeth a commentary upon them. For commentaries are commonly more subject to cavil than the text, and therefore need other commentaries; and so there will be no end of such interpretation. And therefore unless there be an interpreter authorized by the sovereign, from which the subordinate judges are not to recede, the interpreter can be no other than the ordinary judges, in the same manner as they are in cases of the unwritten law; and their sentences are to be taken by them that plead for laws in that particular case, but not to bind other judges in like cases to give like judgements. For a judge may err in the interpretation even of written laws; but no error of a subordinate judge can change the law, which is the general sentence of the sovereign. In written laws men use to make a difference between the letter and the sentence of the law: and when by the letter is meant whatsoever can be gathered from the bare words, it is well distinguished. For the significations of almost all are either in themselves, or in the metaphorical use of them, ambiguous; and may be drawn in argument to make many senses; but there is only one sense of the law. But if by the letter be meant the literal sense, then the letter and the sentence or intention of the law is all one. For the literal sense is that which the legislator intended should by the letter of the law be signified. Now the intention of the legislator is always supposed to be equity: for it were a great contumely for a judge to think otherwise of the sovereign. He ought therefore, if the word of the law do not fully authorize a reasonable sentence, to supply it with the law of nature; or if the case be difficult, to respite judgement till he have received more ample authority. For example, a written law ordaineth that he which is thrust out of his house by force shall be restored by force. It happens that a man by negligence leaves his house empty, and returning is kept out by force, in which case there is no special law ordained. It is evident that this case is contained in the same law; for else there is no remedy for him at all, which is to be supposed against the intention of the legislator. Again, the word of the law commandeth to judge according to the evidence. A man is accused falsely of a fact which the judge himself saw done by another, and not by him that is accused. In this case neither shall the letter of the law be followed to the condemnation of the innocent, nor shall the judge give sentence against the evidence of the witnesses, because the letter of the law is to the contrary; but procure of the sovereign that another be made judge, and himself witness. So that the incommodity that follows the bare words of a written law may lead him to the intention of the law, whereby to interpret the same the better; though no incommodity can warrant a sentence against the law. For every judge of right and wrong is not judge of what is commodious or incommodious to the Commonwealth. The abilities required in a good interpreter of the law, that is to say, in a good judge, are not the same with those of an advocate; namely, the study of the laws. For a judge, as he ought to take notice of the fact from none but the witnesses, so also he ought to take notice of the law from nothing but the statutes and constitutions of the sovereign, alleged in the pleading, or declared to him by some that have authority from the sovereign power to declare them; and need not take care beforehand what he shall judge; for it shall be given him what he shall say concerning the fact, by witnesses; and what he shall say in point of law, from those that shall in their pleadings show it, and by authority interpret it upon the place. The Lords of Parliament in England were judges, and most difficult causes have been heard and determined by them; yet few of them were much versed in the study of the laws, and fewer had made profession of them; and though they consulted with lawyers that were appointed to be present there for that purpose, yet they alone had the authority of giving sentence. In like manner, in the ordinary trials of right, twelve men of the common people are the judges and give sentence, not only of the fact, but of the right; and pronounce simply for the complainant or for the defendant; that is to say, are judges not only of the fact, but also of the right; and in a question of crime, not only determine whether done or not done, but also whether it be murder, homicide, felony, assault, and the like, which are determinations of law: but because they are not supposed to know the law of themselves, there is one that hath authority to inform them of it in the particular case they are to judge of. But yet if they judge not according to that he tells them, they are not subject thereby to any penalty; unless it be made appear they did it against their consciences, or had been corrupted by reward. The things that make a good judge or good interpreter of the laws are, first, a right understanding of that principal law of nature called equity; which, depending not on the reading of other men's writings, but on the goodness of a man's own natural reason and meditation, is presumed to be in those most that had most leisure, and had the most inclination to meditate thereon. Secondly, contempt of unnecessary riches and preferments. Thirdly, to be able in judgement to divest himself of all fear, anger, hatred, love, and compassion. Fourthly, and lastly, patience to hear, diligent attention in hearing, and memory to retain, digest, and apply what he hath heard. The difference and division of the laws has been made in diverse manners, according to the different methods of those men that have written of them. For it is a thing that dependeth on nature, but on the scope of the writer, and is subservient to every man's proper method. In the Institutions of Justinian, we find seven sorts of civil laws:

1. The edicts, constitutions, and epistles of prince; that is, of the emperor, because the whole power of the people was in him. Like these are the proclamations of the kings of England.

2. The decrees of the whole people of Rome, comprehending the Senate, when they were put to the question by the Senate. These were laws, at first, by the virtue of the sovereign power residing in the people; and such of them as by the emperors were not abrogated remained laws by the authority imperial. For all laws that bind are understood to be laws by his authority that has power to repeal them. Somewhat like to these laws are the Acts of Parliament in England.

3. The decrees of the common people, excluding the Senate, when they were put to the question by the tribune of the people. For such of them as were not abrogated by the emperors, remained laws by the authority imperial. Like to these were the orders of the House of Commons in England.

4. Senatus consulta, the orders of the Senate: because when the people of Rome grew so numerous as it was inconvenient to assemble them, it was thought fit by the emperor that men should consult the Senate instead of the people: and these have some resemblance with the Acts of Council.

5. The edicts of praetors, and in some cases of the aediles: such as are the chief justices in the courts of England.

6. Responsa prudentum, which were the sentences and opinions of those lawyers to whom the emperor gave authority to interpret the law, the law, and to give answer to such as in matter of law demanded their advice; which answers the judges in giving judgement were obliged by the constitutions of the emperor to observe: and should be like the reports of cases judged, if other judges be by the law of England bound to observe them. For the judges of the common law of England are not properly judges, but juris consulti; of whom the judges, who are either the lords, or twelve men of the country, are in point of law to ask advice.

7. Also, unwritten customs, which in their own nature are an imitation of law, by the tacit consent of the emperor, in case they be not contrary to the law of nature, are very laws.

Another division of laws is into natural and positive. Natural are those which have been laws from all eternity, and are called not only natural, but also moral laws, consisting in the moral virtues; as justice, equity, and all habits of the mind that conduce to peace and charity, of which I have already spoken in the fourteenth and fifteenth Chapters. Positive are those which have not been from eternity, but have been made laws by the will of those that have had the sovereign power over others, and are either written or made known to men by some other argument of the will of their legislator. Again, of positive laws some are human, some divine: and of human positive laws, some are distributive, some penal. Distributive are those that determine the rights of the subjects, declaring to every man what it is by which he acquireth and holdeth a propriety in lands or goods, and a right or liberty of action: and these speak to all the subjects. Penal are those which declare what penalty shall be inflicted on those that violate the law; and speak to the ministers and officers ordained for execution. For though every one ought to be informed of the punishments ordained beforehand for their transgression; nevertheless the command is not addressed to the delinquent (who cannot be supposed will faithfully punish himself), but to public ministers appointed to see the penalty executed. And these penal laws are for the most part written together with the laws distributive, and are sometimes called judgements. For all laws are general judgements, or sentences of the legislator; as also every particular judgement is a law to him whose case is judged. Divine positive laws (for natural laws, being eternal and universal, are all divine) are those which, being the commandments of God, not from all eternity, nor universally addressed to all men, but only to a certain people or to certain persons, are declared for such by those whom God hath authorized to declare them.

But this authority of man to declare what be these positive of God, how can it be known? God may command a man, by a supernatural way, to deliver laws to other men. But because it is of the essence of law that he who is to be obliged be assured of the authority of him that declareth it, which we cannot naturally take notice to be from God, how can a man without supernatural revelations be assured of the revelation received by the declarer? And how can he be bound to obey bound to obey them? For the first question, how a man can be assured of the revelation of another without a revelation particularly to himself, it is evidently impossible: for though a man may be induced to believe such revelation, from the miracles they see him do, or from seeing the extraordinary sanctity of his life, or from seeing the extraordinary wisdom, or extraordinary felicity of his actions, all which are marks of God's extraordinary favour; yet they are not assured evidences of special revelation. Miracles are marvellous works; but that which is marvellous to one may not be so to another. Sanctity may be feigned; and the visible felicities of this world are most often the work of God by natural and ordinary causes. And therefore no man can infallibly know by natural reason that another has had a supernatural revelation of God's will but only a belief; every one, as the signs thereof shall appear greater or lesser, a firmer or a weaker belief. But for the second, how he can be bound to obey them, it is not so hard. For if the law declared be not against the law of nature, which is undoubtedly God's law, and he undertake to obey it, he is bound by his own act; bound I say to obey it, but not bound to believe it: for men's belief, and interior cogitations, are not subject to the commands, but only to the operation of God, ordinary or extraordinary. Faith of supernatural law is not a fulfilling, but only an assenting to the same; and not a duty that we exhibit to God, but a gift which God freely giveth to whom He pleaseth; as also unbelief is not a breach of any of His laws, but a rejection of them all, except the laws natural. But this that I say will be made yet clearer by, the examples and testimonies concerning this point in Holy Scripture. The covenant God made with Abraham in a supernatural manner was thus, "This is the covenant which thou shalt observe between me and thee and thy seed after thee." [Genesis, 17. 10] Abraham's seed had not this revelation, nor were yet in being; yet they are a party to the covenant, and bound to obey what Abraham should declare to them for God's law; which they could not be but in virtue of the obedience they owed to their parents, who (if they be subject to no other earthly power, as here in the case of Abraham) have sovereign power over their children and servants. Again, where God saith to Abraham, "In thee shall all nations of the earth be blessed: for I know thou wilt command thy children and thy house after thee to keep the way of the Lord, and to observe righteousness and judgement," it is manifest the obedience of his family, who had no revelation, depended on their former obligation to obey their sovereign. At Mount Sinai Moses only went up to God; the people were forbidden to approach on pain of death; yet were they bound to obey all that Moses declared to them for God's law. Upon what ground, but on this submission of their own, "Speak thou to us, and we will hear thee; but let not God speak to us, lest we die"? By which two places it sufficiently appeareth that in a Commonwealth a subject that has no certain and assured revelation particularly to himself concerning the will of God is to obey for such the command of the Commonwealth: for if men were at liberty to take for God's commandments their own dreams and fancies, or the dreams and fancies of private men, scarce two men would agree upon what is God's commandment; and yet in respect of them every man would despise the commandments of the Commonwealth. I conclude, therefore, that in all things not contrary to the moral law (that is to say, to the law of nature), all subjects are bound to obey that for divine law which is declared to be so by the laws of the Commonwealth. Which also is evident to any man's reason; for whatsoever is not against the law of nature may be made law in the name of them that have the sovereign power; there is no reason men should be the less obliged by it when it is propounded in the name of God. Besides, there is no place in the world where men are permitted to pretend other commandments of God than are declared for such by the Commonwealth. Christian states punish those that revolt from Christian religion; and all other states, those that set up any religion by them forbidden. For in whatsoever is not regulated by the Commonwealth, it is equity (which is the law of nature, and therefore an eternal law of God) that every man equally enjoy his liberty. There is also another distinction of laws into fundamental and not fundamental: but I could never see in any author what a fundamental law signifieth. Nevertheless one may very reasonably distinguish laws in that manner. For a fundamental law in every Commonwealth is that which, being taken away, the Commonwealth faileth and is utterly dissolved, as a building whose foundation is destroyed. And therefore a fundamental law is that by which subjects are bound to uphold whatsoever power is given to the sovereign, whether a monarch or a sovereign assembly, without which the Commonwealth cannot stand; such as is the power of war and peace, of judicature, of election of officers, and of doing whatsoever he shall think necessary for the public good. Not fundamental is that, the abrogating whereof draweth not with it the dissolution of the Commonwealth; such as are the laws concerning controversies between subject and subject. Thus much of the division of laws. I find the words lex civilis and jus civile, that is to say, and law and right civil, promiscuously used for the same thing, even in the most learned authors; which nevertheless ought not to be so. For right is liberty, namely that liberty which the civil law leaves us: but civil law is an obligation, and takes from us the liberty which the law of nature gave us. Nature gave a right to every man to secure himself by his own strength, and to invade a suspected neighbour by way of prevention: but the civil law takes away that liberty, in all cases where the protection of the law may be safely stayed for. Insomuch as lex and jus are as different as obligation and liberty. Likewise laws and charters are taken promiscuously for the same thing. Yet charters are donations of the sovereign; and not laws, but exemptions from law. The phrase of a law is jubeo, injungo; I command and enjoin: the phrase of a charter is dedi, concessi; I have given, I have granted: but what is given or granted to a man is not forced upon him by a law. A law may be made to bind all the subjects of a Commonwealth: a liberty or charter is only to one man or some one part of the people. For to say all the people of a Commonwealth have liberty in any case whatsoever is to say that, in such case, there hath been no law made; or else, having been made, is now abrogated.

**CHAPTER XXVII, OF CRIMES, EXCUSES, AND EXTENUATIONS**

A sin is not only a transgression of a law, but also any contempt of the legislator. For such contempt is a breach of all his laws at once, and therefore may consist, not only in the commission of a fact, or in the speaking of words by the laws forbidden, or in the omission of what the law commandeth, but also in the intention or purpose to transgress. For the purpose to break the law is some degree of contempt of him to whom it belonged to see it executed. To be delighted in the imagination only of being possessed of another man's goods, servants, or wife, without any intention to take them from him by force or fraud, is no breach of the law, that saith, "Thou shalt not covet": nor is the pleasure a man may have in imagining or dreaming of the death of him from whose life he expecteth nothing but damage and displeasure, a sin; but the resolving to put some act in execution that tendeth thereto. For to be pleased in the fiction of that which would please a man if it were real is a passion so adherent to the nature both of man and every other living creature, as to make it a sin were to make sin of being a man. Th consideration of this has made me think them too severe, both to themselves and others, that maintain that the first motions of the mind, though checked with the fear of God, be sins. But I confess it is safer to err on that hand than on the other. A crime is a sin consisting in the committing by deed or word of that which the law forbiddeth, or the omission of what it hath commanded. So that every crime is a sin; but not every sin a crime. To intend to steal or kill is a sin, though it never appear in word or fact: for God that seeth the thought of man can lay it to his charge: but till it appear by something done, or said, by which the intention may be argued by a human judge, it hath not the name of crime: which distinction the Greeks observed in the word amartema and egklema or aitia; whereof the former (which is translated sin) signifieth any swerving from the law whatsoever; but the two latter (which are translated crime) signify that sin only whereof one man may accuse another. But of intentions, which never appear by any outward act, there is no place for human accusation. In like manner the Latins by peccatum, which is sin, signify all manner of deviation from the law; but by crimen (which word they derive from cerno, which signifies to perceive) they mean only such sins as may be made appear before a judge, and therefore are not mere intentions. From this relation of sin to the law, and of crime to the civil law, may be inferred, first, that where law ceaseth, sin ceaseth. But because the law of nature is eternal, violation of covenants, ingratitude, arrogance, and all facts contrary to any moral virtue can never cease to be sin. Secondly, that the civil law ceasing, crimes cease: for there being no other law remaining but that of nature, there is no place for accusation; every man being his own judge, and accused only by his own conscience, and cleared by the uprightness of his own intention. When therefore his intention is right, his fact is no sin; if otherwise, his fact is sin, but not crime. Thirdly, that when the sovereign power ceaseth, crime also ceaseth: for where there is no such power, there is no protection to be had from the law; and therefore every one may protect himself by his own power: for no man in the institution of sovereign power can be supposed to give away the right of preserving his own body, for the safety whereof all sovereignty was ordained. But this is to be understood only of those that have not themselves contributed to the taking away of the power that protected them: for that was a crime from the beginning. The source of every crime is some defect of the understanding, or some error in reasoning, or some sudden force of the passions. Defect in the understanding is ignorance; in reasoning, erroneous opinion. Again, ignorance is of three sorts; of the law, and of the sovereign, and of the penalty. Ignorance of the law of nature excuseth no man, because every man that hath attained to the use of reason is supposed to know he ought not to do to another what he would not have done to himself. Therefore into what place soever a man shall come, if he do anything contrary to that law, it is a crime. If a man come from the Indies hither, and persuade men here to receive a new religion, or teach them anything that tendeth to disobedience of the laws of this country, though he be never so well persuaded of the truth of what he teacheth, he commits a crime, and may be justly punished for the same, not only because his doctrine is false, but also because he does that which he would not approve in another; namely, that coming from hence, he should endeavour to alter the religion there. But ignorance of the civil law shall excuse a man in a strange country till it be declared to him, because till then no civil law is binding. In the like manner, if the civil law of a man's own country be not so sufficiently declared as he may know it if he will; nor the action against the law of nature; the ignorance is a good excuse: in other cases ignorance of the civil law excuseth not. Ignorance of the sovereign power the place of a man's ordinary residence excuseth him not, because he ought to take notice of the power by which he hath been protected there. Ignorance of the penalty, where the law is declared, excuseth no man: for in breaking the law, which without a fear of penalty to follow were not a law, but vain words, he undergoeth the penalty, though he know not what it is; because whosoever voluntarily doth any action, accepteth all the known consequences of it; but punishment is a known consequence of the violation of the laws in every Commonwealth; which punishment, if it be determined already by the law, he is subject to that; if not, then is he subject to arbitrary punishment. For it is reason that he which does injury, without other limitation than that of his own will, should suffer punishment without other limitation than that of his will whose law is thereby violated. But when a penalty is either annexed to the crime in the law itself, or hath been usually inflicted in the like cases, there the delinquent is excused from a greater penalty. For the punishment foreknown, if not great enough to deter men from the action, is an invitement to it: because when men compare the benefit of their injustice with the harm of their punishment, by necessity of nature they choose that which appeareth best for themselves: and therefore when they are punished more than the law had formerly determined, or more than others were punished for the same crime, it is the law that tempted and deceiveth them. No law made after a fact done can make it a crime: because if the fact be against the law of nature, the law was before the fact; and a positive law cannot be taken notice of before it be made, and therefore cannot be obligatory. But when the law that forbiddeth a fact is made before the fact be done, yet he that doth the fact is liable to the penalty ordained after, in case no lesser penalty were made known before, neither by writing nor by example, for the reason immediately before alleged. From defect in reasoning (that is to say, from error), men are prone to violate the laws three ways. First, by presumption of false principles: as when men, from having observed how in all places and in all ages unjust actions have been authorised by the force and victories of those who have committed them; and that, potent men breaking through the cobweb laws of their country, the weaker sort and those that have failed in their enterprises have been esteemed the only criminals; have thereupon taken for principles and grounds of their reasoning that justice is but a vain word: that whatsoever a man can get by his own industry and hazard is his own: that the practice of all nations cannot be unjust: that examples of former times are good arguments of doing the like again; and many more of that kind: which being granted, no act in itself can be a crime, but must be made so, not by the law, but by the success of them that commit it; and the same fact be virtuous or vicious fortune pleaseth; so that what Marius makes a crime, Sylla shall make meritorious, and Caesar (the same laws standing) turn again into a crime, to the perpetual disturbance of the peace of the Commonwealth. Secondly, by false teachers that either misinterpret the law of nature, making it thereby repugnant to the law civil, or by teaching for laws such doctrines of their own, or traditions of former times, as are inconsistent with the duty of a subject. Thirdly, by erroneous inferences from true principles; which happens commonly to men that are hasty and precipitate in concluding and resolving what to do; such as are they that have both a great opinion of their own understanding and believe that things of this nature require not time and study, but only common experience and a good natural wit, whereof no man thinks himself unprovided: whereas the knowledge of right and wrong, which is no less difficult, there is no man will pretend to without great and long study. And of those defects in reasoning, there is none that can excuse, though some of them may extenuate, a crime in any man that pretendeth to the administration of his own private business; much less in them that undertake a public charge, because they pretend to the reason upon the want whereof they would ground their excuse. Of the passions that most frequently are the causes of crime, one is vainglory, or a foolish overrating of their own worth; as if difference of worth were an effect of their wit, or riches, or blood, or some other natural quality, not depending on the will of those that have the sovereign authority. From whence proceedeth a presumption that the punishments ordained by the laws, and extended generally to all subjects, ought not to be inflicted on them with the same rigor they are inflicted on poor, obscure, and simple men, comprehended under the name of the vulgar. Therefore it happeneth commonly that such as value themselves by the greatness of their wealth adventure on crimes, upon hope of escaping punishment by corrupting public justice, or obtaining pardon by money or other rewards. And that such as have multitude of potent kindred, and popular men that have gained reputation amongst the multitude, take courage to violate the laws from a hope of oppressing the power to whom it belonged to put them in execution. And that such as have a great and false opinion of their own wisdom take upon them to reprehend the actions and call in question the authority of them that govern, and so to unsettle the laws with their public discourse, as that nothing shall be a crime but what their own designs require should be so. It happeneth also to the same men to be prone to all such crimes as consist in craft, and in deceiving of their neighbours; because they think their designs are too subtle to be perceived. These I say are effects of a false presumption of their own wisdom. For of them that are the first movers in the disturbance of Commonwealth (which can never happen without a civil war), very few are left alive long enough to see their new designs established: so that the benefit of their crimes redoundeth to posterity and such as would least have wished it: which argues they were not so wise as they thought they were. And those that deceive upon hope of not being observed do commonly deceive themselves, the darkness in which they believe they lie hidden being nothing else but their own blindness, and are no wiser than children that think all hid by hiding their own eyes. And generally all vainglorious men, unless they be withal timorous, are subject to anger; as being more prone than others to interpret for contempt the ordinary liberty of conversation: and there are few crimes that may not be produced by anger. As for the passions, of hate, lust, ambition, and covetousness, what crimes they are apt to produce is so obvious to every man's experience and understanding as there needeth nothing to be said of them, saving that they are infirmities, so annexed to the nature, both of man and all other living creatures, as that their effects cannot be hindered but by extraordinary use of reason, or a constant severity in punishing them. For in those things men hate, they find a continual and unavoidable molestation; whereby either a man's patience must be everlasting, or he must be eased by removing the power of that whith molesteth him: the former is difficult; the latter is many times impossible without some violation of the law. Ambition and covetousness are passions also that are perpetually incumbent and pressing; whereas reason is not perpetually present to resist them: and therefore whensoever the hope of impunity appears, their effects proceed. And for lust, what it wants in the lasting, it hath in the vehemence, which sufficeth to weigh down the apprehension of all easy or uncertain punishments. Of all passions, that which inclineth men least to break the laws is fear. Nay, excepting some generous natures, it is the only thing (when there is appearance of profit or pleasure by breaking the laws) that makes men keep them. And yet in many cases a crime may be committed through fear. For not every fear justifies the action it produceth, but the fear only of corporeal hurt, which we call bodily fear, and from which a man cannot see how to be delivered but by the action. A man is assaulted, fears present death, from which he sees not how to escape but by wounding him that assaulteth him; if he wound him to death, this is no crime, because no man is supposed, at the making of a Commonwealth to have abandoned the defence of his life or limbs, where the law cannot arrive time enough to his assistance. But to kill a man because from his actions or his threatenings I may argue he will kill me when he can (seeing I have time and means to demand protection from the sovereign power) is a crime. Again, a man receives words of disgrace, or some little injuries, for which they that made the laws had assigned no punishment, nor thought it worthy of a man that hath the use of reason to take notice of, and is afraid unless he revenge it he shall fall into contempt, and consequently be obnoxious to the like injuries from others; and to avoid this, breaks the law, and protects himself for the future by the terror of his private revenge. This is a crime: for the hurt is not corporeal, but fantastical, and (though, in this corner of the world, made sensible by a custom not many years since begun, amongst young and vain men) so light as a gallant man, and one that is assured of his own courage, cannot take notice of. Also a man may stand in fear of spirits, either through his own superstition or through too much credit given to other men that tell him of strange dreams and visions; and thereby be made believe they will hurt him for doing or omitting diverse things which, nevertheless, to do or omit is contrary to the laws; and that which is so done, or omitted, is not to be excused by this fear, but is a crime. For, as I have shown before in the second Chapter, dreams be naturally but the fancies remaining in sleep, after the impressions our senses had formerly received waking; and, when men are by any accident unassured they have slept, seem to be real visions; and therefore he that presumes to break the law upon his own or another's dream or pretended vision, or upon other fancy of the power of invisible spirits than is permitted by the Commonwealth, leaveth the law of nature, which is a certain offence, and followeth the imagery of his own or another private man's brain, which he can never know whether it signifieth anything or nothing, nor whether he that tells his dream say true or lie; which if every private man should have leave to do (as they must, by the law of nature, if any one have it), there could no law be made to hold, and so all Commonwealth would be dissolved. From these different sources of crimes, it appears already that all crimes are not, as the Stoics of old time maintained, of the same alloy. There is place, not only for excuse, by which that which seemed a crime is proved to be none at all; but also for extenuation, by which the crime, that seemed great, is made less. For though all crimes do equally deserve the name of injustice, as all deviation from a straight line is equally crookedness, which the Stoics rightly observed; yet it does not follow that all crimes are equally unjust, no more than that all crooked lines are equally crooked; which the Stoics, not observing, held it as great a crime to kill a hen, against the law, as to kill one's father. That which totally excuseth a fact, and takes away from it the nature of a crime, can be none but that which, at the same time, taketh away the obligation of the law. For the fact committed once against the law, if he that committed it be obliged to the law, can be no other than a crime. The want of means to know the law totally excuseth: for the law whereof a man has no means to inform himself is not obligatory. But the want of diligence to enquire shall not be considered as a want of means; nor shall any man that pretendeth to reason enough for the government of his own affairs be supposed to want means to know the laws of nature; because they are known by the reason he pretends to: only children and madmen are excused from offences against the law natural. Where a man is captive, or in the power of the enemy (and he is then in the power of the enemy when his person, or his means of living, is so), if it be without his own fault, the obligation of the law ceaseth; because he must obey the enemy, or die, and consequently such obedience is no crime: for no man is obliged (when the protection of the law faileth) not to protect himself by the best means he can. If a man by the terror of present death be compelled to do a fact against the law, he is totally excused; because no law can oblige a man to abandon his own preservation. And supposing such a law were obligatory, yet a man would reason thus: "If I do it not, I die presently; if I do it, I die afterwards; therefore by doing it, there is time of life gained." Nature therefore compels him to the fact. When a man is destitute of food or other thing necessary for his life, and cannot preserve himself any other way but by some fact against the law; as if in a great famine he take the food by force, or stealth, which he cannot obtain for money, nor charity; or in defence of his life, snatch away another man's sword; he is totally excused for the reason next before alleged. Again, facts done against the law, by the authority of another, are by that authority excused against the author, because no man ought to accuse his own fact in another that is but his instrument: but it is not excused against a third person thereby injured, because in the violation of the law both the author and actor are criminals. From hence it followeth that when that man or assembly that hath the sovereign power commandeth a man to do that which is contrary to a former law, the doing of it is totally excused: for he ought not to condemn it himself, because he is the author; and what cannot justly be condemned by the sovereign cannot justly be punished by any other. Besides, when the sovereign commandeth anything to be done against his own former law, the command, as to that particular fact, is an abrogation of the law. If that man or assembly that hath the sovereign power disclaim any right essential to the sovereignty, whereby there accrueth to the subject any liberty inconsistent with the sovereign power; that is to say, with the very being of a Commonwealth; if the subject shall refuse to obey the command in anything, contrary to the liberty granted, this is nevertheless a sin, and contrary to the duty of the subject: for he to take notice of what is inconsistent with the sovereignty, because it was erected by his own consent and for his own defence, and that such liberty as is inconsistent with it was granted through ignorance of the evil consequence thereof. But if he not only disobey, but also resist a public minister in the execution of it, then it is a crime, because he might have been righted, without any breach of the peace, upon complaint. The degrees of crime are taken on diverse scales, and measured, first, by the malignity of the source, or cause: secondly, by the contagion of the example: thirdly, by the mischief of the effect: and fourthly, by the concurrence of times, places, and persons. The same fact done against the law, if it proceed from presumption of strength, riches, or friends to resist those that are to execute the law, is a greater crime than if it proceed from hope of not being discovered, or of escape by flight: for presumption of impunity by force is a root from whence springeth, at all times, and upon all temptations, a contempt of all laws; whereas in the latter case the apprehension of danger that makes a man fly renders him more obedient for the future. A crime which know to be so is greater than the same crime proceeding from a false persuasion that it is lawful: for he that committeth it against his own conscience presumeth on his force, or other power, which encourages him to commit the same again, but he that doth it by error, after the error shown him, is conformable to the law. He whose error proceeds from the authority of a teacher, or an interpreter of the law publicly authorised, is not so faulty as he whose error proceedeth from a peremptory pursuit of his own principles and reasoning: for what is taught by one that teacheth by public authority, the Commonwealth teacheth, and hath a resemblance of law, till the same authority controlleth it; and in all crimes that contain not in them a denial of the sovereign power, nor are against an evident law, excuseth totally; whereas he that groundeth his actions on his private judgement ought, according to the rectitude or error thereof, to stand or fall. The same fact, if it have been constantly punished in other men, is a greater crime than if there have been many precedent examples of impunity. For those examples are so many hopes of impunity, given by the sovereign himself: and because he which furnishes a man with such a hope and presumption of mercy, as encourageth him to offend, hath his part in the offence, he cannot reasonably charge the offender with the whole. A crime arising from a sudden passion is not so great as when the same ariseth from long meditation: for in the former case there is a place for extenuation in the common infirmity of human nature; but he that doth it with premeditation has used circumspection, and cast his eye on the law, on the punishment, and on the consequence thereof to human society; all which in committing the crime he hath contemned and postponed to his own appetite. But there is no suddenness of passion sufficient for a total excuse: for all the time between the first knowing of the law, and the commission of the fact, shall be taken for a time of deliberation, because he ought, by meditation of the law, to rectify the irregularity of his passions. Where the law is publicly, and with assiduity, before all the people read and interpreted, a fact done against it is a greater crime than where men are left without such instruction to enquire of it with difficulty, uncertainty, and interruption of their callings, and be informed by private men: for in this case, part of the fault is discharged upon common infirmity; but in the former there is apparent negligence, which is not without some contempt of the sovereign power. Those facts which the law expressly condemneth, but the lawmaker by other manifest signs of his will tacitly approveth, are less crimes than the same facts condemned both by the law and lawmaker. For seeing the will of the lawmaker is a law, there appear in this case two contradictory laws; which would totally excuse, if men were bound to take notice of the sovereigns approbation, by other arguments than are expressed by his command. But because there are punishments consequent, not only to the transgression of his law, but also to the observing of it he is in part a cause of the transgression, and therefore cannot reasonably impute the whole crime to the delinquent. For example, the law condemneth duels; the punishment is made capital: on the contrary part, he that refuseth duel is subject to contempt and scorn, without remedy; and sometimes by the sovereign himself thought unworthy to have any charge or preferment in war: if thereupon he accept duel, considering all men lawfully endeavour to obtain the good opinion of them that have the sovereign power, he ought not in reason to be rigorously punished, seeing part of the fault may be discharged on the punisher: which I say, not as wishing liberty of private revenges, or any other kind of disobedience, but a care in governors not to countenance anything obliquely which directly they forbid. The examples of princes, to those that see them, are, and ever have been, more potent to govern their actions than the laws themselves. And though it be our duty to do, not what they do, but what they say; yet will that duty never be performed till it please God to give men an extraordinary and supernatural grace to follow that precept. Again, if we compare crimes by the mischief of their effects; first, the same fact when it redounds to the damage of many is greater than when it redounds to the hurt of few. And therefore when a fact hurteth, not only in the present, but also by example in the future, it is a greater crime than if it hurt only in the present: for the former is a fertile crime, and multiplies to the hurt of many; the latter is barren. To maintain doctrines contrary to the religion established in the Commonwealth is a greater fault in an authorised preacher than in a private person: so also is it to live profanely, incontinently, or do any irreligious act whatsoever. Likewise in a professor of the law, to maintain any point, or do any act, that tendeth to the weakening of the sovereign power is a greater crime than in another man: also in a man that hath such reputation for wisdom as that his counsels are followed, or his actions imitated by many, his fact against the law is a greater crime than the same fact in another: for such men not only commit crime, but teach it for law to all other men. And generally all crimes are the greater by the scandal they give; that is to say, by becoming stumbling-blocks to the weak, that look not so much upon the way they go in, as upon the light that other men carry before them. Also facts of hostility against the present state of the Commonwealth are greater crimes than the same acts done to private men: for the damage extends itself to all: such are the betraying of the strengths or revealing of the secrets of the Commonwealth to an enemy; also all attempts upon the representative of the Commonwealth, be it a monarch or an assembly; and all endeavours by word or deed to diminish the authority of the same, either in the present time or in succession: which crimes the Latins understand by crimina laesae majestatis, and consist in design, or act, contrary to a fundamental law. Likewise those crimes which render judgements of no effect are greater crimes than injuries done to one or a few persons; as to receive money to give false judgement or testimony is a greater crime than otherwise to deceive a man of the like or a greater sum; because not only he has wrong, that falls by such judgements, but all judgements are rendered useless, and occasion ministered to force and private revenges. Also robbery and depeculation of the public treasury or revenues is a greater crime than the robbing or defrauding of a private man, because to rob the public is to rob many at once; also the counterfeit usurpation of public ministry, the counterfeiting of public seals, or public coin, than counterfeiting of a private man's person or his seal, because the fraud thereof extendeth to the damage of many. Of facts against the law done to private men, the greater crime is that where the damage, in the common opinion of men, is most sensible. And therefore: To kill against the law is a greater crime than any other injury, life preserved. And to kill with torment, greater than simply to kill. And mutilation of a limb, greater than the spoiling a man of his goods. And the spoiling a man of his goods by terror of death or wounds, than by clandestine surreption. And by clandestine surreption, than by consent fraudulently obtained. And the violation of chastity by force, greater than by flattery. And of a woman married, than of a woman not married. For all these things are commonly so valued; though some men are more, and some less, sensible of the same offence. But the law regardeth not the particular, but the general inclination of mankind. And there-fore the offence men take from contumely, in words or gesture, when they produce no other harm than the present grief of him that is reproached, hath been neglected in the laws of the Greeks, Romans, and other both ancient and modern Commonwealths; supposing the true cause of such grief to consist, not in the contumely (which takes no hold upon men conscious of their own virtue), but in the pusillanimity of him that is offended by it. Also a crime against a private man is much aggravated by the person, time, and place. For to kill one's parent is a greater crime than to kill another: for the parent ought to have the honour of a sovereign (though he have surrendered his power to the civil law), because he had it originally by nature. And to rob a poor man is a greater crime than to rob a rich man, because it is to the poor a more sensible damage. And a crime commit-ted in the time or place appointed for devotion is greater than if committed at another time or place: for it pro-ceeds from a greater contempt of the law. Many other cases of aggravation and extenuation might be added; but by these I have set down, it is obvious to every man to take the altitude of any other crime proposed. Last-ly, because in almost all crimes there is an injury done, not only to some private men, but also to the Com-monwealth, the same crime, when the accusation is in the name of the Commonwealth, is called public crime; and when in the name of a private man, a private crime; and the pleas according thereupon called public, judi-cia publica, pleas of the crown; or private pleas. As in an accusation of murder, if the accuser be a private man, the plea is a private plea; if the accuser be the sovereign, the plea is a public plea.

## CHAPTER XXVIII, OF PUNISHMENTS AND REWARDS

A punishment is an evil inflicted by public authority on him that hath done or omitted that which is judged by the same authority to be a transgression of the law, to the end that the will of men may thereby the better be disposed to obedience. Before I infer anything from this definition, there is a question to be answered of much importance; which is, by what door the right or authority of punishing, in any case, came in. For by that which has been said before, no man is supposed bound by covenant not to resist violence; and consequently it cannot be intended that he gave any right to another to lay violent hands upon his person. In the making of a Com-monwealth every man giveth away the right of defending another, but not of defending himself. Also he obligeth himself to assist him that hath the sovereignty in the punishing of another, but of himself not. But to covenant to assist the sovereign in doing hurt to another, unless he that so covenanteth have a right to do it himself, is not to give him a right to punish. It is manifest therefore that the right which the Commonwealth (that is, he or they that represent it) hath to punish is not grounded on any concession or gift of the subjects. But I have also shown formerly that before the institution of Commonwealth, every man had a right to every-thing, and to do whatsoever he thought necessary to his own preservation; subduing, hurting, or killing any man in order thereunto. And this is the foundation of that right of punishing which is exercised in every Com-monwealth. For the subjects did not give the sovereign that right; but only, in laying down theirs, strengthened him to use his own as he should think fit for the preservation of them all: so that it was not given, but left to him, and to him only; and, excepting the limits set him by natural law, as entire as in the condition of mere na-ture, and of war of every one against his neighbour. From the definition of punishment, I infer, first, that nei-ther private revenges nor injuries of private men can properly be styled punishment, because they proceed not from public authority. Secondly, that to be neglected and unpreferred by the public favour is not a punish-ment, because no new evil is thereby on any man inflicted; he is only left in the estate he was in before. Third-ly, that the evil inflicted by public authority, without precedent public condemnation, is not to be styled by the name of punishment, but of a hostile act, because the fact for which a man is punished ought first to be judged by public authority to be a transgression of the law. Fourthly, that the evil inflicted by usurped power, and judges without authority from the sovereign, is not punishment, but an act of hostility, because the acts of power usurped have not for author the person condemned, and therefore are not acts of public authority. Fifthly, that all evil which is inflicted without intention or possibility of disposing the delinquent or, by his example, other men to obey the laws is not punishment, but an act of hostility, because without such an end no hurt done is contained under that name. Sixthly, whereas to certain actions there be annexed by nature diverse hurtful consequences; as when a man in assaulting another is himself slain or wounded; or when he falleth into sickness by the doing of some unlawful act; such hurt, though in respect of God, who is the author of nature, it may be said to be inflicted, and therefore a punishment divine; yet it is not contained in the name of punishment in respect of men, because it is not inflicted by the authority of man. Seventhly, if the harm inflicted be less than the benefit of contentment that naturally followeth the crime committed, that harm is not within the definition and is rather the price or redemption than the punishment of a crime: because it is of the nature of punishment to have for end the disposing of men to obey the law; which end (if it be less than the benefit of the transgression) it attaineth not, but worketh a contrary effect. Eighthly, if a punishment be determined and prescribed in the law itself, and after the crime committed there be a greater punishment inflicted, the excess is not punishment, but an act of hostility. For seeing the aim of punishment is not a revenge, but terror; and the terror of a great punishment unknown is taken away by the declaration of a less, the unexpected addition is no part of the punishment. But where there is no punishment at all determined by the law, there whatsoever is inflicted hath the nature of punishment. For he that goes about the violation of a law, wherein no penalty is determined, expecteth an indeterminate, that is to say, an arbitrary punishment. Ninthly, harm inflicted for a fact done before there was a law that forbade it is not punishment, but an act of hostility: for before the law, there is no transgression of the law: but punishment supposeth a fact judged to have been a transgression of the law; therefore harm inflicted before the law made is not punishment, but an act of hostility. Tenthly, hurt inflicted on the representative of the Commonwealth is not punishment, but an act of hostility: because it is of the nature of punishment to be inflicted by public authority, which is the authority only of the representative itself. Lastly, harm inflicted upon one that is a declared enemy falls not under the name of punishment: because seeing they were either never subject to the law, and therefore cannot transgress it; or having been subject to it, and professing to be no longer so, by consequence deny they can transgress it, all the harms that can be done them must be taken as acts of hostility. But in declared hostility all infliction of evil is lawful. From whence it followeth that if a subject shall by fact or word wittingly and deliberately deny the authority of the representative of the Commonwealth (whatsoever penalty hath been formerly ordained for treason), he may lawfully be made to suffer whatsoever the representative will: for in denying subjection, he denies such punishment as by the law hath been ordained, and therefore suffers as an enemy of the Commonwealth; that is, according to the will of the representative. For the punishments set down in the law are to subjects, not to enemies; such as are they that, having been by their own act subjects, deliberately revolting, deny the sovereign power. The first and most general distribution of punishments is into divine and human. Of the former I shall have occasion to speak in a more convenient place hereafter. Human are those punishments that be inflicted by the commandment of man; and are either corporal, or pecuniary, or ignominy, or imprisonment, or exile, or mixed of these. Corporal punishment is that which is inflicted on the body directly, and according to the intention of him that inflicteth it: such as are stripes, or wounds, or deprivation of such pleasures of the body as were before lawfully enjoyed. And of these, some be capital, some less than capital. Capital is the infliction of death; and that either simply or with torment. Less than capital are stripes, wounds, chains, and any other corporal pain not in its own nature mortal. For if upon the infliction of a punishment death follow, not in the intention of the inflicter, the punishment is not to be esteemed capital, though the harm prove mortal by an accident not to be foreseen; in which case death is not inflicted, but hastened. Pecuniary punishment is that which consisteth not only in the deprivation of a sum of money, but also of lands, or any other goods which are usually bought and sold for money. And in case the law that ordaineth such a punishment be made with design to gather money from such as shall transgress the same, it is not properly a punishment, but the price of privilege and exemption from the law, which doth not absolutely forbid the fact but only to those that are not able to pay the money: except where the law is natural, or part of religion; for in that case it is not an exemption from the law, but a transgression of it. As where a law exacteth a pecuniary mulct of them that take the name of God in vain, the payment of the mulct is not the price of a dispensation to swear, but the punishment of the transgression of a law indispensable. In like manner if the law impose a sum of money to be paid to him that has been injured, this is but a satisfaction for the hurt done him, and extinguisheth the accusation of the party injured, not the crime of the offender. Ignominy is the infliction of such evil as is made dishonourable; or the deprivation of such good as is made honourable by the Commonwealth. For there be some things honourable by nature; as the effects of courage, magnanimity, strength, wisdom, and other abilities of body and mind: others made honourable by the Commonwealth; as badges, titles, offices, or any other singular mark of the sovereigns favour. The former, though they may fail by nature or accident, cannot be taken away by a law; and therefore the loss of them is not punishment. But the latter may be taken away by the public authority that made them honourable, and are properly punishments: such are, degrading men condemned, of their badges, titles, and offices; or declaring them incapable of the like in time to come. Imprisonment is when a man is by public authority deprived of liberty, and may happen from two diverse ends; whereof one is the safe custody of a man accused; the other is the inflicting of pain on a man condemned. The former is not punishment, because no man is supposed to be punished before he be judicially heard and declared guilty. And therefore whatsoever hurt a man is made to suffer by bonds or restraint before his cause be heard, over and above that which is necessary to assure his custody, is against the law of nature. But the latter is punishment because evil, and inflicted by public authority for somewhat that has by the same authority been judged a transgression of the law. Under this word imprisonment, I comprehend all restraint of motion caused by an external obstacle, be it a house, which is called by the general name of a prison; or an island, as when men are said to be confined to it; or a place where men are set to work, as in old time men have been condemned to quarries, and in these times to galleys; or be it a chain or any other such impediment. Exile (banishment) is when a man is for a crime condemned to depart out of the dominion of the Commonwealth, or out of a certain part thereof, and during a prefixed time, or for ever, not to return into it; and seemeth not in its own nature, without other circumstances, to be a punishment, but rather an escape, or a public commandment to avoid punishment by flight. And Cicero says there was never any such punishment ordained in the city of Rome; but calls it a refuge of men in danger. For if a man banished be nevertheless permitted to enjoy his goods, and the revenue of his lands, the mere change of air is no punishment; nor does it tend to that benefit of the Commonwealth for which all punishments are ordained, that is to say, to the forming of men's wills to the observation of the law; but many times to the damage of the Commonwealth. For a banished man is a lawful enemy of the Commonwealth that banished him, as being no more a member of the same. But if he be withal deprived of his lands, or goods, then the punishment lieth not in the exile, but is to be reckoned amongst punishments pecuniary. All punishments of innocent subjects, be they great or little, are against the law of nature: for punishment is only for transgression of the law, and therefore there can be no punishment of the innocent. It is therefore a violation, first, of that law of nature which forbiddeth all men, in their revenges, to look at anything but some future good: for there can arrive no good to the Commonwealth by punishing the innocent. Secondly, of that which forbiddeth ingratitude: for seeing all sovereign power is originally given by the consent of every one of the subjects, to the end they should as long as they are obedient be protected thereby, the punishment of the innocent is a rendering of evil for good. And thirdly, of the law that commandeth equity; that is to say, an equal distribution of justice, which in punishing the innocent is not observed. But the infliction of what evil soever on an innocent man that is not a subject, if it be for the benefit of the Commonwealth, and without violation of any former covenant, is no breach of the law of nature. For all men that are not subjects are either enemies, or else they have ceased from being so by some precedent covenants. But against enemies, whom the Commonwealth judgeth capable to do them hurt, it is lawful by the original right of nature to make war; wherein the sword judgeth not, nor doth the victor make distinction of nocent and innocent as to the time past, nor has other respect of mercy than as it conduceth to the good of his own people. And upon this ground it is that also in subjects who deliberately deny the authority of the Commonwealth established, the vengeance is lawfully extended, not only to the fathers, but also to the third and fourth generation not yet in being, and consequently innocent of the fact for which they are afflicted: because the nature of this offence consisteth in the renouncing of subjection, which is a relapse into the condition of war commonly called rebellion; and they that so offend, suffer not as subjects, but as enemies. For rebellion is but war renewed. Reward is either of gift or by contract. When by contract, it is called salary and wages; which is benefit due for service performed or promised. When of gift, it is benefit proceeding from the grace of them that bestow it, to encourage or enable men to do them service. And therefore when the sovereign of a Commonwealth appointeth a salary to any public office, he that receiveth it is bound in justice to perform his office; otherwise, he is bound only in honour to acknowledgement and an endeavour of requital. For though men have no lawful remedy when they be commanded to quit their private business to serve the public, without reward or salary, yet they are not bound thereto by the law of nature, nor by the institution of the Commonwealth, unless the service cannot otherwise be done; because it is supposed the sovereign may make use of all their means, insomuch as the most common soldier may demand the wages of his warfare as a debt. The benefits which a sovereign bestoweth on a subject, for fear of some power and ability he hath to do hurt to the Commonwealth, are not properly rewards: for they are not salaries, because there is in this case no contract supposed, every man being obliged already not to do the Commonwealth disservice: nor are they graces, because they be extorted by fear, which ought

126

not to be incident to the sovereign power: but are rather sacrifices, which the sovereign, considered in his natural person, and not in the person of the Commonwealth, makes for the appeasing the discontent of him he thinks more potent than himself; and encourage not to obedience, but, on the contrary, to the continuance and increasing of further extortion. And whereas some salaries are certain, and proceed from the public treasury; and others uncertain and casual, proceeding from the execution of the office for which the salary is ordained; the latter is in some cases hurtful to the Commonwealth, as in the case of judicature. For where the benefit of the judges, and ministers of a court of justice, ariseth for the multitude of causes that are brought to their cognizance, there must needs follow two inconveniences: one is the nourishing of suits; for the more suits, the greater benefit: and another that depends on that, which is contention which is about jurisdiction; each court drawing to itself as many causes as it can. But in offices of execution there are not those inconveniences, because their employment cannot be increased by any endeavour of their own. And thus much shall suffice for the nature of punishment and reward; which are, as it were, the nerves and tendons that move the limbs and joints of a Commonwealth. Hitherto I have set forth the nature of man, whose pride and other passions have compelled him to submit himself to government; together with the great power of his governor, whom I compared to LEVIATHAN, taking that comparison out of the two last verses of the one-and-fortieth of Job; where God, having set forth the great power of Leviathan, calleth him king of the proud. "There is nothing," saith he, "on earth to be compared with him. He is made so as not to be afraid. He seeth every high thing below him; and is king of all the children of pride." But because he is mortal, and subject to decay, as all other earthly creatures are; and because there is that in heaven, though not on earth, that he should stand in fear of, and whose laws he ought to obey; I shall in the next following chapters speak of his diseases and the causes of his mortality, and of what laws of nature he is bound to obey.

**CHAPTER XXIX, OF THOSE THINGS THAT WEAKEN OR TEND TO THE DISSOLUTION OF A COMMONWEALTH**

THOUGH nothing can be immortal which mortals make; yet, if men had the use of reason they pretend to, their Commonwealths might be secured, at least, from perishing by internal diseases. For by the nature of their institution, they are designed to live as long as mankind, or as the laws of nature, or as justice itself, which gives them life. Therefore when they come to be dissolved, not by external violence, but intestine disorder, the fault is not in men as they are the matter, but as they are the makers and orderers of them. For men, as they become at last weary of irregular jostling and hewing one another, and desire with all their hearts to conform themselves into one firm and lasting edifice; so for want both of the art of making fit laws to square their actions by, and also of humility and patience to suffer the rude and cumbersome points of their present greatness to be taken off, they cannot without the help of a very able architect be compiled into any other than a crazy building, such as, hardly lasting out their own time, must assuredly fall upon the heads of their posterity. Amongst the infirmities therefore of a Commonwealth, I will reckon in the first place those that arise from an imperfect institution, and resemble the diseases of a natural body, which proceed from a defectuous procreation. Of which this is one: that a man to obtain a kingdom is sometimes content with less power than to the peace and defence of the Commonwealth is necessarily required. From whence it cometh to pass that when the exercise of the power laid by is for the public safety to be resumed, it hath the resemblance of an unjust act, which disposeth great numbers of men, when occasion is presented, to rebel; in the same manner as the bodies of children gotten by diseased parents are subject either to untimely death, or to purge the ill quality derived from their vicious conception, by breaking out into biles and scabs. And when kings deny themselves some such necessary power, it is not always (though sometimes) out of ignorance of what is necessary to the office they undertake, but many times out of a hope to recover the same again at their pleasure: wherein they reason not well; because such as will hold them to their promises shall be maintained against them by foreign Commonwealths; who in order to the good of their own subjects let slip few occasions to weaken the estate of their neighbours. So was Thomas Becket, Archbishop of Canterbury, supported against Henry the Second by the Pope; the subjection of ecclesiastics to the Commonwealth having been dispensed with by William the Conqueror at his reception, when he took an oath not to infringe the liberty of the Church. And so were the barons, whose power was by William Rufus, to have their help in transferring the succession from his elder brother to himself, increased to a degree inconsistent with the sovereign power, maintained in their rebellion against King John by the French. Nor does this happen in monarchy only. For whereas the style of the ancient

Roman Commonwealth was, "The Senate and People of Rome"; neither senate nor people pretended to the whole power; which first caused the seditions of Tiberius Gracchus, Caius Gracchus, Lucius Saturninus, and others; and afterwards the wars between the senate and the people under Marius and Sylla; and again under Pompey and Caesar to the extinction of their democracy and the setting up of monarchy. The people of Athens bound themselves but from one only action, which was that no man on pain of death should propound the renewing of the war for the island of Salamis; and yet thereby, if Solon had not caused to be given out he was mad, and afterwards in gesture and habit of a madman, and in verse, propounded it to the people that flocked about him, they had had an enemy perpetually in readiness, even at the gates of their city: such damage, or shifts, are all Commonwealths forced to that have their power never so little limited. In the second place, I observe the diseases of a Commonwealth that proceed from the poison of seditious doctrines, whereof one is that every private man is judge of good and evil actions. This is true in the condition of mere nature, where there are no civil laws; and also under civil government in such cases as are not determined by the law. But otherwise, it is manifest that the measure of good and evil actions is the civil law; and the judge the legislator, who is always representative of the Commonwealth. From this false doctrine, men are disposed to debate with themselves and dispute the commands of the Commonwealth, and afterwards to obey or disobey them as in their private judgments they shall think fit; whereby the Commonwealth is distracted and weakened. Another doctrine repugnant to civil society is that whatsoever a man does against his conscience is sin; and it dependeth on the presumption of making himself judge of good and evil. For a man's conscience and his judgement is the same thing; and as the judgement, so also the conscience may be erroneous. Therefore, though he that is subject to no civil law sinneth in all he does against his conscience, because he has no other rule to follow but his own reason, yet it is not so with him that lives in a Commonwealth, because the law is the public conscience by which he hath already undertaken to be guided. Otherwise in such diversity as there is of private consciences, which are but private opinions, the Commonwealth must needs be distracted, and no man dare to obey the sovereign power farther than it shall seem good in his own eyes. It hath been also commonly taught that faith and sanctity are not to be attained by study and reason, but by supernatural inspiration or infusion. Which granted, I see not why any man should render a reason of his faith; or why every Christian should not be also a prophet; or why any man should take the law of his country rather than his own inspiration for the rule of his action. And thus we fall again into the fault of taking upon us to judge of good and evil; or to make judges of it such private men as pretend to be supernaturally inspired, to the dissolution of all civil government. Faith comes by hearing, and hearing by those accidents which guide us into the presence of them that speak to us; which accidents are all contrived by God Almighty, and yet are not supernatural, but only, for the great number of them that concur to every effect, unobservable. Faith and sanctity are indeed not very frequent; but yet they are not miracles, but brought to pass by education, discipline, correction, and other natural ways by which God worketh them in His elect, at such time as He thinketh fit. And these three opinions, pernicious to peace and government, have in this part of the world proceeded chiefly from tongues and pens of unlearned divines; who, joining the words of Holy Scripture together otherwise is agreeable to reason, do what they can to make men think that sanctity and natural reason cannot stand together. A fourth opinion repugnant to the nature of a Commonwealth is this: that he that hath the sovereign power is subject to the civil laws. It is true that sovereigns are all subject to the laws of nature, because such laws be divine and divine and cannot by any man or Commonwealth be abrogated. But to those laws which the sovereign himself, that is, which the Commonwealth, maketh, he is not subject. For to be subject to laws is to be to be subject to the Commonwealth, that is, to the sovereign representative, that is, to himself which is not subjection, but freedom from the laws. Which error, because it setteth the laws above the sovereign, setteth also a judge above him, and a power to punish him; which is to make a new sovereign; and again for the same reason a third to punish the second; and so continually without end, to the confusion and dissolution of the Commonwealth. A fifth doctrine that tendeth to the dissolution of a Commonwealth is that every private man has an absolute propriety in his goods, such as excludeth the right of the sovereign. Every man has indeed a propriety that excludes the right of every other subject: and he has it only from the sovereign power, without the protection whereof every other man should have right to the same. But the right of the sovereign also be excluded, he cannot perform

## CHAPTER XXX, OF THE OFFICE OF THE SOVEREIGN REPRESENTATIVE

THE office of the sovereign, be it a monarch or an assembly, consisteth in the end for which he was trusted with the sovereign power, namely the procuration of the safety of the people, to which he is obliged by the law of nature, and to render an account thereof to God, the Author of that law, and to none but Him. But by safety here is not meant a bare preservation, but also all other contentments of life, which every man by lawful industry, without danger or hurt to the Commonwealth, shall acquire to himself. And this is intended should be done, not by care applied to individuals, further than their protection from injuries when they shall complain; but by a general providence, contained in public instruction, both of doctrine and example; and in the making and executing of good laws to which individual persons may apply their own cases. And because, if the essential rights of sovereignty (specified before in the eighteenth Chapter) be taken away, the Commonwealth is thereby dissolved, and every man returneth into the condition and calamity of a war with every other man, which is the greatest evil that can happen in this life; it is the office of the sovereign to maintain those rights entire, and consequently against his duty, first, to transfer to another or to lay from himself any of them. For he that deserteth the means deserteth the ends; and he deserteth the means that, being the sovereign, acknowledgeth himself subject to the civil laws, and renounceth the power of supreme judicature; or of making war or peace by his own authority; or of judging of the necessities of the Commonwealth; or of levying money and soldiers when and as much as in his own conscience he shall judge necessary; or of making officers and ministers both of war and peace; or of appointing teachers, and examining what doctrines are conformable or contrary to the defence, peace, and good of the people. Secondly, it is against his duty to let the people be ignorant or misinformed of the grounds and reasons of those his essential rights, because thereby men are easy to be seduced and drawn to resist him when the Commonwealth shall require their use and exercise. And the grounds of these rights have the rather need drafter need to be diligently and truly taught, because they cannot be maintained by any civil law or terror of legal punishment. For a civil law that shall forbid rebellion (and such is all resistance to the essential rights of sovereignty) is not, as a civil law, any obligation but by virtue only of the law of nature that forbiddeth the violation of faith; which natural obligation, if men know not, they cannot know the right of any law the sovereign maketh. And for the punishment, they take it but for an act of hostility; which when they think they have strength enough, they will endeavour, by acts of hostility, to avoid. As I have heard some say that justice is but a word, without substance; and that whatsoever a man can by force or art acquire to himself, not only in the condition of war, but also in a Commonwealth, is his own, which I have already shown to be false: so there be also that maintain that there are no grounds, nor principles of reason, to sustain those essential rights which make sovereignty absolute. For if there were, they would have been found out in some place or other; whereas we see there has not hitherto been any Commonwealth where those rights have been acknowledged, or challenged. Wherein they argue as ill, as if the savage people of America should deny there were any grounds or principles of reason so to build a house as to last as long as the materials, because they never yet saw any so well built. Time and industry produce every day new knowledge. And as the art of well building is derived from principles of reason, observed by industrious men that had long studied the nature of materials, and the diverse effects of figure and proportion, long after mankind began, though poorly, to build: so, long time after men have begun to constitute Commonwealths, imperfect and apt to relapse into disorder, there may principles of reason be found out, by industrious meditation, to make their constitution, excepting by external violence, everlasting. And such are those which I have in this discourse set forth: which, whether they come not into the sight of those that have power to make use of them, or be neglected by them or not, concerneth my particular interest, at this day, very little. But supposing that these of mine are not such principles of reason; yet I am sure they are principles from authority of Scripture, as I shall make it appear when I shall come to speak of the kingdom of God, administered by Moses, over the Jews, His peculiar people by covenant. But they say again that though the principles be right, yet common people are not of capacity enough to be made to understand them. I should be glad that the rich and potent subjects of a kingdom, or those that are accounted the most learned, were no less incapable than they. But all men know that the obstructions to this kind of doctrine proceed not so much from the difficulty of the matter, as from the interest of them that are to learn. Potent men digest hardly anything that setteth up a power to bridle their affections; and learned men, anything that discovereth their errors, and thereby their authority: whereas the common people's minds, unless they be tainted with dependence on the potent, or scribbled over with the opinions of their doctors, are like clean paper, fit to receive whatsoever by public authority shall be imprinted in them. Shall whole nations be brought to acquiesce in the great mysteries of Christian religion, which are above reason; and millions of men be made believe that the same body may be in innumerable places at one and the same time, which is against reason; and shall not men be able, by their teaching and preaching, protected by the law, to make that received which is so consonant to reason that any unprejudicated man needs no more to learn it than to hear it? I conclude therefore that in the instruction of the people in the essential rights which are the natural and fundamental laws of sovereignty, there is no difficulty, whilst a sovereign has his power entire, but what proceeds from his own fault, or the fault of those whom he trusteth in the administration of the Commonwealth; and consequently, it is his duty to cause them so to be instructed; and not only his duty, but his benefit also, and security against the danger that may arrive to himself in his natural person from rebellion. And, to descend to particulars, the people are to be taught, first, that they ought not to be in love with any form of government they see in their neighbour nations, more than with their own, nor, whatsoever present prosperity they behold in nations that are otherwise governed than they, to desire change. For the prosperity of a people ruled by an aristocratical or democratical assembly cometh not from aristocracy, nor from democracy, but from the obedience and concord of the subjects: nor do the people flourish in a monarchy because one man has the right to rule them, but because they obey him. Take away in any kind of state the obedience, and consequently the concord of the people, and they shall not only not flourish, but in short time be dissolved. And they that go about by disobedience to do no more than reform the Commonwealth shall find they do thereby destroy it; like the foolish daughters of Peleus, in the fable, which desiring to renew the youth of their decrepit father, did by the counsel of Medea cut him in pieces and boil him, together with strange herbs, but made not of him a new man. This desire of change is like the breach of the first of God's Commandments: for there God says, Non habebis Deos alienos: "Thou shalt not have the Gods of other nations"; and in another place concerning kings, that they are gods. Secondly, they are to be taught that they ought not to be led with admiration of the virtue of any of their fellow subjects, how high soever he stand, nor how conspicuously soever he shine in the Commonwealth; nor of any assembly, except the sovereign assembly, so as to defer to them any obedience or honour appropriate to the sovereign only, whom, in their particular stations, they represent; nor to receive any influence from them, but such as is conveyed by them from the sovereign authority. For that sovereign cannot be imagined to love his people as he ought that is not jealous of them, but suffers them by the flattery of popular men to be seduced from their loyalty, as they have often been, not only secretly, but openly, so as to proclaim marriage with them in facie ecclesiae by preachers, and by publishing the same in the open streets: which may fitly be compared to the violation of the second of the Ten Commandments. Thirdly, in consequence to this, they ought to be informed how great a fault it is to speak evil of the sovereign representative, whether one man or an assembly of men; or to argue and dispute his power, or any way to use his name irreverently, whereby he may be brought into contempt with his people, and their obedience, in which the safety of the Commonwealth consisteth, slackened. Which doctrine the third Commandment by resemblance pointeth to. Fourthly, seeing people cannot be taught this, nor, when it is taught, remember it, nor after one generation past so much as know in whom the sovereign power is placed, without setting apart from their ordinary labour some certain times in which they may attend those that are appointed to instruct them; it is necessary that some such times be determined wherein they may assemble together, and, after prayers and praises given to God, the Sovereign of sovereigns, hear those their duties told them, and the positive laws, such as generally concern them all, read and expounded, and be put in mind of the authority that maketh them laws. To this end had the Jews every seventh day a Sabbath, in which the law was read and expounded; and in the solemnity whereof they were put in mind that their king was God; that having created the world in six days, He rested on the seventh day; and by their resting on it from their labour, that that God was their king, which redeemed them from their servile and painful labour in Egypt, and gave them a time, after they had rejoiced in God, to take joy also in themselves, by lawful recreation. So that the first table of the Commandments is spent all in setting down the sum of God's absolute power; not only as God, but as King by pact, in peculiar, of the Jews; and may therefore give light to those that have sovereign power conferred on them by the consent of men, to see what doctrine they ought to teach their subjects. And because the first instruction of children dependeth on the care of their parents, it is necessary that they should be obedient to them whilst they are under their tuition; and not only so, but that also afterwards, as gratitude requireth, they acknowledge the benefit of their education by external signs of honour. To which end they are to be taught that originally the father of every man was also his sovereign lord, with power over him of life and death; and that the fathers of families, when by instituting a Commonwealth they resigned that absolute power, yet it was never intended they should lose the honour due unto them for their education. For to relinquish such right was not necessary to the institution of sovereign power; nor would there be any reason why any man should desire to have children, or take the care to nourish and instruct them, if they were afterwards to have no other benefit from them than from other men. And this accordeth with the fifth Commandment. Again, every sovereign ought to cause justice to be taught, which, consisting in taking from no man what is his, is as much as to say, to cause men to be taught not to deprive their neighbours, by violence or fraud, of anything which by the sovereign authority is theirs. Of things held in propriety, those that are dearest to a man are his own life and limbs; and in the next degree, in most men, those that concern conjugal affection; and after them riches and means of living. Therefore the people are to be taught to abstain from violence to one another's person by private revenges, from violation of conjugal honour, and from forcible rapine and fraudulent surreption of one another's goods. For which purpose also it is necessary they be shown the evil consequences of false judgment, by corruption either of judges or witnesses, whereby the distinction of propriety is taken away, and justice becomes of no effect: all which things are intimated in the sixth, seventh, eighth, and ninth Commandments. Lastly, they are to be taught that not only the unjust facts, but the designs and intentions to do them, though by accident hindered, are injustice; which consisteth in the pravity of the will, as well as in the irregularity of the act. And this is the intention of the tenth Commandment, and the sum of the second table; which is reduced all to this one commandment of mutual charity, "Thou shalt love thy neighbour as thy self"; as the sum of the first table is reduced to "the love of God"; whom they had then newly received as their king. As for the means and conduits by which the people may receive this instruction, we are to search by what means so many opinions contrary to the peace of mankind, upon weak and false principles, have nevertheless been so deeply rooted in them. I mean those which I have in the precedent the precedent chapter specified: as that men shall judge of what is lawful and unlawful, not by the law itself, but by their own consciences; that is to say, by their own private judgements: that subjects sin in obeying the commands of the Commonwealth, unless they themselves have first judged them to be lawful: that their propriety in their riches is such as to exclude the dominion which the Commonwealth hath the same: that it is lawful for subjects to kill such as they call tyrants: that the sovereign power may be divided, and the like; which come to be instilled into the people by this means. They whom necessity or covetousness keepeth attent on their trades and labour; and they, on the other side, whom superfluity or sloth carrieth after their sensual pleasures (which two sorts of men take up the greatest part of mankind), being diverted from the deep meditation which the of truth, not only in the matter of natural justice, but also of all other sciences necessarily requireth, receive the notions of their duty chiefly from divines in the pulpit, and partly from such of their neighbours or familiar acquaintance as having the faculty of discoursing readily and plausibly seem wiser and better learned in cases of law and conscience than themselves. And the divines, and such others as make show of learning, derive their knowledge from the universities, and from the schools of law, or from the books which by men eminent in those schools and universities have been published. It is therefore manifest that the instruction of the people dependeth wholly on the right teaching of youth in the universities. But are not, may some man say, the universities of England learned enough already to do that? Or is it, you will undertake to teach the universities? Hard questions. Yet to the first, I doubt not to answer: that till towards the latter end of Henry the Eighth, the power of the Pope was always upheld against the power of the Commonwealth, principally by the universities; and that the doctrines by so many preachers against the sovereign power of the king, and by so many lawyers and others that had their education there, is a sufficient argument that, though the universities were not authors of those false doctrines, yet they knew not how to plant the true. For in such a contradiction of opinions, it is most certain that they have not been sufficiently instructed; and it is no wonder, if they yet retain a relish of that subtle liquor wherewith they were first seasoned against the civil authority. But to the lat ter question, it is not fit nor needful for me to say either aye or no: for any man that sees what I am doing may easily perceive what I think. The safety of the people requireth further, from him or them that have the sovereign power, that justice be equally administered to all degrees of people; that is, that as well the rich and mighty, as poor and obscure persons, may be righted of the injuries done them; so as the great may have no greater hope of impunity, when they do violence, dishonour, or any injury to the meaner sort, than when one of these does the like to one of them: for in this consisteth equity; to which, as being a precept of the law of nature, a sovereign is as much subject as any of the meanest of his people. All breaches of the law are offences against the Commonwealth: but there be some that are also against private persons. Those that concern the Commonwealth only may without breach of equity be pardoned; for every man may pardon what is done against himself, according to his own discretion. But an offence against a private man cannot in equity be pardoned without the consent of him that is injured; or reasonable satisfaction. The inequality of subjects proceedeth from the acts of sovereign power, and therefore has no more place in the presence of the sovereign; that is to say, in a court of justice, than the inequality between kings and their subjects in the presence of the King of kings. The honour of great persons is to be valued for their beneficence, and the aids they give to men of inferior rank, or not at all. And the violences, oppressions, and injuries they do are not extenuated, but aggravated, by the greatness of their persons, because they have least need to commit them. The consequences of this partiality towards the great proceed in this manner. Impunity maketh insolence; insolence, hatred; and hatred, an endeavour to pull down all oppressing and contumelious greatness, though with the ruin of the Commonwealth. To equal justice appertaineth also the equal imposition of taxes; the equality whereof dependeth not on the equality of riches, but on the equality of the debt that every man oweth to the Commonwealth for his defence. It is not enough for a man to labour for the maintenance of his life; but also to fight, if need be, for the securing of his labour. They must either do as the Jews did after their return from captivity, in re-edifying the Temple, build with one hand and hold the sword in the other, or else they must hire others to fight for them. For the impositions that are laid on the people by the sovereign power are nothing else but the wages due to them that hold the public sword to defend private men in the exercise of several trades and callings. Seeing then the benefit that every one receiveth thereby is the enjoyment of life, which is equally dear to poor and rich, the debt which a poor man oweth them that defend his life is the same which a rich man oweth for the defence of his; saving that the rich, who have the service of the poor, may be debtors not only for their own persons, but for many more. Which considered, the equality of imposition consisteth rather in the equality of that which is consumed, than of the riches of the persons that consume the same. For what reason is there that he which laboureth much and, sparing the fruits of his labour, consumeth little should be more charged than he that, living idly, getteth little and spendeth all he gets; seeing the one hath no more protection from the Commonwealth than the other? But when the impositions are laid upon those things which men consume, every man payeth equally for what he useth; nor is the Commonwealth defrauded by the luxurious waste of private men. And whereas many men, by accident inevitable, become unable to maintain themselves by their labour, they ought not to be left to the charity of private persons, but to be provided for, as far forth as the necessities of nature require, by the laws of the Commonwealth. For as it is uncharitableness in any man to neglect the impotent; so it is in the sovereign of a Commonwealth, to expose them to the hazard of such uncertain charity. But for such as have strong bodies the case is otherwise; they are to be forced to work; and to avoid the excuse of not finding employment, there ought to be such laws as may encourage all manner of arts; as navigation, agriculture, fishing, and all manner of manufacture that requires labour. The multitude of poor and yet strong people still increasing, they are to be transplanted into countries not sufficiently inhabited; where nevertheless they are not to exterminate those they find there; but constrain them to inhabit closer together, and not range a great deal of ground to snatch what they find, but to court each little plot with art and labour, to give them their sustenance in due season. And when all the world is overcharged with inhabitants, then the last remedy of all is war, which provideth for every man, by victory or death. To the care of the sovereign belongeth the making of good laws. But what is a good law? By a good law, I mean not a just law: for no law can be unjust. The law is made by the sovereign power, and all that is done by such power is warranted and owned by every one of the people; and that which every man will have so, no man can say is

unjust. It is in the laws of a Commonwealth, as in the laws of gaming: whatsoever the gamesters all agree on is injustice to none of them. A good law is that which is needful, for the good of the people, and withal perspicuous. For the use of laws (which are but rules authorized) is not to bind the people from all voluntary actions, but to direct and keep them in such a motion as not to hurt themselves by their own impetuous desires, rashness, or indiscretion; as hedges are set, not to stop travellers, but to keep them in the way. And therefore a law that is not needful, having not the true end of a law, is not good. A law may be conceived to be good when it is for the benefit of the sovereign, though it be not necessary for the people, but it is not so. For the good of the sovereign and people cannot be separated. It is a weak sovereign that has weak subjects; and a weak people whose sovereign wanteth power to rule them at his will. Unnecessary laws are not good laws, but traps for money which, where the right of sovereign power is acknowledged, are superfluous; and where it is not acknowledged, insufficient to defend the people. The perspicuity consisteth not so much in the words of the law itself, as in a declaration of the causes and motives for which it was made. That is it that shows us the meaning of the legislator; and the meaning of the legislator known, the law is more easily understood by few than many words. For all words are subject to ambiguity; and therefore multiplication of words in the body of the law is multiplication of ambiguity: besides it seems to imply, by too much diligence, that whosoever can evade the words is without the compass of the law. And this is a cause of many unnecessary processes. For when I consider how short were the laws of ancient times, and how they grew by degrees still longer, methinks I see a contention between the penners and pleaders of the law; the former seeking to circumscribe the latter, and the latter to evade their circumscriptions; and that the pleaders have got the victory. It belongeth therefore to the office of a legislator (such as is in all Commonwealths the supreme representative, be it one man or an assembly) to make the reason perspicuous why the law was made, and the body of the law itself as short, but in as proper and significant terms, as may be. It belongeth also to the office of the sovereign to make a right application of punishments and rewards. And seeing the end of punishing is not revenge and discharge of choler, but correction either of the offender or of others by his example, the severest punishments are to be inflicted for those crimes that are of most danger to the public; such as are those which proceed from malice to the government established; those that spring from contempt of justice; those that provoke indignation in the multitude; and those which, unpunished, seem authorized, as when they are committed by sons, servants, or favourites of men in authority: for indignation carrieth men, not only against the actors and authors of injustice, but against all power that is likely to protect them; as in the case of Tarquin, when for the insolent act of one of his sons he was driven out of Rome, and the monarchy itself dissolved. But crimes of infirmity; such as are those which proceed from great provocation, from great fear, great need, or from ignorance whether the fact be a great crime or not, there is place many times for lenity, without prejudice to the Commonwealth; and lenity, when there is such place for it, is required by the law of nature. The punishment of the leaders and teachers in a commotion; not the poor seduced people, when they are punished, can profit the Commonwealth by their example. To be severe to people is to punish ignorance which may in great part be imputed to the sovereign, whose fault it was they were no better instructed. In like manner it belongeth to the office and duty of the sovereign to apply his rewards always so as there may arise from them benefit to the Commonwealth: wherein consisteth their use and end; and is then done when they that have well served the Commonwealth are, with as little expense of the common treasury as is possible, so well recompensed as others thereby may be encouraged, both to serve the same as faithfully as they can, and to study the arts by which they may be enabled to do it better. To buy with money or preferment, from a popular ambitious subject to be quiet and desist from making ill impressions in the minds of the people, has nothing of the nature of reward (which is ordained not for disservice, but for service past); nor a sign of gratitude, but of fear; nor does it tend to the benefit, but to the damage of the public. It is a contention with ambition, that of Hercules with the monster Hydra, which, having many heads, for every one that was vanquished there grew up three. For in like manner, when the stubbornness of one popular man is overcome with reward, there arise many more by the example, that do the same mischief in hope of like benefit: and as all sorts of manufacture, so also malice increaseth by being vendible. And though sometimes a civil war may be deferred by such ways as that, yet the danger grows still the greater, and the public ruin more assured. It is therefore against the duty of the sovereign, to whom the public safety is committed, to reward those that aspire to greatness by disturbing the peace of their country, and not rather to oppose the beginnings of such men with a little danger, than after a longer time with greater. Another business of the sovereign is to choose good counsellors; I mean such whose advice he is to take in the government of the Commonwealth. For this word counsel (consilium, corrupted from considium) is of a large signification, and comprehendeth all assemblies of men that sit together, not only to deliberate what is to be done hereafter, but also to judge of facts past, and of law for the present. I take it here in the first sense only: and in this sense, there is no choice of counsel, neither in a democracy nor aristocracy; because the persons counselling are members of the person counselled. The choice of counsellors therefore is proper to monarchy, in which the sovereign that endeavoureth not to make choice of those that in every kind are the most able, dischargeth not his office as he ought to do. The most able counsellors are they that have least hope of benefit by giving evil counsel, and most knowledge of those things that conduce to the peace and defence of the Commonwealth. It is a hard matter to know who expecteth benefit from public troubles; but the signs that guide to a just suspicion is the soothing of the people in their unreasonable or irremediable grievances by men whose estates are not sufficient to discharge their accustomed expenses, and may easily be observed by any one whom it concerns to know it. But to know who has most knowledge of the public affairs is yet harder; and they that know them need them a great deal the less. For to know who knows the rules almost of any art is a great degree of the knowledge of the same art, because no man can be assured of the truth of another's rules but he that is first taught to understand them. But the best signs of knowledge of any art are much conversing in it and constant good effects of it. Good counsel comes not by lot, nor by inheritance; and therefore there is no more reason to expect good advice from the rich or noble in matter of state, than in delineating the dimensions of a fortress; unless we shall think there needs no method in the study of the politics, as there does in the study of geometry, but only to be lookers on; which is not so. For the politics is the harder study of the two. Whereas in these parts of Europe it hath been taken for a right of certain persons to have place in the highest council of state by inheritance, it derived from the conquests of the ancient Germans; wherein many absolute lords, joining together to conquer other nations, would not enter into the confederacy without such privileges as might be marks of difference, in time following, between their posterity and the posterity of their subjects; which privileges being inconsistent with the sovereign power, by the favour of the sovereign they may seem to keep; but contending for them as their right, they must needs by degrees let them go, and have at last no further honour than adhereth naturally to their abilities. And how able soever be the counsellors in any affair, the benefit of their counsel is greater when they give every one his advice, and the reasons of it apart, than when they do it in an assembly by way of orations; and when they have premeditated, than when they speak on the sudden; both because they have more time to survey the consequences of action, and are less subject to be carried away to contradiction through envy, emulation, or other passions arising from the difference of opinion. The best counsel, in those things that concern not other nations, but only the ease and benefit the subjects may enjoy, by laws that look only inward, is to be taken from the general informations and complaints of the people of each province, who are best acquainted with their own wants, and ought therefore, when they demand nothing in derogation of the essential rights of sovereignty, to be diligently taken notice of. For without those essential rights, as I have often before said, the Commonwealth cannot at all subsist. A commander of an army in chief, if he be not popular, shall not be beloved, nor feared as he ought to be by his army, and consequently cannot perform that office with good success. He must therefore be industrious, valiant, affable, liberal and fortunate, that he may gain an opinion both of sufficiency and of loving his soldiers. This is popularity, and breeds in the soldiers both desire and courage to recommend themselves to his favour; and protects the severity of the general, in punishing, when need is, the mutinous or negligent soldiers. But this love of soldiers, if caution be not given of the commander's fidelity, is a dangerous thing to sovereign power; especially when it is in the hands of an assembly not popular. It belongeth therefore to the safety of the people, both that they be good conductors and faithful subjects, to whom the sovereign commits his armies. But when the sovereign himself is popular; that is, reverenced and beloved of his people, there is no danger at all from the popularity of a subject. For soldiers are never so generally unjust as to side with their captain, though they love him, against their sovereign, when they love not only his person, but also his cause. And therefore those who by violence have at any time suppressed the power of their lawful sovereign, before they could settle themselves in his place, have been always put to the trouble of contriving their titles to save the people from the shame of receiving them. To have a known right to sovereign power is so popular a quality as he that has it needs no more, for his own part, to turn the hearts of his subjects to him, but that they see him able absolutely to govern his own family: nor, on the part of his enemies, but a disbanding of their armies. For the greatest and most active part of mankind has never hitherto been well contented with the present. Concerning the offices of one sovereign to another, which are comprehended in that law which is commonly called the law of nations, I need not say anything in this place, because the law of nations and the law of nature is the same thing. And every sovereign hath the same right in procuring the safety of his people, that any particular man can have in procuring the safety of his own body. And the same law that dictateth to men that have no civil government what they ought to do, and what to avoid in regard of one another, dictateth the same to Commonwealths; that is, to the consciences of sovereign princes and sovereign assemblies; there being no court of natural justice, but in the conscience only, where not man, but God reigneth; whose laws, such of them as oblige all mankind, in respect of God, as he is the Author of nature, are natural; and in respect of the same God, as he is King of kings, are laws. But of the kingdom of God, as King of kings, and as King also of a peculiar people, I shall speak in the rest of this discourse.

## CHAPTER XXXI, OF THE KINGDOM OF GOD BY NATURE

THAT the condition of mere nature, that is to say, of absolute liberty, such as is theirs that neither are sovereigns nor subjects, is anarchy and the condition of war: that the precepts, by which men are guided to avoid that condition, are the laws of nature: that a Commonwealth without sovereign power is but a word without substance and cannot stand: that subjects owe to sovereigns simple obedience in all things wherein their obedience is not repugnant to the laws of God, I have sufficiently proved in that which I have already written. There wants only, for the entire knowledge of civil duty, to know what are those laws of God. For without that, a man knows not, when he is commanded anything by the civil power, whether it be contrary to the law of God or not: and so, either by too much civil obedience offends the Divine Majesty, or, through fear of offending God, transgresses the commandments of the Commonwealth. To avoid both these rocks, it is necessary to know what are the laws divine. And seeing the knowledge of all law dependeth on the knowledge of the sovereign power, I shall say something in that which followeth of the KINGDOM OF GOD. "God is King, let the earth rejoice," [Psalms, 97. 1] saith the psalmist. And again, "God is King though the nations be angry; and he that sitteth on the cherubim, though the earth be moved." [Ibid., 99. 1] Whether men will or not, they must be subject always to the divine power. By denying the existence or providence of God, men may shake off their ease, but not their yoke. But to call this power of God, which extendeth itself not only to man, but also to beasts, and plants, and bodies inanimate, by the name of kingdom, is but a metaphorical use of the word. For he only is properly said to reign that governs his subjects by his word and by promise of rewards to those that obey it, by threatening them with punishment that obey it not. Subjects therefore in the kingdom of God are not bodies inanimate, nor creatures irrational; because they understand no precepts as his: nor atheists, nor they that believe not that God has any care of the actions of mankind; because they acknowledge no word for his, nor have hope of his rewards, or fear of his threatenings. They therefore that believe there is a God that governeth the world, and hath given precepts, and propounded rewards and punishments to mankind, are God's subjects; all the rest are to be understood as enemies. To rule by words requires that such words be manifestly made known; for else they are no laws: for to the nature of laws belongeth a sufficient and clear promulgation, such as may take away the excuse of ignorance; which in the laws of men is but of one only kind, and that is, proclamation or promulgation by the voice of man. But God declareth his laws three ways; by the dictates of natural reason, by revelation, and by the voice of some man to whom, by the operation of miracles, he procureth credit with the rest. From hence there ariseth a triple word of God, rational, sensible, and prophetic; to which correspondeth a triple hearing: right reason, sense supernatural, and faith. As for sense supernatural, which consisteth in revelation or inspiration, there have not been any universal laws so given, because God speaketh not in that manner but to particular persons, and to diverse men diverse things. From the difference between the other two kinds of God's word, rational and prophetic, there may be attributed to God a twofold kingdom, natural and prophetic: natural, wherein He governeth as many of mankind as acknowledge His providence, by the natural dictates of right reason; and prophetic, wherein having chosen out one peculiar nation, the Jews, for His subjects, He governed them, and none but them, not only by natural reason, but by positive laws, which He gave them by the mouths of His holy prophets. Of the natural kingdom of God I intend to speak in this chapter. The right of nature whereby God reigneth over men, and punisheth those that break his laws, is to be derived, not from His creating them, as if He required obedience as of gratitude for His benefits, but from His irresistible power. I have formerly shown how the sovereign right ariseth from pact: to show how the same right may arise from nature requires no more but to show in what case it is never taken away. Seeing all men by nature had right to all things, they had right every one to reign over all the rest. But because this right could not be obtained by force, it concerned the safety of every one, laying by that right, to set up men, with sovereign authority, by common consent, to rule and defend them: whereas if there had been any man of power irresistible, there had been no reason why he should not by that power have ruled and defended both himself and them, according to his own discretion. To those therefore whose power is irresistible, the dominion of all men adhereth naturally by their excellence of power; and consequently it is from that power that the kingdom over men, and the right of afflicting men at his pleasure, belongeth naturally to God Almighty; not as Creator and gracious, but as omnipotent. And though punishment be due for sin only, because by that word is understood affliction for sin; yet the right of afflicting is not always derived from men's sin, but from God's power. This question: why evil men often prosper; and good men suffer adversity, has been much disputed by the ancient, and is the same with this of ours: by what right God dispenseth the prosperities and adversities of this life; and is of that difficulty, as it hath shaken the faith, not only of the vulgar, but of philosophers and, which is more, of the saints, concerning the Divine Providence. "How good," saith David, "is the God of Israel to those that are upright in heart; and yet my feet were almost gone, my treadings had wellnigh slipped; for I was grieved at the wicked, when I saw the ungodly in such prosperity." [Psalms, 73. 1-3] And Job, how earnestly does he expostulate with God for the many afflictions he suffered, notwithstanding his righteousness? This question in the case of Job is decided by God Himself, not by arguments derived from Job's sin, but His own power. For whereas the friends of Job drew their arguments from his affliction to his sin, and he defended himself by the conscience of his innocence, God Himself taketh up the matter, and having justified the affliction by arguments drawn from His power, such as this, "Where wast thou when I laid the foundations of the earth," [Job, 38. 4] and the like, both approved Job's innocence and reproved the erroneous doctrine of his friends. Conformable to this doctrine is the sentence of our Saviour concerning the man that was born blind, in these words, "Neither hath this man sinned, nor his fathers; but that the works of God might be made manifest in him." And though it be said, "that death entered into the world by sin," (by which is meant that if Adam had never sinned, he had never died, that is, never suffered any separation of his soul from his body), it follows not thence that God could not justly have afflicted him, though he had not sinned, as well as He afflicteth other living creatures that cannot sin. Having spoken of the right of God's sovereignty as grounded only on nature, we are to consider next what are the divine laws, or dictates of natural reason; which laws concern either the natural duties of one man to another, or the honour naturally due to our Divine Sovereign. The first are the same laws of nature, of which I have spoken already in the fourteenth and fifteenth Chapters of this treatise; namely, equity, justice, mercy, humility, and the rest of the moral virtues. It remaineth therefore that we consider what precepts are dictated to men by their natural reason only, without other word of God, touching the honour and worship of the Divine Majesty. Honour consisteth in the inward thought and opinion of the power and goodness of another: and therefore to honour God is to think as highly of His power and goodness as is possible. And of that opinion, the external signs appearing in the words and actions of men are called worship; which is one part of that which the Latins understand by the word cultus: for cultus signifieth properly, and constantly, that labour which a man bestows on anything with a purpose to make benefit by it. Now those things whereof we make benefit are either subject to us, and the profit they yield followeth the labour we bestow upon them as a natural effect; or they are not subject to us, but answer our labour according to their own wills. In the first sense the labour bestowed on the earth is called culture; and the education of children, a culture of their minds. In the second sense, where men's wills are to be wrought to our purpose, not by force, but by complaisance, it signifieth as much as courting, that is, winning of favour by good offices; as by praises, by acknowledging their power, and by whatsoever is pleasing to them from whom we look for any benefit. And this is properly worship: in which sense publicola is understood for a worshipper of the people; and cultus Dei, for the worship of God. From internal honour, consisting in the opinion of power and goodness, arise three passions; love, which hath reference to goodness; and hope, and fear, that relate to power: and three parts of external worship; praise, magnifying, and blessing: the subject of praise being goodness; the subject of magnifying and blessing being power, and the effect thereof felicity. Praise and magnifying are signified both by words and actions: by words, when we say a man is good or great; by actions, when we thank him for his bounty, and obey his power. The opinion of the happiness of another can only be expressed by words. There be some signs of honour, both in attributes and actions, that be naturally so; as amongst attributes, good, just, liberal, and the like; and amongst actions, prayers, thanks, and obedience. Others are so by institution, or custom of men; and in some times and places are honourable; in others, dishonourable; in others, indifferent: such as are the gestures in salutation, prayer, and thanksgiving, in different times and places, differently used. The former is natural; the latter arbitrary worship. And of arbitrary worship, there be two differences: for sometimes it is commanded, sometimes voluntary worship: commanded, when it is such as he requireth who is worshipped: free, when it is such as the worshipper thinks fit. When it is commanded, not the words or gesture, but the obedience is the worship. But when free, the worship consists in the opinion of the beholders: for if to them the words or actions by which we intend honour seem ridiculous, and tending to contumely; they are no worship, because no signs of honour; and no signs of honour, because a sign is not a sign to him that giveth it, but to him to whom it is made, that is, to the spectator. Again there is a public an private worship. Public is the worship that a Commonwealth performeth, as one person. Private is that which a private person exhibiteth. Public, in respect of the whole Commonwealth, is free; but in respect of particular men it is not so. Private is in secret free; but in the sight of the multitude it is never without some restraint, either from the laws or from the opinion of men; which is contrary to the nature of liberty. The end of worship amongst men is power. For where a man seeth another worshipped, he supposeth him powerful, and is the readier to obey him; which makes his power greater. But God has no ends: the worship we do him proceeds from our duty and is directed according to our capacity by those rules of honour that reason dictateth to be done by the weak to the more potent men, in hope of benefit, for fear of damage, or in thankfulness for good already received from them. That we may know what worship of God is taught us by the light of nature, I will begin with His attributes. Where, first, it is manifest, we ought to attribute to Him existence: for no man can have the will to honour that which he thinks not to have any being. Secondly, that those philosophers who said the world, or the soul of the world, was God spake unworthily of Him, and denied His existence: for by God is understood the cause of the world; and to say the world is God is to say there is no cause of it, that is, no God. Thirdly, to say the world was not created, but eternal, seeing that which is eternal has no cause, is to deny there is a God. Fourthly, that they who, attributing, as they think, ease to God, take from Him the care of mankind, take from Him his honour: for it takes away men's love and fear of Him, which is the root of honour. Fifthly, in those things that signify greatness and power, to say He is finite is not to honour Him: for it is not a sign of the will to honour God to attribute to Him less than we can; and finite is less than we can, because to finite it is easy to add more. Therefore to attribute figure to Him is not honour; for all figure is finite: Nor to say we conceive, and imagine, or have an idea of Him in our mind; for whatsoever we conceive is finite: Nor to attribute to Him parts or totality; which are the attributes only of things finite: Nor to say He is in this or that place; for whatsoever is in place is bounded and finite: Nor that He is moved or resteth; for both these attributes ascribe to Him place: Nor that there be more gods than one, because it implies them all finite; for there cannot be more than one infinite: Nor to ascribe to Him (unless metaphorically, meaning not the passion, but the effect) passions that partake of grief; as repentance, anger, mercy: or of want; as appetite, hope, desire; or of any passive faculty: for passion is power limited by somewhat else. And therefore when we ascribe to God a will, it is not to be understood, as that of man, for a rational appetite; but as the power by which He effecteth everything. Likewise when we attribute to Him sight, and other acts of sense; as also knowledge and understanding; which in us is nothing else but a tumult of the mind, raised by external things that press the organical parts of man's body: for there is no such thing in God, and, being things that depend on natural causes, cannot be attributed to Him. He that will attribute to God nothing but what is warranted by natural reason must either use such negative attributes as infinite, eternal, incomprehensible; or superlatives, as most high, most great, and the like; or indefinite, as good, just, holy, creator; and in such sense as if He meant not to declare what He is (for that were to circumscribe Him within the limits of our fancy), but how much we admire Him, and how ready we would be to obey Him; which is a sign of humility, and of a will to honour Him as much as we can: for there is but one name to signify our conception of His nature, and that is I AM; and but one name of His relation to us, and that is God, in which is contained father, king, and lord. Concerning the actions of divine worship, it is a most general precept of reason that they be signs of the intention to honour God; such as are, first, prayers: for not the carvers, when they made images, were thought to make them gods, but the people that prayed to them. Secondly, thanksgiving; which differeth from prayer in divine worship no otherwise than that prayers precede, and thanks succeed, the benefit, the end both of the one and the other being to acknowledge God for author of all benefits as well past as future. Thirdly, gifts; that is to say, sacrifices and oblations, if they be of the best, are signs of honour, for they are thanksgivings. Fourthly, not to swear by any but God is naturally a sign of honour, for it is a confession that God only knoweth the heart and that no man's wit or strength can protect a man against God's vengeance on the perjured. Fifthly, it is a part of rational worship to speak considerately of God, for it argues a fear of Him, and fear is a confession of His power. Hence followeth, that the name of God is not to be used rashly and to no purpose; for that is as much as in vain: and it is to no purpose unless it be by way of oath, and by order of the Commonwealth, to make judgements certain; or between Commonwealths, to avoid war. And that disputing of God's nature is contrary to His honour, for it is supposed that in this natural kingdom of God, there is no other way to know anything but by natural reason; that is, from the principles of natural science; which are so far from teaching us anything of God's nature, as they cannot teach us our own nature, nor the nature of the smallest creature living. And therefore, when men out of the principles of natural reason dispute of the attributes of God, they but dishonour Him: for in the attributes which we give to God, we are not to consider the signification of philosophical truth, but the signification of pious intention to do Him the greatest honour we are able. From the want of which consideration have proceeded the volumes of disputation about the nature of God that tend not to His honour, but to the honour of our own wits and learning; and are nothing else but inconsiderate and vain abuses of His sacred name. Sixthly, in prayers, thanksgiving, offerings and sacrifices, it is a dictate of natural reason that they be every one in his kind the best and most significant of honour. As, for example, that prayers and thanksgiving be made in words and phrases not sudden, nor light, nor plebeian, but beautiful and well composed; for else we do not God as much honour as we can. And therefore the heathens did absurdly to worship images for gods, but their doing it in verse, and with music, both of voice and instruments, was reasonable. Also that the beasts they offered in sacrifice, and the gifts they offered, and their actions in worshipping, were full of submission, and commemorative of benefits received, was according to reason, as proceeding from an intention to honour him. Seventhly, reason directeth not only to worship God in secret, but also, and especially, in public, and in the sight of men: for without that, that which in honour is most acceptable, the procuring others to honour Him is lost. Lastly, obedience to His laws (that is, in this case to the laws of nature) is the greatest worship of all. For as obedience is more acceptable to God than sacrifice; so also to set light by His commandments is the greatest of all contumelies. And these are the laws of that divine worship which natural reason dictateth to private men. But seeing a Commonwealth is but one person, it ought also to exhibit to God but one worship; which then it doth when it commandeth it to be exhibited by private men, publicly. And this is public worship, the property whereof is to be uniform: for those actions that are done differently by different men cannot said to be a public worship. And therefore, where many sorts of worship be allowed, proceeding from the different religions of private men, it cannot be said there is any public worship, nor that the Commonwealth is of any religion at all. And because words (and consequently the attributes of God) have their signification by agreement and constitution of men, those attributes are to be held significative of honour that men intend shall so be; and whatsoever may be done by the wills of particular men, where there is no law but reason, may be done by the will of the Commonwealth by laws civil. And because a Commonwealth hath no will, nor makes no laws but those that are made by the will of him or them that have the sovereign power, it followeth that those attributes which the sovereign ordaineth in the worship of God for signs of honour ought to be taken and used for such by private men in their public worship. But because not all actions are signs by constitution, but some are naturally signs of honour, others of contumely, these latter, which are those that men are ashamed to do in the sight of them they reverence, cannot be made by human power a part of divine worship; nor the former, such as are decent, modest, humble behaviour, ever be separated from it. But whereas there be an infinite number of actions and gestures of an indifferent nature, such of them as the Commonwealth shall ordain to be publicly and universally in use, as signs of honour and part of God's worship, are to be taken and used for such by the subjects. And that which is said in the Scripture, "It is better to obey God than man," hath place in the kingdom of God by pact, and not by nature. Having thus briefly spoken of the natural kingdom of God, and His natural laws, I will add only to this chapter a short declaration of His natural punishments. There is no action of man in this life that is not the beginning of so long a chain of consequences as no human providence is high enough to give a man a prospect to the end. And in this chain there are linked together both pleasing and unpleasing events; in such manner as he that will do anything for his pleasure, must engage himself to suffer all the pains annexed to it; and these pains are the natural punishments of those actions which are the beginning of more harm than good. And hereby it comes to pass that intemperance is naturally punished with diseases; rashness, with mischances; injustice, with the violence of enemies; pride, with ruin; cowardice, with oppression; negligent government of princes, with rebellion; and rebellion, with slaughter. For seeing punishments are consequent to the breach of laws, natural punishments must be naturally consequent to the breach of the laws of nature, and therefore follow them as their natural, not arbitrary, effects. And thus far concerning the constitution, nature, and right of sovereigns, and concerning the duty of subjects, derived from the principles of natural reason. And now, considering how different this doctrine is from the practice of the greatest part of the world, especially of these western parts that have received their moral learning from Rome and Athens, and how much depth of moral philosophy is required in them that have the administration of the sovereign power, I am at the point of believing this my labour as useless as the Commonwealth of Plato: for he also is of opinion that it is impossible for the disorders of state, and change of governments by civil war, ever to be taken away till sovereigns be philosophers. But when I consider again that the science of natural justice is the only science necessary for sovereigns and their principal ministers, and that they need not be charged with the sciences mathematical, as by Plato they are, further than by good laws to encourage men to the study of them; and that neither Plato nor any other philosopher hitherto hath put into order, and sufficiently or probably proved all the theorems of moral doctrine, that men may learn thereby both how to govern and how to obey, I recover some hope that one time or other this writing of mine may fall into the hands of a sovereign who will consider it himself (for it is short, and I think clear) without the help of any interested or envious interpreter; and by the exercise of entire sovereignty, in protecting the public teaching of it, convert this truth of speculation into the utility of practice.

## THE THIRD PART, OF A CHRISTIAN COMMONWEALTH

## CHAPTER XXXII OF THE PRINCIPLES OF CHRISTIAN POLITICS

I HAVE derived the rights of sovereign power, and the duty of subjects, hitherto from the principles of nature only; such as experience has found true, or consent concerning the use of words has made so; that is to say, from the nature of men, known to us by experience, and from definitions, of such words as are essential to all political reasoning, universally agreed on. But in that I am next to handle, which is the nature and rights of a Christian Commonwealth, whereof there dependeth much upon supernatural revelations of the will of God, the ground of my discourse must be not only the natural word of God, but also the prophetical. Nevertheless, we are not to renounce our senses and experience, nor that which is the undoubted word of God, our natural reason. For they are the talents which he hath put into our hands to negotiate, till the coming again of our blessed Saviour; and therefore not to be folded up in the napkin of an implicit faith, but employed in the purchase of justice, peace, and true religion. For though there be many things in God's word above reason; that is to say, which cannot by natural reason be either demonstrated or confuted; yet there is nothing contrary to it; but when it seemeth so, the fault is either in our unskillful interpretation, or erroneous ratiocination. Therefore, when anything therein written is too hard for our examination, we are bidden to captivate our understanding to the words; and not to labour in sifting out a philosophical truth by logic of such mysteries as are not comprehensible, nor fall under any rule of natural science. For it is with the mysteries of our religion as with wholesome pills for the sick, which swallowed whole have the virtue to cure, but chewed, are for the most part cast up again without effect. But by the captivity of our understanding is not meant a submission of the intellectual faculty to the opinion of any other man, but of the will to obedience where obedience is due. For sense, memory, understanding, reason, and opinion are not in our power to change; but always, and necessarily such, as the things we see, hear, and consider suggest unto us; and therefore are not effects of our will, but our will of them. We then captivate our understanding and reason when we forbear contradiction; when we so speak as, by lawful authority, we are commanded; and when we live accordingly; which, in sum, is trust and faith reposed in him that speaketh, though the mind be incapable of any notion at all from the words spoken. When God speaketh to man, it must be either immediately or by mediation of another man, to whom He had formerly spoken by Himself immediately. How God speaketh to a man immediately may be understood by those well enough to whom He hath so spoken; but how the same should be understood by another is hard, if not impossible, to know. For if a man pretend to me that God hath spoken to him supernaturally, and immediately, and I make doubt of it, I cannot easily perceive what argument he can produce to oblige me to believe it. It is true that if he be my sovereign, he may oblige me to obedience, so as not by act or word to declare I believe him not; but not to think any otherwise than my reason persuades me. But if one that hath not such authority over me shall pretend the same, there is nothing that exacteth either belief or obedience. For to say that God hath spoken to him in the Holy Scripture is not to say God hath spoken to him immediately, but by mediation of the prophets, or of the Apostles, or of the Church, in such manner as He speaks to all other Christian men. To say He hath spoken to him in a dream is no more than to say he dreamed that God spake to him; which is not of force to win belief from any man that knows dreams are for the most part natural, and may proceed from former thoughts; and such dreams as that, from self-conceit, and foolish arrogance, and false opinion of a man's own goodliness, or virtue, by which he thinks he hath merited the favour of extraordinary revelation. To say he hath seen a vision, or heard a voice, is to say that he dreamed between sleeping and waking: for in such manner a man doth many times naturally take his dream for a vision, as not having well observed his own slumbering. To say he speaks by supernatural inspiration is to say he finds an ardent desire to speak, or some strong opinion of himself, for which he can allege no natural and sufficient reason. So that though God Almighty can speak to a man by dreams, visions, voice, and inspiration, yet He obliges no man to believe He hath so done to him that pretends it; who, being a man, may err and, which is more, may lie. How then can he to whom God hath never revealed His will immediately (saving by the way of natural reason) know when he is to obey or not to obey His word, delivered by him that says he is a prophet? Of four hundred prophets, of whom the King of Israel, asked counsel concerning the war he made against Ramoth Gilead, only Micaiah was a true one. [I Kings, 22] The prophet that was sent to prophesy against the altar set up by Jeroboam, [Ibid., 13] though a true prophet, and that by two miracles done in his presence appears to be a prophet sent from God, was yet deceived by another old prophet that persuaded him, as from the mouth of God, to eat and drink with him. If one prophet deceive another, what certainty is there of knowing the will of God by other way than that of reason? To which I answer out of the Holy Scripture that there be two marks by which together, not asunder, a true prophet is to be known. One is the doing of miracles; the other is the not teaching any other religion than that which is already established. Asunder, I say, neither of these is sufficient. "If a prophet rise amongst you, or a dreamer of dreams, and shall pretend the doing of a miracle, and the miracle come to pass; if he say, Let us follow strange gods, which thou hast not known, thou shalt not hearken to him, etc. But that prophet and dreamer of dreams shall be put to death, because he hath spoken to you to revolt from the Lord your God." [Deuteronomy, 13. 1-5] In which words two things are to be observed; first, that God will not have miracles alone serve for arguments to approve the prophet's calling; but (as it is in the third verse) for an experiment of the constancy of our adherence to Himself. For the works of the Egyptian sorcerers, though not so great as those of Moses, yet were great miracles. Secondly, that how great soever the miracle be, yet if it tend to stir up revolt against the king or him that governeth by the king's authority, he that doth such miracle is not to be considered otherwise than as sent to make trial of their allegiance. For these words, revolt from the Lord your God, are in this place equivalent to revolt from your king. For they had made God their king by pact at the foot of Mount Sinai; who ruled them by Moses only; for he only spake with God, and from time to time declared God's commandments to the people. In like manner, after our Saviour Christ had made his Disciples acknowledge him for the Messiah (that is to say, for God's anointed, whom the nation of the Jews daily expected for their king, but refused when he came), he omitted not to advertise them of the danger of miracles. "There shall arise," saith he, "false Christs, and false prophets, and shall do great wonders and miracles, even to the seducing (if it were possible) of the very elect." [Matthew, 24. 24] By which it appears that false prophets may have the power of miracles; yet are we not to take their doctrine for God's word. St. Paul says further to the Galatians that "if himself or an angel from heaven preach another Gospel to them than he had preached, let him be accursed." [Galatians, 1. 8] That Gospel was that Christ was King; so that all preaching against the power of the king received, in consequence to these words, is by St. Paul accursed. For his speech is addressed to those who by his preaching had already received Jesus for the Christ, that is to say, for King of the Jews. And as miracles, without preaching that doctrine which God hath established; so preaching the true doctrine, without the doing of miracles, is an insufficient argument of immediate revelation. For if a man that teacheth not false doctrine should pretend to be a prophet without showing any miracle, he is never the more to be regarded for his pretence, as is evident by Deuteronomy, 18. 21, 22: "If thou say in thy heart, How shall we know that the word" (of the prophet) "is not that which the Lord hath spoken? When the prophet shall have spoken in the name of the Lord, that which shall not come to pass, that is the word which the Lord hath not spoken, but the prophet has spoken it out of the pride of his own heart, fear him not." But a man may here again ask: When the prophet hath foretold a thing, how shall we know whether it will come to pass or not? For he may foretell it as a thing to arrive after a certain long time, longer than the time of man's life; or indefinitely, that it will come to pass one time or other: in which case this mark of a prophet is unuseful; and therefore the miracles that oblige us to believe a prophet ought to be confirmed by an immediate, or a not long deferred event. So that it is manifest that the teaching of the religion which God hath established, and the showing of a present miracle, joined together, were the only marks whereby the Scripture would have a true prophet, that is to say, immediate revelation, to be acknowledged; of them being singly sufficient to oblige any other man to regard what he saith. Seeing therefore miracles now cease, we have no sign left whereby to acknowledge the pretended revelations or inspirations of any private man; nor obligation to give ear to any doctrine, farther than it is conformable to the Holy Scriptures, which since the time of our Saviour supply the place and sufficiently recompense the want of all other prophecy; and from which, by wise and learned interpretation, and careful ratiocination, all rules and precepts necessary to the knowledge of our duty both to God and man, without enthusiasm, or supernatural inspiration, may easily be deduced. And this Scripture is it out of which I am to take the principles of my discourse concerning the rights of those that are the supreme governors on earth of Christian Commonwealths, and of the duty of Christian subjects towards their sovereigns. And to that end, I shall speak, in the next chapter, of the books, writers, scope and authority of the Bible.

## CHAPTER XXXIII, OF THE NUMBER, ANTIQUITY, SCOPE, AUTHORITY, AND INTER-PRETERS OF THE BOOKS OF HOLY SCRIPTURE

BY THE Books of Holy Scripture are understood those which ought to be the canon, that is to say, the rules of Christian life. And because all rules of life, which men are in conscience bound to observe, are laws, the question of the Scripture is the question of what is law throughout all Christendom, both natural and civil. For though it be not determined in Scripture what laws every Christian king shall constitute in his own dominions; yet it is determined what laws he shall not constitute. Seeing therefore I have already proved that sovereigns in their own dominions are the sole legislators; those books only are canonical, that is, law, in every nation, which are established for such by the sovereign authority. It is true that God is the Sovereign of all sovereigns; and therefore, when he speaks to any subject, he ought to be obeyed, whatsoever any earthly potentate command to the contrary. But the question is not of obedience to God, but of when, and what God hath said; which, to subjects that have no supernatural revelation, cannot be known but by that natural reason which guided them for the obtaining of peace and justice to obey the authority of their several Commonwealths; that is to say, of their lawful sovereigns. According to this obligation, I can acknowledge no other books of the Old Testament to be Holy Scripture but those which have been commanded to be acknowledged for such by the authority of the Church of England. What books these are is sufficiently known without a catalogue of them here; and they are the same that are acknowledged by St. Jerome, who holdeth the rest, namely, the Wisdom of Solomon, Ecclesiasticus, Judith, Tobias, the first and the second of Maccabees (though he had seen the first in Hebrew), and the third and fourth of Esdras, for Apocrypha. Of the canonical, Josephus, a learned Jew, that wrote in the time of the Emperor Domitian, reckoneth twenty-two, making the number agree with the Hebrew alphabet. St. Jerome does the same, though they reckon them in different manner. For Josephus numbers five books of Moses, thirteen of prophets that writ the history of their own times (which how it agrees with the prophets writings contained in the Bible we shall see hereafter), and four of Hymns and moral precepts. But St. Jerome reckons five Books of Moses, eight of prophets, and nine of other Holy Writ which he calls of Hagiographa. The Septuagint, who were seventy learned men of the Jews, sent for by Ptolemy, king of Egypt, to translate the Jewish law out of the Hebrew into the Greek, have left us no other for Holy Scripture in the Greek tongue but the same that are received in the Church of England. As for the books of the New Testament, they are equally acknowledged for canon by all Christian churches, and by all sects of Christians that admit any books at all for canonical. Who were the original writers of the several books of Holy Scripture has not been made evident by any sufficient testimony of other history, which is the only proof of matter of fact; nor can be by any arguments of natural reason: for reason serves only to convince the truth, not of fact, but of consequence. The light therefore that must guide us in this question must be that which is held out unto us from the books themselves: and this light, though it show us not the writer of every book, yet it is not useful to give us knowledge of the time wherein they were written. And first, for the Pentateuch, it is not argument enough that they were written by Moses, because they are called the five Books of Moses; no more than these titles, the Book of Joshua, the Book of Judges, the Book of Ruth, and the Books of the Kings, are arguments sufficient to prove that they were written by Joshua, by the Judges, by Ruth, and by the Kings. For in titles of books, the subject is marked as often as the writer. The History of Livy denotes the writer; but the History of Scanderberg is denominated from the subject. We read in the last chapter of Deuteronomy concerning the sepulchre of Moses, "that no man knoweth of his sepulchre to this day," [Deuteronomy, 34. 6] that is, to the day wherein those words were written. It is therefore manifest that those words were written after his interment. For it were a strange interpretation to say Moses spake of his own sepulchre (though by prophecy), that it was not found to that day wherein he was yet living. But it may perhaps be alleged that the last chapter only, not the whole Pentateuch, was written by some other man, but the rest not. Let us therefore consider that which we find in the Book of Genesis, "And Abraham passed through the land to the place of Sichem, unto the plain of Moreh, and the Canaanite was then in the land"; [Genesis, 12. 6] which must needs be the words of one that wrote when the Canaanite was not in the land; and consequently, not of Moses, who died before he came into it. Likewise Numbers, 21. 14, the writer citeth another more ancient book, entitled, The Book of the Wars of the Lord, wherein were registered the acts of Moses, at the Red Sea, and at the brook of Arnon. It is therefore sufficiently evident that the five Books of Moses were written after his time, though how long after it be not so manifest. But though Moses did not compile those books entirely, and in the form we have them; yet he wrote all that which he is there said to have written: as for example, the volume of the law, which is contained, as it seemeth, in the 11th of Deuteronomy, and the following chapters to the 27th, which was also commanded to be written on stones, in their entry into the land of Canaan. And this did Moses himself write, and deliver to the priests and elders of Israel, to be read every seventh year to all Israel, at their assembling in the feast of tabernacles. [Deuteronomy, 21. 9, 10] And this is that law which God commanded that their kings (when they should have established that form of government) should take a copy of from the priests and Levites; and which Moses commanded the priests and Levites to lay in the side of the Ark; [Ibid., 31. 26] and the same which, having been lost, was long time after found again by Hilkiah, [II KIngs, 22. 8] and sent to King Josias, who, causing it to be read to the people, renewed the covenant between God and them. [Ibid., 23. 1- 3] That the Book of Joshua was also written long after the time of Joshua may be gathered out of many places of the book itself. Joshua had set up twelve stones in the midst of Jordan, for a monument of their passage; of which the writer saith thus, "They are there unto this day";[Joshua, 4. 9] for unto this day is a phrase that signifieth a time past, beyond the memory of man. In like manner, upon the saying of the Lord that He had rolled off from the people the reproach of Egypt, the writer saith, "The place is called Gilgal unto this day";[Ibid., 5. 9] which to have said in the time of Joshua had been improper. So also the name of the valley of Achor, from the trouble that Achan raised in the camp, the writer saith, "remaineth unto this day"; [Ibid., 7. 26] which must needs be therefore long after the time of Joshua. Arguments of this kind there be many other; as Joshua, 8. 29, 13. 13, 14. 14, 15. 63. The same is manifest by like arguments of the Book of Judges, 1. 21, 26, 4. 24, 10. 4, 15. 19, 18. 6, and Ruth, 1. 1, but especially Judges, 18. 30. where it said that Jonathan "and his sons were priests to the tribe of Dan, until the day of the captivity of the land." That the Books of Samuel were also written after his own time, there are the like arguments, I Samuel, 5. 5, 7. 13, 15, 27. 6, and 30. 25, where, after David had adjudged equal part of the spoils to them that guarded the ammunition, with them that fought, the writer saith, "He made it a statute and an ordinance to Israel to this day." Again, when David (displeased that the Lord had slain Uzzah for putting out his hand to sustain the Ark) called the place Perezuzzah, the writer saith it is called so "to this day":[II Samuel, 6. 8] the time therefore of the writing of that book must be long after the time of the fact; that is, long after the time of David. As for the two Books of the Kings, and the two Books of the Chronicles, besides the places which mention such monuments, as the writer saith remained till his own days; such as are I Kings, 9. 13, 9. 21, 10. 12, 12. 19; II Kings, 2. 22, 10. 27, 14. 7, 16. 6, 17. 23, 17. 34, 17. 41, and I Chronicles, 4. 41, 5. 26. It is argument sufficient they were written after the captivity in Babylon that the history of them is continued till that time. For the facts registered are always more ancient than the register; and much more ancient than such books as make mention of and quote the register; as these books do in diverse places, referring the reader to the chronicles of the Kings of Judah, to the chronicles of the Kings of Israel, to the books of the prophet Samuel, of the prophet Nathan, of the prophet Ahijah; to the vision of Jehdo, to the books of the prophet Serveiah, and of the prophet Addo. The Books of Esdras and Nehemiah were written certainly after their return from captivity; because their return, the re-edification of the walls and houses of Jerusalem, the renovation of the covenant, and ordination of their policy are therein contained. The history of Queen Esther is of the time of the Captivity; and therefore the writer must have been of the same time, or after it. The Book of Job hath no mark in it of the time wherein it was written: and though it appear sufficiently that he was no feigned person; [Ezekiel, 14. 14 and James, 5. 11] yet the book itself seemeth not to be a history, but a treatise concerning a question in ancient time much disputed: why wicked men have often prospered in this world, and good men have been afflicted; and it is the more probable, because from the beginning to the third verse of the third chapter, where the complaint of Job beginneth, the Hebrew is (as St. Jerome testifies) in prose; and from thence to the sixth verse of the last chapter in hexameter verses; and the rest of that chapter again in prose. So that the dispute is all in verse; and the prose is added, as a preface in the beginning and an epilogue in the end. But verse is no usual style of such as either are themselves in great pain, as Job; or of such as come to comfort them, as his friends; but in philosophy, especially moral philosophy, in ancient time frequent. The Psalms were written the most part by David, for the use of the choir. To these are added some songs of Moses and other holy men; and some of them after the return from the Captivity, as the 137th and the 126th, whereby it is manifest that the Psalter was compiled, and put into the form it now hath, after the return of the Jews from Babylon. The Proverbs, being a collection of wise and godly sayings, partly of Solomon, partly of Agur the son of Jakeh, and partly of the mother of King Lemuel, cannot probably be thought to have been collected by Solomon, rather than by Agur, or the mother of Lemuel; and that, though the sentences be theirs, yet the collection or compiling them into this one book was the work of some other godly man that lived after them all. The Books of Ecclesiastes and the Canticles have nothing that was not Solomon's, except it be the titles or inscriptions. For The Words of the Preacher, the Son of David, King in Jerusalem, and The Song of Songs, which is Solomon's, seem to have been made for distinction's sake, then, when the books of Scripture were gathered into one body of the law; to the end that not the doctrine only, but the authors also might be extant. Of the Prophets, the most ancient are Zephaniah, Jonas, Amos, Hosea, Isaiah, and Micaiah, who lived in the time of Amaziah and Azariah, otherwise Ozias, Kings of Judah. But the Book of Jonah is not properly a register of his prophecy; for that is contained in these few words, "Forty days and Nineveh shall be destroyed"; but a history or narration of his frowardness and disputing God's commandments; so that there is small probability he should be the author, seeing he is the subject of it. But the Book of Amos is his prophecy. Jeremiah, Obadiah, Nahum, and Habakkuk prophesied in the time of Josiah. Ezekiel, Daniel, Haggai, and Zechariah, in the Captivity. When Joel and Malachi prophesied is not evident by their writings. But considering the inscriptions or titles of their books, it is manifest enough that the whole Scripture of the Old Testament was set forth, in the form we have it, after the return of the Jews from their Captivity in Babylon, and before the time of Ptolemaeus Philadelphus, that caused it to be translated into Greek by seventy men, which were sent him out of Judea for that purpose. And if the books of Apocrypha (which are recommended to us by the Church, though not for canonical, yet for profitable books for our instruction) may in this point be credited, the Scripture was set forth in the form we have it in by Esdras, as may appear by that which he himself saith, in the second book, chapter 14, verses 21, 22, etc., where, speaking to God, he saith thus, "Thy law is burnt; therefore no man knoweth the things which thou hast done, or the works that are to begin. But if I have found grace before thee, send down the holy spirit into me, and I shall write all that hath been done in the world, since the beginning, which were written in thy law, that men may find thy path, and that they which will live in the latter days, may live." And verse 45: "And it came to pass, when the forty days were fulfilled, that the Highest spake, saying, The first that thou hast written, publish openly, that the worthy and unworthy may read it; but keep the seventy last, that thou mayst deliver them only to such as be wise among the people." And thus much concerning the time of the writing of the books of the Old Testament. The writers of the New Testament lived all in less than an age after Christ's ascension, and had all of them seen our Saviour, or been his Disciples, except St. Paul and St. Luke; and consequently whatsoever was written by them is as ancient as the time of the Apostles. But the time wherein the books of the New Testament were received and acknowledged by the Church to be of their writing is not altogether so ancient. For, as the books of the Old Testament are derived to us from no higher time than that of Esdras, who by the direction of God's spirit retrieved them when they were lost: those of the New Testament, of which the copies were not many, nor could easily be all in any one private man's hand, cannot be derived from a higher time than that wherein the governors of the Church collected, approved, and recommended them to us as the writings of those Apostles and disciples under whose names they go. The first enumeration of all the books, both of the Old and New Testament, is in the Canons of the Apostles, supposed to be collected by Clement the First (after St. Peter), Bishop of Rome. But because that is but supposed, and by many questioned, the Council of Laodicea is the first we know that recommended the Bible to the then Christian churches for the writings of the prophets and Apostles: and this Council was held in the 364th year after Christ. At which time, though ambition had so far prevailed on the great doctors of the Church as no more to esteem emperors, though Christian, for the shepherds of the people, but for sheep; and emperors not Christian, for wolves; and endeavoured to pass their doctrine, not for counsel and information, as preachers; but for laws, as absolute governors; and thought such frauds as tended to make the people the more obedient to Christian doctrine to be pious; yet I am persuaded they did not therefore falsify the Scriptures, though the copies of the books of the New Testament were in the hands only of the ecclesiastics; because if they had had an intention so to do, they would surely have made them more favorable to their power over Christian princes and civil sovereignty than they are. I see not therefore any reason to doubt but that the Old and New Testament, as we have them now, are the true registers of those things which were done and said by the prophets and Apostles. And so perhaps are some of those books which are called Apocrypha, if left out of the Canon, not for inconformity of doctrine with the rest, but only because they are not found in the Hebrew. For after the conquest of Asia by Alexander the Great, there were few learned Jews that were not perfect in the Greek tongue. For the seventy interpreters that converted the Bible into Greek were all of them Hebrews; and we have extant the works of Philo and Josephus, both Jews, written by them eloquently in Greek. But it is not the writer but the authority of the Church that maketh a book canonical. And although these books were written by diverse men, yet it is manifest the writers were all endued with one and the same spirit, in that they conspire to one and the same end, which is the setting forth of the rights of the kingdom of God, the Father, Son, and Holy Ghost. For the book of Genesis deriveth the genealogy of God's people from the creation of the world to the going into Egypt: the other four Books of Moses contain the election of God for their King, and the laws which he prescribed for their government: the Books of Joshua, Judges, Ruth, and Samuel, to the time of Saul, describe the acts of God's people till the time they cast off God's yoke, and called for a king, after the manner of their neighbour nations: the rest of the history of the Old Testament derives the succession of the line of David to the Captivity, of which line was to spring the restorer of the kingdom of God, even our blessed Saviour, God the Son, whose coming was foretold in the books of the prophets, after whom the Evangelists wrote his life and actions, and his claim to the kingdom, whilst he lived on earth: and lastly, the Acts and Epistles of the Apostles declare the coming of God, the Holy Ghost, and the authority He left with them and their successors, for the direction of the Jews and for the invitation of the Gentiles. In sum, the histories and the prophecies of the Old Testament and the gospels and epistles of the New Testament have had one and the same scope, to convert men to the obedience of God: 1. in Moses and the priests; 2. in the man Christ; and 3. in the Apostles and the successors to apostolical power. For these three at several times did represent the person of God: Moses, and his successors the high priests, and kings of Judah, in the Old Testament: Christ Himself, in the time he lived on earth: and the Apostles, and their successors, from the day of Pentecost (when the Holy Ghost descended on them) to this day. It is a question much disputed between the diverse sects of Christian religion, from whence the Scriptures derive their authority; which question is also propounded sometimes in other terms, as, how we know them to be the word of God, or, why we believe them to be so; and the difficulty of resolving it ariseth chiefly from the improperness of the words wherein the question itself is couched. For it is believed on all hands that the first and original author of them is God; and consequently the question disputed is not that. Again, it is manifest that none can know they are God's word (though all true Christians believe it) but those to whom God Himself hath revealed it supernaturally; and therefore the question is not rightly moved, of our knowledge of it. Lastly, when the question is propounded of our belief; because some are moved to believe for one, and others for other reasons, there can be rendered no one general answer for them all. The question truly stated is: by what authority they are made law. As far as they differ not from the laws of nature, there is no doubt but they are the law of God, and carry their authority with them, legible to all men that have the use of natural reason: but this is no other authority than that of all other moral doctrine consonant to reason; the dictates whereof are laws, not made, but eternal. If they be made law by God Himself, they are of the nature of written law, which are laws to them only to whom God hath so sufficiently published them as no man can excuse himself by saying he knew not they were His. He therefore to whom God hath not supernaturally revealed that they are His, nor that those that published them were sent by Him, is not obliged to obey them by any authority but his whose commands have already the force of laws; that is to say, by any other authority than that of the Commonwealth, residing in the sovereign, who only has the legislative power. Again, if it be not the legislative authority of the Commonwealth that giveth them the force of laws, it must be some other authority derived from God, either private or public: if private, it obliges only him to whom in particular God hath been pleased to reveal it. For if every man should be obliged to take for God's law what particular men, on pretence of private inspiration or revelation, should obtrude upon him (in such a number of men that out of pride and ignorance take their own dreams, and extravagant fancies, and madness for testimonies of God's spirit; or, out of ambition, pretend to such divine testimonies, falsely and contrary to their own consciences), it were impossible that any divine law should be acknowledged. If public, it is the authority of the Commonwealth or of the Church. But the Church, if it be one person, is the same thing with a Commonwealth of Christians; called a Commonwealth because it consisteth of men united in one person, their sovereign; and a Church, because it consisteth in Christian men, united in one Christian sovereign. But if the Church be not one person, then it hath no authority at all; it can neither command nor do any action at all; nor is capable of having any power or right to anything; nor has any will, reason, nor voice; for all these qualities are personal. Now if the whole number of Christians be not contained in one Commonwealth, they are not one person; nor is there a universal Church that hath any authority over them; and therefore the Scriptures are not made laws by the universal Church: or if it be one Commonwealth, then all Christian monarchs and states are private persons, and subject to be judged, deposed, and punished by a universal sovereign of all Christendom. So that the question of the authority of the Scriptures is reduced to this: whether Christian kings, and the sovereign assemblies in Christian Commonwealths, be absolute in their own territories, immediately under God; or subject to one Vicar of Christ, constituted over the universal Church; to be judged condemned, deposed, and put to death, as he shall think expedient or necessary for the common good. Which question cannot be resolved without a more particular consideration of the kingdom of God; from whence also, we are to judge of the authority of interpreting the Scripture. For, whosoever hath a lawful power over any writing, to make it law, hath the power also to approve or disapprove the interpretation of the same.

## CHAPTER XXXIV, OF THE SIGNIFICATION OF SPIRIT, ANGEL, AND INSPIRATION IN THE BOOKS OF HOLY SCRIPTURE

SEEING the foundation of all true ratiocination is the constant signification of words; which, in the doctrine following, dependeth not (as in natural science) on the will of the writer, nor (as in common conversation) on vulgar use, but on the sense they carry in the Scripture; it is necessary, before I proceed any further, to determine, out of the Bible, the meaning of such words as by their ambiguity may render what I am to infer upon them obscure or disputable. I will begin with the words body and spirit, which in the language of the Schools are termed substances, corporeal and incorporeal. The word body, in the most general acceptation, signifieth that which filleth or occupieth some certain room or imagined place; and dependeth not on the imagination, but is a real part of that we call the universe. For the universe, being the aggregate of all bodies, there is no real part thereof that is not also body; nor anything properly a body that is not also part of that aggregate of all bodies, the universe. The same also, because bodies are subject to change, that is to say, to variety of appearance to the sense of living creatures, is called substance, that is to say, subject to various accidents: as sometimes to be moved, sometimes to stand still; and to seem to our senses sometimes hot, sometimes cold; sometimes of one colour, smell, taste, or sound, sometimes of another. And this diversity of seeming, produced by the diversity of the operation of bodies on the organs of our sense, we attribute to alterations of the bodies that operate, and call them accidents of those bodies. And according to this acceptation of the word, substance and body signify the same thing; and therefore substance incorporeal are words which, when they are joined together, destroy one another, as if a man should say, an incorporeal body. But in the sense of common people, not all the universe is called body, but only such parts thereof as they can discern, by the sense of feeling, to resist their force; or, by the sense of their eyes, to hinder them from a farther prospect. Therefore in the common language of men, air and aerial substances use not to be taken for bodies, but, as often as men are sensible of their effects, are called wind, or breath, or (because the same are called in the Latin spiritus) spirits; as when they call that aerial substance which in the body of any living creature gives it life and motion, vital and animal spirits. But for those idols of the brain which represent bodies to us where they are not, as in a looking-glass, in a dream, or to a distempered brain waking, they are (as the Apostle saith generally of all idols) nothing; nothing at all, I say, there where they seem to be; and in the brain itself, nothing but tumult, proceeding either from the action of the objects or from the disorderly agitation of the organs of our sense. And men that are otherwise employed than to search into their causes know not of themselves what to call them; and may therefore easily be persuaded, by those whose knowledge they much reverence, some to call them bodies, and think them made of air compacted by a power supernatural, because the sight judges them corporeal; and some to call them spirits, because the sense of touch discerneth nothing, in the place where they appear, to resist their fingers: so that the proper signification of spirit in common speech is either a subtle, fluid, and invisible body, or a ghost, or other idol or phantasm of the imagination. But for metaphorical significations there be many: for sometimes it is taken for disposition or inclination of the mind, as when for the disposition to control the sayings of other men, we say, a spirit of contradiction; for a disposition to uncleanness, an unclean spirit; for perverseness, a froward spirit; for sullenness, a dumb spirit; and for inclination to godliness and God's service, the Spirit of God: sometimes for any eminent ability, or extraordinary passion, or disease of the mind, as when great wisdom is called the spirit of wisdom; and madmen are said to be possessed with a spirit. Other signification of spirit I find nowhere any; and where none of these can satisfy the sense of that word in Scripture, the place falleth not under human understanding; and our faith therein consisteth, not in our opinion, but in our submission; as in all places where God is said to be a Spirit, or where by the Spirit of God is meant God Himself. For the nature of God is incomprehensible; that is to say, we understand nothing of what He is, but only that He is; and therefore the attributes we give Him are not to tell one another what He is, nor to signify our opinion of His nature, but our desire to honour Him with such names as we conceive most honourable amongst ourselves. "The Spirit of God moved upon the face of the waters." [Genesis, 1. 2] Here if by the Spirit of God be meant God Himself, then is motion attributed to God, and consequently place, which are intelligible only of bodies, and not of substances incorporeal; and so the place is above our understanding that can conceive nothing moved that changes not place or that has not dimension; and whatsoever has dimension is body. But the meaning of those words is best understood by the like place, where when the earth was covered with waters, as in the beginning, God intending to abate them, and again to discover the dry land, useth the like words, "I will bring my Spirit upon the earth, and the waters shall be diminished":[Ibid., 8. 1] in which place by Spirit is understood a wind (that is an air or spirit moved), which might be called, as in the former place, the Spirit of God, because it was God's work. Pharaoh calleth the wisdom of Joseph the Spirit of God. For Joseph having advised him to look out a wise and discreet man, and to set him over the land of Egypt, he saith thus, "Can we find such a man as this is, in whom is the Spirit of God?" [Genesis, 41. 38] And Exodus, 28. 3, "Thou shalt speak," saith God, "to all that are wise hearted, whom I have filled with the spirit of wisdom, to make Aaron garments, to consecrate him." Where extraordinary understanding, though but in making garments, as being the gift of God, is called the Spirit of God. The same is found again, Exod. 31. 3-6, and 35. 31 And Isaiah, 11. 2, 3, where the prophet, speaking of the Messiah, saith, "The Spirit of the Lord shall abide upon him, the spirit of wisdom and understanding, the spirit of counsel, and fortitude, and the spirit of the fear of the Lord." Where manifestly is meant, not so many ghosts, but so many eminent graces that God would give him. In the Book of Judges, an extraordinary zeal and courage in the defence of God's people is called the Spirit of God; as when it excited Othniel, Gideon, Jephtha, and Samson to deliver them from servitude, Judges, 3. 10, 6. 34, 11. 29, 13. 25, 14. 6, 19. And of Saul, upon the news of the insolence of the Ammonites towards the men of Jabesh Gilead, it is said that "The Spirit of God came upon Saul, and his anger" (or, as it is in the Latin, his fury) "was kindled greatly." [I Samuel, 11. 6] Where it is not probable was meant a ghost, but an extraordinary zeal to punish the cruelty of the Ammonites. In like manner by the Spirit of God that came upon Saul, when he was amongst the prophets that praised God in songs and music, [Ibid., 19. 20] is to be understood, not a ghost, but an unexpected and sudden zeal to join with them in their devotion. The false prophet Zedekiah saith to Micaiah, "Which way went the Spirit of the Lord from me to speak to thee?" [I Kings, 22. 24] Which cannot be understood of a ghost; for Micaiah declared before the kings of Israel and Judah the event of the battle as from a vision and not as from a spirit speaking in him. In the same manner it appeareth, in the books of the Prophets, that though they spake by the Spirit of God, that is to say, by a special grace of prediction; yet their knowledge of the future was not by a ghost within them, but by some supernatural dream or vision. It is said, "God made man of the dust of the earth, and breathed into his nostrils (spiraculum vitae) the breath of life, and man was made a living soul." [Genesis, 2. 7] There the breath of life inspired by God signifies no more but that God gave him life; and "as long as the spirit of God is in my nostrils" [Job, 27. 3] is no more than to say, "as long as I live." So in Ezekiel, 1. 20, "the spirit of life was in the wheels," is equivalent to, "the wheels were alive." And "the spirit entered into me, and me, and set me on my feet," [Ezekiel, 2. 30] that is, "I recovered my vital strength"; not that any ghost or incorporeal substance entered into and possessed his body. In the eleventh chapter of Numbers, verse 17, "I will take," saith God, "of the spirit which is upon thee, and will put it upon them, and they shall bear the burden of the people with thee"; that is, upon the seventy elders: whereupon two of the seventy are said to prophesy in the camp; of whom some complained, and Joshua desired Moses to forbid them, which Moses would not do. Whereby it appears that Joshua knew not they had received authority so to do, and prophesied according to the mind of Moses, that is to say, by a spirit or authority subordinate to his own. In the like sense we read that "Joshua was full of the spirit of wisdom, because Moses had laid his hands upon him":[Deuteronomy, 34. 9] that is, because he was ordained by Moses to prosecute the work he had himself begun (namely, the bringing of God's people into the promised land) but, prevented by death, could not finish. In the like sense it is said, "If any man have not the Spirit of Christ, he is none of his":[Romans, 8. 9] not meaning thereby the ghost of Christ, but a submission to his doctrine. As also, "Hereby you shall know the Spirit of God: every spirit that confesseth that Jesus Christ is come in the flesh is of God"; [I John, 4. 2] by which is meant the spirit of unfeigned Christianity, submission to that main article of Christian faith, that Jesus is the Christ; which cannot be interpreted of a ghost. Likewise these words, "And Jesus full of the Holy Ghost"[Luke, 4. 1] (that is, as it is expressed, Matthew, 4. 1, and Mark, 1. 12, "of the Holy Spirit") may be understood for zeal to do the work for which he was sent by God the Father: but to interpret it of a ghost is to say that God Himself (for so our Saviour was) was filled with God; which is very improper and insignificant. How we came to translate spirits by the word ghosts, which signifieth nothing, neither in heaven nor earth, but the imaginary inhabitants of man's brain, I examine not: but this I say, the word spirit in the text signifieth no such thing; but either properly a real substance or, metaphorically, some extraordinary ability or affection of the mind or of the body. The Disciples of Christ, seeing him walking upon the sea[Matthew, 14. 26 and Mark, 6. 49] supposed him to be a spirit, meaning thereby an aerial body, and not a phantasm: for it is said they all saw him; which cannot be understood of the delusions of the brain (which are not common to many at once. as visible bodies are; but singular, because of the differences of fancies), but of bodies only. In like manner, where he was taken for a spirit, by the same Apostles: [Luke, 24. 3, 7] so also when St. Peter was delivered out of prison, it would not be believed; but when the maid said he was at the door, they said it was his angel; [Acts, 12. 15] by which must be meant a corporeal substance, or we must say the disciples themselves did follow the common opinion of both Jews and Gentiles that some such apparitions were not imaginary, but real; and such as needed not the fancy of man for their existence: these the Jews called spirits and angels, good or bad; as the Greeks called the same by the name of demons. And some such apparitions may be real and substantial; that is to say, subtle bodies, which God can form by the same power by which He formed all things, and make use of as ministers and messengers (that is to say, angels), to declare His will, and execute the same when He pleaseth in extraordinary and supernatural manner. But when He hath so formed them they are substances, endued with dimensions, and take up room, and can be moved from place to place, which is peculiar to bodies; and therefore are not ghosts not ghosts incorporeal, that is to say, ghosts that are in no place; that is to say, that are nowhere; that is to say, that, seeming to be somewhat, are nothing. But if corporeal be taken in the most vulgar manner, for such substances as are perceptible by our external senses; then is substance incorporeal a thing not imaginary, but real; namely, a thin substance invisible, but that hath the same dimensions that are in grosser bodies. By the name of angel is signified, generally, a messenger; and most often, a messenger of God: and by a messenger of God is signified anything that makes known His extraordinary presence; that is to say, the extraordinary manifestation of His power, especially by a dream or vision. Concerning the creation of angels, there is nothing delivered in the Scriptures. That they are spirits is often repeated: but by the name of spirit is signified both in Scripture and vulgarly, both amongst Jews and Gentiles, sometimes thin bodies; as the air, the wind, the spirits vital and animal of living creatures; and sometimes the images that rise in the fancy in dreams and visions; which are not real substances, nor last any longer than the dream or vision they appear in; which apparitions, though no real substances, but accidents of the brain; yet when God raiseth them supernaturally, to signify His will, they are not improperly termed God's messengers, that is to say, His angels. And as the Gentiles did vulgarly conceive the imagery of the brain for things really subsistent without them, and not dependent on the fancy; and out of them framed their opinions of demons, good and evil; which because they seemed to subsist really, they called substances; and because they could not feel them with their hands, incorporeal: so also the Jews upon the same ground, without anything in the Old Testament that constrained them thereunto, had generally an opinion (except the sect of the Sadducees) that those apparitions, which it pleased God sometimes to produce in the fancy of men, for His own service, and therefore called them His angels, were substances, not dependent on the fancy, but permanent creatures of God; whereof those which they thought were good to them, they esteemed the angels of God, and those they thought would hurt them, they called evil angels, or evil spirits; such as was the spirit of Python, and the spirits of madmen, of lunatics and epileptics: for they esteemed such as were troubled with such diseases, demoniacs. But if we consider the places of the Old Testament where angels are mentioned, we shall find that in most of them, there can nothing else be understood by the word angel, but some image raised, supernaturally, in the fancy, to signify the presence of God in the execution of some supernatural work; and therefore in the rest, where their nature is not expressed, it may be understood in the same manner. For we read that the same apparition is called not only an angel, but God, where that which is called the angel of the Lord, saith to Hagar, "I will multiply thy seed exceedingly"; [Genesis, 16. 7, 10] that is, speaketh in the person of God. Neither was this apparition a fancy figured, but a voice. By which it is manifest that angel signifieth there nothing but God Himself, that caused Hagar supernaturally to apprehend a voice from heaven; or rather, nothing else but a voice supernatural, testifying God's special presence there. Why therefore may not the angels that appeared to Lot, and are called men; [Ibid., 19. 10] and to whom, though they were two, Lot speaketh as but to one, [Ibid., 19. 18] and that one as God (for the words are, "Lot said unto them, Oh not so my Lord"), be understood of images of men, supernaturally formed in the fancy; as well as before by angel was understood a fancied voice? When the angel called to Abraham out of heaven, to stay his hand from slaying Isaac, [Genesis, 22. 11] there was no apparition, but a voice; which nevertheless was called properly enough a messenger or angel of God, because it declared God's will supernaturally, and saves the labour of supposing any permanent ghosts. The angels which Jacob saw on the ladder of heaven[Ibid., 28. 12] were a vision of his sleep; therefore only fancy and a dream; yet being supernatural, and signs of God's special presence, those apparitions are not improperly called angels. The same is to be understood where Jacob saith thus, "The angel of the Lord appeared to me in my sleep." [, 31. 11] For an apparition made to a man in his sleep is that which all men call a dream, whether such dream be natural or supernatural: and that which there Jacob calleth an angel was God Himself; for the same angel saith, "I am the God of Bethel." [Ibid., 31. 13] Also the angel that went before the army of Israel to the Red Sea, and then came behind it, is the Lord Himself; [Exodus, 14. 19 and He appeared not in the form of a beautiful man, but in form, by day, of a "pillar of cloud," and, by night, in form of a "pillar of fire"; [Ibid., 13. 21] and yet this pillar was all the apparition and angel promised to Moses for the army's guide: for this cloudy pillar is said to have descended and stood at the door of the tabernacle, and to have talked with Moses. [Ibid., 33. 2] There you see motion and speech, which are commonly attributed to angels, attributed to a cloud, because the cloud served as a sign of God's presence; and was no less an angel than if it had had the form of a man or child of never so great beauty; or wings, as usually they are painted, for the false instruction of common people. For it is not the shape, but their use, that makes them angels. But their use is to be significations of God's presence in supernatural operations; as when Moses had desired God to go along with the camp, as He had done always before the making of the golden calf, God did not answer, "I will go," nor "I will send an angel in my stead"; but thus, "My presence shall go with thee."[Exodus, 33. 14] To mention all the places of the Old Testament where the name of angel is found would be too long. Therefore to comprehend them all at once, I say there is no text in that part of the Old Testament which the Church of England holdeth for canonical from which we can conclude there is, or hath been created, any permanent thing (understood by the name of spirit or angel) that hath not quantity, and that may not be by the understanding divided; that is to say, considered by parts; so as one part may be in one place, and the next part in the next place to it; and, in sum, which is not (taking body for that which is somewhat or somewhere) corporeal; but in every place the sense will bear the interpretation of angel for messenger; as John Baptist is called an angel, and Christ the Angel of the Covenant; and as (according to the same analogy) the dove and the fiery tongues, in that they were signs of God's special presence, might also be called angels. Though we find in Daniel two names of angels, Gabriel and Michael; yet it is clear out of the text itself that by Michael is meant Christ, not as an angel, but as a prince: [Daniel, 12. 1] and that Gabriel (as the like apparitions made to other holy men in their sleep) was nothing but a supernatural phantasm, by which it seemed to Daniel in his dream that two saints being in talk, one of them said to the other, "Gabriel, let us make this man understand his vision": for God needeth not to distinguish his celestial servants by names, which are useful only to the short memories of mortals. Nor in the New Testament is there any place out of which it can be proved that angels (except when they are put for such men as God hath made the messengers and ministers of His word or works) are things permanent, and withal incorporeal. That they are permanent may be gathered from the words of our Saviour himself where he saith it shall be said to the wicked in the last day, "Go ye cursed into everlasting fire prepared for the Devil and his angels":[Matthew, 25. 41] which place is manifest for the permanence of evil angels (unless we might think the name of Devil and his angels may be understood of the Church's adversaries and their ministers); but then it is repugnant to their immateriality, because everlasting fire is no punishment to impatible substances, such as are all things incorporeal. Angels therefore are not thence proved to be incorporeal. In like manner where St. Paul says, "Know ye not that we shall judge the angels?" [I Corinthians, 6. 3] And II Peter, 2. 4, "For if God spared not the angels that sinned, but cast them down into hell"; and "And the angels that kept not their first estate, but left their own habitation, he hath reserved in everlasting chains under darkness unto the judgement of the last day";[Jude, 1. 6] though it prove the permanence of angelical nature, it confirmeth also their materiality. And, "In the resurrection men do neither marry, nor give in marriage, but are as the angels of God in heaven":[Matthew, 22. 30] but in the resurrection men shall be permanent, and not incorporeal; so therefore also are the angels. There be diverse other places out of which may be drawn the like conclusion. To men that understand the signification of these words, substance and incorporeal (as incorporeal is taken not for subtle body, but for not body), they imply a contradiction: insomuch as to say, an angel or spirit is in that sense an incorporeal substance is to say, in effect, there is no angel nor spirit at all. Considering therefore the signification of the word angel in the Old Testament, and the nature of dreams and visions that happen to men by the ordinary way of nature, I was inclined to this opinion, that angels were nothing but supernatural apparitions of the fancy, raised by the special and extraordinary operation of God, thereby to make His presence and commandments known to mankind, and chiefly to His own people. But the many places of the New Testament, and our Saviour's own words, and in such texts wherein is no suspicion of corruption of the Scripture, have extorted from my feeble reason an acknowledgement and belief that there be also angels substantial and permanent. But to believe they be in no place, that is to say, nowhere, that is to say, nothing, as they, though indirectly, say that will have them incorporeal, cannot by Scripture be evinced. On the signification of the word spirit dependeth that of the word inspiration; which must either be taken properly, and then it is nothing but the blowing into a man some thin and subtle air or wind in such manner as a man filleth a bladder with his breath; or if spirits be not corporeal, but have their existence only in the fancy, it is nothing but the blowing in of a phantasm; which is improper to say, and impossible; for phantasms are not, but only seem to be, somewhat. That word therefore is used in the Scripture metaphorically only: as where it is said that God inspired into man the breath of life, [Genesis, 2. 7] no more is meant than that God gave unto him vital motion. For we are not to think that God made first a living breath, and then blew it into Adam after he was made, whether that breath were real or seeming; but only as it is "that he gave him life, and breath";[Acts, 17. 25] that is, made him a living creature. And where it is said "all Scripture is given by inspiration from God," [II Timothy, 3. 16] speaking there of the Scripture of the Old Testament, it is an easy metaphor to signify that God inclined the spirit or mind of those writers to write that which should be useful in teaching, reproving, correcting, and instructing men in the way of righteous living. But where St. Peter saith that "Prophecy came not in old time by the will of man, but the holy men of God spake as they were moved by the Holy Spirit," [II Peter, 1. 21] by the Holy Spirit is meant the voice of God in a dream or vision supernatural, which is not inspiration: nor when our Saviour, breathing on His Disciples, said, "Receive the Holy Spirit, was that breath the Spirit, but a sign of the spiritual graces he gave unto them. And though it be said of many, and of our Saviour Himself, that he was full of the Holy Spirit; yet that fullness is not to be understood for infusion of the substance of God, but for accumulation of his gifts, such as are the gift of sanctity of life, of tongues, and the like, whether attained supernaturally or by study and industry; for in all cases they are the gifts of God. So likewise where God says, "I will pour out my Spirit upon all flesh, and your sons and your daughters shall prophesy, your old men shall dream dreams, and your young men shall see visions," [Joel, 2. 28] we are not to understand it in the proper sense, as if his Spirit were like water, subject to effusion or infusion; but as if God had promised to give them prophetical dreams and visions. For the proper use of the word infused, in speaking of the graces of God, is an abuse of it; for those graces are virtues, not bodies to be carried hither and thither, and to be poured into men as into barrels. In the same manner, to take inspiration in the proper sense, or to say that good spirits entered into men to make them prophesy, or evil spirits into those that became phrenetic, lunatic, or epileptic, is not to take the word in the sense of the Scripture; for the Spirit there is taken for the power of God, working by causes to us unknown. As also the wind that is there said to fill the house wherein the Apostles were assembled on the day of Pentecost[Acts, 2. 2] is not to be understood for the Holy Spirit, which is the Deity itself; but for an external sign of God's special working on their hearts to effect in them the internal graces and holy virtues He thought requisite for the performance of their apostleship.

**CHAPTER XXXV, OF THE SIGNIFICATION IN SCRIPTURE OF KINGDOM OF GOD, OF HOLY, SACRED, AND SACRAMENT**

THE kingdom of God in the writings of divines, and specially in sermons and treatises of devotion, is taken most commonly for eternal felicity, after this life, in the highest heaven, which they also call the kingdom of glory; and sometimes for the earnest of that felicity, sanctification, which they term the kingdom of grace; but never for the monarchy, that is to say, the sovereign power of God over any subjects acquired by their own consent, which is the proper signification of kingdom. To the contrary, I find the kingdom of God to signify in most places of Scripture a kingdom properly so named, constituted by the votes of the people of Israel in peculiar manner, wherein they chose God for their king by covenant made with Him, upon God's promising them the possession of the land of Canaan; and but seldom metaphorically; and then it is taken for dominion over sin (and only in the New Testament), because such a dominion as that every subject shall have in the kingdom of God, and without prejudice to the sovereign. From the very creation, God not only reigned over all men naturally by His might, but also had peculiar subjects, whom He commanded by a voice, as one man speaketh to another. In which manner He reigned over Adam and gave him commandment to abstain from the tree of cognizance of good and evil; which when he obeyed not, but tasting thereof took upon him to be as God, judging between good and evil, not by his Creator's commandment, but by his own sense, his punishment was a privation of the estate of eternal life, wherein God had at first created him: and afterwards God punished his posterity for their vices, all but eight persons, with a universal deluge; and in these eight did consist the then kingdom of God. After this, it pleased God to speak to Abraham, and to make a covenant with him in these words, "I will establish my covenant between me and thee and thy seed after thee in their generations for an everlasting covenant, to be a God to thee, and to thy seed after thee; And I will give unto thee, and to thy seed after thee, the land wherein thou art a stranger, all the land of Canaan, for an everlasting possession." [Genesis, 17. 7, 8] In this covenant Abraham promiseth for himself and his posterity to obey, as God, the Lord that spake to him; and God on his part promiseth to Abraham the land of Canaan for an everlasting possession. And for a memorial and a token of this covenant, he ordaineth the sacrament of circumcision. [Ibid., 16. 11] This is it which is called the Old Covenant, or Testament, and containeth a contract between God and Abraham, by which Abraham obligeth himself and his posterity in a peculiar manner to be subject to God's positive law; for to the law moral he was obliged before, as by an oath of allegiance. And though the name of King be not yet given to God; nor of kingdom to Abraham and his seed, yet the thing is the same; namely, an institution by pact of God's peculiar sovereignty over the seed of Abraham, which in the renewing of the same covenant by Moses at Mount Sinai is expressly called a peculiar kingdom of God over the Jews: and it is of Abraham, not of Moses, St. Paul saith that he is the father of the faithful; [Romans, 4. 11] that is, of those that are loyal and do not violate their allegiance sworn to God, then by circumcision, and afterwards in the New Covenant by baptism. This covenant at the foot of Mount Sinai was renewed by Moses where the Lord commandeth Moses to speak to the people in this manner, "If you will obey my voice indeed, and keep my covenant, then ye shall be a peculiar people to me, for all the earth is mine; and ye shall be unto me a sacerdotal kingdom, and an holy nation." [Exodus, 19. 5] For a "peculiar people," the vulgar Latin hath, peculium de cunctis populis: the English translation made in the beginning of the reign of King James hath, a "peculiar treasure unto me above all nations"; and the Geneva French, "the most precious jewel of all nations." But the truest translation is the first, because it is confirmed by St. Paul himself where he saith, [Titus, 2. 14] alluding to that place, that our blessed Saviour "gave Himself for us, that He might purify us to Himself, a peculiar (that is, an extraordinary) people": for the word is in the Greek periousios, which is opposed commonly to the word epiousios: and as this signifieth ordinary, quotidian, or, as in the Lord's Prayer, of daily use; so the other signifieth that which is overplus, and stored up, and enjoyed in a special manner; which the Latins call peculium: and this meaning of the place is confirmed by the reason God rendereth of it, which followeth immediately, in that He addeth, "For all the earth is mine," as if He should say, "All the nations of the world are mine; but it is not so that you are mine, but in a special manner: for they are all mine, by reason of my power; but you shall be mine by your own consent and covenant," which is an addition to his ordinary title to all nations. The same is again confirmed in express words in the same text, "Ye shall be to me a sacerdotal kingdom, and an holy nation." The vulgar Latin hath it, regnum sacerdotale, to which agreeth the translation of that place, sacerdotium regale, a regal priesthood; [I Peter, 2. 9] as also the institution itself, by which no man might enter into the sanctum sanctorum, that is to say, no man might enquire God's will immediately of God Himself, but only the high priest. The English translation before mentioned, following that of Geneva, has, "a kingdom of priests"; which is either meant of the succession of one high priest after another, or else it accordeth not with St. Peter, nor with the exercise of the high priesthood. For there was never any but the high priest only that was to inform the people of God's will; nor any convocation of priests ever allowed to enter into the sanctum sanctorum. Again, the title of a holy nation confirms the same: for holy signifies that which is God's by special, not by general, right. All the earth, as is said in the text, is God's; but all the earth is not called holy, but that only which is set apart for his especial service, as was the nation of the Jews. It is therefore manifest enough by this one place that by the kingdom of God is properly meant a Commonwealth, instituted (by the consent of those which were to be subject thereto) for their civil government and the regulating of their behaviour, not only towards God their king, but also towards one another in point of justice, and towards other nations both in peace and war; which properly was a kingdom wherein God was king, and the high priest was to be, after the death of Moses, his sole viceroy, or lieutenant. But there be many other places that clearly prove the same. As first when the elders of Israel, grieved with the corruption of the sons of Samuel, demanded a king, Samuel, displeased therewith, prayed unto the Lord; and the Lord answering said unto him, "Hearken unto the voice of the people, for they have not rejected thee, but they have rejected me, that I should not reign over them." [I Samuel, 8. 7] Out of which it is evident that God Himself was then their king; and Samuel did not command the people, but only delivered to them that which God from time to time appointed him. Again, where Samuel saith to the people, "When ye saw that Nahash, king of the children of Ammon, came against you, ye said unto me, Nay, but a king shall reign over us; when the Lord your God was your king":[I Samuel, 12. 12] it is manifest that God was their king, and governed the civil state of their Commonwealth. And after the Israelites had rejected God, the prophets did foretell His restitution; as, "Then the moon shall be confounded, and the sun ashamed, when the Lord of hosts shall reign in Mount Zion, and in Jerusalem"; [Isaiah, 24. 23] where he speaketh expressly of His reign in Zion and Jerusalem; that is, on earth. And, "And the Lord shall reign over them in Mount Zion":[Micah, 4. 7] this Mount Zion is in Jerusalem upon the earth. And, "As I live, saith the Lord God, surely with a mighty hand, and a stretched out arm, and with fury poured out, I will rule over you";[Ezekiel, 20. 33] and, "I will cause you to pass under the rod, and I will bring you into the bond of the covenant";[Ibid., 20. 37] that is, I will reign over you, and make you to stand to that covenant which you made with me by Moses, and broke in your rebellion against me in the days of Samuel, and in your election of another king. And in the New the New Testament the angel Gabriel saith of our Saviour, "He shall be great, and be called the Son of the most High, and the Lord shall give him the throne of his father David; and he shall reign over the house of Jacob for ever; and of his kingdom there shall be no end." [Luke, 1. 32, 33] This is also a kingdom upon earth, for the claim whereof, as an enemy to Caesar, he was put to death; the title of his cross was Jesus of Nazareth, King of the Jews; he was crowned in scorn with a crown of thorns; and for the proclaiming of him, it is said of the Disciples "That they did all of them contrary to the decrees of Caesar, saying there was another King, one Jesus." [Acts, 17. 7] The kingdom therefore of God is a real, not a metaphorical kingdom; and so taken, not only in the Old Testament, but the New. When we say, "For thine is the kingdom, the power, and glory," it is to be understood of God's kingdom, by force of our covenant, not by the right of God's power; for such a kingdom God always hath; so that it were superfluous to say in our prayer, "Thy kingdom come," unless it be meant of the restoration of that kingdom of God by Christ which by revolt of the Israelites had been interrupted in the election of Saul. Nor had it been proper to say, "The kingdom of heaven is at hand"; or to pray, "Thy kingdom come," if it had still continued. There be so many other places that confirm this interpretation that it were a wonder there is no greater notice taken of it, but that it gives too much light to Christian kings to see their right of ecclesiastical government. This they have observed, that instead of a sacerdotal kingdom, translate, a kingdom of priests: for they may as well translate a royal priesthood, as it is in St. Peter, into a priesthood of kings. And whereas, for a peculiar people, they put a precious jewel, or treasure, a man might as well call the special regiment or company of a general the general's precious jewel, or his treasure. In short, the kingdom of God is a civil kingdom, which consisted first, in the obligation of the people of Israel to those laws which Moses should bring unto them from Mount Sinai; and which afterwards the high priest, for the time being, should deliver to them from before the cherubim in the sanctum sanctorum; and which kingdom having been cast off in the election of Saul, the prophets foretold, should be restored by Christ; and the restoration whereof we daily pray for when we say in the Lord's Prayer, "Thy kingdom come"; and the right whereof we acknowledge when we add, "For thine is the kingdom, the power, and glory, for ever and ever, Amen"; and the proclaiming whereof was the preaching of the Apostles; and to which men are prepared by the teachers of the Gospel; to embrace which Gospel (that is to say, to promise obedience to God's government) is to be in the kingdom of grace, because God hath gratis given to such the power to be the subjects (that is, children) of God hereafter when Christ shall come in majesty to judge the world, and actually to govern his own people, which is called the kingdom of glory. If the kingdom of God (called also the kingdom of heaven, from the gloriousness and admirable height of that throne) were not a kingdom which God by His lieutenants or vicars, who deliver His commandments to the people, did exercise on earth, there would not have been so much contention and war about who it is by whom God speaketh to us; neither would many priests have troubled themselves with spiritual jurisdiction, nor any king have denied it them. Out of this literal interpretation of the kingdom of God ariseth also the true interpretation of the word holy. For it is a word which in God's kingdom answereth to that which men in their kingdoms use to call public, or the king's. The king of any country is the public person, or representative of all his own subjects. And God the king of Israel was the Holy One of Israel. The nation which is subject to one earthly sovereign is the nation of that sovereign, that is, of the public person. So the Jews, who were God's nation, were called a holy nation. [Exodus, 19. 6] For by holy is always understood either God Himself or that which is God's in propriety; as by public is always meant either the person or the Commonwealth itself, or something that is so the Commonwealth's as no private person can claim any propriety therein. Therefore the Sabbath (God's day) is a holy day; the Temple (God's house), a holy house; sacrifices, tithes, and offerings (God's tribute), holy duties; priests, prophets, and anointed kings, under Christ (God's ministers), holy men; the celestial ministering spirits (God's messengers), holy angels; and the like: and wheresoever the word holy is taken properly, there is still something signified of propriety gotten by consent. In saying "Hallowed be thy name," we do but pray to God for grace to keep the first Commandment of having no other Gods but Him. Mankind is God's nation in propriety: but the Jews only were a holy nation,. Why, but because they became his propriety by covenant? And the word profane is usually taken in the Scripture for the same with common; and consequently their contraries, holy and proper, in the kingdom of God must be the same also. But figuratively, those men also are called holy that led such godly lives, as if they had forsaken all worldly designs, and wholly devoted and given themselves to God. In the proper sense, that which is made holy by God's appropriating or separating it to his own use is said to be sanctified by God, as the seventh day in the fourth Commandment; and as the elect in the New Testament were said to be sanctified when they were endued with the spirit of godliness. And that which is made holy by the dedication of men, and given to God, so as to be used only in his public service, is called also sacred, and said to be consecrated, as temples, and other houses of public prayer, and their utensils, priests, and ministers, victims, offerings, and the external matter of sacraments. Of holiness there be degrees: for of those things that are set apart for the service of God, there may be some set apart again for a nearer and more especial service. The whole nation of the Israelites were a people holy to God; yet the tribe of Levi was amongst the Israelites a holy tribe; and amongst the Levites the priests were yet more holy; and amongst the priests the high priest was the most holy. So the land of Judea was the Holy Land, but the Holy City wherein God was to be worshipped was more holy; and again, the Temple more holy than the city, and the sanctum sanctorum more holy than the rest of the Temple. A sacrament is a separation of some visible thing from common use; and a consecration of it to God's service, for a sign either of our admission into the kingdom of God, to be of the number of his peculiar people, or for a commemoration of the same. In the Old Testament the sign of admission was circumcision; in the New Testament, baptism. The commemoration of it in the Old Testament was the eating (at a certain time, which was anniversary) of the Paschal Lamb, by which they were put in mind of the night wherein they were delivered out of their bondage in Egypt; and in the New Testament, the celebrating of the Lord's Supper, by which we are put in mind of our deliverance from the bondage of sin by our blessed Saviour's death upon the cross. The sacraments of admission are but once to be used, because there needs but one admission; but because we have need of being often put in mind of our deliverance and of our allegiance, the sacraments of commemoration have need to be reiterated. And these are the principal sacraments and, as it were, the solemn oaths we make of our allegiance. There be also other consecrations that may be called sacraments, as the word implieth only consecration to God's service; but as it implies an oath or promise of allegiance to God, there were no other in the Old Testament but circumcision and the Passover; nor are there any other in the New Testament but baptism and the Lord's Supper.

## CHAPTER XXXVI, OF THE WORD OF GOD, AND OF PROPHETS

WHEN there is mention of the word of God, or of man, it doth not signify a part of speech, such as grammarians call a noun or a verb, or any simple voice, without a contexture with other words to make it significative; but a perfect speech or discourse, whereby the speaker affirmeth, denieth, commandeth, promiseth, threateneth, wisheth, or interrogateth. In which sense it is not vocabulum that signifies a word, but sermo (in Greek logos) that is, some speech, discourse, or saying. Again, if we say the word of God, or of man, it may be understood sometimes of the speaker: as the words that God hath spoken, or that a man hath spoken; in which sense, when we say the Gospel of St. Matthew, we understand St. Matthew to be the writer of it: and sometimes of the subject; in which sense, when we read in the Bible, "The words of the days of the kings of Israel, or Judah," it is meant the acts that were done in those days were the subject of those words; and in the Greek, which, in the Scripture, retaineth many Hebraisms, by the word of God is oftentimes meant, not that which is spoken by God, but concerning God and His government; that is to say, the doctrine of religion: insomuch as it is all one to say logos theou, and theologia; which is that doctrine which we usually call divinity, as is manifest by the places following: "The Paul and Barnabas waxed bold, and said, it was necessary that the word of God should first have been spoken to you, but seeing you put it from you, and judge yourselves unworthy of everlasting life, lo, we turn to the Gentiles." [Acts, 13. 46] That which is here called the word of God was the doctrine of Christian religion; as it appears evidently by that which goes before. And where it is said to the Apostles by an angel, "Go stand and speak in the Temple, all the words of this life";[Ibid., 5. 20] by the words of this life is meant the doctrine of the Gospel, as is evident by what they did in the Temple, and is expressed in the last verse of the same chapter. "Daily in the Temple, and in every house, they ceased not to teach and preach Christ Jesus":[Ibid., 15. 7 in which place it is manifest that Jesus Christ was the subject of this "word of life"; or, which is all one, the subject of the "words of this life eternal" that our Saviour offered them. So the word of God is called the word of the Gospel, because it containeth the doctrine of the kingdom of Christ; and the same word is called the word of faith; [Romans, 10. 8, 9] that is, as is there expressed, the doctrine of Christ come and raised from the dead. Also, "When any one heareth the word of the kingdom";[Matthew, 13. 19] that is the doctrine of the kingdom taught by Christ. Again, the same word is said "to grow and to be multiplied";[Acts, 12. 24] which to understand of the evangelical doctrine is easy, but of the voice or speech of God, hard and strange. In the same sense the doctrine of devils I Timothy, 4. 1] signifieth not the words of any devil, but the doctrine of heathen men concerning demons, and those phantasms which they worshipped as gods. Considering these two significations of the word of God, as it is taken in Scripture, it is manifest in this latter sense (where it is taken for the doctrine of Christian religion) that the whole Scripture is the word of God: but in the former sense, not so. For example, though these words, "I am the Lord thy God," etc., to the end of the Ten Commandments, were spoken by God to Moses; yet the preface, "God spake these words and said," is to be understood for the words of him that wrote the holy history. The word of God, as it is taken for that which He hath spoken, is understood sometimes properly, sometimes metaphorically. Properly, as the words He hath spoken to His prophets: metaphorically, for His wisdom, power, and eternal decree, in making the world; in which sense, those fiats, "Let their be light, Let there be a firmament, Let us make man," etc. [Genesis, 1] are the word of God. And in the same sense it is said, "All things were made by it, and without it was nothing made that was made":[John, 1. 3] and "He upholdeth all things by the word of His power";[Hebrews, 1. 3] that is, by the power of His word; that is, by His power: and "The worlds were framed by the word of God";[Ibid., 11. 3] and many other places to the same sense: as also amongst the Latins, the name of fate, which signifieth properly the word spoken, is taken in the same sense. Secondly, for the effect of His word; that is to say, for the thing itself, which by His word is affirmed, commanded, threatened, or promised; as where Joseph is said to have been kept in prison, "till his word was come";[Psalms, 105. 19] that is, till that was come to pass which he had foretold to Pharoah's butler concerning his being restored to his office: [Genesis, 11. 13] for there, by his word was come, is meant the thing itself was come to pass. So also, Elijah saith to God, "I have done all these thy words," [I Kings, 18. 36] instead of "I have done all these things at thy word," or commandment. And, "Where is the word of the Lord"[Jeremiah, 17. 15] is put for "Where is the evil He threatened." And, "There shall none of my words be prolonged any more";[Ezekiel, 12. 28] by words are understood those things which God promised to His people. And in the New Testament, "heaven and earth shall pass away, but my words shall not pass away";[Matthew, 24. 35] that is, there is nothing that I have promised or foretold that shall not come to pass. And in this sense it is that St. John the Evangelist, and, I think, St. John only, calleth our Saviour Himself as in the flesh the Word of God, "And the Word was made flesh";[John, 1. 14] that is to say, the word, or promise, that Christ should come into the world, "who in the beginning was with God": that is to say, it was in the purpose of God the Father to send God the Son into the world to enlighten men in the way of eternal life; but it was not till then put in execution, and actually incarnate; so that our Saviour is there called the Word, not because he was the promise, but the thing promised. They that taking occasion from this place do commonly call him the Verb of God do but render the text more obscure. They might as well term him the Noun of God: for as by noun, so also by verb, men understand nothing but a part of speech, a voice, a sound, that neither affirms, nor denies, nor commands, nor promiseth, nor is any substance corporeal or spiritual; and therefore it cannot be said to be either God or man; whereas our Saviour is both. And this Word which St. John in his Gospel saith was with God is, in his first Epistle, called the "Word of life";[Ibid., 1. 1] and "the Eternal Life, which was with the Father": [Ibid., 1. 2] so that he can be in no other sense called the Word than in that wherein He is called Eternal Life; that is, he that hath procured us eternal life by his coming in the flesh. So also the Apostle, speaking of Christ clothed in a garment dipped in blood, saith his name is "the Word of God," [Apocalypse, 19. 13] which is to be understood as if he had said his name had been "He that was come according to the purpose of God from the beginning, and according to His word and promises delivered by the prophets." So that there is nothing here of the incarnation of a word, but of the incarnation of God the Son, therefore called the Word, because his incarnation was the performance of the promise; in like manner as the Holy Ghost is called the Promise. [Acts, 1. 4; Luke, 24. 49] There are also places of the Scripture where by the Word of God is signified such words as are consonant to reason and equity, though spoken sometimes neither by prophet nor by a holy man. For Pharaoh Necho was an idolater, yet his words to the good King Josiah, in which he advised him by messengers not to oppose him in his march against Carchemish, are said to have proceeded from the mouth of God; and that Josiah, not hearkening to them, was slain in the battle; as is to be read II Chronicles, 35. 21, 22, 23. It is true that as the same history is related in the first Book of Esdras, not Pharaoh, but Jeremiah, spake these words to Josiah from the mouth of the Lord. But we are to give credit to the canonical Scripture whatsoever be written in the Apocrypha. The Word of God is then also to be taken for the dictates of reason and equity, when the same is said in the Scriptures to be written in man's heart; as Psalms, 37. 31; Jeremiah, 31. 33; Deuteronomy, 30. 11, 14, and many other like places. The name of prophet signifieth in Scripture sometimes prolocutor; that is, he that speaketh from God to man, or from man to God: and sometimes predictor, or a foreteller of things to come: and sometimes one that speaketh incoherently, as men that are distracted. It is most frequently used in the sense speaking from God to the people. So Moses, Samuel, Elijah, Isaiah, Jeremiah, and others were prophets. And in this sense the high priest was a prophet, for he only went into the sanctum sanctorum to enquire of God, and was to declare his answer to the people. And therefore when Caiaphas said it was expedient that one man should die for the people, St. John saith that "He spake not this of himself, but being high priest that year, he prophesied that one man should die for the nation." [John, 11. 51] Also they that in Christian congregations taught the people are said to prophesy. [I Corinthians, 14. 3] In the like sense it is that God saith to Moses concerning Aaron, "He shall be thy spokesman to the people; and he shall be to thee a mouth, and thou shalt be to him instead of God":[Exodus, 4. 16] that which here is spokesman is, Exodus, 7. 1, interpreted prophet: "See," saith God, "I have made thee a god to Pharaoh, and Aaron thy brother shall be thy prophet." In the sense of speaking from man to God, Abraham is called a prophet where God in a dream speaketh to Abimelech in this manner, "Now therefore restore the man his wife, for he is a prophet, and shall pray for thee";[Genesis, 20. 7] whereby may be also gathered that the name of prophet may be given not unproperly to them that in Christian churches have a calling to say public prayers for the congregation. In the same sense, the prophets that came down from the high place, or hill of god, with a psaltery, and a tabret, and a pipe, and a harp, Saul amongst them, are said to prophesy, in that they praised God in that manner publicly. [I Samuel, 10. 5, 6, 10] In the like sense is Miriam called a prophetess. [Exodus, 15. 20] So is it also to be taken where St. Paul saith, "Every man that prayeth or prophesieth with his head covered," etc., and every woman that prayeth or prophesieth with her head uncovered":[I Corinthians, 11. 4, 5] for prophecy in that place signifieth no more but praising God in psalms and holy songs, which women might do in the church, though it were not lawful for them to speak to the congregation. And in this signification it is that the poets of the heathen, that composed hymns and other sorts of poems in the honor of their gods, were called vates, prophets, as is well enough known by all that are versed in the books of the Gentiles, and as is evident where St. Paul saith of the Cretans that a prophet of their own said they were liars; [Titus, 1. 12] not that St. Paul held their poets for poets for prophets, but acknowledgeth that the word prophet was commonly used to signify them that celebrated the honour of God in verse. When by prophecy is meant prediction, or foretelling of future contingents, not only they were prophets who were God's spokesmen, and foretold those things to others which God had foretold to them; but also all those impostors that pretend by the help familiar spirits, or by superstitious divination of events past, from false causes, to foretell the like events in time to come: of which (as I have declared already in the twelfth Chapter of this discourse) there be many kinds who gain in the opinion of the common sort of men a greater reputation of prophecy by one casual event that may be but wrested to their purpose, than can be lost again by never so many failings. Prophecy is not an art, nor, when it is taken for prediction, a constant vocation, but an extraordinary and temporary employment from God, most often of good men, but sometimes also of the wicked. The woman of Endor, who is said to have had a familiar spirit, and thereby to have raised a phantasm of Samuel, and foretold Saul his death, was not therefore a prophetess; for neither had she any science whereby she could raise such a phantasm, nor does it appear that God commanded the raising of it, but only guided that imposture to be a means of Saul's terror and discouragement, and by consequent, of the discomfiture by which he fell. And for incoherent speech, it was amongst the Gentiles taken for one sort of prophecy, because the prophets of their oracles, intoxicated with a spirit or vapor from the cave of the Pythian Oracle at Delphi, were for the time really mad, and spake like madmen; of whose loose words a sense might be made to fit any event, in such sort as all bodies are said to be made of materia prima. In the Scripture I find it also so taken in these words, "And the evil spirit came upon Saul, and he prophesied in the midst of the house."[I Samuel, 18. 10] And although there be so many significations in Scripture of the word prophet; yet is that the most frequent in which it is taken for him to whom God speaketh immediately that which the prophet is to say from Him to some other man, or to the people. And hereupon a question may be asked, in what manner God speaketh to such a prophet. Can it, may some say, be properly said that God hath voice and language, when it cannot be properly said He hath a tongue or other organs as a man? The Prophet David argueth thus, "Shall He that made the eye, not see? or He that made the ear, not hear?" [Psalms, 94. 9] But this may be spoken, not, as usually, to signify God's nature, but to signify our intention to honour Him. For to see and hear are honourable attributes, and may be given to God to declare as far as capacity can conceive His almighty power. But if it were to be taken in the strict and proper sense, one might argue from his making of all other parts of man's body that he had also the same use of them which we have; which would be many of them so uncomely as it would be the greatest contumely in the world to ascribe them to Him. Therefore we are to interpret God's speaking to men immediately for that way, whatsoever it be, by which God makes them understand His will: and the ways whereby He doth this are many, and to be sought only in the Holy Scripture; where though many times it be said that God spake to this and that person, without declaring in what manner, yet there be again many places that deliver also the signs by which they were to acknowledge His presence and commandment; and by these may be understood how He spake to many of the rest. In what manner God spake to Adam, and Eve, and Cain, and Noah is not expressed; nor how he spake to Abraham, till such time as he came out of his own country to Sichem in the land of Canaan, and then God is said to have appeared to him. [Genesis, 12. 7] So there is one way whereby God made His presence manifest; that is, by an apparition, or vision. And again, the word of the Lord came to Abraham in a vision";[Ibid., 15. 1] that is to say, somewhat, as a sign of God's presence, appeared as God's messenger to speak to him. Again, the Lord appeared to Abraham by an apparition of three angels; [Ibid., 18. 1] and to Abimelech in a dream; [Ibid., 18. 1] to Lot by an apparition of two angels; [Ibid., 19. 1] and to Hagar by the apparition of one angel; [Ibid., 21. 17] and to Abraham again by the apparition of a voice from heaven; [Ibid., 22. 11] and to Isaac in the night[Ibid., 26. 24] (that is, in his sleep, or by dream); and to Jacob in a dream; [Ibid., 28. 12] that is to say (as are the words of the text), "Jacob dreamed that he saw a ladder," etc. And in a vision of angels; [Ibid., 32. 1] and to Moses in the apparition of a flame of fire out of the midst of a bush; [Exodus, 3. 2] and after the time of Moses, where the manner how God spake immediately to man in the Old Testament is expressed, He spake always by a vision, or by a dream; as to Gideon, Samuel, Eliah, Elisha, Isaiah, Ezekiel, and the rest of the prophets; and often in the New Testament, as to Joseph, to St. Peter, to St. Paul, and to St. John the Evangelist in the Apocalypse. Only to Moses He spake in a more extraordinary manner in Mount Sinai, and in the Tabernacle; and to the high priest in the Tabernacle, and in the sanctum sanctorum of the Temple. But Moses, and after him the high priests, were prophets of a more eminent place and degree in God's favour; and God Himself in express words declareth that to other prophets He spake in dreams and visions, but to His servant Moses in such manner as a man speaketh to his friend. The words are these: "If there be a prophet among you, I the Lord will make Myself known to him in a vision, and will speak unto him in a dream. My servant Moses is not so, who is faithful in all my house; with him I will speak mouth to mouth, even apparently, not in dark speeches; and the similitude of the Lord shall he behold." [Numbers, 12. 6, 7, 8] And, "The Lord spake to Moses face to face, as a man speaketh to his friend." [Exodus, 33. 11] And yet this speaking of God to Moses was by mediation of an angel, or angels, as appears expressly, Acts 7. 35 and 53, and Galatians, 3. 19, and was therefore a vision, though a more clear vision than was given to other prophets. And conformable hereun-

to, where God saith, "If there arise amongst you a prophet, or dreamer of dreams," [Deuteronomy, 13. 1] the latter word is but the interpretation of the former. And, "Your sons and yo
r daughters shall prophesy; your old men shall dream dreams, and your young men shall see visions ":[Joel, 2. 28] where again, the word prophesy is expounded by dream and vision. And in the same manner it was that God spake to Solomon, promising him wisdom, riches, and honour; for the text saith, "And Solomon awoke, and behold it was a dream":[I Kings, 3. 15] so that generally the prophets extraordinary in the Old Testament took notice of the word of God no otherwise than from their dreams or visions that is to say, from the imaginations which they had in their sleep or in an ecstasy: which imaginations in every true prophet were supernatural, but in false prophets were either natural or feigned. The same prophets were nevertheless said to speak by the spirit; as where the prophet, speaking of the Jews, saith, "They made their hearts hard as adamant, lest they should hear the law, and the words which the Lord of Hosts hath sent in His Spirit by the former prophets." [Zechariah, 7. 12] By which it is manifest that speaking by the spirit or inspiration was not a particular manner of God's speaking, different from vision, when they that were said to speak by the Spirit were extraordinary prophets, such as for every new message were to have a particular commission or, which is all one, a new dream or vision. Of prophets that were so by a perpetual calling in the Old Testament, some were supreme and some subordinate: supreme were first Moses, and after him the high priests, every one for his time, as long the priesthood was royal; and after the people of the Jews had rejected God, that He should no more reign over them, those kings which submitted themselves to God's government were also his chief prophets; and the high priest's office became ministerial. And when God was to be consulted, they put on the holy vestments, and enquired of the Lord as the king commanded them, and were deprived of their office when the king thought fit. For King Saul commanded the burnt offering to be brought; [I Samuel, 13. 9] and he commands the priest to bring the Ark near him; [Ibid.,14. 18] and, again, to let it alone, because he saw an advantage upon his enemies. [Ibid., 14. 19] And in the same chapter Saul asketh counsel of God. In like manner King David, after his being anointed, though before he had possession of the kingdom, is said to "enquire of the Lord" whether he should fight against the Philistines at Keilah; [Ibid., 23. 2] and David commandeth the priest to bring him the ephod, to enquire whether he should stay in Keilah or not. [Ibid., 23. 9] And King Solomon took the priesthood from Abiathar, [I Kings, 2. 27] and gave it to Zadok. [Ibid., 2. 35] Therefore Moses, and the high priests, and the pious kings, who enquired of God on all extraordinary occasions how they were to carry themselves, or what event they were to have, were all sovereign prophets. But in what manner God spake unto them is not manifest. To say that when Moses went up to God in Mount Sinai it was a dream, or vision, such as other prophets had, is contrary to that distinction which God made between Moses and other prophets. [Numbers, 12. 6, 7, 8] To say God spake or appeared as He is in His own nature is to deny His infiniteness, invisibility, incomprehensibility. To say he spake by inspiration, or infusion of the Holy Spirit, as the Holy Spirit signifieth the Deity, is to make Moses equal with Christ, in whom only the Godhead, as St. Paul speaketh, dwelleth bodily. [Colossians, 2. 9] And lastly, to say he spake by the Holy Spirit, as it signifieth the graces or gifts of the Holy Spirit, is to attribute nothing to him supernatural. For God disposeth men to piety, justice, mercy, truth, faith, and all manner of virtue, both moral and intellectual, by doctrine, example, and by several occasions, natural and ordinary. And as these ways cannot be applied to God, in His speaking to Moses at Mount Sinai; so also they cannot be applied to Him in His speaking to the high priests from the mercy-seat. Therefore in what manner God spake to those sovereign prophets of the Old Testament, whose office it was to enquire of Him, is not intelligible. In the time of the New Testament there was no sovereign prophet but our Saviour, who was both God that spake, and the prophet to whom He spake. To subordinate prophets of perpetual calling, I find not any place that proveth God spake to them supernaturally, but only in such manner as naturally He inclineth men to piety, to belief, to righteousness, and to other virtues all other Christian men. Which way, though it consist in constitution, instruction, education, and the occasions and invitements men have to Christian virtues, yet it is truly attributed to the operation of the Spirit of God, or Holy Spirit, which we in our language call the Holy Ghost: for there is no good inclination that is not of the operation of God. But these operations are not always supernatural. When therefore a prophet is said to speak in the spirit, or by the Spirit of God, we are to understand no more but that he speaks according to God's will, declared by the supreme prophet. For the most common acceptation of the word spirit is in the signification of a man's intention, mind, or disposition. In the time of Moses, there were seventy men besides himself that prophesied in the camp of the Israelites. In what manner God spake to them is declared in the eleventh Chapter of Numbers, verse 25: "The Lord came down in a cloud, and spake unto Moses, and took of the spirit that was upon him, and gave it to the seventy elders. And it came to pass, when the spirit rested upon them, they prophesied, and did not cease." By which it is manifest, first, that their prophesying to the people was sub-

servient and subordinate to the prophesying of Moses; for that God took of the spirit of Moses put upon them; so that they prophesied as Moses would have them: otherwise they had not been suffered to prophesy at all. For there was a complaint made against them to Moses; [Numbers, 11. 27] and Joshua would have Moses to have forbidden them; which he did not, but said to Joshua "Be not jealous in my behalf." Secondly, that the Spirit of God in that place signifieth nothing but the mind and disposition to obey and assist Moses in the administration of the government. For if it were meant they had the substantial Spirit of God; that is, the divine nature, inspired into them, then they had it in no less manner than Christ himself, in whom only the Spirit of God dwelt bodily. It is meant therefore of the gift and grace of God, that guided them to co-operate with Moses, from whom their spirit was derived. And it appeareth that they were such as Moses himself should appoint for elders and officers of the people: [Ibid., 11. 16] for the words are, "Gather unto me seventy men, whom thou knowest to be elders and officers of the people": where, thou knowest is the same with thou appointest, or hast appointed to be such. For we are told before that Moses, following the counsel of Jethro his father-in-law, did appoint judges and officers over the people such as feared God; [Exodus, 18] and of these were those seventy whom God, by putting upon them Moses' spirit, inclined to aid Moses in the administration of the kingdom: and in this sense the spirit of God is said presently upon the anointing of David to have come upon David, and left Saul; [I Samuel, 16. 13, 14] God giving His graces to him He chose to govern His people, and taking them away from him He rejected. So that by the spirit is meant inclination to God's service, and not any supernatural revelation. God spake also many times by the event of lots, which were ordered by such as He had put in authority over His people. So we read that God manifested by the lots which Saul caused to be drawn the fault that Jonathan had committed in eating a honeycomb, contrary to the oath taken by the people. [I Samuel, 14. 43] And God divided the land of Canaan amongst the Israelites by the "lots that Joshua did cast before the Lord in Shiloh." [Joshua, 18. 10] In the same manner it seemeth to be that God discovered the crime of Achan. [ Ibid., 7. 16, etc.] And these are the ways whereby God declared His will in the Old Testament. All which ways He used also in the New Testament. To the Virgin Mary, by a vision of an angel; to Joseph, in a dream; again to Paul, in the way to Damascus in a vision of our Saviour; and to Peter in the vision of a sheet let down from heaven with diverse sorts of flesh of clean and unclean beasts; and in prison, by vision of an angel; and to all the Apostles and writers of the New Testament, by the graces of His Spirit; and to the Apostles again, at the choosing of Matthias in the place of Judas Iscariot, by lot. Seeing then all prophecy supposeth vision or dream (which two, when they be natural, are the same), or some especial gift of God so rarely observed in mankind as to be admired where observed; and seeing as well such gifts as the most extraordinary dreams and visions may proceed from God, not only by His supernatural and immediate, but also by his natural operation, and by mediation of second causes; there is need of reason and judgement to discern between natural and supernatural gifts, and between natural and supernatural visions or dreams. And consequently men had need to be very circumspect, and wary, in obeying the voice of man that, pretending himself to be a prophet, requires us to obey God in that way which he in God's name telleth us to be the way to happiness. For he that pretends to teach men the way of so great felicity pretends to govern them; that is to say, rule and reign over them; which is a thing that all men naturally desire, and is therefore worthy to be suspected of ambition and imposture; and consequently ought be examined and tried by every man before he yield them obedience, unless he have yielded it them already in the institution of a Commonwealth; as when the prophet is the civil sovereign, or by the civil sovereign authorized. And if this examination of prophets and spirits were not allowed to every one of the people, it had been to no purpose to set out the marks by which every man might be able to distinguish between those whom they ought, and those whom they ought not to follow. Seeing therefore such marks are set out to know a prophet by, [Deuteronomy, 13. 1, etc.] and to know a spirit by; [I John, 4. 1, etc.] and seeing there is so much prophesying in the Old Testament, and so much preaching in the New Testament against prophets, and so much greater a number ordinarily of false prophets than of true; every one is to beware of obeying their directions at their own peril. And first, that there were many more false than true prophets appears by this, that when Ahab consulted four hundred prophets, they were all false impostors, but only one Micaiah. [I Kings, 22] And a little before the time of the Captivity the prophets were generally liars. "The prophets," saith the Lord by Jeremiah, "prophesy lies in my name. I sent them not, neither have I commanded them, nor spake unto them: they prophesy to you a false vision, a thing of naught, and the deceit of their heart." [Jeremiah, 14. 14] Insomuch as God commanded the people by the mouth of the prophet Jeremiah not to obey them. "Thus saith the Lord of Hosts, hearken not unto the words of the prophets that prophesy to you. They make you vain: they speak a vision of their own heart, and not out of the mouth of the Lord." [Ibid., 23. 16] Seeing then there was in the time of the Old Testament such quarrels amongst the visionary prophets, one contesting with another, and asking, "When departed the spirit from me, to go to thee?" as between Micaiah and the rest of the four hundred; and such giving of the lie to one another, as in Jeremiah, 14. 14, and such controversies in the new Testament this day amongst the spiritual prophets: every man then was, and now is, bound to make use of his natural reason to apply to all prophecy those rules which God hath given us to discern the true from the false. Of which rules, in the Old Testament, one was conformable doctrine to that which Moses the sovereign prophet had taught them; and the other, the miraculous power of foretelling what God would bring to pass, as I have already shown out of Deuteronomy, 13. 1, etc. And in the New Testament there was but one only mark, and that was the preaching of this doctrine that Jesus is the Christ, that is, the King of the Jews, promised in the Old Testament. Whosoever denied that article, he was a false prophet, whatsoever miracles he might seem to work; and he that taught it was a true prophet. For St. John, speaking expressly of the means to examine spirits, whether they be of God or not, after he had told them that there would arise false prophets, saith thus, "Hereby know ye the Spirit of God. Every spirit that confesseth that Jesus Christ is come in the flesh, is of God";[I John, 4. 2, etc.] that is, is approved and allowed as a prophet of God: not that he is a godly man, or one of the elect for this that he confesseth, professeth, or preacheth Jesus to be the Christ, but for that he is a prophet avowed. For God sometimes speaketh by prophets whose persons He hath not accepted; as He did by Baalam, and as He foretold Saul of his death by the Witch of Endor. Again in the next verse, "Every spirit that confesseth not that Jesus Christ is come in the flesh, is not of Christ. And this is the spirit of Antichrist." So that the rule is perfect rule is perfect on both sides: that he is a true prophet which preacheth the Messiah already come, in the person of Jesus; and he a false one that denieth him come, and looketh for him in some future impostor that shall take upon him that honour falsely, whom the Apostle there properly calleth Antichrist. Every man therefore ought to consider who is the sovereign prophet; that is to say, who it is that is God's vicegerent on earth, and hath next under God the authority of governing Christian men; and to observe for a rule that doctrine which in the name of God he hath commanded to be taught, and thereby to examine and try out the truth of those doctrines which pretended prophets, with miracle or without, shall at any time advance: and if they find it contrary to that rule, to do as they did that came to Moses and complained that there were some that prophesied in the camp whose authority so to do they doubted of; and leave to the sovereign, as they did to Moses, to uphold or to forbid them, as he should see cause; and if he disavow them, then no more to obey their voice, or if he approve them, then to obey them as men to whom God hath given a part of the spirit of their sovereign. For when Christian men take not their Christian sovereign for God's prophet, they must either take their own dreams for the prophecy they mean to be governed by, and the tumour of their own hearts for the Spirit of God; or they must suffer themselves to be lead by some strange prince, or by some of their fellow subjects that can bewitch them by slander of the government into rebellion, without other miracle to confirm their calling than sometimes an extraordinary success and impunity; and by this means destroying all laws, both divine and human, reduce all order, government, and society to the first chaos of violence and civil war.

## CHAPTER XXXVII, OF MIRACLES AND THEIR USE

BY Miracles are signified the admirable works of God: and therefore they are also called wonders. And because they are for the most part done for a signification of His commandment in such occasions as, without them, men are apt to doubt (following their private natural reasoning) what He hath commanded, and what not, they are commonly, in Holy Scripture, called signs, in the same sense as they are called by the Latins, ostenta and portenta, from showing and foresignifying that which the Almighty is about to bring to pass. To understand therefore what is a miracle, we must first understand what works they are which men wonder at and call admirable. And there be but two things which make men wonder at any event: the one is if it be strange, that is to say, such as the like of it hath never or very rarely been produced; the other is if when it is produced, we cannot imagine it to have been done by natural means, but only by the immediate hand of God. But when we see some possible natural cause of it, how rarely soever the like has been done; or if the like have been often done, how impossible soever it be to imagine a natural means thereof, we no more wonder, nor esteem it for a miracle. Therefore, if a horse or cow should speak, it were a miracle, because both the thing is strange and the natural cause difficult to imagine; so also were it to see a strange deviation of nature in the production of some new shape of a living creature. But when a man, or other animal, engenders his like, though we know no more how this is done than the other; yet because it is usual, it is no miracle. In like manner, if a man be metamorphosed into a stone, or into a pillar, it is a miracle, because strange; but if a piece of wood be so changed, because we see it often it is no miracle: and yet we know no more by what operation of God the one is brought to pass than the other. The first rainbow that was seen in the world was a miracle, because the first, and consequently strange, and served for a sign from God, placed in heaven to assure His people there should be no more a universal destruction of the world by water. But at this day, because they are frequent, they are not miracles, neither to them that know their natural causes, nor to them who know them not. Again, there be many rare works produced by the art of man; yet when we know they are done, because thereby we know also the means how they are done, we count them not for miracles, because not wrought by the immediate hand of God, but by mediation of human industry. Furthermore, seeing admiration and wonder is consequent to the knowledge and experience wherewith men are endued, some more, some less, it followeth that the same thing may be a miracle to one, and not to another. And thence it is that ignorant and superstitious men make great wonders of those works which other men, knowing to proceed from nature (which is not the immediate, but the ordinary work of God), admire not at all; as when eclipses of the sun and moon have been taken for super-natural works by the common people, when nevertheless there were others could, from their natural causes, have foretold the very hour they should arrive; or, as when a man, by confederacy and secret intelligence, get-ting knowledge of the private actions of an ignorant, unwary man, thereby tells him what he has done in for-mer time, it seems to him a miraculous thing; but amongst wise and cautelous men, such miracles as those cannot easily be done. Again, it belongeth to the nature of a miracle that it be wrought for the procuring of credit to God's messengers, ministers, and prophets, that thereby men may know they are called, sent, and em-ployed by God, and thereby be the better inclined to obey them. And therefore, though the creation of the world, and after that the destruction of all living creatures in the universal deluge, were admirable works; yet because they were not done to procure credit to any prophet or other minister of God, they use not to be called miracles. For how admirable soever any work be, the admiration consisteth not in that could be done, because men naturally believe the Almighty can do all things, but because He does it at the prayer or word of a man. But the works of God in Egypt, by the hand of Moses, were properly miracles, because they were done with intention to make the people of Israel believe that Moses came unto them, not out of any design of his own in-terest, but as sent from God Therefore after God had commanded him to deliver the Israelites from the Egyp-tian bondage, when he said, "They will not believe me, but will say the Lord hath not appeared unto me," [Ex-odus, 4. 1] God gave him power to turn the rod he had in his hand into a serpent, and again to return it into a rod; and by putting his hand into his bosom, to make it leprous, and again by pulling it out to make it whole, to make the children of Israel believe that the God of their fathers had appeared unto him: [Ibid., 4. 5] and if that were not enough, He gave him power to turn their waters into blood. And when he had done these mira-cles before the people, it is said that "they believed him." [Ibid., 4. 31] Nevertheless, for fear of Pharaoh, they durst not yet obey him. Therefore the other works which were done to plague Pharaoh and the Egyptians tend-ed all to make the Israelites believe in Moses, and properly miracles. In like manner if we consider all the mir-acles done by the hand of Moses, and all the rest of the prophets till the Captivity, and those of our Saviour and his Apostles afterwards, we shall find their end was always to beget or confirm belief that they came not of their own motion, but were sent by God. We may further observe in Scripture that the end of miracles was to beget belief, not universally in all men, elect and reprobate, but in the elect only; that is to say, in such as God had determined should become His subjects. For those miraculous plagues of Egypt had not for end the conversion of Pharaoh; for God had told Moses before that He would harden the heart of Pharaoh, that he should not let the people go: and when he let them go at last, not the miracles persuaded him, but the plagues forced him to it. So also of our Saviour it is written that He wrought not many miracles in His own country, because of their unbelief; [Matthew, 13. 58] and instead of, "He wrought not many," it is, "He could work none." [Mark, 6. 5] It was not because he wanted power; which, to say, were blasphemy against God; nor that the end of miracles was not to convert incredulous men to Christ; for the end of all the miracles of Moses, of the prophets, of our Saviour and of his Apostles was to add men to the Church; but it was because the end of their miracles was to add to the Church, not all men, but such as should be saved; that is to say, such as God had elected. Seeing therefore our Saviour was sent from His Father, He could not use His power in the con-version of those whom His Father had rejected. They that, expounding this place of St. Mark, say that this word, "He could not," is put for, "He would not," do it without example in the Greek tongue (where would not is put sometimes for could not, in things inanimate that have no will; but could not, for would not, never), and thereby lay a stumbling block before weak Christians, as if Christ could do no miracles but amongst the cred-ulous. From that which I have here set down, of the nature and use of a miracle, we may define it thus: a mira-cle is a work of God (besides His operation by the way of nature, ordained in the Creation) done for the mak-ing manifest to His elect the mission of an extraordinary minister for their salvation. And from this definition, we may infer: first, that in all miracles the work done is not the effect of any virtue in the prophet, because it is the effect of the immediate hand of God; that is to say, God hath done it, without using the prophet therein as a subordinate cause. Secondly, that no devil, angel, or other created spirit can do a miracle. For it must either be by virtue of some natural science or by incantation, that is, virtue of words. For if the enchanters do it by their own power independent, there is some power that proceedeth not from God, which all men deny; and if they do it by power given them, then is the work not from the immediate hand of God, but natural, and consequently no miracle. There be some texts of Scripture that seem to attribute the power of working wonders, equal to some of those immediate miracles wrought by God Himself, to certain arts of magic and incantation. As, for example, when we read that after the rod of Moses being cast on the ground became a serpent, "the magicians of Egypt did the like by their enchantments";[Exodus, 7. 11] and that after Moses had turned the waters of the Egyptian streams, rivers, ponds, and pools of water into blood, "the magicians of Egypt did likewise, with their enchantments";[Ibid., 7. 22] and that after Moses had by the power of God brought frogs upon the land, "the magicians also did so with their enchantments, and brought up frogs upon the land of Egypt";[Ibid., 8. 7] will not man be apt to attribute miracles to enchantments; that is to say, to the efficacy of the sound of words; and think the same very well proved out of this and other such places? And yet there is no place of Scripture that telleth us what an enchantment is. If therefore enchantment be not, as many think it, a working of strange effects by spells and words, but imposture and delusion wrought by ordinary means; and so far from supernatural, as the impostors need not the study so much of natural causes, but the ordinary ignorance, stupidity, and superstition of mankind, to do them; those texts that seem to countenance the power of magic, witchcraft, and enchantment must needs have another sense than at first sight they seem to bear. For it is evident enough that words have no have now effect but on those that understand them, and then they have no other but to signify the intentions or passions of them that speak; and thereby produce hope, fear, or other passions, or conceptions in the hearer. Therefore when a rod seemeth a serpent, or the waters blood, or any other miracle seemeth done by enchantment; if it be not to the edification of God's people, not the rod, nor the water, nor any other thing is enchanted; that is to say, wrought upon by the words, but the spectator. So that all the miracle consisteth in this, that the enchanter has deceived a man; which is no miracle, but a very easy matter to do. For such is the ignorance and aptitude to error generally of all men, but especially of them that have not much knowledge of natural causes, and of the nature and interests of men, as by innumerable and easy tricks to be abused. What opinion of miraculous power, before it was known there was a science of the course of the stars, might a man have gained that should have told the people, this hour, or day, the sun should be darkened? A juggler, by the handling of his goblets and other trinkets, if it were not now ordinarily practised, would be thought to do his wonders by the power at least of the Devil. A man that hath practised to speak by drawing in of his breath (which kind of men in ancient time were called ventriloqui) and so make the weakness of his voice seem to proceed, not from the weak impulsion of the organs of speech, but from distance of place, is able to make very many men believe it is a voice from heaven, whatsoever he please to tell them. And for a crafty man that hath enquired into the secrets and familiar confessions that one man ordinarily maketh to another of his actions and adventures past, to tell them him again is no hard matter; and yet there be many that by such means as that obtain the reputation of being conjurers. But it is too long a business to reckon up the several sorts of those men which the Greeks called thaumaturgi, that is to say, workers of things wonderful; and yet these do all they do by their own single dexterity. But if we look upon the impostures wrought by confederacy, there is nothing how impossible soever to be done that is impossible to be believed. For two men conspiring, one to seem lame, the other to cure him with a charm, will deceive many: but many conspiring, one to seem lame, another so to cure him, and all the rest to bear witness, will deceive many more. In this aptitude of mankind to give too hasty belief to pretended miracles, there can there can be no better nor I think any other caution than that which God hath prescribed, first by Moses (as I have said before in the precedent chapter), in the beginning of the thirteenth and end of the eighteenth of Deuteronomy; that we take not any for prophets that teach any other religion than that which God's lieutenant, which at that time was Moses, hath established; nor any, though he teach the same religion, whose prediction we do not see come to pass. Moses therefore in his time, and Aaron and his successors in their times, and the sovereign governor of God's people next under God Himself, that is to say, the head of the Church in all times, are to be consulted what doctrine he hath established before we give credit to a pretended miracle or prophet. And when that is done, the thing they pretend to be a miracle, we must both see it done and use all means possible to consider whether it be really done; and not only so, but whether it be such as no man can do the like by his natural power, but that it requires the immediate hand of God. And in this also we must have recourse to God's lieutenant, to whom in all doubtful cases we have submitted our private judgements. For example, if a man pretend that after certain words spoken over a piece of bread, that presently God hath made it not bread, but a god, or a man, or both, and nevertheless it looketh still as like bread as ever it did, there is no reason for any man to think it really done, nor consequently to fear him till he enquire of God by his vicar or lieutenant whether it be done or not. If he say not, then followeth that which Moses, saith "he hath spoken it presumptuously; thou shalt not fear him." [Deuteronomy, 18. 22] If he say it is done, then he is not to contradict it. So also if we see not, but only hear tell of a miracle, we are to consult the lawful Church; that is to say, the lawful head thereof, how far we are to give credit to the relators of it. And this is chiefly the case of men that in these days live under Christian sovereigns. For in these times I do not know one man that ever saw any such wondrous work, done by the charm or at the word or prayer of a man, that a man endued but with a mediocrity of reason would think supernatural: and the question is no more whether what we see done be a miracle; whether the miracle we hear, or read of, were a real work, and not the act of a tongue or pen; but in plain terms, whether the report be true, or a lie. In which question we are not every one to make our own private reason or conscience, but the public reason, that is the reason of God's supreme lieutenant, judge; and indeed we have made him judge already, if we have given him a sovereign power to do all that is necessary for our peace and defence. A private man has always the liberty, because thought is free, to believe or not believe in his heart those acts that have been given out for miracles, according as he shall see what benefit can accrue, by men's belief, to those that pretend or countenance them, and thereby conjecture whether they be miracles or lies. But when it comes to confession of that faith, the private reason must submit to the public; that is to say, to God's lieutenant. But who is this lieutenant of God, and head of the Church, shall be considered in its proper place hereafter.

## CHAPTER XXXVIII, OF THE SIGNIFICATION IN SCRIPTURE OF ETERNAL LIFE, HELL, SALVATION, THE WORLD TO COME, AND REDEMPTION

THE maintenance of civil society depending on justice, and justice on the power of life and death, and other less rewards and punishments residing in them that have the sovereignty of the Commonwealth; it is impossible a Commonwealth should stand where any other than the sovereign hath a power of giving greater rewards than life, and of inflicting greater punishments than death. Now seeing eternal life is a greater reward than the life present, and eternal torment a greater punishment than the death of nature, it is a thing worthy to be well considered of all men that desire, by obeying authority, to avoid the calamities of confusion and civil war, what is meant in Holy Scripture by life eternal and torment eternal; and for what offences, and against whom committed, men are to be eternally tormented; and for what actions they are to obtain eternal life. And first we find that Adam was created in such a condition of life as, had he not broken the commandment of God, he had enjoyed it in the Paradise of Eden everlastingly. For there was the tree of life, whereof he was so long allowed to eat as he should forbear to eat of the tree of knowledge of good and evil, which was not allowed him. And therefore as soon as he had eaten of it, God thrust him out of Paradise, "lest he should put forth his hand, and take also of the tree of life, and live forever." [Genesis, 3. 22] By which it seemeth to me (with submission nevertheless both in this, and in all questions whereof the determination dependeth on the Scriptures, to the interpretation of the Bible authorized by the Commonwealth whose subject I am) that Adam, if he had not sinned, had had an eternal life on earth; and that mortality entered upon himself, and his posterity, by his first sin. Not that actual death then entered, for Adam then could never have had children; whereas he lived long after, and saw a numerous posterity ere he died. But where it is said, "In the day that thou eatest thereof, thou shalt surely die," [Ibid., 2. 17] it must needs be meant of his mortality and certitude of death. Seeing then eternal life was lost by Adam's forfeiture, in committing sin, he that should cancel that forefeiture was to recover thereby that life again. Now Jesus Christ hath satisfied for the sins of all that believe in him, and therefore recovered to all believers that eternal life which was lost by the sin of Adam. And in this sense it is that the comparison of St. Paul holdeth: "As by the offence of one, judgement came upon all men to condemnation; even so by the righteousness of one, the free gift came upon all men to justification of life." [Romans, 5. 18, 19] Which is again more perspicuously delivered in these words, "For since by man came death, by man came also the resurrection of the dead. For as in Adam all die, even so in Christ shall all be made alive." [I Corinthians, 15. 21, 22] Concerning the place wherein men shall enjoy that eternal life which Christ hath obtained for them, the texts next before alleged seem to make it on earth. For if, as in Adam, all die, that is, have forfeited Paradise and eternal life on earth, even so in Christ all shall be made alive; then all men shall be made to live on earth; for else the comparison were not proper. Hereunto seemeth to agree that of the Psalmist, "Upon Zion God commanded the blessing, even life for evermore"; [Psalms, 133. 3] for Zion is in Jerusalem upon earth: as also that of St. John, "To him that overcometh I will give to eat of the tree of life, which is in the midst of the Paradise of God." [Revelation, 2. 7] This was the tree of Adam's eternal life; but his life was to have been on earth. The same seemeth to be confirmed again by St. John, where he saith, "I John saw the holy city, new Jerusalem, coming down from God out of heaven, prepared as a bride adorned for her husband": and again, verse 10, to the same effect; as if he should say, the new Jerusalem, the Paradise of God, at the coming again of Christ, should come down to God's people from heaven, and not they go up to it from earth. And this differs nothing from that which the two men in white clothing (that is, the two angels) said to the Apostles that were looking upon Christ ascending: "This same Jesus, who is taken up from you into heaven, shall so come, as you have seen him go up into heaven." Which soundeth as if they had said he should come down to govern them under his Father eternally here, and not take them up to govern them in heaven; and is conformable to the restoration of the kingdom of God, instituted under Moses, which was a political government of the Jews on earth. Again, that saying of our Saviour, "that in the resurrection they neither marry, nor are given in marriage, but are as the angels of God in heaven," is a description of an eternal life, resembling that which we lost in Adam in the point of marriage. For seeing Adam and Eve, if they had not sinned, had lived on earth eternally in their individual persons, it is manifest they should not continually have procreated their kind. For if immortals should have generated, as mankind doth now, the earth in a small time would not have been able to afford them place to stand on. The Jews that asked our Saviour the question, whose wife the woman that had married many brothers should be in the resurrection, knew not what were the consequences of life eternal: and therefore our puts them in mind of this consequence of immortality; that there shall be no generation, and consequently no marriage, no more than there is marriage or generation among the angels. The comparison between that eternal life which Adam lost, and our Saviour by his victory over death hath recovered, holdeth also in this, that as Adam lost eternal life by his sin, and yet lived after it for a time, so the faithful Christian hath recovered eternal life by Christ's passion, though he die a natural death, and remain dead for a time; namely, till the resurrection. For as death is reckoned from the condemnation of Adam, not from the execution; so life is reckoned from the absolution, not from the resurrection of them that are elected in Christ. That the place wherein men are to live eternally, after the resurrection, is the heavens, meaning by heaven those parts of the world which are the most remote from earth, as where the stars are, or above the stars, in another higher heaven, called coelum empyreum (whereof there is no mention in Scripture, nor ground in reason), is not easily to be drawn from any text that I can find. By the Kingdom of Heaven is meant the kingdom of the King that dwelleth in heaven; and His kingdom was the people of Israel, whom He ruled by the prophets, his lieutenants; first Moses, and after him Eleazar, and the sovereign priests, till in the days of Samuel they rebelled, and would have a mortal man for their king after the manner of other nations. And when our Saviour Christ by the preaching of his ministers shall have persuaded the Jews to return, and called the Gentiles to his obedience, then shall there be a new king of heaven; because our King shall then be God, whose throne is heaven, without any necessity evident in the Scripture that man shall ascend to his happiness any higher than God's footstool the earth. On the contrary, we find written that "no man hath ascended into heaven, but he that came down from heaven, even the Son of Man, that is in heaven." Where I observe, by the way, that these words are not, as those which go immediately before, the words of our Saviour, but of St. John himself; for Christ was then not in heaven, but upon the earth. The like is said of David where St. Peter, to prove the Ascension of Christ, using the words of the Psalmist, "Thou wilt not leave my soul in hell, nor suffer thine Holy One to see corruption," saith they were spoken, not of David, but of Christ, and to prove it, addeth this reason, "For David is not ascended into heaven." But to this a man may easily answer and say that, though their bodies were not to ascend till the general day of judgement, yet their souls were in heaven as soon as they were departed from their bodies; which also seemeth to be confirmed by the words of our Saviour, who, proving the resurrection out of the words of Moses, saith thus, "That the dead are raised, even Moses shewed at the bush, when he calleth the Lord, the God of Abraham, and the God of Isaac, and the God of Jacob. For he is not a God of the dead, but of the living; for they all live to him." [Luke, 20. 37, 38] But if these words be to be understood only of the immortality of the soul, they prove not at all that which our Saviour intended to prove, which was the resurrection of the body, that is to say, the immortality of the man. Therefore our Saviour meaneth that those patriarches were immortal, not by a property consequent to the essence and nature of mankind, but by the will of God, that was pleased of His mere grace to bestow eternal life upon the faithful. And though at that time the patriarchs and many other faithful men were dead, yet as it is in the text, they "lived to God"; that is, they were written in the Book of Life with them that were absolved of their sins, and ordained to life eternal at the resurrection. That the soul of man is in its own nature eternal, and a living creature independent on the body; or that any mere man is immortal, otherwise than by the resurrection in the last day, except Enos and Elias, is a doctrine not apparent in Scripture. The whole fourteenth Chapter of Job, which is the speech not of his friends, but of himself, is a complaint of this mortality of nature; and yet no contradiction of the immortality at the resurrection. "There is hope of a tree," saith he, "if it be cast down. Though the root thereof wax old, and the stock thereof die in the ground, yet when it scenteth the water it will bud, and bring forth boughs like a plant. But man dieth, and wasteth away, yea, man giveth up the ghost, and where is he?" [Job, 14. 7] And, verse 12, "man lieth down, riseth not, till the heavens be no more." But when is it that the heavens shall be no more? St. Peter tells us that it is at the general resurrection. For in his second Epistle, third Chapter, verse 7, he saith that "the heavens and the earth that are now, are reserved unto fire against the day of judgement, and perdition of ungodly men," and, verse 12, "looking for and hasting to the coming of God, wherein the heavens shall be on fire, and shall be dissolved, and the elements shall melt with fervent heat. Nevertheless, we according to the promise look for new heavens, and a new earth, wherein dwelleth righteousness." Therefore where Job saith, "man riseth not till the heavens be no more"; it is all one, as if he had said the immortal life (and soul and life in the Scripture do usually signify the same thing) beginneth not in man till the resurrection and day of judgement; and hath for cause, not his specifical nature and generation, but the promise. For St. Peter says not, "We look for new heavens, and a new earth," but "from promise." Lastly, seeing it hath been already proved out of diverse evident places of Scripture, in the thirty-fifth Chapter of this book, that the kingdom of God is a civil Commonwealth, where God Himself is sovereign, by virtue first of the Old, and since of the New, Covenant, wherein He reigneth by His vicar or lieutenant; the same places do therefore also prove that after the coming again of our Saviour in his majesty and glory to reign actually and eternally, the kingdom of God is to be on earth. But because this doctrine, though proved out of places of Scripture not few nor obscure, will appear to most men a novelty, I do but propound it, maintaining nothing in this or any other paradox of religion, but attending the end of that dispute of the sword, concerning the authority (not yet amongst my countrymen decided), by which all sorts of doctrine are to be approved or rejected; and whose commands, both in speech and writing, whatsoever be the opinions of private men, must by all men, that mean to be protected by their laws, be obeyed. For the points of doctrine concerning the kingdom of God have so great influence on the kingdom of man as not to be determined but by them that under God have the sovereign power. As the kingdom of God, and eternal life, so also God's enemies, and their torments after judgement, appear by the Scripture to have their place on earth. The name of the place where all men remain till the resurrection, that were either buried or swallowed up of the earth, is usually called in Scripture by words that signify under ground; which the Latins read generally infernus and inferi, and the Greeks ades; that is to say, a place where men cannot see; and containeth as well the grave as any other deeper place. But for the place of the damned after the resurrection, it is not determined, neither in the Old nor New Testament, by any note of situation, but only by the company: as that it shall be where such wicked men were, as God in former times in extraordinary and miraculous manner had destroyed from off the face of the earth: as for example, that they are in Inferno, in Tartarus, or in the bottomless pit; because Corah, Dathan, and Abiram were swallowed up alive into the earth. Not that the writers of the Scripture would have us believe there could be in the globe of the earth, which is not only finite, but also, compared to the height of the stars, of no considerable magnitude, a pit without a bottom; that is, a hole of infinite depth, such as the Greeks in their demonology (that is to say in their doctrine concerning demons), and after them the Romans, called Tartarus; of which Virgil says, Bis patet in praeceps, tantum tenditque sub umbras, Quantus ad aethereum coeli suspectus Olympum: for that is a thing the proportion of earth to heaven cannot bear: but that we should believe them there, indefinitely, where those men are, on whom God inflicted that exemplary punishment. Again, because those mighty men of the earth that lived in the time of Noah, before the flood (which the Greeks called heroes, and the Scripture giants, and both say were begotten by copulation of the children of God with the children of men), were for their wicked life destroyed by the general deluge, the place of the damned is therefore also sometimes marked out by the company of those deceased giants; as Proverbs, 21. 16, "The man that wandereth out of the way of understanding shall remain in the congregation of the giants," and Job, 26. 5, "Behold the giants groan under water, and they that dwell with them." Here the place of the damned is under the water. And Isaiah, 14. 9, "Hell is troubled how to meet thee" (that is, the King of Babylon) "and will displace the giants for thee": and here again the place of the damned, if the sense be literal, is to be under water. Thirdly, because the cities of Sodom and Gomorrah, by the extraordinary wrath of God, were consumed for their wickedness with fire and brimstone, and together with them the country about made a stinking bituminous lake, the place of the damned is sometimes expressed by fire, and a fiery lake: as in the

Apocalypse, 21. 8, "But the timorous, incredulous, and abominable, and murderers, and whoremongers, and sorcerers, and idolaters, and all liars, shall have their part in the lake that burneth with fire and brimstone; which is the second death." So that it is manifest that hell fire, which is here expressed by metaphor, from the real fire of Sodom, signifieth not any certain kind or place of torment, but is to be taken indefinitely for destruction, as it is in Revelation, 20, at the fourteenth verse, where it is said that "Death and hell were cast into the lake of fire"; that is to say, were abolished and destroyed; as if after the day of judgement there shall be no more dying, nor no more going into hell; that is, no more going to Hades (from which word perhaps our word hell is derived), which is the same with no more dying. Fourthly, from the plague of darkness inflicted on the Egyptians, of which it is written, "They saw not one another, neither rose any man from his place for three days; but all the children of Israel had light in their dwellings";[Exodus, 10. 23] the place of the wicked after judgement is called utter darkness, or, as it is in the original, darkness without. And so it is expressed where the king commandeth his servants, "to bind hand and foot the man that had not on his wedding garment and to cast him into," eis to skotos to exoteron "external darkness," [Matthew, 22. 13] or "darkness without": which, though translated "utter darkness," does not signify how great, but where that darkness is to be; namely, without the habitation of God's elect. Lastly, whereas there was a place near Jerusalem called the Valley of the Children of Hinnon in a part whereof called Tophet the Jews had committed most grievous idolatry, sacrificing their children to the idol Moloch; and wherein also God had afflicted His enemies with most grievous punishments; and wherein Josiah had burnt the priests of Moloch upon their own altars, as appeareth at large in II Kings, Chapter 23; the place served afterwards to receive the filth and garbage which was carried thither out of the city; and there used to be fires made, from time to time, to purify the air and take away the stench of carrion. From this abominable place, the Jews used ever after to call the place of the damned by the name of Gehenna, or Valley of Hinnon. And this Gehenna is that word which is usually now translated hell; and from the fires from time to time there burning, we have the notion of everlasting and unquenchable fire. Seeing now there is none that so interprets the Scripture as that after the day of judgement the wicked are all eternally to be punished in the Valley of Hinnon; or that they shall so rise again as to be ever after underground or underwater; or that after the resurrection they shall no more see one another, nor stir from one place to another; it followeth, methinks, very necessarily, that which is thus said concerning hell fire is spoken metaphorically; and that therefore there is a proper sense to be enquired after (for of all metaphors there is some real ground, that may be expressed in proper words), both of the place of hell, and the nature of hellish torments and tormenters. And first for the tormenters, we have their nature and properties exactly and properly delivered by the names of the enemy, or Satan; the Accuser, or Diabolus; the Destroyer, or Abaddon. Which significant names, Satan, Devil, Abaddon, set not forth to us any individual person, as proper names use to do, but only an office or quality; and are therefore appellatives; which ought not to have been left untranslated, as they are in the Latin and modern Bibles, because thereby they seem to be the proper names of demons; and men are more easily seduced to believe the doctrine of devils, which at that time was the religion of the Gentiles, and contrary to that of Moses and of Christ. And because by the Enemy, the Accuser, and Destroyer is meant the enemy of them that shall be in the kingdom of God; therefore if the kingdom of God after the resurrection be upon the earth (as in the former chapter I have shown by Scripture it seems to be), the enemy and his kingdom must be on earth also. For so also was it in the time before the Jews had deposed God. For God's kingdom was in Palestine; and the nations round about were the kingdoms of the Enemy; and consequently by Satan is meant any earthly enemy of the Church. The torments of hell are expressed sometimes by "weeping, and gnashing of teeth," as Matthew, 8. 12; sometimes, by "the worm of conscience," as Isaiah, 66. 24, and Mark, 9. 44, 46, 48; sometimes, by fire, as in the place now quoted, "where the worm dieth not, and the fire is not quenched," and many places besides: sometimes, by "shame, and contempt," as, "And many of them that sleep in the dust of the earth shall awake; some to everlasting life; and some to shame, and everlasting contempt." [Daniel, 12. 2] All which places design metaphorically a grief and discontent of mind from the sight of that eternal felicity in others which they themselves through their own incredulity and disobedience have lost. And because such felicity in others is not sensible but by comparison with their own actual miseries, it followeth that they are to suffer such bodily pains and calamities as are incident to those who not only live under evil and cruel governors, but have also for enemy the eternal king of the saints, God Almighty. And amongst these bodily pains is to be reckoned also to every one of the wicked a second death. For though the Scripture be clear for a universal resurrection, yet we do not read that to any of the reprobate is promised an eternal life. For whereas St. Paul, to the question concerning what bodies men shall rise with again, saith that "the body is sown in corruption, and is raised in incorruption; it is sown in dishonour, it is raised in glory; it is sown in weakness, it is raised in power";[I Corinthians, 15. 42, 43] glory and power cannot be applied to the bodies of the wicked: nor can the name of second death be applied to those that can never die but once. And although in metaphorical speech a calamitous life everlasting may be called an everlasting death, yet it cannot well be understood of a second death. The fire prepared for the wicked is an everlasting fire: that is to say, the estate wherein no man can be without torture, both of body and mind, after the resurrection, shall endure for ever; and in that sense the fire shall be unquenchable, and the torments everlasting: but it cannot thence be inferred that he who shall be cast into that fire, or be tormented with those torments, shall endure and resist them so as be eternally burnt and tortured, and yet never be destroyed nor die. And though there be many places that affirm everlasting fire and torments, into which men may be cast successively one after another for ever, yet I find none that affirm there shall be an eternal life therein of any individual person; but to the contrary, an everlasting death, which is the second death: "For after death and the grave shall have delivered up the dead which were in them, and every man be judged according to his works; death and the grave shall also be cast into the lake of fire. This is the second death." [Revelation, 20. 13, 14] Whereby it is evident that there is to be a second death of every one that shall be condemned at the day judgement, after which he shall die no more. The joys of life eternal are in Scripture comprehended all under the name of salvation, or being saved. To be saved is to be secured, either respectively, against special evils, or absolutely, against all evil, comprehending want, sickness, and death itself. And because man was created in a condition immortal, not subject to corruption, and consequently to nothing that tendeth to the dissolution of his nature; and fell from that happiness by the sin of Adam; it followeth that to be saved from sin is to be saved from all the evil and calamities that sin hath brought upon us. And therefore in the Holy Scripture, remission of sin, and salvation from death and misery, is the same thing, as it appears by the words of our Saviour, who, having cured a man sick of the palsy, by saying, "Son be of good cheer thy sins be forgiven thee"; [Matthew, 9. 2] and knowing that the scribes took for blasphemy that a man should pretend to forgive sins, asked them "whether it were easier to say, Thy sins be forgiven thee, or, Arise and walk";[Ibid., 9. 5] signifying thereby that it was all one, as to the saving of the sick, to say, "Thy sins are forgiven," and "Arise and walk"; and that he used that form of speech only to show he had power to forgive sins. And it is besides evident in reason that since death and misery were the punishments of sin, the discharge of sin must also be a discharge of death and misery; that is to say, salvation absolute, such as the faithful are to enjoy after the day of judgement, by the power and favour of Jesus Christ, who that cause is called our Saviour. Concerning particular salvations, such as are understood, "as the Lord liveth that saveth Israel," [I Samuel, 14. 39] that is, from their temporary enemies; and, "Thou art my Saviour, thou savest me from violence";[II Samuel, 22. 3] and, "God gave the Israelites a Saviour, and so they were delivered from the hand of the Assyrians," [II Kings, 13. 5] and the like, I need say nothing; there being neither difficulty nor interest to corrupt the interpretation of texts of that kind. But concerning the general salvation, because it must be in the kingdom of heaven, there is great difficulty concerning the place. On one side, by kingdom, which is an estate ordained by men for their perpetual security against enemies and want, it seemeth that this salvation should be on earth. For by salvation is set forth unto us a glorious reign of our king by conquest; not a safety by escape: and therefore there where we look for salvation, we must look also for triumph; and before triumph, for victory; and before victory, for battle; which cannot well be supposed shall be in heaven. But how good soever this reason may be, I will not trust to it without very evident places of Scripture. The state of salvation is described at large, Isaiah, 33. 20, 21, 22, 23, 24: "Look upon Zion, the city of our solemnities; thine eyes shall see Jerusalem a quiet habitation, a tabernacle that shall not be taken down; not one of the stakes thereof shall ever be removed, neither shall any of the cords thereof be broken. "But there the glorious Lord will be unto us a place of broad rivers and streams; wherein shall go no galley with oars, neither shall gallant ship pass thereby. "For the Lord is our judge, the Lord is our lawgiver, the Lord is our king, he will save us. "Thy tacklings are loosed; they could not well strengthen their mast; they could not spread the sail: then is the a great spoil divided; the lame take the prey. "And the inhabitant shall not say, I am sick; the people that shall dwell therein shall be forgiven their iniquity." In which words we have the place from whence salvation is to proceed, "Jerusalem, a quiet habitation"; the eternity of it, "a tabernacle that shall not be taken down," etc.; the Saviour of it, "the Lord, their judge, their lawgiver, their king, he will save us"; the salvation, "the Lord shall be to them as a broad moat of swift waters," etc.; the condition of their enemies, "their tacklings are loose, their masts weak, the lame shall take the spoil of them"; the condition of the saved, "The inhabitant shall not say, I am sick"; and lastly, all this is comprehended in forgiveness of sin, "the people that dwell therein shall be forgiven their iniquity." By which it is evident that salvation shall be on earth, then, when God shall reign, at the coming again of Christ, in Jerusalem; and from Jerusalem shall proceed the salvation of the Gentiles that shall be received into God's kingdom: as is also more expressly declared by the same prophet, "And they" (that is, the Gentiles who had any Jew in bondage) "shall bring all your brethren for an offering to the Lord, out of all nations, upon horses, and in chariots, and in litters, and upon mules, and upon swift beasts, to my holy mountain, Jerusalem, saith the Lord, as the children of Israel bring an offering in a clean vessel into the house of the Lord. And I will also take of them for priests and for Levites, saith the Lord":[Isaiah, 66. 20, 21] whereby it is manifest that the chief seat of God's kingdom, which is the place from whence the salvation of us that were Gentiles shall proceed, shall be Jerusalem: and the same is also confirmed by our Saviour, in his discourse with the woman of Samaria concerning the place of God's worship; to whom he saith that the Samaritans worshipped they knew not what, but the Jews worshipped what they knew, "for salvation is of the Jews" [John, 4. 22] (ex Judaeis, that is, begins at the Jews): as if he should say, you worship God, but know not by whom He will save you, as we do, that know it shall be by one of the tribe of Judah; a Jew, not a Samaritan. And therefore also the woman not impertinently answered him again, "We know the Messias shall come." So that which our Saviour saith, "Salvation is from the Jews,: is the same that Paul says, "The gospel is the power of God to salvation to every one that believeth: to the Jew first, and also to the Greek. For therein is the righteousness of God revealed from faith to faith";[Romans, 1. 16, 17] from the faith of the Jew to the faith of the Gentile. In the like sense the prophet Joel, describing the day of judgement, that God would "shew wonders in heaven, and in earth, blood, and fire, and pillars of smoke. The sun should be turned to darkness, and the moon into blood, before the great and terrible day of the Lord come." [Joel, 2. 30, 31] He addeth, "and it shall come to pass, that whosoever shall call upon the name of the Lord shall be saved. For in Mount Zion and in Jerusalem shall be salvation." [Ibid., 2. 32] And Obadiah, verse 17, saith the same, "Upon Mount Zion shall be deliverance; and there shall be holiness, and the house of Jacob shall possess their possessions," that is, the possessions of the heathen, which possessions he expresseth more particularly in the following verses, by the mount of Esau, the land of the Philistines, the fields of Ephraim, of Samaria, Gilead, and the cities of the South, and concludes with these words, "the kingdom shall be the Lord's." All these places are for salvation, and the kingdom of God, after the day of judgement, upon earth. On the other side, I have not found any text that can probably be drawn to prove any ascension of the saints into heaven; that is to say, into any coelum empyreum, or other ethereal region, saving that it is called the kingdom of heaven: which name it may have because God, that was king of the Jews, governed them by His commands sent to Moses by angels from heaven; and after their revolt, sent His Son from heaven to reduce them to their obedience; and shall send him thence again to rule both them and all other faithful men from the day of judgement, everlastingly: or from that, that the throne of this our Great King is in heaven; whereas the earth is but His footstool. But that the subjects of God should have any place as high as His throne, or higher than His footstool, it seemeth not suitable to the dignity of a king, nor can I find any evident text for it in Holy Scripture. From this that hath been said of the kingdom of God, and of salvation, it is not hard to interpret what is meant by the world to come. There are three worlds mentioned in the Scripture; the old world, the present world, and the world to come. Of the first, St. Peter speaks, "If God spared not the old world, but saved Noah the eighth person, a preacher of righteousness, bringing the flood upon the world of the ungodly," etc. [II Peter, 2. 5] So the first world was from Adam to the general flood. Of the present world, our Saviour speaks, "My kingdom is not of this world." [John, 18. 36] For He came only to teach men the way of salvation, and to renew the kingdom of His Father by His doctrine. Of the world to come, St. Peter speaks, "Nevertheless we according to his promise look for new heavens, and a new earth." [II Peter, 3. 13] This is that world wherein Christ coming down from heaven in the clouds, with great power and glory, shall send His angels, and shall gather together his elect, from the four winds, and from the uttermost parts of the earth, and thenceforth reign over them, under his Father, everlastingly. Salvation of a sinner supposeth a precedent redemption; for he that is once guilty of sin is obnoxious to the penalty of the same; and must pay, or some other for him, such ransom as he that is offended, and has him in his power, shall require. And seeing the person offended is Almighty God, in whose power are all things, such ransom is to be paid before salvation can be acquired, as God hath been pleased to require. By this ransom is not intended a satisfaction for sin equivalent to the offence, which no sinner for himself, nor righteous man can ever be able to make for another: the damage a man does to another he may make amends for by restitution or recompense, but sin cannot be taken away by recompense; for that were to make the liberty to sin a thing vendible. But sins may be pardoned to the repentant, either gratis or upon such penalty as God is pleased to accept. That which God usually accepted, in the Old Testament, was some sacrifice or oblation. To forgive sin is not an act of injustice, though the punishment have been threatened. Even amongst men, though the promise of good bind the promiser; yet threats, that is to say, promises of evil, bind them not; much less shall they bind God, who is infinitely more merciful than men. Our Saviour Christ therefore to redeem us did not in that sense satisfy for the sins of men, as that his death, of its own virtue, could make it unjust in God to punish sinners with eternal death; but did make that sacrifice and oblation of Himself, at His first coming, which God was pleased to require for the salvation at His second coming, of such as in the meantime should repent and believe in Him. And though this act of our redemption be not always in Scripture called a sacrifice and oblation, but sometimes a price; yet by price we are not to understand anything by the value whereof He could claim to a pardon for us from his offended Father; but that price which God the Father was pleased in mercy to demand.

## CHAPTER XXXIX, OF THE SIGNIFICATION IN SCRIPTURE OF THE WORD CHURCH

THE WORD Church (ecclesia) signifieth in the books of Holy Scripture diverse things. Sometimes, though not often, it is taken for God's house, that is to say, for a tem
le wherein Christians assemble to perform holy duties publicly; as, "Let your women keep silence in the churches":[I Corinthians, 14. 34] but this is metaphorically put for the congregation there assembled, and hath been since used for the edifice itself to distinguish between the temples of Christians and idolaters. The Temple of Jerusalem was God's house, and the house of prayer; and so is any edifice dedicated by Christians to the worship of Christ, Christ's house: and therefore the Greek Fathers call it Kuriake, the Lord's house; and thence in our language it came to be called kirk, and church. Church, when not taken for a house, signifieth the same that ecclesia signified in the Grecian Commonwealths; that is to say, a congregation, or an assembly of citizens, called forth to hear the magistrate speak unto them; and which in the Commonwealth of Rome was called concio, as he that spake was called ecclesiastes, and concionator. And when they were called forth by lawful authority, it was ecclesia legitima, a lawful Church, ennomos Ekklesia. [Acts, 19. 39] But when they were excited by tumultuous and seditious clamour, then it was a confused Church, Ekklesia sug-kechumene. It is taken also sometimes for the men that have right to be of the congregation, though not actually assembled; that is to say, for the whole multitude of Christian men, how far soever they be dispersed: as where it is said that "Saul made havoc of the church":[Acts, 8. 3] and in this sense is Christ said to be Head of the Church. And sometimes for a certain part of Christians; as, "Salute the Church that is in his house." [Colossians, 4. 15] Sometimes also for the elect only; as, "A glorious Church, without spot or wrinkle, holy and without blemish"; [Ephesians, 5. 27] which is meant of the Church triumphant, or Church to come. Sometimes, for a congregation assembled of professors of professors of Christianity, whether their profession be true or counterfeit, as it is understood where it is said, "Tell it to the Church, and if he neglect to hear the Church, let him be to thee as a Gentile, or publican." [Matthew, 18. 17] And in this last sense only it is that the Church can be taken for one person; that is to say, that it can be said to have power to will, to pronounce, to command, to be obeyed, to make laws, or to do any other action whatsoever; for without authority from a lawful congregation, whatsoever act be done in a concourse of people, it is the particular act of every one of those that were present, and gave their aid to the performance of it; and not the act of them all in gross, as of one body; much less the act of them that were absent, or that, being present, were not willing it should be done. According to this sense, I define a Church to be: a company of men professing Christian religion, united in the person of one sovereign; at whose command they ought to assemble, and without whose authority they ought not to assemble. And because in all Commonwealths that assembly which is without warrant from the civil sovereign is unlawful; that Church also which is assembled in any Commonwealth that hath forbidden them to assemble is an unlawful assembly. It followeth also that there is on earth no such universal Church as all Christians are bound to obey, because there is no power on earth to which all other Commonwealths are subject. There are Christians in the dominions of several princes and states, but every one of them is subject to that Commonwealth whereof he is himself a member, and consequently cannot be subject to the commands of any other person. And therefore a Church, such a one as is capable to command, to judge, absolve, condemn, or do any other act, is the same thing with a civil Commonwealth consisting of Christian men; and is called a civil state, for that the subjects of it are men; and a Church, for that the subjects thereof are Christians. Temporal and spiritual government are but two words brought into the world to make men see double and mistake their lawful sovereign. It is true that the bodies of the faithful, after the resurrection, shall be not only spiritual, but eternal; but in this life they are gross and corruptible. There is therefore no other government in this life, neither of state nor religion, but temporal; nor teaching of any doctrine lawful to any subject which the governor both of the state and of the religion forbiddeth to be taught. And that governor must be one; or else there must needs follow faction and civil war in the Commonwealth between the Church and State; between spiritualists and temporalists; between the sword of justice and the shield of faith; and, which

is more, in every Christian man's own breast between the Christian and the man. The doctors of the Church are called pastors; so also are civil sovereigns: but if pastors be not subordinate one to another, so as that there may be one chief pastor, men will be taught contrary doctrines, whereof both may be, and one must be, false. Who that one chief pastor is, according to the law of nature, hath been already shown; namely, that it is the civil sovereign: and to whom the Scripture hath assigned that office, we shall see in the chapters following.

## CHAPTER XL, OF THE RIGHTS OF THE KINGDOM OF GOD, IN ABRAHAM, MOSES, THE HIGH PRIESTS, AND THE KINGS OF JUDAH

THE FATHER of the faithful, and first in the kingdom of God by covenant, was Abraham. For with him was the covenant first made; wherein he obliged himself and his seed after him to acknowledge and obey the commands of God; not only such as he could take notice of (as moral laws) by the light of nature; but also such as God should in special manner deliver to him by dreams and visions. For as to the moral law, they were already obliged, and needed not have been contracted withal, by promise of the land of Canaan. Nor was there any contract that could add to or strengthen the obligation by which both they and all men else were bound naturally to obey God Almighty: and therefore the covenant which Abraham made with God was to take for the commandment of God that which in the name of God was commanded him, in a dream or vision, and to deliver it to his family and cause them to observe the same. In this contract of God with Abraham, we may observe three points of important consequence in the government of God's people. First, that at the making of this covenant God spoke only to Abraham, and therefore contracted not with any of his family or seed otherwise than as their wills (which make the essence of all covenants) were before the contract involved in the will of Abraham, who was therefore supposed to have had a lawful power to make them perform all that he covenanted for them. According whereunto God saith, "All the nations of the earth shall be blessed in him, for I know him that he will command his children and his household after him, and they shall keep the way of the Lord." [Genesis, 18. 18, 19] From whence may be concluded this first point, that they to whom God hath not spoken immediately are to receive the positive commandments of God from their sovereign, as the family and seed of Abraham did from Abraham their father and lord and civil sovereign. And consequently in every Commonwealth, they who have no supernatural revelation to the contrary ought to obey the laws of their own sovereign in the external acts and profession of religion. As for the inward thought and belief of men, which human governors can take no notice of (for God only knoweth the heart), they are not voluntary, nor the effect of the laws, but of the unrevealed will and of the power of God, and consequently fall not under obligation. From whence proceedeth another point; that it was not unlawful for Abraham, when any of his subjects should pretend private vision or spirit, or other revelation from God, for the countenancing of any doctrine which Abraham should forbid, or when they followed or adhered to any such pretender, to punish them; and consequently that it is lawful now for the sovereign to punish any man that shall oppose his private spirit against the laws: for he hath the same place in the Commonwealth that Abraham had in his own family. There ariseth also from the same a third point; that as none but Abraham in his family, so none but the sovereign in a Christian Commonwealth, can take notice what is or what is not the word of God. For God spoke only to Abraham, and it was he only that was able to know what God said, and to interpret the same to his family: and therefore also, they that have the place of Abraham in a Commonwealth are the only interpreters of what God hath spoken. The same covenant was renewed with Isaac, and afterwards with Jacob, but afterwards no more till the Israelites were freed from the Egyptians and arrived at the foot of Mount Sinai: and then it was renewed by Moses (as I have said before, Chapter thirty-five), in such manner as they became from that time forward the peculiar kingdom of God, whose lieutenant was Moses for his own time: and the succession to that office was settled upon Aaron and his heirs after him to be to God a sacerdotal kingdom forever. By this constitution, a kingdom is acquired to God. But seeing Moses had no authority to govern the Israelites as a successor to the right of Abraham, because he could not claim it by inheritance, it appeareth not as yet that the people were obliged to take him for God's lieutenant longer than they believed that God spoke unto him. And therefore his authority, notwithstanding the covenant they made with God, depended yet merely upon the opinion they had of his sanctity, and of the reality of his conferences with God, and the verity of his miracles; which opinion coming to change, they were no more obliged to take anything for the law of God which he propounded to them in God's name. We are therefore to consider what other ground there was of their obligation to obey him. For it could not be the commandment of God that could oblige them, because God spoke not to them immediately, but by the mediation of Moses himself: and our Saviour saith of himself, "If I bear witness of myself, my witness is not true";[John, 5. 31] much less if Moses bear witness of himself, especially in a claim of kingly power over God's people, ought his testimony to be received. His authority therefore, as the authority of all other princes, must be grounded on the consent of the people and their promise to obey him. And so it was: for "the people when they saw the thunderings, and the lightnings, and the noise of the trumpet, and the mountain smoking, removed and stood afar off. And they said unto Moses, Speak thou with us, and we will hear, but let not God speak with us lest we die." [Exodus, 20. 18, 19] Here was their promise of obedience; and by this it was they obliged themselves to obey whatsoever he should deliver unto them for the commandment of God. And notwithstanding the covenant constituteth a sacerdotal kingdom, that is to say, a kingdom hereditary to Aaron; yet that is to be understood of the succession after Moses should be dead. For whosoever ordereth and establisheth the policy as first founder of a Commonwealth, be it monarchy, aristocracy, or democracy, must needs have sovereign power over the people all the while he is doing of it. And that Moses had that power all his own time is evidently affirmed in the Scripture. First, in the text last before cited, because the people promised obedience, not to Aaron, but to him. Secondly, "And God said unto Moses, Come up unto the Lord, thou and Aaron, Nadab and Abihu, and seventy of the elders of Israel. And Moses alone shall come near the Lord, but they shall not come nigh, neither shall the people go up with him." [Exodus, 24. 1, 2] By which it is plain that Moses, who was alone called up to God (and not Aaron, nor the other priests, nor the seventy elders, nor the people who were forbidden to come up), was alone he that represented to the Israelites the person of God; that is to say, was their sole sovereign under God. And though afterwards it be said, "Then went up Moses and Aaron, Nadab and Abihu, and seventy of the elders of Israel, and they saw the God of Israel, and there was under His feet as it were a paved work of sapphire stone," [Ibid., 24. 9] etc.; yet this was not till after Moses had been with God before, and had brought to the people the words which God had said to him. He only went for the business of the people; the others, as the nobles of his retinue, were admitted for honour to that special grace which was not allowed to the people; which was, as in the verse after appeareth, to see God and live. "God laid not His hand upon them, they saw God, and did eat and drink" (that is, did live), but did not carry any commandment from Him to the people. Again, it is everywhere said, "The Lord spake unto Moses," as in all other occasions of government, so also in also in the ordering of the ceremonies of religion, contained in the 25th, 26th, 27th, 28th, 29th, 30th, and 31st chapters of Exodus, and throughout Leviticus; to Aaron, seldom. The calf that Aaron made, Moses threw into the fire. Lastly, the question of the authority of Aaron, by occasion of his and Miriam's mutiny against Moses, was judged by God Himself for Moses. [Numbers, 12] So also in the question between Moses and the people, who had the right of governing the people, when Korah, Dathan, and Abiram, and two hundred and fifty princes of the assembly "gathered themselves together against Moses, and against Aaron, and said unto them, ye take too much upon you, seeing all the congregation are holy, every one of them, and the Lord is amongst them, why lift you up yourselves above the congregation of the Lord?" [Ibid., 16. 3] God caused the earth to swallow Korah, Dathan, and Abiram, with their wives and children, alive, and consumed those two hundred and fifty princes with fire. Therefore neither Aaron, nor the people, nor any aristocracy of the chief princes of the people, but Moses alone had next under God the sovereignty over the Israelites: and that not only in causes of civil policy, but also of religion: for Moses only spoke with God, and therefore only could tell the people what it was that God required at their hands. No man upon pain of death might be so presumptuous as to approach the mountain where God talked with Moses. "Thou shalt set bounds," saith the Lord, "to the people round about, and say, Take heed to yourselves that you go not up into the Mount, or touch the border of it; whosoever toucheth the Mount shall surely be put to death." [Exodus, 19. 12] And again, "Go down, charge the people, lest they break through unto the Lord to gaze." [Ibid., 19. 21] Out of which we may conclude that whosoever in Christian Commonwealth holdeth the place of Moses is the sole messenger of God and interpreter of His commandments. And according hereunto, no man ought in the interpretation of the Scripture to proceed further than the bounds which are set by their several sovereigns. For the Scriptures, since God now speaketh in them, are the Mount Sinai, the bounds whereof are the laws of them that represent God's person on earth. To look upon them, and therein to behold the wondrous works of God, and learn to fear Him, is allowed; but to interpret them, that is, to pry into what God saith to him whom He appointeth to govern under Him, and make themselves judges whether he govern as God commandeth him, or not, is to transgress the bounds God hath set us, and to gaze upon God irreverently. There was no prophet in the time of Moses, nor pretender to the spirit of God, but such as Moses had approved and authorized. For there were in his time but seventy men that are said to prophesy by the spirit of God, and these were all of Moses his election; concerning whom God said to Moses, "Gather to me seventy of the elders of Israel, whom thou knowest to be the elders of the people."

[Numbers, 11. 16] To these God imparted His spirit; but it was not a different spirit from that of Moses; for it is said, "God came down in a cloud, and took of the spirit that was upon Moses, and gave it to the seventy elders." [Ibid., 11. 25] But as I have shown before, Chapter thirty-six, by spirit is understood the mind; so that the sense of the place is no other than this, that God endued them with a mind conformable and subordinate to that of Moses, that they might prophesy, that is to say, speak to the people in God's name in such manner as to set forward (as ministers of Moses, and by his authority) such doctrine as was agreeable to Moses his doctrine. For they were but ministers; and when two of them prophesied in the camp, it was thought a new and unlawful thing; and as it is in the 27th and 28th verses of the same chapter, they were accused of it, and Joshua advised Moses to forbid them, as not knowing that it was by Moses his spirit that they prophesied. By which it is manifest that no subject ought to pretend to prophecy, or to the spirit, in opposition to the doctrine established by him whom God hath set in the place of Moses. Aaron being dead, and after him also Moses, the kingdom, as being a sacerdotal kingdom, descended by virtue of the covenant to Aaron's son, Eleazar the high priest: and God declared him, next under Himself, for sovereign, at the same time that He appointed Joshua for the general of their army. For thus God saith expressly concerning Joshua: "He shall stand before Eleazar the priest, who shall ask counsel for him before the Lord; at his word shall they go out, and at his word they shall come in, both he, and all the children of Israel with him." [Numbers, 27. 21] Therefore the supreme power of making war and peace was in the priest. The supreme power of judicature belonged also to the high priest: for the Book of the Law was in their keeping, and the priests and Levites only were the subordinate judges in causes civil, as appears in Deuteronomy, 17. 8, 9, 10. And for the manner of God's worship, there was never doubt made but that the high priest, till the time of Saul, had the supreme authority. Therefore the civil and ecclesiastical power were both joined together in one and the same person, the high priest; and ought to be so, in whosoever governeth by divine right; that is, by authority immediate from God. After the death of Joshua, till the time of Saul, the time between is noted frequently in the Book of Judges, "that there was in those days no king in Israel"; and sometimes with this addition, that "every man did that which was right in his own eyes." By which is to be understood that where it is said, "there was no king," is meant, "there was no sovereign power," in Israel. And so it was, if we consider the act and exercise of such power. For after the death of Joshua and Eleazar, "there arose another generation that knew not the Lord, nor the nor the works which He had done for Israel, but did evil in the sight of the Lord and served Baalim." [Judges, 2. 10] And the Jews had that quality which St. Paul noteth, "to look for a sign," not only before they would submit themselves to the government of Moses, but also after they had obliged themselves by their submission. Whereas signs and miracles had for end to procure faith, not to keep men from violating it when they have once given it, for to that men are obliged by the law of nature. But if we consider not the exercise, but the right of governing, the sovereign power was still in the high priest. Therefore whatsoever obedience was yielded to any of the judges (who were men chosen by God extraordinarily to save His rebellious subjects out of the hands of the enemy), it cannot be drawn into argument against the right the high priest had to the sovereign power in all matters both of policy and religion. And neither the judges nor Samuel himself had an ordinary, but extraordinary, calling to the government, and were obeyed by the Israelites, not out of duty, but out of reverence to their favour with God, appearing in their wisdom, courage, or felicity. Hitherto therefore the right of regulating both the policy and the religion were inseparable. To the judges succeeded kings: and whereas before all authority, both in religion and policy, was in the high priest; so now it was all in the king. For the sovereignty over the people which was, before, not only by virtue of the divine power, but also by a particular pact of the Israelites in God, and next under Him, in the high priest, as His vicegerent on earth, was cast off by the people, with the consent of God Himself. For when they said to Samuel, "make us a king to judge us, like all the nations," [I Samuel, 8. 5] they signified that they would no more be governed by the commands that should be laid upon them by the priest, in the name of God; but by one that should command them in the same manner that all other nations were commanded; and consequently in deposing the high priest of royal authority, they deposed that peculiar government of God. And yet God consented to it, saying to Samuel, "Hearken unto the voice of the people, in all that they shall say unto thee; for they have not rejected thee; but they have rejected me, that I should not reign over them." [Ibid., 8. 7] Having therefore rejected God, in whose right the priests governed, there was no authority left to the priests but such as the king was pleased to allow them; which was more or less, according as the kings were good or evil. And for the government of civil affairs, it is manifest, it was all in the hands of the king. For in the same chapter they say they will be like all the nations; that their king shall be their judge, and go before them, and fight their battles; [Ibid., 8. 20] that is, he shall have the whole authority, both in peace and war. In which is continued also the ordering of religion: for there was no other word of God in that time by which to regulate religion but the Law of Moses, which was their civil law.

Besides, we read that Solomon "thrust out Abiathar from being priest before the Lord":[I Kings, 2. 27] he had therefore authority over the high priest, as over any other subject, which is a great mark of supremacy in religion. And we read also that he dedicated the Temple; that he blessed the people; and that he himself in person made that excellent prayer, used in the consecrations of all churches and houses of prayer; [] which is another great mark of supremacy in religion. Again, we read that when there was question concerning the Book of the Law found in the Temple, the same was not decided by the high priest, but Josiah sent both and others to enquire concerning it, of Huldah, the prophetess; [II Kings, 22] which is another mark of the supremacy in religion. Lastly, we read that David made Hashabiah and his brethren, Hebronites, officers of Israel among them westward, "in all business of the Lord, and in the service of the king." [I Chronicles, 26. 30] Likewise, that he made other Hebronites "rulers over the Reubenites, the Gadites, and the half tribe of Manasseh" (these were the rest of Israel that dwelt beyond Jordan) "for every matter pertaining to God, and affairs of the king." [Ibid., 26. 32] Is not this full power, both temporal and spiritual, as they call it that would divide it? To conclude: from the first institution of God's kingdom, to the Captivity, the supremacy of religion was in the same hand with that of the civil sovereignty; and the priest's office, after the election of Saul, was not magisterial, but ministerial. Notwithstanding the government both in policy and religion were joined, first in the high priests, and afterwards in the kings, so far forth as concerned the right; yet it appeareth by the same holy history that the people understood it not; but there being amongst them a great part, and probably the greatest part, that no longer than they saw great miracles, or, which is equivalent to a miracle, great abilities, or great felicity in the enterprises of their governors, gave sufficient credit either to the fame of Moses or to the colloquies between God and the priests, they took occasion, as oft as their governors displeased them, by blaming sometimes the policy, sometimes the religion, to change the government or revolt from their obedience at their pleasure; and from thence proceeded from time to time the civil troubles, divisions, and calamities of the nation. As for example, after the death of Eleazar and Joshua, the next generation, which had not seen the wonders of God, but were left to their own weak reason, not knowing themselves obliged by the covenant of a sacerdotal kingdom, regarded no more the commandment of the priest, nor any law of Moses, but did every man that which was right in his own eyes; and obeyed in civil affairs such men as from time to time they thought able to deliver them from the neighbour nations that oppressed them; and consulted not with God, as they ought to do, but with such men, or women, as they guessed to be prophets by their predictions of things to come; and though they had an idol in their chapel, yet if they had a Levite for their chaplain, they made account they worshipped the God of Israel. And afterwards when they demanded a king, after the manner of the nations, yet it was not with a design to depart from the worship of God their King; but despairing of the justice of the sons of Samuel, they would have a king to judge them in civil actions; but not that they would allow their king to change the religion which they thought was recommended to them by Moses. So that they always kept in store a pretext, either of justice or religion, to discharge themselves of their obedience whensoever they had hope to prevail. Samuel was displeased with the people, for that they desired a king (for God was their King already, and Samuel had but an authority under Him); yet did Samuel, when Saul observed not his counsel in destroying Agag as God had commanded, anoint another king, namely, David, to take the succession from his heirs. Rehoboam was no idolater; but when the people thought him an oppressor, that civil pretence carried from him ten tribes to Jeroboam an idolater. And generally through the whole history of the kings, as well of Judah as of Israel, there were prophets that always controlled the kings for transgressing the religion, and sometimes also for errors of state; as Jehoshaphat was reproved by the prophet Jehu for aiding the King of Israel against the Syrians; [II Chronicles, 19. 2] and Hezekiah, by Isaiah, for showing his treasures to the ambassadors of Babylon. By all which it appeareth that though the power both of state and religion were in the kings, yet none of them were uncontrolled in the use of it but such as were gracious for their own natural abilities or felicities. So that from the practice of those times, there can no argument be drawn that the right of supremacy in religion was not in the kings, unless we place it in the prophets, and conclude that because Hezekiah, praying to the Lord before the cherubim, was not answered from thence, nor then, but afterwards by the prophet Isaiah, therefore Isaiah was supreme head of the Church; or because Josiah consulted Huldah the prophetess, concerning the Book of the Law, that therefore neither he, nor the high priest, but Huldah the prophetess had the supreme authority in matter of religion, which I think is not the opinion of any doctor. During the Captivity the Jews had no Commonwealth at all; and after their return, though they renewed their covenant with God, yet there was no promise made of obedience, neither to Esdras nor to any other: and presently after they became subjects to the to the Greeks, from whose customs and demonology, and from the doctrine of the Cabalists, their religion became much corrupted: in such sort as nothing can be gathered from their confusion, both in state and religion, concerning the supremacy in either. And therefore so far forth as concerneth the Old Testament, we may conclude that whosoever had the sovereignty of the Commonwealth amongst the Jews, the same had also the supreme authority in matter of God's external worship, and represented God's person; that is, the person of God the Father; though He were not called by the name of Father till such time as He sent into the world His Son Jesus Christ to redeem mankind from their sins, and bring them into his everlasting kingdom to be saved for evermore. Of which we are to speak in the chapter following.

**CHAPTER XLI, OF THE OFFICE OF OUR BLESSED SAVIOUR**


WE FIND in Holy Scripture three parts of the office of the Messiah: the first of a redeemer, or saviour; the second of a pastor, counsellor, or teacher, that is, of a prophet sent from God to convert such as God hath elected to salvation; the third of a king, an eternal king, but under his Father, as Moses and the high priests were in their several times. And to these three parts are correspondent three times. For, our redemption he wrought at his first coming, by the sacrifice wherein he offered up himself for our sins upon the cross; our conversion he wrought partly then in his own person, and partly worketh now by his ministers, and will continue to work till his coming again. And after his coming again shall begin that his glorious reign over his elect which is to last eternally. To the office of a redeemer, that is, of one that payeth the ransom of sin, which ransom is death, it appertaineth that he was sacrificed, and thereby bore upon his own head and carried away from us our iniquities, in such sort as God had required. Not that the death of one man, though without sin, can satisfy for the offences of all men, in the rigour of justice, but in the mercy of God, that ordained such sacrifices for sin as He was pleased in His mercy to accept. In the old law (as we may read, Leviticus, 16) the Lord required that there should, every year once, be made an atonement for the sins of all Israel, both priests and others; for the doing whereof Aaron alone was to sacrifice for himself and the priests a young bullock, and for the rest of the people he was to receive from them two young goats, of which he was to sacrifice one; but as for the other, which was the scapegoat, he was to lay his hands on the head thereof, and by a confession of the iniquities of the people, to lay them all on that head, and then by some opportune man to cause the goat to be led into the wilderness, and there to escape and carry away with him the iniquities of the people. As the sacrifice of the one goat was a sufficient, because an acceptable, price for the ransom of all Israel; so the death of the Messiah is a sufficient price for the sins of all mankind, because there was no more required. Our Saviour Christ's sufferings seem to be here figured as clearly as in the oblation of Isaac, or in any other type of him in the Old Testament. He was both the sacrificed goat and the scapegoat: "He was oppressed, and he was afflicted; he opened not his mouth; he is brought as a lamb to the slaughter, and as a sheep is dumb before the shearer, so opened he not his mouth":[Isaiah, 53. 7] here is the sacrificed goat. "He hath borne our griefs and carried our sorrows";[Ibid.Ibid., 53. 6] and so he is the scapegoat. "He was cut off from the land of the living for the transgression of my people": [Ibid., 53. 8] there again he is the sacrificed goat. And again, "he shall bear their sins":[, 53. 11] he is the scapegoat. Thus is the Lamb of God equivalent to both those goats; sacrificed, in that he died; and escaping, in his resurrection; being raised opportunely by his Father, and removed from the habitation of men in his ascension. For as much therefore as he that redeemeth hath no title to the thing redeemed, before the redemption and ransom paid, and this ransom was the death of the redeemer, it is manifest that our Saviour, as man, was not king of those that he redeemed, before he suffered death; that is, during that time he conversed bodily on the earth. I say he was not then king in present, by virtue of the pact which the faithful make with him in baptism: nevertheless, by the renewing of their pact with God in baptism, they were obliged to obey him for king, under his Father, whensoever he should be pleased to take the kingdom upon him. According whereunto, our Saviour himself expressly saith, "My kingdom is not of this world." [John, 18. 36] Now seeing the Scripture maketh mention but of two worlds; this that is now, and shall remain to the day of judgement, which is therefore also called the last day; and that which shall be after the day of judgement, when there shall be a new heaven and a new earth; the kingdom of Christ is not to begin till the general resurrection. And that is it which our Saviour saith, "The Son of Man shall come in the glory of his Father, with his angels; and then he shall reward every man according to his works." [Matthew, 16. 27] To reward every man according to his works is to execute the office of a king; and this is not to be till he come in the glory of his Father, with his angels. When our Saviour saith, "The Scribes and Pharisees sit in Moses' seat; all therefore whatsoever they bid you do, that observe and do";[Ibid., 23. 2] he declareth plainly that he ascribeth kingly power, for that time, not to himself, but to them. And so he doth also, where he saith, "Who made me a judge or divider over you?" [Luke, 12. 14] And, "I came not to judge the world, but to save the world." [John, 12. 47] And yet our Saviour came into this world that he might be a king and a judge in the world to come: for he was the Messiah, that is, the Christ, that is, the anointed priest and the sovereign prophet of God; that is to say, he was to have all the power that was in Moses the prophet, in the high priests that succeeded Moses, and in the kings that succeeded the priests. And St. John says expressly, "The Father judgeth no man, but hath committed all judgement to the Son." [Ibid., 5. 22] And this is not repugnant to that other place, "I came not to judge the world": for this is spoken of the world present, the other of the world to come; as also where it is said that at the second coming of Christ, "Ye that have followed me, in the regeneration when the Son of man shall sit in the throne of his glory, ye shall also sit on twelve thrones, judging the twelve tribes of Israel." [Matthew, 19. 28] If then Christ, whilst he was on earth, had no kingdom in this world, to what end was his first coming? It was to restore unto God, by a new covenant, the kingdom which, being his by the old covenant, had been cut off by the rebellion of the Israelites in the election of Saul. Which to do, he was to preach unto them that he was the Messiah, that is, the king promised to them by the prophets, and to offer himself in sacrifice for the sins of them that should by faith submit themselves thereto; and in case the nation generally should refuse him, to call to his obedience such as should believe in him amongst the Gentiles. So that there are two parts of our Saviour's office during his abode upon the earth: one to proclaim himself the Christ; and another by teaching, and by working of miracles, to persuade and prepare men to live so as to be worthy of the immortality believers were to enjoy, at such time as he should come in majesty to take posses- sion of his Father's kingdom. And therefore it is that the time of his preaching is often by himself called the regeneration, which is not properly a kingdom, and thereby a warrant to deny obedience to the magistrates that then were; for he commanded to obey those that sat then in Moses' chair, and to pay tribute to Caesar; but only an earnest of the kingdom of God that was to come to those to whom God had given the grace to be his disciples and to believe in him; for which cause the godly are said to be already in the kingdom of grace, as naturalized in that heavenly kingdom. Hitherto therefore there is nothing done or taught by Christ that tendeth to the diminution of the civil right of the Jews or of Caesar. For as touching the Commonwealth which then was amongst the Jews, both they that bore rule amongst them and they that were governed did all expect the Messiah and kingdom of God; which they could not have done if their laws had forbidden him, when he came, to manifest and declare himself. Seeing therefore he did nothing, but by preaching and miracles go about to prove himself to be that Messiah, he did therein nothing against their laws. The kingdom he claimed was to be in another world: he taught all men to obey in the meantime them that sat in Moses' seat: he allowed them to give Caesar his tribute, and refused to take upon himself to be a judge. How then could his words or actions be seditious, or tend to the overthrow of their then civil government? But God having determined his sacrifice for the reduction of His elect to their former covenanted obedience, for the means, whereby He would bring the same to effect, made use of their malice and ingratitude. Nor was it contrary to the laws of Caesar. For though Pilate himself, to gratify the Jews, delivered him to be crucified; yet before he did so, he pronounced openly that he found no fault in him; and put for title of his condemnation, not as the Jews re- quired, "that he pretended to be king," but simply, "that he was King of the Jews"; and notwithstanding their clamour, refused to alter it, saying, "What I have written, I have written." As for the third part of his office, which was to be king, I have already shown that his kingdom was not to begin till the resurrection. But then he shall be king, not only as God, in which sense he is king already, and ever shall be, of all the earth, in virtue of his omnipotence; but also peculiarly of his own elect, by virtue of the pact they make with him in their baptism. And therefore it is that our Saviour saith that his Apostles should sit upon twelve thrones, judg- ing the twelve tribes of Israel, "When the Son of Man shall sit in the throne of his glory":[Loc. cit.] whereby he signified that he should reign then in his human nature; and "The Son of Man shall come in the glory of his Father, with his angels, and then he shall reward every man according to his works." [Ibid., 16. 27] The same we may read, Mark, 13. 26, and 14. 62, and more expressly for the time, Luke, 22. 29, 30, "I appoint unto you a kingdom, as my Father hath appointed to me, that you may eat and drink at my table in my kingdom, and sit on thrones judging the twelve tribes of Israel." By which it is manifest that the kingdom of Christ appointed to him by his Father is not to be before the Son of Man shall come in glory, and make his Apostles judges of the twelve tribes of Israel. But a man may here ask, seeing there is no marriage in the kingdom of heaven, whether men shall then eat and drink. What eating therefore is meant in this place? This is expounded by our Saviour where he saith, "Labour not for the meat which perisheth, but for that meat which endureth unto ever- lasting life, which the Son of Man shall give you." So that by eating at Christ's table is meant the eating of the tree of life; that is to say, the enjoying of immortality, in the kingdom of the Son of Man. By which places, and many more, it is evident that our Saviour's kingdom is to be exercised by him in his human nature. Again, he is to be king then no otherwise than as subordinate or vicegerent of God the Father, as Moses was in the wilderness, and as the high priests were before the reign of Saul, and as the kings were after it. For it is one of the prophecies concerning Christ that he be like, in office, to Moses: "I will raise them up a prophet," saith the Lord, "from amongst their brethren like unto thee, and will put my words into his mouth";[Deuteronomy, 18. 18] and this similitude with Moses is also apparent in the actions of our Saviour himself, whilst he was conversant on earth. For as Moses chose twelve princes of the tribes to govern under him; so did our Saviour choose twelve Apostles, who shall sit on twelve thrones and judge the twelve tribes of Israel: and as Moses authorized seventy elders to receive the Spirit of God, and to prophesy to the people, that is, as I have said before, to speak unto them in the name of God; so our Saviour also ordained seventy disciples to preach his kingdom and salvation to all nations. And as when a complaint was made to Moses against those of the seventy that prophesied in the camp of Israel, he justified them in it as being subservient therein to his government; so also our Saviour, when St. John complained to him of a certain man that cast out devils in his name, justified him therein, saying, "Forbid him not, for he that is not against us is on our part." [Luke, 9. 50] Again, our Saviour resembled Moses in the institution of sacraments, both of admission into the kingdom of God and of commemoration of his deliverance of his elect from their miserable condition. As the children of Israel had for sacrament of their reception into the kingdom of God, before the time of Moses, the rite of circumcision, which rite, having been omitted in the wilderness, was again restored as soon as they came into the Land of Promise; so also the Jews, before the coming of our Saviour, had a rite of baptizing, that is, of washing with water all those that, being Gentiles, embraced the God of Israel. This rite St. John the Baptist used in the reception of all them that gave their names to the Christ, whom he preached to be already come into the world; and our Saviour instituted the same for a sacrament to be taken by all that believed in him. For what cause the rite of baptism first proceeded is not expressed formally in the Scripture, but it may be probably thought to be an imitation of the law of Moses concerning leprosy; wherein the leprous man was commanded to be kept out of the camp of Israel for a certain time; after which time, being judged by the priest to be clean, he was admitted into the camp after a solemn washing. And this may therefore be a type of the washing in baptism, wherein such men as are cleansed of the leprosy of sin by faith are received into the Church with the solemnity of baptism. There is another conjecture drawn from the ceremonies of the Gentiles, in a certain case that rarely happens: and that is, when a man that was thought dead chanced to recover, other men made scruple to converse with him, as they would do to converse with a ghost, unless he were received again into the number of men by washing, as children new born were washed from the uncleanness of their nativity, which was a kind of new birth. This ceremony of the Greeks, in the time that Judaea was under the dominion of Alexander and the Greeks his successors, may probably enough have crept into the religion of the Jews. But seeing it is not likely our Saviour would countenance a heathen rite, it is most likely it proceeded from the legal ceremony of washing after leprosy. And for the other sacrament, of eating the Paschal Lamb, it is manifestly imitated in the sacrament of the Lord's Supper; in which the breaking of the bread and the pouring out of the wine do keep in memory our deliverance from the misery of sin by Christ's Passion, as the eating of the Paschal Lamb kept in memory the deliverance of the Jews out of the bondage of Egypt. Seeing therefore the authority of Moses was but subordinate, and he but a lieutenant to God, it followeth that Christ, whose authority, as man, was to be like that of Moses, was no more but subordinate to the authority of his Father. The same is more expressly signified by that that he teacheth us to pray, "Our Father, let thy kingdom come"; and, "For thine is the kingdom, the power, and the glory"; and by that it is said that "He shall come in the glory of his Father"; and by that which St. Paul saith, "then cometh the end, when he shall have delivered up the kingdom to God, even the Father";[I Corinthians, 15. 24] and by many other most express places. Our Saviour therefore, both in teaching and reigning, representeth, as Moses did, the person God; which God from that time forward, but not before, is called the Father; and, being still one and the same substance, is one person as represented by Moses, and another person as represented by His Son the Christ. For person being a relative to a representer, it is consequent to plurality of representers that there be a plurality of persons, though of one and the same substance.

## CHAPTER XLII, OF POWER ECCLESIASTICAL

FOR the understanding of power ecclesiastical, what and in whom it is, we are to distinguish the time from the ascension of our Saviour into two parts; one before the conversion of kings and men endued with sovereign civil power; the other after their conversion. For it was long after the ascension before any king or civil sovereign embraced and publicly allowed the teaching of Christian religion. And for the time between, it is manifest that the power ecclesiastical was in the Apostles; and after them in such as were by them ordained to preach the gospel, and to convert men to Christianity; and to direct them that were converted in the way of salvation; and after these the power was delivered again to others by these ordained, and this was done by imposition of hands upon such as were ordained; by which was signified the giving of the Holy Spirit, or Spirit of God, to those whom they ordained ministers of God, to advance His kingdom. So that imposition of hands was nothing else but the seal of their commission to preach Christ and teach his doctrine; and the giving of the Holy Ghost by that ceremony of imposition of hands was an imitation of that which Moses did. For Moses used the same ceremony to his minister Joshua, as we read, Deuteronomy, 34. 9, "And Joshua the son of Nun was full of the spirit of wisdom; for Moses had laid his hands upon him." Our Saviour therefore between his resurrection and ascension gave his spirit to the Apostles; first, by breathing on them, and saying, "Receive ye the Holy Spirit";[John, 20. 22] and after his ascension by sending down upon them a "mighty wind, and cloven tongues of fire";[Acts, 2. 2, 3] and not by imposition of hands; as neither did God lay His hands on Moses: and his Apostles afterward transmitted the same spirit by imposition of hands, as Moses did to Joshua. So that it is manifest hereby in whom the power ecclesiastical continually remained in those first times where there was not any Christian Commonwealth; namely, in them that received the same from the Apostles, by successive laying on of hands. Here we have the person of God born now the third time. For Moses and the high priests were God's representative in the Old Testament; and our Saviour himself, as man, during his abode on earth: so the Holy Ghost, that is to say, the Apostles and their successors, in the office of preaching and teaching, that had received the Holy Spirit, have represented him ever since. But a person (as I have shown before, Chapter thirteen) is he that is represented, as of as he is represented; and therefore God, who has been represented (that is, personated) thrice, may properly enough be said to be three persons; though neither the word Person nor Trinity be ascribed to him in the Bible. St. John indeed saith, "There be three that bear witness in heaven, the Father, the Word, and the Holy Spirit; and these three are one":[Luke, 5. 11] but this disagreeth not, but accordeth fitly with three persons in the proper signification of persons; which is that which is represented by another. For so God the Father, as represented by Moses, is one person; and as represented by His Son, another person; and as represented by the Apostles, and by the doctors that taught by authority from them derived, is a third person; and yet every person here is the person of one and the same God. But a man may here ask what it was whereof these three bore witness. St. John therefore tells us that they bear witness that "God hath given us eternal life in His Son." Again, if it should be asked wherein that testimony appeareth, the answer is easy; for He hath testified the same by the miracles He wrought, first by Moses; secondly, by His Son himself; and lastly by His Apostles that had received the Holy Spirit; all which in their times represented the person of God, and either prophesied or preached Jesus Christ. And as for the Apostles, it was the character of the apostleship, in the twelve first and great Apostles, to bear witness of his resurrection, as appeareth expressly where St. Peter, when a new Apostle was to be chosen in the place of Judas Iscariot, useth these words, "Of these men which have companied with us all the time that the Lord Jesus went in and out amongst us, beginning at the baptism of John, unto that same day that he was taken up from us, must one be ordained to be a witness with us of his resurrection":[Acts, 1. 21, 22] which words interpret the "bearing of witness" mentioned by St. John. There is in the same place mentioned another Trinity of witnesses in earth. For he saith, "there are three that bear witness in earth; the Spirit, and the water, and the blood; and these three agree in one": [Ibid., 1. 8] that is to say, the graces of God's Spirit, and the two sacraments, baptism and the Lord's Supper, which all agree in one testimony to assure the consciences of believers of eternal life; of which testimony he saith, "He that believeth on the Son of Man hath the witness in himself." [Ibid., 1. 10] In this Trinity on earth, the unity is not of the thing; for the spirit, the water, and the blood are not the same substance, though they give the same testimony: but in the Trinity of heaven, the persons are the persons of one and the same God, though represented in three different times and occasions. To conclude, the doctrine of the Trinity, as far as can be gathered directly from the Scripture, is in substance this: that God, who is always one and the same, was the person represented by Moses; the person represented by his Son incarnate; and the person represented by the Apostles. As represented by the Apostles, the Holy Spirit by which they spoke is God; as represented by His Son, that was God and man, the Son is that God; as represented by Moses and the high priests, the Father, that is to say, the Father of our Lord Jesus Christ, is that God: from whence we may gather the reason those names Father, Son, and Holy Spirit, in the signification of the godhead, are never used in the Old Testament: for they are persons, that is, they have their names from representing; which could not be till diverse men had represented God's person in ruling or in directing under Him. Thus we see how the power ecclesiastical was left by our Saviour to the Apostles; and how they were (to the end they might the better exercise that power) endued with the Holy Spirit, which is therefore called sometimes in the New Testament paracletus, which signifieth an assister, or one called to for help, though it be commonly translated a comforter. Let us now consider the power itself, what it was, and over whom. Cardinal Bellarmine, in his third general controversy, hath handled a great many questions concerning the ecclesiastical power of the Pope of Rome, and begins with this, whether it ought to be monarchical, aristocratical, or democratical. All which sorts of power are sovereign and coercive. If now it should appear that there is no coercive power left them by our Saviour, but only a power to proclaim the kingdom of Christ, and to persuade men to submit themselves there unto; and, by precepts and good counsel, to teach them that have submitted what they are to do, that they may be received into the kingdom of God when it comes; and that the Apostles, and other ministers of the Gospel, are our schoolmasters, and not our commanders, and their precepts not laws, but wholesome counsels; then were all that dispute in vain. I have shown already, in the last chapter, that the kingdom of Christ is not of this world: therefore neither can his ministers, unless they be kings, require obedience in his name. For if the Supreme King have not his regal power in this world; by what authority can obedience be required to his officers? "As my Father sent me," so saith our Saviour, "I send you." [John, 20. 21] But our Saviour was sent to persuade the Jews to return to, and to invite the Gentiles to receive, the kingdom of his Father, and not to reign in majesty, no not as his Father's lieutenant till the day of judgement. The time between the ascension and the general resurrection is called, not a reigning, but a regeneration; that is, a preparation of men for the second and glorious coming of Christ at the day of judgement, as appeareth by the words of our Saviour, "You that have followed me in the regeneration, when the Son of man shall sit in the throne of his glory, you shall also sit upon twelve thrones";[Matthew, 19. 28] and of St. Paul, "Having your feet shod with the preparation of the gospel of peace";[Ephesians, 6. 15] and is compared by our Saviour to fishing; that is, to winning men to obedience, not by coercion and punishing, but by persuasion. And therefore he said not to his Apostles he would make them so many Nimrods, hunters of men; but fishers of men. It is compared also to leaven, to sowing of seed, and to the multiplication of a grain of mustard-seed; by all which compulsion is excluded; and consequently there can in that time be no actual reigning. The work of Christ's ministers is evangelization; that is, a proclamation of Christ, and a preparation for his second coming; as the evangelization of John the Baptist was a preparation to his first coming. Again, the office of Christ's ministers in this world is to make men believe and have faith in Christ: but faith hath no relation to, nor dependence at all upon, compulsion or commandment; but only upon certainty, or probability of arguments drawn from reason, or from something men believe already. Therefore the ministers of Christ in this world have no power by that title to punish any man for not believing or for contradicting what they say: they have, I say, no power by that title of Christ's ministers to punish such; but if they have sovereign civil power, by politic institution, then they may indeed lawfully punish any contradiction to their laws whatsoever: and St. Paul, of himself and other the then preachers of the Gospel, saith in express words, "We have no dominion over your faith, but are helpers of your joy."[II Corinthians, 1. 24] Another argument, that the ministers of Christ in this present world have no right of commanding, may be drawn from the lawful authority which Christ hath left to all princes, as well Christians as infidels. St. Paul saith, "Children, obey your parents in all things; for this is well pleasing to the Lord." [Colossians, 3. 20] And, "Servants, obey in all things your masters according to the flesh, not with eye-service, as men-pleasers, but in singleness of heart, as fearing the Lord":[Ibid., 3. 22] this is spoken to them whose masters were infidels; and yet they are bidden to obey them in all things. And again, concerning obedience to princes, exhorting "to be subject to the higher powers," he saith, "that all power is ordained of God"; and "that we ought to subject to them not only for" fear of incurring their "wrath, but also for conscience sake." [Romans, 13. 1-6] And St. Peter, "Submit yourselves to every ordinance of man, for the Lord's sake, whether it be to the king, as supreme, or unto governors, as to them that be sent by him for the punishment of evildoers, and for the praise of them that do well; for so is the will of God." [I Peter, 2. 13, 14, 15] And again St. Paul, "Put men in mind to be subject to principalities, and powers, and to obey magistrates." [Titus, 3. 1] These princes and powers whereof St. Peter and St. Paul here speak were all infidels: much more therefore we are to obey those Christians whom God hath ordained to have sovereign power over us. How then can we be obliged to obey any minister of Christ if he should command us to do anything contrary to the command of the king or other sovereign representant of the Commonwealth whereof we are members, and by whom we look to be protected? It is therefore manifest that Christ hath not left to his ministers in this world, unless they be also endued with civil authority, any authority to command other men. But what, may some object, if a king, or a senate, or other sovereign person forbid us to believe in Christ? To this I answer that such forbidding is of no effect; because belief and unbelief never follow men's commands. Faith is a gift of God which man can neither give nor take away by promise of rewards or menaces of torture. And, if it be further asked, what if we be commanded by our lawful prince to say with our tongue we believe not; must we obey such command? Profession with the tongue is but an external thing, and no more than any other gesture whereby we signify our obedience; and wherein a Christian, holding firmly in his heart the faith of Christ, hath the same liberty which the prophet Elisha allowed to Naaman the Syrian. Naaman was converted in his heart to the God of Israel, for he saith, "Thy servant will henceforth offer neither burnt offering nor sacrifice unto other gods, but unto the Lord. In this thing the Lord pardon thy servant, that when my master goeth into the house of Rimmon to worship there, and he leaneth on my hand, and I bow myself in the house of Rimmon; when I bow myself in the house of Rimmon, the Lord pardon thy servant in this thing." [II Kings, 5. 17, 18] This the Prophet approved, and bid him "Go in peace." Here Naaman believed in his heart; but by bowing before the idol Rimmon, he denied the true God in effect as much as if he had done it with his lips. But then what shall we answer to our Saviour's saying, "Whosoever denieth me before men, I will deny him before my Father which is in heaven?" [Matthew, 10. 33] This we may say, that whatsoever a subject, as Naaman was, is compelled to in obedience to his sovereign, and doth it not in order to his own mind, but in order to the laws of his country, that action is not his, but his sovereign's; nor is it he that in this case denieth Christ before men, but his governor, and the law of his country. If any man shall accuse this doctrine as repugnant to true and un-feigned Christianity, I ask him, in case there should be a subject in any Christian Commonwealth that should be inwardly in his heart of the Mahomedan religion, whether if his sovereign command him to be present at the divine service of the Christian church, and that on pain of death, he think that Mahomedan obliged in conscience to suffer death for that cause, rather than to obey that command of his lawful prince. If he say he ought rather to suffer death, then he authorizeth all private men to disobey their princes in maintenance of their religion, true or false: if he say he ought to be obedient, then he alloweth to himself that which he deni-eth to another, contrary to the words of our Saviour, "Whatsoever you would that men should do unto you, that do ye unto them";[Luke, 6. 31] and contrary to the law of nature (which is the indubitable everlasting law of God), "Do not to another that which thou wouldest not he should do unto thee." But what then shall we say of all those martyrs we read of in the history of the Church, that they have needlessly cast away their lives? For answer hereunto, we are to distinguish the persons that have been for that cause put to death; whereof some have received a calling to preach and profess the profess the kingdom of Christ openly; others have had no such calling, nor more has been required of them than their own faith. The former sort, if they have been put to death for bearing witness to this point, that Jesus Christ is risen from the dead, were true martyrs; for a martyr is, to give the true definition of the word, a witness of the resurrection of Jesus the Messiah; which none can be but those that those that conversed with him on earth, and saw him after he was risen: for a wit-ness must have seen what he testifieth, or else his testimony is not good. And that none but such can properly be called martyrs of Christ is manifest out of the words of St. Peter, "Wherefore of these men which have companied with us all the time that the Lord Jesus went in and out amongst us, beginning from the baptism of John unto that same day he was taken up from us, must one be ordained to be a martyr" (that is, a witness) "with us of his resurrection":[Acts, 1. 21, 22] where we may observe that he which is to be a witness of truth of the resurrection of Christ, that is to say, of the truth of this fundamental article of Christian religion, that Je-sus was the Christ, must be some Disciple that conversed with him, and saw him before and after his resurrec-tion; and consequently must be one of his original Disciples: whereas they which were not so can witness no more, but that their antecessors said it, and are therefore but witnesses of other men's testimony, and are but second martyrs, or martyrs of Christ's witnesses. He that to maintain every doctrine which he himself draweth out of the history of our Saviour's life, and of the Acts or Epistles of the Apostles, or which he believeth, upon the authority of a private man, will oppose the laws and authority of the civil state, is very far from being a martyr of Christ, or a martyr of his martyrs. It is one article only, which to die for meriteth so honourable a name, and that article is this, that Jesus is the Christ; that is to say, he that hath redeemed us, and shall come again to give us salvation, and eternal life in his glorious kingdom. To die for every tenet that serveth the am-bition or profit of the clergy is not required; nor is it the death of the witness, but the testimony itself that makes the martyr: for the word signifieth nothing else but the man that beareth witness, whether he be put to death for his testimony, or not. Also he that is not sent to preach this fundamental article, but taketh it upon him of his private authority, though he be a witness, and consequently a martyr, either primary of Christ, or secondary of his Apostles, Disciples, or their successors; yet is he not obliged to suffer death for that cause, because being not called thereto, it is not required at his hands; nor ought he to complain if he loseth the re-ward he expecteth from those that never set him on work. None therefore can be a martyr, neither of the first nor second degree, that have not a warrant to preach Christ come in the flesh; that is to say, none but such as are sent to the conversion of infidels. For no man is a witness to him that already believeth, and therefore needs no witness; but to them that deny, or doubt, or have not heard it. Christ sent his Apostles and his seventy Disciples with authority to preach; he sent not all that believed. And he sent them to unbelievers; "I send you," saith he, "as sheep amongst wolves";[Matthew, 10. 16] not as sheep to other sheep. Lastly, the points of their commission, as they are expressly set down in the gospel, contain none of them any authority over the congregation. We have first that the twelve Apostles were sent "to the lost sheep of the house of Israel," and commanded to preach "that the kingdom of God was at hand." [Matthew, 10. 6, 7] Now preaching, in the original, is that act which a crier, herald, or other officer useth to do publicly in proclaiming of a king. But a crier hath not right to command any man. And the seventy Disciples are sent out as "Labourers, not as lords of the harvest";[Luke, 10. 2] and are bidden to say, "The kingdom of God is come nigh unto you";[Ibid., 10. 9] and by kingdom here is meant, not the kingdom of grace, but the kingdom of glory; for they are bidden to denounce it to those cities which shall not receive them, as a threatening, that it shall be more tolerable in that day for Sodom than for such a city. [Ibid., 10. 11] And our Saviour telleth his Disciples, that sought priority of place, their office was to minister, even as the Son of Man came, not to be ministered unto, but to minister. [Matthew, 20. 28] Preachers therefore have not magisterial, but ministerial power: "Be not called masters," saith our Saviour, "for one is your master, even Christ." [Ibid., 23. 10] Another point of their commission is to "teach all nations"; as it is in Matthew, 28. 19, or as in St. Mark, 16. 15, "Go into all the world, and preach the gospel to every creature." Teaching, therefore, and preaching is the same thing. For they that proclaim the coming of a king must withal make known by what right he cometh, if they mean men shall submit themselves unto him: as St. Paul did to the Jews of Thessalonica, when "three Sabbath days he reasoned with them out of the Scriptures, opening and alleging that Christ must needs have suffered, and risen again from the dead, and that this Jesus is Christ." [Acts, 17. 2, 3] But to teach out of the Old Testament that Jesus was Christ, that is to say, king, and risen from the dead, is not to say that men are bound, after they believe it, to obey those that tell them so, against the laws and commands o

their sovereigns; but that they shall do wisely to expect the coming of Christ hereafter, in patience and faith, with obedience to their present magistrates. Another point of their commission is to "baptize, in the name of the Father, and of the Son, and of the Holy Ghost." What is baptism? Dipping into water. But what is it to dip a man into the water in the name of anything? The meaning of these words of baptism is this. He that is baptized is dipped or washed as a sign of becoming a new man and a loyal subject to that God whose person was represented in old time by Moses, and the high priests, when He reigned over the Jews; and to Jesus Christ, His Son, God and Man, that hath redeemed us, and shall in his human nature represent his Father's person in his eternal kingdom after the resurrection; and to acknowledge the doctrine of the Apostles, who, assisted by the Spirit of the Father and of the Son, were left for guides to bring us into that kingdom, to be the only and assured way thereunto. This being our promise in baptism; and the authority of earthly sovereigns being not to be put down till the day of judgement; for that is expressly affirmed by St. Paul, where he saith, "As in Adam all die, so in Christ all shall be made alive. But every man in his own order, Christ the first fruits, afterward they that are Christ's at his coming; then cometh the end, when he shall have delivered up the kingdom to God, even the Father, when he shall have put down all rule, and all authority and power." [I Corinthians, 15. 22, 23, 24] It is manifest that we do not in baptism constitute over us another authority by which our external actions are to be governed in this life, but promise to take the doctrine of the Apostles for our direction in the way to life eternal. The power of remission and retention of sins, called also the power of loosing and binding, and sometimes the keys of the kingdom of heaven is a consequence of the authority to baptize or refuse to baptize. For baptism is the sacrament of allegiance of them that are to be received into the kingdom of God; that is to say, into eternal life; that is to say, to remission of sin: for as eternal life was lost by the committing, so it is recovered by the remitting of men's sins. The end of baptism is remission of sins: therefore St. Peter, when they that were converted by his sermon on the day of Pentecost asked what they were to do, advised them to "repent, and be baptized in the name of Jesus, for the remission of sins." [Acts, 2. 38] And therefore, seeing to baptize is to declare the reception of men into God's kingdom, and to refuse to baptize is to declare their exclusion, it followeth that the power to declare them cast out, or retained in it, was given to the same Apostles, and their substitutes and successors. And therefore after our Saviour had breathed upon them, saying, "Receive the Holy Ghost," [John, 20. 22] he addeth in the next verse, "Whosoever sins ye remit, they are remitted unto them; and whosoever sins ye retain, they are retained." By which words is not granted an authority to forgive or retain sins, simply and absolutely, as God forgiveth or retaineth them, Who knoweth the heart of man and truth of his penitence and conversion; but conditionally, to the penitent: and this forgiveness, or absolution, in case the absolved have but a feigned repentance, is thereby, without other act or sentence of the absolved, made void, and hath no effect at all to salvation, but, on the contrary, to the aggravation of his sin. Therefore the Apostles and their successors are to follow but the outward marks of repentance; which appearing, they have no authority to deny absolution; and if they appear not, they have no authority to absolve. The same also is to be observed in baptism: for to a converted Jew or Gentile, the Apostles had not the power to deny baptism, nor to grant it to the unpenitent. But seeing no man is able to discern the truth of another man's repentance, further than by external marks taken from his words and actions, which are subject to hypocrisy, another question will arise: who is it that is constituted judge of those marks? And this question is decided by our Saviour himself: "If thy brother," saith he, "shall trespass against thee, go and tell him his fault between thee and him alone; if he shall hear thee, thou hast gained thy brother. But if he will not hear thee, then take with thee one or two more. And if he shall neglect to hear them, tell it unto the Church; but if he neglect to hear the Church, let him be unto thee as an heathen man and a publican." [Matthew, 18. 15, 16, 17] By which it is manifest that the judgement concerning the truth of repentance belonged not to any one man, but to the Church, that is, to the assembly of the faithful, or to them that have authority to be their representant. But besides the judgement, there is necessary also the pronouncing of sentence: and this belonged always to the Apostle, or some pastor of the Church, as prolocutor; and of this our Saviour speaketh in the eighteenth verse, "Whatsoever ye shall bind on earth shall be bound in heaven; and whatsoever ye shall loose on earth shall be loosed in heaven." And conformable hereunto was the practice of St. Paul where he saith, "For I verily, as absent in body, but present in spirit, have determined already, as though I were present, concerning him that hath so done this deed; in the name of our Lord Jesus Christ, when ye are gathered together, and my spirit, with the power of our Lord Jesus Christ, to deliver such a one to Satan";[I Corinthians, 5. 3, 4, 5] that is to say, to cast him out of the Church, as a man whose sins are not forgiven. Paul here pronounceth the sentence, but the assembly was first to hear the cause (for St. Paul was absent), and by consequence to condemn him. But in the same chapter the judgement in such a case is more expressly attributed to the assembly: "But now I have written unto you not to keep company, if any man that is called a brother be a fornicator," etc., "with such a one no not to eat. For what have I to do to judge them that are without? Do not ye judge them that are within?" [Ibid., 5. 11, 12] The sentence therefore by which a man was put out of the Church was pronounced by the Apostle or pastor; but the judgement concerning the merit of the cause was in the Church; that is to say, as the times were before the conversion of kings, and men that had sovereign authority in the Commonwealth, the assembly of the Christians dwelling in the same city; as in Corinth, in the assembly of the Christians of Corinth. This part of the power of the keys by which men were thrust out from the kingdom of God is that which is called excommunication and to excommunicate is, in the original, aposunagogon poiein, to cast out of the synagogue; that is, out of the place of divine service; a word drawn from the custom of the Jews, to cast out of their synagogues such as they thought in manners or doctrine contagious, as lepers were by the law of Moses separated from the congregation of Israel till such time as they should be by the priest pronounced clean. The use and effect of excommunication, whilst it was not yet strengthened with the civil power, was no more than that they who were not excommunicate were to avoid the company of them that were. It was not enough to repute them as heathen, that never had been Christians; for with such they might eat and drink, which with excommunicate persons they might not do, as appeareth by the words of St. Paul where he telleth them he had formerly forbidden them to "company with fornicators";[I Corinthians, 5. 9, 10, etc.] but, because that could not be without going out of the world, he restraineth it to such fornicators and otherwise vicious persons as were of the brethren; "with such a one," he saith, they ought not to keep company, "no not to eat." And this is no more than our Saviour saith, "Let him be to thee as a heathen, and as a publican." [Matthew, 18. 17] For publicans (which signifieth farmers and receivers of the revenue of the Commonwealth) were so hated and detested by the Jews that were to pay it, as that publican and sinner were taken amongst them for the same thing; insomuch as when our Saviour accepted the invitation of Zacchaeus a publican, though it were to convert him, yet it was objected to him as a crime. And therefore, when our Saviour, to heathen, added publican, he did forbid them to eat with a man excommunicate. As for keeping them out of their synagogues, or places of assembly, they had no power to do it but that of the owner of the place, whether he were Christian or heathen. And because all places are by right in the dominion of the Commonwealth, as well he that was excommunicated as he that never was baptized, might enter into them by commission from the civil magistrate; as Paul before his conversion entered into their synagogues at Damascus, to apprehend Christians, men and women, and to carry them bound to Jerusalem, by commission from the high priest.[Acts, 9. 2] By which it appears that upon a Christian that should become an apostate, in a place where the civil power did persecute or not assist the Church, the effect of excommunication had nothing in it, neither of damage in this world nor of terror: not of terror, because of their unbelief; nor of damage, because they returned thereby into the favour of the world; and in the world to come were to be in no worse estate than they which never had believed. The damage redounded rather to the Church, by provocation of them they cast out to a freer execution of their malice. Excommunication therefore had its effect only upon those that believed that Jesus Christ was to come again in glory to reign over and to judge both the quick and the dead, and should therefore refuse entrance into his kingdom to those whose sins were retained; that is, to those that were excommunicated by the Church. And thence it is that St. Paul calleth excommunication a delivery of the excommunicate person to Satan. For without the kingdom of Christ, all other kingdoms after judgement are comprehended in the kingdom of Satan. This is it that the faithful stood in fear of, as long as they stood excommunicate, that is to say, in an estate wherein their sins were not forgiven. Whereby we may understand that excommunication in the time that Christian religion was not authorized by the civil power was used only for a correction of manners, not of errors in opinion: for it is a punishment whereof none could be sensible but such as believed and expected the coming again of our Saviour to judge the world; and they who so believed needed no other opinion, but only uprightness of life, to be saved. There lieth excommunication for injustice; as, if thy brother offend thee, tell it him privately, then with witnesses; lastly, tell the Church, and then if he obey not, "Let him be to thee as an heathen man, and a publican." [Matthew, 18. 15, 16, 17] And there lieth excommunication for a scandalous life, as "If any man that is called a brother be a fornicator, or covetous, or an idolater, or a drunkard, or an extortioner, with such a one ye are not to eat." [I Corinthians, 5. 3, 4, 5] But to excommunicate a man that held this foundation, that Jesus was the Christ, for difference of opinion in other points by which that foundation was not destroyed, there appeareth no authority in the Scripture, nor example in the Apostles. There is indeed in St. Paul a text that seemeth to be to the contrary: "A man that is an heretic, after the first and second admonition, reject." [Ibid., 5. 11, 12] For a heretic is he that, being a member of the Church, teacheth nevertheless some private opinion which the Church has forbidden: and such a one, St. Paul adviseth Titus after the first and second admonition, to reject. But to reject in this place is not to excommunicate the man; but to give over admonishing him, to let him alone, to set by disputing with him, as one that is to be convinced only by himself. The same Apostle saith, "Foolish and unlearned questions avoid":[II Timothy, 2. 23] The word avoid in this place, and reject in the former, is the same in the original, paraitou, but foolish questions may be set by without excommunication. And again, "Avoid foolish questions,: [Titus, 3. 9] where the original periistaso (set them by) is equivalent to the former word, reject. There is no other place that can so much as colourably be drawn to countenance the casting out of the Church faithful men, such as believed the foundation, only for a singular superstructure of their own, proceeding perhaps from a good and pious conscience. But, on the contrary, all such places as command avoiding such disputes are written for a lesson to pastors, such as Timothy and Titus were, not to make new articles of faith by determining every small controversy, which oblige men to a needless burden of conscience, or provoke them to break the union of the Church. Which lesson the Apostles themselves observed well. St. Peter and St. Paul, though their controversy were great, as we may read in Galatians, 2. 11, yet they did not cast one another out of the Church. Nevertheless, during the Apostles' times, there were other pastors that observed it not; as Diotrephes who cast out of the Church such as St. John himself thought fit to be received into it, out of a pride he took in pre-eminence: [3 John, 9, etc.] so early it was that vainglory and ambition had found entrance into the Church of Christ. That a man be liable to excommunication, there be many conditions requisite; as first, that he be a member of some commonalty, that is to say, of some lawful assembly, that is to say, of some Christian Church that hath power to judge of the cause for which he is to be excommunicated. For where there is no community, there can be no excommunication; nor where there is no power to judge, can there be any power to give sentence. From hence it followeth that one Church cannot be excommunicated by another: for either they have equal power to excommunicate each other, in which case excommunication is not discipline, nor an act of authority, but schism, and dissolution of charity; or one is so subordinate to the other as that they both have but one voice, and then they be but one Church; and the part excommunicated is no more a Church, but a dissolute number of individual persons. And because the sentence of excommunication importeth an advice not to keep company nor so much as to eat with him that is excommunicate, if a sovereign prince or assembly be excommunicate, the sentence is of no effect. For all subjects are bound to be in the company and presence of their own sovereign, when he requireth it, by the law of nature; nor can they lawfully either expel him from any place of his own dominion, whether profane or holy; nor go out of his dominion without his leave; much less, if he call them to that honour, refuse to eat with him. And as to other princes and states, because they are not parts of one and the same congregation, they need not any other sentence to keep them from keeping company with the state excommunicate: for the very institution, as it uniteth many men into one community, so it dissociateth one community from another: so that excommunication is not needful for keeping kings and states asunder; nor has any further effect than is in the nature of policy itself, unless it be to instigate princes to war upon one an-other. Nor is the excommunication of a Christian subject that obeyeth the laws of his own sovereign, whether Christian or heathen, of any effect. For if he believe that "Jesus is the Christ, he hath the Spirit of God," [John, 5. 1] "and God dwelleth in him, and he in God." [, 4. 15] But he that hath the Spirit of God; he that dwelleth in God; he in whom God dwelleth, can receive no harm by the excommunication of men. Therefore, he that believeth Jesus to be the Christ is free from all the dangers threatened to persons excommunicate. He that be-lieveth it not is no Christian. Therefore a true and unfeigned Christian is not liable to excommunication: nor he also that is a professed Christian, till his hypocrisy appear in his manners; that is, till his behaviour be con-trary to the law of his sovereign, which is the rule of manners, and which Christ and his Apostles have com-manded us to be subject to. For the Church cannot judge of manners but by external actions, which actions can never be unlawful but when they are against the law of the Commonwealth. If a man's father, or mother, or master be excommunicate, yet are not the children forbidden to keep them company, nor to eat with them; for that were, for the most part, to oblige them not to eat at all, for want of means to get food; and to authorize them to disobey their parents and masters, contrary to the precept of the Apostles. In sum, the power of ex-communication cannot be extended further than to the end for which the Apostles and pastors of the Church have their commission from our Saviour; which is not to rule by command and coercion, but by teaching and direction of men in the way of salvation in the world to come. And as a master in any science may abandon his scholar when he obstinately neglecteth the practice of his rules, but not accuse him of injustice, because he was never bound to obey him: so a teacher of Christian doctrine may abandon his disciples that obstinately continue in an unchristian life; but he cannot say they do him wrong, because they are not obliged to obey him: for to a teacher that shall so complain may be applied the answer of God to Samuel in the like place, "They have not rejected thee, but me." [I Samuel, 8. 7] Excommunication therefore, when it wanteth the assis-tance of the civil power, as it doth when a Christian state or prince is excommunicate by a foreign authority, is without effect, and consequently ought to be without terror. The name of fulmen excommunicationis (that is, the thunderbolt of excommunication) proceeded from an imagination of the Bishop of Rome, which first used it, that he was king of kings, as the heathen made Jupiter king of the gods; and assigned him, in their poems and pictures, a thunderbolt wherewith to subdue and punish the giants that should dare to deny his power: which imagination was grounded on two errors; one, that the kingdom of Christ is of this world, contrary to our Saviour's own words, "My kingdom is not of this world";[John, 18. 36] the other, that he is Christ's vicar, not only over his own subjects, but over all the Christians of the world; whereof there is no ground in Scrip-ture, and the contrary shall be proved in its due place. St. Paul coming to Thessalonica, where was a syna-gogue of the Jews, "as his manner was, went in unto them, and three Sabbath days reasoned with them out of the Scriptures, opening and alleging, that Christ must needs have suffered, and risen again from the dead; and that this Jesus whom he preached was the Christ." [Acts, 17. 2, 3] The Scriptures here mentioned were the Scriptures of the Jews, that is, the Old Testament. The men to whom he was to prove that Jesus was the Christ, and risen again from the dead, were also Jews, and did believe already that they were the word of God. Hereupon, as it is in the fourth verse some of them believed, and, as it is in the fifth verse, some believed not. What was the reason, when they all believed the Scripture, that they did not all believe alike, but that some approved, others disapproved, the interpretation of St. Paul that cited them, and every one interpreted them to himself? It was this: St. Paul came to them without any legal commission, and in the manner of one that would not command, but persuade; which he must needs do, either by miracles, as Moses did to the Israelites in Egypt, that they might see his authority in God's works; or by reasoning from the already received Scrip-ture, that they might see the truth of his doctrine in God's word. But whosoever persuadeth by reasoning from principles written maketh him to whom he speaketh judge; both of the meaning of those principles and also of the force of his inferences upon them. If these Jews of Thessalonica were not, who else was the judge of what St. Paul alleged out of Scripture? If St. Paul, what needed he to quote any places to prove his doctrine? It had been enough to have said, "I find it so in Scripture; that is to say, in your laws, of which I am interpreter, as sent by Christ." The interpreter therefore of the Scripture, to whose interpretation the Jews of Thessalonica were bound to stand, could be none: every one might believe or not believe, according as the allegations seemed to himself to be agreeable or not agreeable to the meaning of the places alleged. And generally in all cases of the world he that pretendeth any proof maketh judge of his proof him to whom he addresseth his speech. And as to the case of the Jews in particular, they were bound by express words to receive the determi-nation of all hard questions from the priests and judges of Israel for the time being. [Deuteronomy, 17] But this is to be understood of the Jews that were yet unconverted. For the conversion of the Gentiles, there was no use of alleging the Scriptures, which they believed not. The Apostles therefore laboured by reason to confute their idolatry; and that done, to persuade them to the faith of Christ by their testimony of his life and resurrection. So that there could not yet be any controversy concerning the authority to interpret Scripture; seeing no man was obliged, during his infidelity, to follow any man's interpretation of any Scripture except his sovereign's interpretation of the laws of his country. Let us now consider the conversion itself, and see what there was therein that could be cause of such an obligation. Men were converted to no other thing than to the belief of that which the Apostles preached: and the Apostles preached nothing but that Jesus was the Christ, that is to say, the King that was to save them and reign over them eternally in the world to come; and consequently that he was not dead, but risen again from the dead, and gone up into heaven, and should come again one day to judge the world (which also should rise again to be judged), and reward every man according to his works. None of them preached that himself, or any other Apostle, was such an interpreter of the Scripture as all that became Christians ought to take their interpretation for law. For to interpret the laws is part of the administration of a present kingdom, which the Apostles had not. They prayed then, and all other pastors since, "Let thy kingdom come"; and exhorted their converts to obey their then ethnic princes. The New Testament was not yet published in one body. Every of the evangelists was interpreter of his own gospel, and every Apostle of his own epistle; and of the Old Testament our Saviour himself saith to the Jews, "Search the Scriptures; for in them ye think to have eternal life, and they are they that testify of me." [John, 5. 39] If he had not meant they should interpret them, he would not have bidden them take thence the proof of his being the Christ: he would either have interpreted them himself, or referred them to the interpretation of the priests. When a difficulty arose, the Apostles and elders of the Church assembled themselves together, and determined what should be preached and taught, and how they should interpret the Scriptures to the people, but took not from the people the liberty to read and interpret them to themselves. The Apostles sent diverse letters to the Churches, and other writings for their instruction; which had been in vain if they had not allowed them to interpret, that is, to consider the meaning of them. And as it was in the Apostles' time, it must be till such time as there should be pastors that could authorize an interpreter whose interpretation should generally be stood to: but that could not be till kings were pastors, or pastors kings. There be two senses wherein a writing may be said to be canonical: for canon signifieth a rule; and a rule is a precept by which a man is guided and directed in any action whatsoever. Such precepts, though given by a teacher to his disciple, or a counsellor to his friend, without power to compel him to observe them, are nevertheless canons, because they are rules. But when they are given by one whom he that receiveth them is bound to obey, then are those canons not only rules, but laws: the question therefore here is of the power to make the Scriptures, which are the rules of Christian faith, laws. That part of the Scripture which was first law was the Ten Commandments, written in two tables of stone and delivered by God Himself to Moses, and by Moses made known to the people. Before that time there was no written law of God, who, as yet having not chosen any people to be His peculiar kingdom, had given no law to men, but the law of nature, that is to say, the precepts of natural reason, written in every man's own heart. Of these two tables, the first containeth the law of sovereignty: 1. That they should not obey nor honour the gods of other nations, in these words, Non habebis deos alienos coram me; that is, "Thou shalt not have for gods, the gods that other nations worship, but only me": whereby they were forbidden to obey or honour as their king and governor any other God than Him that spake unto them by Moses, and afterwards by the high priest. 2. That they "should not make any image to represent Him"; that is to say, they were not to choose to themselves, neither in heaven nor in earth, any representative of their own fancying, but obey Moses and Aaron, whom He had appointed to that office. 3. That "they should not take the name of God in vain"; that is, they should not speak rashly of their King, nor dispute his right, nor the commissions of Moses and Aaron, His lieutenants. 4. That "they should every seventh day abstain from their ordinary labour," and employ that time in doing Him public honour. The second table containeth the duty of one man towards another, as "To honour parents"; "Not to kill"; "Not to commit adultery"; "Not to steal"; "Not to corrupt judgement by false witness"; and finally, "Not so much as to design in their heart the doing of any injury one to another." The question now is who it was that gave to these written tables the obligatory force of laws. There is no doubt but they were made laws by God Himself: but because a law obliges not, nor is law to any but to them that acknowledge it to be the act of the sovereign, how could the people of Israel, that were forbidden to approach the mountain to hear what God said to Moses, be obliged to obedience to all those laws which Moses propounded to them? Some of them were indeed the laws of nature, as all the second table, and therefore to be acknowledged for God's laws; not to the Israelites alone, but to all people: but of those that were peculiar to the Israelites, as those of the first table, the question remains, saving that they had obliged themselves, presently after the propounding of them, to obey Moses, in these words, "Speak thou to us, and we will hear thee; but let not God speak to us, lest we die." [Exodus, 20. 19] It was therefore only Moses then, and after him the high priest, whom, by Moses, God declared should administer this His peculiar kingdom, that had on earth the power to make this short Scripture of the Decalogue to be law in the commonwealth of Israel. But Moses, and Aaron, and the succeeding high priests were the civil sovereigns. Therefore hitherto the canonizing, or making of the Scripture law, belonged to the civil sovereign. The judicial law, that is to say, the laws that God prescribed to the magistrates of Israel for the rule of their administration of justice, and of the sentences or judgements they should pronounce in pleas between man and man; and the Levitical law, that is to say, the rule that God prescribed touching the rites and ceremonies of the priests and Levites, were all delivered to them by Moses only; and therefore also became laws by virtue of the same promise of obedience to Moses. Whether these laws were then written, or not written, but dictated to the people by Moses, after his forty days being with God in the Mount, by word of mouth, is not expressed in the text; but they were all positive laws, and equivalent to Holy Scripture, and made canonical by Moses the civil sovereign. After the Israelites were come into the plains of Moab over against Jericho, and ready to enter into the Land of Promise, Moses to the former laws added diverse others; which therefore are called Deuteronomy; that is, Second Laws; and are, as it is written, "the words of a covenant which the Lord commanded Moses to make with the children of Israel, besides the covenant which he made with them in Horeb." [Deuteronomy, 29. 1] For having explained those former laws, in the beginning of the Book of Deuteronomy, he addeth others, that begin at the twelfth Chapter and continue to the end of the twenty-sixth of the same book. This law they were commanded to write upon great stones plastered over, at their passing over Jordan: [Ibid., 27] this law also was written by Moses himself in a book, and delivered into the hands of the priests, and to the elders of Israel, [Ibid., 31. 9] and commanded "to be put in the side of the Ark";[Ibid., 31. 26] for in the Ark itself was nothing but the Ten Commandments. This was the law which Moses commanded the kings of Israel should keep a copy of: [Ibid., 17. 18] and this is the law which, having been long time lost, was found again in the Temple in the time of Josiah, and by his authority received for the law of God. But both Moses at the writing and Josiah at the recovery thereof had both of them the civil sovereignty. Hitherto therefore the power of making Scripture canonical was in the civil sovereign. Besides this Book of the Law, there was no other book, from the time of Moses till after the Captivity, received amongst the Jews for the law of God. For the prophets, except a few, lived in the time of the Captivity itself; and the rest lived but a little before it, and were so far from having their prophecies generally received for laws as that their persons were persecuted, partly by false prophets, and partly by the kings were seduced by them. And this book itself, which was confirmed by Josiah for the law of God, and with it all the history of the works of God, was lost in the Captivity, and sack of the city of Jerusalem, as appears by that of II Esdras, 14. 21, "Thy law is burnt; therefore no man knoweth the things that are done of Thee, or the works that shall begin." And before the Captivity, between the time when the law was lost (which is not mentioned in the Scripture, but may probably be thought to be the time of Rehoboam when Shishak, King of Egypt, took the spoil of the Temple[I Kings, 14. 26]) and the time of Josiah, when it was found again, they had no written word of God, but ruled according to their own discretion, or by the direction of such as each of them esteemed prophets. From hence we may infer that the Scriptures of the Old Testament, which we have at this day, were not canonical, nor a law unto the Jews, till the renovation of their covenant with God at their return from the Captivity, and restoration of their Commonwealth under Esdras. But from that time forward they were accounted the law of the Jews, and for such translated into Greek by seventy elders of Judaea, and put into the library of Ptolemy at Alexandria, and approved for the word of God. Now seeing Esdras was the high priest, and the high priest was their civil sovereign, it is manifest that the Scriptures were never made laws, but by the sovereign civil power. By the writings of the Fathers that lived in the time before that Christian religion was received and authorized by Constantine the Emperor, we may find that the books we now have of the New Testament were held by the Christians of that time (except a few, in respect of whose paucity the rest were called the Catholic Church, and others heretics) for the dictates of the Holy Ghost; and consequently for the canon, or rule of faith: such was the reverence and opinion they had of their teachers; as generally the reverence that the disciples bear to their first masters in all manner of doctrine they receive from them is not small. Therefore there is no doubt but when St. Paul wrote to the churches he had converted; or any other Apostle or Disciple of Christ, to those which had then embraced Christ; they received those their writings for the true Christian doctrine. But in that time when not the power and authority of the teacher, but the faith of the hearer, caused them to receive it, it was not the Apostles that made their own writings canonical, but every convert made them so to himself. But the question here is not what any Christian made a law or canon to himself, which he might again reject by the same right he received it, but what was so made a canon to them as without injustice they could not do anything contrary thereunto. That the New Testament should in this sense be canonical, that is to say, a law in any place where the law of the

Commonwealth had not made it so, is contrary to the nature of a law. For a law, as hath been already shown, is the commandment of that man, or assembly, to whom we have given sovereign authority to make such rules for the direction of our actions as he shall think fit, and to punish us when we do anything contrary to the same. When therefore any other man shall offer unto us any other rules, which the sovereign ruler hath not prescribed, they are but counsel and advice; which, whether good or bad, he that is counselled may without injustice refuse to observe; and when contrary to the laws already established, without injustice cannot observe, how good soever he conceiveth it to be. I say he cannot in this case observe the same in his actions, nor in his discourse with other men, though he may without blame believe his private teachers and wish he had the liberty to practise their advice, and that it were publicly received for law. For internal faith is in its own nature invisible, and consequently exempted from all human jurisdiction; whereas the words and actions that proceed from it, as breaches of our civil obedience, are injustice both before God and man. Seeing then our Saviour hath denied his kingdom to be in this world, seeing he hath said he came not to judge, but to save the world, he hath not subjected us to other laws than those of the Commonwealth; that is, the Jews to the law of Moses, which he saith he came not to destroy, but to fulfil; [Matthew, 5] and other nations to the laws of their several sovereigns, and all men to the laws of nature; the observing whereof, both he himself and his Apostles have in their teaching recommended to us as a necessary condition of being admitted by him in the last day into his eternal kingdom, wherein shall be protection and life everlasting. Seeing then our Saviour and his Apostles left not new laws to oblige us in this world, but new doctrine to prepare us for the next, the books of the New Testament, which contain that doctrine, until obedience to them was commanded by them that God had given power to on earth to be legislators, were not obligatory canons, that is, laws, but only good and safe advice for the direction of sinners in the way to salvation, which every man might take and refuse at his own peril, without injustice. Again, our Saviour Christ's commission to his Apostles and Disciples was to proclaim his kingdom, not present, but to come; and to teach all nations, and to baptize them that should believe; and to enter into the houses of them that should receive them; and where they were not received, to shake off the dust of their feet against them; but not to call for fire from heaven to destroy them, nor to compel them to obedience by the sword. In all which there is nothing of power, but of persuasion. He sent them out as sheep unto wolves, not as kings to their subjects. They had not in commission to make laws; but to obey and teach obedience to laws made; and consequently they could not make their writings obligatory canons, without the help of the sovereign civil power. And therefore the Scripture of the New Testament is there only law where the lawful civil power hath made it so. And there also the king, or sovereign, maketh it a law to himself; by which he subjecteth himself, not to the doctor or Apostle that converted him, but to God Himself, and His Son Jesus Christ, as immediately as did the Apostles themselves. That which may seem to give the New Testament, in respect of those that have embraced Christian doctrine, the force of laws, in the times and places of persecution, is the decrees they made amongst themselves in their synods. For we read the style of the council of the Apostles, the elders, and the whole Church, in this manner, "It seemed good to the Holy Ghost, and to us, to lay upon you no greater burden than these necessary things," [Acts, 15. 28] etc., which is a style that signifieth a power to lay a burden on them that had received their doctrine. Now "to lay a burden on another" seemeth the same as to oblige, and therefore the acts of that council were laws to the then Christians. Nevertheless, they were no more laws than are these other precepts, "Repent"; "Be baptized"; "Keep the Commandments"; "Believe the Gospel"; "Come unto me"; "Sell all that thou hast"; "Give it to the poor"; and "Follow me"; which are not commands, but invitations and callings of men to Christianity, like that of Isaiah, "Ho, every man that thirsteth, come ye to the waters, come, and buy wine and milk without money." [Isaiah, 55. 1] For first, the Apostles' power was no other than that of our Saviour, to invite men to embrace the kingdom of God; which they themselves acknowledged for a kingdom, not present, but to come; and they that have no kingdom can make no laws. And secondly, if their acts of council were laws, they could not without sin be disobeyed. But we read not anywhere that they who received not the doctrine of Christ did therein sin, but that they died in their sins; that is, that their sins against the laws to which they owed obedience were not pardoned. And those laws were the laws of nature, and the civil laws of the state, whereto every Christian man had by pact submitted himself. And therefore by the burden which the Apostles might lay on such as they had converted are not to be understood laws, but conditions, proposed to those that sought salvation; which they might accept or refuse at their own peril, without a new sin, though not without the hazard of being condemned and excluded out of the kingdom of God for their sins past. And therefore of infidels, St. John saith not, the wrath of God shall come upon them, but the wrath of God remaineth upon them; [John, 3. 36] and not that they shall he condemned, but that they are condemned already. [Ibid., 3. 18] Nor can it be conceived that the benefit of faith is remission of sins, unless we conceive withal that the damage of infidelity is the retention of the same sins. But to what end is it, may some man ask, that the Apostles and other pastors of the Church, after their time, should meet together to agree upon what doctrine should be taught, both for faith and manners, if no man were obliged to observe their decrees? To this may be answered that the Apostles and elders of that council were obliged, even by their entrance into it, to teach the doctrine therein concluded, and decreed to be taught, so far forth as no precedent law, to which they were obliged to yield obedience, was to the contrary; but not that all other Christians should be obliged to observe what they taught. For though they might deliberate what each of them should teach, yet they could not deliberate what others should do, unless their assembly had had a legislative power, which none could have but civil sovereigns. For though God be the sovereign of all the world, we are not bound to take for His law whatsoever is propounded by every man in His name; nor anything contrary to the civil law, which God hath expressly commanded us to obey. Seeing then the acts of council of the Apostles were then no laws, but counsels; much less are laws the acts of any other doctors or councils since, if assembled without the authority of the civil sovereign. And consequently, the books of the New Testament, though most perfect rules of Christian doctrine, could not be made laws by any other authority than that of kings or sovereign assemblies. The first council that made the Scriptures we now have canon is not extant: for that collection of the canons of the Apostles, attributed to Clemens, the first bishop of Rome after St. Peter, is subject to question: for though the canonical books be there reckoned up; yet these words, Sint vobis omnibus Clericis & Laicis Libri venerandi, etc., contain a distinction of clergy and laity that was not in use so near St. Peter's time. The first council for settling the canonical Scripture that is extant is that of Laodicea, Can. 59, which forbids the reading of other books than those in the churches; which is a mandate that is not addressed to every Christian, but to those only that had authority to read anything publicly in the Church; that is, to ecclesiastics only. Of ecclesiastical officers in the time of the Apostles, some were magisterial, some ministerial. Magisterial were the offices of preaching of the gospel of the kingdom of God to infidels; of administering the sacraments and divine service; and of teaching the rules of faith and manners to those that were converted. Ministerial was the office of deacons, that is, of them that were appointed to the administration of the secular necessities of the Church, at such time as they lived upon a common stock of money, raised out of the voluntary contributions of the faithful. Amongst the officers Amongst the officer magisterial, the first and principal were the Apostles, whereof there were at first but twelve; and these were chosen and constituted by our Saviour himself; and their office was not only to preach, teach, and baptize, but also to be martyrs (witnesses of our Saviour's resurrection). This testimony was the specifical and essential mark whereby the apostleship was distinguished from other magistracy ecclesiastical; as being necessary for an Apostle either to have seen our Saviour after his resurrection or to have conversed with him before, and seen his works, and other arguments of his divinity, whereby they might be taken for sufficient witnesses. And therefore at the election of a new Apostle in the place of Judas Iscariot, St. Peter saith, "Of these men that have companied with us, all the time that the Lord Jesus went in and out among us, beginning from the baptism of John unto that same day that he was taken up from us, must one be ordained to be a witness with us of his resurrection":[Acts, 1. 21, 22] where by this word must is implied a necessary property of an Apostle, to have companied with the first and prime Apostles in the time that our Saviour manifested himself in the flesh. The first Apostle of those which were not constituted by Christ in the time he was upon the earth was Matthias, chosen in this manner: there were assembled together in Jerusalem about one hundred and twenty Christians. [Acts, 1. 15] These appointed two, Joseph the Just and Matthias, [Ibid., 1. 23] and caused lots to be drawn; "and the lot fell on Matthias, and he was numbered with the apostles." [Ibid., 1. 26] So that here we see the ordination of this Apostle was the act of the congregation, and not of St. Peter, nor of the eleven, otherwise than as members of the assembly. After him there was never any other Apostle ordained, but Paul and Barnabas, which was done, as we read, in this manner: "There were in the church that was at Antioch, certain prophets and teachers; as Barnabas, and Simeon that was called Niger, and Lucius of Cyrene, and Manaen; which had been brought up with Herod the Tetrarch, and Saul. As they ministered unto the Lord, and fasted, the Holy Ghost said, Separate me Barnabas and Saul for the work whereunto I have called them. And when they had fasted, and prayed, and laid their hands on them, they sent them away."[Acts, 13. 1, 2, 3\] By which it is manifest that though they were called by the Holy Ghost, their calling was declared unto them, and their mission authorized by the particular church of Antioch. And that this their calling was to the apostleship is apparent by that, that they are both called Apostles: [Acts, 14. 14] and that it was by virtue of this act of the church of Antioch that they were Apostles, St. Paul declareth plainly in that he useth the word, which the Holy Ghost used at his calling, for he styleth himself, "An apostle separated unto the gospel of God," [Romans, 1. 1] alluding to the words of the Holy Ghost, "Separate me Barnabas and Saul," etc. But seeing the work of an Apostle was to be a witness of the resurrection of Christ, a man may here ask how St. Paul, that conversed not with our Saviour before his Passion, could know he was risen. To which is easily answered that our Saviour himself appeared to him in the way to Damascus, from heaven, after his ascension; "and chose him for a vessel to bear his name before the Gentiles, and kings, and children of Israel"; and consequently, having seen the Lord after his Passion, was a competent witness of his resurrection: and as for Barnabas, he was a disciple before the Passion. It is therefore evident that Paul and Barnabas were Apostles, and yet chosen and authorized, not by the first Apostles alone, but by the Church of Antioch; as Matthias was chosen and authorized by the Church of Jerusalem. Bishop, a word formed in our language out of the Greek episcopus, signifieth an overseer or superintendent of any business, and particularly a pastor or shepherd; and thence by metaphor was taken, not only amongst the Jews that were originally shepherds, but also amongst the heathen, to signify the office of a king, or any other ruler or guide of people, whether he ruled by laws or doctrine. And so the Apostles were the first Christian bishops, instituted by Christ himself: in which sense the apostleship of Judas is called "his bishoprick." [Acts, 1. 20] And afterwards, when there were constituted elders in the Christian churches, with charge to guide Christ's flock by their doctrine and advice, these elders were also called bishops. Timothy was an elder (which word elder, in the New Testament, is a name of office as well as of age); yet he was also a bishop. And bishops were then content with the title of elders. Nay, St. John himself, the Apostle beloved of our Lord, beginneth his Second Epistle with these words, "The elder to the elect lady." By which it is evident that bishop, pastor, elder, doctor, that is to say, teacher, were but so many diverse names of the same office in the time of the Apostles. For there was then no government by coercion, but only by doctrine and persuading. The kingdom of God was yet to come, in a new world; so that there could be no authority to compel in any church till the Commonwealth had embraced the Christian faith; and consequently no diversity of authority, though there were diversity of employments. Besides these magisterial employments in the Church; namely, apostles, bishops, elders, pastors, and doctors, whose calling was to proclaim Christ to the Jews and infidels, and to direct and teach those that believed, we read in the New Testament of no other. For by the names of evangelists and prophets is not signified any office, but several gifts by which several men were profitable to the Church: as evangelists, by writing the life and acts of our Saviour; such as were St. Matthew and St. John Apostles, and St. Mark and St. Luke Disciples, and whosoever else wrote of that subject (as St. Thomas and St. Barnabas are said to have done, though the Church have not received the books that have gone under their names); and as prophets, by the gift of interpreting the Old Testament, and sometimes by declaring their special revelations to the Church. For neither these gifts, nor the gifts of languages, nor the gift of casting out devils, nor of curing other diseases, nor anything else did make an officer in the save only the due calling and election to the charge of teaching. As the Apostles Matthias, Paul, and Barnabas were not made by our Saviour himself, but were elected by the Church, that is, by the assembly of Christians; namely, Matthias by the church of Jerusalem, and Paul and Barnabas by the church of Antioch; so were also the presbyters and pastors in other cities, elected by the churches of those cities. For proof whereof, let us consider, first, how St. Paul proceeded in the ordination of presbyters in the cities where he had converted men to the Christian faith, immediately after he and Barnabas had received their apostleship. We read that "they ordained elders in every church";[Acts, 14. 23] which at first sight may be taken for an argument that they themselves chose and gave them their authority: but if we consider the original text, it will be manifest that they were authorized and chosen by the assembly of the Christians of each city. For the words there are cheirotonesantes autois presbuterous kat ekklesian, that is, "when they had ordained them elders by the holding up of hands in every congregation." Now it is well enough known that in all those cities the manner of choosing magistrates and officers was by plurality of suffrages; and, because the ordinary way of distinguishing the affirmative votes from the negatives was by holding up of hands, to ordain an officer in any of the cities was no more but to bring the people together to elect by plurality of votes, whether it were by plurality of elevated hands, or by plurality of voices, or plurality of balls, or beans, or small stones, of which every man cast in one, into a vessel marked for the affirmative or negative; for diverse cities had diverse customs in that point. It was therefore the assembly that elected their own elders: the Apostles were only presidents of the assembly to call them together for such election, and to pronounce them elected, and to give them the benediction, which now is called consecration. And for this cause they that were presidents of the assemblies, as in the absence of the Apostles the elders were, were called proestotes and in Latin antistites; which words signify the principal person of the assembly, whose office was to number the votes, and to declare thereby who was chosen; and where the votes were equal, to decide the matter in question by adding his own which is the office of a president in council. And, because all the churches had their presbyters ordained in the same manner, where the word is constitute, as ina katasteses kata polin presbuterous, "For this cause left I thee in Crete, that thou shouldest constitute elders in every city," [Titus, 1. 5] we are to understand the same thing; namely, that he should call the faithful together, and ordain them presbyters by plurality of suffrages. It had been a strange thing if in a town where men perhaps had never seen any magistrate otherwise chosen than by an assembly, those of the town, becoming Christians, should so much as have thought on any other way of election of their teachers and guides, that is to say, of their presbyters (otherwise called bishops), than this of plurality of suffrages, intimated by St. Paul in the word cheirotonesantes. [Acts, 14. 23] Nor was there ever any choosing of bishops, before the emperors found it necessary to regulate them in order to the keeping of the peace amongst them, but by the assemblies of the Christians in every several town. The same is also confirmed by the continual practice even to this day in the election of the bishops of Rome. For if the bishop of any place had the right of choosing another to the succession of the pastoral office, in any city, at such time as he went from thence to plant the same in another place; much more had he had the right to appoint his successor in that place in which he last resided and died: and we find not that ever any bishop of Rome appointed his successor. For they were a long time chosen by the people, as we may see by the sedition raised about the election between Damasus and Ursinus; which Ammianus Marcellinus saith was so great that Juventius the Praefect, unable to keep the peace between them, was forced to go out of the city; and that there were above a hundred men found dead upon that occasion in the church itself. And though they afterwards were chosen, first, by the whole clergy of Rome, and afterwards by the cardinals; yet never any was appointed to the succession by his predecessor. If therefore they pretended no right to appoint their own successors, I think I may reasonably conclude they had no right to appoint the successors of other bishops without receiving some new power; which none could take from the Church to bestow on them, but such as had a lawful authority, not only to teach, but to command the Church, which none could do but the civil sovereign. The word minister in the original, diakonos, signifieth one that voluntarily doth the business of another man, and differeth from a servant only in this, that servants are obliged by their condition to what is commanded them; whereas ministers are obliged only by their undertaking, and bound therefore to no more than that they have undertaken: so that both they that teach the word of God and they that administer the secular affairs of the Church are both ministers, but they are ministers of different persons. For the pastors of the Church, called "the ministers of the word," [Acts, 6. 4] are ministers of Christ, whose word it is: but the ministry of a deacon, which is called "serving of tables," [Ibid., 6. 2] is a service done to the church or congregation: so that neither any one man nor the whole Church could ever of their pastor say he was their minister; but of a deacon, whether the charge he undertook were to serve tables or distribute maintenance to the Christians when they lived in each city on a common stock, or upon collections, as in the first times, or to take a care of the house of prayer, or of the revenue, or other worldly business of the Church, the whole congregation might properly call him their minister. For their employment as deacons was to serve the congregation, though upon occasion they omitted not to preach the Gospel, and maintain the doctrine of Christ, every one according to his gifts, as St. Stephen did; and both to preach and baptize, as Philip did: for that Philip, which preached the Gospel at Samaria, [Acts, 8. 5] and baptized the eunuch, [Ibid., 8. 38] was Philip the Deacon, not Philip the Apostle. For it is manifest that when Philip preached in Samaria, the Apostles were at Jerusalem, [Ibid., 8. 1] and "when they heard that Samaria had received the word of God, sent Peter and John to them";[Ibid., 8. 14] by imposition of whose hands they that were baptized received (which before by the baptism of Philip they had not received) the Holy Ghost. [Ibid., 8. 15] For it was necessary for the conferring of the Holy Ghost that their baptism should be administered or confirmed by a minister of the word, not by a minister of the Church. And therefore to confirm the baptism of those that Philip the Deacon had baptized, the Apostles sent out of their own number from Jerusalem to Samaria, Peter and John, who conferred on them that before were but baptized, those graces that were signs of the Holy Spirit, which at that time did accompany all true believers; which what they were may be understood by that which St. Mark saith, "These signs follow them that believe in my name; they shall cast out devils; they shall speak with new tongues; they shall take up serpents; and if they drink any deadly thing, it shall not hurt them; they shall lay hands on the sick, and they shall recover." [Mark, 16. 17] This to do was it that Philip could not give, but the Apostles could and, as appears by this place, effectually did to every man that truly believed, and was by a minister of Christ himself baptized: which power either Christ's ministers in this age cannot confer, or else there are very few true believers, or Christ hath very few ministers. That the first deacons were chosen, not by the Apostles, but by a congregation of the disciples; that is, of Christian men of all sorts, is manifest out of Acts, 6, where we read that the Twelve, after the number of disciples was multiplied, called them together, and having told them that it was not fit that the Apostles should leave the word of God, and serve tables, said unto them, "Brethren look you out among you seven men of honest report, full of the Holy Ghost, and of wisdom, whom we may appoint over this business." [Acts, 6. 3] Here it is manifest that though the Apostles declared them elected, yet the congregation chose them; which also is more expressly said where it is written that "the saying pleased the whole multitude, and they seven," etc. [Ibid., 6. 5] Under the Old Testament, the tribe of Levi were only capable of the priesthood and other inferior offices of the Church. The land was divided amongst the other tribes, Levi excepted, which by the subdivision of the tribe of Joseph into Ephraim and Manasseh were still twelve. To the tribe of Levi were assigned certain cities for their habitation, with the suburbs for their cattle; but for their portion they were to have the tenth of the fruits of the land of their brethren. Again, the priests for their maintenance had the tenth of that tenth, together with part of the oblations and sacrifices. For God had said to Aaron, "Thou shalt have no inheritance in their land, neither shalt thou have any part amongst them; I am thy part and thine inheritance amongst the children of Israel." [Numbers, 18. 20] For God being then King, and having constituted the tribe of Levi to be His public ministers, He allowed them for their maintenance the public revenue, that is to say, the part that God had reserved to Himself; which were tithes and offerings: and that is it which is meant where God saith, "I am thine inheritance." And therefore to the Levites might not unfitly be attributed the name of clergy, from Kleros, which signifieth lot or inheritance; not that they were heirs of the kingdom of God, more than other; but that God's inheritance was their maintenance. Now seeing in this time God Himself was their King, and Moses, Aaron, and the succeeding high priests were His lieutenants; it is manifest that the right of tithes and offerings was constituted by the civil power. After their rejection of God in the demanding of a king, they enjoyed still the same revenue; but the right thereof was derived from that, that the kings did never take it from them: for the public revenue was at the disposing of him that was the public person; and that, till the Captivity, was the king. And again, after the return from the Captivity, they paid their tithes as before to the priest. Hitherto therefore Church livings were determined by the civil sovereign. Of the maintenance of our Saviour and his Apostles, we read only they had a purse (which was carried by Judas Iscariot); and that of the Apostles such as were fishermen did sometimes use their trade; and that when our Saviour sent the twelve Apostles to preach, he forbade them to carry gold, and silver, and brass in their purses, "for that the workman is worthy of his hire":[Matthew, 10. 9, 10] by which it is probable their ordinary maintenance was not unsuitable to their employment; for their employment was "freely to give, because they had freely received";[ Ibid., 10. 8] and their maintenance was the free gift of those that believed the good tiding they carried about of the coming of the Messiah their Saviour. To which we may add that which was contributed out of gratitude by such as our Saviour had healed of diseases; of which are mentioned "certain women which had been healed of evil spirits and infirmities; Mary Magdalen, out of whom went seven devils; and Joanna the wife of Chuza, Herod's steward; and Susanna, and many others, which ministered unto him of their substance." [Luke, 8. 2, 3] After our Saviour's ascension, the Christians of every city lived in common upon the money which was made of the sale of their lands and possessions, and laid down at the feet of the Apostles, of good will, not of duty; [Acts, 4. 34, 35] for "whilst the land remained." saith St. Peter to Ananias, "was it not thine? And after it was sold, was it not in thy power?" [Ibid., 5. 4] Which showeth he needed not have saved his land, nor his money by lying, as not being bound to contribute anything at all unless he had pleased. And as in the time of the Apostles, so also all the time downward, till after Constantine the Great, we shall find that the maintenance of the bishops and pastors of the Christian Church was nothing but the voluntary contribution of them that had embraced their doctrine. There was yet no mention of tithes: but such was in the time of Constantine and his sons the affection of Christians to their pastors, as Ammianus Marcellinus saith, describing the sedition of Damasus and Ursinus about the bishopric, that it was worth their contention, in that the bishops of those times by the liberality of their flock, and especially of matrons, lived splendidly, were carried in coaches, and were sumptuous in their fare and apparel. But here may some ask whether the pastor were then bound to live upon voluntary contribution, as upon alms, "For who," saith St. Paul, "goeth to war at his own charges? or who feedeth a flock, and eateth not of the milk of the flock?" [I Corinthians, 9. 7] And again, "Do ye not know that they which minister about holy things live of the things of the Temple; and they which wait at the altar partake with the altar";[Ibid., 9. 13] that is to say, have part of that which is offered at the altar for their maintenance? And then he concludeth, "Even so hath the Lord appointed that they which preach the gospel should live of the gospel." From which place may be inferred, indeed, that the pastors of the Church ought to be maintained by their flocks; but not that the pastors were to determine either the quantity or the kind of their own allowance, and be, as it were, their own carvers. Their allowance must needs therefore be determined either by the gratitude and liberality of every particular man of their flock or by the whole congregation. By the whole congregation it could not be, because their acts were then no laws: therefore the maintenance of pastors before emperors and civil sovereigns had made laws to settle it was nothing but benevolence. They that served at the altar lived on what was offered. So may the pastors also take what is offered them by their flock, but not exact what is not offered. In what court should they sue for it who had no tribunals? Or if they had arbitrators

amongst themselves, who should execute their judgements when they had no power to arm their officers? It remaineth therefore that there could be no certain maintenance assigned to any pastors of the Church, but by the whole congregation; and then only when their decrees should have the force, not only of canons, but also of laws; which laws could not be made but by emperors, kings, or other civil sovereigns. The right of tithes in Moses' Law could not be applied to then ministers of the Gospel, because Moses and the high priests were the civil sovereigns of the people under God, whose kingdom amongst the Jews was present; whereas the kingdom of God by Christ is yet to come. Hitherto hath been shown what the pastors of the Church are; what are the points of their commission, as that they were to preach, to teach, to baptize, to be presidents in their several congregations; what is ecclesiastical censure, viz., excommunication, that is to say, in those places where Christianity was forbidden by the civil laws, a putting of themselves out of the company of the excommunicate, and where Christianity was by the civil law commanded, a putting the excommunicate out of the congregations of Christians; who elected the pastors and of the Church, that it the congregation; who consecrated and blessed them, that it was the pastor; what was their due revenue, that it was none but their own possessions, and their own labour, and the voluntary contributions of devout and grateful Christians. We are to consider now what office in the Church those persons have who, being civil sovereigns, have embraced also the Christian faith. And first, we are to remember that the right of judging what doctrines are fit for peace, and to be taught the subjects, is in all Commonwealths inseparably annexed (as hath been already proved, Chapter eighteen) to the sovereign power civil, whether it be in one man or in one assembly of men. For it is evident to the meanest capacity that men's actions are derived from the opinions they have of the good or ev
l which from those actions redound unto themselves; and consequently, men that are once possessed of an opinion that their obedience to the sovereign power will be more hurtful to them than their disobedience will disobey the laws, and thereby overthrow the Commonwealth, and introduce confusion and civil war; for the avoiding whereof, all civil government was ordained. And therefore in all Commonwealths of the heathen, the sovereigns have had the name of pastors of the people, because there was no subject that could lawfully teach the people, but by their permission and authority. This right of the heathen kings cannot be thought taken from them by their conversion to the faith of Christ, who never ordained that kings, for believing in him, should be deposed, that is, subjected to any but himself, or, which is all one, be deprived of the power necessary for the conservation of peace amongst their subjects and for their defence against foreign enemies. And therefore Christian kings are still the supreme pastors of their people, and have power to ordain what pastors they please, to teach the Church, that is, to teach the people committed to their charge. Again, let the right of choosing them be, as before the conversion of kings, in the Church, for so it was in the time of the Apostles themselves (as hath been shown already in this chapter); even so also the right will be in the civil sovereign, Christian. For in that he is a Christian, he allows the teaching; and in that he is the sovereign (which is as much as to say, the Church by representation), the teachers he elects are elected by the Church. And when an assembly of Christians choose their pastor in a Christian Commonwealth, it is the sovereign that electeth him, because it is done by his authority; in the same manner as when a town choose their mayor, it is the act of him that hath the sovereign power: for every act done is the act of him without whose consent it is invalid. And therefore whatsoever examples may be drawn out of history concerning the election of pastors by the people or by the clergy, they are no arguments against the right of any civil sovereign, because they that elected them did it by his authority. Seeing then in every Christian Commonwealth the civil sovereign is the supreme pastor, to whose charge the whole flock of his subjects is committed, and consequently that it is by his authority that all other pastors are made, and have power to teach and perform all other pastoral offices, it followeth also that it is from the civil sovereign that all other pastors derive their right of teaching, preaching, and other functions pertaining to that office, and that they are but his ministers; in the same manner as magistrates of towns, judges in courts of justice, and commanders of armies are all but ministers of him that is the magistrate of the whole Commonwealth, judge of all causes, and commander of the whole militia, which is always the civil sovereign. And the reason hereof is not because they that teach, but because they that are to learn, are his subjects. For let it be supposed that a Christian king commit the authority of ordaining pastors in his dominions to another king (as diverse Christian kings allow that power to the Pope), he doth not thereby constitute a pastor over himself, nor a sovereign pastor over his people; for that were to deprive himself of the civil power; which, depending on the opinion men have of their duty to him, and the fear they have of punishment in another world, would depend also on the skill and loyalty of doctors who are no less subject, not only to ambition, but also to ignorance, than any other sort of men. So that where a stranger hath authority to appoint teachers, it is given him by the sovereign in whose dominions he teacheth. Christian doctors are our schoolmasters to Christianity; but kings are fathers of families, and may receive schoolmasters for their subjects

from the recommendation of a stranger, but not from the command; especially when the ill teaching them shall redound to the great and manifest profit of him that recommends them: nor can they be obliged to retain them longer than it is for the public good, the care of which they stand so long charged withal as they retain any other essential right of the sovereignty. If a man therefore should ask a pastor, in the execution of his office, as the chief priests and elders of the people asked our Saviour, "By what authority doest thou these things, and who gave thee this authority?": [Matthew, 21. 23] he can make no other just answer but that he doth it by the authority of the Commonwealth, given him by the king or assembly that representeth it. All pastors, except the supreme, execute their charges in the right, that is, by the authority of the civil sovereign, that is, jure civili. But the king, and every other sovereign, executeth his office of supreme pastor by immediate authority from God, that is to say, in God's right, or jure divino. And therefore none but kings can put into their titles, a mark of their submission to God only, Dei gratia Rex, etc. Bishops ought to say in the beginning of their mandates, "By the favour of the King's Majesty, Bishop of such a diocese"; or as civil ministers, "In His Majesty's name." For in saying, Divina providentia, which is the same with Dei gratia, though disguised, they deny to have received their authority from the civil state, and slyly slip off the collar of their civil subjection, contrary to the unity and defence of the Commonwealth. But if every Christian sovereign be the supreme pastor of his own subjects, it seemeth that he hath also the authority, not only to preach, which perhaps no man will deny, but also to baptize, and to administer sacrament of administer the sacrament of the Lord's Supper and to consecrate both temples and pastors to God's service; which most men deny, partly because they use not to do it, and partly because the administration of sacraments, and consecration of persons and places to holy uses, requireth the imposition of such men's hands as by the like imposition successively from the time of the Apostles have been ordained to the like ministry. For proof therefore that Christian kings have power to baptize and to consecrate, I am to render a reason both why they use not to do it, and how, without the ordinary ceremony of imposition of hands, they are made capable of doing it when they will. There is no doubt but any king, in case he were skilful in the sciences, might by the same right of his office read lectures of them himself by which he authorizeth others to read them in the universities. Nevertheless, because the care of the sum of the business of the Commonwealth taketh up his whole time, it were not convenient for him to apply himself in person to that particular. A king may also, if he please, sit in judgement to hear and determine all manner of causes, as well as give others authority to do it in his name; but that the charge that lieth upon him of command and government constrain him to be continually at the helm, and to commit the ministerial offices to others under him. In the like manner our Saviour, who surely had power to baptize, baptized none himself, but sent his Apostles and Disciples to baptize. [John, 4. 2] So also St. Paul, by the necessity of preaching in diverse and far distant places, baptized few: amongst all the Corinthians he baptized only Crispus, Gaius, and Stephanas; [I Corinthians, 1. 14, 16] and the reason was because his principal charge was to preach. [Ibid., 1. 17] Whereby it is manifest that the greater charge, such as is the government of the Church, is a dispensation for the less. The reason therefore why Christian kings use not to baptize is evident, and the same for which at this day there are few baptized by bishops, and by the Pope fewer. And as concerning imposition of hands, whether it be needful for the authorizing of a king to baptize and consecrate, we may consider thus. Imposition of hands was a most ancient public ceremony amongst the Jews, by which was designed, and made certain, the person or other thing intended in a man's prayer, blessing, sacrifice, consecration, condemnation, or other speech. So Jacob, in blessing the children of Joseph, "Laid his right hand on Ephraim the younger, and his left hand on Manasseh the firstborn";[Genesis, 48. 14] and this he did wittingly (though they were so presented to him by Joseph as he was forced in doing it to stretch out his arms across) to design to whom he whom he intended the greater blessing. So also in the sacrificing of the burnt offering, Aaron is commanded "to lay his hands on the head of the bullock";[Exodus, 29. 10] and "to lay his hand on the head of the ram." [Ibid., 29. 15] The same is also said again, Leviticus, 1. 4, and 8. 14. Likewise Moses when he ordained Joshua to be captain of the Israelites, that is, consecrated him to God's service, "laid his hands upon him, and gave him his charge," [Numbers, 27. 23] designing and rendering certain who it was they were to obey in war. And in the consecration of the Levites God commanded that "the children of Israel should put their hands the Levites." [Ibid., 8. 10] And in the condemnation of him that had blasphemed the Lord, God commanded that "all that heard him should lay their hands on his head, and that all the congregation should stone him." [Leviticus, 24. 14] And why should they only that heard him lay their hands upon him, and not rather a priest, Levite, or other minister of justice, but that none else were able to design and demonstrate to the eyes of the congregation who it was that had blasphemed and ought to die? And to design a man, or any other thing, by the hand to the eye is less subject to mistake than when it is done to the ear by a name. And so much was this ceremony observed that in blessing the whole congregation at once, which cannot be done by laying on of hands, yet Aaron "did lift up his hand towards the people when he blessed them." [Leviticus, 9. 22] And we read also of the like ceremony of consecration of temples amongst the heathen, as that the priest laid his hands on some post of the temple, all the while he was uttering the words of consecration. So natural it is to design any individual thing rather by the hand, to assure the eyes, than by words to inform the ear, in matters of God's public service. This ceremony was not therefore new in our Saviour's time. For Jairus, whose daughter was sick, besought our Saviour not to heal her, but "to lay his hands upon her, that she might be healed." [Mark, 5. 23] And "they brought unto him little children, that he should put his hands on them, and pray." [Matthew, 19. 13] According to this ancient rite, the Apostles and presbyters and the presbytery itself laid hands on them whom they ordained pastors, and withal prayed for them that they might receive the Holy Ghost; and that not only once, but sometimes oftener, when a new occasion was presented: but the end was still the same, namely a punctual and religious designation of the person ordained either to the pastoral charge in general or to a particular mission. So "The Apostles prayed, and laid their hands"[Acts, 6. 6] on the seven deacons; which was done, not to give them the Holy Ghost (for they were full of the Holy Ghost before they were chosen, as appeareth immediately before[Ibid., 6. 3]), but to design them to that office. And after Philip the Deacon had converted certain persons in Samaria, Peter and John went down "and laid their hands on them, and they received the Holy Ghost." [Ibid., 8. 17] And not only an Apostle, but a presbyter had this power: for St. Paul adviseth Timothy, "Lay hands suddenly on no man";[I Timothy, 5. 22] that is, design no man rashly to the office of a pastor. The whole presbytery laid their hands on Timothy, as we read, I Timothy, 4. 14, but this is to be understood as that some did it by the appointment of the presbytery, and most likely their proestos, or prolocutor, which it may be was St. Paul himself. For in his second Epistle to Timothy, verse 6, he saith to him, "Stir up the gift of God which is in thee, by the laying on of my hands": [Acts, 9. 17, 18] where note, by the way, that by the Holy Ghost is not meant the third person in the Trinity, but the gifts necessary to the pastoral office. We read also that St. Paul had imposition of hands twice; once from Ananias at Damascus at the time of his baptism; and again at Antioch, when he was first sent out to preach. [Ibid., 13. 3] The use then of this ceremony considered in the ordination of pastors was to design the person to whom they gave such power. But if there had been then any Christian that had had the power of teaching before, the baptizing of him, that is, the making him a Christian, had given him no new power, but had only caused him to preach true doctrine, that is, to use his power aright; and therefore the imposition of hands had been unnecessary; baptism itself had been sufficient. But every sovereign, before Christianity, had the power of teaching and ordaining teachers; and therefore Christianity gave them no new right, but only directed them in the way of teaching truth; and consequently they needed no imposition of hands (besides that which is done in baptism) to authorize them to exercise any part of the pastoral function, as namely, to baptize and consecrate. And in the Old Testament, though the priest only had right to consecrate, during the time that the sovereignty was in the high priest, yet it was not so when the sovereignty was in the king: for we read that Solomon blessed the people, consecrated the Temple, and pronounced that public prayer, [I Kings, 8] which is the pattern now for consecration of all Christian churches and chapels: whereby it appears he had not only the right of ecclesiastical government, but also of exercising ecclesiastical functions. From this consolidation of the right politic and ecclesiastic in Christian sovereigns, it is evident they have all manner of power over their subjects that can be given to man for the government of men's external actions, both in policy and religion, and may make such laws as themselves shall judge fittest, for the government of their own subjects, both as they are the Commonwealth and as they are the Church: for both State and Church are the same men. If they please, therefore, they may, as many Christian kings now do, commit the government of their subjects in matters of religion to the Pope; but then the Pope is in that point subordinate to them, and exerciseth that charge in another's dominion jure civili, in the right of the civil sovereign; not jure divino, in God's right; and may therefore be discharged of that office when the sovereign for the good of his subjects shall think it necessary. They may also, if they please, commit the care of religion to one supreme pastor, or to an assembly of pastors, and give them what power over the Church, or one over another, they think most convenient; and what titles of honor, as of bishops, archbishops, priests, or presbyters, they will; and make such laws for their maintenance, either by tithes or otherwise, as they please, so they do it out of a sincere conscience, of which God only is the judge. It is the civil sovereign that is to appoint judges and interpreters of the canonical scriptures; for it is he that maketh them laws. It is he also that giveth strength to excommunications; which but for such laws and punishments as may humble obstinate libertines, and reduce them to union with the rest of the Church, would be contemned. In sum, he hath the supreme power in all causes, as well ecclesiastical as civil, as far as concerneth actions and words, for those only are known and may be accused; and of that which cannot be accused, there is no judge at all, but God, that knoweth the heart. And these rights are incident to all sovereigns, whether monarchs or assemblies: for they that are the representants of a Christian people are representants of the Church: for a Church and a Commonwealth of Christian people are the same thing. Though this that I have here said, and in other places of this book, seem clear enough for the asserting of the supreme ecclesiastical power to Christian sovereigns, yet because the Pope of Rome's challenge to that power universally hath been maintained chiefly, and I think as strongly as is possible, by Cardinal Bellarmine in his controversy DeSummo Pontifice, I have thought it necessary, as briefly as I can, to examine the grounds and strength of his discourse. Of five books he hath written of this subject, the first containeth three questions: one, which is simply the best government, monarchy, aristocracy, or democracy, and concludeth for neither, but for a government mixed of all three; another, which of these is the best government of the Church, and concludeth for the mixed, but which should most participate of monarchy; the third, whether in this mixed monarchy, St. Peter had the place of monarch. Concerning his first conclusion, I have already sufficiently proved (Chapter eighteen) that all governments, which men are bound to obey, are simple and absolute. In monarchy there is but one man supreme, and all other men that have any kind of power in the state have it by his commission, during his pleasure, and execute it in his name; and in aristocracy and democracy, but one supreme assembly, with the same power that in monarchy belongeth to the monarch, which is not a mixed, but an absolute sovereignty. And of the three sorts, which is the best is not to be disputed where any one of them is already established; but the present ought always to be preferred, maintained, and accounted best, because it is against both the law of nature and the divine positive law to do anything tending to the subversion thereof. Besides, it maketh nothing to the power of any pastor (unless he have the civil sovereignty) what kind of government is the best, because their calling is not to govern men by commandment, but to teach them and persuade them by arguments, and leave it to them to consider whether they shall embrace or reject the doctrine taught. For monarchy, aristocracy, and democracy do mark out unto us three sorts of sovereigns, not of pastors; or, as we may say, three sorts of masters of families, not three sorts of schoolmasters for their children. And therefore the second conclusion, concerning the best form of government of the Church, is nothing to the question of the Pope's power without his own dominions: for in all other Commonwealths his power, if he have any at all, is that of the schoolmaster only, and not of the master of the family. For the third conclusion, which is that St. Peter was monarch of the Church, he bringeth for his chief argument the place of St. Matthew, "Thou art Peter, and upon this rock I will build my church," etc. "And I will give thee the keys of heaven; whatsoever thou shalt bind on earth shall be bound in heaven, and whatsoever thou shalt loose on earth shall be loosed in heaven." [Matthew, 16. 18, 19] Which place, well considered, proveth no more but that the Church of Christ hath for foundation one only article; namely, that which Peter, in the name of all the Apostles professing, gave occasion to our Saviour to speak the words here cited. Which that we may clearly understand, we are to consider, that our Saviour preached by himself, by John Baptist, and by his Apostles, nothing but this article of faith, "that he was the Christ"; all other articles requiring faith no otherwise than as founded on that. John began first, preaching only this, "The kingdom of God is at hand." [Ibid., 3. 2] Then our Saviour himself preached the same: [Matthew, 4. 17] and to his twelve Apostles, when he gave them their commission, there is no mention of preaching any other article but that. [Ibid., 10. 7] This was the fundamental article, that is the foundation of the Church's faith. Afterwards the Apostles being returned to him, he asketh them all, not Peter only, who men said he was; and they answered that some said he was John the Baptist, some Elias, and others Jeremias, or one of the Prophets; [Ibid., 16. 13] then he asked them all again, not Peter only, "Whom say ye that I am?" [Ibid., 16. 15] Therefore St. Peter answered for them all, "Thou art Christ, the Son of the living God"; which I said is the foundation of the faith of the whole Church; from which our Saviour takes the occasion of saying, "upon this stone I will build my Church": by which it is manifest that by the foundation-stone of the Church was meant the fundamental article of the Church's faith. But why then, will some object, doth our Saviour interpose these words, "Thou art Peter"? If the original of this text had been rigidly the reason would easily have appeared. We are therefore to consider that the Apostle Simon was surnamed Stone (which is the signification of the Syriac word cephas, and of the Greek word petrus). Our Saviour therefore after the confession of that fundamental article, alluding to his name, said (as if it were in English) thus, "Thou art Stone, and upon this Stone I will build my Church": which is as much as to say, "This article, that I am the Christ, is the foundation of all the faith I require in those that are to be members my Church." Neither is this allusion to a name an unusual thing in common speech: but it had been a strange and obscure speech, if our Saviour, intending to build his Church on the person of St. Peter, had said, "Thou art a stone, and upon this stone I will build my Church," when it was so obvious, without ambiguity, to have said, "I will build my Church on thee"; and yet there had been still the same allusion to his name. And for the following words, "I will give thee the keys of heaven," etc., it is no more than what our Saviour gave also to all the rest of his Disciples, "Whatsoever ye shall bind on earth shall be bound in heaven. And whatsoever ye shall loose on earth shall be loosed in heaven." [Matthew, 18. 18] But howsoever this be interpreted, there is no doubt but the power here granted belongs to all supreme pastors; such as are all Christian civil sovereigns in their own dominions. Insomuch as if St. Peter, or our Saviour himself, had converted any of them to believe him and to acknowledge his kingdom; yet because his kingdom is not of this world, he had left the supreme care of converting his subjects to none but him; or else he must have deprived him of the sovereignty to which the right of teaching is inseparably annexed. And thus much in refutation of his first book, wherein he would prove St. Peter to have been the monarch universal of the Church, that is to say, of all the Christians in the world. The second book hath two conclusions: one, that St. Peter was Bishop of Rome, and there died; the other, that the Popes of Rome are his successors; both which have been disputed by others. But supposing them true; yet if by Bishop of Rome be understood either the monarch of the Church, or the supreme pastor of it, not Silvester, but Constantine (who was the first Christian emperor) was that bishop; and as Constantine, so all other Christian emperors were of right supreme bishops of the Roman Empire. I say, of the Roman Empire, not of all Christendom, for other Christian sovereigns had the same right in their several territories, as to an office essentially adherent to their sovereignty: which shall serve for answer to his second book. In the third book he handleth the question whether the Pope be Antichrist. For my part, I see no argument that proves he is so, in that sense the Scripture useth the name: nor will I take any argument from the quality of Antichrist to contradict the authority he exerciseth, or hath heretofore exercised, in the dominions of any other prince or state. It is evident that the prophets of the Old Testament foretold, and the Jews expected, a Messiah, that is, a Christ, that should re-establish amongst them the kingdom of God, which had been rejected by them in the time of Samuel when they required a king after the manner of other nations. This expectation of theirs made them obnoxious to the imposture of all such as had both the ambition to attempt the attaining of the kingdom, and the art to deceive the people by counterfeit miracles, by hypocritical life, or by orations and doctrine plausible. Our Saviour therefore, and his Apostles, forewarned men of false prophets and of false Christs. False Christs are such as pretend to be the Christ, but are not, and are called properly Antichrists, in such sense as when there happeneth a schism in the Church by the election of two Popes, the one the one calleth the other Antipapa, or the false Pope. And therefore Antichrist in the proper signification hath two essential marks: one, that he denieth Jesus to be Christ; and another that he professeth himself to be Christ. The first mark is set down by St. John in his first Epistle, 4. 3, "Every spirit that confesseth not that Jesus Christ is come in the flesh is not of God; and this is the spirit of Antichrist." The other mark is expressed in the words of our Saviour, "Many shall come in my name, saying, I am Christ";[Matthew, 24. 5] and again, "If any man shall say unto you, Lo, here is Christ, there is Christ, believe it not." And therefore Antichrist must be a false Christ; that is, some one of them that shall pretend themselves to be Christ. And out of these two marks, to deny Jesus to be the Christ and to affirm himself to be the Christ, it followeth that he must also be an adversary of Jesus the true Christ, which is another usual signification of the word Antichrist. But of these many Antichrists, there is one special one, o Antichristos, the Antichrist, or Antichrist definitely, as one certain person; not indefinitely an Antichrist. Now seeing the Pope of Rome neither pretendeth himself, nor denieth Jesus to be the Christ, I perceive not how he can be called Antichrist; by which word is not meant one that falsely pretendeth to be his lieutenant, or vicar general, but to be He. There is also some mark of the time of this special Antichrist, as when that abominable destroyer, spoken of by Daniel, [Daniel, 9. 27] shall stand in the holy place, [Matthew, 24. 15] and such tribulation as was not since the beginning of the world, nor ever shall be again, insomuch as if it were to last long, no flesh could be saved; but for the elect's sake those days shall be shortened," [Ibid., 24. 22] (made fewer). But that tribulation is not yet come; for it is to be followed immediately by a darkening of the sun and moon, a falling of the stars, a concussion of the heavens, and the glorious coming again of our Saviour in the clouds. [Ibid., 24. 29] And therefore the Antichrist is not yet come; whereas many Popes are both come and gone. It is true, the Pope, in taking upon him to give laws to all Christian kings and nations, usurpeth a kingdom in this world, which Christ took not on him: but he doth it not as Christ, but as for Christ, wherein there is nothing of the Antichrist. In the fourth book, to prove the Pope to be the supreme judge in all questions of faith and manners, which is as much as to be the absolute monarch of all Christians in the world, he bringeth three propositions: the first, that his judgements are infallible; the second, that he can make very laws, and punish those that observe them not; the third, that our Saviour conferred all jurisdiction ecclesiastical on the Pope of Rome. For the infallibility of his judgements, he allegeth the Scriptures: the first, that of Luke, 22. 31, "Simon, Simon, Satan hath desired you that he may sift you as wheat; but I have prayed for thee, that thy faith fail not; and when thou art converted, strengthen thy brethren." This, according to Bellarmine's exposition, is that Christ gave here to Simon Peter two privileges: one, that neither his faith should fail, nor the faith of any of his successors; the other, that neither he nor any of his successors should ever define any point concerning faith or manners erroneously, or contrary to the definition of a former Pope: which is a strange and very much strained interpretation. But he that with attention readeth that chapter shall find there is no place in the whole Scripture that maketh more against the Pope's authority than this very place. The priests and scribes, seeking to kill our Saviour at the Passover, and Judas possessed with a resolution to betray him, and the day of killing the Passover being come, our Saviour celebrated the same with his Apostles, which he said, till the kingdom of God was come he would do no more, and withal told them that one of them was to betray him. Hereupon they questioned which of them it should be; and withal, seeing the next Passover their master would celebrate should be when he was king, entered into a contention who should then be the greatest man. Our Saviour therefore told them that the kings of the nations had dominion over their subjects, and are called by a name in Hebrew that signifies bountiful; "but I cannot be so to you; you must endeavour to serve one another; I ordain you a kingdom, but it is such as my Father hath ordained me; a kingdom that I am now to purchase with my blood, and not to possess till my second coming; then ye shall eat and drink at my table, and sit on thrones, judging the twelve tribes of Israel." And then addressing himself to St. Peter, he saith, "Simon, Simon, Satan seeks, by suggesting a present domination, to weaken your faith of the future; but I have prayed for thee, that thy faith shall not fail; thou therefore note this: being converted, and understanding my kingdom as of another world, confirm the same faith in thy brethren." To which St. Peter answered (as one that no more expected any authority in this world), "Lord, I am ready to go with thee, not only to prison, but to death." Whereby it is manifest, St. Peter had not only no jurisdiction given him in this world, but a charge to teach all the other Apostles that they also should have none. And for the infallibility of St. Peter's sentence definitive in matter of faith, there is no more to be attributed to it out of this text than that Peter should continue in the belief of this point, namely, that Christ should come again and possess the kingdom at the day of judgement; which was not given by this text to all his successors; for we see they claim it in the world that now is. The second place is that of Matthew 16. 18, "Thou art Peter, and upon this rock I will build my Church, and the gates of hell shall not prevail against it." By which, as I have already shown in this chapter, is proved no more than that the gates of hell shall not prevail against the confession of Peter, which gave occasion to that speech; namely this, that Jesus is Christ the Son of God. The third text is John, 21. 16, 17, "Feed my sheep"; which contains no more but a commission of teaching. And if we grant the rest of the Apostles to be contained in that name of sheep, then it is the supreme power of teaching: but it was only for the time that there were no Christian sovereigns already possessed of that supremacy. But I have already proved that Christian sovereigns are in their own dominions the supreme pastors, and instituted thereto by virtue of their being baptized, though without other imposition of hands. For such imposition, being a ceremony of designing the person, is needless when he is already designed to the power of teaching what doctrine he will, by his institution to an absolute power over his subjects. For as I have proved before, sovereigns are supreme teachers, in general, by their office, and therefore oblige themselves, by their baptism, to teach the doctrine of Christ: and when they suffer others to teach their people, they do it at the peril of their own souls; for it is at the hands of the heads of families that God will require the account of the instruction of His children and servants. It is of Abraham himself, not of a hireling, that God saith, "I know him that he will command his children, and his household after him, that they keep the way of the Lord, and do justice and judgement."[Genesis, 18. 19] The fourth place is that of Exodus, 28. 30, "Thou shalt put in the breastplate of judgement, the Urim and the Thummim": which he saith is interpreted by the Septuagint, delosin kai aletheian, that is, evidence and truth: and thence concludeth, God hath given evidence and truth, which is almost infallibility, to the high priest. But be it evidence and truth itself that was given; or be it but admonition to the priest to endeavour to inform himself clearly, and give judgement uprightly; yet in that it was given to the high priest, it was given to the civil sovereign (for such next under God was the high priest in the Commonwealth of Israel), and is an argument for evidence and truth, that is, for the ecclesiastical supremacy of civil sovereigns over their own subjects, against the pretended power of the Pope. These are all the texts he bringeth for the infallibility of the judgement of the Pope, in point of faith. For the infallibility of his judgement concerning manners, he bringeth one text, which is that of John, 16. 13, "When the Spirit of truth is come, he will lead you into all truth": where, saith he, by all truth is meant, at least, all truth necessary to salvation. But with this mitigation, he attributeth no more infallibility to the Pope than to any man that professeth Christianity, and is not to be damned: for if any man err in any point, wherein not to err is necessary to salvation, it is impossible he should be saved; for that only is necessary to salvation without which to be saved is impossible. What points these are I shall declare out of the Scripture in the chapter following. In this place I say no more but that though it were granted the Pope could not possibly teach any error at all, yet doth not this entitle him to any jurisdiction in the dominions of another prince, unless we shall also say a man is obliged in conscience to set on work upon all occasions the best workman, even then also when he hath formerly promised his work to another. Besides the text, he argueth from reason, thus. If the Pope could err in necessaries, then Christ hath not sufficiently provided for the Church's salvation, because he hath commanded her to follow the Pope's directions. But this reason is invalid, unless he show when and where Christ commanded that, or took at all any notice of a Pope. Nay, granting whatsoever was given to St. Peter was given to the Pope, yet seeing there is in the Scripture no command to any man to obeyeth him when his commands are contrary to those of his lawful sovereign. Lastly, it hath not been declared by the Church, nor by the Pope himself, that he is the civil of all the Christians in the world; and therefore all Christians are not bound to acknowledge his jurisdiction in point of manners. For the civil sovereignty, and supreme judicature in controversies of manners, are the same thing: and the makers of civil laws are not only declarers, but also makers of the justice and injustice of actions; there being nothing in men's manners that makes them righteous or unrighteous, but their conformity with the law of the sovereign. And therefore when the Pope challengeth supremacy in controversies of manners, he teacheth men to disobey the civil sovereign; which is an erroneous doctrine, contrary to the many precepts of our Saviour and his Apostles delivered to us in the Scripture. To prove the Pope has power to make laws, he allegeth many places; as first, Deuteronomy, 17. 12, "The man that will do presumptuously, and will not hearken unto the priest, that standeth to minister there before the Lord thy God, or unto the judge, even that man shall die, and thou shalt put away the evil from Israel." For answer whereunto we are to remember that the high priest, next and immediately under God, was the civil sovereign; and all judges were to be constituted by him. The words alleged sound therefore thus, "The man that will presume to disobey the civil sovereign for the time being, or any of his officers, in the execution of their places, that man shall die," etc., which is clearly for the civil sovereignty, against the universal power of the Pope. Secondly, he allegeth that of Matthew, 16, "Whatsoever ye shall bind," etc., and interpreteth it for such binding as is attributed to the Scribes and Pharisees, "They bind heavy burdens, and grievous to be borne, and lay them on men's shoulders"; [Matthew, 23. 4] by which is meant, he says, making of laws; and concludes thence that the Pope can make laws. But this also maketh only for the legislative power of civil sovereigns: for the Scribes and Pharisees sat in Moses' chair, but Moses next under God was sovereign of the people of Israel: and therefore our Saviour commanded them to do all that they should say, but not all that they should do; that is, to obey their laws, but not follow their example. The third place is John, 21. 16, "Feed my sheep"; which is not a power to make laws, but a command to teach. Making laws belongs to the lord of the family, who by his own discretion chooseth his chaplain, as also a schoolmaster to teach his children. The fourth place, John, 20. 21, is against him. The words are, "As my Father sent me, so send I you." But our Saviour was sent to redeem by his death such as should believe; and by his own and his Apostles' preaching to prepare them for their entrance into his kingdom; which he himself saith is not of this world, and hath taught us to pray for the coming of it hereafter, though he refused to tell his Apostles when it should come; [Acts, 1. 6, 7] and in which, when it comes, the twelve Apostles shall sit on twelve thrones (every one perhaps as high as that of St. Peter), to judge the twelve tribes of Israel. Seeing then God the Father sent not our Saviour to make laws in this present world, we may conclude from the text that neither did our Saviour send St. Peter to make laws here, but to persuade men to expect his second coming with a steadfast faith; and in the meantime, if subjects, to obey their princes; and if princes, both to believe it themselves and to do their best to make their subjects do the same, which is the office of a bishop. Therefore this place maketh most strongly for the joining of the ecclesiastical supremacy to the civil sovereignty, contrary to that which Cardinal Bellarmine allegeth it for. The fifth is Acts, 15. 28, "It hath seemed good to the Holy Spirit, and to us, to lay upon you no greater burden than these necessary things, that ye abstain from meats offered to idols, and from blood, and from things strangled, and from fornication." Here he notes the word "laying of burdens" for the legislative power. But who is there that, reading this text, can say this style of the Apostles may not as properly be used in giving counsel as in making laws? The style of a law is, "we command": but, "we think good," is the ordinary style of them that but give advice; and they lay a burden that give advice, though it be conditional, that is, if they to whom they give it will attain their ends: and such is the burden of abstaining from things strangled, and from blood, not absolute, but in case they will not err. I have shown before (Chapter twenty-five) that law is distinguished from counsel in this, that the reason of a law is taken from the design and benefit of him that prescribeth it; but the reason of a counsel, from the design and benefit of him to whom the counsel is given. But here, the Apostles aim only at the benefit of the converted Gentiles, namely, their salvation; not at their own benefit; for having done their endeavour, they shall have their reward, whether they be obeyed or not. And therefore the acts of this council were not laws, but counsels. The sixth place is that of Romans, 13, "Let every soul be subject to the higher powers, for there is no power but of God"; which is meant, he saith, not only of secular, but also of ecclesiastical princes. To which I answer, first, that there are no ecclesiastical princes but those that are also civil sovereigns, and their principalities exceed not the compass of their civil sovereignty; without those bounds, though they may be received for doctors, they cannot be acknowledged for princes. For if the Apostle had meant we should be subject both to our own princes and also to the Pope, he had taught us a doctrine which Christ himself hath told us is impossible, namely, to serve two masters. And though the Apostle say in another place, "I write these things being absent, lest being present I should use sharpness, according to the power which the Lord hath given me";[II Corinthians, 13. 10] it is not that he challenged a power either to put to death, imprison, banish, whip, or fine any of them, which are punishments; but only to excommunicate, which, without the civil power, is no more but a leaving of their company, and having no more to do with them than with a heathen man or a publican; which in many occasions might be a greater pain to the excommunicant than to the excommunicate. The seventh place is I Corinthians, 4. 21, "Shall I come unto you with a rod, or in love, and the spirit of lenity?" But here again, it is not the power of a magistrate to punish offenders, that is meant by a rod; but only the power of excommunication, which is not in its own nature a punishment, but only a denouncing of punishment, that Christ shall inflict, when he shall be in possession of his kingdom, at the day of judgement. Nor then also shall it be properly a punishment, as upon a subject that hath broken the law; but a revenge, as upon an enemy, or revolter, that denyeth the right of our saviour to the kingdom: and therefore this proveth not the legislative power of any bishop that has not also the civil power. The eighth place is Timothy, 3. 2, "A bishop must be the husband but of one wife, vigilant, sober," etc., which he saith was a law. I thought that none could make a law in the Church but the monarch of the Church, St. Peter. But suppose this precept made by the authority of St. Peter; yet I see no reason why to call it a law, rather than an advice, seeing Timothy was not a subject, but a disciple of St. Paul; nor the flock under the charge of Timothy, his subjects in the kingdom, but his scholars in the school of Christ. If all the precepts he giveth Timothy be laws, why is not this also a law, "Drink no longer water, but use a little wine for health's sake"? And why are not also the precepts of good physicians so many laws, but that it is not the imperative manner of speaking, but an absolute subjection to a person, that maketh his precepts laws? In like manner, the ninth place, I Timothy, 5. 19, "Against an elder receive not an accusation, but before two or three witnesses," is a wise precept, but not a law. The tenth place is Luke, 10. 16, "He that heareth you, heareth me; and he that despiseth you, despiseth me." And there is no doubt but he that despiseth the counsel of those that are sent by Christ despiseth the counsel of Christ himself. But who are those now that are sent by Christ but such as are ordained pastors by lawful authority? And who are lawfully ordained that are not ordained by the sovereign pastor? And who is ordained by the sovereign pastor in a Christian Commonwealth that is not ordained by the authority of the sovereign thereof? Out of this place therefore it followeth that he which heareth his sovereign, being a Christian, heareth Christ; and he that despiseth the doctrine which his king, being a Christian, authorizeth despiseth the doctrine of Christ, which is not that which Bellarmine intendeth here to prove, but the contrary. But all this is nothing to a law. Nay more, a Christian king, a pastor and teacher of his subjects makes not thereby his doctrines laws. He cannot oblige men to believe, though as a civil sovereign he may make laws suitable to his doctrine, which may oblige men to certain actions, and sometimes to such as they would not otherwise do, and which he ought not to command; and yet when they are commanded, they are laws; and the external actions done in obedience to them, without the inward approbation, are the actions of the sovereign, and not of the subject, which is in that case but as an instrument, without any motion of his own at all, because God hath commanded to obey them. The eleventh is every place where the Apostle, for counsel, putteth some word by which men use to signify command, or calleth the following of his counsel by the name of obedience. And therefore they are alleged out of I Corinthians, 11. 2, "I commend you for keeping my precepts as I delivered them to you." The Greek is, "I commend you for keeping those things I delivered to you, as I delivered them": which is far from signifying that they were laws, or anything else, but good counsel. And that of I Thessalonians, 4. 2, "You know what commandments we gave you": where the Greek word is paraggelias edokamen, equivalent to paredokamen, "what we delivered to you," as in the place next before alleged, which does not prove the traditions of the Apostles to be any more than counsels; though as is said in the eighth verse, "he that despiseth them, despiseth not man, but God": for our Saviour himself came not to judge, that is, to be king in this world; but to sacrifice himself for sinners, and leave doctors in his Church, to lead, not to drive men to Christ, who never accepteth forced actions (which is all the law produceth), but the inward conversion of the heart, which is not the work of laws, but of counsel and doctrine. And that of II Thessalonians, 3. 14, "If any man obey not our word by this epistle, note that man, and have no company with him, that he may be ashamed": where from the word obey, he would infer that this epistle was a law to the Thessalonians. The epistles of the emperors were indeed laws. If therefore the Epistle of St. Paul were also a law, they were to obey two masters. But the word obey, as it is in the Greek upakouei, signifieth hearkening to, or putting in practice, not only that which is commanded by him that has right to punish, but also that which is delivered in a way of counsel for our good; and therefore St. Paul does not bid kill him that disobeys; nor beat, nor imprison, nor amerce him, which legislators may all do; but avoid his company, that he may be ashamed: whereby it is evident it was not the empire of an Apostle, but his reputation amongst the faithful, which the Christians stood in awe of. The last place is that of Hebrews, 13. 17, "Obey your leaders, and submit yourselves to them, for they watch for your souls, as they that must give account": and here also is intended by obedience, a following of their counsel: for the reason of our obedience is not drawn from the will and command of our pastors, but from our own benefit, as being the salvation of our souls they watch for, and not for the exaltation of their own power and authority. If it were meant here that all they teach were laws, then not only the Pope, but every pastor in his parish should have legislative power. Again, they that are bound to obey their pastors have no power to examine their commands. What then shall we say to St. John, who bids us "not to believe every spirit, but to try the spirits whether they are of God, because many false prophets are gone out into the world?" [I John, 4. 1] It is therefore manifest that we may dispute the doctrine of our pastors, but no man can dispute a law. The commands of civil sovereigns are on all sides granted to be laws: if any else can make a law besides himself, all Commonwealth, and consequently all peace and justice, must cease; which is contrary to all laws, both divine and human. Nothing therefore can be drawn from these or any other places of Scripture to prove the decrees of the Pope, where he has not also the civil sovereignty, to be laws. The last point he would prove is this, that our Saviour Christ has committed ecclesiastical jurisdiction immediately to none but the Pope. Wherein he handleth not the question of supremacy between the Pope and Christian kings, but between the Pope and other bishops. And first, he says it is agreed that the jurisdiction of bishops is at least in the general de jure divino, that is, in the right of God; for which he alleges St. Paul, Ephesians, 4. 11, where he says that Christ, after his ascension into heaven, "gave gifts to men, some Apostles, some prophets, and some evangelists, and some pastors, and some teachers"; and thence infers they have indeed their jurisdiction in God's right, but will not grant they have it immediately from God, but derived through the Pope. But if a man may be said to have his jurisdiction de jure divino, and yet not immediately; what lawful jurisdiction, though but civil, is there in a Christian Commonwealth that is not also de jure divino? For Christian kings have their civil power from God immediately; and the magistrates under Him exercise their several charges in virtue of His commission; wherein that which they do is no less de jure divino mediato than that which the bishops do in virtue of the Pope's ordination. All lawful power is of God, immediately in the supreme governor, and mediately in those that have authority under him: so that either he must grant every constable in the state to hold his office in the right of God, or he must not hold that any bishop holds his so, besides the Pope himself. But this whole dispute, whether Christ left the jurisdiction to the Pope only, or to other bishops also, if considered out of those places where the Pope has the civil sovereignty, is a contention de lana caprina: for none of them, where they are not sovereigns, has any jurisdiction at all. For jurisdiction is the power of hearing and determining causes between man and man, and can belong to none but him that hath the power to prescribe the rules of right and wrong; that is, to make laws; and with the sword of justice to compel men to obey his decisions, pronounced either by himself or by the judges he ordaineth thereunto, which none can lawfully do but the civil sovereign. Therefore when he allegeth, out of the sixth chapter of Luke, that our Saviour called his disciples together, and chose twelve of them, which he named Apostles, he proveth that he elected them (all, except Matthias, Paul, and Barnabas), and gave them power and command to preach, but not to judge of causes between man and man: for that is a power which he refused to take upon himself, saying, "Who made me a judge, or a divider, amongst you?" and in another place, "My kingdom is not of this world." But he that hath not the power to hear and determine causes between man and man cannot be said to have any jurisdiction at all. And yet this hinders not but that our Saviour gave them power to preach and baptize in all parts of the world, supposing they were not by their own lawful sovereign forbidden: for to our own sovereigns Christ himself and his Apostles have in sundry places expressly commanded us in all things to be obedient. The arguments by which he would prove that bishops receive their jurisdiction from the Pope (seeing the Pope in the dominions of other princes hath no jurisdiction himself) are all in vain. Yet because they prove, on the contrary, that all bishops receive jurisdiction, when they have it, from their civil sovereigns, I will not omit the recital of them. The first is from Numbers, 11, where Moses, not being able alone to undergo the whole burden of administering the affairs of the people of Israel, God commanded him to choose seventy elders, and took part of the spirit of Moses, to put it upon those seventy elders: by which is understood, not that God weakened the spirit of Moses, for that had not eased him at all, but that they had all of them their authority from him; wherein he doth truly and ingenuously interpret that place. But seeing Moses had the entire sovereignty in the Commonwealth of the Jews, it is manifest that it is thereby signified that they had their authority from the civil sovereign: and therefore that place proveth that bishops in every Christian Commonwealth have their authority from the civil sovereign; and from the Pope in his own territories only, and not in the territories of any other state. The second argument is from the nature of monarchy, wherein all authority is in one man, and in others by derivation from him. But the government of the Church, he says, is monarchical. This also makes for Christian monarchs. For they are really monarchs of their own people; that is, of their own Church (for the Church is the same thing with a Christian people); whereas the power of the Pope, though he were St. Peter, is neither monarchy, nor hath anything of archical nor cratical, but only of didactical; for God accepteth not a forced, but a willing obedience. The third is from that the See of St. Peter is called by St. Cyprian, the head, the source, the root, the sun, from whence the authority of bishops is derived. But by the law of nature, which is a better principle of right and wrong than the word of any doctor that is but a man, the civil sovereign in every Commonwealth is the head, the source, the root, and the sun, from which all jurisdiction is derived. And therefore the jurisdiction of bishops is derived from the civil sovereign. The fourth is taken from the inequality of their jurisdictions: for if God, saith he, had given it them immediately, He had given as well equality of jurisdiction, as of order: but we see some are bishops but of one town, some of a hundred towns, and some of many whole provinces; which differences were not determined by the command of God: their jurisdiction therefore is not of God, but of man: and one has a greater, another a less, as it pleaseth the Prince of the Church. Which argument, if he had proved before that the Pope had had a universal jurisdiction over all Christians, had been for his purpose. But seeing that hath not been proved, and that it is notoriously known the large jurisdiction of the Pope was given him by those that had it, that is, by the emperors of Rome (for the Patriarch of Constantinople, upon the same title, namely, of being bishop of the capital city of the Empire, and seat of the emperor, claimed to be equal to him), it followeth that all other bishops have their jurisdiction from the sovereigns of the place wherein they exercise the same: and as for that cause they have not their authority de jure divino; so neither hath the Pope his de jure divino, except only where he is also the civil sovereign. His fifth argument is this: "If bishops have their jurisdiction immediately from God, the Pope could not take it from them, for he can do nothing contrary to God's ordination"; and this consequence is good and well proved. "But," saith he, "the Pope can do this, and has done it." This also is granted, so he do it in his own dominions, or in the dominions of any other prince that hath given him that power; but not universally, in right of the popedom: for that power belongeth to every Christian sovereign, within the bounds of his own empire, and is inseparable from the sovereignty. Before the people of Israel had, by the commandment of God to Samuel, set over themselves a king, after the manner of other nations, the high priest had the civil government; and none but he could make nor depose an inferior priest. But that power was afterwards in the king, as may be proved by this same argument of Bellarmine; for if the priest, be he the high priest or any other, had his jurisdiction immediately from God, then the king could not take it from him; for he could do nothing contrary to God's ordinance. But it is certain that King Solomon deprived Abiathar the high priest of his office, [I Kings, 2. 26, 27] and placed Zadok in his room. [Ibid., 2. 35] Kings therefore may in the like manner ordain and deprive bishops, as they shall think fit, for the well governing of their subjects. His sixth argument is this: if bishops have their jurisdiction de jure divino, that is, immediately from God, they that maintain it should bring some word of God to prove it: but they can bring none. The argument is good; I have therefore nothing to say against it. But it is an argument no less good to prove the Pope himself to have no jurisdiction in the dominion of any other prince. Lastly, he bringeth for argument the testimony of two Popes, Innocent and Leo; and I doubt not but he might have alleged, with as good reason, the testimonies of all the Popes almost since St. Peter: for, considering the love of power naturally implanted in mankind, whosoever were made Pope, he would be tempted to uphold the same opinion. Nevertheless, they should therein but do as Innocent and Leo did, bear witness of themselves, and therefore their witness should not be good. In the fifth book he hath four conclusions. The first is that the Pope is not lord of all the world; the second, that the Pope is not lord of all the Christian world; the third, that the Pope, without his own territory, has not any temporal jurisdiction directly. These three conclusions are easily granted. The fourth is that the Pope has, in the dominions of other princes, the supreme temporal power indirectly: which is denied; unless he mean by indirectly that he has gotten it by indirect means, then is that also granted. But I understand that when he saith he hath it indirectly, he means that such temporal jurisdiction belongeth to him of right, but that this right is but a consequence of his pastoral authority, the which he could not exercise, unless he have the other with it: and therefore to the pastoral power, which he calls spiritual, the supreme power civil is necessarily annexed; and that thereby he hath a right to change kingdoms, giving them to one, and taking them from another, when he shall think it conduces to the salvation of souls. Before I come to consider the arguments by which he would prove this doctrine, it will not be amiss to lay open the consequences of it, that princes and states that have the civil sovereignty in their several Commonwealths may bethink themselves whether it be convenient for them, and conducing to the good of their subjects of whom they are to give an account at the day of judgement, to admit the same. When it is said the Pope hath not, in the territories of other states, the supreme civil power directly, we are to understand he doth not challenge it, as other civil sovereigns do, from the original submission thereto of those that are to be governed. For it is evident, and has already been sufficiently in this treatise demonstrated, that the right of all sovereigns is derived originally from the consent of every one of those that are to be governed; whether they that choose him do it for it for their common defence against an enemy, as when they agree amongst themselves to appoint a man or an assembly of men to protect them, or whether they do it to save their lives, by submission to a conquering enemy. The Pope therefore, when he disclaimeth the supreme civil power over other states directly, denieth no more but that his right cometh to him by that way; he ceaseth not for all that to claim it another way; and that is, without the consent of them that are to be governed, by a right given him by God, which he calleth indirectly, in his assumption to the papacy. But by what way soever he pretend, the power is the same; and he may, if it be granted to be his right, depose princes and states, as often as it is for the salvation of souls, that is, as often as he will: for he claimeth also the sole power to judge whether it be to the salvation of men's souls, or not. And this is the doctrine, not only that Bellarmine here, and many other doctors teach in their sermons and books, but also that some councils have decreed, and the Popes have accordingly, when the occasion hath served them, put in practice. For the fourth council of Lateran, held under Pope Innocent the Third (in the third Chapter, De Haereticis), hath this canon: "If a king, at the Pope's admonition, do not purge his kingdom of heretics, and being excommunicate for the same, make not satisfaction within a year, his subjects are absolved of their obedience." And the practice hereof hath been seen on diverse occasions: as in the deposing of Childeric, King of France; in the translation of the Roman Empire to Charlemagne; in the oppression of John, King of England; in transferring the kingdom of Navarre; and of late years, in the league against Henry the Third of France, and in many more occurrences. I think there be few princes that consider not this as unjust and inconvenient; but I wish they would all resolve to be kings or subjects. Men cannot serve two masters. They ought therefore to ease them, either by holding the reins of government wholly in their own hands, or by wholly delivering them into the hands of the Pope, that such men as are willing to be obedient may be protected in their obedience. For this distinction of temporal and spiritual power is but words. Power is as really divided, and as dangerously to all purposes, by sharing with another indirect power, as with a direct one. But to come now to his arguments. The first is this, "The civil power is subject to the spiritual: therefore he that hath the supreme power spiritual hath right to command temporal princes, and dispose of their temporals in order to the spiritual." As for the distinction of temporal and spiritual, let us consider in what sense it may be said intelligibly that the temporal or civil power is subject to the spiritual. There be but two ways that those words can be made sense. For when we say one power is subject to another power, the meaning either is that he which hath the one is subject to him that hath the other; or that the one power is to the other as the means to the end. For we cannot understand that one power hath power over another power; or that one power can have right or command over another: for subjection, command, right, and power are accidents, not of powers, but of persons. One power may be subordinate to another, as the art of a saddler to the art of a rider. If then it be granted that the civil government be ordained as a means to bring us to a spiritual felicity, yet it does not follow that if a king have the civil power, and the Pope the spiritual, that therefore the king is bound to obey the Pope, more than every saddler is bound to obey every rider. Therefore as from subordination of an art cannot be inferred the subjection of the professor; so from the subordination of a government cannot be inferred the subjection of the governor. When therefore he saith the civil power is subject to the spiritual, his meaning is that the civil sovereign is subject to the spiritual sovereign. And the argument stands thus: the civil sovereign is subject to the spiritual; therefore the spiritual prince may command temporal princes, (where the conclusion is the same with the antecedent he should have proved). But to prove it, he allegeth first, this reason, "Kings and popes, clergy and laity, make but one Commonwealth; that is to say, but one Church: and in all bodies the members depend one upon another: but things spiritual depend not of things temporal: therefore temporal depend on spiritual, and therefore are subject to them." In which argumentation there be two gross errors: one is that all Christian kings, popes, clergy, and all other Christian men make but one Commonwealth: for it is evident that France is one Commonwealth, Spain another, and Venice a third, etc. And these consist of Christians, and therefore also are several bodies of Christians; that is to say, several churches: and their several sovereigns represent them, whereby they are capable of commanding and obeying, of doing and suffering, as a natural man; which no

general or universal Church is, till it have a representant, which it hath not on earth: for if it had, there is no doubt but that all Christendom were one Commonwealth, whose sovereign were that representant, both in things spiritual and temporal: and the Pope, to make himself this representant, wanteth three things that our Saviour hath not given him, to command, and to judge, and to punish, otherwise than, by excommunication, to run from those that will not learn of him: for though the Pope were Christ's only vicar, yet he cannot exercise his government till our Saviour's second coming: and then also it is not the Pope, but St. Peter himself, with the other Apostles, that are to be judges of the world. The other error in this his first argument is that he says the members of every Commonwealth, as of a natural body, depend one of another. It is true they cohere together, but they depend only on the sovereign, which is the soul of the Commonwealth; which failing, the Commonwealth is dissolved into a civil war, no one man so much as cohering to another, for want of a common dependence on a known sovereign; just as the members of the natural body dissolve into earth for want of a soul to hold them together. Therefore there is nothing in this similitude f
om whence to infer a dependence of the laity on the clergy, or of the temporal officers on the spiritual, but of both on the civil sovereign; which ought indeed to direct his civil commands to the salvation of souls; but is not therefore subject to any but God Himself. And thus you see the laboured fallacy of the first argument, to deceive such men as distinguish not between the subordination of actions in the way to the end; and the subjection of persons one to another in the administration of the means. For to every end, the means are determined by nature, or by God Himself supernaturally: but the power to make men use the means is in every nation resigned, by the law of nature, which forbiddeth men to violate their faith given, to the civil sovereign. His second argument is this: "Every Commonwealth, because it is supposed to be perfect and sufficient in itself, may command any other Commonwealth not subject to it, and force it to change the administration of the government; nay depose the prince, and set another in his room, if it cannot otherwise defend itself against the injuries he goes about to do them: much more may a spiritual Commonwealth command a temporal one to change the administration of their government, and may depose princes, and institute others, when they cannot otherwise defend the spiritual good." That a Commonwealth, to defend itself against injuries, may lawfully do all that he hath here said is very true; and hath already in that which hath gone before been sufficiently demonstrated. And if it were also true that there is now in this world a spiritual Commonwealth, distinct from a civil Commonwealth, then might the prince thereof, upon injury done him, or upon want of caution that injury be not done him in time to come, repair and secure himself by war; which is, in sum, deposing, killing, or subduing, or doing any act of hostility. But by the same reason, it would be no less lawful for a civil sovereign, upon the like injuries done, or feared, to make war upon the spiritual sovereign; which I believe is more than Cardinal Bellarmine would have inferred from his own proposition. But spiritual Commonwealth there is none in this world: for it is the same thing with the kingdom of Christ; which he himself saith is not of this world, but shall be in the next world, at the resurrection, when they that have lived justly, and believed that he was the Christ, shall, though they died natural bodies, rise spiritual bodies; and then it is that our Saviour shall judge the world, and conquer his adversaries, and make a spiritual Commonwealth. In the meantime, seeing there are no men on earth whose bodies are spiritual, there can be no spiritual Commonwealth amongst men that are yet in the flesh; unless we call preachers, that have commission to teach and prepare men for their reception into the kingdom of Christ at the resurrection, a Commonwealth; which I have proved already to be none. The third argument is this: "It is not lawful for Christians to tolerate an infidel or heretical king, in case he endeavour to draw them to his heresy, or infidelity. But to judge whether a king draw his subjects to heresy, or not, belongeth to the Pope. Therefore hath the Pope right to determine whether the prince be to be deposed, or not deposed." To this I answer that both these assertions false. For Christians, or men of what religion soever, if they tolerate not their king, whatsoever law he maketh, though it be concerning religion, do violate their faith, contrary to the divine law, both natural and positive: nor is there any judge of heresy amongst subjects but their own civil sovereign. For heresy is nothing else but a private opinion, obstinately maintained, contrary to the opinion which the public person (that is to say, the representant of the Commonwealth) hath commanded to be taught. By which it is manifest that an opinion publicly appointed to be taught cannot be heresy; nor the sovereign princes that authorize them, heretics. For heretics are none but private men that stubbornly defend some doctrine prohibited by their lawful sovereigns. But to prove that Christians are not to tolerate infidel or heretical kings, he allegeth a place in Deuteronomy where God forbiddeth the Jews, when they shall set a king over themselves, to choose a stranger: [Deuteronomy, 17] and from thence inferreth that it is unlawful for a Christian to choose a king that is not a Christian. And it is true that he that is a Christian, that is, he that hath already obliged himself to receive our Saviour, when he shall come, for his king, shall tempt God too much in choosing for king in this world one that he knoweth will endeavour, both by terror and persua-

sion, to make him violate his faith. But, it is, saith he, the same danger to choose one that is not a Christian for king, and not to depose him when he is chosen. To this I say, the question is not of the danger of not deposing; but of the justice of deposing him. To choose him may in some cases be unjust; but to depose him, when he is chosen, is in no case just. For it is always violation of faith, and consequently against the law of nature, which is the eternal law of God. Nor do we read that any such doctrine was accounted Christian in the time of the Apostles; nor in the time of the Roman Emperors, till the popes had the civil sovereignty of Rome. But to this he hath replied that the Christians of old deposed not Nero, nor Dioclesian, nor Julian, nor Valens, an Arian, for this cause only, that they wanted temporal forces. Perhaps so. But did our Saviour, who for calling for might have had twelve legions of immortal, invulnerable angels to assist him, want forces to depose Caesar, or at least Pilate, that unjustly, without finding fault in him, delivered him to the Jews to be crucified? Or ff the Apostles wanted temporal forces to depose Nero, was it therefore necessary for them in their epistles to the new made Christians to teach them, as they did, to obey the powers constituted over them, whereof Nero in that time was one, and that they ought to obey them, not for fear of their wrath, but for conscience sake? Shall we say they did not only obey, but also teach what they meant not, for want of strength? It is not therefore for want of strength, but for conscience sake, that Christians are to tolerate their heathen princes, or princes (for I cannot call any one whose doctrine is the public doctrine, a heretic) that authorize the teaching of an error. And whereas for the temporal power of the Pope, he allegeth further that St. Paul appointed judges under the heathen princes of those times, such as were not ordained by those princes; [I Corinthians, 6] it is not true. For St. Paul does but advise them to take some of their brethren to compound their differences, as arbitrators, rather than to go to law one with another before the heathen judges; which is a wholesome precept, and full of charity, fit to be practised also in the best Christian Commonwealths. And for the danger that may arise to religion, by the subjects tolerating of a heathen, or an erring prince, it is a point of which a subject is no competent judge; or if he be, the Pope's temporal subjects may judge also of the Pope's doctrine. For every Christian prince, as I have formerly proved, is no less supreme pastor of his own subjects than the Pope of his. The fourth argument is taken from the baptism of kings; wherein, that they may be made Christians, they submit their sceptres to Christ, and promise to keep and defend the Christian faith. This is true; for Christian kings are no more but Christ's subjects: but they may, for all that, be the Pope's fellows; for they are supreme pastors of their own subjects; and the Pope is no more but king and pastor, even in Rome itself. The fifth argument is drawn from the words spoken by our Saviour, "Feed my sheep"; by which was given all power necessary for a pastor; as the power to chase away wolves, such as are heretics; the power to shut up rams, if they be mad, or push at the other sheep with their horns, such as are evil, though Christian, kings; and power to give the flock convenient food: from whence he inferreth that St. Peter had these three powers given him by Christ. To which I answer that the last of these powers is no more than the power, or rather command, to teach. For the first, which is to chase away wolves, that is, heretics, the place he quoteth is, "Beware of false prophets which come to you in sheep's clothing, but inwardly are ravening wolves." [Matthew, 7. 15] But neither are heretics false prophets, or at all prophets: nor (admitting heretics for the wolves there meant) were the Apostles commanded to kill them, or if they were kings, to depose them; but to beware of, fly, and avoid them. Nor was it to St. Peter, nor to any of the Apostles, but to the multitude of the Jews that followed him into the mountain, men for the most part not yet converted, that he gave this counsel, to beware of false prophets: which therefore, if it confer a power of chasing away kings, was given not only to private men, but to men that were not at all Christians. And as to the power of separating and shutting up of furious rams, by which he meaneth Christian kings that refuse to submit themselves to the Roman pastor, our Saviour refused to take upon him that power in this world himself, but advised to let the corn and tares grow up together till the day of judgement: much less did he give it to St. Peter, or can St. Peter give it to the Popes. St. Peter, and all other pastors, are bidden to esteem those Christians that disobey the Church, that is, that disobey the Christian sovereign, as heathen men and as publicans. Seeing then men challenge to the Pope no authority over heathen princes, they ought to challenge none over those that are to be esteemed as heathen. But from the power to teach only, he inferreth also a coercive power in the Pope over kings. The pastor, saith he, must give his flock convenient food: therefore food: therefore the pope may and ought to compel kings to do their duty. Out of which it followeth that the Pope, as pastor of Christian men, is king of kings: which all Christian kings ought indeed either to confess, or else they ought to take upon themselves the supreme pastoral charge, every one in his own dominion. His sixth and last argument is from examples. To which I answer, first, that examples prove nothing; secondly, that the examples he allegeth make not so much as a probability of right. The fact of Jehoiada in killing Athaliah[II Kings, 11] was either by the authority of King Joash, or it was a horrible crime in the high priest, which ever after the election of King Saul was a mere subject. The fact of St. Ambrose in excommunicating Theodosius the Emperor, if it were true he did so, was a capital crime. And for the Popes, Gregory I, Gregory II, Zachary, and Leo III, their judgements are void, as given in their own cause; and the acts done by them conformably to this doctrine are the greatest crimes, especially that of Zachary, that are incident to human nature. And thus much of power ecclesiastical; wherein I had been more brief, forbearing to examine these arguments of Bellarmine, if they had been his as a private man, and not as the champion of the Papacy against all other Christian princes and states.

## CHAPTER XLIII, OF WHAT IS NECESSARY FOR A MAN'S RECEPTION INTO THE KINGDOM OF HEAVEN

THE most frequent pretext of sedition and civil war in Christian Commonwealths hath a long time proceeded from a difficulty, not yet sufficiently resolved, of obeying at once both God and man then when their commandments are one contrary to the other. It is manifest enough that when a man receiveth two contrary commands, and knows that one of them is God's, he ought to obey that, and not the other, though it be the command even of his lawful sovereign (whether a monarch or a sovereign assembly), or the command of his father. The difficulty therefore consisteth in this, that men, when they are commanded in the name of God, know not in diverse cases whether the command be from God, or whether he that commandeth do but abuse God's name for some private ends of his own. For as there were in the Church of the Jews many false prophets that sought reputation with the people by feigned dreams and visions; so there have been in all times, in the Church of Christ, false teachers that seek reputation with the people by fantastical and false doctrines; and by such reputation, as is the nature of ambition, to govern them for their private benefit. But this difficulty of obeying both God and the civil sovereign on earth, to those that can distinguish between what is necessary and what is not necessary for their reception into the kingdom of God, is of no moment. For if the command of the civil sovereign be such as that it may be obeyed without the forfeiture of life eternal, not to obey it is unjust; and the precept of the apostle takes place: "Servants, obey your masters in all things"; and "Children, obey your parents in all things"; and the precept of our Saviour, "The Scribes and Pharisees sit in Moses' chair; all therefore they shall say, that observe, and do." But if the command be such as cannot be obeyed, without being damned to eternal death, then it were madness to obey it, and the counsel of our Saviour takes place, "Fear not those that kill the body, but cannot kill the soul." [Matthew, 10. 28] All men therefore that would avoid both the punishments that are to be in this world inflicted for disobedience to their earthly sovereign, and those that shall be inflicted in the world to come for disobedience to God, have need be taught to distinguish well between what is, and what is not, necessary to eternal salvation. All that is necessary to salvation is contained in two virtues, faith in Christ, and obedience to laws. The latter of these, if it were perfect, were enough to us. But because we are all guilty of disobedience to God's law, not only originally in Adam, but also actually by our own transgressions, there is required at our hands now, not only obedience for the rest of our time, but also a remission of sins for the time past; which remission is the reward of our faith in Christ. That nothing else is necessarily required to salvation is manifest from this, that the kingdom of heaven is shut to none but to sinners; that is to say, to the disobedient, or transgressors of the law; nor to them, in case they repent, and believe all the articles of Christian faith necessary to salvation. The obedience required at our hands by God, that accepteth in all our actions the will for the deed, is a serious endeavour to obey Him; and is called also by all such names as signify that endeavour. And therefore obedience is sometimes called by the names of charity and love, because they imply a will to obey; and our Saviour himself maketh our love to God, and to one another, a fulfilling of the whole law; and sometimes by the name of righteousness, for righteousness is but the will to give to every one his own, that is to say, the will to obey the laws; and sometimes by the name of repentance, because to repent implieth a turning away from sin, which is the same with the return of the will to obedience. Whosoever therefore unfeignedly desireth to fulfil the commandments of God, or repenteth him truly of his transgressions, or that loveth God with all his heart, and his neighbour as himself, hath all the obedience necessary to his reception into the kingdom of God: for if God should require perfect innocence, there could no flesh be saved. But what commandments are those that God hath given us? Are all those laws which were given to the Jews by the hand of Moses the commandments of God? If they be, why are not Christians taught to obey them? If they be not, what others are so, besides the law of nature? For our Christ hath not given us new laws, but counsel to observe those we are subject to; that is to say, the laws of nature, and the laws of our several sovereigns: nor did he make any new law to the Jews in his Sermon on the

Mount, but only expounded the laws of Moses, to which they were subject before. The laws of God therefore are none but the laws of nature, whereof the principal is that we should not violate our faith, that is, a commandment to obey our civil sovereigns, which we constituted over us by mutual pact one with another. And this law of God, that commandeth obedience to the law civil, commandeth by consequence obedience to all the precepts of the Bible; which, as I have proved in the precedent chapter, is there only law where the civil sovereign hath made it so; and in other places but counsel, which a man at his own peril may without injustice refuse to obey. Knowing now what is the obedience necessary to salvation, and to whom it is due, we are to consider next, concerning faith, whom and why we believe, and what are the articles or points necessarily to be believed by them that shall be saved. And first, for the person whom we believe, because it is impossible to believe any person before we know what he saith, it is necessary he be one that we have heard speak. The person therefore whom Abraham, Isaac, Jacob, Moses, and the prophets believed was God Himself, that spake unto them supernaturally; and the person whom the Apostles and Disciples that conversed with Christ believed, was our Saviour himself. But of them, to whom neither God the Father nor our Saviour ever spake, it cannot be said that the person whom they believed was God. They believed the Apostles, and after them the pastors and doctors of the Church that recommended to their faith the history of the Old and New Testament: so that the faith of Christians ever since our Saviour's time hath had for foundation, first, the reputation of their pastors, and afterward, the authority of those that made the Old and New Testament to be received for the rule of faith; which none could do but Christian sovereigns, who are therefore the supreme pastors, and the only persons whom Christians now hear speak from God; except such as God speaketh to in these days supernaturally. But because there be many false prophets gone out into the world, other men are to examine such spirits, as St. John adviseth us, "whether they be of God, or not." [I John, 4. 1] And, therefore, seeing the examination of doctrines belongeth to the supreme pastor, the person which all they that have no special revelation are to believe is, in every Commonwealth, the supreme pastor, that is to say, the civil sovereign. The causes why men believe any Christian doctrine are various: for faith is the gift of God, and He worketh it in each several man by such ways as it seemeth good unto Himself. The most ordinary immediate cause of our belief, concerning any point of Christian faith, is that we believe the Bible to be the word of God. But why we believe the Bible to be the word of God is much disputed, as all questions must needs be that are not well stated. For they make not the question to be, why we believe it, but how we know it; as if believing and knowing were all one. And thence while one side ground their knowledge upon the infallibility of the Church, and the other side on the testimony of the private spirit, neither side concludeth what it pretends. For how shall a man know the infallibility of the Church but by knowing first the infallibility of the Scripture? Or how shall a man know his own private spirit to be other than a belief grounded upon the authority and arguments of his teachers or upon a presumption of his own gifts? Besides, there is nothing in the Scripture from which can be inferred the infallibility of the Church; much less, of any particular Church; and least of all, the infallibility of any particular man. It is manifest, therefore, that Christian men do not know, but only believe the Scripture to be the word of God; and that the means of making them believe, which God is pleased to afford men ordinarily, is according to the way of nature, that is to say, from their teachers. It is the doctrine of St. Paul concerning Christian faith in general, "Faith cometh by hearing," [Romans, 10. 17] that is, by hearing our lawful pastors. He saith also, "How shall they believe in him of whom they have not heard? And how shall they hear without a preacher? And how shall they preach, except they be sent?" [Ibid., 10. 14, 15] Whereby it is evident that the ordinary cause of believing that the Scriptures are the word of God is the same with the cause of the believing of all other articles of our faith, namely, the hearing of those that are by the law allowed and appointed to teach us, as our parents in their houses, and our pastors in the churches: which also is made more manifest by experience. For what other cause can there be assigned why in Christian Commonwealths all men either believe or at least profess the Scripture to be the word of God, and in other Commonwealths scarce any, but that in Christian Commonwealths they are taught it from their infancy, and in other places they are taught otherwise? But if teaching be the cause of faith, why do not all believe? It is certain therefore that faith is the gift of God, and He giveth it to whom He will. Nevertheless, because to them to whom He giveth it, He giveth it by the means of teachers, the immediate cause of faith is hearing. In a school, where many are taught, and some profit, others profit not, the cause of learning in them that profit is the master; yet it cannot be thence inferred that learning is not the gift of God. All good things proceed from God; yet cannot all that have them say they are inspired; for that implies a gift supernatural, and the immediate hand of God; which he that pretends to, pretends to be a prophet, and is subject to the examination of the Church. But whether men know, or believe, or grant the Scriptures to be the word of God, if out of such places of them as are without obscurity I shall show what articles of faith are necessary, and only necessary, for salvation, those men must needs know, believe, or grant the same. The unum necessarium, only article of faith, which the Scripture maketh simply necessary to salvation is this, that Jesus is the Christ. By the name of Christ is understood the King which God had before promised by the prophets of the Old Testament to send into the world, to reign (over the Jews and over such of other nations as should believe in him) under Himself eternally; and to give them that eternal life which was lost by the sin of Adam. Which, when I have proved out of Scripture, I will further show when, and in what sense, some other articles may be also called necessary. For proof that the belief of this article, Jesus is the Christ, is all the faith required to salvation, my first argument shall be from the scope of the evangelists; which was, by the description of the life of our Saviour, to establish that one article, Jesus is the Christ. The sum of St. Matthew's Gospel is this, that Jesus was of the stock of David, born of a virgin, which are the marks of the true Christ; that the Magi came to worship him as King of the Jews; that Herod for the same cause sought to kill him; that John the Baptist proclaimed him; that he preached by himself and his Apostles that he was that King; that he taught the law, not as a scribe, but as a man of authority; that he cured diseases by his word only, and did many other miracles, which were foretold the Christ should do; that he was saluted King when he entered into Jerusalem; that he forewarned them to beware of all others that should pretend to be Christ; that he was taken, accused, and put to death for saying he was King; that the cause of his condemnation, written on the cross, was JESUS OF NAZARETH, THE KING OF THE JEWS. All which tend to no other end than this, that men should believe that Jesus is the Christ. Such therefore was the scope of St. Matthew's Gospel. But the scope of all the evangelists, as may appear by reading them, was the same. Therefore the scope of the whole Gospel was the establishing of that only article. And St. John expressly makes it his conclusion, "These things are written, that you may know that Jesus is the Christ, the Son of the living God."[John, 20. 31] My second argument is taken from the subject of the sermons of the Apostles, both whilst our Saviour lived on earth, and after his ascension. The Apostles in our Saviour's time were sent to preach the kingdom of God: [Luke, 9. 2] for neither there, nor Matthew, 10. 7, giveth he any commission to them other than this, "As ye go, preach, saying, the kingdom of heaven is at hand"; that is, that Jesus is the Messiah, the Christ, the King which was to come. That their preaching also after his ascension was the same is manifest out of the Acts, 17. 6, "They drew," saith St. Luke, "Jason and certain brethren unto the rulers of the city, crying, These that have turned the world upside down are come hither also, whom Jason hath received. And these all do contrary to the decrees of Caesar, saying that there is another king, one Jesus." And out of the second and third verses of the same chapter, where it is said that St. Paul, "as his manner was, went in unto them; and three Sabbath days reasoned with them out of the Scriptures; opening and alleging that Christ must needs have suffered, and risen again from the dead, and that this Jesus is Christ." The third argument is from those places of Scripture by which all the faith required to salvation is declared to be easy. For if an inward assent of the mind to all the doctrines concerning Christian faith now taught, whereof the greatest part are disputed, were necessary to salvation, there would be nothing in the world so hard as to be a Christian. The thief upon the cross, though repenting, could not have been saved for saying, "Lord, remember me when thou comest into thy kingdom"; by which he testified no beliefs of any other article, but this, that Jesus was the King. Nor could it be said, as it is, Matthew, 11. 30, that "Christ's yoke is easy, and his burden light": nor that "little children believe in him," as it is, Matthew, 18. 6. Nor could St. Paul have said (I Cor., 1. 21), "It pleased God by the foolishness of preaching, to save them that believe":[I Corinthians, 1. 21] nor could St. Paul himself have been saved, much less have been so great a doctor of the Church so suddenly, that never perhaps thought of transubstantiation, nor purgatory, nor many other articles now obtruded. The fourth argument is taken from places express, and such as receive no controversy of interpretation; as first, John, 5. 39, "Search the Scriptures, for in them ye think ye have eternal life, and they are they that testify of me." Our Saviour here speaketh of the Scriptures only of the Old Testament; for the Jews at that time could not search the Scriptures of the New Testament, which were not written. But the Old Testament hath nothing of Christ but the marks by which men might know him when he came; as that he should descend from David; be born at Bethlehem, and of a virgin; do great miracles, and the like. Therefore to believe that this Jesus was, he was sufficient to eternal life: but more than sufficient is not necessary; and consequently no other article is required. Again, "Whosoever liveth and believeth in me shall not die eternally." [John, 11. 26] Therefore to believe in Christ is faith sufficient to eternal life; and consequently no more faith than that is necessary. But to believe in Jesus, and to believe that Jesus is the Christ, is all one, as appeareth in the verses immediately following. For when our Saviour had said to Martha, "Believest thou this?" [Ibid.] she answereth, "Yea, Lord, I believe that thou art the Christ, the Son of God, which should come into the world." [Ibid., 11. 27] Therefore this article alone is faith sufficient to life eternal, and more than sufficient is not necessary. Thirdly, John, 20. 31, "These things are written that ye might believe, that Jesus is the Christ, the Son of God, and that believing ye might have life through his name." There, to believe that Jesus is the Christ is faith sufficient to the obtaining of life; and therefore no other article is necessary. Fourthly, I John, 4. 2, "Every spirit that confesseth that Jesus Christ is come in the flesh is of God." And I John, 5. 1, "Whosoever believeth that Jesus is the Christ is born of God." And verse 5, "Who is he that overcometh the world, but he that believeth that Jesus is the Son of God?" Fifthly, Acts, 8. 36, 37, "See," saith the eunuch, "here is water, what doth hinder me to be baptized? And Philip said, If thou believest with all thy heart thou mayst. And he answered and said, I believe that Jesus Christ is the Son of God." Therefore this article believed, Jesus is the Christ, is sufficient to baptism, that is to say, to our reception into the kingdom of God, and, by consequence, only necessary. And generally in all places where our Saviour saith to any man, "Thy faith hath saved thee," the cause he saith it is some confession which directly, or by consequence, implieth a belief that Jesus is the Christ. The last argument is from the places where this article is made the foundation of faith: for he that holdeth the foundation shall be saved. Which places are first, Matthew, 24. 23, "If any man shall say unto you, Lo, here is Christ, or there, believe it not, for there shall arise false Christs, and false prophets, and shall shew great signs, and wonders," etc. Here, we see, this article, Jesus is the Christ, must be held, though he that shall teach the contrary should do great miracles. The second place is Galatians, 1. 8, "Though we, or an angel from heaven, preach any other gospel unto you than that we have preached unto you, let him be accursed." But the gospel which Paul and the other Apostles preached was only this article, that Jesus is the Christ: therefore for the belief of this article, we are to reject the authority of an angel from heaven; much more of any mortal man, if he teach the contrary. This is therefore the fundamental article of Christian faith. A third place is I John, 4. 1, "Beloved, believe not every spirit. Hereby ye shall know the Spirit of God; every spirit that confesseth that is come in the flesh is of God." By which it is evident that this article is the measure and rule by which to estimate and examine all other articles, and is therefore only fundamental. A fourth is Matthew, 16. 18, where, after St. Peter had professed this article, saying to our Saviour, "Thou art Christ the Son of the living God," our Saviour answered, "Thou art Peter, and upon this rock I will build my Church": from whence I infer that this article is that on which all other doctrines of the Church are built, as on their foundation. A fifth is I Corinthians, 3. 11, 12, etc., "Other foundation can no man lay than that which is laid, Jesus is the Christ. Now if any man build upon this foundation, gold, silver, precious stones, wood, hay, stubble; every man's work shall be made manifest; for the day shall declare it, because it shall be revealed by fire, and the fire shall try every man's work, what sort it is. If any man's work abide which he hath built thereupon, he shall receive a reward. If any man's work shall be burnt, he shall suffer loss; but he himself shall be saved, yet so as by fire." Which words, being partly plain and easy to understand, and partly allegorical and difficult, out of that which is plain may be inferred that pastors that teach this foundation, that Jesus is the Christ, though they draw from it false consequences (which all men are sometimes subject to), they may nevertheless be saved; much more that they may be saved, who, being no pastors, but hearers, believe that which is by their lawful pastors taught them. Therefore the belief of this article is sufficient; and by consequence, there is no other article of faith necessarily required to salvation. Now for the part which is allegorical, as that "the fire shall try every man's work," and that they "shall be saved, but so as by fire," or "through fire" (for the original is dia puros), it maketh nothing against this conclusion which I have drawn from the other words that are plain. Nevertheless, because upon this place there hath been an argument taken to prove the fire of purgatory, I will also here offer you my conjecture concerning the meaning of this trial of doctrines and saving of men as by fire. The Apostle here seemeth to allude to the words of the Prophet Zechariah, who, speaking of the restoration of the kingdom of God, saith thus, "Two parts therein shall be cut off, and die, but the third shall be left therein; and I will bring the third part through the fire, and will refine them as silver is refined, and will try them as gold is tried; they shall call on the name of the Lord, and I will hear them." [Zechariah, 13. 8, 9] The day of judgement is the day of the restoration of the kingdom of God; and at that day it is that St. Peter tells us shall be the conflagration of the world, wherein the wicked shall perish; but the remnant which God will save shall pass through that fire unhurt, and be therein (as silver and gold are refined by the fire from their dross) tried, and refined from their idolatry, and be made to call upon the name of the true God. [II Peter, 3] Alluding whereto, St. Paul here saith that "the day" (that is, the day of judgement, the great day of our Saviour's coming to restore the kingdom of God in Israel) shall try every man's doctrine, by judging which are gold, silver, precious stones, wood, hay, stubble; and then they that have built false consequences on the true foundation shall see their doctrines condemned; nevertheless they themselves shall be saved, and pass unhurt through this universal fire, and live eternally, to call upon the name of the true and only God. In which sense there is nothing that accordeth not with the rest of Holy Scripture, or any glimpse of the fire of purgatory. But a man may here ask whether it be not as necessary to salvation to believe that God is Omnipotent Creator of the world; that Jesus Christ is risen; and that all men else shall rise again from the dead at the last day; as to believe that Jesus is the Christ. To which I answer, they are; and so are many more articles; but they are such as are contained in this one, and may be deduced from it, with more or less difficulty. For who is there that does not see that they who believe Jesus to be the Son of the God of Israel, and that the Israelites had for God the Omnipotent Creator of all things, do therein also believe that God is the Omnipotent Creator of all things? Or how can a man believe that Jesus is the king that shall reign eternally, unless he believe him also risen again from the dead? For a dead man cannot exercise the office of a king. In sum, he that holdeth this foundation, Jesus is the Christ, holdeth expressly all that he seeth rightly deduced from it, and implicitly all that is consequent thereunto, though he have not skill enough to discern the consequence. And therefore it holdeth still good that the belief of this one article is sufficient faith to obtain remission of sins to the penitent, and consequently to bring them into the kingdom of heaven. Now that I have shown that all the obedience required to salvation consisteth in the will to obey the law of God, that is to say, in repentance; and all the faith required to the same is comprehended in the belief of this article, Jesus is the Christ; I will further allege those places of the Gospel that prove that all that is necessary to salvation is contained in both these joined together. The men to whom St. Peter preached on the day of Pentecost, next after the ascension of our Saviour, asked him, and the rest of the Apostles, saying, "Men and brethren, what shall we do?" [Acts, 2. 37] To whom St. Peter answered, "Repent, and be baptized every one of you, for the remission of sins, and ye shall receive the gift of the Holy Ghost." [Ibid., 2. 38] Therefore repentance and baptism, that is, believing that Jesus is the Christ, is all that is necessary to salvation. Again, our Saviour being asked by a certain ruler, "What shall I do to inherit eternal life?" [Luke, 18. 18] answered, "Thou knowest the commandments, Do not commit adultery, Do not kill, Do not steal, Do not bear false witness, Honour thy father and thy mother":[Ibid., 18. 20] which when he said he had observed, our Saviour added, "Sell all thou hast, give it to the poor, and come and follow me": which was as much as to say, rely on me that am the king. Therefore to fulfil the law, and to believe that Jesus is the king, is all that is required to bring a man to eternal life. Thirdly, St. Paul saith, "The just shall live by faith";[Romans, 1. 17] not every one, but the just; therefore faith and justice (that is, the will to be just, or repentance) are all that is necessary to life eternal. And our Saviour preached, saying, "The time is fulfilled, and the kingdom of God is at hand; repent and believe the Evangel," [Mark, 1. 15] that is, the good news that the Christ was come. Therefore to repent, and to believe that Jesus is the Christ, is all that is required to salvation. Seeing then it is necessary that faith and obedience (implied in the word repentance) do both concur to our salvation, the question by which of the two we are justified is impertinently disputed. Nevertheless, it will not be impertinent to make manifest in what manner each of them contributes thereunto, and in what sense it is said that we are to be justified by the one and by the other. And first, if by righteousness be understood the justice of the works themselves, there is no man that can be saved; for there is none that hath not transgressed the law of God. And therefore when we are said to be justified by works, it is to be understood of the will, which God doth always accept for the work itself, as well in good as in evil men. And in this sense only it is that a man is called just, or unjust; and that his justice justifies him, that is, gives him the title, in God's acceptation of just, and renders him capable of living by his faith, which before he was not. So that justice justifies in that sense in which to justify is the same as that to denominate a man just; and not in the signification of discharging the law, whereby the punishment of his sins should be unjust. But a man is then also said to be justified when his plea, though in itself insufficient, is accepted; as when we plead our will, our endeavour to fulfil the law, and repent us of our failings, and God accepteth it for the performance itself. And because God accepteth not the will for the deed, but only in the faithful, it is therefore, faith that makes good our plea; and in this sense it is that faith only justifies: so that faith and obedience are both necessary to salvation, yet in several senses each of them is said to justify. Having thus shown what is necessary to salvation, it is not hard to reconcile our obedience to God with our obedience to the civil sovereign, who is either Christian or infidel. If he be a Christian, he alloweth the belief of this article, that Jesus is the Christ; and of all the articles that are contained in, or are by evident consequence deduced from it: which is all the faith necessary to salvation. And because he is a sovereign, he requireth obedience to all his own, that is, to all the civil laws; in which also are contained all the laws of nature, that is, all the laws of God: for besides the laws of nature, and the laws of the Church, which are part of the civil law (for the Church that can make laws is the Commonwealth), there be no other laws divine. Whosoever therefore obeyeth his Christian sovereign is not thereby hindered neither from believing nor from obeying God. But suppose that a Christian king should from this foundation, Jesus is the Christ, draw some false consequences, that is to say, make some superstructions of hay or stubble, and command the teaching of the same; yet seeing St. Paul says he shall be saved; much more shall he be saved that teacheth them by his command; and much more yet, he that teaches not, but only believes his lawful teacher. And in case a subject be forbidden by the civil sovereign to profess some of those his opinions, upon what just ground can he disobey? Christian kings may err in deducing a consequence, but who shall judge? Shall a private man judge, when the question is of his own obedience? Or shall any man judge but he that is appointed thereto by the Church, that is, by the civil sovereign that representeth it? Or if the Pope or an Apostle judge, may he not err in deducing of a consequence? Did not one of the two, St. Peter or St. Paul, err in a superstructure, when St. Paul withstood St. Peter to his face? There can therefore be no contradiction between the laws of God and the laws of a Christian Commonwealth. And when the civil sovereign is an infidel, every one of his own subjects that resisteth him sinneth against the laws of God (for such are the laws of nature), and rejecteth the counsel of the Apostles that admonisheth all Christians to obey their princes, and all children and servants to obey their parents and masters in all things. And for their faith, it is internal and invisible; they have the license that Naaman had, and need not put themselves into danger for it. But if they do, they ought to expect their reward in heaven, and not complain of their lawful sovereign, much less make war upon him. For he that is not glad of any just occasion of martyrdom has not the faith he professeth, but pretends it only, to set some colour upon his own contumacy. But what infidel king is so unreasonable as, knowing he has a subject that waiteth for the second coming of Christ, after the present world shall be burnt, and intendeth then to obey Him (which is the intent of believing that Jesus is the Christ), and in the meantime thinketh himself bound to obey the laws of that infidel king, which all Christians are obliged in conscience to do, to put to death or to persecute such a subject? And thus much shall suffice, concerning the kingdom of God and policy ecclesiastical. Wherein I pretend not to advance any position of my own, but only to show what are the consequences that seem to me deducible from the principles of Christian politics (which are the Holy Scriptures), in confirmation of the power of civil sovereigns and the duty of their subjects. And in the allegation of Scripture, I have endeavoured to avoid such texts as are of obscure or controverted interpretation, and to allege none but in such sense as is most plain and agreeable to the harmony and scope of the whole Bible, which was written for the re-establishment of the kingdom of God in Christ. For it is not the bare words, but the scope of the writer, that giveth the true light by which any writing is to be interpreted; and they that insist upon single texts, without considering the main design, can derive no thing from them clearly; but rather, by casting atoms of Scripture as dust before men's eyes, make everything more obscure than it is, an ordinary artifice of those that seek not the truth, but their own advantage.

## THE FOURTH PART, OF THE KINGDOM OF DARKNESS

## CHAPTER XLIV, OF SPIRITUAL DARKNESS FROM MISINTERPRETATION OF SCRIPTURE

Besides these sovereign powers, divine and human, of which I have hitherto discoursed, there is mention in Scripture of another power, namely, that of "the rulers of the darkness of this world," [Ephesians, 6. 12] "the kingdom of Satan," [Matthew, 12. 26] and "the principality of Beelzebub over demons," [Ibid., 9. 34] that is to say, over phantasms that appear in the air: for which cause Satan is also called "the prince of the power of the air";[Ephesians, 2. 2] and, because he ruleth in the darkness of this world, "the prince of this world":[John, 16. 11] and in consequence hereunto, they who are under his dominion, in opposition to the faithful, who are the "children of the light," are called the "children of darkness." For seeing Beelzebub is prince of phantasms, inhabitants of his dominion of air and darkness, the children of darkness, and these demons, phantasms, or spirits of illusion, signify allegorically the same thing. This considered, the kingdom of darkness, as it is set forth in these and other places of the Scripture, is nothing else but a confederacy of deceivers that, to obtain dominion over men in this present world, endeavour, by dark and erroneous doctrines, to extinguish in them the light, both of nature and of the gospel; and so to disprepare them for the kingdom of God to come. As men that are utterly deprived from their nativity of the light of the bodily eye have no idea at all of any such light; and no man conceives in his imagination any greater light than he hath at some time or other perceived by his outward senses: so also is it of the light of the gospel, and of the light of the understanding, that no man can conceive there is any greater degree of it than that which he hath already attained unto. And from hence it comes to pass that men have no other means to acknowledge their own darkness but only by reasoning from the unforeseen mischances that befall them in their ways. The darkest part of the kingdom of Satan is that which is without the Church of God; that is to say, amongst them that believe not in Jesus Christ. But we cannot say that therefore the Church enjoyeth, as the land of Goshen, all the light which to the performance of the work enjoined us by God is necessary. Whence comes it that in Christendom there has been, almost from the time of the Apostles, such jostling of one another out of their places, both by foreign and civil war; such stumbling at every little asperity of their own fortune, and every little eminence of that of other men; and such diversity of ways in running to the same mark, felicity, if it be not night amongst us, or at least a mist? We are therefore yet in the dark. The enemy has been here in the night of our natural ignorance, and sown the tares of spiritual errors; and that, first, by abusing and putting out the light of the Scriptures: for we err, not knowing the Scriptures. Secondly, by introducing the demonology of the heathen poets, that is to say, their fabulous doctrine concerning demons, which are but idols, or phantasms of the brain, without any real nature of their own, distinct from human fancy; such as are dead men's ghosts, and fairies, and other matter of old wives' tales. Thirdly, by mixing with the Scripture diverse relics of the religion, and much of the vain and erroneous philosophy of the Greeks, especially of Aristotle. Fourthly, by mingling with both these, false or uncertain traditions, and feigned or uncertain history. And so we come to err, by giving heed to seducing spirits, and the demonology of such as speak lies in hypocrisy, or, as it is in the original, "of those that play the part of liars," [I Timothy, 4. 1, 2] with a seared conscience, that is, contrary to their own knowledge. Concerning the first of these, which is the seducing of men by abuse of Scripture, I intend to speak briefly in this chapter. The greatest and main abuse of Scripture, and to which almost all the rest are either consequent or subservient, is the wresting of it to prove that the kingdom of God, mentioned so often in the Scripture, is the present Church, or multitude of Christian men now living, or that, being dead, are to rise again at the last day: whereas the kingdom of God was first instituted by the ministry of Moses, over the Jews only; who were therefore called his peculiar people; and ceased afterward, in the election of Saul, when they refused to be governed by God any more, and demanded a king after the manner of the nations; which God Himself consented unto, as I have more at large proved before, in the thirty-fifth Chapter. After that time, there was no other kingdom of God in the world, by any pact or otherwise, than He ever was, is, and shall be king of all men and of all creatures, as governing according to His will, by His infinite power. Nevertheless, He promised by His prophets to restore this His government to them again, when the time He hath in His secret counsel appointed for it shall be fully come, and when they shall turn unto Him by repentance and amendment of life. And not only so, but He invited also the Gentiles to come in, and enjoy the happiness of His reign, on the same conditions of conversion and repentance. And He promised also to send His Son into the world, to expiate the sins of them all by his death, and to prepare them by his doctrine to receive him at his second coming: which second coming not yet being, the kingdom of God is not yet come, and we are not now under any other kings by pact but our civil sovereigns; saving only that Christian men are already in the kingdom of grace, inasmuch as they have already the promise of being received at his coming again. Consequent to this error, that the present Church is Christ's kingdom, there ought to be some one man, or assembly, by whose mouth our Saviour, now in heaven, speaketh, giveth law, and which representeth his person to all Christians; or diverse men, or diverse assemblies that do the same to diverse parts of Christendom. This power regal under Christ being challenged universally by the Pope, and in particular Commonwealths by assemblies of the pastors of the place (when the Scripture gives it to none but to civil sovereigns), comes to be so passionately disputed that it putteth out the light of nature, and causeth so great a darkness in men's understanding that they see not who it is to whom they have engaged their obedience. Consequent to this claim of the Pope to vicar general of Christ in the present Church (supposed to be that kingdom of his to which we are addressed in the gospel) is the doctrine that it is necessary for a Christian king to receive his crown by a bishop; as if it were from that ceremony that he derives the clause of Dei gratia in his title; and that then only is he made king by the favour of God when he is crowned by the authority of God's universal vicegerent on earth; and that every bishop, whosoever be his sovereign, taketh at his consecration an oath of absolute obedience to the Pope. Consequent to the same is the doctrine of the fourth Council of Lateran, held under Pope Innocent the Third (Chapter 3, De Haereticis), "That if a king, at the pope's admonition, do not purge his kingdom of heresies, and being excommunicate for the same, do not give satisfaction within a year, his subjects are absolved of the bond of their obedience." Whereby heresies are understood all opinions which the Church of Rome hath forbidden to be maintained. And by this means, as often as there is any repugnancy between the political designs of the Pope and other Christian princes, as there is very often, there ariseth such a mist amongst their subjects, that they know not a stranger that thrusteth himself into the throne of their lawful prince, from him whom they had themselves placed there; and, in this darkness of mind, are made to fight one against another, without discerning their enemies from their friends, under the conduct of another man's ambition. From the same opinion, that the present Church is the kingdom of God, it proceeds that pastors, deacons, and all other ministers of the Church take the name to themselves of the clergy; giving to other Christians the name of laity, that is, simply people.

For clergy signifies those whose maintenance is that revenue which God, having reserved to Himself during His reign over the Israelites, assigned to the tribe of Levi (who were to be His public ministers, and had no portion of land set them out to live on, as their brethren) to be their inheritance. The Pope therefore (pretending the present Church to be, as the realms of Israel, the kingdom of God), challenging to himself and his subordinate ministers the like revenue as the inheritance of God, the name of clergy was suitable to that claim. And thence it is that tithes and other tributes paid to the Levites as God's right, amongst the Israelites, have a long time been demanded and taken of Christians by ecclesiastics, jure divino, that is, in God's right. By which means, the people everywhere were obliged to a double tribute; one to the state, another to the clergy; whereof that to the clergy, being the tenth of their revenue, is double to that which a king of Athens (and esteemed a tyrant) exacted of his subjects for the defraying of all public charges: for he demanded no more but the twentieth part, and yet abundantly maintained therewith the Commonwealth. And in the kingdom of the Jews, during the sacerdotal reign of God, the tithes and offerings were the whole public revenue. From the same mistaking of the present Church for the kingdom of God came in the distinction between the civil and the canon laws: the civil law being the acts of sovereigns in their own dominions, and the canon law being the acts of the Pope in the same dominions. Which canons, though they were but canons, that is, rules propounded, and but voluntarily received by Christian princes, till the translation of the Empire to Charlemagne; yet afterwards, as the power of the Pope increased, became rules commanded, and the emperors themselves, to avoid greater mischiefs, which the people blinded might be led into, were forced to let them pass for laws. From hence it is that in all dominions where the Pope's ecclesiastical power is entirely received, Jews, Turks, and Gentiles are in the Roman Church tolerated in their religion as far forth as in the exercise and profession thereof they offend not against the civil power: whereas in a Christian, though a stranger, not to be of the Roman religion is capital, because the Pope pretendeth that all Christians are his subjects. For otherwise it were as much against the law of nations to persecute a Christian stranger for professing the religion of his own country, as an infidel; or rather more, inasmuch as they that are not against Christ are with him. From the same it is that in every Christian state there are certain men that are exempt, by ecclesiastical liberty, from the tributes and from the tribunals of the civil state; for so are the secular clergy, besides monks and friars, which in many places bear so great a proportion to the common people as, if need were, there might be raised out of them alone an army sufficient for any war the Church militant should employ them in against their own or other princes. A second general abuse of Scripture is the turning of consecration into conjuration, or enchantment. To consecrate is, in Scripture, to offer, give, or dedicate, in pious and decent language and gesture, a man or any other thing to God, by separating of it from common use; that is to say, to sanctify, or make it God's, and to be used only by those whom God hath appointed to be His public ministers (as I have already proved at large in the thirty-fifth Chapter), and thereby to change, not the thing consecrated, but only the use of it, from being profane and common, to be holy, and peculiar to God's service. But when by such words the nature or quality of the thing itself is pretended to be changed, it is not consecration, but either an extraordinary work of God, or a vain and impious conjuration. But seeing, for the frequency of pretending the change of nature in their consecrations, it cannot be esteemed a work extraordinary, it is no other than a conjuration or incantation, whereby they would have men to believe an alteration of nature that is not, contrary to the testimony of man's sight and of all the rest of his senses. As for example, when the priest, instead of consecrating bread and wine to God's peculiar service in the sacrament of the Lord's Supper (which is but a separation of it from the common use to signify, that is, to put men in mind of, their redemption by the Passion of Christ, whose body was broken and blood shed upon the cross for our transgressions), pretends that by saying of the words of our Saviour, "This is my body," and "This is my blood," the nature of bread is no more there, but his very body; notwithstanding there appeareth not to the sight or other sense of the receiver anything that appeared not before the consecration. The Egyptian conjurers, that are said to have turned their rods to serpents, and the water into blood, are thought but to have deluded the senses of the spectators by a false show of things, yet are esteemed enchanters. But what should we have thought of them if there had appeared in their rods nothing like a serpent, and in the water enchanted nothing like blood, nor like anything else but water, but that they had faced down the king, that they were serpents that looked like rods, and that it was blood that seemed water? That had been both enchantment and lying. And yet in this daily act of the priest, they do the very same, by turning the holy words into the manner of a charm, which produceth nothing new to the sense; but they face us down, that it hath turned the bread into a man; nay, more, into a God; and require men to worship it as if it were our Saviour himself present, God and Man, and thereby to commit most gross idolatry. For if it be enough to excuse it of idolatry to say it is no more bread, but God; why should not the same excuse serve the Egyptians, in case they had the faces to say the leeks and onions they worshipped were not very

208

leeks and onions, but a divinity under their species or likeness? The words, "This is my body," are equivalent to these, "This signifies, or represents, my body"; and it is an ordinary figure of speech: but to take it literally is an abuse; nor, though so taken, can it extend any further than to the bread which Christ himself with his own hands consecrated. For he never said that of what bread soever any priest whatsoever should say, "This is my body," or "This is Christ's body," the same should presently be transubstantiated. Nor did the Church of Rome ever establish this transubstantiation, till the time of Innocent the Third; which was not above five hundred years ago, when the power of Popes was at the highest, and the darkness of the time grown so great, as men discerned not the bread that was given them to eat, especially when it was stamped with the figure of Christ upon the cross, as if they would have men believe it were transubstantiated, not only into the body of Christ, but also into the wood of his cross, and that they did eat both together in the sacrament. The like incantation, instead of consecration, is used also in the sacrament of baptism: where the abuse of God's name in each several person, and in the whole Trinity, with the sign of the cross at each name, maketh up the charm. As first, when they make the holy water, the priest saith, "I conjure thee, thou creature of water, in the name of God the Father Almighty, and in the name of Jesus Christ His only Son our Lord, and in virtue of the Holy Ghost, that thou become conjured water, to drive away all the powers of the enemy, and to eradicate, and supplant the enemy," etc. And the same in the benediction of the salt to be mingled with it, "That thou become conjured salt, that all phantasms and knavery of the Devil's fraud may fly and depart from the place wherein thou art sprinkled; and every unclean spirit be conjured by him that shall come to judge the quick and the dead." The same in the benediction of the oil, "That all the power of the enemy, all the host of the Devil, all assaults and phantasms of Satan, may be driven away by this creature of oil." And for the infant that is to be baptized, he is subject to many charms: first, at the church door the priest blows thrice in the child's face, and says, "Go out of him, unclean spirit, and give place to the Holy Ghost the Comforter." As if all children, till blown on by the priest, were demoniacs. Again, before his entrance into the church, he saith as before, "I conjure thee, etc., to go out, and depart from this servant of God"; and again the same exorcism is repeated once more before he be baptized. These and some other incantations are those that are used instead of benedictions and consecrations in administration of the sacraments of baptism and the Lord's Supper; wherein everything that serveth to those holy uses, except the unhallowed spittle of the priest, hath some set form of exorcism. Nor are the other rites, as of marriage, of extreme unction, of visitation of the sick, of consecrating churches, and churchyards, and the like, exempt from charms; inasmuch as there is in them the use of enchanted oil and water, with the abuse of the cross, and of the holy word of David, asperges me Domine hyssopo, as things of efficacy to drive away phantasms and imaginary spirits. Another general error is from the misinterpretation of the words eternal life, everlasting death, and the second death. For though we read plainly in Holy Scripture that God created Adam in an estate of living for ever, which was conditional, that is to say, if he disobeyed not His commandment; which was not essential to human nature, but consequent to the virtue of the tree of life, whereof he had liberty to eat, as long as he had not sinned; and that he was thrust out of Paradise after he had sinned, lest he should eat thereof, and live for ever; and that Christ's Passion is a discharge of sin to all that believe on Him, and by consequence, a restitution of eternal life to all the faithful, and to them only: yet the doctrine is now and hath been a long time far otherwise; namely, that every man hath eternity of life by nature, inasmuch as his soul is immortal. So that the flaming sword at the entrance of Paradise, though it hinder a man from coming to the tree of life, hinders him not from the immortality which God took from him for his sin, nor makes him to need the sacrificing of Christ for the recovering of the same; and consequently, not only the faithful and righteous, but also the wicked and the heathen, shall enjoy eternal life, without any death at all, much less a second and everlasting death. To salve this, it is said that by second and everlasting death is meant a second and everlasting life, but in torments; a figure never used but in this very case. All which doctrine is founded only on some of the obscurer places of the New Testament; which nevertheless, the whole scope of the Scripture considered, are clear enough in a different sense, and unnecessary to the Christian faith. For supposing that when a man dies, there remaineth nothing of him but his carcass; cannot God, that raised inanimated dust and clay into a living creature by His word, as easily raise a dead carcass to life again, and continue him alive for ever, or make him die again by another word? The soul, in Scripture, signifieth always either the life or the living creature; and the body and soul jointly, the body alive. In the fifth day of the Creation, God said, Let the waters produce reptile animae viventis, the creeping thing that hath in it a living soul; the English translate it, "that hath life." And again, God created whales, et omnem animam viventem; which in the English is, "every living creature." And likewise of man, God made him of the dust of the earth, and breathed in his face the breath of life, et factus est homo in animam viventem, that is, "and man was made a living creature." And after Noah came out of the ark, God saith, He will no more smite omnem animam viventem, that is, "every living creature." And, "Eat not the blood, for the blood is the soul"; that is, the life. From which places, if by soul were meant a substance incorporeal, with an existence separated from the body, it might as well be inferred of any other living creature, as of man. But that the souls of the faithful are not of their own nature, but by God's special grace, to remain in their bodies from the resurrection to all eternity, I have already, I think, sufficiently proved out of the Scriptures, in the thirty-eighth Chapter. And for the places of the New Testament where it is said that any man shall be cast body and soul into hell fire, it is no more than body and life; that is to say, they shall be cast alive into the perpetual fire of Gehenna. This window it is that gives entrance to the dark doctrine, first, of eternal torments, and afterwards of purgatory, and consequently of the walking abroad, especially in places consecrated, solitary, or dark, of the ghosts of men deceased; and thereby to the pretences of exorcism and conjuration of phantasms, as also of invocation of men dead; and to the doctrine of indulgences; that is to say, of exemption for a time, or for ever, from the fire of purgatory, wherein these incorporeal substances are pretended by burning to be cleansed and made fit for heaven. For men being generally possessed, before the time of our Saviour, by contagion of the demonology of the Greeks, of an opinion that the souls of men were substances distinct from their bodies; and therefore that when the body was dead, the soul of every man, whether

odly or wicked, must subsist somewhere by virtue of its own nature, without acknowledging therein any supernatural gift of God's; the doctors of the Church doubted a long time what was the place which they were to abide in, till they should be reunited to their bodies in the resurrection, supposing for a while, they lay under the altars: but afterward the Church of Rome found it more profitable to build for them this place of purgatory, which by some other Churches, in this later age, has been demolished. Let us now consider what texts of Scripture seem most to confirm these three general errors I have here touched. As for those which Cardinal Bellarmine hath alleged for the present kingdom of God administered by the Pope (than which there are none that make a better show of proof), I have already answered them; and made it evident that the kingdom of God, instituted by Moses, ended in the election of Saul: after which time the priest of his own authority never deposed any king. That which the high priest did to Athaliah was not done in his own right, but in the right of the young King Joash, her son: But Solomon in his own right deposed the high priest Abiathar, and set up another in his place. The most difficult place to answer, of all those that can be brought to prove the kingdom of God by Christ is already in this world, is alleged, not by Bellarmine, nor any other of the Church of Rome, but by Beza, that will have it to begin from the resurrection of Christ. But whether he intend thereby to entitle the presbytery to the supreme power ecclesiastical in the Commonwealth of Geneva, and consequently to every presbytery in every other Commonwealth, or to princes and other civil sovereigns, I do not know. For the presbytery hath challenged the power to excommunicate their own kings, and to be the supreme moderators in religion, in the places where they have that form of Church government, no less than the Pope challengeth it universally. The words are, "Verily I say unto you, that there be some of them that stand here, which shall not taste of death, till they have seen the kingdom of God come with power." [Mark, 9. 1] Which words, if taken grammatically, make it certain that either some of those men that stood by Christ at that time are yet alive, or else that the kingdom of God must be now in this present world. And then there is another place more difficult: for when the Apostles after our Saviour's resurrection, and immediately before his ascension, asked our Saviour, saying, "Wilt thou at this time restore again the kingdom to Israel?" he answered them, "It is not for you to know the times and the seasons, which the Father hath put in His own power; but ye shall receive power by the coming of the Holy Ghost upon you, and ye shall be my witnesses both in Jerusalem, and in all Judaea, and in Samaria, and unto the uttermost part of the earth":[Acts, 1. 6] which is as much as to say, My kingdom is not yet come, nor shall you foreknow when it shall come; for it shall come as a thief in the night; but I will send you the Holy Ghost, and by him you shall have power to bear witness to all the world, by your preaching of my resurrection, and the works I have done, and the doctrine I have taught, that they may believe in me, and expect eternal life, at my coming again. How does this agree with the coming of Christ's kingdom at the resurrection? And that which St. Paul says, "That they turned from idols, to serve the living and true God, and to wait for His Son from heaven";[I Thessalonians, 1. 9, 10] where "to wait for His Son from heaven" is to wait for his coming to be king in power; which were not necessary if his kingdom had been then present. Again, if the kingdom of God began, as Beza on that place would have it, at the resurrection; what reason is there for Christians ever since the resurrection to say in their prayers, "Let thy kingdom come"? It is therefore manifest that the words of St. Mark are not so to be interpreted. There be some of them that stand here, saith our Saviour, that shall not taste of death till they have seen the kingdom of God come in power. If then this kingdom were to come at the resurrection of Christ, why is it said, some of them, rather than all? For they all lived till after Christ was risen. But they that require an exact interpretation of this text, let them interpret first the like words of our Saviour to St. Peter concerning St. John, "If I will that he tarry till I come, what is that to thee?" [John, 21. 22] upon which was grounded a report that he should not die. Nevertheless the truth of that report was neither confirmed, as well grounded; nor refuted, as ill grounded on those words; but left as a saying not understood. The same difficulty is also in the place of St. Mark. And if it be lawful to conjecture at their meaning, by that which immediately follows, both here and in St. Luke, where the same is again repeated, it is not improbable to say they have relation to the Transfiguration, which is described in the verses immediately following, where it is said that "After six days Jesus taketh with him Peter, and James, and John" (not all, but some of his Disciples), "and leadeth them up into an high mountain apart by themselves, and was transfigured before them. And his raiment became shining, exceeding white as snow; so as no fuller on earth can white them. And there appeared unto them Elias with Moses, and they were talking with Jesus," etc. So that they saw Christ in glory and majesty, as he is to come; insomuch as "they were sore afraid." And thus the promise of our Saviour was accomplished by way of vision. For it was a vision, as may probably be inferred out of St. Luke, that reciteth the same story, and saith that Peter and they that were with him were heavy with sleep: [Luke, 9. 28] but most certainly out of Matthew 17. 9 where the same is again related; for our Saviour charged them, saying, "Tell no man the vision until the Son of Man be risen from the dead." Howsoever it be, yet there can from thence be taken no argument to prove that the kingdom of God taketh beginning till the day of judgement. As for some other texts to prove the Pope's power over civil sovereigns (besides those of Bellarmine), as that the two swords that Christ and his Apostles had amongst them were the spiritual and the temporal sword, which they say St. Peter had given him by Christ; and that of the two luminaries, the greater signifies the Pope, and the lesser the king; one might as well infer out of the first verse of the Bible that by heaven is meant the Pope, and by earth the king: which is not arguing from Scripture, but a wanton insulting over princes that came in fashion after the time the popes were grown so secure of their greatness as to contemn all Christian kings; and treading on the necks of emperors, to mock both them and the Scripture, in the words of the ninetyfirst Psalm, "Thou shalt tread upon the lion and the adder; the young lion and the dragon thou shalt trample under thy feet." As for the rites of consecration, though they depend for the most part upon the discretion and judgement of the governors of the Church, and not upon the Scriptures; yet those governors are obliged to such direction as the nature of the action itself requireth; as that the ceremonies, words, gestures be both decent and significant, or at least conformable to the action. When Moses consecrated the tabernacle, the altar, and the vessels belonging to them, he anointed them with the oil which God had commanded to be made for that purpose: [Exodus, 40] and they were holy. There was nothing exorcized, to drive away phantasms. The same Moses (the civil sovereign of Israel), when he consecrated Aaron (the high priest) and his sons, did wash them with water (not exorcized water), put their garments upon them, and anointed them with oil; and they were sanctified, to minister unto the Lord in the priest's office, which was a simple and decent cleansing and adorning them before he presented them to God, to be His servants. When King Solomon (the civil sovereign of Israel) consecrated the temple he had built, he stood before all the congregation of Israel; and having blessed them, he gave thanks to God for putting into the heart of his father to build it, and for giving to himself the grace to accomplish the same; and then prayed unto Him, first, to accept that house, though it were not suitable to His infinite greatness, and to hear the prayers of His servants that should pray therein, or (if they were absent) towards it; and lastly, he offered a sacrifice of peace offering, and the house was dedicated. [II Kings, 8] Here was no procession; the King stood still in his first place; no exorcized water; no Asperges me, nor other impertinent application of words spoken upon another occasion; but a decent and rational speech, and such as in making to God a present of his new-built house was most conformable to the occasion. We read not that St. John did exorcize the water of Jordan; nor Philip the water of the river wherein he baptized the eunuch; nor that any pastor in the time of the Apostles did take his spittle and put it to the nose of the person to be baptized, and say, in odorem suavitatis, that is, "for a sweet savour unto the Lord"; wherein neither the ceremony of spittle, for the uncleanness; nor the application of that Scripture, for the levity, can by any authority of man be justified. To prove that the soul, separated from the body, liveth eternally, not only the souls of the elect, by especial grace, and restoration of the eternal life which Adam lost by sin, and our Saviour restored by the sacrifice of himself to the faithful; but also the souls of reprobates, as a property naturally consequent to the essence of mankind, without other grace of God but that which is universally given to all mankind; there are diverse places which at the first sight seem sufficiently to serve the turn: but such as when I compare them with that which I have before (Chapter thirty-eight) alleged out of the fourteenth of Job seem to me much more subject to a diverse interpretation than the words of Job. And first there are the words of Solomon, "Then shall the dust return to dust, as it was, and the spirit shall return to God that gave it." [Ecclesiastes, 12. 7] Which may bear well enough (if there be no other text directly against it) this interpretation, that God only knows, but man not, what becomes of a man's spirit when he expireth; and the same Solomon, in the same book, delivereth the same sentence in the sense I have given it. His words are, "All go to the same place; all are of the dust, and all turn to dust again; who knoweth that the spirit of man goeth upward, and that the spirit of the beast goeth downward to the earth?" [Ibid., 3. 20, 21] That is, none knows but God; nor is it an unusual phrase to say of things we understand not, "God knows what," and "God knows where." That of Genesis, 5. 24, "Enoch walked with God, and he was not; for God took him"; which is expounded, Hebrews, 11. 5, "He was translated, that he should not die; and was not found, because God had translated him. For before his translation, he had this testimony, that he pleased God," making as much for the immortality of the body as of the soul, proveth that this his translation was peculiar to them that please God; not common to them with the wicked; and depending on grace, not on nature. But on the contrary, what interpretation shall we give, besides the literal sense of the words of Solomon, "That which befalleth the sons of men befalleth beasts, even one thing befalleth them; as the one dieth, so doth the other; yea, they have all one breath; so that a man hath no pre-eminence above a beast, for all is vanity." [Ibid., 3. 19] By the literal sense, here is no natural immortality of the soul; nor yet any repugnancy with the life eternal, which the elect shall enjoy by grace. And, "Better is he that hath not yet been than both they"; [Ibid., 4. 3] that is, than they that live or have lived; which, if the soul of all them that have lived were immortal, were a hard saying; for then to have an immortal soul were worse than to have no soul at all. And again, "The living know they shall die, but the dead know not anything";[Ibid., 9. 5] that is, naturally, and before the resurrection of the body. Another place which seems to make for a natural immortality of the soul is that where our Saviour saith that Abraham, Isaac, and Jacob are living: but this is spoken of the promise of God, and of their certitude to rise again, not of a life then actual; and in the same sense that God said to Adam that on the day he should eat of the forbidden fruit, he should certainly die; from that time forward he was a dead man by sentence; but not by execution, till almost a thousand years after. So Abraham, Isaac, and Jacob were alive by promise, then, when Christ spoke; but are not actually till the resurrection. And the history of Dives and Lazarus make nothing against this, if we take it, as it is, for a parable. But there be other places of the New Testament where an immortality seemeth to be directly attributed to the to the wicked. For it is evident that they shall all rise to judgement. And it is said besides, in many places, that they shall go into "everlasting fire, everlasting torments, everlasting punishments; and that the worm of conscience never dieth"; and all this is comprehended in the word everlasting death, which is ordinarily interpreted "everlasting life in torments": and yet I can find nowhere that any man shall live in torments everlastingly. Also, it seemeth hard to say that God, who is the Father of mercies, that doth in heaven and earth all that He will; that hath the hearts of all men in His disposing; that worketh in men both to do and to will; and without whose free gift a man hath neither inclination to good nor repentance of evil, should punish men's transgressions without any end of time, and with all the extremity of torture that men can imagine, and more. We are therefore to consider what the meaning is of everlasting fire, and other the like phrases of Scripture. I have shown already that the kingdom of God by Christ beginneth at the day of judgement: that in that day, the faithful shall rise again, with glorious and spiritual bodies and be his subjects in that his kingdom, which shall be eternal: that they shall neither marry, nor be given in marriage, nor eat and drink, as they did in their natural bodies; but live for ever in their individual persons, without the specific eternity of generation: and that the reprobates also shall rise again, to receive punishments for their sins: as also that those of the elect, which shall be alive in their earthly bodies at that day, shall have their bodies suddenly changed, and made spiritual and immortal. But that the bodies of the reprobate, who make the kingdom of Satan, shall also be glorious or spiritual bodies, or that they shall be as the angels of God, neither eating, nor drinking, nor engendering; or that their life shall be eternal in their individual persons, as the life of every faithful man is, or as the life of Adam had been if he had not sinned, there is no place of Scripture to prove it; save only these places concerning eternal torments, which may otherwise be interpreted. From whence may be inferred that, as the elect after the resurrection shall be restored to the estate wherein Adam was before he had sinned; so the reprobate shall be in the estate that Adam and his posterity were in after the sin committed; saving that God promised a redeemer to Adam, and such of his seed as should trust in him and repent, but not to them that should die in their sins, as do the reprobate. These things considered, the texts that mention "eternal fire," "eternal torments," or "the worm that never dieth," contradict not the doctrine of a second and everlasting death, in the proper and natural sense of the word death. The fire or torments prepared for the wicked in Gehenna, Tophet, or in what place soever, may continue forever; and there may never want wicked men to be tormented in them, though not every nor any one eternally. For the wicked, being left in the estate they were in after Adam's sin, may at the resurrection live as they did, marry, and give in marriage, and have gross and corruptible bodies, as all mankind now have; and consequently may engender perpetually, after the resurrection, as they did before: for there is no place of Scripture to the contrary. For St. Paul, speaking of the resurrection, understandeth it only of the resurrection to life eternal, and not the resurrection to punishment. [I Corinthians, 15] And of the first, he saith that the body is "sown in corruption, raised in incorruption; sown in dishonour, raised in honour; sown in weakness, raised in power; sown a natural body, raised a spiritual body." There is no such thing can be said of the bodies of them that rise to punishment. So also our Saviour, when he speaketh of the nature of man after the resurrection, meaneth the resurrection to life eternal, not to punishment. The text is Luke, 20, verses 34, 35, 36, a fertile text: "The children of this world marry, and are given in marriage; but they that shall be counted worthy to obtain that world, and the resurrection from the dead, neither marry, nor are given in marriage: neither can they die any more; for they are equal to the angels, and are the children of God, being the children of the resurrection." The children of this world, that are in the estate which Adam left them in, shall marry and be given in marriage; that is, corrupt and generate successively; which is an immortality of the kind, but not of the persons of men: they are not worthy to be counted amongst them that shall obtain the next world, an absolute resurrection from the dead; but only a short time, as inmates of that world; and to the end only to receive condign punishment for their contumacy. The elect are the only children of the resurrection; that is to say, the sole heirs of eternal life: they only can die no more. It is they that are equal to the angels, and that are the children of God, and not the reprobate. To the reprobate there remaineth after the resurrection a second and eternal death, between which resurrection and their second and eternal death is but a time of punishment and torment, and to last by succession of sinners thereunto as long as the kind of man by propagation shall endure, which is eternally. Upon this doctrine of the natural eternity of separated souls is founded, as I said, the doctrine of purgatory. For supposing eternal life by grace only, there is no life but the life of the body; and no immortality till the resurrection. The texts for purgatory alleged by Bellarmine out of the canonical Scripture of the Old Testament are, first, the fasting of David for Saul and Jonathan, mentioned II Samuel, 1. 12, and again, II Samuel, 3. 35, for the death of Abner. This fasting of David, he saith, was for the obtaining of something for them at God's hands, after their death: because after he had fasted to procure the recovery of his own child, as soon as he knew it was dead, he called for meat. Seeing then the soul hath an existence separate from the body, and nothing can be obtained by men's fasting for the souls that are already either in heaven or hell, it followeth that there be some souls of dead men that are neither in heaven nor in hell; and therefore they must be in some third place, which must be purgatory. And thus with hard straining, he has wrested those places to the proof of a purgatory: whereas it is manifest that the ceremonies of mourning and fasting, when they are used for the death of men whose life was not profitable to the mourners, they are used for honour's sake to their persons; and when it is done for the death of them by whose life the mourners had benefit, it proceeds from their particular damage: and so David honoured Saul and Abner with his fasting; and, in the death of his own child, recomforted himself by receiving his ordinary food. In the other places which he allegeth out of the Old Testament, there is not so much as any show or colour of proof. He brings in every text wherein there is the word anger, or fire, or burning, or purging, or cleansing, in case any of the fathers have but in a sermon rhetorically applied it to the doctrine of purgatory, already believed. The first verse of Psalm 37, "O Lord, rebuke me not in thy wrath, nor chasten me in thy hot displeasure": what were this to purgatory, if Augustine had not applied the wrath to the fire of hell, and the displeasure to that of purgatory? And what is it to purgatory, that of Psalm, 66. 12 "We went through fire and water, and thou broughtest us to a moist place"; and other the like texts, with which the doctors of those times intended to adorn or extend their sermons or commentaries, haled to their purposes by force of wit? But he allegeth other places of the New Testament that are not so easy to be answered. And first that of Matthew, 12. 32, "Whosoever speaketh a word against the Son of Man, it shall be forgiven him; but whosoever speaketh against the Holy Ghost, it shall not be forgiven him neither in this world, nor in the world to come"; where he will have purgatory to be the world to come, wherein some sins may be forgiven which in this world were not forgiven: notwithstanding that it is manifest there are but three worlds; one from the creation to the flood, which was destroyed by water, and is called in Scripture "the old world"; another from the flood to the day of judgement, which is "the present world, and shall be destroyed by fire; and the third, which shall be from the day of judgement forward, everlasting, which is called "the world to come"; and in which it agreed by all there shall be no purgatory: and therefore the world to come, and purgatory, are inconsistent. But what then can be the meaning of those our Saviour's words? I confess they are very hardly to be reconciled with all the doctrines now unanimously received: nor is it any shame to confess the profoundness of the Scripture to be too great to be sounded by the shortness of human understanding. Nevertheless, I may propound such things to the consideration of more learned divines, as the text itself suggesteth. And first, seeing to speak against the Holy Ghost, as being the third person of the Trinity, is to speak against the Church, in which

213

the Holy Ghost resideth; it seemeth the comparison is made between the easiness of our Saviour in bearing with offences done to him while he himself taught the world, that is, when he was on earth, and the severity of the pastors after him, against those which should deny their authority, which was from the Holy Ghost. As if he should say, you that deny my power; nay, you that shall crucify me, shall be pardoned by me, as often as you turn unto me by repentance: but if you deny the power of them that teach you hereafter, by virtue of the Holy Ghost, they shall be inexorable, and shall not forgive you, but persecute you in this world, and leave you without absolution (though you turn to me, unless you turn also to them), to the punishments, as much as lies in them, of the world to come. And so the words may be taken as a prophecy or prediction concerning the times, as they have long been in the Christian Church: or if this be not the meaning (for I am not peremptory in such difficult places), perhaps there may be place left after the resurrection for the repentance of some sinners. And there is also another place that seemeth to agree therewith. For considering the words of St. Paul, "What shall they do which are baptized for the dead, if the dead rise not at all? Why also are they baptized for the dead?" [I Corinthians, 15. 29] a man may probably infer, as some have done, that in St. Paul's time there was a custom, by receiving baptism for the dead, (as men that now believe are sureties and undertakers for the faith of infants that are not capable of believing) to undertake for the persons of their deceased friends, that they should be ready to obey and receive our Saviour for their king at his coming again; and then the forgiveness of sins in the world to come has no need of a purgatory. But in both these interpretations, there is so much of paradox that I trust not to them, but propound them to those that are thoroughly versed in the Scripture, to inquire if there be no clearer place that contradicts them. Only of thus much, I see evident Scripture to persuade me that there is neither the word nor the thing of purgatory, neither in this nor any other text; nor anything that can prove a necessity of a place for the soul without the body; neither for the soul of Lazarus during the four days he was dead; nor for the souls of them which the Roman Church pretend to be tormented now in purgatory. For God, that could give a life to a piece of clay, hath the same power to give life again to a dead man, and renew his inanimate and rotten carcass into a glorious, spiritual, and immortal body. Another place is that of I Corinthians, 3, where it is said that they which build stubble, hay, etc., on the true foundation, their work shall perish; but "they themselves shall be saved; but as through fire": this fire he will have to be the fire of purgatory. The words, as I have said before, are an allusion to those of Zechariah, 13. 9, where he saith, "I will bring the third part through the fire, and refine them as silver is refined, and will try them as gold is tried": which is spoken of the coming of the Messiah in power and glory; that is, at the day of judgement, and conflagration of the present world; wherein the elect shall not be consumed, but be refined; that is, depose their erroneous doctrines and traditions, and have them, as it were, singed off; and shall afterwards call upon the name of the true God. In like manner, the Apostle saith of them that, holding this foundation, Jesus is the Christ, shall build thereon some other doctrines that be erroneous, that they shall not be consumed in that fire which reneweth the world, but shall pass through it to salvation; but so as to see and relinquish their former errors. The builders are the pastors; the foundation, that Jesus is the Christ; the stubble and hay, false consequences drawn from it through ignorance or frailty; the gold, silver, and precious stones are their true doctrines; and their refining or purging, the relinquishing of their errors. In all which there is no colour at all for the burning of incorporeal, that is to say, impatible souls. A third place is that of I Corinthians, 15. 29, before mentioned, concerning baptism for the dead: out of which he concludeth, first, that prayers for the dead are not unprofitable; and out of that, that there is a fire of purgatory: but neither of them rightly. For of many interpretations of the word baptism, he approveth this in the first place, that by baptism is meant, metaphorically, a baptism of penance; and that men are in this sense baptized when they fast, and pray, and give alms; and so baptism for the dead, and prayer for the dead, is the same thing. But this is a metaphor, of which there is no example, neither in the Scripture nor in any other use of language; and which is also discordant to the harmony and scope of the Scripture. The word baptism is used for being dipped in one's own blood, as Christ was upon the cross, and as most of the Apostles were, for giving testimony of him. [Mark, 10. 38, and Luke, 12. 50] But it is hard to say that prayer, fasting, and alms have any similitude with dipping. The same is used also, Matthew, 3. 11 (which seemeth to make somewhat for purgatory), for a purging with fire. But it is evident the fire and purging here mentioned is the same whereof the Prophet Zechariah speaketh, "I will bring the third part through the fire, will refine them," etc. [Zechariah, 13. 9] And St. Peter after him, "That the trial of your faith, which is much more precious than of gold that perisheth, though it be tried with fire, might be found unto praise, and honour, and glory at the appearing of Jesus Christ"; [I Epistle, 1. 7] and St. Paul, "The fire shall try every man's work of what sort it is." [I Corinthians, 3. 13] But St. Peter and St. Paul speak of the fire that shall be at the second appearing of Christ; and the Prophet Zechariah, of the day of judgement. And therefore this place of St. Matthew may be interpreted of the same, and then there will be no necessity of the fire of purgatory. Another interpretation of baptism for the dead is that which I have before mentioned, which he preferreth to the second place of probability: and thence also he inferreth the utility of prayer for the dead. For if after the resurrection such as have not heard of Christ, or not believed in him, may be received into Christ's kingdom, it is not in vain, after their death, that their friends should pray for them till they should be risen. But granting that God, at the prayers of the faithful, may convert unto him some of those that have not heard Christ preached, and consequently cannot have rejected Christ, and that the charity of men in that point cannot be blamed; yet this concludeth nothing for purgatory, because to rise from death to life is one thing; to rise from purgatory to life is another; as being a rising from life to life, from a life in torments to a life in joy. A fourth place is that of Matthew, 5. 25: "Agree with thine adversary quickly, whilst thou art in the way with him, lest at any time the adversary deliver thee to the judge, and the judge deliver thee to the officer, and thou be cast into prison. Verily I say unto thee, Thou shalt by no means come out thence, till thou hast paid the uttermost farthing." In which allegory, the offender is the sinner; both the adversary and the judge is God; the way is this life; the prison is the grave; the officer, death; from which the sinner shall not rise again to life eternal, but to a second death, till he have paid the utmost farthing, or Christ pay it for him by his Passion, which is a full ransom for all manner of sin, as well lesser sins as greater crimes, both being made by the Passion of Christ equally venial. The fifth place is that of Matthew, 5. 22: "Whosoever is angry with his brother without a cause shall be guilty in judgement. And whosoever shall say to his brother, Raca, shall be guilty in the council. But whosoever shall say, Thou fool, shall be guilty to hell fire." From which words he inferreth three sorts of sins, and three sorts of punishments; and that none of those sins, but the last, shall be punished with hell fire; and consequently, that after this life there is punishment of lesser sins in purgatory. Of which inference there is no colour in any interpretation that hath yet been given of them. Shall there be a distinction after this life of courts of justice, as there was amongst the Jews in our Saviour's time, to hear and determine diverse sorts of crimes, as the judges and the council? Shall not all judicature appertain to Christ and his Apostles? To understand therefore this text, we are not to consider it solitarily, but jointly with the words precedent and subsequent. Our Saviour in this chapter interpreteth the Law of Moses, which the Jews thought was then fulfilled when they had not transgressed the grammatical sense thereof, howsoever they had transgressed against the sentence or meaning of the legislator. Therefore, whereas they thought the sixth Commandment was not broken but by killing a man; nor the seventh, but when a man lay with a woman not his wife; our Saviour tells them, the inward anger of a man against his brother, if it be without just cause, is homicide. You have heard, saith he, the Law of Moses, "Thou shalt not kill," and that "Whosoever shall kill shall be condemned before the judges," or before the session of the Seventy: but I say unto you, to be angry with one's brother without cause, or to say unto him Raca, or Fool, is homicide, and shall be punished at the day of judgement, and session of Christ and his Apostles, with hell fire. So that those words were not used to distinguish between diverse crimes, and diverse courts of justice, and diverse punishments; but to tax the distinction between sin and sin, which the Jews drew not from the difference of the will in obeying God, but from the difference of their temporal courts of justice; and to show them that he that had the will to hurt his brother, though the effect appear but in reviling, or not at all, shall be cast into hell fire by the judges and by the session, which shall be the same, not different, courts at the day of judgement. This considered, what can be drawn from this text to maintain purgatory, I cannot imagine. The sixth place is Luke, 16. 9: "Make ye friends of the unrighteous mammon, that when ye fail, they may receive you into everlasting tabernacles." This he alleges to prove invocation of saints departed. But the sense is plain, that we should make friends, with our riches, of the poor; and thereby obtain their prayers whilst they live. "He that giveth to the poor lendeth to the Lord." The seventh is Luke, 23. 42: "Lord, remember me when thou comest into thy kingdom." Therefore, saith he, there is remission of sins after this life. But the consequence is not good. Our Saviour then forgave him, and, at his coming again in glory, will remember to raise him again to life eternal. The eighth is Acts, 2. 24, where St. Peter saith of Christ, "that God had raised him up, and loosed the pains of death, because it was not possible he should be holden of it": which he interprets to be a descent of Christ into purgatory, to loose some souls there from their torments: whereas it is manifest that it was Christ that was loosed. It was he that could not be holden of death or the grave, and not the souls in purgatory. But if that which Beza says in his notes on this place be well observed, there is none that will not see that instead of pains, it should be bands; and then there is no further cause to seek for purgatory in this text.

## CHAPTER XLV, OF DEMONOLOGY AND OTHER RELICS OF THE RELIGION OF THE GENTILES

THE impression made on the organs of sight by lucid bodies, either in one direct line or in many lines, reflected from opaque, or refracted in the passage through diaphanous bodies, produceth in living creatures, in whom God hath placed such organs, an imagination of the object from whence the impression proceedeth; which imagination is called sight, and seemeth not to be a mere imagination, but the body itself without us; in the same manner as when a man violently presseth his eye, there appears to him a light without, and before him, which no man perceiveth but himself, because there is indeed no such thing without him, but only a motion in the interior organs, pressing by resistance outward, that makes him think so. And the motion made by this pressure, continuing after the object which caused it is removed, is that we call imagination, and memory, and, in sleep, and sometimes in great distemper of the organs by sickness or violence, a dream, of which things I have already spoken briefly in the second and third Chapters. This nature of sight having never been discovered by the ancient pretenders to natural knowledge, much less by those that consider not things so remote (as that knowledge is) from their present use, it was hard for men to conceive of those images in the fancy and in the sense otherwise than of things really without us: which some, because they vanish away, they know not whither nor how, will have to be absolutely incorporeal, that is to say, immaterial, or forms without matter (colour and figure, without any coloured or figured body), and that they can put on airy bodies, as a garment, to make them visible when they will to our bodily eyes; and others say, are bodies and living and living creatures, but made of air, or other more subtle and ethereal matter, which is, then, when they will be seen, condensed. But both of them agree on one general appellation of them, demons. As if the dead of whom they dreamed were not inhabitants of their own brain, but of the air, or of heaven, or hell; not phantasms, but ghosts; with just as much reason as if one should say he saw his own ghost in a looking-glass, or the ghosts of the stars in a river; or call the ordinary apparition of the sun, of the quantity of about a foot, the demon or ghost of that great sun that enlighteneth the whole visible world: and by that means have feared them, as things of an unknown, that is, of an unlimited power to do them good or harm; and consequently, given occasion to the governors of the heathen Commonwealths to regulate this their fear by establishing that demonology (in which the poets, as principal priests of the heathen religion, were specially employed or reverenced) to the public peace, and to the obedience of subjects necessary thereunto; and to make some of them good demons, and others evil; the one as a spur to the observance, the other as reins to withhold them from violation of the laws. What kind of things they were to whom they attributed the name of demons appeareth partly in the genealogy of their gods, written by Hesiod, one of the most ancient poets of the Grecians, and partly in other histories, of which I have observed some few before, in the twelfth Chapter of this discourse. The Grecians, by their colonies and conquests communicated their language and writings into Asia, Egypt, and Italy; and therein, by necessary consequence, their demonology, or, as St. Paul calls it, their doctrines of devils: and by that means the contagion was derived also to the Jews, both of Judaea and Alexandria, and other parts, whereinto they were dispersed. But the name of demon they did not, as the Grecians, attribute to spirits both good and evil; but to the evil only: and to the good demons they gave the name of the Spirit of God, and esteemed those into whose bodies they entered to be prophets. In sum, all singularity, if good, they attributed to the Spirit of God; and if evil, to some demon, but a kakodaimen, an evil demon, that is, a devil. And therefore, they called demoniacs, that is, possessed by the devil, such as we call madmen or lunatics, or such as had the falling-sickness; or that spoke anything which they, for want of understanding, thought absurd. As also of an unclean person in a notorious degree, they used to say he had an unclean spirit; of a dumb man, that he had a dumb devil; and of John the Baptist, for the singularity of his fasting, that he had a devil; [Matthew, 11. 18] and of our Saviour, because he said, he that keepeth his sayings should not see death in aeternum, "Now we know thou hast a devil; Abraham is dead, and the prophets are dead." [John, 8. 52] And again, because he said they went about to kill him, the people answered, "Thou hast a devil: who goeth about to kill thee?" [John, 7. 20] Whereby it is manifest that the Jews had the same opinions concerning phantasms; namely, that they were not phantasms, that is, idols of the brain, but things real, and independent on the fancy. Which doctrine, if it be not true, why, may some say, did not our Saviour contradict it, and teach the contrary? Nay, why does He use on diverse occasions such forms of speech as seem to confirm it? To this I answer that, first, where Christ saith, "A spirit hath not flesh and bone," [Luke, 24. 39] though he show that there be spirits, yet he denies not that they are bodies. And where St. Paul says, "We shall rise spiritual bodies," [I Corinthians, 15. 44] he acknowledgeth the nature of spirits, but that they are bodily spirits; which is not difficult to understand. For air and many other things are bodies, though not flesh and bone, or any other gross body to be discerned by the eye. But when our Saviour speaketh to the devil, and commandeth him to go out of a man, if by the devil be meant a disease, as frenzy, or lunacy, or a corporeal spirit, is not the speech improper? Can diseases hear? Or can there be a corporeal spirit in a body of flesh and bone, full already of vital and animal spirits? Are there not therefore spirits, that neither have bodies, nor are mere imaginations? To the first I answer that the addressing of our Saviour's command to the madness or lunacy he cureth is no more improper than was his rebuking of the fever, or of the wind and sea; for neither do these hear: or than was the command of God to the light, to the firmament, to the sun, and stars, when He commanded them to be; for they could not hear before they had a being. But those speeches are not improper, because they signify the power of God's word: no more therefore is it improper to command madness or lunacy, under the appellation of devils by which they were then commonly understood, to depart out of a man's body. To the second, concerning their being incorporeal, I have not yet observed any place of Scripture from whence it can be gathered that any man was ever possessed with any other corporeal spirit but that of his own by which his body is naturally moved. Our Saviour, immediately after the Holy Ghost descended upon Him in the form of a dove, is said by St. Matthew to have been "led up by the Spirit into the wilderness";[Matthew, 4. 1] and the same is recited, Luke, 4. 1, in these words, "Jesus being full of the Holy Ghost, was led in the Spirit into the wilderness": whereby it is evident that by Spirit there is meant the Holy Ghost. This cannot be interpreted for a possession; for Christ and the Holy Ghost are but one and the same substance, which is no possession of one substance, or body, by another. And whereas in the verses following he is said "to have been taken up by the devil into the holy city, and set upon a pinnacle of the temple," shall we conclude thence that he was possessed of the devil, or carried thither by violence? And again, "carried thence by the devil into an exceeding high mountain, who showed him thence all the kingdoms of the world": wherein we are not to believe he was either possessed or forced by the devil; nor that any mountain is high enough, according to the literal sense to show him one whole hemisphere. What then can be the meaning of this place, other than that he went of himself into the wilderness; and that this carrying of him up and down, from the wilderness to the city, and from thence into a mountain, was a vision? Conformable whereunto is also the phrase of St. Luke, that he was led into the wilderness, not by, but in the Spirit: whereas, concerning his being taken up into the mountain, and unto the pinnacle of the temple, he speaketh as St. Matthew doth, which suiteth with the nature of a vision. Again, where St. Luke says of Judas Iscariot that "Satan entered into him, and thereupon that he went and communed with the chief priests, and captains, how he might betray Christ unto them";[Luke, 22. 3, 4] it may be answered that by the entering of Satan (that is, the enemy) into him is meant the hostile and traitorous intention of selling his Lord and Master. For as by the Holy Ghost is frequently in Scripture understood the graces and good inclinations given by the Holy Ghost; so by the entering of Satan may be understood the wicked cogitations and designs of the adversaries of Christ and his Disciples. For as it is hard to say that the devil was entered into Judas, before he had any such hostile design; so it is impertinent to say he was first Christ's enemy in his heart, and that the devil entered into him afterwards. Therefore the entering of Satan, and his wicked purpose, was one and the same thing. But if there be no immaterial spirit, nor any possession of men's bodies by any spirit corporeal, it may again be asked why our Saviour his Apostles did not teach the people so, and in such clear words as they might no more doubt thereof. But such questions as these are more curious than necessary for a Christian man's salvation. Men may as well ask why Christ, that could have given to all men faith, piety, and all manner of moral virtues, gave it to some only, and not to all: and why he left the search of natural causes and sciences to the natural reason and industry of men, and did not reveal it to all, or any man supernaturally; and many other such questions, of which nevertheless there may be alleged probable and pious reasons. For as God, when He brought the Israelites into the Land of Promise, did not secure them therein by subduing all the nations round about them, but left many of them, as thorns in their sides, to awaken from time to time their piety and industry: so our Saviour, in conducting us toward his heavenly kingdom, did not destroy all the difficulties of natural questions, but left them to exercise our industry and reason; the scope of his preaching being only to show us this plain and direct way to salvation, namely, the belief of this article, that he was the Christ, the Son of the living God, sent into the world to sacrifice himself for our sins, and, at his coming again, gloriously to reign over his elect, and to save them from their enemies eternally: to which the opinion of possession by spirits or phantasms is no impediment in the way, though it be to some an occasion of going out of the way, and to follow their own inventions. If we require of the Scripture an account of all questions which may be raised to trouble us in the performance of God's commands, we may as well complain of Moses for not having set down the time of the creation of such spirits, as well as of the creation of the earth and sea, and of men and beasts. To conclude, I find in Scripture that there be angels and spirits, good and evil; but not that they are incorporeal, as are the apparitions men see in the dark, or in a dream or vision, which the Latins call spectra, and took for demons. And I find that there are spirits corporeal, though subtle and invisible; but not that any man's body was possessed or inhabited by them, and that the bodies of the saints shall be such, namely, spiritual bodies, as St. Paul calls them. Nevertheless, the contrary doctrine, namely, that there be incorporeal spirits, hath hitherto so prevailed in the Church that the use of exorcism (that is to say, of ejection of devils by conjuration) is thereupon built; and, though rarely and faintly practised, is not yet totally given over. That there were many demoniacs in the primitive Church, and few madmen, and other such singular diseases; whereas in these times we hear of, and see many madmen, and few demoniacs, proceeds not from the change of nature, but of names. But how it comes to pass that whereas heretofore the Apostles, and after them for a time the pastors of the Church, did cure those singular diseases, which now they are not seen to do; as likewise, why it is not in the power of every true believer now to do all that the faithful did then, that is to say, as we read "in Christ's name to cast out devils, to speak with new tongues, to take up serpents, to drink deadly poison without harm taking, and to cure the sick by the laying on of their hands," [Mark, 16. 17] and all this without other words but "in the name of Jesus," is another question. And it is probable that those extraordinary gifts were given to the Church for no longer a time than men trusted wholly to Christ, and looked for their felicity only in his kingdom to come; and consequently, that when they sought authority and riches, and trusted to their own subtlety for a kingdom of this world, these supernatural gifts of God were again taken from them. Another relic of Gentilism is the worship of images, neither instituted by Moses in the Old, nor by Christ in the New Testament; nor yet brought in from the Gentiles; but left amongst them, after they had given their names to Christ. Before our Saviour preached, it was the general religion of the Gentiles to worship for gods those appearances that remain in the brain from the impression of external bodies upon the organs of their senses, which are commonly called ideas, idols, phantasms, conceits, as being representations of those external bodies which cause them, and have nothing in them of reality, no more than there is in the things that seem to stand before us in a dream. And this is the reason why St. Paul says, "We know that an idol is nothing": not that he thought that an image of metal, stone, or wood was nothing; but that the thing which they honored or feared in the image, and held for a god, was a mere figment, without place, habitation, motion, or existence, but in the motions of the brain. And the worship of these with divine honour is that which is in the Scripture called idolatry, and rebellion against God. For God being King of the Jews, and His lieutenant being first Moses, and afterward the high priest, if the people had been permitted to worship and pray to images (which are representations of their own fancies), they had had no further dependence on the true God, of whom there can be no similitude; nor on His prime ministers, Moses and the high priests; but every man had governed himself according to his own appetite, to the utter eversion of the Commonwealth, and their own destruction for want of union. And therefore the first law of God was: they should not take for gods, alienos deos, that is, the gods of other nations, but that only true God, who vouchsafed to commune with Moses, and by him to give them laws and directions for their peace, and for their salvation from their enemies. And the second was that they should not make to themselves any image to worship, of their own invention. For it is the same deposing of a king to submit to another king, whether he be set up by a neighbour nation or by ourselves. The places of Scripture pretended to countenance the setting up of images to worship them, or to set them up at all in the places where God is worshipped, are, first, two examples; one of the cherubim over the Ark of God; the other of the brazen serpent: secondly, some texts whereby we are commanded to worship certain creatures for their relation to God; as to worship His footstool: and lastly, some other texts, by which is authorized a religious honouring of holy things. But before I examine the force of those places, to prove that which is pretended, I must first explain what is to be understood by worshipping, and what by images and idols. I have already shown, in the twentieth Chapter of this discourse, that to honour is to value highly the power of any person, and that such value is measured by our comparing him with others. But because there is nothing to be compared with God in power, we honour Him not, but dishonour Him, by any value less than infinite. And thus honour is properly of its own nature secret, and internal in the heart. But the inward thoughts of men, which appear outwardly in their words and actions, are the signs of our honouring, and these go by the name of worship; in Latin, cultus. Therefore, to pray to, to swear by, to obey, to be diligent and officious in serving; in sum, all words and actions that betoken fear to offend, or desire to please, is worship, whether those words and actions be sincere or feigned: and because they appear as signs of honouring are ordinarily also called honour. The worship we exhibit to those we esteem to be but men, as to kings and men in authority, is civil worship: but the worship we exhibit to that which we think to be God, whatsoever the words, ceremonies, gestures, or other actions be, is divine worship. To fall prostrate before a king, in him that thinks him but a man, is but civil worship: and he that but putteth off his hat in the church, for this cause, that he thinketh it the house of God, worshippeth with divine worship. They that seek the distinction of divine and civil worship, not in the intention of the worshipper, but in the words douleia and latreia, deceive themselves. For whereas there be two sorts of servants: that sort which is of those that are absolutely in the power of their masters, as slaves taken in war, and their issue, whose bodies are not in their own power (their lives depending on the will of their masters, in such manner as to forfeit them upon the least disobedience), and that are bought and sold as beasts, were called Douloi, that is properly, slaves, and their service, Douleia; the other, which is of those that serve for hire, or in hope of benefit from their masters voluntarily, are called Thetes, that is, domestic servants; to whose service the masters have no further right than is contained in the covenants made betwixt them. These two kinds of servants have thus much common to them both, that their labour is appointed them by another: and the word Latris is the general name of both, signifying him that worketh for another, whether as a slave or a voluntary servant. So that latreia signifieth generally all service; but douleia the service of bondmen only, and the condition of slavery: and both are used in Scripture, to signify our service of God, promiscuously. Douleia, because we are God's slaves; latreia, because we serve Him: and in all kinds of service is contained, not only obedience, but also worship; that is, such actions, gestures, and words as signify honour. An image, in the most strict signification of the word, is the resemblance of something visible: in which sense the fantastical forms, apparitions, or seemings of visible bodies to the sight, are only images; such as are the show of a man or other thing in the water, by reflection or refraction; or of the sun or stars by direct vision in the air; which are nothing real in the things seen, nor in the place where they seem to be; nor are their magnitudes and figures the same with that of the object, but changeable, by the variation of the organs of sight, or by glasses; and are present oftentimes in our imagination, and in our dreams, when the object is absent; or changed into other colours, and shapes, as things that depend only upon the fancy. And these are the images which are originally and most properly called ideas and idols, and derived from the language of the Grecians, with whom the word eido signifieth to see. They are also called phantasms, which is in the same language, apparitions. And from these images it is that one of the faculties of man's nature is called the imagination. And from hence it is manifest that there neither is, nor can be, any image made of a thing invisible. It is also evident that there can be no image of a thing infinite: for all the images and phantasms that are made by the impression of things visible are figured. But figure is quantity every way determined, and therefore there can be no image of God, nor of the soul of man, nor of spirits; but only of bodies visible, that is, bodies that have light in themselves, or are by such enlightened. And whereas a man can fancy shapes he never saw, making up a figure out of the parts of diverse creatures, as the poets make their centaurs, chimeras, and other monsters never seen: so can he also give matter to those shapes, and make them in wood, clay, or metal. And these are also called images, not for the resemblance of any corporeal thing, but for the resemblance of some fantastical inhabitants of the brain of the maker. But in these idols, as they are originally in the brain, and as they are painted, carved, moulded, or molten in matter, there is a similitude of the one to the other, for which the material body made by art may be said to be the image of the fantastical idol made by nature. But in a larger use of the word image is contained also any representation of one thing by another. So an earthly sovereign may be called the image of God, and an inferior magistrate the image of an earthly sovereign. And many times in the idolatry of the Gentiles there was little regard to the similitude of their material idol to the idol in their fancy, and yet it was called the image of it. For a stone unhewn has been set up for Neptune, and diverse other shapes far different from the shapes they conceived of their gods. And at this day we see many images of the Virgin Mary, and other saints, unlike one another, and without correspondence to any one man's fancy; and yet serve well enough for the purpose they were erected for, which was no more but by the names only to represent the persons mentioned in the history; to which every man applieth a mental image of his own making, or none at all. And thus an image, in the largest sense, is either the resemblance or the representation of some thing visible; or both together, as it happeneth for the most part. But the name of idol is extended yet further in Scripture, to signify also the sun, or a star, or any other creature, visible or invisible, when they are worshipped for gods. Having shown what is worship, and what an image, I will now put them together, and examine what that idolatry is which is forbidden in the second Commandment, and other places of the Scripture. To worship an image is voluntarily to do those external acts which are signs of honouring either the matter of the image (which is wood, stone, metal, or some other visible creature), or the phantasm of the brain for the resemblance or representation whereof the matter was formed and figured, or both together as one animate body composed of the matter and the phantasm, as of a body and soul. To be uncovered, before a man of power and authority, or before the throne of a prince, or in such other places as he ordaineth to that purpose in his absence, is to worship that man or prince with civil worship; as being a sign, not of honouring the stool or place, but the person, and is not idolatry. But if he that doth it should suppose the

219

soul of the prince to be in the stool, or should present a petition to the stool, it were divine worship, and idolatry. To pray to a king for such things as he is able to do for us, though we prostrate ourselves before him, is but civil worship, because we acknowledge no other power in him but human: but voluntarily to pray unto him for fair weather, or for anything which God only can do for us, is divine worship, and idolatry. On the other side, if a king compel a man to it by the terror of death, or other great corporal punishment, it is not idolatry; for the worship which the sovereign commandeth to be done unto himself by the terror of his laws is not a sign that he that obeyeth him does inwardly honour him as a god, but that he is desirous to save himself from death, or from a miserable life: and that which is not a sign of internal honour is no worship, and therefore no idolatry. Neither can it be said that he that does it scandalizeth or layeth any stumbling block before his brother: because how wise or learned soever he be that worshippeth in that manner, another man cannot from thence argue that he approveth it, but that he doth it for fear; and that it is not his act, but the act of his sovereign. To worship God in some peculiar place, or turning a man's face towards an image or determinate place, is not to worship or honour the place or image, but to acknowledge it holy; that is to say, to acknowledge the image or the place to be set apart from common use, for that is the meaning of the word holy; which implies no new quality in the place or image, but only a new relation by appropriation to God, and therefore is not idolatry; no more than it was idolatry to worship God before the brazen serpent; or for the Jews, when they were out of their own country, to turn their faces, when they prayed, toward the temple of Jerusalem; or for Moses to put off his shoes when he was before the flaming bush, the ground appertaining to Mount Sinai, which place God had chosen to appear in, and to give His laws to the people of Israel, and was therefore holy ground, not by inherent sanctity, but by separation to God's use; or for Christians to worship in the churches which are once solemnly dedicated to God for that purpose by the authority of the king or other true representant of the Church. But to worship God as inanimating or inhabiting such image or place; that is to say, an infinite substance in a finite place, is idolatry: for such finite gods are but idols of the brain, nothing real, and are commonly called in the Scripture by the names of vanity, and lies, and nothing. Also to worship God, not as inanimating, or present in the place or image, but to the end to be put in mind of Him, or of some works of His, in case the place or image be dedicated or set up by private authority, and not by the authority of them that are our sovereign pastors, is idolatry. For the Commandment is, "Thou shalt not make to thyself any graven image." God commanded Moses to set up the brazen serpent; he did not make it to himself; it was not therefore against the Commandment. But the making of the golden calf by Aaron and the people, as being done without authority from God, was idolatry; not only because they held it for God, but also because they made it for a religious use, without warrant either from God their Sovereign, or from Moses that was His lieutenant. The Gentiles worshipped, for gods, Jupiter and others that, living, were men perhaps that had done great and glorious acts; and, for the children of God, diverse men and women, supposing them gotten between an immortal deity and a mortal man. This was idolatry, because they made them so to themselves, having no authority from God, neither in His eternal law of reason, nor in His positive and revealed will. But though our Saviour was a man, whom we also believe to be God immortal and the Son of God, yet this is no idolatry, because we build not that belief upon our own fancy or judgement, but upon the word of God revealed in the Scriptures. And for the adoration of the Eucharist, if the words of Christ, "This is my body," signify that he himself, and the seeming bread in his hand, and not only so, but that all the seeming morsels of bread that have ever since been, and any time hereafter shall be, consecrated by priests, be so many Christ's bodies, and yet all of them but one body, then is that no idolatry, because it is authorized by our Saviour: but if that text do not signify that (for there is no other that can be alleged for it), then, because it is a worship of human institution, it is idolatry. For it is not enough to say, God can transubstantiate the bread into Christ's body, for the Gentiles also held God to be omnipotent, and might upon that ground no less excuse their idolatry, by pretending, as well as others, a transubstantiation of their wood and stone into God Almighty. Whereas there be, that pretend divine inspiration to be a supernatural entering of the Holy Ghost into a man, and not an acquisition of God's graces by doctrine and study, I think they are in a very dangerous dilemma. For if they worship not the men whom they believe to be so inspired, they fall into impiety, as not adoring God's supernatural presence. And again, if they worship them they commit idolatry, for the Apostles would never permit themselves to be so worshipped. Therefore the safest way is to believe that by the descending of the dove upon the Apostles, and by Christ's breathing on them when he gave them the Holy Ghost, and by the giving of it by imposition of hands, are understood the signs which God hath been pleased to use, or ordain to be used, of his promise to assist those persons in their study to preach His kingdom, and in their conversation, that it might not be scandalous, but edifying to others. Besides the idolatrous worship of images, there is also a scandalous worship of them, which is also a sin, but not idolatry. For idolatry is to worship by signs of an internal and real honour; but scandalous worship is but seeming worship, and may sometimes be joined with an inward and hearty detestation, both of the image and of the fantastical demon or idol to which it is dedicated; and proceed only from the fear of death or other grievous punishment; and is nevertheless a sin in them that so worship, in case they be men whose actions are looked at by others as lights to guide them by; because following their ways, they cannot but stumble and fall in the way of religion: whereas the example of those we regard not, works not on us at all, but leaves us to our own diligence and caution, and consequently are no causes of our falling. If therefore a pastor lawfully called to teach and direct others, or any other, of whose knowledge there is a great opinion, do external honour to an idol for fear; unless he make his fear and unwillingness to it as evident as the worship, he scandalizeth his brother by seeming to approve idolatry. For his brother arguing from the action of his teacher, or of him whose knowledge he esteemeth great, concludes it to be lawful in itself. And this scandal is sin, and a scandal given. But if one being no pastor, nor of eminent reputation for knowledge in Christian doctrine, do the same, and another follow him, this is no scandal given (for he had no cause to follow such example), but is a pretence of scandal which he taketh of himself for an excuse before men. For an unlearned man that is in the pow

r of an idolatrous king or state, if commanded on pain of death to worship before an idol, he detesteth the idol in his heart: he doth well; though if he had the fortitude to suffer death, rather than worship it, he should do better. But if a pastor, who as Christ's messenger has undertaken to teach Christ's doctrine to all nations, should do the same, it were not only a sinful scandal, in respect of other Christian men's consciences, but a perfidious forsaking of his charge. The sum of that which I have said hitherto, concerning the worship of images, is this, that he that worshippeth in an image, or any creature, either the matter thereof, or any fancy of his own which he thinketh to dwell in it; or both together; or believeth that such things hear his prayers, or see his devotions, without ears or eyes, committeth idolatry. And he that counterfeiteth such worship for fear of punishment, if he be a man whose example hath power amongst his brethren, committeth a sin. But he that worshippeth the Creator of the world before such an image, or in such a place as he hath not made or chosen of himself, but taken from the commandment of God's word, as the Jews did in worshipping God before the cherubim, and before the brazen serpent for a time, and in or towards the temple of Jerusalem, which was also but for a time, committeth not idolatry. Now for the worship of saints, and images, and relics, and other things at this day practised in the Church of Rome, I say they are not allowed by the word of God, nor brought into the Church of Rome from the doctrine there taught; but partly left in it at the first conversion of the Gentiles, and afterwards countenanced, and confirmed, and augmented by the bishops of Rome. As for the proofs alleged out of Scripture; namely, those examples of images appointed by God to be set up; they were not set up for the people or any man to worship, but that they should worship God Himself before them; as before the cherubim over the Ark, and the brazen serpent. For we read not that the priest or any other did worship the cherubim. But contrarily we read that Hezekiah broke in pieces the brazen serpent which Moses had set up, [II Kings, 18. 4] because the people burnt incense to it. Besides, those examples are not put for our imitation, that we also should set up images, under pretence of worshipping God before them; because the words of the second Commandment, "Thou shalt not make to thyself any graven image," etc., distinguish between the images that God commanded to be set up, and those which we set up to ourselves. And therefore from the cherubim or brazen serpent, to the images of man's devising; and from the worship commanded by God, to the will-worship of men, the argument is not good. This also is to be considered, that as Hezekiah broke in pieces the brazen serpent, because the Jews did worship it, to the end they should do so no more; so also Christian sovereigns ought to break down the images which their subjects have been accustomed to worship, that there be no more occasion of such idolatry. For at this day the ignorant people, where images are worshipped, do really believe there is a divine power in the images; and are told by their pastors that some of them have spoken, and have bled; and that miracles have been done by them; which they apprehend as done by the saint, which they think either is the image itself, or in it. The Israelites, when they worshipped the calf, did think they worshipped the God that brought them out of Egypt, and yet it was idolatry, because they thought the calf either was that God, or had Him in his belly. And though some man may think it impossible for people to be so stupid as to think the image to be God, or a saint, or to worship it in that notion, yet it is manifest in Scripture to the contrary; where, when the golden calf was made, the people said, "These are thy gods, O Israel";[Exodus, 32] and where the images of Laban are called his gods. [Genesis, 31. 30] And we see daily by experience in all sorts of people that such men as study nothing but their food and ease are content to believe any absurdity, rather than to trouble themselves to examine it, holding their faith as it were by entail unalienable, except by an express and new law. But they infer from some other places that it is lawful to paint angels, and also God Himself: as from God's walking in the garden; from Jacob's seeing God at the top of the ladder; and from other visions and dreams. But visions and dreams, whether natural or supernatural, are but phantasms: and he that painteth an image of any of them, maketh not an image of God, but of his own phantasm, which is making of an idol. I say not, that to draw a picture after a fancy is a sin; but when it is drawn, to hold it for a representation of God is against the second Commandment and can be of no use but to worship. And the same may be said of the images of angels, and of men dead; unless as monuments of friends, or of men worthy remembrance: for such use of an image is not worship of the image, but a civil honouring of the person; not that is, but that was: but when it is done to the image which we make of a saint, for no other reason but that we think he heareth our prayers, and is pleased with the honour we do him, when dead and without sense, we attribute to him more than human power, and therefore it is idolatry. Seeing therefore there is no authority, neither in the Law of Moses nor in the Gospel, for the religious worship of images or other representations of God which men set up to themselves, or for the worship of the image of any creature in heaven, or earth, or under the earth; and whereas Christian kings, who are living representants of God, are not to be worshipped by their subjects by any act that signifieth a greater esteem of his power than the nature of mortal man is capable of; it cannot be imagined that the religious worship now in use was brought into the Church by misunderstanding of the Scripture. It resteth therefore that it was left in it by not destroying the images themselves in the conversion of the Gentiles that worshipped them. The cause whereof was the immoderate esteem and prices set upon the workmanship of them, which made the owners, though converted from worshipping them as they had done religiously for demons, to retain them still in their houses, upon pretence of doing it in the honor of Christ, of the Virgin Mary, and of the Apostles, and other the pastors of the primitive Church; as being easy, by giving them new names, to make that an image of the Virgin Mary and of her Son our Saviour, which before perhaps was called the image of Venus and Cupid; and so of a Jupiter to make a Barnabas, and of Mercury, a Paul, and the like. And as worldly ambition, creeping by degrees into the pastors, drew them to an endeavour of pleasing the new-made Christians; and also to a liking of this kind of honour, which they also might hope for after their decease, as well as those that had already gained it: so the worshipping of the images of Christ and his Apostles grew more and more idolatrous; save that somewhat after the time of Constantine diverse emperors, and bishops, and general councils observed and opposed the unlawfulness thereof, but too late or too weakly. The canonizing of saints is another relic of Gentilism: it is neither a misunderstanding of Scripture, nor a new invention of the Roman Church, but a custom as ancient as the Commonwealth of Rome itself. The first that ever was canonized at Rome was Romulus, and that upon the narration of Julius Proculus, that swore before the Senate he spoke with him after his death, and was assured by him he dwelt in heaven, and was there called Quirinus, and would be propitious to the state of their new city: and thereupon the Senate gave public testimony of his sanctity. Julius Caesar, and other emperors after him, had the like testimony; that is, were canonized for saints: for by such testimony is canonization now defined, and is the same with the apotheosis of the heathen. It is also from the Roman heathen that the popes have received the name and power of Pontifex Maximus. This was the name of him that in the ancient Commonwealth of Rome had the supreme authority under the Senate and people of regulating all ceremonies and doctrines concerning their religion: and when Augustus Caesar changed the state into a monarchy, he took to himself no more but this office, and that of tribune of the people (that is to say, the supreme power both in state and religion); and the succeeding emperors enjoyed the same. But when the Emperor Constantine lived, who was the first that professed and authorized Christian religion, it was consonant to his profession to cause religion to be regulated, under his authority, by the bishop of Rome: though it do not appear they had so soon the name of Pontifex; but rather that the succeeding bishops took it of themselves, to countenance the power they exercised over the bishops of the Roman provinces. For it is not any privilege of St. Peter, but the privilege of the city of Rome, which the emperors were always willing to uphold, that gave them such authority over other bishops; as may be evidently seen by that, that the bishop of Constantinople, when the Emperor made that city the seat of the Empire, pretended to be equal to the bishop of Rome; though at last, not without contention, the Pope carried it, and became the Pontifex Maximus; but in right only of the Emperor, and not without the bounds of the Empire, nor anywhere after the Emperor had lost his power in Rome, though it were the Pope himself that took his power from him. From whence we may by the way observe that there is no place for the superiority of the Pope over other bishops, except in the territories whereof he is himself the civil sovereign; and where the emperor, having sovereign power civil, hath expressly chosen the Pope for the chief pastor under himself of his Christian subjects. The carrying about of images in procession is another relic of the religion of the Greeks and Romans, for they also carried their idols from place to place, in a kind of chariot, which was peculiarly dedicated to that use, which the Latins called thensa, and vehiculum Deorum; and the image was placed in a frame, or shrine, which they called ferculum. And that which they called pompa is the same that now is named procession; according whereunto, amongst the divine honours which were given to Julius Caesar by the Senate, this was one, that in the pomp, or procession, at the Circaean games, he should have thensam et ferculum, a sacred chariot and a shrine; which was as much as to be carried up and down as a god, just as at this day the popes are carried by Switzers under a canopy. To these processions also belonged the bearing of burning torches and candles before the images of the gods, both amongst the Greeks and Romans. For afterwards the emperors of Rome received the same honor; as we read of Caligula, that at his reception to the Empire he was carried from Misenum to Rome in the midst of a throng of people, the ways beset with altars, and beasts for sacrifice, and burning torches; and of Caracalla, that was received into Alexandria with incense, and with casting of flowers, and dadouchiais, that is, with torches; for dadochoi were they that amongst the Greeks carried torches lighted in the processions of their gods. And in process of time the devout but ignorant people did many times honour their bishops with the like pomp of wax candles, and the images of our Saviour and the saints, constantly, in the church itself. And thus came in the use of wax candles and was also established by some of the ancient councils. The heathens had also their aqua lustralis, that is to say, holy water. The Church of Rome imitates them also in their holy days. They had their bacchanalia, and we have our wakes, answering to them; they their saturnalia, and we our carnivals and Shrove Tuesday's liberty of servants; they their procession of Priapus, we our fetching in, erection, and dancing about Maypoles; and dancing is one kind of worship. They had their procession called Ambarvalia, and we our procession about the fields in the Rogation week. Nor do I think that these are all the ceremonies that have been left in the Church, from the first conversion of the Gentiles, but they are all that I can for the present call to mind. And if a man would well observe that which is delivered in the histories, concerning the religious rites of the Greeks and Romans, I doubt not but he might find many more of these old empty bottles of Gentilism which the doctors of the Roman Church, either by negligence or ambition, have filled up again with the new wine of Christianity, that will not fail in time to break them.

## CHAPTER XLVI, OF DARKNESS FROM VAIN PHILOSOPHY AND FABULOUS TRADITIONS

BY philosophy is understood the knowledge acquired by reasoning, from the manner of the generation of anything, to the properties; or from the properties, to some possible way of generation of the same; to the end to be able to produce, as far as matter and human force permit, such effects as human life requireth. So the geometrician, from the construction of figures, findeth out many properties thereof; and from the properties, new ways of their construction, by reasoning; to the end to be able to measure land and water; and for infinite other uses. So the astronomer, from the rising, setting, and moving of the sun and stars in diverse parts of the heavens, findeth out the causes of day and night, and of the different seasons of the year, whereby he keepeth an account of time; and the like of other sciences. By which definition it is evident that we are not to account as any part thereof that original knowledge called experience, in which consisteth prudence, because it is not attained by reasoning, but found as well in brute beasts as in man; and is but a memory of successions of events in times past, wherein the omission of every little circumstance, altering the effect frustrateth the expectation of the most prudent: whereas nothing is produced by reasoning aright, but general, eternal, and immutable truth. Nor are we therefore to give that name to any false conclusions; for he that reasoneth aright in words he understandeth can never conclude an error: Nor to that which any man knows by supernatural revelation; because it is not acquired by reasoning: Nor that which is gotten by reasoning from the authority of books; because it is not by reasoning from the cause to the effect, nor from the effect to the cause; and is not knowledge, but faith. The faculty of reasoning being consequent to the use of speech, it was not possible but that there should have been some general truths found out by reasoning, as ancient almost as language itself. The savages of America are not without some good moral sentences; also they have a little arithmetic, to add and divide in numbers not too great; but they are not therefore philosophers. For as there were plants of corn and wine in small quantity dispersed in the fields and woods, before men knew their virtue, or made use of them for their nourishment, or planted them apart in fields and vineyards; in which time they fed on acorns and drank water: so also there have been diverse true, general, and profitable speculations from the beginning, as being the natural plants of human reason. But they were at first but few in number; men lived upon gross experience; there was no method; that is to say, no sowing nor planting of knowledge by itself, apart from the weeds and common plants of error and conjecture. And the cause of it being the want of leisure from procuring the necessities of life, and defending themselves against their neighbours, it was impossible, till the erecting of great Commonwealths, it should be otherwise. Leisure is the mother of philosophy; and Commonwealth, the mother of peace and leisure. Where first were great and flourishing cities, there was first the study of philosophy. The Gymnosophists of India, the Magi of Persia, and the Priests of Chaldaea and Egypt are counted the most ancient philosophers; and those countries were the most ancient of kingdoms. Philosophy was not risen to the Grecians and other people of the West, whose Commonwealths, no greater perhaps than Lucca or Geneva, had never peace but when their fears of one another were equal; nor the leisure to observe anything but one another. At length, when war had united many of these Grecian lesser cities into fewer and greater, then began seven men, of several parts of Greece, to get the reputation of being wise; some of them for moral and politic sentences, and others for the learning of the Chaldaeans and Egyptians, which was astronomy and geometry. But we hear not yet of any schools of philosophy. After the Athenians, by the overthrow of the Persian armies, had gotten the dominion of the sea; and thereby, of all the islands and maritime cities of the archipelago, as well of Asia as Europe; and were grown wealthy; they that had no employment, neither at home nor abroad, had little else to employ themselves in but either, as St. Luke says, "in telling and hearing news," [Acts, 17. 21] or in discoursing of philosophy publicly to the youth of the city. Every master took some place for that purpose: Plato, in certain public walks called Academia, from one Academus; Aristotle in the walk of the temple of Pan, called Lycaeum; others in the Stoa, or covered walk, wherein the merchants' goods were brought to land; others in other places, where they spent the time of their leisure in teaching or in disputing of their opinions; and some in any place where they could get the youth of the city together to hear them talk. And this was it which Carneades also did at Rome, when he was ambassador, which caused Cato to advise the Senate to dispatch him quickly, for fear of corrupting the manners of the young men that delighted to hear him speak, as they thought, fine things. From this it was that the place where any of them taught and disputed was called schola, which in their tongue signifieth leisure; and their disputations, diatribae, that is to say, passing of the time. Also the philosophers themselves had the name of their sects, some of them, from these their schools: for they that followed Plato's doctrine were called Academics; the followers of Aristotle, Peripatetics, from the walk he taught in; and those that Zeno taught, Stoics, from the Stoa: as if we should denominate men from More-fields, from Paul's Church, and from the Exchange, because they meet there often to prate and loiter. Nevertheless, men were so much taken with this custom, that in time it spread itself over all Europe, and the best part of Africa; so as there were schools, publicly erected and maintained, for lectures and disputations, almost in every Commonwealth. There were also schools, anciently, both before and after the time of our Saviour, amongst the Jews: but they were schools of their law. For though they were called synagogues, that is to say, congregations of the people; yet, inasmuch as the law was every Sabbath day read, expounded, and disputed in them, they differed not in nature, but in name only, from public schools; and were not only in Jerusalem, but in every city of the Gentiles where the Jews inhabited. There was such a school at Damascus, whereinto Paul entered, to persecute. There were others at Antioch, Iconium and Thessalonica, whereinto he entered, to dispute. And such was the synagogue of the Libertines, Cyrenians, Alexandrians, Cilicians, and those of Asia; that is to say, the school of Libertines, and of Jews, that were strangers in Jerusalem: and of this school they were that disputed with St. Stephen.[Acts, 6. 9] But what has been the utility of those schools? What science is there at this day acquired by their readings and disputings? That we have of geometry, which is the mother of all natural science, we are not indebted for it to the schools. Plato, that was the best philosopher of the Greeks, forbade entrance into his school to all that were not already in some measure geometricians. There were many that studied that science to the great advantage of mankind: but there is no mention of their schools; nor was there any sect of geometricians; nor did they then pass under the name of philosophers. The natural philosophy of those schools was rather a dream than science, and set forth in senseless and insignificant language, which cannot be avoided by those that will teach philosophy without having first attained great knowledge in geometry. For nature worketh by motion; the ways and degrees whereof cannot be known without the knowledge of the proportions and properties of lines and figures. Their moral philosophy is but a description of their own passions. For the rule of manners, without civil government, is the law of nature; and in it, the law civil, that determineth what is honest and dishonest; what is just and unjust; and generally what is good and evil. Whereas they make the rules of good and bad by their own liking and disliking; by which means, in so great diversity of taste, there is nothing generally agreed on; but every one doth, as far as he dares, whatsoever seemeth good in his own eyes, to the subversion of Commonwealth. Their logic, which should be the method of reasoning, is nothing else but captions of words, and inventions how to puzzle such as should go about to pose them. To conclude, there is nothing so absurd that the old philosophers (as Cicero saith, who was one of them) have not some of them maintained. And I believe that scarce anything can be more absurdly said in natural philosophy than that which now is called Aristotle's

Metaphysics; nor more repugnant to government than much of that he hath said in his Politics, nor more igno-rantly, than a great part of his Ethics. The school of the Jews was originally a school of the law of Moses, who commanded that at the end of every seventh year, at the Feast of the Tabernacles, it should be read to all the people, that they might hear and learn it. [Deuteronomy, 31. 10] Therefore the reading of the law (which was in use after the Captivity) every Sabbath day ought to have had no other end but the acquainting of the people with the Commandments which they were to obey, and to expound unto them the writings of the prophets. But it is manifest, by the many reprehensions of them by our Saviour, that they corrupted the text of the law with their false commentaries, and vain traditions; and so little understood the prophets that they did neither acknowledge Christ, nor the works he did, of which the prophets prophesied. So that by their lectures and dis-putations in their synagogues, they turned the doctrine of their law into a fantastical kind of philosophy, con-cerning the incomprehensible nature of God and of spirits; which they compounded of the vain philosophy and theology of the Grecians, mingled with their own fancies, drawn from the obscurer places of the Scrip-ture, and which might most easily be wrested to their purpose; and from the fabulous traditions of their ances-tors. That which is now called a University is a joining together, and an incorporation under one government, of many public schools in one and the same town or city, in which the principal schools were ordained for the three professions; that is to say, of the Roman religion, of the Roman law, and of the art of medicine. And for the study of philosophy it hath no otherwise place than as a handmaid to the Roman religion: and since the au-thority of Aristotle is only current there, that study is not properly philosophy (the nature whereof dependeth not on authors), but Aristotelity. And for geometry, till of very late times it had no place at all, as being sub-servient to nothing but rigid truth. And if any man by the ingenuity of his own nature had attained to any de-gree of perfection therein, he was commonly thought a magician, and his art diabolical. Now to descend to the particular tenets of vain philosophy, derived to the Universities, and thence into the Church, partly from Aris-totle, partly from blindness of understanding; I shall first consider their principles. There is a certain philosophia prima on which all other philosophy ought to depend; and consisteth principally in right limiting of the significations of such appellations, or names, as are of all others the most universal; which limitations serve to avoid ambiguity and equivocation in reasoning, and are commonly called definitions; such as are the definitions of body, time, place, matter, form, essence, subject, substance, accident, power, act, finite, infinite, quantity, quality, motion, action, passion, and diverse others, necessary to the explaining of a man's concep-tions concerning the nature and generation of bodies. The explication (that is, the settling of the meaning) of which, and the like terms, is commonly in the Schools called metaphysics; as being a part of the philosophy of Aristotle, which hath that for title. But it is in another sense; for there it signifieth as much as "books writ-ten or placed after his natural philosophy": but the Schools take them for books of supernatural philosophy: for the word metaphysics will bear both these senses. And indeed that which is there written is for the most part so far from the possibility of being understood, and so repugnant to natural reason, that whosoever thin-keth there is anything to be understood by it must needs think it supernatural. From these metaphysics, which are mingled with the Scripture to make School divinity, we are told there be in the world certain essences sep-arated from bodies, which they call abstract essences, and substantial forms; for the interpreting of which jar-gon, there is need of somewhat more than ordinary attention in this place. Also I ask pardon of those that are not used to this kind of discourse for applying myself to those that are. The world (I mean not the earth only, that denominates the lovers of it "worldly men," but the universe, that is, the whole mass of all things that are) is corporeal, that is to say, body; and hath the dimensions of magnitude, namely, length, breadth, and depth: also every part of body is likewise body, and hath the like dimensions; and consequently every part of the uni-verse is body, and that which is not body is no part of the universe: and because the universe is all that which is no part of it is nothing, and consequently nowhere. Nor does it follow from hence that spirits are nothing: for they have dimensions and are therefore really bodies; though that name in common speech be given to such bodies only as are visible or palpable; that is, that have some degree of opacity: but for spirits, they call them incorporeal, which is a name of more honour, and may therefore with more piety be attributed to God Himself; in whom we consider not what attribute expresseth best His nature, which is incomprehensible, but what best expresseth our desire to honour Him. To know now upon what grounds they say there be essences abstract, or substantial forms, we are to consider what those words do properly signify. The use of words is to register to ourselves, and make manifest to others, the thoughts and conceptions of our minds. Of which words, some are the names of the things conceived; as the names of all sorts of bodies that work upon the senses and leave an impression in the imagination: others are the names of the imaginations themselves; that is to say, of those ideas or mental images we have of all things we see or remember: and others again are names of names, or of different sorts of speech; as universal, plural, singular, are the names of names; and definition, affirmation, negation, true, false, syllogism, interrogation, promise, covenant, are the names of certain forms of speech. Others serve to show the consequence or repugnance of one name to another; as when one saith, "a man is a body," he intendeth that the name of body is necessarily consequent to the name of man, as being but serval name of the same thing, man; which consequence is signified by coupling them together with the word is. And as we use the verb is; so the Latins use their verb est, and the Greeks their esti through all its declinations. Whether all other nations of the world have in their several languages a word that answereth to it, or not, I cannot tell; but I am sure they have not need of it: for the placing of two names in order may serve to signify their consequence, if it were the custom (for custom is it that gives words their force), as well as the words is, or be, or are, and the like. And if it were so, that there were a language without any verb answerable to est, or is, or be; yet the men that used it would be not a jot the less capable of inferring, concluding, and of all kind of reasoning, than were the Greeks and Latins. But what then would become of these terms, of entity, essence, essential, essentiality, that are derived from it, and of many more that depend on these, applied as most commonly they are? They are therefore no names of things; but signs, by which we make known that we conceive the consequence of one name or attribute to another: as when we say, "a man is a living body," we mean not that the man is one thing, the living body another, and the is, or being, a third; but that the man and the living body is the same thing, because the consequence, "If he be a man, he is a living body," is a true consequence, signified by that word is. Therefore, to be a body, to walk, to be speaking, to live, to see, and the like infinitives; also corporeity, walking, speaking, life, sight, and the like, that signify just the same, are the names of nothing; as I have elsewhere more amply expressed. But to what purpose, may some man say, is such subtlety in a work of this nature, where I pretend to nothing but what is necessary to the doctrine of government and obedience? It is to this purpose, that men may no longer suffer themselves to be abused by them that by this doctrine of "separated essences," built on the vain philosophy of Aristotle, would fright them from obeying the laws of their country, with empty names; as men fright birds from the corn with an empty doublet, a hat, and a crooked stick. For it is upon this ground that, when a man is dead and buried, they say his soul, that is his life, can walk separated from his body, and is seen by night amongst the graves. Upon the same ground, they say that the figure, and colour, and taste of a piece of bread has a being, there, where they say there is no bread: and upon the same ground they say that faith, and wisdom, and other virtues are sometimes poured into a man, sometimes blown into him, from heaven; if the virtuous and their virtues could be asunder; and a great many other things that serve to lessen the dependence of subjects on the sovereign power of their country. For who will endeavour to obey the laws, if he expect obedience to be poured or blown into him? Or who will not obey a priest, that can make God, rather than his sovereign; nay, than God Himself? Or who that is in fear of ghosts will not bear great respect to those that can make the holy water that drives them from him? And this shall suffice for an example of the errors which are brought into the Church from the entities and essences of Aristotle: which it may be he knew to be false philosophy, but wrote it as a thing consonant to, and corroborative of, their religion; and fearing the fate of Socrates. Being once fallen into this error of "separated essences," they are thereby necessarily involved in many other absurdities that follow it. For seeing they will have these forms to be real, they are obliged to assign them some place. But because they hold them incorporeal, without all dimension of quantity, and all men know that place is dimension, and not to be filled but by that which is corporeal, they are driven to uphold their credit with a distinction, that they are not indeed anywhere circumscriptive, but definitive: which terms being mere words, and in this occasion insignificant, pass only in Latin, that the vanity of them may be concealed. For the circumscription of a thing is nothing else but the determination or defining of its place; and so both the terms of the distinction are the same. And in particular, of the essence of a man, which, they say, is his soul, they affirm it to be all of it in his little finger, and all of it in every other part, how small soever, of his body; and yet no more soul in the whole body than in any one of those parts. Can any man think that God is served with such absurdities? And yet all this is necessary to believe, to those that will believe the existence of an incorporeal soul, separated from the body. And when they come to give account how an incorporeal substance can be capable of pain, and be tormented in the fire of hell or purgatory, they have nothing at all to answer, but that it cannot be known how fire can burn souls. Again, whereas motion is change of place, and incorporeal substances are not capable of place, they are troubled to make it seem possible how a soul can go hence, without the body, to heaven, hell, or purgatory; and how the ghosts of men (and I may add, of their clothes which they appear in) can walk by night in churches, churchyards, and other places of sepulture. To which I know not what they can answer, unless they will say, they walk definitive, not circumscriptive, or spiritually, not temporally: for such egregious distinctions are equally applicable to any difficulty whatsoever. For the meaning of eternity, they will not have it to be an endless succession of time; for then they should not be able to render a reason how God's will and pre-ordaining of things to come should not be before His prescience of the same, as the efficient cause before the effect, or agent before the action; nor of many other their bold opinions concerning the incomprehensible nature of God. But they will teach us that eternity is the standing still of the present time, a nunc-stans, as the Schools call it; which neither they nor any else understand, no more than they would a hic-stans for an infinite greatness of place. And whereas men divide a body in their thought, by numbering parts of it, and in numbering those parts, number also the parts of the place it filled; it cannot be but in making many parts, we make also many places of those parts; whereby there cannot be conceived in the mind of any man more or fewer parts than there are places for: yet they will have us believe that by the Almighty power of God, one body may be at one and the same time in many places; and many bodies at one and the same time in one place; as if it were an acknowledgement of the Divine Power to say, that which is, is not; or that which has been, has not been. And these are but a small part of the incongruities they are forced to, from their disputing philosophically, instead of admiring and adoring of the divine and incomprehensible Nature; whose attributes cannot signify what He is, but ought to signify our desire to honour Him with the best appellations we can think on. But they that venture to reason of His nature, from these attributes of honour, losing their understanding in the very first attempt, fall from one inconvenience into another, without end and without number; in the same manner as when a man ignorant of the ceremonies of court, coming into the presence of a greater person than he is used to speak to, and stumbling at his entrance, to save himself from falling, lets slip his cloak; to recover his cloak, lets fall his hat; and, with one disorder after another, discovers his astonishment and rusticity. Then for physics, that is, the knowledge of the subordinate and secondary causes of natural events, they render none at all but empty words. If you desire to know why some kind of bodies sink naturally downwards toward the earth, and others go naturally from it, the Schools will tell you, out of Aristotle, that the bodies that sink downwards are heavy; and that this heaviness is it that causes them to descend. But if you ask what they mean by heaviness, they will define it to be an endeavour to go to the center of the earth: so that the cause why things sink downward is an endeavour to be below; which is as much as to say that bodies descend, or ascend, because they do. Or they will tell you the center of the earth is the place of rest and conservation for heavy things, and therefore they endeavour to be there: as if stones and metals had a desire, or could discern the place they would be at, as man does; or loved rest, as man does not; or that a piece of glass were less safe in the window than falling into the street. If we would know why the same body seems greater, without adding to it, one time than another; they say, when it seems less, it is condensed; when greater, rarefied. What is that condensed and rarefied? Condensed is when there is in the very same matter less quantity than before; and rarefied, when more. As if there could be matter that had not some determined quantity; when quantity is nothing else but the determination of matter; that is to say, of body, by which we say one body is greater or lesser than another by thus, or thus much. Or as if a body were made without any quantity at all, and that afterwards more or less were put into it, according as it is intended the body should be more or less dense. For the cause of the soul of man, they say, creatur infundendo and creando infunditur: that is, "It is created by pouring it in," and "poured in by creation." For the cause of sense, an ubiquity of species; that is, of the shows or apparitions of objects; which when they be apparitions to the eye is sight; when to the ear, hearing; to the palate, taste; to the nostril, smelling; and to the rest of the body, feeling. For cause of the will to do any particular action, which is called volitio, they assign the faculty, that is to say, the capacity in general, that men have to will sometimes one thing, sometimes another, which is called voluntas; making the power the cause of the act: as if one should assign for cause of the good or evil acts of men their ability to do them. And in many occasions they put for cause of natural events, their own ignorance, but disguised in other words: as when they say, fortune is the cause of things contingent; that is, of things whereof they know no cause: and as when they attribute many effects to occult qualities; that is, qualities not known to them, and therefore also, as they think, to no man else: and to sympathy, antipathy, antiperistasis, specifical qualities, and other like terms, which signify neither the agent that produceth them, nor the operation by which they are produced. If such metaphysics and physics as this be not vain philosophy, there was never any; nor needed St. Paul to give us warning to avoid it. And for their moral and civil philosophy, it hath the same or greater absurdities. If a man do an action of injustice, that is to say, an action contrary to the law, God, they say, is the prime cause of the law and also the prime cause of that and all other actions; but no cause at all of the injustice; which is the inconformity of the action to the law. This is vain philosophy. A man might as well say that one man maketh both a straight line and a crooked, and another maketh their incongruity. And such is the philosophy of all men that resolve of their conclusions before they know their premises, pretending to comprehend that which is incomprehensible; and of attributes of honour to make attributes of nature; as this distinction was made to maintain the doctrine of free will, that is, of a will of man not subject to the will of God.

Aristotle and other heathen philosophers define good and evil by the appetite of men; and well enough, as long as we consider them governed every one by his own law: for in the condition of men that have no other law but their own appetites, there can be no general rule of good and evil actions. But in a Commonwealth this measure is false: not the appetite of private men, but the law, which is the will and appetite of the state, is the measure. And yet is this doctrine still practised, and men judge the goodness or wickedness of their own and of other men's actions, and of the actions of the Commonwealth itself, by their own passions; and no man calleth good or evil but that which is so in his own eyes, without any regard at all to the public laws; except only monks and friars, that are bound by vow to that simple obedience to their superior to which every subject ought to think himself bound by the law of nature to the civil sovereign. And this private measure of good is a doctrine, not only vain, but also pernicious to the public state. It is also vain and false philosophy to say the work of marriage is repugnant to chastity or continence, and by consequence to make them moral vices; as they do that pretend chastity and continence for the ground of denying marriage to the clergy. For they confess it is no more but a constitution of the Church that requireth in those holy orders, that continually attend the altar and administration of the Eucharist, a continual abstinence from women, under the name of continual chastity, continence, and purity. Therefore they call the lawful use of wives want of chastity and continence; and so make marriage a sin, or at least a thing so impure and unclean as to render a man unfit for the altar. If the law were made because the use of wives is incontinence, and contrary to chastity, then all marriage is vice: if because it is a thing too impure and unclean for a man consecrated to God, much more should other natural, necessary, and daily works, which all men do, render men unworthy to be priests, because they are more unclean. But the secret foundation of this prohibition of marriage of priests is not likely to have been laid so slightly as upon such errors in moral philosophy; nor yet upon the preference of single life to the estate of matrimony; which proceeded from the wisdom of St. Paul, who perceived how inconvenient a thing it was for those that in those times of persecution were preachers of the gospel, and forced to fly from one country to another, to be clogged with the care of wife and children; but upon the design of the popes and priests of after times, to make themselves, (the clergy, that is to say,) sole heirs of the kingdom of God in this world, to which it was necessary to take from them the use of marriage, because our Saviour saith that at the coming of his kingdom the children of God "shall neither marry, nor be given in marriage, but shall be as the angels in heaven"; that is to say, spiritual. Seeing then they had taken on them the name of spiritual, to have allowed themselves, when there was no need, the propriety of wives, had been an incongruity. From Aristotle's civil philosophy, they have learned to call all manner of Commonwealths but the popular (such as was at that time the state of Athens), tyranny. All kings they called tyrants; and the aristocracy of the thirty governors set up there by the Lacedaemonians that subdued them, the thirty tyrants: as also to call the condition of the people under the democracy, liberty. A tyrant originally signified no more, simply, but a monarch. But when afterwards in most parts of Greece that kind of government was abolished, the name began to signify, not only the thing it did before, but with it the hatred which the popular states bore towards it: as also the name of king became odious after the deposing of the kings in Rome, as being a thing natural to all men to conceive some great fault to be signified in any attribute that is given in despite, and to a great enemy. And when the same men shall be displeased with those that have the administration of the democracy, or aristocracy, they are not to seek for disgraceful names to express their anger in; but call readily the one anarchy, and the other oligarchy, or the tyranny of a few. And that which offendeth the people is no other thing but that they are governed, not as every one of them would himself, but as the public representant, be it one man or an assembly of men, thinks fit; that is, by an arbitrary government: for which they give evil names to their superiors, never knowing (till perhaps a little after a civil war) that without such arbitrary government, such war must be perpetual; and that it is men and arms, not words and promises, that make the force and power of the laws. And therefore this is another error of Aristotle's politics, that in a well-ordered Commonwealth, not men should govern, but the laws. What man that has his natural senses, though he can neither write nor read, does not find himself governed by them he fears, and believes can kill or hurt him when he obeyeth not? Or that believes the law can hurt him; that is, words and paper, without hands and swords of men? And this is of the number of pernicious errors: for they induce men, as oft as they like not their governors, to adhere to those that call them tyrants, and to think it lawful to raise war against them: and yet they are many times cherished from the pulpit, by the clergy. There is another error in their civil philosophy (which they never learned of Aristotle, nor Cicero, nor any other of the heathen), to extend the power of the law, which is the rule of actions only, to the very thoughts and consciences of men, by examination and inquisition of what they hold, notwithstanding the conformity of their speech and actions. By which men are either punished for answering the truth of their thoughts, or constrained to answer an untruth for fear of punishment. It is true that the civil magistrate, intending to employ a minister in the charge of teaching, may enquire of him if he be content to preach such and such doctrines; and, in case of refusal, may deny him the employment: but to force him to accuse himself of opinions, when his actions are not by law forbidden, is against the law of nature; and especially in them who teach that a man shall be damned to eternal and extreme torments, if he die in a false opinion concerning an article of the Christian faith. For who is there (that knowing there is so great danger in an error) whom the natural care of himself compelleth not to hazard his soul upon his own judgement, rather than that of any other man that is unconcerned in his damnation? For a private man, without the authority of the Commonwealth; that is to say, without permission from the representant thereof, to interpret the law by his own spirit, is another error in the politics: but not drawn from Aristotle, nor from any other of the heathen philosophers. For none of them deny but that in the power of making laws is comprehended also the power of explaining them when there is need. And are not the Scriptures, in all places where they are law, made law by the authority of the Commonwealth and, consequently, a part of the civil law? Of the same kind it is also when any but the sovereign restraineth in any man that power which the Commonwealth hath not restrained; as they do that impropriate the preaching of the gospel to one certain order of men, where the laws have left it free. If the state give me leave to preach or teach; that is, if it forbid me not, no man can forbid me. If I find myself amongst the idolaters of America, shall I that am a Christian, though not in orders, think it a sin to preach Jesus Christ, till I have received orders from Rome? Or when I have preached, shall not I answer their doubts and expound the Scriptures to them; that is, shall I not teach? But for this may some say, as also for administering to them the sacraments, the necessity shall be esteemed for a sufficient mission; which is true. But this is true also, that for whatsoever a dispensation is due for the necessity, for the same there needs no dispensation when there is no law that forbids it. Therefore to deny these functions to those to whom the civil sovereign hath not denied them is a taking away of a lawful liberty, which is contrary to the doctrine of civil government. More examples of vain philosophy, brought into religion by the doctors of School divinity, might be produced; but other men may if they please observe them of themselves. I shall only add this, that the writings of School divines are nothing else, for the most part, but insignificant trains of strange and barbarous words, or words otherwise used than in the common use of the Latin tongue; such as would pose Cicero, and Varro, and all the grammarians of ancient Rome. Which, if any man would see proved, let him (as I have said once before) see whether he can translate any School divine into any of the modern tongues, as French, English, or any other copious language: for that which cannot in most of these be made intelligible is not intelligible in the Latin. Which insignificancy of language, though I cannot note it for false philosophy, yet it hath a quality, not only to hide the truth, but also to make men think they have it, and desist from further search. Lastly, for the errors brought in from false or uncertain history, what is all the legend of fictitious miracles in the lives of the saints; and all the histories of apparitions and ghosts alleged by the doctors of the Roman Church, to make good their doctrines of hell and purgatory, the power of exorcism, and other doctrines which have no warrant, neither in reason nor Scripture; as also all those traditions which they call the unwritten word of God; but old wives' fables? Whereof, though they find dispersed somewhat in the writings of the ancient Fathers, yet those Fathers were men that might too easily believe false reports. And the producing of their opinions for testimony of the truth of what they believed hath no other force with them that, according to the counsel of St. John, [I John, 4. 1] examine spirits than in all things that concern the power of the Roman Church (the abuse whereof either they suspected not, or had benefit by it), to discredit their testimony in respect of too rash belief of reports; which the most sincere men without great knowledge of natural causes, such as the Fathers were, are commonly the most subject to: for naturally, the best men are the least suspicious of fraudulent purposes. Gregory the Pope and St. Bernard have somewhat of apparitions of ghosts that said they were in purgatory; and so has our Bede: but nowhere, I believe, but by report from others. But if they, or any other, relate any such stories of their own knowledge, they shall not thereby confirm the more such vain reports, but discover their own infirmity or fraud. With the introduction of false, we may join also the suppression of true philosophy by such men as neither by lawful authority nor sufficient study are competent judges of the truth. Our own navigations make manifest, and all men learned in human sciences now acknowledge, there are antipodes: and every day it appeareth more and more that years and days are determined by motions of the earth. Nevertheless, men that have in their writings but supposed such doctrine, as an occasion to lay open the reasons for and against it, have been punished for it by authority ecclesiastical. But what reason is there for it? Is it because such opinions are contrary to true religion? That cannot be, if they be true. Let therefore the truth be first examined by competent judges, or confuted by them that pretend to know the contrary. Is it because they be contrary to the religion established? Let them be silenced by the laws of those to whom the teachers of them are subject; that is, by the laws civil: for disobedience may lawfully be punished in them that against the laws teach even true philosophy. Is it because they tend to disorder in government, as countenancing rebellion or sedition? Then let them be silenced, and the teachers punished, by virtue of his power to whom the care of the public quiet is committed; which is the authority civil. For whatsoever power ecclesiastics take upon themselves (in any place where they are subject to the state) in their own right, though they call it God's right, is but usurpation.

## CHAPTER XLVII, OF THE BENEFIT THAT PROCEEDETH FROM SUCH DARKNESS, AND TO WHOM IT ACCRUETH

CICERO maketh honourable mention of one of the Cassii, a severe judge amongst the Romans, for a custom he had in criminal causes, when the testimony of the witnesses was not sufficient, to ask the accusers, cui bono; that is to say, what profit, honour, or other contentment the accused obtained or expected by the fact. For amongst presumptions, there is none that so evidently declareth the author as doth the benefit of the action. By the same rule I intend in this place to examine who they may be that have possessed the people so long in this part of Christendom with these doctrines contrary to the peaceable societies of mankind. And first, to this error that the present Church, now militant on earth, is the kingdom of God (that is, the kingdom of glory, or the land of promise; not the kingdom of grace, which is but a promise of the land), are annexed these worldly benefits: first, that the pastors and teachers of the Church are entitled thereby, as God's public ministers, to a right of governing the Church; and consequently, because the Church and Commonwealth are the same persons, to be rectors and governors of the Commonwealth. By this title it is that the Pope prevailed with the subjects of all Christian princes to believe that to disobey him was to disobey Christ himself; and in all differences between him and other princes (charmed with the word power spiritual) to abandon their lawful sovereigns; which is in effect a universal monarchy over all Christendom. For though they were first invested in the right of being supreme teachers of Christian doctrine, by and under Christian emperors within the limits of the Roman Empire (as is acknowledged by themselves), by the title of Pontifex Maximus, who was an officer subject to the civil state; yet after the Empire was divided and dissolved, it was not hard to obtrude upon the people already subject to them, another title, namely, the right of St. Peter; not only to save entire their pretended power, but also to extend the same over the same Christian provinces, though no more united in the Empire of Rome. This benefit of a universal monarchy, considering the desire of men to bear rule, is a sufficient presumption that the Popes that pretended to it, and for a long time enjoyed it, were the authors of the doctrine by which it was obtained; namely, that the Church now on earth is the kingdom of Christ. For that granted, it must be understood that Christ hath some lieutenant amongst us by whom we are to be told what are his commandments. After that certain Churches had renounced this universal power of the Pope, one would expect, in reason, that the civil sovereigns in all those Churches should have recovered so much of it as (before they had unadvisedly let it go) was their own right and in their own hands. And in England it was so in effect; saving that they by whom the kings administered the government of religion, by maintaining their employment to be in God's right, seemed to usurp, if not a supremacy, yet an independency on the civil power: and they but seemed to usurp it, inasmuch as they acknowledged a right in the king to deprive them of the exercise of their functions at his pleasure. But in those places where the presbytery took that office, though many other doctrines of the Church of Rome were forbidden to be taught; yet this doctrine, that the kingdom of Christ is already come, and that it began at the resurrection of our Saviour, was still retained. But cui bono? What profit did they expect from it? The same which the popes expected: to have a sovereign power over the people. For what is it for men to excommunicate their lawful king, but to keep him from all places of God's public service in his own kingdom; and with force to resist him when he with force endeavoureth to correct them? Or what is it, without authority from the civil sovereign, to excommunicate any person, but to take from him his lawful liberty, that is, to usurp an unlawful power over their brethren? The authors therefore of this darkness in religion are the Roman and the Presbyterian clergy. To this head, I refer also all those doctrines that serve them to keep the possession of this spiritual sovereignty after it is gotten. As first, that the Pope, in his public capacity, cannot err. For who is there that, believing this to be true, will not readily obey him in whatsoever he commands? Secondly, that all other bishops, in what Commonwealth soever, have not their right, neither immediately from God, nor mediately from their civil sovereigns, but from the Pope, is a doctrine by which there comes to be in every Christian Commonwealth many potent men (for so are Bishops) that have their dependence on the Pope, owe obedience to him, though he be a foreign prince; by which means he is able, as he hath done many times, to raise a civil war against the state that submits not itself to be governed according to his pleasure and interest. Thirdly, the exemption of these and of all other priests, and of all monks and friars, from the power of the civil laws. For by this means, there is a great part of every Commonwealth that enjoy the benefit of the laws and are protected by the power of the civil state, which nevertheless pay no part of the public expense; nor are liable to the penalties, as other subjects, due to their crimes; and, consequently, stand not in fear of any man, but the Pope; and adhere to him only, to uphold his universal monarchy. Fourthly, the giving to their priests (which is no more in the New Testament but presbyters, that is, elders) the name of sacerdotes, that is, sacrificers, which was the title of the civil sovereign, and his public ministers, amongst the Jews, whilst God was their king. Also, the making the Lord's Supper a sacrifice serveth to make the people believe the Pope hath the same power over all Christians that Moses and Aaron had over the Jews; that is to say, all power, both civil and ecclesiastical, as the high priest then had. Fifthly, the teaching that matrimony is a sacrament giveth to the clergy the judging of the lawfulness of marriages; and thereby, of what children are legitimate; and consequently, of the right of succession to hereditary kingdoms. Sixthly, the denial of marriage to priests serveth to assure this power of the Pope over kings. For if a king be a priest, he cannot marry and transmit his kingdom to his posterity; if he be not a priest, then the Pope pretendeth this authority ecclesiastical over him, and over his people. Seventhly, from auricular confession they obtain, for the assurance of their power, better intelligence of the designs of princes and great persons in the civil state than these can have of the designs of the state ecclesiastical. Eighthly, by the canonization of saints, and declaring who are martyrs, they assure their power in that they induce simple men into an obstinacy against the laws and commands of their civil sovereigns, even to death, if by the Pope's excommunication they be declared heretics or enemies to the Church; that is, as they interpret it, to the Pope. Ninthly, they assure the same, by the power they ascribe to every priest of making Christ; and by the power of ordaining penance, and of remitting and retaining of sins. Tenthly, by the doctrine of purgatory, of justification by external works, and of indulgences, the clergy is enriched. Eleventhly, by their demonology, and the use of exorcism, and other things appertaining thereto, they keep, or think they keep, the people more in awe of their power. Lastly, the metaphysics, ethics, and politics of Aristotle, the frivolous distinctions, barbarous terms, and obscure language of the Schoolmen, taught in the universities (which have been all erected and regulated by the Pope's authority), serve them to keep these errors from being detected, and to make men mistake the ignis fatuus of vain philosophy for the light of the Gospel. To these, if they sufficed not, might be added other of their dark doctrines, the profit whereof redoundeth manifestly to the setting up of an unlawful power over the lawful sovereigns of Christian people; or for the sustaining of the same when it is set up; or to the worldly riches, honour, and authority of those that sustain it. And therefore by the aforesaid rule of cui bono, we may justly pronounce for the authors of all this spiritual darkness, the Pope, and Roman clergy, and all those besides that endeavour to settle in the minds of men this erroneous doctrine, that the Church now on earth is that kingdom of God mentioned in the Old and New Testament. But the emperors, and other Christian sovereigns, under whose government these errors and the like encroachments of ecclesiastics upon their office at first crept in, to the disturbance of their possessions and of the tranquillity of their subjects, though they suffered the same for want of foresight of the sequel, and of insight into the designs of their teachers, may nevertheless be esteemed accessaries to their own and the public damage. For without their authority there could at first no seditious doctrine have been publicly preached. I say they might have hindered the same in the beginning: but when the people were once possessed by those spiritual men, there was no human remedy to be applied that any man could invent. And for the remedies that God should provide, who never faileth in His good time to destroy all the machinations of men against the truth, we are to attend His good pleasure that suffereth many times the prosperity of His enemies, together with their ambition, to grow to such a height as the violence thereof openeth the eyes, which the wariness of their predecessors had before sealed up, and makes men by too much grasping let go all, as Peter's net was broken by the struggling of too great a multitude of fishes; whereas the impatience of those that strive to resist such encroachment, before their subjects' eyes were opened, did but increase the power they resisted. I do not therefore blame the Emperor Frederick for holding the stirrup to our countryman Pope Adrian; for such was the disposition of his subjects then, as if he had not done it, he was not likely to have succeeded in the empire. But I blame those that, in the beginning, when their power was entire, by suffering such doctrines to be forged in the universities of their own dominions, have held the stirrup to all the succeeding popes, whilst they mounted into the thrones of all Christian sovereigns, to ride and tire both them and their people, at their pleasure. But as the inventions of men are woven, so also are they ravelled out; the way is the same, but the order is inverted. The web begins at the first elements of power, which are wisdom, humility, sincerity, and other virtues of the Apostles, whom the people, converted, obeyed out of reverence, not by obligation. Their consciences were free, and their words and actions subject to none but the civil power. Afterwards the presbyters, as the flocks of Christ increased, assembling to consider what they should teach, and thereby obliging themselves to teach nothing against the decrees of their assemblies, made it to be thought the people were thereby obliged to follow their doctrine, and, when they refused, refused to keep them company (that was then called excommunication), not as being infidels, but as being disobedient: and this was the first knot upon their liberty. And the number of presbyters increasing, the presbyters of the chief city or province got themselves an authority over the parochial presbyters, and appropriated to themselves the names of bishops: and this was a second knot on Christian liberty. Lastly, the bishop of Rome, in regard of the Imperial City, took upon him an authority (partly by the wills of the emperors themselves, and by the title of Pontifex Maximus, and at last when the emperors were grown weak, by the privileges of St. Peter) over all other bishops of the Empire: which was the third and last knot, and the whole synthesis and construction of the pontifical power. And therefore the analysis or resolution is by the same way, but beginneth with the knot that was last tied; as we may see in the dissolution of the preterpolitical Church government in England. First, the power of the popes was dissolved totally by Queen Elizabeth; and the bishops, who before exercised their functions in right of the Pope, did afterwards exercise the same in right of the Queen and her successors; though by retaining the phrase of jure divino they were thought to demand it by immediate right from God: and so was untied the first knot. After this, the Presbyterians lately in England obtained the putting down of Episcopacy: and so was the second knot dissolved. And almost at the same time, the power was taken also from the Presbyterians: and so we are reduced to the indepe

dency of the primitive Christians to follow Paul, or Cephas, or Apollos, every man as he liketh best: which if it be without contention, and without measuring the doctrine of Christ by our affection to the person of his minister (the fault which the Apostle reprehended in the Corinthians), is perhaps the best: first, because there ought to be no power over the consciences of men, but of the word itself, working faith in every one, not always according to the purpose of them that plant and water, but of God Himself, that giveth the increase. And secondly, because it is unreasonable in them, who teach there is such danger in every little error, to require of a man endued with reason of his own to follow the reason of any other man, or of the most voices of many other men, which is little better than to venture his salvation at cross and pile. Nor ought those teachers to be displeased with this loss of their ancient authority: for there is none should know better than they that power is preserved by the same virtues by which it is acquired; that is to say, by wisdom, humility, clearness of doctrine, and sincerity of conversation; and not by suppression of the natural sciences, and of the morality of natural reason; nor by obscure language; nor by arrogating to themselves more knowledge than they make appear; nor by pious frauds; nor by such other faults as in the pastors of God's Church are not only faults, but also scandals, apt to make men stumble one time or other upon the suppression of their authority. But after this doctrine, that the Church now militant is the kingdom of God spoken of in the Old and New Testament, was received in the world, the ambition and canvassing for the offices that belong thereunto, and especially for that great office of being Christ's lieutenant, and the pomp of them that obtained therein the principal public charges, became by degrees so evident that they lost the inward reverence due to the pastoral function: insomuch as the wisest men of them that had any power in the civil state needed nothing but the authority of their princes to deny them any further obedience. For, from the time that the Bishop of Rome had gotten to be acknowledged for bishop universal, by pretence of succession to St. Peter, their whole hierarchy, or kingdom of darkness, may be compared not unfitly to the kingdom of fairies; that is, to the old wives' fables in England concerning ghosts and spirits, and the feats they play in the night. And if a man consider the original of this great ecclesiastical dominion, he will easily perceive that the papacy is no other than the ghost of the deceased Roman Empire, sitting crowned upon the grave thereof: for so did the papacy start up on a sudden out of the ruins of that heathen power. The language also which they use, both in the churches and in their public acts, being Latin, which is not commonly used by any nation now in the world, what is it but the ghost of the old Roman language? The fairies in what nation soever they converse have but one universal king, which some poets of ours call King Oberon; but the Scripture calls Beelzebub, prince of demons. The ecclesiastics likewise, in whose dominions soever they be found, acknowledge but one universal king, the Pope. The ecclesiastics are spiritual men and ghostly fathers. The fairies are spirits and ghosts. Fairies and ghosts inhabit darkness, solitudes, and graves. The ecclesiastics walk in obscurity of doctrine, in monasteries, churches, and churchyards. The ecclesiastics have their cathedral churches, which, in what town soever they be erected, by virtue of holy water, and certain charms called exorcisms, have the power to make those towns, cities, that is to say, seats of empire. The fairies also have their enchanted castles, and certain gigantic ghosts, that domineer over the regions round about them. The fairies are not to be seized on, and brought to answer for the hurt they do. So also the ecclesiastics vanish away from the tribunals of civil justice. The ecclesiastics take from young men the use of reason, by certain charms compounded of metaphysics, and miracles, and traditions, and abused Scripture, whereby they are good for nothing else but to execute what they command them. The fairies likewise are said to take young children out of their cradles, and to change them into natural fools, which common people do therefore call elves, and are apt to mischief. In what shop or operatory the fairies make their enchantment, the old wives have not determined. But the operatories of the clergy are well enough known to be the universities, that received their discipline from authority pontifical. When the fairies are displeased with anybody, they are said to send their elves to pinch them. The ecclesiastics, when they are displeased with any civil state, make also their elves, that is, superstitious, enchanted subjects, to pinch their princes, by preaching sedition; or one prince, enchanted with promises, to pinch another. The fairies marry not; but there be amongst them incubi that have copulation with flesh and blood. The priests also marry not. The ecclesiastics take the cream of the land, by donations of ignorant men that stand in awe of them, and by tithes: so also it is in the fable of fairies, that they enter into the dairies, and feast upon the cream, which they skim from the milk. What kind of money is current in the kingdom of fairies is not recorded in the story. But the ecclesiastics in their receipts accept of the same money that we do; though when they are to make any payment, it is in canonizations, indulgences, and masses. To this and such like resemblances between the papacy and the kingdom of fairies may be added this, that as the fairies have no existence but in the fancies of ignorant people, rising from the traditions of old wives or old poets: so the spiritual power of the Pope (without the bounds of his own civil dominion) consisteth only in the fear that seduced people stand in of their excommunications, upon hearing of false miracles, false traditions, and false interpretations of the Scripture. It was not therefore a very difficult matter for Henry the Eighth by his exorcism; nor for Queen Elizabeth by hers, to cast them out. But who knows that this spirit of Rome, now gone out, and walking by missions through the dry places of China, Japan, and the Indies, that yield him little fruit, may not return; or rather, an assembly of spirits worse than he enter and inhabit this clean-swept house, and make the end thereof worse than the beginning? For it is not the Roman clergy only that pretends the kingdom of God to be of this world, and thereby to have a power therein, distinct from that of the civil state. And this is all I had a design to say, concerning the doctrine of the POLITICS. Which, when I have reviewed, I shall willingly expose it to the censure of my country.


## A REVIEW AND CONCLUSION


FROM the contrariety of some of the natural faculties of the mind, one to another, as also of one passion to another, and from their reference to conversation, there has been an argument taken to infer an impossibility that any one man should be sufficiently disposed to all sorts of civil duty. The severity of judgement, they say, makes men censorious and unapt to pardon the errors and infirmities of other men: and on the other side, celerity of fancy makes the thoughts less steady than is necessary to discern exactly between right and wrong. Again, in all deliberations, and in all pleadings, the faculty of solid reasoning is necessary: for without it, the resolutions of men are rash, and their sentences unjust: and yet if there be not powerful eloquence, which procureth attention and consent, the effect of reason will be little. But these are contrary faculties; the former being grounded upon principles of truth; the other upon opinions already received, true or false; and upon the passions and interests of men, which are different and mutable. And amongst the passions, courage (by which I mean the contempt of wounds and violent death) inclineth men to private revenges, and sometimes to endeavour the unsettling of the public peace: and timorousness many times disposeth to the desertion of the public defence. Both these, they say, cannot stand together in the same person. And to consider the contrariety of men's opinions and manners in general, it is, they say, impossible to entertain a constant civil amity with all those with whom the business of the world constrains us to converse: which business consisteth almost in nothing else but a perpetual contention for honour, riches, and authority. To which I answer that these are indeed great difficulties, but not impossibilities: for by education and discipline, they may be, and are sometimes, reconciled. Judgement and fancy may have place in the same man; but by turns; as the end which he aimeth at requireth. As the Israelites in Egypt were sometimes fastened to their labour of making bricks, and other times were ranging abroad to gather straw: so also may the judgement sometimes be fixed upon one certain consideration, and the fancy at another time wandering about the world. So also reason and eloquence (though not perhaps in the natural sciences, yet in the moral) may stand very well together. For wheresoever there is place for adorning and preferring of error, there is much more place for adorning and preferring of truth, if they have it to adorn. Nor is there any repugnancy between fearing the laws, and not fearing a public enemy; nor between abstaining from injury, and pardoning it in others. There is therefore no such inconsistence of human nature with civil duties, as some think. I have known clearness of judgement, and largeness of fancy; strength of reason, and graceful elocution; a courage for the war, and a fear for the laws, and all eminently in one man; and that was my most noble and honoured friend, Mr. Sidney Godolphin; who, hating no man, nor hated of any, was unfortunately slain in the beginning of the late civil war, in the public quarrel, by an undiscerned and an undiscerning hand. To the Laws of Nature declared in the fifteenth Chapter, I would have this added: that every man is bound by nature, as much as in him lieth, to protect in war the authority by which he is himself protected in time of peace. For he that pretendeth a right of nature to preserve his own body, cannot pretend a right of nature to destroy him by whose strength he is preserved: it is a manifest contradiction of himself. And though this law may be drawn by consequence from some of those that are there already mentioned, yet the times require to have it inculcated and remembered. And because I find by diverse English books lately printed that the civil wars have not yet sufficiently taught men in what point of time it is that a subject becomes obliged to the conqueror; nor what is conquest; nor how it comes about that it obliges men to obey his laws: therefore for further satisfaction of men therein, I say, the point of time wherein a man becomes subject to a conqueror is that point wherein, having liberty to submit to him, he consenteth, either by express words or by other sufficient sign, to be his subject. When it is that a man hath the liberty to submit, I have shown before in the end of the twenty-first Chapter; namely, that for him that hath no obligation to his former sovereign but that of an ordinary subject, it is then when the means of his life is within the guards and garrisons of the enemy; for it is then that he hath no longer protection from him, but is protected by the adverse party for his contribution. Seeing therefore such contribution is everywhere, as a thing inevitable, notwithstanding it be an assistance to the enemy, esteemed lawful; a total submission, which is but an assistance to the enemy, cannot be esteemed unlawful. Besides, if a man consider that they submit, assist the enemy but with part of their estates, whereas they that refuse, assist him with the whole, there is no reason to call their submission or composition an assistance, but rather a detriment, to the enemy. But if a man, besides the obligation of a subject, hath taken upon him a new obligation of a soldier, then he hath not the liberty to submit to a new power, as long as the old one keeps the field and giveth him means of subsistence, either in his armies or garrisons: for in this case, he cannot complain of want of protection and means to live as a soldier. But when that also fails, a soldier also may seek his protection wheresoever he has most hope to have it, and may lawfully submit himself to his new master. And so much for the time when he may do it lawfully, if he will. It therefore he do it, he is undoubtedly bound to be a true subject: for a contract lawfully made cannot lawfully be broken. By this also a man may understand when it is that men may be said to be conquered; and in what the nature of conquest, and the right of a conqueror consisteth: for this submission is it implieth them all. Conquest is not the victory itself; but the acquisition, by victory, of a right over the persons of men. He therefore that is slain is overcome, but not conquered: he that is taken and put into prison or chains is not conquered, though overcome; for he is still an enemy, and may save himself if he can: but he that upon promise of obedience hath his life and liberty allowed him, is then conquered and a subject; and not before. The Romans used to say that their general had pacified such a province, that is to say, in English, conquered it; and that the country was pacified by victory when the people of it had promised imperata facere, that is, to do what the Roman people commanded them: this was to be conquered. But this promise may be either express or tacit: express, by promise; tacit, by other signs. As, for example, a man that hath not been called to make such an express promise, because he is one whose power perhaps is not considerable; yet if he live under their protection openly, he is understood to submit himself to the government: but if he live there secretly, he is liable to anything that may be done to a spy and enemy of the state. I say not, he does any injustice (for acts of open hostility bear not that name); but that he may be justly put to death. Likewise, if a man, when his country is conquered, be out of it, he is not conquered, nor subject: but if at his return he submit to the government, he is bound to obey it. So that conquest, to define it, is the acquiring of the right of sovereignty by victory. Which right is acquired in the people's submission, by which they contract with the victor, promising obedience, for life and liberty. In the twenty-ninth Chapter I have set down for one of the causes of the dissolutions of Commonwealths their imperfect generation, consisting in the want of an absolute and arbitrary legislative power; for want whereof, the civil sovereign is fain to handle the sword of justice unconstantly, and as if it were too hot for him to hold: one reason whereof (which I have not there mentioned) is this, that they will all of them justify the war by which their power was at first gotten, and whereon, as they think, their right dependeth, and not on the possession. As if, for example, the right of the kings of England did depend on the goodness of the cause of William the Conqueror, and upon their lineal and directest descent from him; by which means, there would perhaps be no tie of the subjects' obedience to their sovereign at this day in all the world: wherein whilst they needlessly think to justify themselves, they justify all the successful rebellions that ambition shall at any time raise against them and their successors. Therefore I put down for one of the most effectual seeds of the death of any state, that the conquerors require not only a submission of men's actions to them for the future, but also an approbation of all their actions past; when there is scarce a Commonwealth in the world whose beginnings can in conscience be justified. And because the name of tyranny signifieth nothing more nor less than the name of sovereignty, be it in one or many men, saving that they that use the former word are understood to be angry with them they call tyrants; I think the toleration of a professed hatred of tyranny is a toleration of hatred to Commonwealth in general, and another evil seed, not differing much from the former. For to the justification of the cause of a conqueror, the reproach of the cause of the conquered is for the most part necessary: but neither of them necessary for the obligation of the conquered. And thus much I have thought fit to say upon the review of the first and second part of this discourse. In the thirty-fifth Chapter, I have sufficiently declared out of the Scripture that in the Commonwealth of the Jews, God Himself was made the Sovereign, by pact with the people; who were therefore called His "peculiar people," to distinguish them from the rest of the world, over whom God reigned, not by their consent, but by His own power: and that in this kingdom Moses was God's lieutenant on earth; and that it was he that told them what laws God appointed them to be ruled by. But I have omitted to set down who were the officers appointed to do execution; especially in capital punishments; not then thinking it a matter of so necessary consideration as I find it since. We know that generally in all Commonwealths, the execution of corporeal punishments was either put upon the guards, or other soldiers of the sovereign power, or given to those in whom want of means, contempt of honour, and hardness of heart concurred to make them sue for such an office. But amongst the Israelites it was a positive law of God their Sovereign that he that was convicted of a capital crime should be stoned to death by the people; and that the witnesses should cast the first stone, and after the witnesses, then the rest of the people. This was a law that designed who were to be the executioners; but not that any one should throw a stone at him before conviction and sentence, where the congregation was judge. The witnesses were nevertheless to be heard before they proceeded to execution, unless the fact were committed in the presence of the congregation itself, or in sight of the lawful judges; for then there needed no other witnesses but the judges themselves. Nevertheless, this manner of proceeding, being not thoroughly understood, hath given occasion to a dangerous opinion, that any man may kill another, in some cases, by a right of zeal; as if the executions done upon offenders in the kingdom of God in old time proceeded not from the sovereign command, but from the authority of private zeal: which, if we consider the texts that seem to favour it, is quite contrary. First, where the Levites fell upon the people that had made and worshipped the golden calf, and slew three thousand of them, it was by the commandment of Moses from the mouth of God; as is manifest, Exodus, 32. 27. And when the son of a woman of Israel had blasphemed God, they that heard it did not kill him, but brought him before Moses, who put him under custody, till God should give sentence against him; as appears, Leviticus, 24. 11, 12. Again, when Phinehas killed Zimri and Cozbi, [Numbers, 25. 6, 7] it was not by right of private zeal: their crime was committed in the sight of the assembly; there needed no witness; the law was known, and he the heir apparent to the sovereignty; and, which is the principal point, the lawfulness of his act depended wholly upon a subsequent ratification by Moses, whereof he had no cause to doubt. And this presumption of a future ratification is sometimes necessary to the safety of a Commonwealth; as in a sudden rebellion any man that can suppress it by his own power in the country where it begins, without express law or commission, may lawfully do it, and provide to have it ratified, or pardoned, whilst it is in doing, or after it is done. Also, it is expressly said, "Whosoever shall kill the murderer shall kill him upon the word of witnesses":[Ibid., 35. 30] but witnesses suppose a formal judicature, and consequently condemn that pretence of jus zelotarum. The Law of Moses concerning him that enticeth to idolatry, that is to say, in the kingdom of God to a renouncing of his allegiance, forbids to conceal him, and commands the accuser to cause him to be put to death, and to cast the first stone at him; [Deuteronomy, 13. 8] but not to kill him before he be condemned. And the process against idolatry is exactly set down: for God there speaketh to the people as Judge, and commandeth them, when a man is accused of idolatry, to enquire diligently of the fact, and finding it true, then to stone him; but still the hand of the witness throweth the first stone. [Ibid., 17. 4, 5, 6] This is not private zeal, but public condemnation. In like manner when a father hath a rebellious son, the law is that he shall bring him before the judges of the town, and all the people of the town shall stone him. [Ibid., 21. 18-21] Lastly, by pretence of these laws it was that St. Stephen was stoned, and not by pretence of private zeal: for before he was carried away to execution, he had pleaded his cause before the high priest. There is nothing in all this, nor in any other part of the Bible, to countenance executions by private zeal; which, being oftentimes but a conjunction of ignorance and passion, is against both the justice and peace of a Commonwealth. In the thirty-sixth Chapter I have said that it is not declared in what manner God spoke supernaturally to Moses: not that He spoke not to him sometimes by dreams and visions, and by a supernatural voice, as to other prophets; for the manner how He spoke unto him from the mercy seat is expressly set down in these words, "From that time forward, when Moses entered into Tabernacle of the congregation to speak with God, he heard a voice which spake unto him from over the mercy seat, which is over the Ark of the testimony; from between the cherubims he spake unto him." [Numbers, 7. 89] But it is not declared in what consisted the pre-eminence of the manner of God's speaking to Moses, above that of His speaking to other prophets, as to Samuel and to Abraham, to whom He also spoke by a voice (that is, by vision), unless the difference consist in the clearness of the vision. For "face to face," and "mouth to mouth," cannot be literally understood of the infiniteness and incomprehensibility of the Divine Nature. And as to the whole doctrine, I see not yet, but the principles of it are true and proper, and the ratiocination solid. For I ground the civil right of sovereigns, and both the duty and liberty of subjects, upon the known natural inclinations of mankind, and upon the articles of the law of nature; of which no man, that pretends but reason enough to govern his private family, ought to be ignorant. And for the power ecclesiastical of the same sovereigns, I ground it on such texts as are both evident in themselves and consonant to the scope of the whole Scripture, and therefore am persuaded that he that shall read it with a purpose only to be informed, shall be informed by it. But for those that by writing or public discourse, or by their eminent actions, have already engaged themselves to the maintaining of contrary opinions, they will not be so easily satisfied. For in such cases, it is natural for men, at one and the same time, both to proceed in reading and to lose their attention in the search of objections to that they had read before: of which, in a time wherein the interests of men are changed (seeing much of that doctrine which serveth to the establishing of a new government must needs be contrary to that which conduced to the dissolution of the old), there cannot choose but be very many.

In that part which treateth of a Christian Commonwealth, there are some new doctrines which, it may be, in a state where the contrary were already fully determined, were a fault for a subject without leave to divulge, as being a usurpation of the place of a teacher. But in this time that men call not only for peace, but also for truth, to offer such doctrines as I think true, and that manifestly tend to peace and loyalty, to the consideration of those that are yet in deliberation, is no more but to offer new wine, to be put into new casks, that both may be preserved together. And I suppose that then, when novelty can breed no trouble nor disorder in a state, men are not generally so much inclined to the reverence of antiquity as to prefer ancient errors before new and well-proved truth. There is nothing I distrust more than my elocution, which nevertheless I am confident (excepting the mischances of the press) is not obscure. That I have neglected the ornament of quoting ancient poets, orators, and philosophers, contrary to the custom of late time, whether I have done well or ill in it, proceedeth from my judgement, grounded on many reasons. For first, all truth of doctrine dependeth either upon reason or upon Scripture; both which give credit to many, but never receive it from any writer. Secondly, the matters in question are not of fact, but of right, wherein there is no place for witnesses. There is scarce any of those old writers that contradicteth not sometimes both himself and others; which makes their testimonies insufficient. Fourthly, such opinions as are taken only upon credit of antiquity are not intrinsically the judgement of those that cite them, but words that pass, like gaping, from mouth to mouth. Fifthly, it is many times with a fraudulent design that men stick their corrupt doctrine with the cloves of other men's wit. Sixthly, I find not that the ancients they cite took it for an ornament to do the like with those that wrote before them. Seventhly, it is an argument of indigestion, when Greek and Latin sentences unchewed come up again, as they use to do, unchanged. Lastly, though I reverence those men of ancient time that either have written truth perspicuously, or set us in a better way to find it out ourselves; yet to the antiquity itself I think nothing due. For if we will reverence the age, the present is the oldest: if the antiquity of the writer, I am not sure that generally they to whom such honour is given, were more ancient when they wrote than I am that am writing: but if it be well considered, the praise of ancient authors proceeds not from the reverence of the dead, but from the competition and mutual envy of the living. To conclude, there is nothing in this whole discourse, nor in that I wrote before of the same subject in Latin, as far as I can perceive, contrary either to the word of God or to good manners; or to the disturbance of the public tranquillity. Therefore I think it may be profitably printed, and more profitably taught in the Universities, in case they also think so, whom the judgement of the same belongeth. For seeing the Universities are the fountains of civil and moral doctrine, from whence the preachers and the gentry, drawing such water as they find, use to sprinkle the same (both from the pulpit and in their conversation) upon the people, there ought certainly to be great care taken, to have it pure, both from the venom of heathen politicians, and from the incantation of deceiving spirits. And by that means the most men, knowing their duties, will be the less subject to serve the ambition of a few discontented persons in their purposes against the state, and be the less grieved with the contributions necessary for their peace and defence; and the governors themselves have the less cause to maintain at the common charge any greater army than is necessary to make good the public liberty against the invasions and encroachments of foreign enemies. And thus I have brought to an end my discourse of civil and ecclesiastical government, occasioned by the disorders of the present time, without partiality, without application, and without other design than to set before men's eyes the mutual relation between protection and obedience; of which the condition of human nature, and the laws divine, both natural and positive, require an inviolable observation. And though in the revolution of states there can be no very good constellation for truths of this nature to be born under (as having an angry aspect from the dissolvers of an old government, and seeing but the backs of them that erect a new); yet I cannot think it will be condemned at this time, either by the public judge of doctrine, or by any that desires the continuance of public peace. And in this hope I return to my interrupted speculation of bodies natural; wherein, if God give me health to finish it, I hope the novelty will as much please as in the doctrine of this artificial body it useth to offend. For such truth as opposeth no man's profit nor pleasure is to all men welcome.


THE END.

**The Two Treatises of Government from 1689**


In the Former, The False Principles and Foundation of Sir Robert Filmer, and His Followers, Are Detected and Overthrown: The Latter, Is an Essay Concerning the Original, Extent, and End, of Civil Government

by John Locke


**The Frist Treatise**


Reader.

Thou hast here the beginning and end of a discourse concerning government; what fate has otherwise disposed of the papers that should have filled up the middle, and were more than all the rest, it is not worth while to tell thee. These which remain I hope are sufficient to establish the throne of our great restorer, our present king William; to make good his title in else consent of the people; which being the only one of all lawful governments, he has more fully and clearly than any prince in Christendom; and to justify to the world the people of England, whose love of their just and natural rights? with their resolution to preserve them, saved the nation when it war on the very brink of slavery and ruin. If these papers have that evidence I flatter myself is to be found in them, there will be no great miss of those which are lost, and my reader may be satisfied without them. For I imagine I shall have neither the time nor inclination to repeat my pains, and fill up the wanting part of my answer, by tracing sir Robert again through all the windings and obscurities which are to be met with in the several branches of his wonderful system. The king, and body of the nation, have since so thoroughly confuted his hypothesis, that I suppose nobody hereafter will have either the confidence to appear against our common safety, and be again an advocate for slavery; or the weakness to be deceived with contradictions dressed up in a popular style and well turned periods. For if any one will be at the pains himself, in those parts which are here untouched, to strip sir Robert's discourses of the flourish of doubtful expressions, and endeavour to reduce his words to direct, positive, intelligible propositions, and then compare them one with another, he will quickly be satisfied there was never so much glib nonsense put together in well sounding English. If he think it not worth while to examine his works all through, let him make an experiment in that part where he treats of usurpation; and let him try whether he can, with all his skill, make sir Robert intelligible and consistent with himself, or common sense. I should not speak so plainly of a gentleman, long since past answering, had not the pulpit, of late years, publicly owned his doctrine, and made it the current divinity of the times. It is necessary those men who, taking on them to be teachers, have so dangerously misled others, should be openly showed of what authority this their patriarch is, whom they have so blindly followed; that so they may either retract what upon so ill grounds they have vented, and cannot be maintained; or else justify those principles which they have preached up for Gospel, though they had no better an author than an English courtier. For I should not have writ against sir Robert, or taken the pains to show his mistakes, inconsistencies, and avant of (what he so much boasts of, and pretends wholly to build on) Scripture-proofs, were there not men amongst us who, by crying up his books, and espousing his doctrine, save me from the reproach of writing against a dead adversary. They have been so zealous in this point, that if I have done him any wrong, I cannot hope they should spare me. I wish, where they have done the truth and the public wrong, they would be as ready to redress it, and allow its just weight to this reflection, viz., that there cannot be done a greater mischief to prince and people, than the propagating wrong notions concerning government; that so at last all times might not have reason to complain of the "drum ecclesiastic." If any one really concerned for truth undertake the confutation of my hypothesis, I promise him either to recant my mistake, upon fair conviction, or to answer his difficulties. But he must remember two things. First, That cavilling here and there at some expression or little incident of my discourse, is not an answer to my book. Secondly, That I shall not take railing for arguments, nor think either of these worth my notice: though I shall always look on myself as bound to give satisfaction to any one who shall appear to be conscientiously scrupulous in the point, and shall show any just grounds for his scruples. I have nothing more but to advertise the reader, that A. stands for our author, O. for his Observations on Hobbes, Milton, &c. And that a bare quotation of pages always means pages of his Patriarcha, edit. 1680.

**Chapter I**

**§1.**

Slavery is so vile and miserable an estate of man, and so directly opposite to the generous temper and courage of our nation, that it is hardly to be conceived that an Englishman, much less a gentleman, should plead for it. And truly I should have taken sir Robert Filmer's Patriarcha, as any other treatise, which would persuade all mere that they are slaves, and ought to be so, for such another exercise of wit as was his who writ the encomium of Nero; rather than for a serious discourse, meant in earnest: had not the gravity of the title and epistle, the picture in the front of the book, and the applause that followed it, required me to believe that the author and publisher were both in earnest. I therefore took it into my hands with all the expectation, and read it through with all the attention due to a treatise that made such a noise at its coming abroad; and cannot but confess myself mightily surprised that in a book, which was to provide chains for all mankind, I should find nothing but a rope of sand; useful perhaps to such whose skill and business it is to wise a dust, and would blind the people, the better to mislead them; but in truth not of any force to draw those into bondage who have their eyes open, and so much sense about them, as to consider that chains are but an ill wearing, how much care soever hath been taken to file and polish them.

**§2.**

If any one think I take too much liberty in speaking so freely of a man who is the great champion of absolute power, and the idol of those who worship it; I beseech him to make this small allowance for once, to one who, even after the reading of sir Robert's book, cannot but think himself; as the laws allow him a free man: and I know no fault it is to do so, unless any one, better skilled in the fate of it than I, should have it revealed to him that this treatise, which has lain dormant so long, was, The False Principles and Foundation of Sir Robert Filmer, and His Followers, Are Detected and Overthrown plan it appeared in the world, to carry, by strength of its arguments, all liberty out or it; and that, from thenceforth, our author's short model was to be the pattern in the mount, and the perfect standard of politics for the future. His system lies in a little compass; it is no more but this, "That all government is absolute monarchy." And the ground he builds on is this. "That no man is born free."

**§3.**

In this last age a generation of men has sprung up amongst us, that would flatter princes with an opinion, that they have a divine right to absolute power, let the laws by which they are constituted and are to govern, and the conditions under which they enter upon their authority, be what they will; and their engagements to observe them ever so well ratified by solemn oaths and promises. To make way for this doctrine, they have denied mankind a right to natural freedom; whereby they have not only, as much as in them lies, exposed all subjects to the utmost misery of tyranny and oppression, but have also unsettled the titles and shaken the thrones of princes: (for they too, by these men's system, except only one, are all born slaves, and by divine right are subjects to Adam's right heir); as if they had designed to make war upon all government, and subvert the very foundations of human society, to serve their present turn.

§4.

However we must believe them upon their own bare words, when they tell us, "We are all born slaves, and we must continue so;" there is no remedy for it; life and thraldom we entered into together, and can never be quit of the one till we part with the other. Scripture or reason, I am sure, do not any where say so, notwithstanding the noise of divine right, as if divine authority hath subjected us to the unlimited will of another. An admirable state of mankind, and that which they have not lead wit enough to find out till this latter age! For however sir Robert Filmier seems to condemn the novelty of the contrary opinion, Patr. p. 3, yet I believe it will be hard for him to find any other age, or country of the world, but this, which has asserted monarchy to be jure divine. And he confesses, Patr. p. 4, that "Heyward, Blackwood, Barclay, and others, that have bravely vindicated the right of kings in most points, never thought of this; but, with one consent, admitted the natural liberty and equality of mankind."

§5.

By whom this doctrine came at first to be broached, and brought in fashion amongst us, and what sad elects it gave rise to, I leave to historians to relate, or to the memory of those who were contemporaries with Sibthorp and Manwaring to recollect. My business at present is only to consider what sir Robert Filmer, who is allowed to have carried this argument farthest, and is supposed to have brought it to perfection, has said in it: for from him every one, who would be as fashionable as French was at court, has learned and runs away with this short system of politics, viz., "Men are not born free, and therefore could never have the liberty to choose either governors, or forms of government." Princes have their power absolute, and by divine right; for slaves could never have a right to compact or consent. Adam was an absolute monarch, and so are all princes ever since.

**Chapter II, Of paternal and regal Power.**

§6.

Sir Robert Filmer's great position is, that "men are not naturally free." This is the foundation on which his absolute monarchy stands, and from which it erects itself to an height, that its power is above every power: caput inter nubila, so high above all earthly and human things, that thought can scarce reach it; that promises and oaths, which tie the infinite Deity, cannot confine it. But if this foundation fails, all his fabric falls with it, and governments must be left again to the old way of being made by contrivance and the consent of men making use of their reason to unite together into society. To prove this grand position of his, he tells us, p. 12, "Men are born in subjection to their parents," and therefore cannot be free. And this authority of parents he calls "royal authority," p. 12,14, "fatherly authority, right of fatherhood," p. 12, 20. One would have thought he would, in the beginning of such a work as this, on which was to depend the authority of princes, and the obedience of subjects, have told us expressly what that fatherly authority is, have definer it, though not limited it, because in some other treatises of his he tells us, it is unlimited, and unlimitable;1 he should at least have given us such an account of it, that we might have had an entire notion of this fatherhood, or fatherly authority, whenever it came in our way, in his writings: this I expected to have found in the first chapter of his Patriarchal But instead thereof, having, 1. En passant, made his obeisance to the arcana imperii, p. 5; 2. Made his compliment to the "rights and liberties of this or any other nation," p. 6, which he is going presently to null and destroy; and 3. Made his leg to those learned men who did not see so far into the matter as himself; p. 7: he comes to fall on Bellarmine, p. 8, and by a victory over him establishes his fatherly authority beyond any question. Bellarmine being routed by his own confession, p. 11, the day is clear got, and there is no more need of any forces: for having done that, I observe not that he states the question, or rallies up any arguments to make good his opinion, but rather tells us the story as he thinks fit of this strange kind of domineering phantom called the fatherhood, which whoever could catch presently got empire, and unlimited absolute power. He acquaints us how this fatherhood liege in Adam, continued its course, and kept the world in order all the time of the patriarchs till the flood; got out of the ark with Noah and his sons, made and supported all the kings of the earth till the captivity of the Israelites in Egypt; and then the poor fatherhood was under hatches, till "God, by giving the Israelites kings, re-established the ancient and prime right of the lineal succession in paternal government." This is his business from p. 12 to 19. And then, obviating au objection, and clearing a difficulty or two with one-half reason, p. 23, "to confirm the natural right of regal power," he ends the first chapter. I hope it is no injury to call an half quotation an half reason; for God says, "Honour thy father and mother;" but our author contents himself with half, leaves out "thy mother" quite, as little serviceable to his purpose. But of that more in another place.

## §7.

I do not think our author so little skilled in the way of writing discourses of this nature, nor so careless of the point in hand, that he by oversight commits the fault that he himself, in his "anarchy of a mixed monarchy," p. 239, objects to Mr. Hunton in these words: "Where first I charge the A. that he hath not given us any definition or description of monarchy in general; for by the rules of method he should have first defined." And by the like rule of method, sir Robert should have told us what his fatherhood, or fatherly authority is, before he had told us in whom it w as to be found, and talked so much of it. But, perhaps, sir Robert found, that this fatherly authority, this power of fathers, and of kings, for he makes them both the same, p. 24, would make a very odd and frightful figure, and very disagreeing with what either children imagine of their parents, or subjects of their kings, if he should have given us the whole draught together, in that gigantic form he had painted it in his own fancy; and therefore, like a wary physician, when he would have his patient swallow some harsh or corrosive liquor, he mingles it with a large quantity of that which may dilute it, that the scattered parts may go down with less feeling, and cause less aversion.

## §8.

Let us then endeavour to find what account he gives us of this  fatherly authority, as it lies scattered in the several parts of his writings. And first, as it was vested in Adam, he says, "Not only Adam, but the succeeding patriarchs, had, by right of fatherhood, royal authority over their children, p. 12. This lordship, which Adam by command had over the wholes world, and by right descending from him the patriarchs did enjoy, was as large and ample as the absolute dominion of any monarch which hath been since the creation, p. 15. Dominion of life and death, making war, and concluding peace, p. 13. Adam and the patriarchs had absolute power of life and death, p. 35. Kings, in the right of parents, succeed to the exercise of supreme jurisdiction, p. 19. As kingly power is by the law of God, so it hath no inferior law to limit it; Adam was lord of all, p. 40. The father of a family governs by no other law than by his own will, p. 78. The superiority of princes is above laws, p. 79. The unlimited jurisdiction of kings is so amply described by Samuel, p. 80. Kings are above the laws," p. 93. And to this purpose see a great deal more, which our A. delivers in Bodin's words: "It is certain, that all laws, privileges, and grants of princes, have no force but during their life, if they be not ratified by the express consent, or by sufferance of the prince following, especially privileges, O. p. 279. The reason why laws have been also made by kings, was this: when kings were either busied with wars, or distracted with public cares, so that every private man could not have access to their persons, to learn their wills and pleasure, then were laws of necessity invented, that so every particular subject might find his prince's pleasure deciphered unto him in the tables of his laws, p. 92. In a monarchy, the lying must by necessity be above the laws, p. 100. A perfect kingdom is that, wherein the king rules all things, according to his own will, p. 100. Neither common nor statute laws are, or can be, any diminution of that general power, which kings have over their peon pie, by right of fatherhood, p. 115. Adam was the father, king, and lord over his family; a son, a subject, and a servant or slave, were one and the same thing at first. The father had power to dispose or sell his children or servants; whence we find, that, in the first reckoning up of goods in Scripture, the man-servant and the maid-servant are numbered among the possessions and substance of the owner, as other goods were, O. pref. God also hath given to the father a right or liberty to alien his power over his children to any other; whence we find the sale and gift of children to have been much in use in the beginning of the world, when men had their servants for a possession and an inheritance, as well as other goods; whereupon we find the power of castrating and making eunuchs much in use in old times, O. p. 155. Law is nothing else but the will of him that hath the power of the supreme father, O. p. 223. It was God's ordinance that the supremacy should be unlimited in Adam, and as large as all the acts of his will; and as in him, so in all others that have supreme power," O. p. 245.

## §9.

I have been fain to trouble my reader with these several quotations in our A.'s own words, that in them might be seen his own description of his fatherly authority, as it lies scattered up and down in his writings, which he supposes was first vested in Adam, and by right belongs to all princes ever since. This fatherly authority there, or right of fatherhood, in our A.'s sense, is a divine unalterable right of sovereignty, whereby a father or a prince hath an absolute, arbitrary, unlimited, and unlimitable power over the lives, liberties, and estates of his children and subjects; so that he may take or alienate their estates, sell, castrate, or use their persons as he pleases, they being all his slaves, and he lord or proprietor of every thing, and his unbounded will their law.

## §10.

Our A. having placed such a mighty power in Adam, and upon that supposition founded all government and all power of princes, it is reasonable to expect that he should have proved this with arguments clear and evident, suitable to the weightiness of the cause. That since men had nothing else left them, they might in slavery have such undeniable proofs of its necessity, that their consciences might be convinced, and oblige them to submit peaceably to that absolute dominion, which their governors had a right to exercise over them. Without this, what good could our A. do, or pretend to do, by erecting such an unlimited power, but flatter the natural vanity and ambition of men, too apt of itself to grow and increase with the possession of any power? And by persuading those, who, by the consent of their fellow-men, are advanced to great but limited degrees of it, that by that part which is given them, they have a right to all that was not so; and therefore may do what they please, because they have authority to do more than others, and so tempt them to do what is neither for their own, nor the good of those under their care; whereby great mischief cannot but follow.

## §11.

The sovereignty of Adam being that on which, as a sure basis, our A. builds his mighty absolute monarchy, I expected, that, in his Patriarcha, this his main supposition would have been proved and established with all that evidence of arguments that such a fundamental tenet required; and that this, which the great stress of the business depends, would have been made out, with reasons sufficient to justify the confidence with which it was assumed. But, In all that treatise, I could find very little tending that way; the thing is there so taken for granted, without proof, that I could scarce believe myself, when, upon attentive reading that treatise, I found there so mighty a structure raised upon the bare supposition of this foundation. For it is scarce credible, that in a discourse, where he pretends to confute the erroneous principle of man's natural freedom, he should do it by a bare supposition of Adam's authority, without offering any proof for that authority. Indeed, he confidently says, that Adam had "royal authority, p. 12 and 13. Absolute lordship and dominion of life and death, p. 13. An universal monarchy, p. 83. Absolute power of life and death," p. 35. He is very frequent in such assertions; but, what is strange, in all his whole Patriarcha, I find not one presence of a reason to establish this his great foundation of government; not any thing that looks like an argument, but these words: "To confirm this natural right of regal power, we find in the decalogue, that the law which enjoins obedience to kings, is delivered ill the terms, Honour thy father; as if all power were originally in the father." And why may I not add as well, that in the decalogue the law that enjoins obedience to queens, is delivered in the terms of "Honour thy mother," as if all power were originally in the mother? The argument, as sir Robert puts it, will hold as well for one as the other; but of this more in its due place.

## §12.

All that I take notice of here is, that this is all our A. says, in this first, or any of the following chapters, to prove the absolute power of Adam, which is his great principle: and yet, as if he had there settled it upon sure demonstration, he begins his second chapter with these words, "By conferring these proofs and reasons, drawn from the authority of the Scripture." Where those proofs and reasons for Adam's sovereignty are, bating that of Honour thy father, above-mentioned, I confess, I cannot find; unless what he says, p. 11, "In these words we have an evident confession," viz., of Bellarmine, "that creation made man prince of his posterity," must be taken for proofs and reasons drawn from Scripture, or for any sort of proof at all: though from thence, by a new way of inference, in the words immediately following, he concludes the royal authority of Adam sufficiently settled in him.

## §13.

If he has in that chapter, or any where in the whole treatise, given any other proofs of Adam's royal authority, other than by often repeating it, which, among some men, goes for argument, I desire any body for him to show me the place and page, that I may be convinced of my mistake, and acknowledge my oversight. If no such arguments are to be found, I beseech those men, who have so much cried up this book, to consider, whether they do not give the world cause to suspect that it is not the force of reason and argument that makes them for absolute monarchy, but some other by interest, and therefore are resolved to applaud any author that writes in favour of this doctrine, whether he support it with reason or no. But I hope they do not expect, that rational and indifferent men should be brought over to their opinion, because this their great doctor of it, In a discourse made on purpose to set up the absolute monarchical power of Adam, in opposition to the natural freedom of mankind, has said so little to prove it, from whence it is rather naturally to be concluded, that there is little to be said.

## §14.

But that I might omit no care to inform myself in our author's full sense, I consulted his Observations on Aristotle, Hobbes, &c. to see whether in disputing with others he made use of any arguments for this his darling tenet of Adam's sovereignty; since in his treatise of the Natural Power of Kings, he hath been so sparing of them. In his Observations on Mr. Hobbes's Leviathan, I think he has put, in short, all those arguments for it together, which in his writings I find him any where to make use of: his words are these: "If God created only Adam, and of a piece of him made the woman, and if by generation from them two, as parts of them, all mankind be propagated: if also God gave to Adam not only the dominion over the woman and the children that should issue from them, but also over all the earth to subdue it, and over all the creatures on it, so that, as long as Adam lived, no man could claim or enjoy any thing but by donation, assignation, or permission from him, I wonder," &c. Obs. 165. Here we have the sum of all his arguments, for Adam's sovereignty, and against natural freedom, which I find up and down In his other treatises: and they are these following; "God s creation of Adam, the dominion he gave him over Eve, an the dominion he had as father over his children; all which I shall particularly consider.

## Chapter III, Of Adam's Title to Sovereignty by Creation.

## §15.

Sir Robert, in his preface to his Observations on Aristotle's Politics, tells us, "A natural freedom of mankind cannot be supposed, without the denial of the creation of Adam:" but how Adam's being created, which was nothing but his receiving a being, immediately from Omnipotency, and the hand of God, gave Adam a sovereignty over any thing, I cannot see; nor consequently understand, how a supposition of natural freedom is a denial of Adam's creation; and would be glad any body else (since our A. did not vouchsafe us the favour) would make it out for him. For I find no difficulty to suppose the freedom of mankind, though I have always believed the creation of Adam. He was created, or began to exist, by God's immediate power, without the intervention of parents, or the pre-existence of any of the same species to beget him, when it pleased God he should; and so did the lion, the king of beasts, before him, by the same creating power of God: and if bare existence by that power, and in that way, will give dominion, without any more ado, our A. by this argument, will make the lion have as good a title to it as he, and certainly the ancienter. No; for Adam had his title "by the appointment of God," says our A. in another place. Then bare creation gave him not dominion, and one might have supposed mankind free, without the denying the creation of Adam, since it was God's appointment made him monarch.

## §16.

But let us see how he puts his creation and this appointment together. "By the appointment of God, says sir Robert, as soon as Adam was created, he was monarch of the world, though he had no subjects; for though there could not be actual government till there were subjects, yet by the right of nature it was due to Adam to be governor of his posterity: though not in act, yet at least in habit, Adam was a king from his creation." I wish he had told us here, what he meant by God's appointment. For whatsoever providence orders, or the law of nature directs, or positive revelation declares, may be said to be by God's appointment: but I suppose it cannot be meant here in the first sense, i.e., by providence; because that would be to say no more, but that as soon as Adam was created, he was de facto monarch, because by right of nature it was due to Adam to be governor of his posterity. But he could not, de facto, be by providence constituted the governor of the world, at a time when there was actually no government, no subjects to be governed, which our A. here confesses. Monarch of the world is also differently used by our A., for sometimes he means by it a proprietor of all the world, exclusive of the rest of mankind, and thus he does in the same page of his preface before cited: "Adam, says he, being commanded to multiply and people the earth, and subdue it, and having dominion given him over all creatures, was thereby the monarch of the whole world; none of his posterity had any right to possess any thing but by his grant or permission, or by succession from him." 2. Let us understand then, by monarch, proprietor of the world, and, by appointment, God's actual donation, and revealed positive grant made to Adam, Gen. i. 28, as we see sir Robert himself does in this parallel place; and then his argument wills tend thus: "by the positive grant of God: as soon as Adam was created, he was proprietor of the world, because by the right of nature it was due to Adam to be governor of his posterity." In which way of arguing there are two manifest falsehoods. First, it is false, that God made that grant to Adam, as soon as he was created, since, though it stands in the text immediately after his creation, yet it is plain it could not be spoken to Adam till after Eve was made and brought to him; and how then could he be monarch by appointment as soon as created, especially since he calls, if I mistake not, that which God says to Eve, Gen. iii. 16, the original grant of government, which not being till after the fall, when Adam was somewhat, at least in time, and very much distant in condition, from his creation, I cannot see, how our A. can say in this sense, that, "by God's appointment, as soon as Adam was created, he was monarch of the world." Secondly, were it true, that God's actual donation "appointed Adam monarch of the world, as soon as he was created," yet the reason here given for it would not prove it; but it would always be a false inference that God, by a positive donation, "appointed Adam monarch of the world, because by right of nature it was due to Adam to be governor of his posterity:" for having given him the right of government by nature, there was no need of a positive donation; at least it will never be a proof of such a donation.

## §17.

On the other side, the matter will not be much mended, if we understand by God's appointment the law of nature, (though it be a pretty harsh expression for it in this place) and by monarch of the world, sovereign ruler of mankind: for then the sentence under consideration must run thus: "By the law of nature, as soon as Adam was created he was governor of mankind, for by right of nature it divas due to Adam to be governor of his posterity;" which amounts to this, he was governor by right of nature, because he was governor by right of nature. But supposing we should grant, that a man is by nature governor of his children, Adam could not hereby be monarch as soon as created: for this right of nature being founded in his being their father, how Adam could have a natural right to be governor, before he was a father, Men by being a father only he had that right, is, methinks, hard to conceive, unless he would have him to be a father before he was a father, and have a title before he had it.

## §18.

To this foreseen objection, our A. answers very logically, "He was governor in habit, and not in act:" a very pretty way of being a governor without government, a father without children, and a king without subjects. And thus sir Robert was an author before he writ his book; not in act, it is true, but in habit; for when he had once published it, it was due to him, by the right of nature, to be an author, as much as it was to Adam to be governor of his children, when he had begot them; and if to be such a monarch of the world, an absolute monarch in habit, but not in act, will serve the turn, I should not much envy it to any of sir Robert's friends, that he thought fit graciously to bestow it upon; though even this of act and habit, if it signified any thing but our A.'s skill in distinctions be not to his purpose in this place. For the question is not here about Adam's actual exercise of government, but actually having a title to be governor. Government, says our A. was "due to Adam by the right of nature:" what is this right of nature? A right fathers have over their children by begetting them; generatione jus acquiritur parentibus in liberos, says our A. out of Grotius, de J. B. P. L. 2. C. 5. S. 1. The right then follows the begetting as arising from it; so that, according to this way of reasoning or distinguishing of our A. Adam, as soon as he was created, had a title only in habit, and not in act, which in plain English is, he had actually no title at all.

## §19.

To speak less learnedly, and more intelligibly, one may say of Adam, he was in a possibility of being governor, since it was possible he might beget children, laid thereby acquire that right of nature, be it what it will, to govern them, that accrues from thence: but what connexion has this with Adam's creation, to make him say, that "as soon as he was created, he was monarch of the world?" For it may as well be said of Noah, that as soon as he was born he was monarch of the world, since he was in possibility (which in our A.'s sense is enough to make a monarch, "a monarch in habit,") to outlive all mankind but his own posterity. What such necessary connexion there is betwixt Adam's creation and his right to government, so that a "natural freedom of mankind cannot be supposed without the denial of the creation of Adam," I confess for my part I do not see; nor how those words, "by the appointment," &c. Obs. 254, however explained, can be put together, to make any tolerable sense, at least to establish this position, with which they end, viz., "Adam was a king from his creation;" a king, says our author, "not in act, but in habit," i.e., actually no king at all.

## §20.

I fear I have tired my reader's patience, by dwelling longer on this passage than the weightiness of any argument in it seems to require: but I have unavoidably been engaged in it by our author's way of writing, who, huddling several suppositions together, and that in doubtful and general terms, makes such a medley and confusion, that it is impossible to show his mistakes, without examining the several senses wherein his words may be taken, and without seeing how, in any of these various meanings, they will consist together, and have any truth in then: for in this present passage before us, how can any one argue against this position of his, "that Adam was a king from his creation," unless one examine, whether the words, "from his creation," be to be taken, as they may, for the time of the commencement of his government, as the fore going words import, "as soon as he was created he was monarch;" or, for the cause of it, as he says, p. 11, "creation made man prince of his posterity?" How farther can one judge of the truth of his being thus king, till one has examined whether king be to be taken, as the words in the beginning of this passage would persuade, on supposition of his private dominion which was, lay God's positive grant, "monarch of the world by appointment;" or king on supposition of lies fatherly power over his offspring, which was by nature, "due by the right of nature;" whether, I say, king be to be taken in both, or one only of these two senses, or in neither of then, but only this, that creation made him prince, in a way different from both the other? For though this assertion, that "Adam was king from his creation," be true in no sense, yet it stands here as an evident conclusion drawn from the preceding words, though in truth it be but a bare assertion joined to other assertions of the same kind, which confidently put together in words of undetermined and dubious meaning, look like a sort of arguing, when there is indeed neither proof nor connexion; a way very familiar with our author; of which having given the reader a taste here, I shall, as much as the argument will permit me, avoid touching on hereafter; and should not have done it here, were it not to let the world see, how incoherences in matter, and suppositions without proofs, put handsomely together in good words and a plausible style, are apt to pass for strong reason and good sense, till they come to be looked into with attention.

## Chapter IV, Of Adam's Title to Sovereignty, by Donation, Gen. i. 28.

### §21.

Having at last got through the foregoing passage, where we have been so long detained, not by the force of arguments and opposition, but by the intricacy of the words, and the doubtfulness of the meaning; let us go on to his next argument, for Adam's sovereignty. Our author tells us in the words of Mr. Selden, that "Adam by donation from God, Gen. i. 28, was made the general lord of all things, not without such a private dominion to himself, as without his grant did exclude his children. This determination of Mr. Selden, says our author, is consonant to the history of the Bible, and natural reason," Obs. 910. And in his Pref. to his Observations on Aristotle, he says thus, "The first government in the world was monarchical in the father of all flesh, Adam being commanded to multiply and people the earth, and to subdue it, and having dominion given him over all creatures, was thereby the monarch of the whole world. None of his posterity had any right to possess any thing, but by his grant or permission, or by succession from him. The earth, saith the Psalmist, hath he given to the children of men, which shows the title comes from fatherhood."

### §22.

Before I examine this argument, and the text on which it is founded, it is necessary to desire the reader to observe, that our author, according to his usual method, begins in one sense, and concludes in another; he begins here with Adam's propriety, or private dominion, by donation; and his conclusion is, "which shows the title comes from fatherhood."

### §23.

But let us see the argument. The words of the text are these: "And God blessed them, and God said unto them, Be fruitful and multiply, and replenish the earth and subdue it, and have dominion over the fish of the sea, and over the fowl of the air, and over every living thing that moveth upon the earth," Gen. i. 28; from whence our author concludes, "that Adam, having here dominion given him over all creatures, was thereby the monarch of the whole world:" whereby must be meant, that either this grant of God gave Adam property, or, as our author calls it, private dominion over the earth, and all inferior or irrational creatures, and so consequently that he was thereby monarch; or, 2dly, that it gave him rule and dominion over all earthly creatures whatsoever, and thereby over his children; and so he was monarch: for, as Mr. Selden has properly worded it, "Adam was made general lord of all things," one may very clearly understand him, that he means nothing to be granted to Adam here but property, and therefore he says not one word of Adam's monarchy. But our author says, "Adam was hereby monarch of the world," which, properly speaking, signifies Sovereign ruler of all the men in the world; and so Adam, by this grant, must be constituted such a ruler. If our author means otherwise, he might with much clearness have said, that "Adam was hereby proprietor of the whole world." But he begs your pardon in that point: clear distinct speaking not serving every where to his purpose, you must not expect it in him, as in Mr. Selden, or other such writers.

## §24.

In opposition, therefore, to our author's doctrine, that "Adam was monarch of the whole world," founded on this place, I shall show 1. That by this grant, Gen. i. 28, God gave no immediate power to Adam over men, over his children, over those of his own species; and so he was not made ruler, or monarch, by this charter. 2. That by this grant God gave him not private dominion over the inferior creatures, but right in common with all mankind; so neither was he monarch upon the account of the property here given him.

## §25.

1. That this donation, Gen. i. 28, gave Adam no power over men, will appear if we consider the words of it: for since all positive grants convey no more than the express words they are made in will carry, let us see which of them here will comprehend mankind or Adam's posterity; and those I imagine, if any, must be these, "every living thing that moveth:" the words in Hebrew are הרמשת חיה i.e., bestiam reptantem, of which words the Scripture itself is the best interpreter: God having created the fishes and fowls the 5th day, the beginning of the 6th, he creates the irrational inhabitants of the dry land, which, ver. 24, are described in these words, "Let the earth bring forth the living creature after his kind; cattle and creeping thins, and beasts of the earth, after his kind; and ver. 2, and God made the beasts of the earth after his kind, and cattle after their kind, and every thing that creepeth on the earth after his kind:" here, in the creation of the brute inhabitants of the earth, he first speaks of them all under one general name, of living creatures, and then afterwards divides them into three ranks,
1. Cattle, or such creatures as were or might be tame, and so be the private possession of particular men; חיה which, ver. 24, 25, in our Bible, is translated beasts, and by the Septuagint, wild beasts, and is the same word, that here in our text, ver. 28, where we have this great charter to Adam, is translated living thing, and is also the same word used, Gen. ix. 2, where this grant is renewed to Noah, and there likewise translated beast.
3. The third rank were the creeping animals, which, ver. 24, 25, are comprised under the word, הרמשת the same that is used here, ver. 28, and is translated moving, but in the former verses creeping, and by the Septuagint in all these places, pet, or reptiles; from whence it appears, that the words which we translate here in God's donation, ver. 28, "living creatures moving," are the same, which in the history of the creation, ver. 24, 25, signify two ranks of terrestrial creatures, viz., wild beasts and reptiles, and are so understood by the Septuagint.

## §26.

When God had made the irrational animals of the world, divided into three kinds, from the places of their habitation, viz., fishes of the sea, fowls of the air, and living creatures of the earth, and these again into cattle, wild beasts, and reptiles; he considers of making man, and the dominion he should have over the terrestrial world, ver. 26, and then he reckons up the inhabitants of these three kingdoms, but in the terrestrial leaves out the second rank חַיָּה or wild beasts: but here, ver. 28, where he actually exercises this design, and gives him this dominion, the text mentions the fishes of the sea, and fowls of the air, and the terrestrial creatures in the words that signify the wild beasts and reptiles, though translated living thing that moveth, leaving out cattle. In both which places, though the word that signifies wild beasts be omitted in one, and that which signifies cattle in the other, yet, since God certainly executed in one lilacs, what he declares he designed in the other, we cannot but understand the same in both places, and have here only an account how the terrestrial irrational animals, which were already created and reckoned up at their creation, in three distinct ranks of cattle, wild beasts, and reptiles, were here, ver. 28, actually put under the dominion of man, as they were designed, ver. 26; nor do these words contain in them the least appearance of any thing that can be wrested to signify God's giving to one man dominion over another, to Adam over his posterity.

## §27.

And this further appears front Gen. ix. 2, where God renewing this charter to Noah and his sons, he gives them dominion over the fowls of the air, and the fishes of the sea, and the terrestrial creatures, expressed by דרמש ח'ה wild beasts and reptiles, the same words that in the text before us, Gen. i. 28, are translated every moving thing that moveth on the earth, which by no means can comprehend man, the grant being made to Noah and his sons, all the men then living, and not to one part of men over another; which is yet more evident from the very next words, ver. 3, where God gives every רמש "every moving thing," the very words used ch. i. 28, to them for food. By all which it is plain that God's donation to Adam, ch. i. 28, and his designation, ver. 26, and his grant again to Noah and his sons; refer to, and contain in them, neither more nor less than the works of the creation the fifth day, and the beginning of the sixth, as they are set down from the both to 26th ver. inclusively of the 1st ch. and so comprehend all the species of irrational animals of the terraqueous globe; though all the words, whereby they are expressed in the history of their creation, are nowhere used in any of the following grants, but some of them omitted in one, and some in another From whence I think it is past all doubt that man can not be comprehended in this grant, nor any dominion over those of his own species be conveyed to Adam. All the terrestrial irrational creatures are enumerated at their creation, ver. 25, under the names, "beasts of the earth, cattle, and creeping things;" but man, being not then created, was not contained under any of those names; and therefore, whether we understand the Hebrew words right or no, they cannot be supposed to comprehend man, in the very same history, and the very next verses following, especially since that Hebrew word רמש which, if any in this donation to Adam, ch. i. 28, must comprehend man, is so plainly used in contradistinction to him, as Gen. vi. 20. vii. 14, 21, 28. Gen. viii. 17, 19. And if God made all mankind slaves to Adam and his heirs, by giving Adam dominion over "every living thing that moveth on the earth," ch. i. 28, as our author would have it; methinks sir Robert should leave carried his monarchical power one step higher, and satisfied the world that princes might eat their subjects too, since God gave as full power to Noah and his heirs, ch. ix. 2, to eat "every living thing that moveth," as he did to Adam to have dominion over them; the Hebrew word in both places being the same.

§28.

David, who might be supposed to understand the donation of God in this text, and the right of kings too, as well as our author, in his comment on this place, as the learned and judicious Ainsworth calls it, in the 8th Psalm, finds here no such charter of monarchical power: his words are, "Thou hast made him, i.e., man, the son of man, a little lower than the angels; thou madest him to have dominion over the works of thy hands; thou hast put all things under his feet, all sheep and oxen, and the beasts of the field, and fowls of the air, and fish of the sea, and whatsoever passeth through the paths of the sea." In which words, if any one can find out, that there is meant any monarchical power of one man over another, but only the dominion of the whole species of mankind over the inferior species of creatures, he may, for aught I know, deserve to be one of sir Robert's monarchs in habit, for the rareness of the discovery. And by this time, I hope it is evident, that he that gave "dominion over every hying thing that moveth on the earth," gave Adam no monarchical power over those of his own species, which will yet appear more fully in the next thing I am to show.

§29.

Whatever God gave by the words of this grant Gen. i. 28, it was not to Adam in particular, exclusive of all other men: whatever dominion he had thereby, it was not a private dominion, but a dominion in common with the rest of mankind. That this donation was not made in particular to Adam, appears evidently from the words of the text, it being made to more than one; for it was spoken in the plural number, God blessed them, and said unto them, have dominion. God says unto Adam and Eve, have dominion; thereby, says our author, "Adam was monarch of the world:" but the grant being to them, i.e., spoken to Eve also, as many interpreters think with reason, that these words were not spoken till Adam had his wife, must not she thereby be lady, as well as he lord of the world? If it be said that Eve was subjected to Adam, it seems she was not so subjected to him as to hinder her dominion over the creatures, or property in them for shall we say that God ever made a joint grant to two, and one only was to have the benefit of it?

**§30.**

But perhaps it will be said Eve was not made till afterward: grant it so, what advantage will our author get by it? The text will be only the more directly against him, and show that God, in this donation, gave the world to mankind in common, and not to Adam in particular. The word them in the text must include the species of man, for it is certain them can by no means signify Adam alone. In the 26th verse, where God declares his intention to give this dominion, it is plain he meant that he would make a species of creatures that should have dominion over the other species of this terrestrial globe. The words are, "And God said, let us make man in our image, after our likeness, and let them have dominion over the fish," &c. They then were to have dominion. Who? even those who were to have the image of God, the individuals of that species of man that he was going to make; for that them should signify Adam singly, of the rest that should be in the world with him, is against both Scripture and all reason: and it cannot possibly be made sense, if man in the former part of the verse do not signify the same with them in the latter; only man there, as is usual, is taken for the species, and them the individuals of that species: and we leave a reason in the very text. God makes him "in his own image, after his own likeness; makes him an intellectual creature, and so capable of dominion:" for wherein soever else the image of God consisted, the intellectual nature was certainly a part of it, and belonged to the whole species, and enabled them to have dominion over the inferior creatures; and therefore David says, in the 8th Psalm above cited, "Thou hast made him little longer than the angels; thou hast made him to have dominion." It is not of Adam king David speaks here; for, verse 4, it is plain it is of man, and the son of man, of the species of mankind.

**§31.**

And that this grant spoken to Adam was made to him, and the whole species of man, is clear from our author's own proof out of the Psalmist. "The earth, saith the Psalmist, hath he given to the children of men, which shows the title comes from fatherhood." These are sir Robert's words in the preface before cited, and a strange inference it is he makes: "God hath given the earth to the children of men, ergo the title comes from fatherhood." It is pity the propriety of the Hebrew tongue had not used fathers of men, instead of children of men, to express mankind: then indeed our author might have had the countenance of talc socials of the words to have placed the title in the fatherhood. But to conclude, that the fatherhood lead the right to the earth, because God gave it to the children of men, is a way of arguing peculiar to our author: and a man must have a great mind to go contrary to the sound as well as sense of the words before he could light on it. But the sense is yet harder, and more remote from our author's purpose: for as it stands in his preface it is to prove Adam's being monarch, and his reasoning is thus, "God gave the partly to the children of men, ergo Adam was monarch of the world." I defy any man try make a more pleasant conclusion than this, which cannot be excused from the most obvious absurdity, till it can be shown that by children of men, he who had no father, Adam alone is signified; but whatever our author does, the Scripture speaks not nonsense.

**§32.**

To maintain this property and private dominion of Adam, our author labours in the following page to destroy the community granted to Noah and his sons, in that parallel place, Gen. ix. 1, 2, 3; and he endeavours to do it two ways. 1. Sir Robert would persuade us, against the express words of the Scripture, that what was here granted to Noah, was not granted to his sons in common with him. His words are, "As for the general community between Noah and his sons, which Mr. Selden will have to be granted to them, Gen. ix. 2, the text cloth not warrant it." What warrant our author would have when the plain express words of Scripture, not capable of another meaning, will not satisfy him, who pretends to build wholly on Scripture, is not easy to imagine. The text says, "God blessed Noah and his sons, and said unto them, i.e., as our author would have it, unto him: for, saith he, although the sons are there unmentioned with Noah in the blessing, yet it may best be understood, with a subordination or benediction m succession," O. 211. That indeed is best for our author to be understood, which best serves to his purpose; but that truly may best be understood by any body else, which best agrees with the plain construction of the words, and arises from the obvious meaning of the place; and then with subordination and in succession will not be lest understood in a grant of God, where he himself put them not, nor mentions any such limitation. But yet our author has reasons why it may best he understood so.

"The blessing, says he in the following words, might truly be fulfilled, if the sons, either under or after their father, enjoyed a private dominion," O. 211; That is to say, that a grant, whose express words give a joint title in present (for the text says, into your hands they are delivered) may best be understood with a subordination or in succession; because it is possible that in subordination, in succession, it may be enjoyed. Which is all one as to say, that a grant of any thing in present possession may best be understood of reversion; because it is possible one may live to enjoy it in reversion. If the grant be indeed to a father and to his sons after him, who is so kind as to let his children enjoy it presently in common with him, one may truly say, as to the event one will be as good as the other; but it can never be true that what the express words grant in possession, and in common, may best be understood to be in reversion. The sum of all his reasoning amounts to this: God did not give to the sons of Noah the world in common with their father, because it was possible they might enjoy it under or after him. A very good sort of argument against an express text of Scripture: but God must not be believed, though he speaks it himself, when he says he does any thing which will not consist with sir Robert's hypothesis.

## §33.

For it is plain, however he would exclude them, that part of this benediction, as he would have it in succession, must needs be meant to the sons, and not to Noah himself at all: "Be fruitful and multiply, and replenish the earth," says God in this blessing This part of the benediction, as appears by the sequel, concerned not Noah himself at all: for we read not of any children he had after the flood; and in the following chapter, where his posterity is reckoned up, there is no mention of any; and so this benediction in succession was not to take place till 350 years after: and to save our author's imaginary monarchy, the peopling of the world must be deferred 350 years; for this part of the benediction cannot be understood with subordination, unless our author will say that they must ask leave of their father Noah to lie with their wives. But in this one point our author is constant to himself in all his discourses; he takes care there should be monarchs in the world, but very little that there should be people; and indeed his way of government is not the way to people the world: for how much absolute monarchy helps to fulfil this great and primary blessing of God Almighty, "Be fruitful and multiply, and replenish the earth," which contains in it the improvement too of arts and sciences, and the conveniencies of life; may be seen in those large and rich countries which are happy under the Turkish government, where are not now to be found one-third, nay in many, if not most parts of them, one-thirtieth, perhaps I might say not one-hundredth of the people, that were formerly, as will easily appear to any one, who will compare the accounts we have of it at this time with ancient history But this by the by.

## §34.

The other parts of this benediction or grant are so expressed, that they must needs be understood to belong equally to them all; as much to Noah's sons as to Noah himself, and not to his sons with a subordination, or in succession. "The fear of you, and the dread of you, says God, shall be upon every beast," &c. Will any body but our author say that the creatures feared and stood in awe of Noah only, and not of his sons without his leave, or till after his death? And the following words, "into your hands they are delivered," are they to be understood as our author says, if your father please, or they shall be delivered into your hands hereafter? If this be to argue from Scripture, I know not what may not be proved by it; and I can scarce see how much this dithers from that fiction and fancy, or how much a surer foundation it will prove than the opinions of philosophers and poets, which our author so much condemns in his preface.

## §35.

But our author goes on to prove, that "it may best be understood with a subordination, or a benediction in succession; for, says he, it is not probable that the private dominion which God gave to Adam, and by his donation, assignation, or cession to his children, was abrogated, and a community of all things instituted between Noah and his sons—Noah was left the sole heir of the world; why should it be thought that God would disinherit him of his birth right, and make him of all men in the world the only tenant in common with his children?" O. 211.

§36.

The prejudices of our own ill-grounded opinions, however by us called probable, cannot authorize us to understand Scripture contrary to the direct and plain meaning of the words. I grant it is not probable that Adam's private dominion was here abrogated; because it is more than improbable (for it will never be proved) that Adam had any such private dominion: and since parallel places of Scripture are most probable to make us know how they may be best understood, there needs but the comparing this blessing here to Noah and his sons, after the flood, with that to Adam after the creation, Gen. i. 28, to assure any one that God gave Adam no such private dominion. It is probable, I confess, that Noah should have the same title, the same property and dominion after the flood, that Adam had before it: but since private dominion cannot consist with the blessing and grant God gave to him and his sons in common, it is a sufficient reason to conclude that Adam had none, especially since, in the donation made to him, there are no words that express it, or do in the least favour it; and then let my reader judge whether it may best be understood, when in the one place there is not one word for it, not to say what has been above proved, that the test itself proves the contrary; and in the other, the words and sense are directly against it.

§37.

But our author says, "Noah was the sole heir of the world; why should it be thought that God would disinherit him of his birth right?" Heir indeed, in England, signifies the eldest son, who is by the law of England to have all his father's land: but where God ever appointed any such heir of the world, our author would have done well to have showed us; and how God disinherited him of his birth right, or what harm was done him if God gave his sons a right to make use of a part of the earth for support of themselves and families, when the whole was not only more than Noah himself, but infinitely more than they all could make use of, and the possessions of one could not at all prejudice, or, as to any use, straiten that of the other.

§38.

Our author probably foreseeing he might not be very successful in persuading people out of their senses, and, say what he could, men would be apt to believe the plain words of Scripture, and think, as they say, that the grant was spoken to Noah and his sons jointly; he endeavours to insinuate, as if this grant to Noah conveyed no property, no dominion; because "subduing the earth and dominion over the creatures are therein omitted, nor the earth once named." And therefore, says he, "there is a considerable difference between these two texts; the first blessing gave Adam a dominion over the earth and all creatures the latter allows Noah liberty to use the living creatures for food: here is no alteration or diminishing of his title to a property of all things, but an enlargement only of his commons," O. 211. So that, in our author's sense, all that was said here to Noah and his sons, gave them no dominion, no property, but only enlarged the commons; their commons, I should say, since God says, "to you are they given;" though our author says his; for as to Noah's sons, they, it seems, by sir Robert's appointment, during their father's lifetime, were to keep fasting-days.

§39.

Any one but our author would be mightily suspected to be blinded with prejudice, that in all this blessing to Noah and his sons, could see nothing but only an enlargement of commons: for as to dominion which our author thinks omitted, "the fear of you, and the dread of you, says God, shall be upon every beast," which I suppose expresses the dominion, or superiority, was designed man over the living creatures, as fully as may be; for in that fear and dread seems chiefly to consist what was given to Adam over the inferior animals, who, as absolute a monarch as he was could not make bold with a lark or rabbit to satisfy his hunger, and had the herbs but in common with the besets, as is plain from Gen. i. 2, 9, and 30. In the next place, it is manifest that in this blessing to Noah and his sons, property is not only given in clear words, but in a larger extent than it was to Adam. "Into your hands they are given," says God to Noah and his sons; which words, if they give not property, nay, property in possession, it will be hard to find words that can; since there is not a way to express a man's being possessed of any thing more natural, nor more certain, than to say, it is delivered into his hands. And ver. 3, to show, that they had then given them the utmost property man is capable of, which is to have a right to destroy any thing by using it: "Every moving thing that liveth, saith God, shall be meat for you;" which was not allowed to Adam in his charter. This our author calls "a liberty of using them for food, and also an enlargement of commons, but no alteration of property," O. 211. What other property man can have in the creatures, but the "liberty of using them," is hard to be understood: so that if the first blessing, as our author says, gave Adam " dominion over the creatures," and the blessing to Noah and his sons gave them "such a liberty to use them" as Adam had not; it must needs give them something that Adam with all his sovereignty wanted, something that one would be apt to take for a greater property; for certainly he has no absolute dominion over even the brutal part of the creatures, and the property he has in them is very narrow and scanty, who cannot make that use of them which is permitted to another. Should any one, who is absolute lord of a country, have bidden our author subdue the earth, and given him dominion over the creatures in it, but not have permitted him to have taken a kid or a lamb out of the flock to satisfy his hunger, I guess he would scarce leave thought himself lord or proprietor of that land, or the cattle on it; but would have found the difference between "having dominion," which a shepherd may have, and having full property as an owner. So that, had it been his own case, sir Robert, I believe, would have thought here was an alteration, nay an enlarging of property; and that Noah and his children had by this grant not only property given them, but such a property given them in the creatures, as Adam had not: for however, in respect of one another, Slice may lo allowed to have propriety in their distinct portions of the creatures; yet in respect of God the maker of heaven and earth, who is sole lord and proprietor of the whole world, man's propriety in the creatures is nothing but that "liberty to use them," which God has permitted; and so man's property may be altered and enlarged, as we see it here, after the flood, when other uses of them are allowed, which before were not. From all which I suppose it is clear, that neither Adam, nor Noah, had any "private dominion," any property in the creatures, exclusive of his posterity, as they should successively grow up into need of them, and come to be able to make use of them.

§40.

Thus we have examined our author's argument for Adams monarchy, founded on the blessing pronounced, Gen. i. 28. Wherein I think it is impossible for any sober reader to find any other but the setting of mankind above the other kinds of creatures in this habitable earth of ours. It is nothing but the giving to, the whole species of man, as the chief inhabitant, who is the image of his Maker, the dominion over the other creatures. This lies so obvious in the plain words, that any one but our author would have thought it necessary to have shown, how these words, that seemed to say the quite contrary, gave "Adam monarchical absolute power" over other men, or the sole property in all the creatures; and methinks in a business of this moment, and that whereon he builds all that follows, he should have done something more than barely cite words, which apparently make against him; for I confess, I cannot see any thing in them tending to Adam's monarchy, or private dominion, but quite the contrary. And I the less deplore the dulness of my apprehension herein, since I find the apostle seems to have as little notion of any such "private dominion of Adam" as I, when he says, "God gives us all things richly to enjoy;" which he could not do, if it were all given away already to monarch Adam, and the monarchs his heirs and successors. To conclude, this text is so far from proving Adam sole proprietor, that, on the contrary, it is a confirmation of the original community of all things amongst the sons of men, which appearing from this donation of God, as well as other places of Scripture, the sovereignty of Adam, built upon his "private dominion," must fall, not having any foundation to support it.

§41.

But yet, if after all any one will needs have it so, that by this donation of God Adam was made sole proprietor of the whole earth, what will this be to his sovereignty? and how will it appear, that propriety in land gives a man power over the life of another? or how will the possession even of the whole earth give any one a sovereign arbitrary authority over the persons of men? The most specious thing to be said is, that he that is proprietor of the whole world, may deny all the rest of mankind food, and so at his pleasure starve them, if they will not acknowledge his sovereignty, and obey his will. If this were true, it would be a good argument to prove, that there never was any such property, that God never gave any such private dominion; since it is more reasonable to think, that God, who bid mankind increase and multiply, should rather himself give them all a right to make use of the food and raiment, and other conveniencies of life, the materials whereof he had so plentifully provided for them; than to make them depend upon the will of a man for their subsistence, who should have power to destroy them all when he pleased, and who, being no better than other men, was in succession likelier, by want and the dependence of a scanty fortune, to tie them to hard service, than by liberal allowance of the conveniencies of life to promote the great design of God, "increase and multiply:" he that doubts this, let him look into the absolute monarchies of the world, and see what becomes of the conveniencies of life, and the multitudes of people.

### §42.

But we know God hath not left one man so to the mercy of another, that he may starve him if he please: God, the Lord and Father of all, has given no one of his children such a property in his peculiar portion of the things of this world, but that he has given his needy brother a right to the surplusage of his goods; so that it cannot justly be denied him, when his pressing wants call for it: and therefore no man could ever have a just power over the life of another by right of property in land or possessions; since it would always be a sin, in any man of estate, to let his brother perish for want of affording him relief out of his plenty. As justice gives every man a title to the product of his honest industry, and the fair acquisitions of his ancestors descended to him; so charity gives every man a title to so much out of another's plenty as will keep him from extreme want, where he has no means to subsist otherwise: and a man can no mare justly make use of another's necessity to force him to become his vassal, by withholding that relief God requires him to afford to the wants of his brother, than he that has more strength can seize upon a weaker, master him to his obedience, and with a dagger at his throat offer him death or slavery.

### §43.

Should any one make so perverse an use of God's blessings poured on him with a liberal hand; should any one be cruel and uncharitable to that extremity; yet all this would not prove that propriety ill land, even in this case, gave any authority over the persons of men, but only that compact might since the authority of the rich proprietor, and the subjections of the needy beggar, began not from the possession of the lord, but the consent of the poor man, who preferred being his subject to starving. And the man he thus submits to, can pretend to no more power over him than he has consented to, upon compact. Upon this ground a man's having his stores filled in a time of scarcity, having money in his pocket, being in a vessel at sea, being able to swim, &c. may as well be the foundation of rule and dominion, as being possessor of all the land in the world: any of these being sufficient to enable me to save a man's life, who would perish, if such assistance were denied him; and any thing, by this rule, that may be an occasion of working upon another's necessity to sale his life, or any thing dear to him, at the of his freedom, may be made a foundation of sovereignty, as well as property. From all which it is clear, that though God should have given Adam private dominion, yet that private dominion could give him no sovereignty: but we have already sufficiently proved that God gave him no "private dominion."

**Chapter V, Of Adam's Title to Sovereignty, by the Subjection of Eve**

### §44.

The next place of Scripture we find our author builds his monarchy of Adam on, is Gen. iii. 26. "And thy desire shall be to thy husband, and he shall rule over thee. Here we have (says he) the original grant of government," from whence he concludes, in the following part of the page, O. 244, "That the supreme power is settled in the fatherhood, and limited to one kind of government, that is, to monarchy." For let his premises be what they will, this is always the conclusion; let rule, in any text, be but once named, and presently absolute monarchy is by divine right established. If any one will but carefully read our author's own reasoning from these words, O. 244, and consider, among other things, "the line and posterity of Adam," as he there brings them in, he will find some difficulty to make sense of what he says; but we will allow this at present to his peculiar way of writing, and consider the force of the text in hand. The words are the curse of God upon the woman for having been the first and forwardest in the disobedience; and if we will consider the occasion of what God says here to our first parents, that he was denouncing judgment, and declaring his wrath against them both for their disobedience, we cannot suppose that this was the time wherein God was granting Adam prerogatives and privileges, investing him with dignity and authority, elevating him to dominion and monarchy: for though, as a holster in the temptation, live was laid below him, and so he had accidentally a superiority over her, for her greater punishment; yet he too had his share in the fall, as well as the sin, and was laid lower, as may be seen in the following verses: and it would be hard to imagine, that Gall, in the same breath, should make him universal monarch over all mankind, and a day-labourer for his life; turn lain out of "paradise to till the ground," ver. 23, and at the same time advance him to a throne, and all the privileges and case of absolute power.

## §45.

This was not a time when Adam could expect any favours, any grant of privileges, from his offended Maker. If this be "the original grant of government," as our author tells us, and Adam was now made monarch, whatever sir Robert would have him, it is plain, God made him but a very poor monarch, such an one as our author himself would have counted it no great privilege to be. God sets him to work for his living, and seems rather to give him a spade into his hand to subdue the earth, than a sceptre to rule over its inhabitants. "In the sweat of thy face thou shalt eat thy bread," says God to him, ver. 19. This was unavoidable, may it perhaps be answered, because he was yet without subjects, and had nobody to work for him; but afterwards, living as he did above 900 years, he might have people enough, whom he might command to work for him: no, says God, not only whilst thou art without other help, save thy wife, but as long as thou livest, shalt thou live by thy labour, "In the sweat of thy face shalt thou eat thy bread, till thou return unto the ground, for out of it west thou taken; for dust thou art, and unto dust shalt thou return," ver. 19. It will perhaps be answered again in favour of our author, that these words are not spoken personally to Adam, but in him, as their representative, to all mankind, this being a curse upon mankind, because of the fall.

## §46.

God, I believe, speaks differently from men, because he speaks with more truth, more certainty: but when he vouchsafes to speak to men, l do not think he speaks differently from them, in crossing the rules of language in use amongst them: this would not be to condescend to their capacities, when he humbles himself to speak to them, but to lose his design in speaking what, thus spoken, they could not understand. And fact thus must we think of God, if the interpretations of Scripture, necessary to maintain our author's doctrine, must be received for good: for by the ordinary rules of language, it will be very hard to understand what God says, if what he speckles here, in the singular number, to Adam, must be understood to be spoken to all mankind; and what he says in the plural number, Gen. i. 20 and 28, must be understood of Adam alone, exclusive of all others; and what he says to Noah and his sons jointly, must be understood to be meant to Noah alone, Gen. ix.

## §47.

Farther it is to be noted, that these words here of Gen. iii. 16, which our author calls "the original grant of government," were not spoken to Adam, neither indeed was there any grant in them Snide to Adam, but a punishment laid upon Eve: and if we will take them as they were directed in particular to her, or in her, as their representative. to all other women, they will at most concern the female sex only, and im port no more, but that subjection they should ordinarily be in to their husbands: but there is here no more law to oblige a woman to such subjection, if the circumstances either of her condition, or contract with her husband, should exempt her from it, than there is, that she should bring forth her children in sorrow and pain, if there could be found a remedy for it,which is also a part of the same curse upon her: for the whole verse runs thus, "Unto the woman he said, I will greatly multiply thy sorrow and thy conception; in sorrow thou shalt bring forth child-ren, and thy desire shall be to thy husband, and he shall rule over thee." It would, I think, have been a hard matter for any body, but our author, to have found out a grant of "monarchical government to Adam" in these words, which were neither spoken to, nor of him: neither will any one, I suppose, by these words, think the weaker sex, as by a law, so subjected to the curse contained in them, that it is their duty not to endeavour to avoid it. find will any one say that Eve, or any other woman, sinned, if she were brought to bed without those multiplied pains God threatens her here with? or that either of our queens, Mary or Elizabeth, had they mar-ried any of their subjects, had been by this text put into a political subjection to him? or that he should thereby have had monarchical rule over her? God, in this text, gives note that I see, any authority to Adam over Eve, or to men over their wives, but only foretell what should be the woman's lot; how by his providence he would order it so, that she should be subject to her husband, as we see that generally the Laws of mankind and cus-toms of nations leave ordered it so: and there is, I grant, a foundation in nature for it.

## §48.

Thus when God says of Jacob and Esau, "that the elder should serve the younger," Gen. xxv. 23, nobody sup-poses that God hereby made Jacob Esau's sovereign, but foretold what should de facto come to pass. But if these words here spoken to Eve must needs be understood as a law to bind her and all other women to subjec-tion, it can be no other subjection than what every wife owes her husband; and then if this be the "original grant of government, and the foundation of monarchical power," there will be as many monarchs as there are husbands: if therefore these words give any power to Adam, it can be only a conjugal power, not political; the power that every husband hath to order the things of private concernment in his family, as proprietor of the goods and land there, and to have his will take place before that of his wife in all things of their common con-cernment; but not a political power of life and death over her, much less over any body else

## §49.

This I am sure: if our author will have this text to be a "grant, the original grant of government," political gov-ernment, he ought to have proved it by some better arguments than by barely saying, that "thy desire shall be unto thy husband," was a law whereby Eve, and "all that should come of her," were subjected to the absolute monarchical power of Adam and his heirs. "Thy desire shall be to thy husband," is too doubtful an expression, of whose signification interpreters are not agreed, to build so confidently on, and in a matter of such moment, and so great and general concernment: but our author, according to his way of writing, having once named the text, concludes presently, without any more ado, that the meaning is as he would have it. Let the words rule and subject be but found in the text or margin, and it immediately signifies the duty of a subject to his prince; the relation is changed, and though God says husband, sir Robert will have it king; Adam has presently abso-lute monarchical power over Eve, and not only over love, but "all that should come of her," though the Scrip-ture says not a word of it, nor our author a word to prove it. But Adam must for all that be an absolute monarch, and so down to the end of the chapter. And here I leave my reader to consider whether my bare say-ing, without offering any reasons to evince it, that this text gave not Adam that absolute monarchical power, our author supposes, be not as sufficient to destroy that power, as his bare assertion is to establish it, since the text mentions neither prince nor people, speckles nothing of absolute or monarchical power, but the subjection of Eve to Adam, a wife to her husband. And he that would trace our author so all through, would make a short and sufficient answer to the greatest part of the grounds he proceeds on, and abundantly confute them by bare-ly denying; it being a sufficient answer to assertions without proof, to deny them without giving a reason. And therefore should I have said nothing, but barely denied that by this text "the supreme power was settled and founded by God himself, in the fatherhood, limited to monarchy, and that to Adam's person and heirs," all which our author notably concludes from these words, as may be seen in the same page, O. 244., it had been a sufficient answer: should I have desired any sober man only to have read the text, and considered to whom and on what occasion it was spoken, he would no doubt have wondered how our author found out monarchi-cal absolute power in it, had he not had an exceeding good faculty to find it himself, where he could not show it others. And thus we have examined the two places of Scripture, all that I remember our author brings to prove Adam's sovereignty, that supremacy which he says "it was God's ordinance should be unlimited in Adam, and as large as all the acts of his will," O. 254, viz. Gen. i. 28, and Gen. iii. 16; one whereof signifies only the subjection of the inferior ranks of creatures to mankind, and the other the subjection that is due from a wife to her husband; both far enough from that which subjects owe the governors of political societies.

**Chapter VI, Of Adam's Title to Sovereignty by Fatherhood.**

## §50.

There is one thing more, and then I think I have given you all that our author brings for proof of Adam's sovereignty, and that is a supposition of a natural right of dominion over his children, by being their father: and this title of fatherhood he is so pleased with, that you will find it brought in almost in every page; particularly he says, "not only Adam, but the succeeding patriarchs had, by right of fatherhood, royal authority over their children," p. 12. And in the same page, "this subjection of children being the fountain of all regal authority," &c. This being, as one would think by his so frequent mentioning it, the main basis of all his frame, we may well expect clear and evident reason for it, since he lays it down as a position necessary to his purpose, that "every man that is born is so far from being free, that by his very birth he becomes a subject of him that begets him," O. 156. So that Adam being the only man created, and all ever since being begotten, nobody has been born free. If we ask how Adam comes by this power over his children, he tells us here it is lay begetting them: and so again, O.223, "This natural dominion of Adam," says he, "may be proved out of Grotius himself, who teacheth that 'generations jus acquiritur parentibus in liberos.'" And indeed the act of begetting being that which makes a man a father, his right of a father over his children can naturally arise from nothing else.

## §51.

Grotius tells us Lot here how far this "jus in liberos," this power of parents over their children extends; but our author, always very clear in the point, assures us it is supreme power, and like that of absolute monarchs over their slaves, absolute power of life and death. He that should demand of him how, or for what reason it is, that begetting a child gives the father such an absolute power over him, will find him answer nothing: we are to take his word for this, as well as several other things, and by that the laws of nature and the constitutions of government must stand or fall. Had he been an absolute monarch, this way of talking might have suited well enough; "pro ratione voluntas," might have been of force in his mouth; but in the way of proof or argument is very unbecoming, and will little advantage his plea for absolute monarchy. Sir Robert has too much lessened a subject's authority to leave himself the hopes of establishing any thing by his bare saying it; one slave's opinion without proof, is not of weight enough to dispose of the liberty and fortunes of all mankind. If all men are not, as I think they are, naturally equal, I am sure all slaves are; and then I may without presumption oppose my single opinion to his; and be confident that my saying, "that begetting of children makes them not slaves to their fathers," as certainly sets all mankind free, as his affirming the contrary makes them all slaves. But that this position, which is the foundation of all their doctrine, who would have monarchy to be "jure divino," may have all fair play, let us hear what reasons others give for it, since our author offers none.

## §52.

The argument I leave heard others make use of to prove that fathers, by begetting them, come by an absolute power over their children, is this, that "fathers have a power over the lives of their children, because they give them life and being," which is the only proof it is capable of: since there can be no reason why naturally one man should have any claim or presence of right over that in another, which was never his, which he bestowed not, but was received from the bounty of another. 1. I answer, that every one who gives another any thing, has not always thereby a right to take it away again. But, 2. They who say the father gives life to children, are so dazzled with the thoughts of monarchy, that they do not, as they ought, remember God, who is "the author and giver of life: it is in him alone we live, move, and have our being." How can he be thought to give life to another, that knows not wherein his own life consists Philosophers are at a loss about it, after their most diligent inquiries; and anatomists, after their whole lives and studies spent in dissections, and diligent examining the bodies of men, confess their ignorance in the structure and use of many parts of man's body, and in that operation wherein life consists in the whole. And doth the rude ploughman, or the more ignorant voluptuary, frame or fashion such an admirable engine as this is, and then put life and sense into it? Can any man say he formed the parts that are necessary to the life of his child? or can he suppose himself to give the life, and yet not know what subject is fit to receive it, nor what actions or organs are necessary for its reception or preservation?

## §53.

To give life to that which has yet no being, is to frame and make a living creature, fashion the parts, and mould and suit them to their uses; and having proportioned and fitted them together, to put into them a hying soul. He that could do this, might indeed have some presence to destroy his own workmanship But is there any one so bold that dares thus far arrogate to himself the incomprehensible works of the Almighty? Who alone did at first, and continues still to make a living soul, he alone can breathe in the greatly of life. If any one thinks himself an artist at this, let lain number up the parts of his child's body will he hath made, tell me their uses and operations, and when the living and rational soul began to inhabit this curious structure, when sense began, and how this engine, which he has framed, thinks and reasons: if he made it, let him, when it is out of order, mend it, at least tell wherein the defects lie. "Shall he that made the eye not see?" says the Psalmist, Psalm xciv. 9. See these men's vanities; the structure of that one part is sufficient to convince us of an all-wise Contriver, and he has so visible a claim to us as his workmanship, that one of the ordinary appellations of God in Scripture is, "God our maker," and "the Lord our maker." And therefore though our author, for the magnifying his fatherhood, be pleased to say, O. 159, "That even the power which God himself exerciseth over mankind is by right of fatherhood," yet this fatherhood is such an one as utterly excludes all presence of title in earthly parents; for he is king, because he is indeed maker of us all, which no parents can pretend to be of their children.

## §54.

But had men skill and power to make their children, it is not so slight a piece of workmanship, that it can be imagined they could make them without designing it. What father of a thousand, when he begets a child, thinks farther than the satisfying his prey sent appetite? God in his infinite wisdom has put strong desires of copulation into the constitution of men, thereby to continue the race of mankind, which he doth most commonly without the intention, and often against the consent and will of the begetter. And indeed those who desire and design children, are but the occasions of their being, and, when they design and wish to beget them, do little more towards their making than Deucalion and his wife in the fable did towards the making of mankind, by throwing pebbles over their heads.

## §55.

But grant that the parents made their children, gave them life and being, and that hence there followed an absolute power. This would give the father but a joint dominion with the mother over them: for nobody can deny but that the woman lath an equal share, if not the greater, as nourishing the child a long time in her own body out of her own substance: there it is fashioned, and from her it receives the materials and principles of its constitution: and it is so hard to imagine the rational soul should presently inhabit the yet unformed embryo, as soon as the father has done his part in the act of generation, that if it must be supposed to derive any thing from the parents, it must certainly owe most to the mother. But be that as it will, the mother cannot be denied an equal share in begetting of the child nod so the absolute authority of the father will not arise from hence. Our author indeed is of another mind; for he says, "we know that God at the creation gave the sovereignty to the man over the woman, as being the nobler and principal agent in generation," O.172. I remember not this in my Bible; and when the place is brought where God at the creation gave the sovereignty to man over the woman, and that for this reason, because "he is the nobler and principal agent in generation," it will be time enough to consider, and answer it. But it is no new thing for our author to tell us his own fancies for certain and divine truths, though there be often a great deal of difference between his and divine revelations; for God in the Scripture says, "his father and his mother that begot him."

## §56.

They who allege the practice of mankind, for exposing or selling their children, as a proof of their power over them, are with sir Robert happy arguers; and cannot but recommend their opinion, by founding it on the most shameful action, and most unnatural murder human nature is capable of. The dens of lions and nurseries of wolves know no such cruelty as this: these savage inhabitants of the desert obey God and nature in being tender and careful of their offspring: they will hunt, watch, fight, and almost starve for the preservation of their young; never part with them never forsake them, till they are able to shift for themselves. And is it the privilege of man alone to act more contrary to nature than the wild and most untamed part of the creation? doth God forbid us under the severest penalty, that of death, to take away the life of any man, a stranger, and upon provocation? and does he permit us to destroy those he has given us the charge and care of; and by the dictates of nature and reason, as well as his revealed command, requires us to preserve? He has in all the parts of creation taken a peculiar care to propagate and continue the several species of creatures, anal makes the individuals act so strongly to this end, that they sometimes neglect their own private good for it, and seem to forget that general rule, which nature teaches all things, of self-preservation; and the preservation of their young, as the strongest principle in them, over-rules the constitution of their particular natures. Thus we see, when their young stand in need of it, the timorous become valiant, the fierce and savage kind, and the ravenous, tender and liberal.

## §57.

But if the example of what hath been done be the rule of what ought to be, history would have furnished our author with instances of this absolute fatherly power in its height and perfection, and he might have showed us in Peru people that begot children on purpose to fatten and eat them. The story is so remarkable, that I cannot but set it down in the author's words: "In some provinces, says he, they were so liquorish after man's flesh, that they would not have the patience to stay till the breath was out of the body, but would suck the blood as it ran from the wounds of the dying man; they had public shambles of man's flesh, and their madness herein was to that degree, that they spared not their own children, which they had begot on strangers taken in war: for they made their captives their mistresses, and choicely nourished the children they lead by them, till about thirteen years old they butchered and eat them; and they served the mothers after the same fashion, when they grew past child-bearing, and ceased to bring them any more roasters." Garcilasso de la Vega, Hist. des Yncas de Peru, 1. i. c. 12.

## §58.

Thus far can the busy mind of man carry him to a brutality below the level of beasts, when he quits his reason, which places him almost equal to angels. Nor can it be otherwise in a creature, whose thoughts are more than the sands, and wider than the ocean where fancy and passion must needs run him into strange courses, if reason, which is his only star and compass, be not that he steers by. The imagination is always restless, and suggests variety of thoughts, and the will, reason being laid afield, is ready for every extravagant project; and in this state he that goes farthest out of the way, is thought fittest to lead, and is sure of most followers: and when fashion hath once established what folly or craft began, custom makes it sacred, and it will be thought impudence, or madness, to contradict or question it. He that will impartially survey the nations of the world, will find so much of their religions governments, and manners, brought in and continued amongst them by these means, that he will have but little reverence for the practices which are in use and credit amongst men; and will have reason to think, that the woods and forests, where the irrational untaught inhabitants keep right by following nature, are fitter to give us rules, than cities and palaces, where those that call themselves civil and rational, go out of their way, by the authority of example. If precedents are sufficient to establish a rule in this case, our author might have found in holy writ children sacrificed by their parents, and this amongst the people of God themselves the Psalmist tells us, Psalm cvi. 38, "They shed innocent blood, even the blood of their sons and of their daughters, whom they sacrificed unto the idols of Canaan." But God judged not of this by our author's rule, nor allowed of the authority of practice against his righteous law; but, as it follows there, "the land was polluted with blood; therefore was the wrath of the Lord kindled against his people, insomuch that he abhorred his own inheritance." The killing of their children, though it were fashionable, was charged on them as innocent blood, and so had in the account of God the guilt of murder, as the offering them to idols had the guilt of idolatry.

## §59.

Be it then, as sir Robert says, that anciently it was usual for men "to sell and castrate their children," O. 155. Let it be, that they exposed them; add to it, if you please, for this is still greater power, that they begat them for their tables, to fat and eat them: if this proves a right to do so, we may, by the same argument, justify adultery, incest, and sodomy, for there are examples of these too, both ancient and modern; sins, which I suppose have their principal aggravation from this, that they cross the main intention of nature, which willeth the increase of mankind, and the continuation of the species in the highest perfection, and the distinction of families, with the security of the marriage-bed, as necessary "hereunto.

## §60.

In confirmation of this natural authority of the father, our author brings a lame proof from the positive command of God in Scripture: his words are, "To confirm the natural right of regal power, we find in the decalogue, that the law which enjoins obedience to kings, is delivered in the terms, Honour thy father, p. 23. Whereas many confess, that government only in the abstract, is the ordinance of God, they are not able to prove any such ordinance in the Scripture, but only in the fatherly power; and therefore we find the commandment, that enjoins obedience to superiors, given in the terms, Honour thy father; so that not only the power and right of government, but the form of the power governing, and the person having the power, are all the ordinances of God. The first father had not only simply power, but power monarchical, as he was father immediately from God," O. 254,. To the same purpose, the same law is cited lay our author in several other places, and just after the same fashion; that is, "and mother," as apocryphal words, are always left out; a great argument of our author's ingenuity, and the goodness of his cause, which required in its defender zeal to a degree of warmth, able to warp the sacred rule of the word of God, to make it comply with his present occasion; a way of proceeding not unusual to those who embrace not truths because reason and revelation offer them, but espouse tenets and parties for ends deferent from truth, and then resolve at any rate to defend then; and so do with the words and sense of authors, they would fit to their purpose, just as Procrustes did with his guests, lop or stretch them, as clay best fit them to the size of their notions; and they always prove, like those so served, deformed, lame, and useless.

## §61.

For had our author set down this command without garbling, as God gave it, and joined another to father, every reader would have seen, that it had made directly against him, and that it was so far from establishing the "monarchical power of the father," that it set up the mother equal with him, and enjoined zing but was due In common to both father and mother: for that is the constant tenour of the Scripture. "Honour thy father and thy another," Exod. xx. "He that smiteth his father or mother, shall surely be put to death, xx. 15. "He that curseth his father or mother, shall surely be put to death," ver. 17. repeated Lev. xx 9, and by our Saviour, Matth. xv. 4. "Ye shall fear every man his mother and his father," Lev. xix. 3. "If any man have a rebellious son, which will not obey the voice of his father or the voice of his mother; then shall his father and his mother lay hold an him, and say, This our son is stubborn and rebellious, he will not obey our voice," Deut. xxi. 18, 19, 20, 21. "Cursed be he that setteth light by his father or his mother," xxvii. 16. "My son, hear the instructions of thy father, and forsake not the law of thy mother," are the words of Solomon, a king who was not ignorant of what belonged to him as a father or a king; and yet he joins father and mother together, in all the instructions he gives children quite through his book of Proverbs. "Woe unto him, that saith unto his father, What begettest thou? or to the woman, What hast thou brought forth?" Isa. xiv. 10. "In thee have they set light by father and mother," Ezeli. xxii. 7. "And it shall come to pass, that when any shall yet prophesy, then his father and his mother that begat him shall say unto him, Thou shalt not live; and his father anti his mother that begat him shall thrust him through when he prophesieth." Zech. xiii. 3. Here not the father only, but the father and mother jointly, had power in this case of life and death. Thus ran the law of the Old Testament, and in the New they are likewise joined, in the obedience of their children, Eph. vi. 1. The rule is, "Children, obey your parents;" and 1 do not remember, that I any where read, "Children, obey your father," and no more: the Scripture joins mother too in that homage which is due from children; and had there been any text, where the honour or obedience of children had been directed to the father alone, it is not likely that our author, who pretends to build all upon Scripture, would have omitted it: nay, the Scripture makes the authority of father and mother, in respect of those they have begot, so equal, that in some places it neglects even the priority of order, which is thought due to the father, and the mother is put first, as Lev. xix. A. From which so constantly joining father and mother together, as is found quite through Scripture, we may conclude that the honour they have a title to from their children is one common right belonging so equally to them both, that neither can claim it wholly, neither can be excluded.

## §62.

One would wonder then how our author infers from the fifth commandment, that all "power was originally in the father;" how he finds "monarchical power of government settled and fixed by the commandment, Honour thy father and thy mother." If all the honour due by the commandment, be it what it will, be the only right of the father, because he, as our author says, "has the sovereignty over the woman, as being the nobler and principal agent in generation," why did God afterwards all along join the mother with him, to share in his honour? Can the father, by this sovereignty of his, discharge the child front paying this honour to his mother? The Scripture gave no such licence to the Jews, anal yet there were often breaches wide enough betwixt husband and wife, even to divorce and separation: and, I think, nobody will say a child may withhold honour from his mother, or, as the Scripture terms it, "set light by her," though his father should command him to do so; no more than the mother could dispense with him for neglecting to honour his father: whereby it is plain, that this command of God gives the father no sovereignty, no supremacy.

## §63.

I agree with our author that the title to this honour is vested in the parents by nature, and is a right which accrues to them by their having begotten their children, and God by many positive declarations has confirmed it to them: I also allow our author's rule, "that in grants and gifts, that have their original from God and nature, as the power of the father," (let me add "and mother," for whom God hath joined together let no man put asunder) "no inferior power of men can limit, nor make any law of prescription against them," O. 158: so that the mother having, by this law of God, a right to honour from her children, which is not subject to the will of her husband, we see this "absolute monarchical popover of the father" Can neither be founded on it, nor consist with it; and he has a power very far from monarchical, very far from that absoluteness our author contends for, when another has over his subjects the same power he hath, and by the same title: and therefore he cannot forbear saying himself that "he cannot see how any man's children can be free from subjection to their parents," p. 12, which, in common speech, I think, signifies mother as well as father, or if parents here signifies only father, it is the first time I ever yet knew it to do so, and by such an use of words one may say any thing.

## §64.

By our author's doctrine, the father having absolute jurisdiction over his children, has also the same over their issue; and the consequence is good, were it true that the father had such a power: and yet I ask our author whether the grandfather, by his sovereignty, could discharge the grandchild from paying to his father the honour due to him by the fifth commandment. If the grandfather hath, by "right of fatherhood," sole sovereign power in him, and that obedience which is due to the supreme magistrate he commanded in these words, "Honour thy father," it is certain the grandfather might dispense with the grandson's honouring his father, which since it is evident in common sense he cannot, it follows from hence, that "honour thy father and mother" cannot mean an absolute subjection to a sovereign power, but something else. belie right therefore which parents have by nature, and which is confirmed to them by the fifth commandment, cannot be that political dominion which our author would derive from it: for that being in every civil society supreme somewhere, can discharge any subject from any political obedience to any one of his fellow-subjects. But what law of the magistrate can give a child liberty not to "honour his father and mother?" It is an eternal law, annexed purely to the relation of parents and children, and so contains nothing of the magistrate's power in it, nor is subjected to it.

## §65.

Our author says, "God hath given to a father a right or liberty to alien his power over his children to any other," O. 155. I doubt whether he can alien wholly the right of honour that is due from them; but be that as it will, this I am sure, he cannot alien and retain the same power. If therefore the magistrate's sovereignty be, as our author would have it, "nothing but the authority of a supreme father," p. 23, it is unavoidable, that if the magistrate hath all this paternal right, as he must have if fatherhood be the fountain of all authority; then the subjects, though fathers, can have no power over their children, no right to honour from them: for it cannot be all in another's hands, and a part remain with the parents. So that, according to our author's own doctrine, "Honour thy father and mother" cannot possibly be understood of political subjection and obedience: since the laws both in the Old and New Testament, that commanded children to "honour and obey their parents," were given to such, whose fathers were under civil government and fellow-subjects with them in political societies; and to have bid them "honour and obey their parents," in our author's sense, had been to bid them be subjects to those who had no title to it: the right to obedience from subjects being all vested in another; and instead of teaching obedience, this had been to foment sedition, by setting up powers that were not. If therefore this command, "Honour thy father and mother," concern political dominion, it directly overthrows our author's monarchy: since it being to be paid by every child to his father, even in society, every father must necessarily have political dominion, and there will be as many sovereigns as there are fathers: besides that the mother too hath her title, which destroys the sovereignty of one supreme monarch. But if "Honour thy father and mother" mean something distinct from political power, as necessarily it must, it is besides our author's business, and serves nothing to his purpose.

## §66.

"The law that enjoins obedience to kings is delivered," says our author, "in the terms, Honour thy father, as if all power were originally in the father," O. 254: and that law is also delivered, say I, in the term, "Honour thy mother," as if all power were originally in the mother. I appeal whether the argument be not as good on one side as the other, father and mother being joined all along in the Old and New Testament wherever honour or obedience is enjoined children. Again, our author tells us, O. 254, "that this command, Honour thy father, gives the right to govern, anal makes the form of government monarchical." To which I answer, that if by "Honour thy father" be meant obedience to the political power of the magistrate, it concerns not any duty we owe to our natural fathers, who are subjects; because they, by our author's doctrine, are divested of all that power, it being placed wholly in the prince, and so being equally subjects and slaves with their children, can have no light, by that title, to any such honour or obedience is contains in it political subjection: if "Honour thy father and mother" signifies the duty we owe our natural parents, as by our Saviour's interpretation, Matth. xv. 4, and tall the other mentioned places, it is plain it does: then it; cannot concern political obedience, but a duty that it owing to persons who have no title to sovereignty, nor any political authority as magistrates ever subjects, For the person of a private father, and a title to obedience, due ho the supreme magistrate, are things inconsistent; and therefore this command, which must necessarily comprehend the persons of natural fathers, must mean a duty we owe them distinct from, our obedience to the magistrate, and from which the most absolute poorer of princes cannot absolve us. What this duty is, we shall in its due place examine.

## §67.

And thus we have at last got through all, that in our author looks like an argument for that absolute unlimited sovereignty described, sect. 8, which he sup. poses in Adam, so that mankind have ever since been all born slaves, without any title to freedom. But if creation, which gave nothing but a being, made not Adam prince of his posterity: if Adam, Gen. i. 28, was not constituted lord of mankind, nor had a private dominion given him exclusive of his children, but only a right and power over the earth and inferior creatures in common with the children of men: if also, Gen. iii 16, God gave not any particular power to Adam over his wife and children, but only subjected Eve to Adam, as a punishment, or foretold the subjection of the weaker sex, in the ordering the common concernments of their families, but gave not thereby to Adam, as to the husband, power of life and death, which necessarily bet longs to the magistrate: if fathers by begetting their children acquire no such power over them; and if the command, "Honour thy father and mother," give it not, but only enjoins a duty owing to parents equally whether subjects or not, and to the mother as well as the father: if all this be so, as I think by what has been said is very evident; then man has a natural freedom, notwithstanding all our author confidently says to the contrary; since all that share in the same common nature, faculties, and powers, are in nature equal, and ought to partake in the same common rights and privileges, till the manifest appointment of God, who is "Lord over all, blessed for ever," can be produced show any particular person's supremacy; or a man's own consent subjects him to a superior. This is so plain, that our author confesses that sir John Hayward, Blackwood, and Barclay, "the great vindicators of the right of kings," could not deny it, "but admit with one consent the natural liberty and equality of mankind," for a truth unquestionable. And our author hath been so far from producing any thing that may make good his great position, "that Adam was absolute monarch," and so "men are not naturally free," that even his own proofs make against him; so that, to use his own way of arguing, "the first erroneous principle failing, the whole fabric of this vast engine of absolute power and tyranny drops down of itself," and there needs no more to be said in answer to all that he builds upon so false and frail a foundation.

## §68.

But to save others the pains, were there any need, he is not sparing himself to show, by his own contradictions, the weakness of his own doctrine Adam's absolute and sole dominion is that which he is every where full of, and all along builds on, and yet he tells us, p. 12, "that as Adam was lord of his children, so his children under him had a command and power over their own children." The unlimited and undivided sovereignty of Adam's fatherhood, by our author's computation, stood but a little while, only during the first generation; but as soon as he had grandchildren, sir Robert could give but a very ill account of it. "Adam, as father of his children," saith he, "hath an absolute, unlimited, royal power over them, and by virtue thereof over those that they begot, and so to all generations;" and yet his children, viz., Cain and Seth, have a paternal power over their children at the same time; so that they are at the same time absolute lords,.and yet vassals and slaves; Adam has all the authority, as "grandfather of the people," and they have a part of it as fathers of a part of them: he is absolute over them and their posterity, by having begotten them, and yet they are absolute over their children by the same title. "No," says our author, "Adam's children under him had power over their own children, but still with subordination to the first parent." A good distinction, that sounds well; and it is pity it signifies nothing, nor can be reconciled with our author's words. I readily grant, that supposing Adam's absolute power over his posterity, any of his children might hare from him a delegated, and so a subordinate power over a part, or all the rest: but that cannot be the power our author speaks of here; it is not a power by grant and commission, but the natural paternal power he supposes a father to have over his children. for, 1. He says, "As Adam was lord of his children, so his children under him had a power over their own children:" they were then lords over their own children after the same manner, and by the same title, that Adam was; i.e., by right of generation, by right of fatherhood. 2. It is plain he means the natural power of fathers, because he limits it to be only "over their own children;" a delegated power has no such limitation as only over their own children; it might be over others, is well as their own children. 3. If it were a delegated power, it must appear in Scripture; but there is no ground in Scripture to affirm, that Adam's children had any other power over theirs than what they naturally had as fathers.

## §69.

But that he means here paternal power, and no other, is past doubt, from the inference he makes ill these words immediately following, "I see not then how the children of Adam, or of any man else, can be free from subjection to their parents." Whereby it appears that the power on one side, and the subjection on the other, our author here speaks of, is that natural power and subjection between parents and children: for that which every men's children owed could be no other; and that our author always affirms to be absolute and unlimited.

This natural power of parents over their children Adam had over his posterity, says our author; and this power of parents over their children, his children had over theirs in his lifetime, says our author also; so that Adam, by a natural right of father, had an absolute, unlimited power over all his Posterity, anal at the saline time his children had by the same right absolute, unlimited power over theirs. Here then are two absolute, unlimited powers existing together, which I would love any body reconcile one to another, or to common sense. For the salvo he has put in of subordination makes it more absurd: to have one absolute, unlimited, nay unlimitable power in subordination to another, is so manifest a contradiction, that nothing can be more. "Adam is absolute prince, with the un limited authority of fatherhood over all his posterity;" all his posterity are then absolutely his subjects; anal as our author says, his slaves, children, and grandchildren, are equally in this state of subjection and slavery; and yet, says our author, "the children of Adam have paternal, i.e., absolute, unlimited power over their own children:" which in plain English is, they are slaves and absolute princes at the same time, and in the same government; and one part of the sum jects have an absolute, unlimited power over the other by the natural right of parentage.

## §70.

If any one will suppose in favour of our author, that he here meant that parents, who are in subjection themselves to the absolute authority of their father, have yet some power over their children; I confess he is something nearer the truth: but he will not at all hereby help our author: for he nowhere speaking of the paternal power, but as an absolute, unlimited authority, cannot be supposed to understand any thing else here, unless he himself had limited it, and showed how far it reached; and that he means here paternal authority in that large extent, is plain from the immediately following words: "This subjection of children being," says he, "the foundation of all regal authority," p. 12. The subjection then that in the former line, he says, "every man is in to his parents," and consequently what Adam's grandchildren were in to their parents, was that which was the fountain of all regal authority, i.e., according to our author, absolute, unlimitable authority. And thus Adam's children had regal authority over their children, whilst they themselves were subjects to their father, and fellow-subjects with their children. But him mean as he pleases, it is plain he allows "Adam's children to have paternal power," p. 12, as also all other fathers to have "paternal power over their children." O. 156. From whence one of these two things will necessarily follow, that either Adam's children, even in his life time, had, and so all other fathers have, as he phrases it, p. 12, "by right of fatherhood, royal authority over their children," or else that Adam, "by right of fatherhood, had not royal authority." For it cannot be lout that paternal power does, or does not, give royal authority to them that have it: if it does not, then Adam could not be sovereign by this title, nor any body else; and then there is an end of all our author's politics at once: if it does give royal authority, then every one that has paternal power has royal authority; and then, by our author's patriarchal government, there will be as many kings as there are fathers.

## §71.

An I thus what a monarchy he hath set up, let him and his disciples consider. Princes certainly will have great reason to thank him for these new politics, which set up as many absolute kings in every country as there are fathers of children. And yet who can blame our author for it, it lying unavoidably in the way of one discoursing upon our author's principles? For having placed an "absolute power in fathers by right of begetting," he could not easily resolve how much of this power belonged to a son over the children he had begotten; and so it fell out to be a very hard matter to give all the power, as he does, to Adam, and yet allow a part in his life time to his children when they were parents, and which he knew not well how to deny them. This makes him so doubtful in his expressions, and so uncertain where to place this absolute natural power which he calls fatherhood. Sometimes Adam alone has it all, as p. 13, O. 244, 245, and Pref. Sometimes parents have it, which word scarce signifies the father alone, p. 12,19. Sometimes children during their father's lifetime, as p. 12. Sometimes fathers of families, as p,. 78, 79. Sometimes fathers indefinitely, O. 155. Sometimes the heir to Adam, O. 258. Sometimes the posterity of Adam, 244, 246. Sometimes prime fathers, all sons of grandchildren of Noah, O. 244. Sometimes the eldest parents, p. 12. Sometimes all kings, p. 19. Sometimes all that have supreme power, O. 245. Sometimes heirs to those first progenitors who were at first the natural parents of the whole people, p. 19, Sometimes an elective king, p. 23. Sometimes those, whether a few or a multitude, that govern the commonweath, p. 23. Sometimes he that can catch it, an usurper, p. 23. O. 155.

§72.

Thus this new nothing, that is to carry with it all power, authority, and government; this fatherhood, which is to design the person, and establish the throne of monarchs, whom the people are to obey; may, according to sir Robert, come into any hands, any how, and so by his politics give to democracy royal authority, and make an usurper a lawful prince. And if it will do all these fine feats, much good do our author and all his followers with their omnipotent fatherhood, which can serve for nothing but to unsettle and destroy all the lawful governments in the world, and to establish in their room disorder, tyranny, and usurpation.

**Chapter VII, Of Fatherhood and Property considered together as Fountains of Sovereignty**

§73.

In the foregoing chapters we have seen what Adam's monarchy was in our author's opinion, and upon what titles he founded it. The foundations which he lays the chief stress on, as those from which he thinks he may best derive monarchical power to future princes, are two, viz., "fatherhood and property:" and therefore the way he proposes to "remove the absurdities and inconveniencies of the doctrine of natural freedom is, to maintain the natural and private dominion of Adam," O. 222. Conformable hereunto, he tell us, "the grounds and principles of government necessarily depend upon the original of property," O. 108. "The subjection of children to their parents is the fountain of all regal authority," p. 12. "And all power on earth is either derived or usurped from the fatherly power, there being no other original to be found of any power whatsoever," O. 158. I will not stand here to examine how it can be said without a contradiction, that the "first grounds and principles of government necessarily depend upon the original of property," and yet, "that there is no other original of any power whatsoever but that of the father:" it being hard to understand how there can be "no other original but fatherhood," and yet that the "grounds and principles of government depend upon the original of property;" property and fatherhood being as far different as lord of a manor and father of children. Nor do I see how they will either of them agree with what our author says, O. 244, of God's sentence against Eve, Gen. iii. 16, "that it is the original grant of government:" so that if that were the original, government had not its original, by our author's own confession, either from property or fatherhood; and this text, which he brings as a proof of Adam's power over Eve, necessarily contradicts what he says of the fatherhood, that it is the "sole fountain of all power:" for if Adam had any such regal power over Eve as our author contends for, it must be by some other title than that of begetting.

§74.

But I leave him to reconcile these contradictions, as well as many others, which may plentifully be found in him by any one, who will but read him with a little attention; and shall come now to consider, how these two originals of government, "Adam's natural and private dominion," will consist and serve to make out and establish the titles of succeeding monarchs, who, as our author obliges them, must all derive their popover from these fountains. Let us then suppose Adam made, "by God's donation," lord and sole proprietor of the whole earth, in as large and ample a manner as sir Robert could wish; let us suppose him also, "by right of fatherhood," absolute ruler over his children with an unlimited supremacy; I ask then, upon Adam's death, what becomes of both his natural and private domination? and I doubt not it will be answered, that they descended to his next heir, as our author tells us in several places. But this way, it is plain, cannot possibly convey both his natural and private dominion to the same person: for should we allow that all the property, all the estate of the father, ought to descend to the eldest son, (which will need some proof to establish it) and so he has by that title all the private dominion of the father, yet the father's natural dominion, the paternal power, cannot descend to him by inheritance: for it being a right that accrues to a man only by begetting, no man can have this natural dominion over any one he does not beget; unless it can be supposed that a man can have a right to any thing, without doing that upon which that right is solely founded: for if a father by begetting, and no other title, has natural dominion over his children, he that does not beget them cannot have this natural dominion over them; and therefore be it true or false, that our author says, O. 156, That "every man that is born, by his very birth, becomes a subject to him that begets him," this necessarily follows, viz., That a man by his birth cannot become a subject to his brother, who did not beget him; unless it can be supposed that a man by the very same title can come to be under the "natural and absolute dominion" of two different men at once; or it be sense to say, that a man by birth is under the natural dominion of his father, only because he begat him, and a man by birth also is under the natural dominion of his eldest brother, though he did not beget him.

§75.

If then the private dominion of Adam, i.e., his property in the creatures, descended at his death all entirely to his eldest son, his heir; (for, if it did not, there is presently an end of all sir Robert's monarchy) and his natural dominion, the dominion a father has over his children by begetting them, belonged, immediately upon Adam's decease, equally to all his sons who had children, by the same title their father had it, the sovereignty founded upon property, and the sovereignty founded upon fatherhood, come to be divided; since Cain, as heir, had that of property alone; Seth, and the other sons, that of fatherhood equally with him, This is the best can be made of our author's doctrine, and of the two titles of sovereignty he sets up in Adam; one of them will either signify nothing; or, if they both must stand, they can serve only to confound the rights of princes, and disorder government in his posterity: for by building upon two titles to dominion, which cannot descend together, and which he allows may be separated, (for he yields that "Adam's children had their distinct territories by right of private dominion," O. 210, p. 40) he makes it perpetually a doubt upon his principles where the sovereignty is, or to whom we owe our obedience; since fatherhood and property are distinct titles, and began presently upon Adam's death to be in distinct persons. And which then was to give way to the other?

§76.

Let us take the account of it, as he himself gives it us. He tells us out of Grotius, that "Adams children, by donation, assignation, or some kind of cession before he was dead, had their distinct territories by right of private dominion; Abel had his flocks, and pastures for them: Cain had his fields for corn, and the land of Nod, where he built him a city," O. 210. Here it is obvious to demand, which of these two after Adam's death was sovereign? Cain, says our author, p. 19. By what title? "As heir; for heirs to progenitors, who were natural parents of their people, are not only lords of their own children, but also of their brethren," says our author, p. 19 What was Cain heir to? Not the entire possessions not all that which Adam had private dominion in; for our author allows that Abel, by a title derived from his father, "had his distinct territory for pasture by right of private dominion." What then Abel had by private dominion, was exempt from Cain's dominion: for he could not have private dominion over that which was under the private dominion of another, and therefore his sovereignty over his brother is gone with this private dominion, and so there are presently two sovereigns, and his imaginary title of fatherhood is out of doors, and Cain is no prince over his brother: or else if Cain retain his sovereignty over Abel, notwithstanding his private dominion, it will follow, that the "first grounds and principles of government" have nothing to do with property, whatever our author says to the contrary. It is true, Abel did not outlive his father Adam; but that makes nothing to the argument, which will hold good against sir Robert in Abel's issue, or in Seth, or any of the posterity of Adam, not descended from Cain.

§77.

The same inconvenience he runs into about the three sons of Noah, who, as he says, p. 13, "had the whole world divided amongst them by their father." I ask then, in which of the three we shall find "the establishment of regal power" after Noah's death? If in all three, as our author there seems to say, then it will follow, that regal power is founded in property of land, and follows private dominion, and not in paternal power or natural dominion; and so there is an end of paternal power as the fountain of regal authority and the so much magnified fatherhood quite vanishes If the regal power descended to Shem as eldest, and heir to his father, then "Noah's division of the world by lot to his sons, or his ten years' sailing about the Mediterranean to appoint each son his part," which our author tells of, p. 15, was labour lost; his division of the world to them, was to ill, or to no purpose: for his grant to Cham and Japhet was little worth, if Shem, notwithstanding this grant, as soon as Noah was dead, was to be lord over them. Or, if this grant of private dominion to them, over their assigned territories' were good, here were set up two distinct sorts of power, not subordinate one to the other, with all those inconveniencies which he musters up against the "power of the people," O.158, which I shall set down in his own words, only changing property or people: "All power on earth is either derived or usurper! from the fatherly power, there being no other original to be found of any power whatsoever: for if there should be granted two sorts of power, without any subordination of one to the other, they would be in perpetual strife which should be supreme, for two supremes cannot agree: if the fatherly power be supreme, then the power grounded on private dominion must be subordinate, and depend on it; and if the power grounded on property be supreme, then the fatherly power must submit to it, and cannot be exercised without the licence of the proprietors, which must quite destroy the frame and course of nature." This is his own arguing against two distinct independent powers, which I have set down in his own words, only putting power rising from property, for power of the people; and when he has answered what he himself has urged here against two distinct powers, we shall be better able to see how, with any tolerable sense, he can derive all regal authority "from the natural anal private dominion of Adam," from fatherhood and property together, which are distinct titles, that do not always meet in the same persons; and it is plain, by his own confession, presently separated as soon both as Adam's and Noah's death makes way for succession: though our author frequently in his writings jumbles them together, and omits not to make use of either, where he thinks it will sound best to his purpose. But the absurdities of this will more fully appear in the next chapter, where we shall examine the ways of coveyance of the sovereignty of Adam to princes that were to reign after him.

**Chapter VIII, Of the Conveyance of Adam's sovereigns monarchical Power**

§78.

Sir Robert, having not been very happy in any proof he brings for the sovereignty of Adam, is not much more fortunate in conveying it to future princes; who, if his politics be true, must all derive their titles from that first monarch. The ways he has assigned, as they lie scattered up and down in his writings, I will set down in his own words: in his preface he tells us, that "Adam being monarch of the whole world, none of his posterity had any right to possess any thing, but by his grant or permission, or by succession from him." Here he snakes two ways of conveyance of any thing Adam stood possessed of; and those are grants, or succession. Again he says, "All kings either are, or arc to be reputed, the next heirs to those first progenitors, who were at first the natural parents of the whole people," p. 19.— "there cannot be any multitude of men whatsoever but that in it, considered by itself, there is one man amongst them, that in nature hath a right to be the king of all the rest, as being the next heir to Adam," O. 253. Here in these places inheritance is the only way he allows of conveying monarchical power to princes. In other places he tells us, O. 155, "All power on earth is either derived or usurped from the fatherly power," O.158. "All kings that now are, or ever were, are or were either fathers of their people, or heirs of such fathers, or usurpers of the right of such fathers," O. 253. And here he makes inheritance or usurpation the only way whereby kings come by this original power: but yet he tells us. "this fatherly empire, as it was of itself hereditary, so it was alienable by patent, and seizable by an usurper," O. 190. So then here inheritance, grant, or usurpation, will convey it. And last of all, which is most admirable, he tells us, p. 100, "It skills not which way kings come by their power, whether by election, donation, succession, or by any other means; for it is still the manner of the government by supreme popover that makes them properly kings, and not the means of obtaining their crowns." Which I think is a full answer to all his whole hypothesis and discourse about Adam's royal authority, as the fountain from which all princes were to derive theirs: and he might have spared the trouble of speaking so much as he does, up and down, of heirs and inheritance, if to make any one properly a king needs no more but "governing by supreme power, and it matters not by what means he came by it."

§79.

By this notable way, our author may make Oliver as properly king as any one else he could think of: and had he had the happiness to live under Massaniello's government, he could not by this his own rule have forborne to have done homage to him, with "O king live for ever," since the manner of his government by supreme power made him properly king, who was but the day before properly a fisherman. And if Don Quixote had taught his squire to govern with supreme authority, our author no doubt could have made a most loyal subject in Sancho Pancha's island; he must needs have deserved some preferment in such governments, since I think he is the first politician who, pretending to settle government upon its true basis, renal to establish the thrones of lawful princes, ever told the world, that he was "properly a king, whose manner of government was by supreme power, by what means soever he obtained it;" which in plain English is to say, that regal and supreme power is properly and truly his, who can by any means seize upon it: and if this be to be properly a king, I wonder how he came to think of, or where he will find, an usurper.

§80.

This is so strange a doctrine, that the surprise of it hath made me pass by, without their due reflection, the contradictions he runs into, by making sometimes inheritance alone, sometimes only grant or inheritance, sometimes only inheritance or usurpation, sometimes all these three, and at last election, or any other means, added to them, the ways whereby Adam's royal authority, that is, his right to supreme rule, could be conveyed down to future kings and governors, so as to give them a title to the obedience and subjection of the people. But these contradictions lie so open, that the very reading of our author's own words will discover them to any ordinary understanding; and though what I have quoted out of him (with abundance more of the same strain and coherence, which might be found in him) might well excuse me from any farther treble in this argument, yet having proposed to myself to examine the main parts of his doctrine, I shall a little more particularly consider how inheritance, grant, usurpation, or election, can any way make out government in the world upon his principles; or derive to any one a right of empire, froin this regal authority of Adam) had it been ever so well proved that he had been absolute monarch, and lord of the whole world.

**Chapter IX, Of Monarchy by Inheritance from Adam**

§81.

Though it be ever so plain, that there ought to be government in the world, nay, should all men be of our author's mind, that divine appointment had ordained it to be monarchical; yet, since men cannot obey any thing that cannot command; and ideas of government in the fancy, though ever so perfect, though ever so right, cannot give laws, nor prescribe rules to the actions of men; it would be of no behoof for the settling of order, and establishment of government in its exercise and use amongst men, unless there were a way also taught how to know the person, to whom it belonged to have this power, and exercise this dominion over others. It is in vain then to talk of subjection and obedience without telling us whom we are to obey: for were I ever so fully persuaded that there ought to be magistracy and rule in the world; yet I am nevertheless at liberty still, till it appears who is the person that hath right to my obedience; since, if there be no marks to know him by, and distinguish him that hath right to rule from other men, it may be myself, as well as any other; and therefore, though submission to government be every one's duty, yet since that signifies nothing but submitting to the direction and laws of such men as have authority to command, it is not enough to make a man a subject, to convince him that there is regal power in the world; but there must be ways of designing, and knowing the person to whom this regal power of right belongs; and a man can never be obliged in conscience to submit to any power, unless he can be satisfied who is the person who has a right to exercise that power over him. If this were not so, there would be no distinction between pirates and lawful princes; he that has force is without any more ado to be obeyed, and crowns and sceptres would become the inheritance only of violence and rapine. Men too might as often and as innocently change their governors, as they do their physicians, if the person cannot be known who has a right to direct me, and whose prescriptions I am bound to follow. To settle therefore men's consciences, under an obligation to obedience, it is necessary that they know not only that there is a power somewhere in the world, but the person who by right is vested with this power over them.

§82.

How successful our author has been in his attempts to set up a monarchical absolute power in Adam, the reader may judge by what has been already said; but were that absolute monarchy as clear as our author would desire it, as I presume it is the contrary, yet it could be of no use to the government of mankind now in the world, unless he also make out these two things. First, that this power of Adam was not to end with him, but was upon his decease conveyed entire to some other person, and so on to posterity. Secondly, that the princes and rulers now on earth are possessed of this power of Adam, by a right way of conveyance derived to them.

§83.

If the first of these fail, the power of Adam, were it ever so great, ever so certain, will signify nothing to the present government and societies in the world; but we must seek out some other original of power for the government of polities than this of Adam, or else there will be none at all in the world. If the latter fail, it will destroy the authority of the present governors, and absolve the people from subjection to them, since they, having no better claim than others to that power, which is alone the fountain of all authority, can have no title to rule over them.

§84.

Our author, having fancied an absolute sovereignty in Adam, mentions several ways of its conveyance to princes, that were to be his successors; but that which he chiefly insists on is that of inheritance, which occurs so often in his several discourses; and I having in the foregoing chapter quoted several of these passages, I shall not need here again to repeat them. This sovereignty he erects, as has been said, upon a double foundation, viz., that of property, and that of fatherhood. One was the right he was supposed to have in all creatures, a right to possess the earth with the beasts, and other inferior ranks of things in it, for his private use, exclusive of all other men. The other was the right he was supposed to have to rule and govern men, all the rest of mankind.

§85.

In both these rights, there being supposed an exclusion of all other men, it must be upon some reason peculiar to Adam, that they must both be founded. That of his property our author supposes to rise from God's immediate donation, Gen. i. 98, and that of fatherhood from the act of begetting. Now in all inheritance, if the heir succeed not to the reason upon which his father's right was founded, he cannot succeed to the right which followeth from it. For example, Adam had a right of property in the creatures upon the donation and grant of God Almighty, who was lord and proprietor of them all: let this be so as our author tells us, yet upon his death his heir can have no title to them, no such right of property in them, unless the same reason, viz., God's donation, vested a right in the heir too: for if Adam could have had no property in, nor use of the creatures, without this positive donation from God, and this donation were only personally to Adam, his heir could have no right by it; but upon his death it must revert to God, the lord and owner again; for positive grants give no title farther than the express words convey it, and by which only it is held. And thus, if, as our author himself contends, that donation, Gen. i. 28, were made only to Adam personally, his heir could not succeed to his property in the creatures: and if it were a donation to any but Adam, let it be shown that it was to his heir in our author's sense, i.e., to one of his children, exclusive of all the rest.

§86.

But not to follow our author too far out of the way, the plain of the case is this: God having made man, and planted in him, as in all other animals, a strong desire of self-preservation, and furnished the world with things fit for food and raiment, and other necessaries of life, subservient to his design, that man should live and abide for some time upon the face of the earth, and not that so curious and wonderful a piece of workmanship, by his own negligence, or want of necessaries, should perish again, presently after a few moments continuance; God, I say, having made man and the world thus, spoke to him, (that is) directed him by his senses and reason, as he did the inferior animals by their sense and Instinct, which were serviceable for his subsistence, and given him as the means of his preservation; and therefore I could not, but before these words were pronounced, Gen. i. 28, 29, (if they must be understood literally to have been spoken) and without any such verbal donation, man had a right to an use of the creatures, by the will and grant of God: for the desire, strong desire, of preserving his life and being, having been planted in him as a principle of action by God himself, reason, "which was the voice of God in him," could not but teach him and assure him that pursuing that natural inclination he had to preserve his being, he followed the will of his Maker, and therefore had a right to make use of those creatures which by his rear son or senses he could discover would be serviceable thereunto. And thus man's property in the creatures was founded upon the right he had to make use of those things that were necessary or useful to his being.

## §87.

This being the reason and foundation of Adam's property, gave the same title on the same ground to all his children, not only after his death, but in his life time: so that here was no privilege of his heir above his other children, which could exclude them from an equal right to the use of the inferior creatures, for the comfort-able preservation of their beings, which is all the property man hath in them; and so Adam's sovereignty built on property, or, as our author calls it, private dominion, comes to nothing. Every man had a right to the crea-tures by the same title Adam had, viz., by the right every one had to take care of and provide for their subsis-tence: and thus men had a right in common, Adam's children in common with him. But if any one lead begun, and made himself a property in any particular thing, (which how he, or any one else, could do, shall be shown in another place) that thing, that possession, if he disposed not otherwise of it by his positive grant, descended naturally to his children, and they had a right to succeed to it and possess it.

## §88.

It might reasonably be asked here, how cone children by this right of possessing, before any other, the proper-ties of their parent's upon their decease? for it being personally the parents, when they die, without actually transferring their right to another, why does it not return again to the common stock of mankind? It perhaps be answered, that common consent hath disposed of it to their children. Common practice, we see indeed, does so dispose of it; but we cannot say that it is the common consent of mankind; for that hath never been asked, nor actually given; and it common tacit consent hath established it, it would make but a positive, and not a natural right of children to inherit the goods of their parents: but where the practice is universal, it is reasonable to think the cause is natural. The ground then I think to be this: the first and strongest desire God planted in men, and wrought into the very principles of their nature, being that of self-preservation, that is the foundation of a right to the creatures for the particular support and use of each individual person himself. But, next to this, God planted in men a strong desire also of propagating their kind, and continuing themselves in their posteri-ty; and this gives children a title to share in the property of their parents, and a right to inherit their posses-sions. Men are not proprietors of what they have, merely for themselves; their children have a title to part of it, and have their kind of right joined with their parents in the possession, which comes to be wholly theirs, when death, having put an end to their parents' use of it, hath taken them from their possessions; and this eve call inheritance men being by a like obligation bound to preserve what they have begotten, as to preserve themselves, their issue come to have a right in the goods they are possessed of. That children have such a right is plain from the laws of God; and that men arc convinced that children have surly a right is evident from the law of the land; both which laws require parents to provide for their children.

## §89.

For children being by the course of nature born weak, and unable to provide for themselves, they have by the appointment of God himself, who hath thus ordered the course of nature, a right to be nourished and main-tained by their parents; nay, a right not only to a bare subsistence, but to the convenicncics and comforts of life, as far as the conditions of their parents can afford it. Hence it comes, that when their parents leave the world, and so the care due to their children ceases, the effects of it are to extend as far as possibly they can, and the provisions they have made in their lifetime are understood to be intendecl, as nature requires they should, for their children, whom, after themselves, they are bound to provide for: though the dying parents, by express words, declare nothing about them, nature appoints the descent of their property to their children, who thus come to have a title, and natural right of inheritance to their fathers' goods, which the rest of mankind cannot pretend to.

## §90.

Were it not for this right of being nourished and maintained by their parents, which God and nature has given to children, and obliged parents to as a duty, it would be reasonable that the father should inherit the estate of his son, and be preferred in the inheritance before his grandchild: for to the grandfather there is due a long score of care and expenses laid out upon the breeding and education of his son, which one would think in justice ought to be paid. But that haying teen done in obedience to the same law, whereby he received nourishment and education from his own parents; this score of education, received from a man's father, is paid by taking care and providing for his own children; is paid, I say, as much as is required of payment by alteration of property, unless present necessity of the parents require a return of goods for their necessary support and subsistence: for we are not now speaking of that reverence, acknowledgment, respect, and honour, that is always due from children to their parents; but of possessions and commodities of life valuable by money. But though it be incumbent on parents to bring up and provide for their children, yet this debt to their children does not quite cancel the score to their parents; but only is made by nature preferable to it: for the debt a man owes his father takes place, and gives the father a right to inherit the son's goods, where, for want of issue, the right of issue doth not exclude that title; and therefore a man having a right to be maintained by his children, where he needs it, and to enjoy also the comforts of life from them, when the necessary provision due to them end their children will afford it; if his son die without issue, the father has a right in nature to possess his goods and inherit his estate, (whatever the municipal laws of some countries may absurdly direct otherwise); and so again his children and their issue from him; or, for want of such, his father and his issue. But where no such are to be found, i.e., no kindred, there we see the possessions of a private man revert to the community, and so in politic societies come into the hands of the public magistrate; but in the state of nature become again perfectly common, nobody having a right to inherit them: nor can any one have a property in them, otherwise than in any other things common by nature; of which I shall speak in its due place.

## §91.

I have been the larger, in showing upon what ground children have a right to succeedto the possession of their fathers' properties, not only because by it, it will appear, that if Addend had a property (a titular, insignificant, useless property; for it could be no better, for he was bound to nourish and maintain his children and posterity out of it) in the whole earth and its product; yet all his children coming to have, by the law of nature, and right of inheritance, a joint title, and a right of property in it after his death, it could convey no right of sovereignty to any one of his posterity over the rest; since every one having a right of inheritance to his portion, they might enjoy their inheritance, or any part of it, in common, or share it, or some parts of it, by division, as it best liked them. But no one could pretend to the whole inheritance, or any sovereignty supposed to accompany it; since a right of inheritance gave every one of the rest, as well as any one, a title to share in the goods of his father. Not only upon this account, I say, have I been so particular in examining the reason of children's inheriting the property of their fathers, but also because it will give us farther light in the inheritance of rule and power, which in countries where their particular municipal laws give the whole possession of land entirely to the first-born, and descent of power has gone so to men by this custom, that some have been apt to be deceived into an opinion, that there was a natural or divine right of primogeniture to both estate and power; and that the Inheritance of both rule over men, and property in things, sprang from the same original, and were to descend by the same rules.

**§92.**

Property, whose original is from the right a man has to use any of the inferior creatures, for the subsistence and comfort of his life, is for the benefit and sole advantage of the proprietor, so that he may even destroy the thing, that he has property in by his use of it, where need requires: but government being for the preservation of every man's right and property, by preserving him from the violence or injury of others, is for the good of the governed: for the magistrate's sword being for a "terror to evil doers," and by that terror to enforce men to observe the positive laws of the society, made conformable to the laws of nature, for the public good, i.e., the good of every particular member of that society, as far as by common rules it can be provided for; the sword is not given the magistrate for his own good alone.

**§93.**

Children, therefore, as has been showed, by the dependence they have on their parents for subsistence, have a right of inheritance to their fathers' property, as that which belongs to them for their proper good and behoof, and therefore are fitly termed goods, wherein the firstborn has not a sole or peculiar right by any law of God and nature, the younger children having an equal title with him, founded on that right they all have to mainte-nance, support, and comfort from their parents, and on nothing else. But government being for the benefit of the governed, and not the sole advantage of the governors, (but only for theirs with the rest, as they make a part of that politic body, each of whose parts and members are taken care of, and directed in its peculiar func-tions for the good of the whole, by the laws of society) cannot be inherited by the same title that children have to the goods of their father. The right a son has to be maintained and provided with the necessaries and conve-niencies of life out of his father's stock, gives him a right to succeed to his father's property for his own good; but this can give him no right to succeed also to the rule which his father had over other men. All that a child has right to claim from his father is nourishment and education, and the things nature furnishes for the support of life: but he has no right to demand rule or dominion from him: he can subsist and receive from him the por-tion of good things and advantages of education naturally due to him, without empire and dominion. That (if his father hath any) was vested in him, for the good and behoof of others: and therefore the son cannot claim or inherit it by a title, which is founded wholly on his own private good and advantage.

**§94.**

We must know low the first ruler, from whom any one claims, came by his authority, upon what ground any one has empire, what his title is to it, before we can know who has a right to succeed him in it, and inherit it from him: if the agreement and consent of men first gave a sceptre into any one's hand, or put a crown on his head, that also must direct its descent and conveyance; for the same authority, that made the first a lawful ruler, must make the second too, and so give right of succession: in this case inheritance, or primogeniture, can in itself have no right, no presence to it, any farther than that consent, which established the form of the government, hath so settled the succession. And thus we see the succession of crowns, in several countries, places it on different heads, and he comes by right of succession to be a prince in one place, who would be a subject in another.

**§95.**

If God, by his positive grant and revealed declaration, first gave rule and dominion to any man, he that will claim by that title, must have the same positive grant of God for his succession: for if that has not directed the course of its descent and conveyance clown to others, nobody can succeed to this title of the first ruler. Chil-dren have no right of inheritance to this, and primogeniture can lay no claim to it, unless God, the Author of this constitution, hath so ordained it. Thus we see the pretensions of Saul's family, who received his crown from the immediate appointment of God, ended with his reign; and David, by the same title that Saul reigned, viz., God's appointment, succeeded in his throne, to the exclusion of Jonathan, and all pretensions of paternal inheritance: and if Solomon had a right to succeed his father, it must be by some other title than that of primogeniture. A cadet, or sister's son, must have the preference in succession, if he has the same title the first lawful prince had: and in dominion that has its foundation only in the positive appointment of God himself, Benjamin, the youngest, must have the inheritance of the crown, if God so direct, as well as one of that tribe had the first possession.

## §96.

If paternal right, the act of begetting, give a man rule and dominion, inheritance or primogeniture can give no title; for he that cannot succeed to his father's title, which was begetting, cannot succeed to that power over his brethren, which his father had by paternal right over them. But of this I shall have occasion to say more in another place. This is plain in the meantime, that any government, whether supposed to be at first founded in paternal right, consent of the people, or the positive appointment of God himself, which can supersede either of the other, and so begin a new government upon a new foundation; I say, any government began upon either of these, can by right of succession come to those only, who have the title of him they succeed to: power founded on contract can descend only to him who has right by that contract: power founded on begetting, he only can have that begets; and power founded on the positive grant or donation of God, he only can have by right of succession to whom that grant directs it.

## §97.

From what I have said, I think this is clear that a right to the use of the creatures, being founded originally in the right a man has to subsist and enjoy the conveniencies of life; and the natural right children have to inherit the goods of their parents being founded in the right they have to the same subsistence and commodities of life, out of the stock of their parents, who are therefore taught by natural love and tenderness to provide for them, as a part of themselves; and all this being only for the good of the proprietor or heir; it can be no reason for children's inheriting of rule and dominion, which has another original and a different end. Nor can primogeniture have any presence to a right of solely inheriting either property or power, as we shall, in its due place, see more fully. It is enough to have showed here, that Adam's property or private dominion could not convey any sovereignty or rule to his heir, who not having a right to inherit all his father's possessions, could not thereby come to have any sovereignty over his brethren: and therefore, if any sovereignty on account of his property had been vested in Adam, which in truth there was not, yet it would have died with him.

## §98.

As Adam's sovereignty, if, by virtue of being proprietor of the world, he had any authority over men, could not have been inherited by any of his children over the rest, because they had the same title to divide the inheritance, and every one had a right to a portion of his father's possessions: so neither could Adam's sovereignty by right of fatherhood, if any such he had, descend to any one of his children: for it being, in our author's account, a right acquired by begetting, to rule over those he had begotten, it was not a power possible to be inherited, because the right being consequent to, and built on, an act perfectly personal, made that power so too, and impossible to be inherited: for paternal power, being a natural right rising only from the relation of father and son, is as impossible to be inherited as the relation itself; and a man may pretend as well to inherit the conjugal power of the husband, whose heir he is, had over his wife, as he can to inherit the paternal power a father over his children: for the power of the husband being founded on contract, and the power of the father on begetting, he may as well inherit the power obtained by the conjugal contract, which was only personal, as he may the power obtained by begetting, which could reach no farther than the person of the begetter, unless begetting can be a title to power in him that does not beget

## §99.

Which makes it a reasonable question to ask, Whether Adam, dying before Eve, his heir, (suppose Cain or Seth) should have by right of inheriting Adam's fatherhood, sovereign power over Eve his mother? for Adam's father hood being nothing but a right he had to govern his children, because he begot them, he that inherits Adam's fatherhood, inherits nothing, even in our author's sense, but the right Adam had to govern his children, because he begot them: so that the monarchy of the heir would not have taken in Eve; or if it did, it being nothing but the fatherhood of Adam descended by inheritance, the heir must have right to govern love, because Adam begot her; for fatherhood s nothing else.

## §100.

Perhaps it will be said with our author, that a man can alien his power over his child; and what may be transferred by compact, may be possessed by inheritance. I answer, a father cannot alien the power he has over his child: he may perhaps to some degrees forfeit it, but cannot transfer it; and if any other man acquire it, it Is not by the father's grant, but by some act of his own. For example, a father, unnaturally careless of his child, sells or gives him to another man and he again exposes him; a third man finding him breeds him up, cherishes, and provides for him as his own: I think in this case, nobody will doubt, but that the greatest part of filial duty and subjection was here owing, and to be paid to this foster-father; and if any thing could be demanded from the child by either of the other, it could be only due to his natural father, who perhaps might have forfeited his right to much of that duty comprehended in the command, "Honour your parents," but could transfer none of it to another. He that purchased and neglected the child, got by his purchase and grant of the father no title to duty or honour from the child; but only he acquired it, who by his own authority, performing the office and care of a father to the forlorn and perishing infant, made himself, by paternal care, a title to proportionable degrees of paternal power. This will be more easily admitted, upon considerations of the nature of paternal power, for which I refer my reader to the second book.

## §101.

To return to the argument in hand; this is evident, That paternal power arising only from begetting, for in that our author places it alone, can neither be transferred nor inherited: and he that does not beget, can no more have paternal power, which arises from thence, than he can have a right to any thing, who performs not the condition, to which only it is annexed. If one should ask, by what law has a father power over his children? it will be answered, no doubt, by the law of nature, which gives such a power over them to him that begets them. If one should ask likewise, by what law does our author's heir come by a right to inherit? I think it would be answered, by the law of nature too: for I find not that our author brings one word of Scripture to prove the right of such an heir he speaks of. Why then the law of nature gives fathers paternal power over their children, because they did beget them: and the same law of nature gives the paternal power to the heir over his brethren who did not beget them: whence it follows, that either the father has not his paternal power by begetting, or else that the heir has it not at all; for it is hard to understand how the law of nature, which is the law of reason, can give the paternal power to the father over his children, for the only reason of begetting; and to the first-born over his brethren without this only reason, i.e., for no reason at all: and if the eldest, by the law of nature, can inherit this paternal power, without the only reason that gives a title to it, so may the youngest as well as he, and a stranger as well as either; for where there is no reason for any one, as there is not, but for him that begets, all have an equal title. I am sure our author offers no reason; and when any body does, we shall see whether it will hold or no.

## §102.

In the mean time it is as good sense to say, that by the law of nature a man has right to inherit the property of another, because he is of kin to him, and is known to be of his bloods and therefore, by the same law of nature, an utter stranger to his blood has right to inherit his estate; as to say that, by the law of nature, he that begets them has paternal power over his children, and therefore, by the law of nature, the heir that begets them not, has this paternal power over them: or supposing the law of the land gave absolute power over their children, to such only who nursed them, and fed their children themselves, could any body pretend that this law gave any one, who did no such thing, absolute power over those who were not his children?

§103.

When therefore it can be showed that conjugal power can belong to him that is not an husband, it will also I believe be proved, that our author's paternal power, acquired by begetting, may be inherited by a son; and that a brother, as heir to his father's power, may have paternal power over his brethren, and by the same rule conjugal power too: but till then I think we may rest satisfied that the paternal power of Adam, this sovereign authority of fatherhood, were there any such, could not descend to, nor be inherited by his next heir. Fatherly power, I easily grant our author, if it will do him any good, can never be lost, because it will be as long in the world as there are fathers: but none of then will have Adam's paternal power, or derive theirs from him; but every one will have his own by the same title Adam had his, viz., by begetting, but not by inheritance or succession, no more than husbands have their conjugal power by inheritance from Adam. And thus we see, as Adam had no such property, no such paternal power, as gave him sovereign jurisdiction over mankind; so likewise his sovereignty built upon either of these titles, if he had any such, could not have descended to his heir, but must have ended with him. Adam therefore, as has been proved, being neither monarch, nor his imaginary monarchy hereditable, the power which is now in the world is not that which was Adam's; since all that Adam could have, upon our author's grounds, either of property or fatherhood, necessarily cried with him, and could not be conveyed to posterity by inheritance. In the next place we will consider whether Adam had any such heir to inherit his power as our author talks of.

**Chapter X, Of the Heir to Adam's Monarchical Power.**

§104.

Our author tells us, O. 258, "That it is a truth undeniable, that there cannot be any multitude of men whatsoever, either great or small, though gathered together from the several corners and remotest regions of the world, but that in the same multitude, considered by itself, there is one man amongst them that in nature hath a right to be king of all the rest, as being the next heir to Adam, and all the other subjects to him: every man by nature is a king or a subject." And again, p. 20, "If Adam himself were still living, and now ready to die, it is certain that there is one man, and but one in the world, who is next heir." Let this multitude of men be, if our author pleases, all the princes upon the earth, there will then be, by our author's rule, "one amongst them that in nature hath a right to be king of all the rest, as being the right heir to Adam;" an excellent way to establish the thrones of princes, and settle the obedience of their subjects, by setting up an hundred, or perhaps a thousand titles (if there be so many princes in the world) against any king now reigning, each as good, upon our author's grounds, as his who wears the crown. If this right of heir carrier any weight with it, if it be the ordinance of God, as our author seems to tell us, O. 244, must not all be subject to it, from the highest to the lowest? Can those who wear the name of princes, without having, the right of being heirs to Adam, demand obedience from their subjects by this title, and not be bound to pay it by the same law? Either governments in the world are not to be claimed, and held by this title of Adam's heir; and then the starting of it is to no purpose, the being or not being Adam's heir signifies nothing as to the title of dominion: or if it really be, as our author says, the true title to government and sovereignty; the first thing to be done is to find out this true heir of Adam, seat him in his throne, and then all the kings and princes of the world ought to come and resign up their crowns and sceptres to him, as things that belong no more to them than to any of their subjects.

§105.

for either this right in nature of Adam's heir to be king over all the race of men, (for all together they make one multitude) is a right not necessary to the making of a lawful king, and so there may be lawful kings without it, and then kings' titles and pointer depend not on it; or else all the kings in the world but one are not lawful kings, and so have no right to obedience: either this title of heir to Adam is that whereby kings hold their crowns, and have a right to subjection from their subjects, and then one only can have it, and the rest being subjects can require no obedience from other men w ho are but their fellow-subjects; or else it is not the title whereby kings rule, and have a right to obedience from their subjects, and then kings are kings without it, and this dream of the natural sovereignty of Adam's heir is of no use to obedience and government: for if kings be a right to dominion and the obedience of their subjects who are not, nor can possibly be, heirs to Adam, what use is there of such a title, when we are obliged to obey without it? If kings, who are not heirs to Adam, have no right to sovereignty, we are all free, till our author, or any body for him, will show us Adam's right heir. If there be but one heir of Adam, there can be but one lawful king in the world, and noborly in conscience can be obliged to obedience till it be resolved who that is; for it may be any one, who is notknown to be of a younger house, and all others have equal titles. If there be more than one heir of Adam, every one is his heir, and so every one has regal power: for if two sons can be heirs together, then all the sons equally are heirs, and so all are heirs, being all sons, or sons' sons of Adam. Betwixt these two the right of heir cannot stand; for by it either but one only man, or all men are kings. Take which you please, it dissolves the bonds of government and obedience; since if all men are heirs, they can owe obedience to nobody; if only one, nobody can be obliged to pay obedience to him till he be known, and his title made out.

**Chapter XI, Who Heir?**

**§106.**

The great question which in all ages has disturbed mankind, and brought on them the greatest part of those mischiefs which have ruined cities, depopulated countries, and disordered the peace of the world, has been, not whether there be power in the world, nor whence it came, but who should have it. The settling of this point being, of no smaller moment than the security of princes, and the peace and welfare of their estates and kingdoms, a reformer of politics, one would think, should lay this sure, and be very clear in it: for if this re-main disputable, all the rest will be to very little purpose; and the skill used in dressing up power with all the splendor and temptation absoluteness can add to it, without showing who has a right to have it, will serve only to give a greater edge to man's natural ambition, which of itself is but too keen. What can this do but set men on the more eagerly to scramble, and so lay a sure and lasting foundation of endless contention and disorder, instead of that peace and tranquillity, which is the blurriness of government, and the end of human society?

**§107.**

This designation of the person our author is more than ordinary obliged to take care of, because he affirming that "the assignment of civil power is by divine institution," hath made the conveyance as well as the power itself sacred: so that no consideration, no act or art of man, can divert it from that person to whom, by this divine right, it is assigned; no necessity, or contrivance can substitute another person in his room. For if the "assignment of civil power be by divine institution," and Adam's heir be he to whom it is thus assigned, as in the foregoing chapter our author tells us, it would be as much sacrilege for any one to be king, who was not Adam's heir, as it would have been amongst the Jews for any one to have been priest who had not been of Aaron's posterity: for not only the priesthood in general being by divine institution, but the assignment of it" to the sole line and posterity of Aaron, made it impossible to be enjoyed or exercised by any one but those persons who revere else offspring of Aaron: whose succession therefore was carefully observed, and by that the persons who had a right to the priesthood certainly known.

**§108.**

Let us see then what care our author has taken to make us know who is "this heir, who by divine institution leas a right to be king over all men." The first account of him we meet with is p. 12, in these words: "This subjection of children being the fountain of all regal authority, by the ordination of God himself'; it follows that civil power, not only in general, is by divine institution, but even the assignment of it, specifically to the eldest parents." Matters of such consequence as this is should be in plain words, as little liable as might be to doubt or equivocation; and I think if language be capable of expressing any thing distinctly and clearly, that of kindred, and the several degrees of nearness of blood, is one. It were therefore to be wished that our author had used a little more intelligible expressions here, that we might have better known who it is to whom the assignment of civil power is made by divine institution; or at least would have told us what he meant by eldest parents: for I believe if land had been assigned or granted to him, and the eldest parents of his family, he would have thought it had needed an interpreter; and it would scarce have been known to whom next it belonged.

## §109.

In propriety of speech, (and certainly propriety of speech is necessary in a discourse of this nature) eldest parents signifies either the eldest men and women that have had children, or those who have longest had issue; and then our author's assertion will be, that those fathers and mothers who have been longest in the world, or longest fruitful, have by divine institution a right to civil power. If there be any absurdity in this, our author must answer for it: and if his meaning be different from my explication, he is to be blamed, that he would not speak it plainly. This I am sure, parents cannot signify heirs male, nor eldest parents an infant child: who yet may sometimes be the true heir, if there can be but one. And we are hereby still as much at a loss who civil power belongs to, notwithstanding this "assignment by divine institution," as if there had been no such assignment at all, or our author had said nothing of it. This of eldest parents leaving us more in the dark, who by divine institution has a right to civil power, than those who never heard any thing at all of heir or descent, of which our author is so full. And though the chief matter of his writing be to teach obedience to those who have a right to it, which he tells us is conveyed by descent; yet who those are, to whom this right by descent belongs, he leaves like the philosopher's stone in politics, out of the reach of any one to discover from his writings

## §110.

This obscurity cannot be imputed to want of language in so great a master of style as sir Robert is, when he is resolved with himself what he would say: and therefore, I fear, finding how hard it would be to settle rules of descent by divine institution, and how little it would be to his purpose, or conduce to the clearing and establishing the titles of princes, if such rules of descent were settled, he chose rather to content himself with doubtful and general terms, which might make no ill sound in men's ears who were willing to he pleased with them; rather than offer any clear rules of descent of this fatherhood of Adam, by which men's consciences might be satisfied to whom it descended, and know the persons who had a right to regal power, and with it to their obedience.

## §111.

How else is it possible, that laying so much stress, as he does, upon descent, and Adam's heir, next heir, true heir, he should never tell us what heir means, nor the way to know who the next or true heir is? This I do not remember he does any where expressly handle; but, where it comes in his way, very warily and doubtfully touches; though it be so necessary, that without it all discourses of government and obedience upon his principles would be to no purpose, and fatherly power, ever so well made out, will be of no use to any body. Hence he tells us, O. 244, "That not only the constitution of power in general, but the limitation of it to one kind, i.e., monarchy, and the determination of it to the individual person and line of Adam, are all three ordinances of God; neither Eve nor her children could either limit Adam's power, or join others with him; and what was given unto Adam was given in his person to his posterity." Here again our author inform us, that the divine ordinance hath limited the descent of Aclam's monarchical power. To whom? To Adam's line and posterity," says our author. A notable limitation, a limitation to all mankind: for if our author can find any one amongst mankind that is not of the line and posterity of Adam, he may perhaps tell him who this next heir of Adam is: but for us, I despair how this limitation of Adam's empire to his line and posterity will help us to find out one heir. This limitation indeed of our author will save those the labour who would look for him amongst the race of brutes, if any such there were; but will very little contribute to the discovery of one next heir amongst men, though it make a short and easy determination of the question about the descent of Adam's regal power, by telling us that the line and posterity of Adam is to have it, that is, in plain English, any one may have it, since there is no person living that hath not the title of being of the line and posterity of Adam and while it keeps there, it keeps within our author's limitation by God's ordinance. Indeed, p. 19, he tells us, "that such heirs are not only lords of their own children, but of their brethren;" whereby, and by the words following, which we shall consider anon, he seems to insinuate that the eldest son is heir; but he nowhere, that I know, says it in direct words, but by the instances of Cain and Jacob, that there follow, we may allow this to be so far his opinion concerning heirs, that where there are divers children, the eldest son has the right to be heir. That primogeniture cannot give any title to paternal power, we have already showed. That a father may have a natural right to some kind of power over his children, is easily granted; but that an elder brother has so over his brethren, remains to be proved: God or nature has not any where, that I know, placed such jurisdiction in the first born; nor can reason find any such natural superiority amongst brethren. The law of Moses gave a double portion of the goods and possessions to the eldest; but we find not any "here that naturally, or by God's institution, superiority or dominion belonged to him; and the instances there brought by our author are but slender proofs of a right to civil power and dominion in the first born, and do rather show the contrary.

§112.

His words are in the forecited place: "And therefore we find God told Cain of his brother Abel, his desire shall be subject unto thee, and thou shalt rule over him." To which I answer, 1. These words of God to Cain are by many interpreters, with great reason, understood in a quite different sense than what our author uses them in. 2. Whatever was meant by them, it could not be that Cain, as elder, had a natural dominion over Abel; for the words are conditional, "If thou dost well;" and so personal to Cain: and whatever was signified by them did depend on his carriage, and not follow his birthright; and therefore could by no means be an establishment of dominion in the firstborn in general: for before this Abel had his "distinct territories by right of private dominion," as our author himself confesses, O. 210, which he could not have had to the prejudice of the heir's title, "if by divine institution" Cain as heir were to inherit all his father's dominion. 3. If this were intended by God as the charter of primogeniture, and the grant of dominion to the elder brothers in general as such, by right of inheritance, we might expect it should have included all his brethren: for we may well suppose, Adam, from whom the world was to be peopled, had by this time, that these were grown up to be men, more sons than these two: whereas Abel himself is not so much as named; and the words in the original can scarce, with any good construction, be applied to him. 4. It is too much to build a doctrine of so mighty consequence upon so doubtful and obscure a place of Scripture, which may well, nay better, be understood in a quite different sense, and so can be but an ill proof, being as doubtful as the thing to be proved by it; especially when there is nothing else in Scripture or reason to be found, that favours or supports it.

§113.

It follows, p. 19, "accordingly when Jacob bought his brother's birthright, Isaac blessed him thus; Be lord over thy brethren, and let the sons of thy mother bow before thee." Another instance, take it, brought by our author to evince dominion due to birthright, and an admirable one it is: for it must be no ordinary way of reasoning in a man, that is pleading for the natural power of kings, and against all compact, to bring, for proof of it, an example, where his own account of it founds all the right upon compact, and settles empire in the younger brother, unless buying and selling be no compact; for he tells us, "when Jacob bought his birthright." But passing by that, let us consider the history itself, with what use our author makes of it, and we shall find the following mistakes about it. 1. That our author reports this, as if Isaac given Jacob this blessing immediately upon his purchasing the birthright; for he says, "when Jacob bought, Isaac blessed him;" which is plainly otherwise in the Scripture: for it appears, there was a distance of time between, and if we will take the story in the order it lies, it must be no small distance: all Isaac's sojourning in Gerar, and transactions with Abimelech, Gen. xxvi. coming between; Rebecca being then beautiful, and consequently young: but Isaac, when he blessed Jacob, was old and decrepit: and Esau also complains of Jacob, Gen. xxvii. 36, that two times he had supplanted him; "he took away my birthrighllt, (says he) and behold now he hath taken away my blessing;" words, that I think signify distance of time and difference of action. 2. Another mistake of our author's is, that he supposes Isaac gave Jacob the blessing, and bid him be "lord over his brethren," because he had the birthright; for our author brings this example to prove, that he that has the birthright, has thereby a right to "be lord over his brethren." But it is also manifest by the text, that Isaac had no consideration of Jacob's having bought the birthright; for when he blessed him, he considered him not as Jacob, but took him for Esau. Nor did Esau understand any such connexion between birthright and the blessing; for he says, "He hath supplanted me these two times; he took away my birthright, and behold now he hath taken away my blessing:" whereas had the blessing, which was to be "lord over his brethren," belonged to the birthright, Esau could not have complained of this second as a cheat, Jacob having got nothing but what Esau had sold him, when he sold him his birthright; so that it is plain, dominion, if these words signify it, was not understood to belong to the birthright.

## §114.

And that, in those days of the patriarchs, dominion was not understood to be the right of the heir, but only a greater portion of goods, is plain from Gen. xxi. 10; for Sarah, taking Isaac to be heir, says, "cast out this bondwoman and her son, for the son of this bondwoman shall not be heir with my son:" whereby could be meant nothing, but that he should not have a presence to an equal share of his father's estate after his death, but should have his portion presently, and be gone. Accordingly we read, Gen. xxv. 5, 6, "That Abraham gave all that he had unto Isaac: but unto the sons of the concubines which Abraham had, Abraham gave gifts, and sent them away from Isaac his son, while he yet lived." That is, Abraham having given portions to all his other sons, and sent them away, that which he had reserved, being the greatest part of his substance, Isaac as heir possessed after his death: but by being heir, he had no right to be "lord over his children;" for if he had, why should Sarah endeavour to rob him of one of his subjects, or lessen the number of his slaves, by desiring to have Ishmael sent away.

## §115.

Thus, as under the law, the privilege of birthright was nothing but a double portion: so we see that before Moses, in the patriarchs' time, from whence our author pretends to take his model, there vas no knowledge, no thought, that birthright gave rule or empire, paternal or kingly authority, to any one over his brethren. If this be not plain enough in the story of Isaac and Ishmael, he that will look into 1 Chron. v. 1, may there read these words: "Reuben as the first-born: but forasmuch as he defiled his father's bed, his birthright was given unto the sons of Joseph, the son of Israel: and the genealogy is not to be reckoned after the birthright; for Judah prevailed above his brethren, and of him came the chief ruler; but the birthright was Joseph's." What this birthright was, Jacob blessing Joseph, Gen. xlviii. 22, telleth us in these words, "Moreover I have given thee one portion above thy brethren, which I took out of the hand of the Amorite, with my sword and with my bow." Whereby it is not only plain that the birthright was nothing but a double portion, but the text in Chronicles is express against our author's doctrine, and shows that dominion was no part of the birthright; for it tells us, that Joseph the birthright, but Judah the dominion. One would think our author were very fond of the very name of birthright, when he brings this instance of Jacob and Esau, to prove that dominion belongs to the heir over his brethren.

## §116.

1. Because it will be but an ill example to prove, that dominion by God's ordination belonged to the eldest son, because Jacob the youngest here had it, let him come by it how he would: for if it prove any thing, it can only prove, against our author, that the "assignment of dominion to the eldest is not by divine institution," which would then be unalterable: for if by the law of God, or nature, absolute power and empire belongs to the eldest son and his heirs, so that they are supreme monarchs, and all the rest of their brethren slaves, our author gives us reason to doubt whether the eldest son has a popover to part with it, to the prejudice of his posterity, since he tells us, O. 158, "That in grants and gifts that have their original from God or nature, no inferior power of man can limit, or make any law of prescription against them."

## §117.

2. Because this place, Gen. xxvii. 29, brought by our author, concerns not at all the dominion of one brother over the other, nor the subjection of Esau to Jacob: for it is plain in history, that Esau was never subject to Jacob, but lived apart in mount Seir, where he founded a distinct people and government, and was himself prince over them, as much as Jacob was in his own family. The text, if considered, can never be understood of Esau himself, or the personal dominion of Jacob over him: for the words brethren and sons of thy mother, could not be used literally by Isaac, who knew Jacob had only one brother; and these words are so far from being true in a literal sense, or establishing any dominion in Jacob over Esau, that in the story we find the quite contrary; for Gen. xxxii. Jacob several times calls Esau lord, and himself his servant; and Gen. xxxiii. "he bowed himself seven times to the ground to Esau." Whether Esau then were a subject and vassal (my, as our author tells us, all subjects are slaves to Jacob), and Jacob his sovereign prince by birthright, I leave the reader to judge; and to believe, if he can, that these words of Isaac, "be lord over thy brethren, and let thy mother's sons bow down to thee," confirmed Jacob in a sovereignty over Esau, upon the account of the birthright he had got from him.

## §118.

He that reads the story of Jacob and Esau, will find there never was any jurisdiction or authority, that either of them had over the other, after their father's death: they lived with the friendship and equality of brethren, neither lord, neither slave to his brother; but independent of each other, were both heads of their distinct families, where they received no laws from one another, but lived separately, and were the roots out of which sprang two distinct people under two distinct governments. This blessing then of Isaac, whereon our author would build the dominion of the elder brother, signifies no more, but what Rebecca had been told from God, Gen. xxv. 23, "Two nations are in thy womb, and two manner of people shall be separated from thy bowels; and the one people shall be stronger than the other people, and the elder shall serve the younger:" and so Jacob blessed Judah, Gen. xlix, and gave him the sceptre and dominion; from whence our author might have argued as well, that jurisdiction and dominion belongs to the third son over his brethren, as well as from this blessing of Isaac, that it belonged to Jacob: both these places contain only predictions of what should long after happen to their posterities, and not any declaration of the right of inheritance to dominion in either. And thus we have our author's two great and only arguments to prove, that "heirs are lords over their brethren." 1. Because God tells Cain, Gen. iv. that however sin might set upon him, he ought or might be master of it: for the most learned interpreters understood the words of sin, and not of Abel, anal give so strong, reasons for it, that nothing can convincingly be inferred from so doubtful a text to our author's purpose. 2. Because in this of Gen. xxvii. Isaac foretell that the Israelites, the posterity of Jacob, should have dominion over the Edomites, the posterity of Esau; therefore, says our author,"heirs are lords of their brethren:" I leave any one to judge of the conclusion.

**§119.**

And now we see our author has provided for the descending, and conveyance down of Adam's monarchical power, or paternal dominion, to posterity, by the inheritance of his heir, succeeding to all his father's authority, and becoming upon his death as much lord as his father was, "not only over his own children, but over his brethren," and all descended from his father, and so in infinitum. But yet who this heir is, he does not once tell us; and all the light we have from him in this so fundamental a point, is only that in his instance of Jacob, by using the word birthright, as that which passed from Esau to Jacob, he leaves us to guess, that by heir he means the eldest son; though I do not remember he any where mentions expressly the title of the first-born, but all along keeps himself under the shelter of the indefinite term heir. But taking it to be has meaning, that the eldest son is heir (for if the eldest be not, there will be no presence why the sons should not be all heirs alike) and so by right of primogeniture has dominion over his brethren; this is but one step towards the settlement of succession, and the difficulties remain still as much as ever, till he can show us who is meant by right heir, in all those cases which may happen where the present possessor hath no son. This he silently passes over, and perhaps wisely too: for what can be wiser, after one has affirmed, that "the person having that power, as well as the power and form of government, is the ordinance of God, and by divine institution," viz. O. 254, p. 12, than to be careful, not to start any question concerning the person, the resolution whereof will certainly lead him into a confession, that God and nature hath determined nothing about him? And if our author cannot show who by right of nature, or a clear positive law of God, has the next right to inherit the dominion of this natural monarch he has been at such pains about, when he died without a son, he might have spared his pains in all the rest; it being more necessary for the settling men's consciences, and determining their subjection and allegiance, to show them who, by original right, superior and antecedent to the will, or any act of men, hath a title to this paternal jurisdiction, than it is to show that by nature there was such a jurisdiction; it being to no purpose for me to know there is such a paternal power, which I ought, and am disposal to obey, unless where there are many pretenders, I also know the person that is rightfully invested and endowed with it.

**§120.**

For the main matter in question being concerning the duty of my obedience, and the obligation of conscience I am under to pay it to him that is of right my lord and ruler, I must know the person that this right of paternal power resides in, and so empowers him to claim obedience from me. For let it be true what he says, p. 12, "that civil power not only in general is by divine institution, but even the assignment of it specially to the eldest parents;" and O. 254, "That not only the power or right of government, but the form of the power of governing, and the person having that power, are all the ordinance of God;" yet unless he show us in all cases who is this person ordained by God, who is this eldest parent: all his abstract notions of monarchical power will signify just nothing, when they are to be reduced to practice, and men are conscientiously to pay their obedience: for paternal jurisdiction being not the thing to be obeyed, because it cannot command, but is only that which gives one man a right which another hath not, and if it come by inheritance, another man cannot have, to command and be obeyed; it is ridiculous to say, I pay obedience to the paternal power, when I obey him, to whom paternal power gives no right to my obedience: for he can have no divine right to my obedience, who cannot show his divine right to the power of ruling over me, as well as that by divine right there is such a power in the world.

**§121.**

And hence not being able to make out any prince's title to government, as heir to Adam, which therefore is of no use, and had been better let alone, he is fain to resolve all into present possession, and makes civil obedience as due to an usurper as to a lawful king; and thereby the usurper's title as good. His words are, O. 253, and they deserve to be remembered: "If an usurper dispossess the true heir, the subjects' obedience to the fatherly popover must go along, and wait upon God's providence." But I shall leave his title of usurpers to be examined in its due place, and desire my sober reader to consider what thanks princes owe such politics as this, which can suppose paternal popover, i.e., a right to government in the hands of a Cade or a Cromwell; and so all obedience being due to paternal power, the obedience of subjects will be due to them, by the same right, and upon as good grounds, as it is to lawful princes; and yet this, as dangerous a doctrine as it is, must necessarily follow from making all political power to be nothing else but Adam's paternal power by right and divine institution, descending from him without being able to show to whom it descended, or who is heir to it.

### §122.

To settle government in the world, and to lay obligations to obedience on any man's conscience, it is as necessary (supposing with our author that all power be nothing but the being possessed of Adam's fatherhood) to satisfy him, who has a right to this power, this fatherhood, when the possessor dies, without sons to succeed immediately to it; as it was to tell him, that upon the death of the father, the eldest son had a right to it: for it is still to be remembered, that the great question is, (and that which our author would be thought to contend for, if he did not sometimes forget it) what persons have a right to be obeyed, and not whether there be a power in the world, which is to be called paternal, without knowing in whom it resides: for so it be a popover, i.e., right to govern, it matters not, whether it be termed paternal or regal, natural or acquired; whether you call it supreme fatherhood, or supreme brotherhood, will be all one, provided we know who has it.

### §123.

I go on then to ask, whether in the inheriting of this paternal power, this supreme fatherhood, the grandson by a daughter hath a right before a nephew by a brother? Whether the grandson by the eldest son, being an infant, before the younger son, a man and able? Whether the daughter before the uncle? or any other man, descended by a male line? Whether a grandson, by a younger daughter, before a grand-daughter by an elder daughter? Whether the elder son by a concubine, before a younger son by a wife? From whence also will arise many questions of legitimation, and what in nature is the difference betwixt a wife and a concubine? For as to the municipal or positive laws of men, they can signify nothing here. It may farther be asked Whether the eldest son, being a fool, shall inherit this paternal power, before the younger, a wise man? and what degree of folly it must be that shall exclude him? and who shall be judge of it? Whether the son of a fool, excluded for his folly, before the son of his wise brother who reigned? Who has the paternal power whilst the widow-queen is with child by the deceased king, and nobody knows whether it will be a son or a daughter? Which shall be heir of the two male twins, who by the dissection of the mother were laid open to the world? Whether a sister by the half-blood, before a brother's daughter by the whole blood ?

### §124.

These, and many more such doubts, might be proposed about the titles of succession, and the right of inheritance; and that not as idle speculations, but such as in history we shall find have concerned the inheritance of crowns and kingdoms; and if our's want them, we need not go farther for famous examples of it than the other kingdom in this very island, which having been fully related by the ingenious and learned author of Patriarcha non Monarcha, I need say no more of. Till our author hath resolved all the doubts that mall arise about the next heir, and showed that they are plainly determined by the law of nature, or the revealed law of God, all his suppositions of a monarchical, absolute, supreme, paternal power in Adam, and the descent of that power to his heirs, would not be of the least use to establish the authority, or make out the title of any one prince now on earth; but would rather unsettle and bring all into question: for let our author tell us as long as he pleases, and let all men believe it too, that Adam had a paternal, and thereby a monarchical power; that this (the only power in the world) descended to his heirs; and that there is no other power in the world but this: lot this be all as clear demonstration, as it is manifest error; yet if it be not past doubt to whom this paternal power descends, and whose now it is, nobody can be under any obligation of obedience; unless any one will say that I am bound to pay obedience to paternal power in a man who has no more paternal power than I myself; which is all one as to say, I obey a man, because he has a right to govern; and if I be asked how I know he has a right to govern, I should answer it cannot be known that he has any at all: for that cannot be the reason of my obedience, which I know not to be so; much less can that be a reason of my obedience, which nobody at all can know to be so.

## §125.

And therefore all this ado about Adam's fatherhood, the greatness of its power, and the necessity of its supposal, helps nothing to establish the power of those that govern, or to determine the obedience of subjects who are to obey, if they cannot tell whom they are to obey, or it cannot be known who are to govern, and who to obey. In the state the world is now, it is irrecoverably ignorant who is Adam's heir. This fatherhood, this monarchical power of Adam, descending to his heirs, would be of no more use to the government of mankind, than it would be to the quieting of men s consciences, or securing their healths, if our author had assured them that Adam had a power to forgive sins, or cure diseases, which by divine institution descended to his heir, whilst this heir is impossible to be known. And should not he do as rationally, who upon this assurance of our author went and confessed his sins, and expected a good absolution; or took physic with expectation of health, from any one who had taken on himself the name of priest or physician, or thrust himself into those employments, saying, I acquiesce in the absolving power descending from Adam, or I shall be cured by the medicinal power descending from Adam; as he who says, I submit to and obey the paternal lower descending from Adam, when it is confessed all these powers descend only to his single heir, and that heir is unknown?

## §126.

It is true the civil lawyers have pretended to determine some of these cases concerning the succession of princes; but by our author's principles they have meddled in a matter that belongs not to them: for if all political power be derived only from Adam, and be to descend only to his successive heirs, by the ordinance of God and divine institution, this is a right antecedent and paramount to all government; and therefore the positive laws of men cannot determine that which is itself the foundation of all law and government, and is to receive its rule only from the law of God and nature. And that being silent in the case, I am apt to think there is no such right to be conveyed this way: I am sure it would be to no purpose if there were, and men would be more at a loss concerning government, and obedience to governors, than if there were no such right; since by positive laws and compact, which divine institution (if there be any) shuts out, all these endless inextricable doubts can be safely provided against: but it can never be understood how a divine natural right, and that of such moment as is all order and peace in the world, should be conveyed down to posterity, without any plain natural or divine rule concerning it. And there would be an end of all civil government, if the assignment of civil power were by divine institution to the heir, and yet by that divine institution the person of the heir could not be known. This paternal regal power being by divine right only his, it leaves no room for human prudence, or consent, to place it any where else; for if only one man hath a divine right to the obedience of mankind, nobody curl claim bleat obedience but he that can show that right; nor can men's consciences by any other presence he obliged to it. And thus this doctrine cuts up all government by the roots.

## §127.

Thus we see how our author, laying it for a sure foundation, that the very person that is. to rule is the ordinance of God, and by divine institution; tells us at large only that this person is the heir, but who this heir is he leaves us to guess; and so this divine institution, which assigns it to a person whom vie have no rule to know, is just as good as an assignment to nobody at all. But whatever our author does, divine institution makes no such ridiculous assignments: nor can God be supposed to make it a sacred law, that one certain person should have a right to something, and yet not give rules to mark out, and know that person by; or give an heir a divine right to power, and yet not point out who that heir is. It is rather to be thought that an heir had no such right by divine institution, than that God should give such a right to the heir, but yet leave it doubtful and undeterminable who such heir is.

## §128.

If God lead given the land of Canaan to Abraham, and in general terms to somebody after him, without naming his seed, whereby it might be known who that somebody was; it would have been as good and useful an assignment to determine the right to the land of Canaan, as it would be the determining the right of crowns, to give empire to Adam and his successive heirs after him, without telling who his heir is: for the word heir, without a rule to know who it is, signifies no more than somebody, I know not whom. God making it a divine institution that men should not marry those who were of near kin, thinks it not enough to say, "none of you shall approach to any that is near of kin to him, to uncover albeit nakedness;" but moreover gives rules to know who are those near of kin, forbidden by divine institution; or else that law would have been of no use; it being to no purpose to lay restraint or give privileges to men, in such general terms, as the particular person concerned cannot be known by. But God not having any where said the next heir shall inherit all his father's estate or dominion, we are not to wonder that he hath nowhere appointed who that heir should be; for never having intended any such thing, never designed any heir in that sense, we cannot expect he should any where nominate or appoint any person to it, as we might, had it been otherwise. And therefore in Scripture, though the word heir occur; yet there is no such thing as heir in our author's sense, one that was by right of nature to inherit all that his father had; exclusive of his brethren. Hence Sarah supposes that if Ishmael staid in the house to share in Abraham's estate after his death, this son of a bond-woman might be heir with Isaac; and therefore, says she, "cast out this bond-woman and her son, for the son of this bondwoman shall not be heir with my son:" but this cannot excuse our author, who telling us there is, in every number of men, one who is right and next heir to Adam, ought to have told us what the laws of den scent are: but he having been so sparing to instruct us by rules how to know who is heir; let us see in the next place what his history out of Scripture, on which he pretends wholly to build his government, gives us in this necessary and fundamental point.

## §129.

Our author, to make good the title of his look, p. 13, begins his history of the descent of Adam's regal power, p. 13, in these words: "This lordship which Adam by command had over the whole world, and by right descending from him, the patriarchs did enjoy, was a large," &c. How does he prove that the patriarchs by descent did enjoy it? for "dominion of life and deaths says he, we find Judah the father pronounced sentence of death against Thamar his daughter-in-law for playing the harlot," p. 13. How does this prove that Judah had absolute and sovereign authority? "he pronounced sentence of death." The pronouncing of sentence of death is not a certain mark of sovereignty; but usually the office of inferior magistrates. The power of making laws of life and death is indeed a mark of sovereignty; but pronouncing, the sentence according to those laws may be done by others, and therefore this will but ill prove that he had sovereign authority: as if one should say, judge Jefferies pronounced sentence of death in the late times, therefore judge Jefferies had sovereign authority. But it will be said Judah did it not by commission from another and therefore did it in his own right. Who knows whether he had any right at all? Heat of passion might carry him to do that which he had no authority to do. "Judah had dominion of life and death:" how does that appear? He exercised it, he "pronounced sentence of death against Thamar." Our author thinks it is very good proof that because he did it, therefore he had a right to do it. He lay with her also; by the same way of proof he had a right to do that too. If the consequence be good from doing, to a right of doing, Absalom too may be reckoned amongst our author's sovereigns; for he pronounced such a sentence of death against his brother Amnon, and much upon a like occasion, and had it executed too, if that be sufficient to prove a dominion of life and death. But allowing this all to be clear demonstration of sovereign power, who was it that had this "lordship by right descending to him from Adam, as large and ample as the absolutest dominion of any monarch?" Judah, says our author, Judah, a younger son of Jacob, his father and elder brethren living; so that if our author's own proof be to be taken, a younger brother may, in the life of his father and elder brothers, "by right of descent, enjoy Adam's monarchical power;" and if one so qualified may be a monarch by descent, why may not every man? If Judah, his father and elder brethren living, were one of Adam's heirs, I know not who can be excluded from this inheritance; all men by inheritance may be monarchs as well as Judah.

§130.

"Touching war, we see that Abraham commanded an army of 318 soldiers of his own family, and Esau met his brother Jacob with 400 men at arms: for matter of peace, Abraham made a league with Abimelech," &c. p. 13. Is it not possible for a man to have 318 men in his family without being heir to Adam? A planter in the West Indies has more, and might, if he pleased (who doubts?) muster them up and lead them out against the Indians to seek reparation upon any injury received from them; and an this without the "absolute dominion of a monarch, descending to him from Adam." Would it not be an admirable argument to prove, that all power by God's institution descended from Adam by inheritance, and that the very person and power of this planter were the ordinance of God, because he had power in his family over servants born in his house, and bought with his money? For this was just Abraham's case; those who were rich in the patriarch's days, as in the West Indies now, bought men and maid-servants, and by their increase, as well as purchasing of new, came to have large and numerous families, which though they made use of in war or peace, can it be thought the power they had over them was an inheritance descended from Adam, when it was the purchase of their money? A man's riding, in an expedition against an enemy, his horse bought in a fair, would be as good a proof that the owner enjoyed the lordship which Adam by command had over the whole world, by right descending to him," as Abraham's leading out the servants of his family is, that the patriarchs enjoyed this lordship by descent from Adam: since the title to the power the master had in both cases, whether over slaves or horses, was only from his purchase; and the getting a dominion over any thing by bargain and money, is a new way of proving one had it by descent and inheritance.

§131.

"But making war and peace are marks of sovereignty." Let it be so in politic societies: may not therefore a man in the West Indies, who hath with him sons of his own, friends or companions, soldiers under pay; or slaves bought with money, or perhaps a band made up of all these, make war and peace, if there should be occasion, and "ratify the articles too with an oath, without being a sovereign, an absolute king over those who went with him? He that says he cannot, must then allow many masters of ships, many private planters, to be absolute monarchs, for as much as this they have done. War and peace cannot be made for politic societies, but by the supreme power of such societies; because war and peace giving a different motion to the force of such a politic body, none can make war or peace but that which has the direction of the force of the whole body, and that in politic societies is only the supreme power. In voluntary societies for the time, he that has such a power by consent may make war and peace, and so may a single man for himself, the state of war not consisting in the number of partisans, but the enmity of the parties, where they have no superior to appeal to.

§132.

The actual making of war or peace is no proof of any other power, but only of disposing those to exercise or cease acts of enmity for whom he makes it, and this power in many cases any one may have without any politic supremacy: and therefore the making of war or peace will not prove that every one that does so is a politic ruler, much less a king; for then commonwealths must be kings too, for they do as certainly make war and peace as monarchical government.

§133.

But granting this a "mark of sovereignty in Abraham," is it a proof of the descent to him of Adam's sovereignty over the whole world? If it be, it will surely be as good a proof of the descent of Adam's lordship to others too. And then commonwealths, as well as Abraham, will be heirs of Adam, for they make war and peace as well as he. If you say that the "lordship of Adam" doth not by right descend to commonwealths, though they male war and peace, the same say I of Abraham, and then there is an end of your argument: if you stand to your argument, and say those that do make war and peace, as commonwealths do without doubt, "do inherit Adam's lordship," there is an end of your monarchy, unless you will say that commonwealths "by descent enjoying Adam's lordship" are monarchies; and that indeed would be a new way of making all the governments in the world monarchical.

§134.

To give our author the honour of this new invention, for I confess it is not I have first found it out by tracing his principles, and so charged it on him, it is fit my readers know that (as absurd as it may seem) he teaches it himself, p. 28, where he ingenuously says, "In all kingdoms and commonwealths in the world, whether the prince be the supreme father of the people, or but the true heir to such a father, or come to the crown by usurpation or election, or whether some few or a multitude govern the commonwealth; yet still the authority that is in any one, or in many, or in all these, is the only right and natural authority of a supreme father;" which right of fatherhood, he often tells us, is "regal and royal authority;" as particularly p. 12, the page immediately preceding this instance of Abraham. This regal authority, he says, those that govern commonwealths have; and if it be true, that regal and royal authority be in those that govern commonwealths, it is as true that commonwealths are governed by kings; for if regal authority be in him that governs, he that governs must needs be a king, and so all commonwealths are nothing but downright monarchies; and then what need any more ado about the matter? The governments of the world are as they should be, there is nothing but monarchy in it. This, without doubt, was the surest way our author could have found to turn all other governments, but monarchical, out of the world.

§135.

But all this scarce proves Abraham to have been a king as heir to Adam. If by inheritance he kind been king, Lot, who was of the same family, must needs have been his subject by that title, before the servants in his family; but we see they lived as friends and equals, and when their herdsmen could not agree, there was no presence of jurisdiction or superiority between them, but they parted by consent, Gen. xiii. hence he is called, both by Abraham and by the text, Abraham's brother; the name of friendship and equality, and not of jurisdiction and authority, though he were really but his nephew. And if our author knows that Abraham was Adam's heir, and a king, it was more, it seems, than Abraham himself knew, or his servant whom he sent a wooing for his son; for when he sets out the advantages of the match, Gen. xxiv. 35, thereby to prevail with the young woman and her friends, he says, "I am Abraham's servant, and the Lord hath blessed my master greatly, and he is become great; and he hath given him flocks and herds, and silver and gold, and men-servants and maid--servants, and camels and asses; and Sarah, my master's wife, bare a son to my master when she was old, and unto him hath he given all he hath." Can one think that a discreet servant, that was thus particular to set out his master's greatness, would have omitted the crown Isaac was to have, if he had known of any such? Can it be imagined he should have neglected to have told them, on such an occasion as this, that Abraham was a king, a name well known at that time, for he had nine of them his neighbours, if he or his master had thought any such thing, the likeliest matter of all the rest, to make his errand successful?

§136.

But this discovery it seems was reserved for our author to make two or 3000 years after, and let him enjoy the credit of it; only he should have taken care that some of Adam's land should have descended to this his heir; as well as all Adam's lordship: for though this lordship which Abraham, (if we may believe our author) as well as the other patriarchs, "by right descending to him, did enjoy, was as large and ample as the absolutest dominion of any monarch which hath been since the creation;" yet his estate, his territories, his dominions, were very narrow and scanty; for he had not the possession of a foot of land, till he bought a field and a cave of the sons of Heth to bury Sarah in.

§137.

The instance of Esau joined with this of Abraham, to prove that the "lordship which Adam had over the whole world, by right descending from him, the patriarchs did enjoy," is yet more pleasant than the former. "Esau met his brother Jacob with 400 men at arms;" he therefore was a king by right of heir to Adam. Four hundred armed men then, however got together, are enough to prove him that leads them to be a king, and Adam's heir. There have been Tories in Ireland, (whatever there are in other countries) who would have thanked our author for so honourable an opinion of them, especially if there had been nobody near with a better title of 500 armed men, to question their royal authority of 400. It is a shame for men to trifle so, to say no worse of it, in so serious an argument. Here Esau is brought as a proof that Adam's lordship, "Adam's absolute dominion, as large as that of any monarch, descended by right to the patriarchs;" and in this very chap. p. 19, Jacob is brought as an instance of one, that by "birthright was lord over his brethren." So we have here two brothers absolute monarchs by the same title, and at the same time heirs to Adam; the eldest, heir to Adam, because he met his brother with 400 men; and the youngest heir to Adam by birth right: "Esau enjoyed the lordship which Adam had over the whole world by right descending to him, in as large and ample manner as the absolutest dominion of any monarch; and at the same time, Jacob lord over him, by the right heirs have to be lords over their brethren." Risum teneatis? I never, I confess, met with any man of parts so dexterous as sir Robert at this way of arguing: but it w as his misfortune to light upon an hypothesis that could not be accommodated to the nature of things, and human affairs; his principles could not be made to agree with that constitution and order which God lead settled in the world, and therefore must needs often clash with common sense and experience.

§138.

In the next section, he tells us, "This patriarchal power continued not only till the flood, but after it, as the name patriarch cloth in part prove." The word patriarch cloth more than in part prove, that patriarchal power continued in the world as long as there were patriarchs; for it is necessary that patriarchal power should be whilst there are patriarchs, as it is necessary there should be paternal or conjugal power whilst there are fathers or husbands; but this is but playing with names. That which he would fallaciously insinuate is the thing in question to be proved viz. that the "lordship which Adam had over the world, the supposed absolute universal dominion of Adam by right descending from him, the patriarchs did enjoy." If he affirms such an absolute monarchy continued to the flood in the world, I would be glad to know what records he has it from; for I confess I cannot find a word of it in my Bible: if by patriarchal power he means any thing else, it is nothing to the matter in hand. And how the name patriarch in some part proves, that those who are called by that name had absolute monarchical power, I confess I do not see, and therefore I think needs no answer till the argument from it be made out a little clearer.

## §139.

"The three sons of Noah had the world," says our author, "divided amongst them by their father, for of them was the whole world overspread," p. 14. The world might be overspread by the offspring of Noah's sons, though he never divided the world amongst them; for the earth might be replenished without being divided: so that all our author's argument here proves no such division. However, I allow it to him, and then ask, the world being divided amongst them, which of the three was Adam's heir? If Adam's lordship, Adam's monarchy, by right descended only to the eldest, then the other two could be but his subjects, his slaves if by right it descended to all three brothers, by the same right it will descend to all mankind; and then it will be impossible what he says, p. 19, that "heirs are lords of their brethren," should be true; but all brothers, and consequently all men, will be equal and independent, all heirs to Adam's monarchy, and consequently all monarchs too, one as much as another. But it will be said, Noah their father divided the world amongst them; so that our author will allow more to Noah than he will to God Almighty, for O. 211, he thought it hard, that God himself should give the world to Noah and his sons, to the prejudice of Noah's birthright. His words are, "Noah was left sole heir to the world: why should it be thought that God would disinherit him of his birthright, and make him, of all men in the world, the only tenant in common with his children?" and yet he here thinks it fit that Noah should disinherit Shem of his birthright, and divide the world betwixt him and his brethren; so that his birthright, when our author pleases, must, and when he pleases, must not, be sacred and inviolable.

## §140.

If Noah did divide the world between his sons, and his assignment of dominions to them were good, there is an end of divine institution; all our author's discourse of Adam's heir, with whatsoever he builds on it, is quite out of doors; the natural power of kings falls to the ground; and then "the form of the power governing, and the person having that power, will not be (as he says they are, O. 254.), the ordinance of God, but they will he ordinances of man:" for if the right of the heir be the ordinance of God, a divine right; no man, father or not father, can alter it: if it be not a divine right, it is only human, depending on the will of man: and so where human institution gives it not, the first-born has no right at all above his brethren; and men may put government into what hands, and under what form they please.

## §141.

He goes on, "most of the civilest nations of the earth labour to fetch their original from some of the sons or nephews of Noah," p. 14. How many do most of the civilest nations amount to? and who are they? I fear the Chinese, a very great and civil people, as well as several other people of the East, West) North, and South, trouble not themselves much about this matter. All that believe the Bible, which I believe are our author's "most of the civilest nations," must necessarily derive themselves from Noah; but for the rest of the world, they think little of his sons or nephews. But if the heralds and antiquaries of all nations, for it is these men generally that labour to find out the originals of nations, or all the nations themselves, "stout labour to fetch their original from some of the sons or nephews of Noah," what would this be to prove, that the "lordship which Adam had over the whole world, by a right descended to the patriarchs?" Whoever, nations, or races of men, "labour to fetch their original from," may be concluded to be thought by them men of renown, famous to posterity for the greatness of their virtues and actions; but beyond these they look not, nor consider who they were heirs to, but look on them as such as raised themselves by their own virtue to a degree that would give lustre to those who in future ages could pretend to derive themselves from them. But if it were Ogyges, Hercules, Brama Tamerlain, Pharamond; nay, if Jupiter and Saturn were the names, from whence divers races of men, both ancient and modern, have laboured to derive their original; will that prove, that those men "enjoyed the lordship of Adam by right descending to them?" If not, this is but a flourish of our author's to mislead his reader, that in itself signifies nothing.

## §142.

To as much purpose is what he tells us, p. 15, concerning this division of the world, "That some say it was by lot, and others that Noah sailed round the Mediterranean in ten years, and divided the world into Asia, Afric, and Europe, portions for his three sons." America then, it seems, was left to be his that could catch it. Why our author takes such pains to prove the division of the world by Noah to his sons, and will not leave out an imagination, though no better than a dream, that he can find any where to favour it, is hard to guess, since such a division, if it prove any thing, must necessarily take away the title of Adam's heir; unless three brothers can all together be heirs of Adam; and therefore the following words, "howsoever the manner of this division be uncertain, yet it is most certain the division was by families from Noah and his children, over which the parents were heads and princes," p. 15, if allowed him to be true, and of any force to prove, that all the power in the world is nothing but the lordship of Adam's descending by right, they will only prove, that the fathers of the children are all heirs to this lordship of Adam: for if in those days Cham and Japhet, and other parents, besides the eldest son, were heads and princes over their families, and had a right to divide the earth by families what hinders younger brothers, being fathers of families, from having the same right? If Cham and Japhet were princes by right descending to them, notwithstanding any title of heir in their eldest brother, younger brothers by the same right descending to them are princes now; and so all our author's natural power of kings will reach no farther than their own children; and no kingdom, by this natural right, can be bigger than a family: for either this lordship of Adam over the whole world, by right descends only to the eldest son, and then there can be but one heir, as our author says p. 19; or else it by right descends to all the sons equally, and then every father of a family will have it, as well as the three sons of Noah: take which you will, it destroys the present governments and kingdoms, that are now in the world; since whoever has this natural power of a king, by right descending to him, must have it, either as our author tells us Cain had it, and be lord over his brethren, and so be alone king of the whole world; or else, as he tells us here, Shem, Cham, and Japhet had it, three brothers, and so be only prince of his own family, and all families independent one of another: all the world must be only one empire by the right of the next heir, or else every family be a distinct government of itself, by the "lordship of Adam's descending to parents of families." And to this only tend all the proofs he here gives us of the descent of Adam's lordship: for continuing his story of this descent, he says,

## §143.

"In the dispersion of Babel, we must certainly find the establishment of royal power, throughout the kingdoms of the world," p. 14. If you must find it, pray do, and you will help us to a new piece of history: but you must show it us before we shall be bound to believe, that regal power was established in the world upon your principles: for, that regal power was established "in the kingdoms of the world," I think nobody will dispute; but that there should be kingdoms in the world, whose several kings enjoyed their crowns, "by right descending to them from "Adam," that we think not only apocryphal, but also utterly impossible. If our author has no better foundation for his monarchy than a supposition of what was done at the dispersion of Babel, the monarchy he erects thereon, whose top is to reach to heaven to unite mankind, will serve only to divide and scatter them as that tower did; and, instead of establishing civil government and order in the world, will produce nothing but effusion.

## §144.

For he tells us, the nations they were divided into "were distinct families, which had fathers for rulers over them; whereby it appears, that even in the confusion, God was careful to preserve the fatherly authority, by distributing the diversity of languages according to the diversity of families," p. 14. It would have been a hard matter for any one but our author to have found out so plainly, in the text he here brings, that all the nations in that dispersion were governed by fathers, and that "God was careful to preserve the fatherly authority." The words of the text are, "These are the sons of Shem after their families, after their tongues in their lands, after their stations;" and the same thing is said of Cham and Japhet, after an enumeration of their posterities: in all which there is not one word said of their governors, or forms of government; of fathers, or fatherly authority. But our author, who is very quicksighted to spy out fatherhood, where nobody else could see any the least glimpses of it, tells us positively their "rulers were fathers, and God was careful to preserve the fatherly authority;" and why? Because those of the same family spoke the same language, and so of necessity in the division kept together. Just as if one should argue thus: Hannibal in his army, consisting of divers nations, kept those of the same language together; therefore fathers were captains of each band, and Hannibal was careful of the fatherly authority: or in peopling of Carolina, the English, French, Scotch, and Welsh, that are there plant themselves together, and by them the country is divided "in their lands after their tongues, after their families, after their nations;" therefore care was taken of the fatherly authority: or because, in many parts of America, every little tribe was a distinct people, with a different language, one should infer that therefore "God was careful to preserve the fatherly authority," or that therefore their rulers "enjoyed Adam's lordship by right descending to them," though we know not who were their governors, nor what their form of government: but only that they were divided into little independent societies, speaking different languages.

### §145.

The Scripture says not a word of their rulers or forms of government, but only gives an account how mankind came to be divided into distinct languages and nations; and therefore it is not to argue from the authority of Scripture, to tell us positively fathers were their rulers, when the Scripture says no such thing; but to set up fancies in one's own brain, when we confidently aver matter of fact, where records are utterly silent. Upon a like ground, i.e., none at all, he says, "That they were not confused multitudes without heads and governors, and at liberty to choose what governors or governments they pleased."

### §146.

For I demand, when mankind were all yet of one language, all congregated in the plain of Shinar, were they then all under one monarch, "who enjoyed else lordship of Adam by right descending to him?" If they were not, there were then no thoughts, it is plain, of Adam's heir, no right to government known then upon that title; no care taken, by God or man, of Adam's fatherly authority. If when mankind were but one people, dwelt altogether, and were of one language, and were upon building a city together; and when it is plain they could not but know the right heir; for Shem lived till Isaac's time, a long while after the division at Babel; if then, I say, they were not under the monarchical government of Adam's fatherhood, by right descending to the heir, it is plain there w as no regard had to the fatherhood, no monarchy acknowledged due to Adam's heir, no empire of Shem's in Asia, and consequently no such division of the world by Noah, as our author has talked of. As far as we can conclude any thing from Scripture in this matter, it seems from this place, that if they had any government, it was rather a commonwealth than an absolute monarchy: for the Scripture tells us, Gen. xi. "They said:" it was not a prince commanded the building of this city and tower, it was not by the command of one monarch, but by the consultation of many, a free people; "let us build us a city:" they built it for themselves as free men, not as slaves for their lord and master: "that we be not scattered abroad;" having a city once built, and fixed habitations to settle our abodes and families. This was the consultation and design of a people, that were at liberty to part asunder, but desired to keep in one body; and could not have been either necessary or likely in men tied together under the government of one monarch, who if they had been, as our author tells us, all slaves under the absolute dominion of a monarch, needed not have taken such care to hinder themselves from wandering out of the reach of his dominion. I demand whether this be not plainer in Scripture than any thing of Adam's heir or fatherly authority?

### §147.

But if being, as God says, Gen. xi. 6, one people, they had one ruler, one king by natural right, absolute and supreme over them," what care had God to preserve the paternal authority of the supreme fatherhood," if on a sudden he suffer 72 (for so many our author talks of) distinct nations to be erected out of it, under distinct governors, and at once to withdraw themselves from the obedience of their sovereign? This is to intitle God's care how, and to what we please. Can it be sense to say, that God was careful to preserve the fatherly authority in those who had it not? For if these were subjects under a supreme prince, what authority had they? Was it an instance of God's care to preserve the fatherly authority, when he took away the true supreme fatherhood of the natural monarch? Can it be reason to say, that God, for the preservation of fatherly authority, lets several new governments with their governors start up, who could not all have fatherly authority? And is it not as much reason to say, that God is careful to destroy fatherly authority, when he supers one, who is in possession of it, to have his government torn in pieces, and shared by several of his subjects? Would it not be an argument just like this, for monarchical government to say, when any monarchy was shattered to pieces, and divided amongst revolted subjects, that God was careful to preserve monarchical popover, by rending a settled empire into a multitude of little governments? If any one will say, that what happens in providence to be preserved, God is careful to preserve as a thing therefore to be esteemed by men as necessary or useful; it is a peculiar propriety of speech, which every one will not think fit to imitate: but this I an; sure is impossible to be either proper or true speaking, that Shem, for example (for he wa

then alive), should have fatherly authority, or sovereignty by right of fatherhood, over that one people at Babel, and that the next moment, Shem yet living, 72 others should have fatherly authority, or sovereignty by right of fatherhood, over the same people, divided into so many distinct governments: either these 72 fathers actually were rulers, just before the confusion, and then they were not one people, but that God himself says they were; or else they were a commonwealth, and then where was monarchy? or else these 72 fathers had fatherly authority, but knew it not. Strange! that fatherly authority should be the only original of government amongst men, and yet all mankind not know it; and stranger yet, that the confusion of tongues should reveal it to them all of a sudden, that in an instant these 72 should know that they had fatherly power, and all others know that they were to obey it in them, and every one know that particular fatherly authority to which he was a subject. He that can think this arguing from Scripture, may from thence make out what model of an Utopia will best suit with his fancy or interest; and this fatherhood, thus disposed of; will justify both a prince who claims an universal monarchy, and his subjects, who, being fathers of families, shall quit subjection to him, and canton his empire into less governments for themselves: for it will always remain a doubt in which of these the fatherly authority resided, till our outlook resolves us, whether Shem, who was then alive, or these 72 new princes, beginning so many new empires in his dominions, and over his subjects, had right to govern; since our author tells us, that both one and the other had fatherly, which is supreme authority, and are brought in by him as instances of those who did "enjoy the lordships of Adam by right descending to them, which was as large and ample as the absolutest dominion of any monarch." This at least is unavoidable, that if "God was careful to preserve the fatherly authority, in the 72 new-erected nations," it necessarily follows, that he was as careful to destroy all pretences of Adam's heir; since he took care, and therefore did preserve the fatherly authority in so many, at least 71, that could not possibly be Adam's heirs, when the right heir (if God had ever ordained any such inheritance) could not but be known; Shem then living, and they being all one people.

§148.


Nimrod is his next instance of enjoying this patriarchal power, p. 16, but I know not for what reason our author seems a little unkind to him, and says, that he "against right enlarged his empire, by seizing violently on the rights of other lords of families." These lords of families here revere called fathers of families, in his account of the dispersion at Babel: but it matters not how they were called, so we know who they are; for this fatherly authority must be in them, either as heirs to Adam, and so there could not be 72, nor above one at once; or else as natural parents over their children, and so every father will have paternal authority over his children by the same right, and in as large extent as those 72 had, and so be independent princes over their own offspring. Taking his lords of families in this latter sense (as it is hard to give those words any other sense in this place), he gives us a very pretty account of the original of monarchy, in these following words, p. 16. "And in this sense he may be said to be the author and founder of monarchy," viz., As against right seizing violently on the rights of fathers over their children; which paternal authority, if it be in them, by right of nature (for else how could those 72 come by it?) nobody can take from them without their own consents; and then I desire our author and his friends to consider, how far this will concern other princes, and whether it will not, according, to his conclusion of that paragraph, resolve all regal power of those, whose dominions extend beyond their families, either into tyranny and usurpation, or election and consent of fathers of families, which will differ very little from consent of the people.

## §149.

All his instances, in the next section, p. 17, of the 12 dukes of Edom, the nine kings in a little corner of Asia in Abraham's days, the 31 kings in Canaan destroyed by Joshua, and the care he takes to prove that these were all sovereign princes, and that every town in those days had a king, are so many direct proofs against him, that it was not the lordship of Adam by right descending to them, that made kings: for if they had held their royalties by that title, either there must have been but one sovereign over them all, or else every father of a family had been as good a prince, and had as good a claim to royalty, as these: for if all the sons of Esau had each of them, the younger as well as the eldest, the right of fatherhood, and so were sovereign princes after their father's death; the same right had their sons after them, and so on to all posterity; which will limit all the natural power of fatherhood, only to be over the issue of their own bodies, and their descendents; which power of fatherhood dies with the head of each family, and makes way for the like power of fatherhood to take place in each of his sons over their respective posterities: whereby the power of fatherhood will be preserved indeed, and is intelligible, but will not be at all to our author's purpose. None of the instances he brings are proofs of any power they had, as heirs of Adam's paternal authority, by the title of his fatherhood descending to them; no, nor of any power they had by virtue of their own: for Adam's fatherhood being over all mankind, it could descend to but one at once, and from him to his right, heir only. and so there could by that title be but one king in the world at a time: and by right of fatherhood, not descending from Adam, it must be only as they themselves were fathers, end so could be over none but their own posterity. So that if those 12 dukes of Edom; if Abraham and the nine kings his neighbours; if Jacob and Esau, and the 31 kings in Canaan, the 72 kings mutilated by Adonibeseck, the 32 kings that came to Benhadad, the 70 kings of Greece making war at Troy; were, as our author contends, all of them sovereign princes; it is evident that kings derived their power from some other original than fatherhood,.since some of these had power over more than their own posterity; and it is demonstration, they could not be all heirs to Adam: for I challenge any man to make any presence to power by right of fatherhood either intelligible or possible in any one, otherwise, than either as Adam's heir, or as progenitor over his own descendents, naturally sprung from him. And if our author could show that any one of these princes, of which he gives us here so large a catalogue, had his authority by either of these titles, I think I might yield him the cause; though it is manifest they are all impertinent, and directly contrary to what he brings them to prove, viz., "That the lordship which Adam had over the world by right descended to the patriarchs."

## §150.

Having told us, p. 16, That "the patriarchal government continued. in Abraham, Isaac, and Jacob, until the Egyptian bondage," p. 17, he tells us, "by manifest footsteps we may trace this paternal government unto the Israelites coming into Egypt,. Allure the exercise of the supreme patriarchal government was intermitted, because they were in subjection to a stronger prince." What these footsteps are of paternal government, in our author's sense, i.e., of absolute monarchical power descending from Adam, and exercised by right of fatherhood, we have seen; that is, for 2290 years no footsteps at all; since in all that time he cannot produce any one example of any person who claimed or exercised regal authority by right of fatherhood; or show any one who being a king was Adam's heir: all that his proofs amount to is only this, that there were fathers, patriarchs, and kings, in that age of the world; but that the fathers and patriarchs had any absolute arbitrary power, or by what titles those kings had theirs, and of what extent it was, the Scripture is wholly silent; it is manifest by right of fatherhood they neither did, nor could claim any title to dominion or empire.

## §151.

To say, "That the exercise of supreme patriarchal government was intermitted, because they were in subjection to a stronger prince," proves nothing but what I before suspected, viz., "That patriarchal jurisdiction or government" is a fallacious expression, and does not in our author signify (what he would yet insinuate by it) paternal and regal power, such an absolute sovereignty as he supposes was in Adam.

§152.

For how can he say that patriarchal jurisdiction was intermitted in Egypt, where there was a king, under whose regal government the Israelites were, if patriarchal were absolute monarchical jurisdiction? And if it were not, but something else, why does he make such ado about a power not in question, and nothing to the purpose? The exercise of patriarchal jurisdiction, if patriarchal be regal, was not intermitted whilst the Israelites were in Egypt. It is true, the exercise of regal power was not then in the hands of any of the promised seeds of Abraham, nor before neither that I know: but what is that to the intermission of regal authority, as descending from Adam; unless our author will have it, that this chosen line of Abraham had the right of inheritance to Adam's lordship? and then to what purpose are his instances of the 72 rulers, in whom the fatherly authority was preserved in the confusion at Isabel? Why does he bring the 12 princes sons of Ishmael, and the dukes of Edom, and join them with Abraham, Isaac, and Jacob, as examples of the exercise of true patriarchal government, if the exercise of patriarchal jurisdiction were intermitted in the world, whenever the heirs of Jacob had not supreme power? I fear, supreme patriarchal jurisdiction was not only intermitted, but from the time of the Egyptian bondage quite lost in the world; since it will be hard to find, from that time downwards, any one who exercised it as an inheritance descending to him from the patriarchs, Abraham, Isaac, and Jacob. I imagined monarchical government would have served his turn in the hands of Pharaoh, or any body. one cannot easily discover in all places what his discourse tends to, as, particularly in this place, it is not obvious to guess what he drives at, when he says, "the exercise of supreme patriarchal jurisdiction in Egypt," or how this serves to make out the descent of Adam's lordship to the patriarchs, or any body else.

§153.

For I thought he had been giving us out of Scripture proofs and examples of monarchical government, founded on paternal authority, descending from Adam; and not an history of the Jews: amongst whom yet we find no kings, till many years after they were a people: and when kings were their rulers, there is not the least mention or room for a presence that they were heirs to Adam, or kings by paternal authority. I expected, talking so much as he does of Scripture, that he would have produced thence a series of monarchs, whose titles were clear to Adam's fatherhood, and who, as heirs to him, owned and exercised paternal jurisdiction over their subjects, and that this was the true patriarchal government: whereas he neither proves thee the patriarchs were kings, nor that either kings or patriarchs were heirs to Adam, or so much as pretended to it: and one may as well prove that the patriarchs were all absolute monarchs; that the power both of patriarchs and kings was only paternal; and that this power descended to them from Adam: I say all these propositions may be as well proved by a confused account of a multitude of little kinds in the West-Indies, out of Ferdinando Soto, or any of our late histories of the Northern America, or by our author's 70 kings of Greece, out of Homer, as by any thing he brings out of Scripture, in that multitude of kings he has reckoned up.

§154.

And methinks he should have let Homer and his wars of Troy alone, since his great zeal to truth or monarchy carried him to such a pitch of transport against philosophers and poets, that he tells us in his preface, that "there are too many in these days who please themselves in running after the opinions of philosophers and poets, to find out such an original of government as might promise them some title to liberty, to the great scandal of Christianity and bringing in of atheism." And yet these heathens, philosopher Aristotle, and poet Homer, are not rejected by our zealous Christian politician, whenever they over any thing that seems to serve his turn: whether "to the great scandal of Christianity and bringing in of atheism," let him look. This I cannot but observe in authors who it is visible write not for truth, how ready zeal for interest and party is to entitle Christianity to their designs, and to charge atheism on those who will not, without examining, submit to their doctrines, and blindly swallow their nonsense. But to return to his Scripture history, our author farther tells us, p. 18, that "after the return of the Israelites out of bondage, God, out of a special care of them, chose Moses and

Joshua successively to govern as princes in the place and stead of the supreme fathers." If it be true that they returned out of bondage, it must be in a state of freedom, and must imply, that both before and after this bondage they were free; unless our author will say that changing of masters is returning out of bondage; or that a slave returns out of bondage when he is removed from one gaily to another. If then they returned out of bondage, it is plain that in those days, whatever our author in his preface says to the contrary, there was a difference between a son, a subject, and a slave; and that neither the patriarchs before, nor their rulers after this "Egyptian bondage, numbered their sons or subjects amongst their possessions," and disposed of them with as absolute a dominion, as they did their other goods.

## §155.

This is evident in Jacob to whom Reuben offered his two sons as pledges; and Judah was at last surety for Benjamin's safe return out of Egypt: which all had been vain, superfluous, and but a sort of mockery, if Jacob had had the same power over every one of his family as he had over his ox or his ass, as an owner over his substance; and the offers that Reuben or Judah made had been such a security for returning of Benjamin, as if a man should take two lambs out of his lord's flock, and offer one as security that he will safely restore the other.

## §156.

When they were out of this bondage, what then? "God out of a special care of them, the Israelites." It is well that once in his book he will allow God to have any care of the people: for in other places he speaks of mankind as if God had no care of any part of them, but only of their monarchs, and that the rest of the people, the societies of men, were made as so many herds of cattle, only for the service, use, and pleasure of their princes.

## §157.

"Chose Moses and Joshua successively to govern as princes;" a shrewd argument our author has found out to prove God's care of the fatherly authority, and Adam's heirs, that here, as an expression of his care of his own people, he chooses those for princes over them that had not the least presence to either. The persons chosen were Moses, of the tribe of Levi, and Joshua of the tribe of Ephraim, neither of which had any title of fatherhood. But, says our author, they were in the place and stead of the supreme fathers. If God had any where as plainly declared his choice of such fathers to be rulers, as he did of Moses and Joshua, we might believe Moses and Joshua were in their place and stead: but that being the question in debate, till that be better proved, Moses being chosen by God to be ruler of his people, will no more prove that government belonged to Adam's heir, or to the fatherhood, than God's choosing Aaron of the tribe of Levi to be priest, will prove that the priesthood belonged to Adam's heir, or the prime fathers; since God would choose Aaron to be priest, and Moses ruler in Israel, though neither of those offices were settled on Adam's heir or the fatherhood.

## §158.

Our author goes on, "And after them likewise for a time he raised up judges, to defend his people in time of peril," p. 18. This proves fatherly authority to be the original of government, and that it descended from Adam to his heirs just as well as what went before: only here our author seems to confess that these judges, who were all the governors they then had, were only men of velour, whom they made their generals to defend them in time of peril; and cannot God raise up such men, unless fatherhood have a title to government?

## §159.

But says our author, "when God gave the Israelites kings, he re-established the ancient and prime right of lineal succession to paternal government." p. 18.

## §160.

How did God re-establish it? by a law, a positive command? We find no such thing. Our author means then, that when God gave theta a king, in giving them a king, he re-established the right, &c. To re-establish defacto the right of lineal succession to Paternal government is to put a man in possession of that government which his fathers did enjoy, and he by lineal succession had a right to: for, first, if it were another government than what his ancestor had, it was not succeeding to an ancient right, but beginning a new one: for if a prince should give a man, besides his ancient patrimony, which for some ages his family had been disseised of, an additional estate, never before in the possession of his ancestors, he could not be said to re-establish the right of lineal succession to any more than what had been formerly enjoyed by his ancestors If therefore the power the kings of Israel had were any thing more than Isaac or Jacob had, it was not the re-establishing in them the right of succession to a power, but giving them a new power, however you please to call it, paternal or not: and whether Isaac and Jacob had the same power that the kings of Israel had, I desire any one, by what has been above said, to consider; and I do not think he will find that either Abraham Isaac, or Jacob, had any regal power at all.

## §161.

Next, there can be "no reestablishment of the prime and ancient right of lineal succession" to any thing, unless he that is put in possession of it has the right to succeed, and be the true and next heir to him he succeeds to. Can that be a re-establishment which begins in a new family? or that the "re-establishment of an ancient right of lineal succession," when a crown is given to one who has no right of succession to it; and who, if the lineal succession had gone on, had been out of all possibility of presence to it, Saul, the first king God gave the Israelites, was of the tribe of Benjamin. Was the "ancient and prime right of lineal succession re-established" in him? The next was David, the youngest son of Jesse, of the posterity of Judah, Jacob's third son. Was the "ancient and prime right of lineal succession to paternal government reestablished in him?" or in Solomon, his younger son and successor in the throne? or in Jeroboam over the ten tribes? or in Athaliah, a woman who reigned six years, an utter stranger to the royal blood? "If the ancient and prime right of lineal succession to paternal government were re-established" in any of these or their posterity, "the ancient and prime right of lineal succession to paternal government" belongs to younger brothers as well as elder, and may be re-established in any man living: for whatever younger brothers, "by ancient and prime right of lineal succession," may have as well as the elder, that every man living may have a right to by lineal succession, and Sir Robert as well as any other. And so what a brave right of lineal succession to his paternal or regal government our author has re-established, for the securing the rights and inheritance of crowns, where every one may have it, let the world consider.

## §162.

But says our author, however, p. 19, "Whensoever God made choice of any special person to be king, he intended that the issue also should have benefit thereof, as being comprehended sufficiently in the person of the father, although the father was only named in the grant." This yet will not help out succession: for if, as our author says, the benefit of the grant be intended to the issue of the grantee, this will not direct the succession; since, if God give any thing to a man and his issue in general, the claim cannot be to any one of that issue in particular; every one that is of his race will have an equal right. If it be said, our author meant heir, I believe our author was as willing as any body to have used that word, if it would have served his turn: but Solomon, who succeeded David in the throne, being no more his heir than Jeroboam, who succeeded him in the government of the ten tribes, was his issue, our author had reason to avoid saying, that God intended it to the heirs, when that would not hold in a succession, which our author could not except against; and so he has left his succession as undetermined, as if he had said nothing about it: for if the regal power be given by God to a man and his issue, as the land of Canaan was to Abraham and his seed, must they not all have a title to it, all share in it? And one may as well say, that by God's grant to Abraham and his seed, the land of Canaan was to belong only to one of his seed, exclusive of all others, as by God's grant of dominion to a man and his issue, this dominion was to belong in peculiar to one of his issue exclusive of all others.

§163.

But how will our author prove that whensoever God made choice of any special person to be a king he intended that "the (I suppose he means his) issue also should have benefit thereof?" has he so soon forgot Moses and Joshua, whom in this very section, he says, "God out of a special care chose to govern as princes," and the judges that God raised up? Had not these princes, having the same authority of the supreme fatherhood, the same power that the kings had; and being specially chosen by God himself, should not their issue have the benefit of that choice, as well as David's or Solomon's? If these had the paternal authority put into their hands immediately by God, why had not their issue the benefit of this grant in a succession to this power? Or if they had it as Adam's heirs, why did not their heirs enjoy it after them by right descending to them? for they could not be heirs to one another. Was the power the same, and from the same original, in Moses, Joshua, and the Judges, as it was in David and the kings; and was it inheritable in one and not in the other? If it was not paternal authority, then God's own people were governed by those that had not paternal authority, and those governors did well enough without it: if it were paternal authority, and God chose the persons that were to exercise it, our author's rule fails, that "whensoever God makes choice of any person to be supreme ruler," (for I suppose the name king has no spell in it, it is not the title, but the power makes the difference), "he intends that the issue also should have the benefit of it," since from their coming out of Egypt to David's time, 400 years, the issue was never "so sufficiently comprehended in the person of the father," as that any son, after the death of his father, succeeded to the government amongst all those judges that judged Israel. If to avoid this, it be said, God always chose the person of the successor, and so, transferring the fatherly authority to him, excluded his issue from succeeding to it, that is manifestly not so in the story of Jephthah, where he articled with the people, and they made him judge over them, as is plain, Judg. xi.

§164.

It is in vain then to say, that "whensoever God chooses any special person to have the exercise of paternal authority," (for if that be not to be king, I desire to know the difference between a king and one having the exercise of paternal authority), "he intends the issue also should have the benefit of it," since we find the authority the judges had ended with them, and descended not to their issue; and if the judges had not paternal authority, I fear it will trouble our author, or any of the friends to his principles, to tell who had then the paternal authority, that is, the government and supreme power amongst the Israelites: and I suspect they must confess that the chosen people of God continued a people several hundreds of years, without any knowledge or thought of this paternal authority, or any appearance of monarchical government at all.

§165.

To be satisfied of this, he need but read the story of the Levite, and the war thereupon with the Benjamites, in the three last chapters of Judges; and when he finds, that the Levite appeals to the people for justice, that it was the tribes and the congregation that debated, resolved, and directed all that was done on that occasion; he must conclude, either that God was not "careful to preserve the fatherly authority" amongst his own chosen people; or else that the fatherly authority may be preserved where there is no monarchical government: if the latter, then it will follow, that though fatherly authority be ever so well proved, yet it will not infer a necessity of monarchical government; if the former, it will seem very strange and improbable, that God should ordain fatherly authority to be so sacred amongst the sons of men, that there could be no power or government without it, and yet that amongst us own people, even whilst he is providing a government for them, and therein prescribes rules to the several states and relations of men, this great and fundamental one, this most material and necessary of all the rest, should he concealed, and lie neglected for 400 years after.

## §166.

Before I leave this, I must ask flow our author knows that "whensoever God makes choice of any special person to be king, he intends that the issue should have the benefit thereof?" Does God by the law of nature or revelation say so? By the same law also he must say, which of his issue must enjoy the crown in succession, and so point out the heir, or else leave his issue to divide or scramble for the government: both mike absurd, and such as will destroy the benefit of such grant to the issue. When any such declaration of God's intention is produced, it will be our duty to believe God intends it so; but till that be done, our author must show us some better warrant, before we shall be obliged to receive lain as the authentic revealer of God's intentions.

## §167.

"The issue;" says our author, "is comprehended sufficiently in the person of the father, although the father only was named in the grant:" and yet God, when he gave the land of Canaan to Abraham, Gen. xiii. 15, thought fit to put his seed into the grant too: so the priesthood was given to Aaron and his seed; and the crown God gave not only to David, but his seed also: and however our author assures us that "God intends that the issue should have the benefit of it, when he chooses any person to be king," yet we see that the kingdom which he gave to Saul, without mentioning his seed after him, never came to any of his issue: and why, when God chose a person to be king, he should intend that his issue should have the benefit of it, more than when he chose one to be judge in Israel, I would fain know a reason; or why does a errant of fatherly authority to a king more comprehend the issue, than when a like grant is made to a judge? Is paternal authority by right to descend to the issue of one, and not of the other? There will need some reason to be shown of this difference more than the name, when the thing given is the same fatherly authority, and the manner of giving it, God's choice of the person, the same too; for I suppose our author, when he says, "God raised up judges," will by no means allow they were chosen by the people.

## §168.

But since our author has so confidently assured us of the care of God to preserve the fatherhood, and pretends to build all he says upon the authority of the Scripture, we may well expect that that people, whose law, constitution, and history are chiefly contained in the Scripture, should furnish him with the clearest instances of God's care of preserving the fatherly authority in that people who it is agreed he had a most peculiar care of. Let us see then what state this paternal authority or government was in amongst the Jews from their beginning to be a people. It was omitted by our author's confession, from their coming into Egypt, till their return out of that bondage, above 200 years: from thence till God gave the Israelites a king, about 400 years more, our author gives but a very slender account of it; nor indeed all that time are there the least footsteps of paternal or regal government amongst them. But then, says our author, "God re-established the ancient and prime right of lineal succession to paternal government."

## §169.

What a "lineal succession to paternal government" was then established we have already seen. I only now consider how long this lasted, and that was to their captivity, about 500 years: from thence to their destruction by the Romans, above 650 years after, the "ancient and prime right of lineal succession to paternal government" was again lost, and they continued a people in the promised land without it. So that of 1750 years that they were God's peculiar people, they had hereditary kingly government amongst them not one-third of the time; and of that time there is not the least footstep of one moment of "paternal government, nor the re-establishment of the ancient and prime right of lineal succession to it," whether we suppose it to be derived, as from its fountain, from David, Saul, Abraham, or, which upon our author's principles is the only true, from Adam. Notes 1. "In grants and gifts that have their original from God or nature, as the power of the father hath, no inferior power of man can limit, nor shake any law of prescription against them." Obs. 158. "The Scripture teaches that supreme power was originally in the father, without any limitation." Obs. 245.

**The Second Treatise**

**Chapter I, Of Political Power**

1. It having been shown in the foregoing discourse: Firstly. That Adam had not, either by natural right of fatherhood or by positive donation from God, any such authority over his children, nor dominion over the world, as is pretended. Secondly. That if he had, his heirs yet had no right to it. Thirdly. That if his heirs had, there being no law of Nature nor positive law of God that determines which is the right heir in all cases that may arise, the right of succession, and consequently of bearing rule, could not have been certainly determined. Fourthly. That if even that had been determined, yet the knowledge of which is the eldest line of Adam's posterity being so long since utterly lost, that in the races of mankind and families of the world, there remains not to one above another the least pretence to be the eldest house, and to have the right of inheritance. All these promises having, as I think, been clearly made out, it is impossible that the rulers now on earth should make any benefit, or derive any the least shadow of authority from that which is held to be the fountain of all power, "Adam's private dominion and paternal jurisdiction"; so that he that will not give just occasion to think that all government in the world is the product only of force and violence, and that men live together by no other rules but that of beasts, where the strongest carries it, and so lay a foundation for perpetual disorder and mischief, tumult, sedition, and rebellion (things that the followers of that hypothesis so loudly cry out against), must of necessity find out another rise of government, another original of political power, and another way of designing and knowing the persons that have it than what Concerning the True Original Extent and End of Civil Government Sir Robert Filmer hath taught us.

2. To this purpose, I think it may not be amiss to set down what I take to be political power. That the power of a magistrate over a subject may be distinguished from that of a father over his children, a master over his servant, a husband over his wife, and a lord over his slave. All which distinct powers happening sometimes together in the same man, if he be considered under these different relations, it may help us to distinguish these powers one from another, and show the difference betwixt a ruler of a commonwealth, a father of a family, and a captain of a galley.

3. Political power, then, I take to be a right of making laws, with penalties of death, and consequently all less penalties for the regulating and preserving of property, and of employing the force of the community in the execution of such laws, and in the defence of the commonwealth from foreign injury, and all this only for the public good.

**Chapter II, Of the State of Nature**

4. To understand political power aright, and derive it from its original, we must consider what estate all men are naturally in, and that is, a state of perfect freedom to order their actions, and dispose of their possessions and persons as they think fit, within the bounds of the law of Nature, without asking leave or depending upon the will of any other man. A state also of equality, wherein all the power and jurisdiction is reciprocal, no one having more than another, there being nothing more evident than that creatures of the same species and rank, promiscuously born to all the same advantages of Nature, and the use of the same faculties, should also be equal one amongst another, without subordination or subjection, unless the lord and master of them all should,

by any manifest declaration of his will, set one above another, and confer on him, by an evident and clear appointment, an undoubted right to dominion and sovereignty.

5. This equality of men by Nature, the judicious Hooker looks upon as so evident in itself, and beyond all question, that he makes it the foundation of that obligation to mutual love amongst men on which he builds the duties they owe one another, and from whence he derives the great maxims of justice and charity. His words are: "The like natural inducement hath brought men to know that it is no less their duty to love others than themselves, for seeing those things which are equal, must needs all have one measure; if I cannot but wish to receive good, even as much at every man's hands, as any man can wish unto his own soul, how should I look to have any part of my desire herein satisfied, unless myself be careful to satisfy the like desire, which is undoubtedly in other men weak, being of one and the same nature: to have anything offered them repugnant to this desire must needs, in all respects, grieve them as much as me; so that if I do harm, I must look to suffer, there being no reason that others should show greater measure of love to me than they have by me showed unto them; my desire, therefore, to be loved of my equals in Nature, as much as possible may be, imposeth upon me a natural duty of bearing to themward fully the like affection. From which relation of equality between ourselves and them that are as ourselves, what several rules and canons natural reason hath drawn for direction of life no man is ignorant." (Eccl. Pol. i.)

6. But though this be a state of liberty, yet it is not a state of licence; though man in that state have an uncontrollable liberty to dispose of his person or possessions, yet he has not liberty to destroy himself, or so much as any creature in his possession, but where some nobler use than its bare preservation calls for it. The state of Nature has a law of Nature to govern it, which obliges every one, and reason, which is that law, teaches all mankind who will but consult it, that being all equal and independent, no one ought to harm another in his life, health, liberty or possessions; for men being all the workmanship of one omnipotent and infinitely wise Maker; all the servants of one sovereign Master, sent into the world by His order and about His business; they are His property, whose workmanship they are made to last during His, not one another's pleasure. And, being furnished with like faculties, sharing all in one community of Nature, there cannot be supposed any such subordination among us that may authorise us to destroy one another, as if we were made for one another's uses, as the inferior ranks of creatures are for ours. Every one as he is bound to preserve himself, and not to quit his station wilfully, so by the like reason, when his own preservation comes not in competition, ought he as much as he can to preserve the rest of mankind, and not unless it be to do justice on an offender, take away or impair the life, or what tends to the preservation of the life, the liberty, health, limb, or goods of another.

7. And that all men may be restrained from invading others' rights, and from doing hurt to one another, and the law of Nature be observed, which willeth the peace and preservation of all mankind, the execution of the law of Nature is in that state put into every man's hands, whereby every one has a right to punish the transgressors of that law to such a degree as may hinder its violation. For the law of Nature would, as all other laws that concern men in this world, be in vain if there were nobody that in the state of Nature had a power to execute that law, and thereby preserve the innocent and restrain offenders; and if any one in the state of Nature may punish another for any evil he has done, every one may do so. For in that state of perfect equality, where naturally there is no superiority or jurisdiction of one over another, what any may do in prosecution of that law, every one must needs have a right to do.

8. And thus, in the state of Nature, one man comes by a power over another, but yet no absolute or arbitrary power to use a criminal, when he has got him in his hands, according to the passionate heats or boundless extravagancy of his own will, but only to retribute to him so far as calm reason and conscience dictate, what is proportionate to his transgression, which is so much as may serve for reparation and restraint. For these two are the only reasons why one man may lawfully do harm to another, which is that we call punishment. In transgressing the law of Nature, the offender declares himself to live by another rule than that of reason and common equity, which is that measure God has set to the actions of men for their mutual security, and so he becomes dangerous to mankind; the tie which is to secure them from injury and violence being slighted and broken by him, which being a trespass against the whole species, and the peace and safety of it, provided for by the law of Nature, every man upon this score, by the right he hath to preserve mankind in general, may restrain, or where it is necessary, destroy things noxious to them, and so may bring such evil on any one who hath transgressed that law, as may make him repent the doing of it, and thereby deter him, and, by his example, others from doing the like mischief. And in this case, and upon this ground, every man hath a right to punish the offender, and be executioner of the law of Nature.

9. I doubt not but this will seem a very strange doctrine to some men; but before they condemn it, I desire them to resolve me by what right any prince or state can put to death or punish an alien for any crime he com-

mits in their country? It is certain their laws, by virtue of any sanction they receive from the promulgated will of the legislature, reach not a stranger. They speak not to him, nor, if they did, is he bound to hearken to them. The legislative authority by which they are in force over the subjects of that commonwealth hath no power over him. Those who have the supreme power of making laws in England, France, or Holland are, to an Indian, but like the rest of the world—men without authority. And therefore, if by the law of Nature every man hath not a power to punish offences against it, as he soberly judges the case to require, I see not how the magistrates of any community can punish an alien of another country, since, in reference to him, they can have no more power than what every man naturally may have over another.

10. Besides the crime which consists in violating the laws, and varying from the right rule of reason, whereby a man so far becomes degenerate, and declares himself to quit the principles of human nature and to be a noxious creature, there is commonly injury done, and some person or other, some other man, receives damage by his transgression; in which case, he who hath received any damage has (besides the right of punishment common to him, with other men) a particular right to seek reparation from him that hath done it. And any other person who finds it just may also join with him that is injured, and assist him in recovering from the offender so much as may make satisfaction for the harm he hath suffered.

11. From these two distinct rights (the one of punishing the crime, for restraint and preventing the like offence, which right of punishing is in everybody, the other of taking reparation, which belongs only to the injured party) comes it to pass that the magistrate, who by being magistrate hath the common right of punishing put into his hands, can often, where the public good demands not the execution of the law, remit the punishment of criminal offences by his own authority, but yet cannot remit the satisfaction due to any private man for the damage he has received. That he who hath suffered the damage has a right to demand in his own name, and he alone can remit. The damnified person has this power of appropriating to himself the goods or service of the offender by right of self-preservation, as every man has a power to punish the crime to prevent its being committed again, by the right he has of preserving all mankind, and doing all reasonable things he can in order to that end. And thus it is that every man in the state of Nature has a power to kill a murderer, both to deter others from doing the like injury (which no reparation can compensate) by the example of the punishment that attends it from everybody, and also to secure men from the attempts of a criminal who, having renounced reason, the common rule and measure God hath given to mankind, hath, by the unjust violence and slaughter he hath committed upon one, declared war against all mankind, and therefore may be destroyed as a lion or a tiger, one of those wild savage beasts with whom men can have no society nor security. And upon this is grounded that great law of nature, "Whoso sheddeth man's blood, by man shall his blood be shed." And Cain was so fully convinced that every one had a right to destroy such a criminal, that, after the murder of his brother, he cries out, "Every one that findeth me shall slay me," so plain was it writ in the hearts of all mankind.

12. By the same reason may a man in the state of Nature punish the lesser breaches of that law, it will, perhaps, be demanded, with death? I answer: Each transgression may be punished to that degree, and with so much severity, as will suffice to make it an ill bargain to the offender, give him cause to repent, and terrify others from doing the like. Every offence that can be committed in the state of Nature may, in the state of Nature, be also punished equally, and as far forth, as it may, in a commonwealth. For though it would be beside my present purpose to enter here into the particulars of the law of Nature, or its measures of punishment, yet it is certain there is such a law, and that too as intelligible and plain to a rational creature and a studier of that law as the positive laws of commonwealths, nay, possibly plainer; as much as reason is easier to be understood than the fancies and intricate contrivances of men, following contrary and hidden interests put into words; for truly so are a great part of the municipal laws of countries, which are only so far right as they are founded on the law of Nature, by which they are to be regulated and interpreted.

13. To this strange doctrine—viz., That in the state of Nature every one has the executive power of the law of Nature—I doubt not but it will be objected that it is unreasonable for men to be judges in their own cases, that self-love will make men partial to themselves and their friends; and, on the other side, ill-nature, passion, and revenge will carry them too far in punishing others, and hence nothing but confusion and disorder will follow, and that therefore God hath certainly appointed government to restrain the partiality and violence of men. I easily grant that civil government is the proper remedy for the inconveniences of the state of Nature, which must certainly be great where men may be judges in their own case, since it is easy to be imagined that he who was so unjust as to do his brother an injury will scarce be so just as to condemn himself for it. But I shall desire those who make this objection to remember that absolute monarchs are but men; and if government is to be the remedy of those evils which necessarily follow from men being judges in their own cases, and the state of Nature is therefore not to be endured, I desire to know what kind of government that is, and how

much better it is than the state of Nature, where one man commanding a multitude has the liberty to be judge in his own case, and may do to all his subjects whatever he pleases without the least question or control of those who execute his pleasure? and in whatsoever he doth, whether led by reason, mistake, or passion, must be submitted to? which men in the state of Nature are not bound to do one to another. And if he that judges, judges amiss in his own or any other case, he is answerable for it to the rest of mankind.

14. It is often asked as a mighty objection, where are, or ever were, there any men in such a state of Nature? To which it may suffice as an answer at present, that since all princes and rulers of "independent" governments all through the world are in a state of Nature, it is plain the world never was, nor never will be, without numbers of men in that state. I have named all governors of "independent" communities, whether they are, or are not, in league with others; for it is not every compact that puts an end to the state of Nature between men, but only this one of agreeing together mutually to enter into one community, and make one body politic; other promises and compacts men may make one with another, and yet still be in the state of Nature. The promises and bargains for truck, etc., between the two men in Soldania, in or between a Swiss and an Indian, in the woods of America, are binding to them, though they are perfectly in a state of Nature in reference to one another for truth, and keeping of faith belongs to men as men, and not as members of society.

15. To those that say there were never any men in the state of Nature, I will not oppose the authority of the judicious Hooker (Eccl. Pol. i. 10), where he says, "the laws which have been hitherto mentioned"— i.e., the laws of Nature—"do bind men absolutely, even as they are men, although they have never any settled fellowship, never any solemn agreement amongst themselves what to do or not to do; but for as much as we are not by ourselves sufficient to furnish ourselves with competent store of things needful for such a life as our Nature doth desire, a life fit for the dignity of man, therefore to supply those defects and imperfections which are in us, as living single and solely by ourselves, we are naturally induced to seek communion and fellowship with others; this was the cause of men uniting themselves as first in politic societies." But I, moreover, affirm that all men are naturally in that state, and remain so till, by their own consents, they make themselves members of some politic society, and I doubt not, in the sequel of this discourse, to make it very clear.

**Chapter III, Of the State of War**

16. The state of war is a state of enmity and destruction; and therefore declaring by word or action, not a passionate and hasty, but sedate, settled design upon another man's life puts him in a state of war with him against whom he has declared such an intention, and so has exposed his life to the other's power to be taken away by him, or any one that joins with him in his defence, and espouses his quarrel; it being reasonable and just I should have a right to destroy that which threatens me with destruction; for by the fundamental law of Nature, man being to be preserved as much as possible, when all cannot be preserved, the safety of the innocent is to be preferred, and one may destroy a man who makes war upon him, or has discovered an enmity to his being, for the same reason that he may kill a wolf or a lion, because they are not under the ties of the common law of reason, have no other rule but that of force and violence, and so may be treated as a beast of prey, those dangerous and noxious creatures that will be sure to destroy him whenever he falls into their power.

17. And hence it is that he who attempts to get another man into his absolute power does thereby put himself into a state of war with him; it being to be understood as a declaration of a design upon his life. For I have reason to conclude that he who would get me into his power without my consent would use me as he pleased when he had got me there, and destroy me too when he had a fancy to it; for nobody can desire to have me in his absolute power unless it be to compel me by force to that which is against the right of my freedom—i.e. make me a slave. To be free from such force is the only security of my preservation, and reason bids me look on him as an enemy to my preservation who would take away that freedom which is the fence to it; so that he who makes an attempt to enslave me thereby puts himself into a state of war with me. He that in the state of Nature would take away the freedom that belongs to any one in that state must necessarily be supposed to have a design to take away everything else, that freedom being the foundation of all the rest; as he that in the state of society would take away the freedom belonging to those of that society or commonwealth must be supposed to design to take away from them everything else, and so be looked on as in a state of war.

18. This makes it lawful for a man to kill a thief who has not in the least hurt him, nor declared any design upon his life, any farther than by the use of force, so to get him in his power as to take away his money, or what he pleases, from him; because using force, where he has no right to get me into his power, let his pretence be what it will, I have no reason to suppose that he who would take away my liberty would not, when he

had me in his power, take away everything else. And, therefore, it is lawful for me to treat him as one who has put himself into a state of war with me—i.e., kill him if I can; for to that hazard does he justly expose himself whoever introduces a state of war, and is aggressor in it.

19. And here we have the plain difference between the state of Nature and the state of war, which however some men have confounded, are as far distant as a state of peace, goodwill, mutual assistance, and preservation; and a state of enmity, malice, violence and mutual destruction are one from another. Men living together according to reason without a common superior on earth, with authority to judge between them, is properly the state of Nature. But force, or a declared design of force upon the person of another, where there is no common superior on earth to appeal to for relief, is the state of war; and it is the want of such an appeal gives a man the right of war even against an aggressor, though he be in society and a fellow-subject. Thus, a thief whom I cannot harm, but by appeal to the law, for having stolen all that I am worth, I may kill when he sets on me to rob me but of my horse or coat, because the law, which was made for my preservation, where it cannot interpose to secure my life from present force, which if lost is capable of no reparation, permits me my own defence and the right of war, a liberty to kill the aggressor, because the aggressor allows not time to appeal to our common judge, nor the decision of the law, for remedy in a case where the mischief may be irreparable. Want of a common judge with authority puts all men in a state of Nature; force without right upon a man's person makes a state of war both where there is, and is not, a common judge.

20. But when the actual force is over, the state of war ceases between those that are in society and are equally on both sides subject to the judge; and, therefore, in such controversies, where the question is put, "Who shall be judge?" it cannot be meant who shall decide the controversy; every one knows what Jephtha here tells us, that "the Lord the Judge" shall judge. Where there is no judge on earth the appeal lies to God in Heaven. That question then cannot mean who shall judge, whether another hath put himself in a state of war with me, and whether I may, as Jephtha did, appeal to Heaven in it? Of that I myself can only judge in my own conscience, as I will answer it at the great day to the Supreme Judge of all men.

**Chapter IV, Of Slavery**

21. The natural liberty of man is to be free from any superior power on earth, and not to be under the will or legislative authority of man, but to have only the law of Nature for his rule. The liberty of man in society is to be under no other legislative power but that established by consent in the commonwealth, nor under the dominion of any will, or restraint of any law, but what that legislative shall enact according to the trust put in it. Freedom, then, is not what Sir Robert Filmer tells us: "A liberty for every one to do what he lists, to live as he pleases, and not to be tied by any laws"; but freedom of men under government is to have a standing rule to live by, common to every one of that society, and made by the legislative power erected in it. A liberty to follow my own will in all things where that rule prescribes not, not to be subject to the inconstant, uncertain, unknown, arbitrary will of another man, as freedom of nature is to be under no other restraint but the law of Nature.

22. This freedom from absolute, arbitrary power is so necessary to, and closely joined with, a man's preservation, that he cannot part with it but by what forfeits his preservation and life together. For a man, not having the power of his own life, cannot by compact or his own consent enslave himself to any one, nor put himself under the absolute, arbitrary power of another to take away his life when he pleases. Nobody can give more power than he has himself, and he that cannot take away his own life cannot give another power over it. Indeed, having by his fault forfeited his own life by some act that deserves death, he to whom he has forfeited it may, when he has him in his power, delay to take it, and make use of him to his own service; and he does him no injury by it. For, whenever he finds the hardship of his slavery outweigh the value of his life, it is in his power, by resisting the will of his master, to draw on himself the death he desires.

23. This is the perfect condition of slavery, which is nothing else but the state of war continued between a lawful conqueror and a captive, for if once compact enter between them, and make an agreement for a limited power on the one side, and obedience on the other, the state of war and slavery ceases as long as the compact endures; for, as has been said, no man can by agreement pass over to another that which he hath not in himself —a power over his own life. I confess, we find among the Jews, as well as other nations, that men did sell themselves; but it is plain this was only to drudgery, not to slavery; for it is evident the person sold was not under an absolute, arbitrary, despotical power, for the master could not have power to kill him at any time, whom at a certain time he was obliged to let go free out of his service; and the master of such a servant was so

far from having an arbitrary power over his life that he could not at pleasure so much as maim him, but the loss of an eye or tooth set him free (Exod. 21.).

**Chapter V, Of Property**

24. Whether we consider natural reason, which tells us that men, being once born, have a right to their preservation, and consequently to meat and drink and such other things as Nature affords for their subsistence, or "revelation," which gives us an account of those grants God made of the world to Adam, and to Noah and his sons, it is very clear that God, as King David says (Psalm 115. 16), "has given the earth to the children of men," given it to mankind in common. But, this being supposed, it seems to some a very great difficulty how any one should ever come to have a property in anything, I will not content myself to answer, that, if it be difficult to make out "property" upon a supposition that God gave the world to Adam and his posterity in common, it is impossible that any man but one universal monarch should have any "property" upon a supposition that God gave the world to Adam and his heirs in succession, exclusive of all the rest of his posterity; but I shall endeavour to show how men might come to have a property in several parts of that which God gave to mankind in common, and that without any express compact of all the commoners.

25. God, who hath given the world to men in common, hath also given them reason to make use of it to the best advantage of life and convenience. The earth and all that is therein is given to men for the support and comfort of their being. And though all the fruits it naturally produces, and beasts it feeds, belong to mankind in common, as they are produced by the spontaneous hand of Nature, and nobody has originally a private dominion exclusive of the rest of mankind in any of them, as they are thus in their natural state, yet being given for the use of men, there must of necessity be a means to appropriate them some way or other before they can be of any use, or at all beneficial, to any particular men. The fruit or venison which nourishes the wild Indian, who knows no enclosure, and is still a tenant in common, must be his, and so his— i.e., a part of him, that another can no longer have any right to it before it can do him any good for the support of his life.

26. Though the earth and all inferior creatures be common to all men, yet every man has a "property" in his own "person." This nobody has any right to but himself. The "labour" of his body and the "work" of his hands, we may say, are properly his. Whatsoever, then, he removes out of the state that Nature hath provided and left it in, he hath mixed his labour with it, and joined to it something that is his own, and thereby makes it his property. It being by him removed from the common state Nature placed it in, it hath by this labour something annexed to it that excludes the common right of other men. For this "labour" being the unquestionable property of the labourer, no man but he can have a right to what that is once joined to, at least where there is enough, and as good left in common for others.

27. He that is nourished by the acorns he picked up under an oak, or the apples he gathered from the trees in the wood, has certainly appropriated them to himself. Nobody can deny but the nourishment is his. I ask, then, when did they begin to be his? when he digested? or when he ate? or when he boiled? or when he brought them home? or when he picked them up? And it is plain, if the first gathering made them not his, nothing else could. That labour put a distinction between them and common. That added something to them more than Nature, the common mother of all, had done, and so they became his private right. And will any one say he had no right to those acorns or apples he thus appropriated because he had not the consent of all mankind to make them his? Was it a robbery thus to assume to himself what belonged to all in common? If such a consent as that was necessary, man had starved, notwithstanding the plenty God had given him. We see in commons, which remain so by compact, that it is the taking any part of what is common, and removing it out of the state Nature leaves it in, which begins the property, without which the common is of no use. And the taking of this or that part does not depend on the express consent of all the commoners. Thus, the grass my horse has bit, the turfs my servant has cut, and the ore I have digged in any place, where I have a right to them in common with others, become my property without the assignation or consent of anybody. The labour that was mine, removing them out of that common state they were in, hath fixed my property in them.

28. By making an explicit consent of every commoner necessary to any one's appropriating to himself any part of what is given in common. Children or servants could not cut the meat which their father or master had provided for them in common without assigning to every one his peculiar part. Though the water running in the fountain be every one's, yet who can doubt but that in the pitcher is his only who drew it out? His labour hath taken it out of the hands of Nature where it was common, and belonged equally to all her children, and hath thereby appropriated it to himself.

29. Thus this law of reason makes the deer that Indian's who hath killed it; it is allowed to be his goods who hath bestowed his labour upon it, though, before, it was the common right of every one. And amongst those who are counted the civilised part of mankind, who have made and multiplied positive laws to determine property, this original law of Nature for the beginning of property, in what was before common, still takes place, and by virtue thereof, what fish any one catches in the ocean, that great and still remaining common of mankind; or what amber-gris any one takes up here is by the labour that removes it out of that common state Nature left it in, made his property who takes that pains about it. And even amongst us, the hare that any one is hunting is thought his who pursues her during the chase. For being a beast that is still looked upon as common, and no man's private possession, whoever has employed so much labour about any of that kind as to find and pursue her has thereby removed her from the state of Nature wherein she was common, and hath begun a property.

30. It will, perhaps, be objected to this, that if gathering the acorns or other fruits of the earth, etc., makes a right to them, then any one may engross as much as he will. To which I answer, Not so. The same law of Nature that does by this means give us property, does also bound that property too. "God has given us all things richly." Is the voice of reason confirmed by inspiration? But how far has He given it us—"to enjoy"? As much as any one can make use of to any advantage of life before it spoils, so much he may by his labour fix a property in. Whatever is beyond this is more than his share, and belongs to others. Nothing was made by God for man to spoil or destroy. And thus considering the plenty of natural provisions there was a long time in the world, and the few spenders, and to how small a part of that provision the industry of one man could extend itself and engross it to the prejudice of others, especially keeping within the bounds set by reason of what might serve for his use, there could be then little room for quarrels or contentions about property so established.

31. But the chief matter of property being now not the fruits of the earth and the beasts that subsist on it, but the earth itself, as that which takes in and carries with it all the rest, I think it is plain that property in that too is acquired as the former. As much land as a man tills, plants, improves, cultivates, and can use the product of, so much is his property. He by his labour does, as it were, enclose it from the common. Nor will it invalidate his right to say everybody else has an equal title to it, and therefore he cannot appropriate, he cannot enclose, without the consent of all his fellow-commoners, all mankind. God, when He gave the world in common to all mankind, commanded man also to labour, and the penury of his condition required it of him. God and his reason commanded him to subdue the earth—i.e., improve it for the benefit of life and therein lay out something upon it that was his own, his labour. He that, in obedience to this command of God, subdued, tilled, and sowed any part of it, thereby annexed to it something that was his property, which another had no title to, nor could without injury take from him.

32. Nor was this appropriation of any parcel of land, by improving it, any prejudice to any other man, since there was still enough and as good left, and more than the yet unprovided could use. So that, in effect, there was never the less left for others because of his enclosure for himself. For he that leaves as much as another can make use of does as good as take nothing at all. Nobody could think himself injured by the drinking of another man, though he took a good draught, who had a whole river of the same water left him to quench his thirst. And the case of land and water, where there is enough of both, is perfectly the same.

33. God gave the world to men in common, but since He gave it them for their benefit and the greatest conveniencies of life they were capable to draw from it, it cannot be supposed He meant it should always remain common and uncultivated. He gave it to the use of the industrious and rational (and labour was to be his title to it); not to the fancy or covetousness of the quarrelsome and contentious. He that had as good left for his improvement as was already taken up needed not complain, ought not to meddle with what was already improved by another's labour; if he did it is plain he desired the benefit of another's pains, which he had no right to, and not the ground which God had given him, in common with others, to labour on, and whereof there was as good left as that already possessed, and more than he knew what to do with, or his industry could reach to.

34. It is true, in land that is common in England or any other country, where there are plenty of people under government who have money and commerce, no one can enclose or appropriate any part without the consent of all his fellow-commoners; because this is left common by compact—i.e., by the law of the land, which is not to be violated. And, though it be common in respect of some men, it is not so to all mankind, but is the joint propriety of this country, or this parish. Besides, the remainder, after such enclosure, would not be as good to the rest of the commoners as the whole was, when they could all make use of the whole; whereas in the beginning and first peopling of the great common of the world it was quite otherwise. The law man was

under was rather for appropriating. God commanded, and his wants forced him to labour. That was his property, which could not be taken from him wherever he had fixed it. And hence subduing or cultivating the earth and having dominion, we see, are joined together. The one gave title to the other. So that God, by commanding to subdue, gave authority so far to appropriate. And the condition of human life, which requires labour and materials to work on, necessarily introduce private possessions.

35. The measure of property Nature well set, by the extent of men's labour and the conveniency of life. No man's labour could subdue or appropriate all, nor could his enjoyment consume more than a small part; so that it was impossible for any man, this way, to entrench upon the right of another or acquire to himself a property to the prejudice of his neighbour, who would still have room for as good and as large a possession (after the other had taken out his) as before it was appropriated. Which measure did confine every man's possession to a very moderate proportion, and such as he might appropriate to himself without injury to anybody in the first ages of the world, when men were more in danger to be lost, by wandering from their company, in the then vast wilderness of the earth than to be straitened for want of room to plant in.

36. The same measure may be allowed still, without prejudice to anybody, full as the world seems. For, supposing a man or family, in the state they were at first, peopling of the world by the children of Adam or Noah, let him plant in some inland vacant places of America. We shall find that the possessions he could make himself, upon the measures we have given, would not be very large, nor, even to this day, prejudice the rest of mankind or give them reason to complain or think themselves injured by this man's encroachment, though the race of men have now spread themselves to all the corners of the world, and do infinitely exceed the small number was at the beginning. Nay, the extent of ground is of so little value without labour that I have heard it affirmed that in Spain itself a man may be permitted to plough, sow, and reap, without being disturbed, upon land he has no other title to, but only his making use of it. But, on the contrary, the inhabitants think themselves beholden to him who, by his industry on neglected, and consequently waste land, has increased the stock of corn, which they wanted. But be this as it will, which I lay no stress on, this I dare boldly affirm, that the same rule of propriety—viz., that every man should have as much as he could make use of, would hold still in the world, without straitening anybody, since there is land enough in the world to suffice double the inhabitants, had not the invention of money, and the tacit agreement of men to put a value on it, introduced (by consent) larger possessions and a right to them; which, how it has done, I shall by and by show more at large.

37. This is certain, that in the beginning, before the desire of having more than men needed had altered the intrinsic value of things, which depends only on their usefulness to the life of man, or had agreed that a little piece of yellow metal, which would keep without wasting or decay, should be worth a great piece of flesh or a whole heap of corn, though men had a right to appropriate by their labour, each one to himself, as much of the things of Nature as he could use, yet this could not be much, nor to the prejudice of others, where the same plenty was still left, to those who would use the same industry. Before the appropriation of land, he who gathered as much of the wild fruit, killed, caught, or tamed as many of the beasts as he could— he that so employed his pains about any of the spontaneous products of Nature as any way to alter them from the state Nature put them in, by placing any of his labour on them, did thereby acquire a propriety in them; but if they perished in his possession without their due use—if the fruits rotted or the venison putrefied before he could spend it, he offended against the common law of Nature, and was liable to be punished: he invaded his neighbour's share, for he had no right farther than his use called for any of them, and they might serve to afford him conveniencies of life.

38. The same measures governed the possession of land, too. Whatsoever he tilled and reaped, laid up and made use of before it spoiled, that was his peculiar right; whatsoever he enclosed, and could feed and make use of, the cattle and product was also his. But if either the grass of his enclosure rotted on the ground, or the fruit of his planting perished without gathering and laying up, this part of the earth, notwithstanding his enclosure, was still to be looked on as waste, and might be the possession of any other. Thus, at the beginning, Cain might take as much ground as he could till and make it his own land, and yet leave enough to Abel's sheep to feed on: a few acres would serve for both their possessions. But as families increased and industry enlarged their stocks, their possessions enlarged with the need of them; but yet it was commonly without any fixed property in the ground they made use of till they incorporated, settled themselves together, and built cities, and then, by consent, they came in time to set out the bounds of their distinct territories and agree on limits between them and their neighbours, and by laws within themselves settled the properties of those of the same society. For we see that in that part of the world which was first inhabited, and therefore like to be best peopled, even as low down as Abraham's time, they wandered with their flocks and their herds, which was their substance, freely up and down—and this Abraham did in a country where he was a stranger; whence it is plain that, at least, a great part of the land lay in common, that the inhabitants valued it not, nor claimed property in

any more than they made use of; but when there was not room enough in the same place for their herds to feed together, they, by consent, as Abraham and Lot did (Gen. xiii. 5), separated and enlarged their pasture where it best liked them. And for the same reason, Esau went from his father and his brother, and planted in Mount Seir (Gen. 36. 6).

39. And thus, without supposing any private dominion and property in Adam over all the world, exclusive of all other men, which can no way be proved, nor any one's property be made out from it, but supposing the world, given as it was to the children of men in common, we see how labour could make men distinct titles to several parcels of it for their private uses, wherein there could be no doubt of right, no room for quarrel.

40. Nor is it so strange as, perhaps, before consideration, it may appear, that the property of labour should be able to overbalance the community of land, for it is labour indeed that puts the difference of value on everything; and let any one consider what the difference is between an acre of land planted with tobacco or sugar, sown with wheat or barley, and an acre of the same land lying in common without any husbandry upon it, and he will find that the improvement of labour makes the far greater part of the value. I think it will be but a very modest computation to say, that of the products of the earth useful to the life of man, nine-tenths are the effects of labour. Nay, if we will rightly estimate things as they come to our use, and cast up the several expenses about them—what in them is purely owing to Nature and what to labour—we shall find that in most of them ninety-nine hundredths are wholly to be put on the account of labour.

41. There cannot be a clearer demonstration of anything than several nations of the Americans are of this, who are rich in land and poor in all the comforts of life; whom Nature, having furnished as liberally as any other people with the materials of plenty—i.e., a fruitful soil, apt to produce in abundance what might serve for food, raiment, and delight; yet, for want of improving it by labour, have not one hundredth part of the conveniencies we enjoy, and a king of a large and fruitful territory there feeds, lodges, and is clad worse than a day labourer in England.

42. To make this a little clearer, let us but trace some of the ordinary provisions of life, through their several progresses, before they come to our use, and see how much they receive of their value from human industry. Bread, wine, and cloth are things of daily use and great plenty; yet notwithstanding acorns, water, and leaves, or skins must be our bread, drink and clothing, did not labour furnish us with these more useful commodities. For whatever bread is more worth than acorns, wine than water, and cloth or silk than leaves, skins or moss, that is wholly owing to labour and industry. The one of these being the food and raiment which unassisted Nature furnishes us with; the other provisions which our industry and pains prepare for us, which how much they exceed the other in value, when any one hath computed, he will then see how much labour makes the far greatest part of the value of things we enjoy in this world; and the ground which produces the materials is scarce to be reckoned in as any, or at most, but a very small part of it; so little, that even amongst us, land that is left wholly to nature, that hath no improvement of pasturage, tillage, or planting, is called, as indeed it is, waste; and we shall find the benefit of it amount to little more than nothing.

43. An acre of land that bears here twenty bushels of wheat, and another in America, which, with the same husbandry, would do the like, are, without doubt, of the same natural, intrinsic value. But yet the benefit mankind receives from one in a year is worth five pounds, and the other possibly not worth a penny; if all the profit an Indian received from it were to be valued and sold here, at least I may truly say, not one thousandth. It is labour, then, which puts the greatest part of value upon land, without which it would scarcely be worth anything; it is to that we owe the greatest part of all its useful products; for all that the straw, bran, bread, of that acre of wheat, is more worth than the product of an acre of as good land which lies waste is all the effect of labour. For it is not barely the ploughman's pains, the reaper's and thresher's toil, and the baker's sweat, is to be counted into the bread we eat; the labour of those who broke the oxen, who digged and wrought the iron and stones, who felled and framed the timber employed about the plough, mill, oven, or any other utensils, which are a vast number, requisite to this corn, from its sowing to its being made bread, must all be charged on the account of labour, and received as an effect of that; Nature and the earth furnished only the almost worthless materials as in themselves. It would be a strange catalogue of things that industry provided and made use of about every loaf of bread before it came to our use if we could trace them; iron, wood, leather, bark, timber, stone, bricks, coals, lime, cloth, dyeing-drugs, pitch, tar, masts, ropes, and all the materials made use of in the ship that brought any of the commodities made use of by any of the workmen, to any part of the work, all which it would be almost impossible, at least too long, to reckon up.

44. From all which it is evident, that though the things of Nature are given in common, man (by being master of himself, and proprietor of his own person, and the actions or labour of it) had still in himself the great foun-

dation of property; and that which made up the great part of what he applied to the support or comfort of his being, when invention and arts had improved the conveniences of life, was perfectly his own, and did not belong in common to others.

45. Thus labour, in the beginning, gave a right of property, wherever any one was pleased to employ it, upon what was common, which remained a long while, the far greater part, and is yet more than mankind makes use of Men at first, for the most part, contented themselves with what unassisted Nature offered to their necessities; and though afterwards, in some parts of the world, where the increase of people and stock, with the use of money, had made land scarce, and so of some value, the several communities settled the bounds of their distinct territories, and, by laws, within themselves, regulated the properties of the private men of their society, and so, by compact and agreement, settled the property which labour and industry began. And the leagues that have been made between several states and kingdoms, either expressly or tacitly disowning all claim and right to the land in the other's possession, have, by common consent, given up their pretences to their natural common right, which originally they had to those countries; and so have, by positive agreement, settled a property amongst themselves, in distinct parts of the world; yet there are still great tracts of ground to be found, which the inhabitants thereof, not having joined with the rest of mankind in the consent of the use of their common money, lie waste, and are more than the people who dwell on it, do, or can make use of, and so still lie in common; though this can scarce happen amongst that part of mankind that have consented to the use of money.

46. The greatest part of things really useful to the life of man, and such as the necessity of subsisting made the first commoners of the world look after—as it doth the Americans now—are generally things of short duration, such as—if they are not consumed by use- will decay and perish of themselves. Gold, silver, and diamonds are things that fancy or agreement hath put the value on, more than real use and the necessary support of life. Now of those good things which Nature hath provided in common, every one hath a right (as hath been said) to as much as he could use; and had a property in all he could effect with his labour; all that his industry could extend to, to alter from the state Nature had put it in, was his. He that gathered a hundred bushels of acorns or apples had thereby a property in them; they were his goods as soon as gathered. He was only to look that he used them before they spoiled, else he took more than his share, and robbed others. And, indeed, it was a foolish thing, as well as dishonest, to hoard up more than he could make use of If he gave away a part to anybody else, so that it perished not uselessly in his possession, these he also made use of And if he also bartered away plums that would have rotted in a week, for nuts that would last good for his eating a whole year, he did no injury; he wasted not the common stock; destroyed no part of the portion of goods that belonged to others, so long as nothing perished uselessly in his hands. Again, if he would give his nuts for a piece of metal, pleased with its colour, or exchange his sheep for shells, or wool for a sparkling pebble or a diamond, and keep those by him all his life, he invaded not the right of others; he might heap up as much of these durable things as he pleased; the exceeding of the bounds of his just property not lying in the largeness of his possession, but the perishing of anything uselessly in it.

47. And thus came in the use of money; some lasting thing that men might keep without spoiling, and that, by mutual consent, men would take in exchange for the truly useful but perishable supports of life.

48. And as different degrees of industry were apt to give men possessions in different proportions, so this invention of money gave them the opportunity to continue and enlarge them. For supposing an island, separate from all possible commerce with the rest of the world, wherein there were but a hundred families, but there were sheep, horses, and cows, with other useful animals, wholesome fruits, and land enough for corn for a hundred thousand times as many, but nothing in the island, either because of its commonness or perishableness, fit to supply the place of money. What reason could any one have there to enlarge his possessions beyond the use of his family, and a plentiful supply to its consumption, either in what their own industry produced, or they could barter for like perishable, useful commodities with others? Where there is not something both lasting and scarce, and so valuable to be hoarded up, there men will not be apt to enlarge their possessions of land, were it never so rich, never so free for them to take. For I ask, what would a man value ten thousand or an hundred thousand acres of excellent land, ready cultivated and well stocked, too, with cattle, in the middle of the inland parts of America, where he had no hopes of commerce with other parts of the world, to draw money to him by the sale of the product? It would not be worth the enclosing, and we should see him give up again to the wild common of Nature whatever was more than would supply the conveniences of life, to be had there for him and his family.

49. Thus, in the beginning, all the world was America, and more so than that is now; for no such thing as money was anywhere known. Find out something that hath the use and value of money amongst his neighbours, you shall see the same man will begin presently to enlarge his possessions.

50. But, since gold and silver, being little useful to the life of man, in proportion to food, raiment, and carriage, has its value only from the consent of men—whereof labour yet makes in great part the measure— it is plain that the consent of men have agreed to a disproportionate and unequal possession of the earth—I mean out of the bounds of society and compact; for in governments the laws regulate it; they having, by consent, found out and agreed in a way how a man may, rightfully and without injury, possess more than he himself can make use of by receiving gold and silver, which may continue long in a man's possession without decaying for the overplus, and agreeing those metals should have a value.

51. And thus, I think, it is very easy to conceive, without any difficulty, how labour could at first begin a title of property in the common things of Nature, and how the spending it upon our uses bounded it; so that there could then be no reason of quarrelling about title, nor any doubt about the largeness of possession it gave. Right and conveniency went together. For as a man had a right to all he could employ his labour upon, so he had no temptation to labour for more than he could make use of. This left no room for controversy about the title, nor for encroachment on the right of others. What portion a man carved to himself was easily seen; and it was useless, as well as dishonest, to carve himself too much, or take more than he needed.

**Chapter VI, Of Paternal Power**

52. It may perhaps be censured an impertinent criticism in a discourse of this nature to find fault with words and names that have obtained in the world. And yet possibly it may not be amiss to offer new ones when the old are apt to lead men into mistakes, as this of paternal power probably has done, which seems so to place the power of parents over their children wholly in the father, as if the mother had no share in it; whereas if we consult reason or revelation, we shall find she has an equal title, which may give one reason to ask whether this might not be more properly called parental power? For whatever obligation Nature and the right of generation lays on children, it must certainly bind them equal to both the concurrent causes of it. And accordingly we see the positive law of God everywhere joins them together without distinction, when it commands the obedience of children: "Honour thy father and thy mother" (Exod. 20. 12); "Whosoever curseth his father or his mother" (Lev. 20. 9); "Ye shall fear every man his mother and his father" (Lev. 19. 3); "Children, obey your parents" (Eph. 6. 1), etc., is the style of the Old and New Testament.

53. Had but this one thing been well considered without looking any deeper into the matter, it might perhaps have kept men from running into those gross mistakes they have made about this power of parents, which however it might without any great harshness bear the name of absolute dominion and regal authority, when under the title of "paternal" power, it seemed appropriated to the father; would yet have sounded but oddly, and in the very name shown the absurdity, if this supposed absolute power over children had been called parental, and thereby discovered that it belonged to the mother too. For it will but very ill serve the turn of those men who contend so much for the absolute power and authority of the fatherhood, as they call it, that the mother should have any share in it. And it would have but ill supported the monarchy they contend for, when by the very name it appeared that that fundamental authority from whence they would derive their government of a single person only was not placed in one, but two persons jointly. But to let this of names pass.

54. Though I have said above (2) "That all men by nature are equal," I cannot be supposed to understand all sorts of "equality." Age or virtue may give men a just precedency. Excellency of parts and merit may place others above the common level. Birth may subject some, and alliance or benefits others, to pay an observance to those to whom Nature, gratitude, or other respects, may have made it due; and yet all this consists with the equality which all men are in respect of jurisdiction or dominion one over another, which was the equality I there spoke of as proper to the business in hand, being that equal right that every man hath to his natural freedom, without being subjected to the will or authority of any other man.

55. Children, I confess, are not born in this full state of equality, though they are born to it. Their parents have a sort of rule and jurisdiction over them when they come into the world, and for some time after, but it is but a temporary one. The bonds of this subjection are like the swaddling clothes they are wrapt up in and supported

by in the weakness of their infancy. Age and reason as they grow up loosen them, till at length they drop quite off, and leave a man at his own free disposal.

56. Adam was created a perfect man, his body and mind in full possession of their strength and reason, and so was capable from the first instance of his being to provide for his own support and preservation, and govern his actions according to the dictates of the law of reason God had implanted in him. From him the world is peopled with his descendants, who are all born infants, weak and helpless, without knowledge or understanding. But to supply the defects of this imperfect state till the improvement of growth and age had removed them, Adam and Eve, and after them all parents were, by the law of Nature, under an obligation to preserve, nourish and educate the children they had begotten, not as their own workmanship, but the workmanship of their own Maker, the Almighty, to whom they were to be accountable for them.

57. The law that was to govern Adam was the same that was to govern all his posterity, the law of reason. But his offspring having another way of entrance into the world, different from him, by a natural birth, that produced them ignorant, and without the use of reason, they were not presently under that law. For nobody can be under a law that is not promulgated to him; and this law being promulgated or made known by reason only, he that is not come to the use of his reason cannot be said to be under this law; and Adam's children being not presently as soon as born under this law of reason, were not presently free. For law, in its true notion, is not so much the limitation as the direction of a free and intelligent agent to his proper interest, and prescribes no farther than is for the general good of those under that law. Could they be happier without it, the law, as a useless thing, would of itself vanish; and that ill deserves the name of confinement which hedges us in only from bogs and precipices. So that however it may be mistaken, the end of law is not to abolish or restrain, but to preserve and enlarge freedom. For in all the states of created beings, capable of laws, where there is no law there is no freedom. For liberty is to be free from restraint and violence from others, which cannot be where there is no law; and is not, as we are told, "a liberty for every man to do what he lists." For who could be free, when every other man's humour might domineer over him? But a liberty to dispose and order freely as he lists his person, actions, possessions, and his whole property within the allowance of those laws under which he is, and therein not to be subject to the arbitrary will of another, but freely follow his own.

58. The power, then, that parents have over their children arises from that duty which is incumbent on them, to take care of their offspring during the imperfect state of childhood. To inform the mind, and govern the actions of their yet ignorant nonage, till reason shall take its place and ease them of that trouble, is what the children want, and the parents are bound to. For God having given man an understanding to direct his actions, has allowed him a freedom of will and liberty of acting, as properly belonging thereunto within the bounds of that law he is under. But whilst he is in an estate wherein he has no understanding of his own to direct his will, he is not to have any will of his own to follow. He that understands for him must will for him too; he must prescribe to his will, and regulate his actions, but when he comes to the estate that made his father a free man, the son is a free man too.

59. This holds in all the laws a man is under, whether natural or civil. Is a man under the law of Nature? What made him free of that law? what gave him a free disposing of his property, according to his own will, within the compass of that law? I answer, an estate wherein he might be supposed capable to know that law, that so he might keep his actions within the bounds of it. When he has acquired that state, he is presumed to know how far that law is to be his guide, and how far he may make use of his freedom, and so comes to have it; till then, somebody else must guide him, who is presumed to know how far the law allows a liberty. If such a state of reason, such an age of discretion made him free, the same shall make his son free too. Is a man under the law of England? what made him free of that law—that is, to have the liberty to dispose of his actions and possessions, according to his own will, within the permission of that law? a capacity of knowing that law. Which is supposed, by that law, at the age of twenty-one, and in some cases sooner. If this made the father free, it shall make the son free too. Till then, we see the law allows the son to have no will, but he is to be guided by the will of his father or guardian, who is to understand for him. And if the father die and fail to substitute a deputy in this trust, if he hath not provided a tutor to govern his son during his minority, during his want of understanding, the law takes care to do it: some other must govern him and be a will to him till he hath attained to a state of freedom, and his understanding be fit to take the government of his will. But after that the father and son are equally free, as much as tutor and pupil, after nonage, equally subjects of the same law together, without any dominion left in the father over the life, liberty, or estate of his son, whether they be only in the state and under the law of Nature, or under the positive laws of an established government.

60. But if through defects that may happen out of the ordinary course of Nature, any one comes not to such a degree of reason wherein he might be supposed capable of knowing the law, and so living within the rules of

it, he is never capable of being a free man, he is never let loose to the disposure of his own will; because he knows no bounds to it, has not understanding, its proper guide, but is continued under the tuition and government of others all the time his own understanding is incapable of that charge. And so lunatics and idiots are never set free from the government of their parents: "Children who are not as yet come unto those years whereat they may have, and innocents, which are excluded by a natural defect from ever having." Thirdly: "Madmen, which, for the present, cannot possibly have the use of right reason to guide themselves, have, for their guide, the reason that guideth other men which are tutors over them, to seek and procure their good for them," says Hooker (Eccl. Pol., lib. i., s. 7). All which seems no more than that duty which God and Nature has laid on man, as well as other creatures, to preserve their offspring till they can be able to shift for themselves, and will scarce amount to an instance or proof of parents' regal authority.

61. Thus we are born free as we are born rational; not that we have actually the exercise of either: age that brings one, brings with it the other too. And thus we see how natural freedom and subjection to parents may consist together, and are both founded on the same principle. A child is free by his father's title, by his father's understanding, which is to govern him till he hath it of his own. The freedom of a man at years of discretion, and the subjection of a child to his parents, whilst yet short of it, are so consistent and so distinguishable that the most blinded contenders for monarchy, "by right of fatherhood," cannot miss of it; the most obstinate cannot but allow of it. For were their doctrine all true, were the right heir of Adam now known, and, by that title, settled a monarch in his throne, invested with all the absolute unlimited power Sir Robert Filmer talks of, if he should die as soon as his heir were born, must not the child, notwithstanding he were never so free, never so much sovereign, be in subjection to his mother and nurse, to tutors and governors, till age and education brought him reason and ability to govern himself and others? The necessities of his life, the health of his body, and the information of his mind would require him to be directed by the will of others and not his own; and yet will any one think that this restraint and subjection were inconsistent with, or spoiled him of, that liberty or sovereignty he had a right to, or gave away his empire to those who had the government of his nonage? This government over him only prepared him the better and sooner for it. If anybody should ask me when my son is of age to be free, I shall answer, just when his monarch is of age to govern. "But at what time," says the judicious Hooker (Eccl. Pol., lib. i., s. 6), "a man may be said to have attained so far forth the use of reason as sufficeth to make him capable of those laws whereby he is then bound to guide his actions; this is a great deal more easy for sense to discern than for any one, by skill and learning, to determine."

62. Commonwealths themselves take notice of, and allow that there is a time when men are to begin to act like free men, and therefore, till that time, require not oaths of fealty or allegiance, or other public owning of, or submission to, the government of their countries.

63. The freedom then of man, and liberty of acting according to his own will, is grounded on his having reason, which is able to instruct him in that law he is to govern himself by, and make him know how far he is left to the freedom of his own will. To turn him loose to an unrestrained liberty, before he has reason to guide him, is not the allowing him the privilege of his nature to be free, but to thrust him out amongst brutes, and abandon him to a state as wretched and as much beneath that of a man as theirs. This is that which puts the authority into the parents' hands to govern the minority of their children. God hath made it their business to employ this care on their offspring, and hath placed in them suitable inclinations of tenderness and concern to temper this power, to apply it as His wisdom designed it, to the children's good as long as they should need to be under it.

64. But what reason can hence advance this care of the parents due to their offspring into an absolute, arbitrary dominion of the father, whose power reaches no farther than by such a discipline as he finds most effectual to give such strength and health to their bodies, such vigour and rectitude to their minds, as may best fit his children to be most useful to themselves and others, and, if it be necessary to his condition, to make them work when they are able for their own subsistence; but in this power the mother, too, has her share with the father.

65. Nay, this power so little belongs to the father by any peculiar right of Nature, but only as he is guardian of his children, that when he quits his care of them he loses his power over them, which goes along with their nourishment and education, to which it is inseparably annexed, and belongs as much to the foster-father of an exposed child as to the natural father of another. So little power does the bare act of begetting give a man over his issue, if all his care ends there, and this be all the title he hath to the name and authority of a father. And what will become of this paternal power in that part of the world where one woman hath more than one husband at a time? or in those parts of America where, when the husband and wife part, which happens frequently, the children are all left to the mother, follow her, and are wholly under her care and provision? And if the

father die whilst the children are young, do they not naturally everywhere owe the same obedience to their mother, during their minority, as to their father, were he alive? And will any one say that the mother hath a legislative power over her children that she can make standing rules which shall be of perpetual obligation, by which they ought to regulate all the concerns of their property, and bound their liberty all the course of their lives, and enforce the observation of them with capital punishments? For this is the proper power of the magistrate, of which the father hath not so much as the shadow. His command over his children is but temporary, and reaches not their life or property. It is but a help to the weakness and imperfection of their nonage, a discipline necessary to their education. And though a father may dispose of his own possessions as he pleases when his children are out of danger of perishing for want, yet his power extends not to the lives or goods which either their own industry, or another's bounty, has made theirs, nor to their liberty neither when they are once arrived to the enfranchisement of the years of discretion. The father's empire then ceases, and he can from thenceforward no more dispose of the liberty of his son than that of any other man. And it must be far from an absolute or perpetual jurisdiction from which a man may withdraw himself, having licence from Divine authority to "leave father and mother and cleave to his wife."

66. But though there be a time when a child comes to be as free from subjection to the will and command of his father as he himself is free from subjection to the will of anybody else, and they are both under no other restraint but that which is common to them both, whether it be the law of Nature or municipal law of their country, yet this freedom exempts not a son from that honour which he ought, by the law of God and Nature, to pay his parents, God having made the parents instruments in His great design of continuing the race of mankind and the occasions of life to their children. As He hath laid on them an obligation to nourish, preserve, and bring up their offspring, so He has laid on the children a perpetual obligation of honouring their parents, which, containing in it an inward esteem and reverence to be shown by all outward expressions, ties up the child from anything that may ever injure or affront, disturb or endanger the happiness or life of those from whom he received his, and engages him in all actions of defence, relief, assistance, and comfort of those by whose means he entered into being and has been made capable of any enjoyments of life. From this obligation no state, no freedom, can absolve children. But this is very far from giving parents a power of command over their children, or an authority to make laws and dispose as they please of their lives or liberties. It is one thing to owe honour, respect, gratitude, and assistance; another to require an absolute obedience and submission. The honour due to parents a monarch on his throne owes his mother, and yet this lessens not his authority nor subjects him to her government.

67. The subjection of a minor places in the father a temporary government which terminates with the minority of the child; and the honour due from a child places in the parents a perpetual right to respect, reverence, support, and compliance, to more or less, as the father's care, cost, and kindness in his education has been more or less, and this ends not with minority, but holds in all parts and conditions of a man's life. The want of distinguishing these two powers which the father hath, in the right of tuition, during minority, and the right of honour all his life, may perhaps have caused a great part of the mistakes about this matter. For, to speak properly of them, the first of these is rather the privilege of children and duty of parents than any prerogative of paternal power. The nourishment and education of their children is a charge so incumbent on parents for their children's good, that nothing can absolve them from taking care of it. And though the power of commanding and chastising them go along with it, yet God hath woven into the principles of human nature such a tenderness for their offspring, that there is little fear that parents should use their power with too much rigour; the excess is seldom on the severe side, the strong bias of nature drawing the other way. And therefore God Almighty, when He would express His gentle dealing with the Israelites, He tells them that though He chastened them, "He chastened them as a man chastens his son" (Deut. 8. 5)—i.e., with tenderness and affection, and kept them under no severer discipline than what was absolutely best for them, and had been less kindness, to have slackened. This is that power to which children are commanded obedience, that the pains and care of their parents may not be increased or ill-rewarded.

68. On the other side, honour and support all that which gratitude requires to return; for the benefits received by and from them is the indispensable duty of the child and the proper privilege of the parents. This is intended for the parents' advantage, as the other is for the child's; though education, the parents' duty, seems to have most power, because the ignorance and infirmities of childhood stand in need of restraint and correction, which is a visible exercise of rule and a kind of dominion. And that duty which is comprehended in the word "honour" requires less obedience, though the obligation be stronger on grown than younger children. For who can think the command, "Children, obey your parents," requires in a man that has children of his own the same submission to his father as it does in his yet young children to him, and that by this precept he were bound to obey all his father's commands, if, out of a conceit of authority, he should have the indiscretion to treat him still as a boy?

69. The first part, then, of paternal power, or rather duty, which is education, belongs so to the father that it terminates at a certain season. When the business of education is over it ceases of itself, and is also alienable before. For a man may put the tuition of his son in other hands; and he that has made his son an apprentice to another has discharged him, during that time, of a great part of his obedience, both to himself and to his mother. But all the duty of honour, the other part, remains nevertheless entire to them; nothing can cancel that. It is so inseparable from them both, that the father's authority cannot dispossess the mother of this right, nor can any man discharge his son from honouring her that bore him. But both these are very far from a power to make laws, and enforcing them with penalties that may reach estate, liberty, limbs, and life. The power of commanding ends with nonage, and though after that honour and respect, support and defence, and whatsoever gratitude can oblige a man to, for the highest benefits he is naturally capable of be always due from a son to his parents, yet all this puts no sceptre into the father's hand, no sovereign power of commanding. He has no dominion over his son's property or actions, nor any right that his will should prescribe to his son's in all things; however, it may become his son in many things, not very inconvenient to him and his family, to pay a deference to it.

70. A man may owe honour and respect to an ancient or wise man, defence to his child or friend, relief and support to the distressed, and gratitude to a benefactor, to such a degree that all he has, all he can do, cannot sufficiently pay it. But all these give no authority, no right of making laws to any one over him from whom they are owing. And it is plain all this is due, not to the bare title of father, not only because as has been said, it is owing to the mother too, but because these obligations to parents, and the degrees of what is required of children, may be varied by the different care and kindness trouble and expense, is often employed upon one child more than another.

71. This shows the reason how it comes to pass that parents in societies, where they themselves are subjects, retain a power over their children and have as much right to their subjection as those who are in the state of Nature, which could not possibly be if all political power were only paternal, and that, in truth, they were one and the same thing; for then, all paternal power being in the prince, the subject could naturally have none of it. But these two powers, political and paternal, are so perfectly distinct and separate, and built upon so different foundations, and given to so different ends, that every subject that is a father has as much a paternal power over his children as the prince has over his. And every prince that has parents owes them as much filial duty and obedience as the meanest of his subjects do to theirs, and can therefore contain not any part or degree of that kind of dominion which a prince or magistrate has over his subject.

72. Though the obligation on the parents to bring up their children, and the obligation on children to honour their parents, contain all the power, on the one hand, and submission on the other, which are proper to this relation, yet there is another power ordinarily in the father, whereby he has a tie on the obedience of his children, which, though it be common to him with other men, yet the occasions of showing it, almost constantly happening to fathers in their private families and in instances of it elsewhere being rare, and less taken notice of, it passes in the world for a part of "paternal jurisdiction." And this is the power men generally have to bestow their estates on those who please them best. The possession of the father being the expectation and inheritance of the children ordinarily, in certain proportions, according to the law and custom of each country, yet it is commonly in the father's power to bestow it with a
more sparing or liberal hand, according as the behaviour of this or that child hath comported with his will and humour.

73. This is no small tie to the obedience of children; and there being always annexed to the enjoyment of land a submission to the government of the country of which that land is a part, it has been commonly supposed that a father could oblige his posterity to that government of which he himself was a subject, that his compact held them; whereas, it being only a necessary condition annexed to the land which is under that government, reaches only those who will take it on that condition, and so is no natural tie or engagement, but a voluntary submission; for every man's children being, by Nature, as free as himself or any of his ancestors ever were, may, whilst they are in that freedom, choose what society they will join themselves to, what commonwealth they will put themselves under. But if they will enjoy the inheritance of their ancestors, they must take it on the same terms their ancestors had it, and submit to all the conditions annexed to such a possession. By this power, indeed, fathers oblige their children to obedience to themselves even when they are past minority, and most commonly, too, subject them to this or that political power. But neither of these by any peculiar right of fatherhood, but by the reward they have in their hands to enforce and recompense such a compliance, and is no more power than what a Frenchman has over an Englishman, who, by the hopes of an estate he will leave him, will certainly have a strong tie on his obedience; and if when it is left him, he will enjoy it, he must cer-

tainly take it upon the conditions annexed to the possession of land in that country where it lies, whether it be France or England.

74. To conclude, then, though the father's power of commanding extends no farther than the minority of his children, and to a degree only fit for the discipline and government of that age; and though that honour and respect, and all that which the Latins called piety, which they indispensably owe to their parents all their life-time, and in all estates, with all that support and defence, is due to them, gives the father no power of governing—i.e., making laws and exacting penalties on his children; though by this he has no dominion over the property or actions of his son, yet it is obvious to conceive how easy it was, in the first ages of the world, and in places still where the thinness of people gives families leave to separate into unpossessed quarters, and they have room to remove and plant themselves in yet vacant habitations, for the father of the family to become the prince of it;1 he had been a ruler from the beginning of the infancy of his children; and when they were grown up, since without some government it would be hard for them to live together, it was likeliest it should, by the express or tacit consent of the children, be in the father, where it seemed, without any change, barely to continue. And when, indeed, nothing more was required to it than the permitting the father to exercise alone in his family that executive power of the law of Nature which every free man naturally hath, and by that permission resigning up to him a monarchical power whilst they remained in it. But that this was not by any paternal right, but only by the consent of his children, is evident from hence, that nobody doubts but if a stranger, whom chance or business had brought to his family, had there killed any of his children, or committed any other act, he might condemn and put him to death, or otherwise have punished him as well as any of his children. which was impossible he should do by virtue of any paternal authority over one who was not his child, but by virtue of that executive power of the law of Nature which, as a man, he had a right to; and he alone could punish him in his family where the respect of his children had laid by the exercise of such a power, to give way to the dignity and authority they were willing should remain in him above the rest of his family.

75. Thus it was easy and almost natural for children, by a tacit and almost natural consent, to make way for the father's authority and government. They had been accustomed in their childhood to follow his direction, and to refer their little differences to him; and when they were men, who was fitter to rule them? Their little properties and less covetousness seldom afforded greater controversies; and when any should arise, where could they have a fitter umpire than he, by whose care they had every one been sustained and brought up. and who had a tenderness for them all? It is no wonder that they made no distinction betwixt minority and full age, nor looked after one-and-twenty, or any other age, that might make them the free disposers of themselves and fortunes, when they could have no desire to be out of their pupilage. The government they had been under during it continued still to be more their protection than restraint; and they could nowhere find a greater security to their peace, liberties, and fortunes than in the rule of a father.

76. Thus the natural fathers of families, by an insensible change, became the politic monarchs of them too; and as they chanced to live long, and leave able and worthy heirs for several successions or otherwise, so they laid the foundations of hereditary or elective kingdoms under several constitutions and manors, according as chance, contrivance, or occasions happened to mould them. But if princes have their titles in the father's right, and it be a sufficient proof of the natural right of fathers to political authority, because they commonly were those in whose hands we find, de facto, the exercise of government, I say, if this argument be good, it will as strongly prove that all princes, nay, princes only, ought to be priests, since it is as certain that in the beginning "the father of the family was priest, as that he was ruler in his own household."

**Chapter VII, Of Political or Civil Society**

77. God, having made man such a creature that, in His own judgment, it was not good for him to be alone, put him under strong obligations of necessity, convenience, and inclination, to drive him into society, as well as fitted him with understanding and language to continue and enjoy it. The first society was between man and wife, which gave beginning to that between parents and children, to which, in time, that between master and servant came to be added. And though all these might, and commonly did, meet together, and make up but one family, wherein the master or mistress of it had some sort of rule proper to a family, each of these, or all together, came short of "political society," as we shall see if we consider the different ends, ties, and bounds of each of these.

78. Conjugal society is made by a voluntary compact between man and woman, and though it consist chiefly in such a communion and right in one another's bodies as is necessary to its chief end, procreation, yet it

draws with it mutual support and assistance, and a communion of interests too, as necessary not only to unite their care and affection, but also necessary to their common offspring, who have a right to be nourished and maintained by them till they are able to provide for themselves.

79. For the end of conjunction between male and female being not barely procreation, but the continuation of the species, this conjunction betwixt male and female ought to last, even after procreation, so long as is necessary to the nourishment and support of the young ones, who are to be sustained by those that got them till they are able to shift and provide for themselves. This rule, which the infinite wise Maker hath set to the works of His hands, we find the inferior creatures steadily obey. In those vivaporous animals which feed on grass the conjunction between male and female lasts no longer than the very act of copulation, because the teat of the dam being sufficient to nourish the young till it be able to feed on grass. the male only begets, but concerns not himself for the female or young, to whose sustenance he can contribute nothing. But in beasts of prey the conjunction lasts longer because the dam, not being able well to subsist herself and nourish her numerous offspring by her own prey alone (a more laborious as well as more dangerous way of living than by feeding on grass), the assistance of the male is necessary to the maintenance of their common family, which cannot subsist till they are able to prey for themselves, but by the joint care of male and female. The same is observed in all birds (except some domestic ones, where plenty of food excuses the cock from feeding and taking care of the young brood), whose young, needing food in the nest, the cock and hen continue mates till the young are able to use their wings and provide for themselves.

80. And herein, I think, lies the chief, if not the only reason, why the male and female in mankind are tied to a longer conjunction than other creatures—viz., because the female is capable of conceiving, and, de facto, is commonly with child again, and brings forth too a new birth, long before the former is out of a dependency for support on his parents' help and able to shift for himself and has all the assistance due to him from his parents, whereby the father, who is bound to take care for those he hath begot, is under an obligation to continue in conjugal society with the same woman longer than other creatures, whose young, being able to subsist of themselves before the time of procreation returns again, the conjugal bond dissolves of itself, and they are at liberty till Hymen, at his usual anniversary season, summons them again to choose new mates. Wherein one cannot but admire the wisdom of the great Creator, who, having given to man an ability to lay up for the future as well as supply the present necessity, hath made it necessary that society of man and wife should be more lasting than of male and female amongst other creatures, that so their industry might be encouraged, and their interest better united, to make provision and lay up goods for their common issue, which uncertain mixture, or easy and frequent solutions of conjugal society, would mightily disturb.

81. But though these are ties upon mankind which make the conjugal bonds more firm and lasting in a man than the other species of animals, yet it would give one reason to inquire why this compact, where procreation and education are secured and inheritance taken care for, may not be made determinable, either by consent, or at a certain time, or upon certain conditions, as well as any other voluntary compacts, there being no necessity, in the nature of the thing, nor to the ends of it, that it should always be for life—I mean, to such as are under no restraint of any positive law which ordains all such contracts to be perpetual.

82. But the husband and wife, though they have but one common concern, yet having different understandings, will unavoidably sometimes have different wills too. It therefore being necessary that the last determination (i.e., the rule) should be placed somewhere, it naturally falls to the man's share as the abler and the stronger. But this, reaching but to the things of their common interest and property, leaves the wife in the full and true possession of what by contract is her peculiar right, and at least gives the husband no more power over her than she has over his life; the power of the husband being so far from that of an absolute monarch that the wife has, in many cases, a liberty to separate from him where natural right or their contract allows it, whether that contract be made by themselves in the state of Nature or by the customs or laws of the country they live in, and the children, upon such separation, fall to the father or mother's lot as such contract does determine.

83. For all the ends of marriage being to be obtained under politic government, as well as in the state of Nature, the civil magistrate doth not abridge the right or power of either, naturally necessary to those ends—viz., procreation and mutual support and assistance whilst they are together, but only decides any controversy that may arise between man and wife about them. If it were otherwise, and that absolute sovereignty and power of life and death naturally belonged to the husband, and were necessary to the society between man and wife, there could be no matrimony in any of these countries where the husband is allowed no such absolute authority. But the ends of matrimony requiring no such power in the husband, it was not at all necessary to it. The condition of conjugal society put it not in him; but whatsoever might consist with procreation and support of

the children till they could shift for themselves—mutual assistance, comfort, and maintenance—might be varied and regulated by that contract which first united them in that society, nothing being necessary to any society that is not necessary to the ends for which it is made.

84. The society betwixt parents and children, and the distinct rights and powers belonging respectively to them, I have treated of so largely in the foregoing chapter that I shall not here need to say anything of it; and I think it is plain that it is far different from a politic society.

85. Master and servant are names as old as history, but given to those of far different condition; for a free man makes himself a servant to another by selling him for a certain time the service he undertakes to do in exchange for wages he is to receive; and though this commonly puts him into the family of his master, and under the ordinary discipline thereof, yet it gives the master but a temporary power over him, and no greater than what is contained in the contract between them. But there is another sort of servant which by a peculiar name we call slaves, who being captives taken in a just war are, by the right of Nature, subjected to the absolute dominion and arbitrary power of their masters. These men having, as I say, forfeited their lives and, with it, their liberties, and lost their estates, and being in the state of slavery, not capable of any property, cannot in that state be considered as any part of civil society, the chief end whereof is the preservation of property.

86. Let us therefore consider a master of a family with all these subordinate relations of wife, children, servants and slaves, united under the domestic rule of a family, with what resemblance soever it may have in its order, offices, and number too, with a little commonwealth, yet is very far from it both in its constitution, power, and end; or if it must be thought a monarchy, and the paterfamilias the absolute monarch in it, absolute monarchy will have but a very shattered and short power, when it is plain by what has been said before, that the master of the family has a very distinct and differently limited power both as to time and extent over those several persons that are in it; for excepting the slave (and the family is as much a family, and his power as paterfamilias as great, whether there be any slaves in his family or no) he has no legislative power of life and death over any of them, and none too but what a mistress of a family may have as well as he. And he certainly can have no absolute power over the whole family who has but a very limited one over every individual in it. But how a family, or any other society of men, differ from that which is properly political society, we shall best see by considering wherein political society itself consists.

87. Man being born, as has been proved, with a title to perfect freedom and an uncontrolled enjoyment of all the rights and privileges of the law of Nature, equally with any other man, or number of men in the world, hath by nature a power not only to preserve his property— that is, his life, liberty, and estate, against the injuries and attempts of other men, but to judge of and punish the breaches of that law in others, as he is persuaded the offence deserves, even with death itself, in crimes where the heinousness of the fact, in his opinion, requires it. But because no political society can be, nor subsist, without having in itself the power to preserve the property, and in order thereunto punish the offences of all those of that society, there, and there only, is political society where every one of the members hath quitted this natural power, resigned it up into the hands of the community in all cases that exclude him not from appealing for protection to the law established by it. And thus all private judgment of every particular member being excluded, the community comes to be umpire, and by understanding indifferent rules and men authorised by the community for their execution, decides all the differences that may happen between any members of that society concerning any matter of right, and punishes those offences which any member hath committed against the society with such penalties as the law has established; whereby it is easy to discern who are, and are not, in political society together. Those who are united into one body, and have a common established law and judicature to appeal to, with authority to decide controversies between them and punish offenders, are in civil society one with another; but those who have no such common appeal, I mean on earth, are still in the state of Nature, each being where there is no other, judge for himself and executioner; which is, as I have before showed it, the perfect state of Nature.

88. And thus the commonwealth comes by a power to set down what punishment shall belong to the several transgressions they think worthy of it, committed amongst the members of that society (which is the power of making laws), as well as it has the power to punish any injury done unto any of its members by any one that is not of it (which is the power of war and peace); and all this for the preservation of the property of all the members of that society, as far as is possible. But though every man entered into society has quitted his power to punish offences against the law of Nature in prosecution of his own private judgment, yet with the judgment of offences which he has given up to the legislative, in all cases where he can appeal to the magistrate, he has given up a right to the commonwealth to employ his force for the execution of the judgments of the commonwealth whenever he shall be called to it, which, indeed, are his own judgements, they being made by himself or his representative. And herein we have the original of the legislative and executive power of civil

society, which is to judge by standing laws how far offences are to be punished when committed within the commonwealth; and also by occasional judgments founded on the present circumstances of the fact, how far injuries from without are to be vindicated, and in both these to employ all the force of all the members when there shall be need.

89. Wherever, therefore, any number of men so unite into one society as to quit every one his executive power of the law of Nature, and to resign it to the public, there and there only is a political or civil society. And this is done wherever any number of men, in the state of Nature, enter into society to make one people one body politic under one supreme government: or else when any one joins himself to, and incorporates with any government already made. For hereby he authorises the society, or which is all one, the legislative thereof, to make laws for him as the public good of the society shall require, to the execution whereof his own assistance (as to his own decrees) is due. And this puts men out of a state of Nature into that of a commonwealth, by setting up a judge on earth with authority to determine all the controversies and redress the injuries that may happen to any member of the commonwealth, which judge is the legislative or magistrates appointed by it. And wherever there are any number of men, however associated, that have no such decisive power to appeal to, there they are still in the state of Nature.

90. And hence it is evident that absolute monarchy, which by some men is counted for the only government in the world, is indeed inconsistent with civil society, and so can be not form of civil government at all. For the end of civil society being to avoid and remedy those inconveniences of the state of Nature which necessarily follow from every man's being judge in his own case, by setting up a known authority to which every one of that society may appeal upon any injury received, or controversy that may arise, and which every one of the society ought to obey.[2] Wherever any persons are who have not such an authority to appeal to, and decide any difference between them there, those persons are still in the state of Nature. And so is every absolute prince in respect of those who are under his dominion.

91. For he being supposed to have all, both legislative and executive, power in himself alone, there is no judge to be found, no appeal lies open to any one, who may fairly and indifferently, and with authority decide, and from whence relief and redress may be expected of any injury or inconveniency that may be suffered from him, or by his order. So that such a man, however entitled, Czar, or Grand Signior, or how you please, is as much in the state of Nature, with all under his dominion, as he is with the rest of mankind. For wherever any two men are, who have no standing rule and common judge to appeal to on earth, for the determination of controversies of right betwixt them, there they are still in the state of Nature, and under all the inconveniencies of it, with only this woeful difference to the subject, or rather slave of an absolute prince.[3] That whereas, in the ordinary state of Nature, he has a liberty to judge of his right, according to the best of his power to maintain it; but whenever his property is invaded by the will and order of his monarch, he has not only no appeal, as those in society ought to have, but, as if he were degraded from the common state of rational creatures, is denied a liberty to judge of, or defend his right, and so is exposed to all the misery and inconveniencies that a man can fear from one, who being in the unrestrained state of Nature, is yet corrupted with flattery and armed with power.

92. For he that thinks absolute power purifies men's blood, and corrects the baseness of human nature, need read but the history of this, or any other age, to be convinced to the contrary. He that would have been insolent and injurious in the woods of America would not probably be much better on a throne, where perhaps learning and religion shall be found out to justify all that he shall do to his subjects, and the sword presently silence all those that dare question it. For what the protection of absolute monarchy is, what kind of fathers of their countries it makes princes to be, and to what a degree of happiness and security it carries civil society, where this sort of government is grown to perfection, he that will look into the late relation of Ceylon may easily see.

93. In absolute monarchies, indeed, as well as other governments of the world, the subjects have an appeal to the law, and judges to decide any controversies, and restrain any violence that may happen betwixt the subjects themselves, one amongst another. This every one thinks necessary, and believes; he deserves to be thought a declared enemy to society and mankind who should go about to take it away. But whether this be from a true love of mankind and society, and such a charity as we owe all one to another, there is reason to doubt. For this is no more than what every man, who loves his own power, profit, or greatness, may, and naturally must do, keep those animals from hurting or destroying one another who labour and drudge only for his pleasure and advantage; and so are taken care of, not out of any love the master has for them, but love of himself, and the profit they bring him. For if it be asked what security, what fence is there in such a state against the violence and oppression of this absolute ruler, the very question can scarce be borne. They are ready to tell

you that it deserves death only to ask after safety. Betwixt subject and subject, they will grant, there must be measures, laws, and judges for their mutual peace and security. But as for the ruler, he ought to be absolute, and is above all such circumstances; because he has a power to do more hurt and wrong, it is right when he does it. To ask how you may be guarded from or injury on that side, where the strongest hand is to do it, is presently the voice of faction and rebellion. As if when men, quitting the state of Nature, entered into society, they agreed that all of them but one should be under the restraint of laws; but that he should still retain all the liberty of the state of Nature, increased with power, and made licentious by impunity. This is to think that men are so foolish that they take care to avoid what mischiefs may be done them by polecats or foxes, but are content, nay, think it safety, to be devoured by lions.

94. But, whatever flatterers may talk to amuse people's understandings, it never hinders men from feeling; and when they perceive that any man, in what station soever, is out of the bounds of the civil society they are of, and that they have no appeal, on earth, against any harm they may receive from him, they are apt to think themselves in the state of Nature, in respect of him whom they find to be so; and to take care, as soon as they can, to have that safety and security, in civil society, for which it was first instituted, and for which only they entered into it. And therefore, though perhaps at first, as shall be showed more at large hereafter, in the following part of this discourse, some one good and excellent man having got a pre-eminency amongst the rest, had this deference paid to his goodness and virtue, as to a kind of natural authority, that the chief rule, with arbitration of their differences, by a tacit consent devolved into his hands, without any other caution but the assurance they had of his uprightness and wisdom; yet when time giving authority, and, as some men would persuade us, sacredness to customs, which the negligent and unforeseeing innocence of the first ages began, had brought in successors of another stamp, the people finding their properties not secure under the government as then it was4 (whereas government has no other end but the preservation of property), could never be safe, nor at rest, nor think themselves in civil society, till the legislative was so placed in collective bodies of men, call them senate, parliament, or what you please, by which means every single person became subject equally with other the meanest men, to those laws, which he himself, as part of the legislative, had established; nor could any one, by his own authority, avoid the force of the law, when once made, nor by any pretence of superiority plead exemption, thereby to license his own, or the miscarriages of any of his dependants. No man in civil society can be exempted from the laws of it. For if any man may do what he thinks fit and there be no appeal on earth for redress or security against any harm he shall do, I ask whether he be not perfectly still in the state of Nature, and so can be no part or member of that civil society, unless any one will say the state of Nature and civil society are one and the same thing, which I have never yet found any one so great a patron of anarchy as to affirm.

**Chapter VIII, Of the Beginning of Political Societies**

95. Men being, as has been said, by nature all free, equal, and independent, no one can be put out of this estate and subjected to the political power of another without his own consent, which is done by agreeing with other men, to join and unite into a community for their comfortable, safe, and peaceable living, one amongst another, in a secure enjoyment of their properties, and a greater security against any that are not of it. This any number of men may do, because it injures not the freedom of the rest; they are left, as they were, in the liberty of the state of Nature. When any number of men have so consented to make one community or government, they are thereby presently incorporated, and make one body politic, wherein the majority have a right to act and conclude the rest.

96. For, when any number of men have, by the consent of every individual, made a community, they have thereby made that community one body, with a power to act as one body, which is only by the will and determination of the majority. For that which acts any community, being only the consent of the individuals of it, and it being one body, must move one way, it is necessary the body should move that way whither the greater force carries it, which is the consent of the majority, or else it is impossible it should act or continue one body, one community, which the consent of every individual that united into it agreed that it should; and so every one is bound by that consent to be concluded by the majority. And therefore we see that in assemblies empowered to act by positive laws where no number is set by that positive law which empowers them, the act of the majority passes for the act of the whole, and of course determines as having, by the law of Nature and reason, the power of the whole.

97. And thus every man, by consenting with others to make one body politic under one government, puts himself under an obligation to every one of that society to submit to the determination of the majority, and to be

concluded by it; or else this original compact, whereby he with others incorporates into one society, would signify nothing, and be no compact if he be left free and under no other ties than he was in before in the state of Nature. For what appearance would there be of any compact? What new engagement if he were no farther tied by any decrees of the society than he himself thought fit and did actually consent to? This would be still as great a liberty as he himself had before his compact, or any one else in the state of Nature, who may submit himself and consent to any acts of it if he thinks fit.

98. For if the consent of the majority shall not in reason be received as the act of the whole, and conclude every individual, nothing but the consent of every individual can make anything to be the act of the whole, which, considering the infirmities of health and avocations of business, which in a number though much less than that of a commonwealth, will necessarily keep many away from the public assembly; and the variety of opinions and contrariety of interests which unavoidably happen in all collections of men, it is next impossible ever to be had. And, therefore, if coming into society be upon such terms, it will be only like Cato's coming into the theatre, tantum ut exiret. Such a constitution as this would make the mighty leviathan of a shorter duration than the feeblest creatures, and not let it outlast the day it was born in, which cannot be supposed till we can think that rational creatures should desire and constitute societies only to be dissolved. For where the majority cannot conclude the rest, there they cannot act as one body, and consequently will be immediately dissolved again.

99. Whosoever, therefore, out of a state of Nature unite into a community, must be understood to give up all the power necessary to the ends for which they unite into society to the majority of the community, unless they expressly agreed in any number greater than the majority. And this is done by barely agreeing to unite into one political society, which is all the compact that is, or needs be, between the individuals that enter into or make up a commonwealth. And thus, that which begins and actually constitutes any political society is nothing but the consent of any number of freemen capable of majority, to unite and incorporate into such a society. And this is that, and that only, which did or could give beginning to any lawful government in the world.

100. To this I find two objections made: 1. That there are no instances to be found in story of a company of men, independent and equal one amongst another, that met together, and in this way began and set up a government. 2. It is impossible of right that men should do so, because all men, being born under government, they are to submit to that, and are not at liberty to begin a new one.

101. To the first there is this to answer: That it is not at all to be wondered that history gives us but a very little account of men that lived together in the state of Nature. The inconveniencies of that condition, and the love and want of society, no sooner brought any number of them together, but they presently united and incorporated if they designed to continue together. And if we may not suppose men ever to have been in the state of Nature, because we hear not much of them in such a state, we may as well suppose the armies of Salmanasser or Xerxes were never children, because we hear little of them till they were men and embodied in armies. Government is everywhere antecedent to records, and letters seldom come in amongst a people till a long continuation of civil society has, by other more necessary arts, provided for their safety, ease, and plenty. And then they begin to look after the history of their founders, and search into their original when they have outlived the memory of it. For it is with commonwealths as with particular persons, they are commonly ignorant of their own births and infancies; and if they know anything of it, they are beholding for it to the accidental records that others have kept of it. And those that we have of the beginning of any polities in the world, excepting that of the Jews, where God Himself immediately interposed, and which favours not at all paternal dominion, are all either plain instances of such a beginning as I have mentioned, or at least have manifest footsteps of it.

102. He must show a strange inclination to deny evident matter of fact, when it agrees not with his hypothesis, who will not allow that the beginning of Rome and Venice were by the uniting together of several men, free and independent one of another, amongst whom there was no natural superiority or subjection. And if Josephus Acosta's word may be taken, he tells us that in many parts of America there was no government at all. "There are great and apparent conjectures," says he, "that these men [speaking of those of Peru] for a long time had neither kings nor commonwealths, but lived in troops, as they do this day in Florida— the Cheriquanas, those of Brazil, and many other nations, which have no certain kings, but, as occasion is offered in peace or war, they choose their captains as they please" (lib. i. cap. 25). If it be said, that every man there was born subject to his father, or the head of his family. that the subjection due from a child to a father took away not his freedom of uniting into what political society he thought fit, has been already proved; but be that as it will, these men, it is evident, were actually free; and whatever superiority some politicians now would place in any

of them, they themselves claimed it not; but, by consent, were all equal, till, by the same consent, they set rulers over themselves. So that their politic societies all began from a voluntary union, and the mutual agreement of men freely acting in the choice of their governors and forms of government.

103. And I hope those who went away from Sparta, with Palantus, mentioned by Justin, will be allowed to have been freemen independent one of another, and to have set up a government over themselves by their own consent. Thus I have given several examples out of history of people, free and in the state of Nature, that, being met together, incorporated and began a commonwealth. And if the want of such instances be an argument to prove that government were not nor could not be so begun, I suppose the contenders for paternal empire were better let it alone than urge it against natural liberty; for if they can give so many instances out of history of governments begun upon paternal right, I think (though at least an argument from what has been to what should of right be of no great force) one might, without any great danger, yield them the cause. But if I might advise them in the case, they would do well not to search too much into the original of governments as they have begun de facto, lest they should find at the foundation of most of them something very little favourable to the design they promote, and such a power as they contend for.

104. But, to conclude: reason being plain on our side that men are naturally free; and the examples of history showing that the governments of the world, that were begun in peace, had their beginning laid on that foundation, and were made by the consent of the people; there can be little room for doubt, either where the right is, or what has been the opinion or practice of mankind about the first erecting of governments.

105. I will not deny that if we look back, as far as history will direct us, towards the original of commonwealths, we shall generally find them under the government and administration of one man. And I am also apt to believe that where a family was numerous enough to subsist by itself, and continued entire together, without mixing with others, as it often happens, where there is much land and few people, the government commonly began in the father. For the father having, by the law of Nature, the same power, with every man else, to punish, as he thought fit, any offences against that law, might thereby punish his transgressing children, even when they were men, and out of their pupilage; and they were very likely to submit to his punishment, and all join with him against the offender in their turns, giving him thereby power to execute his sentence against any transgression, and so, in effect, make him the law-maker and governor over all that remained in conjunction with his family. He was fittest to be trusted; paternal affection secured their property and interest under his care, and the custom of obeying him in their childhood made it easier to submit to him rather than any other. If, therefore, they must have one to rule them, as government is hardly to be avoided amongst men that live together, who so likely to be the man as he that was their common father, unless negligence, cruelty, or any other defect of mind or body, made him unfit for it? But when either the father died. and left his next heir—for want of age, wisdom, courage, or any other qualities—less fit for rule, or where several families met and consented to continue together, there, it is not to be doubted, but they used their natural freedom to set up him whom they judged the ablest and most likely to rule well over them. Conformable hereunto we find the people of America, who—living out of the reach of the conquering swords and spreading domination of the two great empires of Peru and Mexico— enjoyed their own natural freedom, though, caeteris paribus, they commonly prefer the heir of their deceased king; yet, if they find him any way weak or incapable, they pass him by, and set up the stoutest and bravest man for their ruler.

106. Thus, though looking back as far as records give us any account of peopling the world, and the history of nations, we commonly find the government to be in one hand, yet it destroys not that which I affirm—viz., that the beginning of politic society depends upon the consent of the individuals to join into and make one society, who, when they are thus incorporated, might set up what form of government they thought fit. But this having given occasion to men to mistake and think that, by Nature, government was monarchical, and belonged to the father, it may not be amiss here to consider why people, in the beginning, generally pitched upon this form, which, though perhaps the father's pre-eminency might, in the first institution of some commonwealths, give a rise to and place in the beginning the power in one hand, yet it is plain that the reason that continued the form of government in a single person was not any regard or respect to paternal authority, since all petty monarchies- that is, almost all monarchies, near their original, have been commonly, at least upon occasion, elective.

107. First, then, in the beginning of things, the father's government of the childhood of those sprung from him having accustomed them to the rule of one man, and taught them that where it was exercised with care and skill, with affection and love to those under it, it was sufficient to procure and preserve men (all the political happiness they sought for in society), it was no wonder that they should pitch upon and naturally run into that form of government which, from their infancy, they had been all accustomed to, and which, by experience,

they had found both easy and safe. To which if we add, that monarchy being simple and most obvious to men, whom neither experience had instructed in forms of government, nor the ambition or insolence of empire had taught to beware of the encroachments of prerogative or the inconveniencies of absolute power, which monarchy, in succession, was apt to lay claim to and bring upon them; it was not at all strange that they should not much trouble themselves to think of methods of restraining any exorbitances of those to whom they had given the authority over them, and of balancing the power of government by placing several parts of it in different hands. They had neither felt the oppression of tyrannical dominion, nor did the fashion of the age, nor their possessions or way of living, which afforded little matter for covetousness or ambition, give them any reason to apprehend or provide against it; and, therefore, it is no wonder they put themselves into such a frame of government as was not only, as I said, most obvious and simple, but also best suited to their present state and condition, which stood more in need of defence against foreign invasions and injuries than of multiplicity of laws where there was but very little property, and wanted not variety of rulers and abundance of officers to direct and look after their execution where there were but few trespassers and few offenders. Since, then, those who liked one another so well as to join into society cannot but be supposed to have some acquaintance and friendship together, and some trust one in another, they could not but have greater apprehensions of others than of one another; and, therefore, their first care and thought cannot but be supposed to be, how to secure themselves against foreign force. It was natural for them to put themselves under a frame of government which might best serve to that end, and choose the wisest and bravest man to conduct them in their wars and lead them out against their enemies, and in this chiefly be their ruler.

108. Thus we see that the kings of the Indians, in America, which is still a pattern of the first ages in Asia and Europe, whilst the inhabitants were too few for the country, and want of people and money gave men no temptation to enlarge their possessions of land or contest for wider extent of ground, are little more than generals of their armies; and though they command absolutely in war, yet at home, and in time of peace, they exercise very little dominion, and have but a very moderate sovereignty, the resolutions of peace and war being ordinarily either in the people or in a council, though the war itself, which admits not of pluralities of governors, naturally evolves the command into the king's sole authority.

109. And thus, in Israel itself, the chief business of their judges and first kings seems to have been to be captains in war and leaders of their armies, which (besides what is signified by "going out and in before the people," which was, to march forth to war and home again at the heads of their forces) appears plainly in the story of Jephtha. The Ammonites making war upon Israel, the Gileadites, in fear, send to Jephtha, a bastard of their family, whom they had cast off, and article with him, if he will assist them against the Ammonites, to make him their ruler, which they do in these words: "And the people made him head and captain over them" (Judges 11. 11), which was, as it seems, all one as to be judge. "And he judged Israel" (Judges 12. 7)—that is, was their captain-general- "six years." So when Jotham upbraids the Shechemites with the obligation they had to Gideon, who had been their judge and ruler, he tells them: "He fought for you, and adventured his life for, and delivered you out of the hands of Midian" (Judges 9. 17). Nothing mentioned of him but what he did as a general, and, indeed, that is all is found in his history, or in any of the rest of the judges. And Abimelech particularly is called king, though at most he was but their general. And when, being weary of the ill-conduct of Samuel's sons, the children of Israel desired a king, "like all the nations, to judge them, and to go out before them, and to fight their battles" (1 Sam. 8. 20), God, granting their desire, says to Samuel, "I will send thee a man, and thou shalt anoint him to be captain over my people Israel, that he may save my people out of the hands of the Philistines" (ch. 9. 16). As if the only business of a king had been to lead out their armies and fight in their defence; and, accordingly, at his inauguration, pouring a vial of oil upon him, declares to Saul that "the Lord had anointed him to be captain over his inheritance" (ch. 10. 1). And therefore those who, after Saul being solemnly chosen and saluted king by the tribes at Mispah, were unwilling to have him their king, make no other objection but this, "How shall this man save us?" (ch. 10. 27), as if they should have said: "This man is unfit to be our king, not having skill and conduct enough in war to be able to defend us." And when God resolved to transfer the government to David, it is in these words: "But now thy kingdom shall not continue: the Lord hath sought Him a man after His own heart, and the Lord hath commanded him to be captain over His people" (ch. 13. 14.). As if the whole kingly authority were nothing else but to be their general; and therefore the tribes who had stuck to Saul's family, and opposed David's reign, when they came to Hebron with terms of submission to him, they tell him, amongst other arguments, they had to submit to him as to their king, that he was, in effect, their king in Saul's time, and therefore they had no reason but to receive him as their king now. "Also," say they, "in time past, when Saul was king over us, thou wast he that leddest out and broughtest in Israel, and the Lord said unto thee, Thou shalt feed my people Israel, and thou shalt be a captain over Israel."

110. Thus, whether a family, by degrees, grew up into a commonwealth, and the fatherly authority being continued on to the elder son, every one in his turn growing up under it tacitly submitted to it, and the easiness

and equality of it not offending any one, every one acquiesced till time seemed to have confirmed it and settled a right of succession by prescription; or whether several families, or the descendants of several families, whom chance, neighbourhood, or business brought together, united into society; the need of a general whose conduct might defend them against their enemies in war, and the great confidence the innocence and sincerity of that poor but virtuous age, such as are almost all those which begin governments that ever come to last in the world, gave men one of another, made the first beginners of commonwealths generally put the rule into one man's hand, without any other express limitation or restraint but what the nature of the thing and the end of government required. It was given them for the public good and safety, and to those ends, in the infancies of commonwealths, they commonly used it; and unless they had done so, young societies could not have subsisted. Without such nursing fathers, without this care of the governors, all governments would have sunk under the weakness and infirmities of their infancy, the prince and the people had soon perished together.

111. But the golden age (though before vain ambition, and amor sceleratus habendi, evil concupiscence had corrupted men's minds into a mistake of true power and honour) had more virtue, and consequently better governors, as well as less vicious subjects; and there was then no stretching prerogative on the one side to oppress the people, nor, consequently, on the other, any dispute about privilege, to lessen or restrain the power of the magistrate; and so no contest betwixt rulers and people about governors or government.6 Yet, when ambition and luxury, in future ages, would retain and increase the power, without doing the business for which it was given, and aided by flattery, taught princes to have distinct and separate interests from their people, men found it necessary to examine more carefully the original and rights of government, and to find out ways to restrain the exorbitances and prevent the abuses of that power, which they having entrusted in another's hands, only for their own good, they found was made use of to hurt them.

112. Thus we may see how probable it is that people that were naturally free, and, by their own consent, either submitted to the government of their father, or united together, out of different families, to make a government, should generally put the rule into one man's hands, and choose to be under the conduct of a single person, without so much, as by express conditions, limiting or regulating his power, which they thought safe enough in his honesty and prudence; though they never dreamed of monarchy being jure Divino, which we never heard of among mankind till it was revealed to us by the divinity of this last age, nor ever allowed paternal power to have a right to dominion or to be the foundation of all government. And thus much may suffice to show that, as far as we have any light from history, we have reason to conclude that all peaceful beginnings of government have been laid in the consent of the people. I say "peaceful," because I shall have occasion, in another place, to speak of conquest, which some esteem a way of beginning of governments. The other objection, I find, urged against the beginning of polities, in the way I have mentioned, is this, viz.:

113. "That all men being born under government, some or other, it is impossible any of them should ever be free and at liberty to unite together and begin a new one, or ever be able to erect a lawful government." If this argument be good, I ask, How came so many lawful monarchies into the world? For if anybody, upon this supposition, can show me any one man, in any age of the world, free to begin a lawful monarchy, I will be bound to show him ten other free men at liberty, at the same time, to unite and begin a new government under a regal or any other form. It being demonstration that if any one born under the dominion of another may be so free as to have a right to command others in a new and distinct empire, every one that is born under the dominion of another may be so free too, and may become a ruler or subject of a distinct separate government. And so, by this their own principle, either all men, however born, are free, or else there is but one lawful prince, one lawful government in the world; and then they have nothing to do but barely to show us which that is, which, when they have done, I doubt not but all mankind will easily agree to pay obedience to him.

114. Though it be a sufficient answer to their objection to show that it involves them in the same difficulties that it doth those they use it against, yet I shall endeavour to discover the weakness of this argument a little farther. "All men," say they, "are born under government, and therefore they cannot be at liberty to begin a new one. Every one is born a subject to his father or his prince, and is therefore under the perpetual tie of subjection and allegiance." It is plain mankind never owned nor considered any such natural subjection that they were born in, to one or to the other, that tied them, without their own consents, to a subjection to them and their heirs.

115. For there are no examples so frequent in history, both sacred and profane, as those of men withdrawing themselves and their obedience from the jurisdiction they were born under, and the family or community they were bred up in, and setting up new governments in other places, from whence sprang all that number of petty commonwealths in the beginning of ages, and which always multiplied as long as there was room enough, till the stronger or more fortunate swallowed the weaker; and those great ones, again breaking to pieces, dis-

solved into lesser dominions; all which are so many testimonies against paternal sovereignty, and plainly prove that it was not the natural right of the father descending to his heirs that made governments in the beginning; since it was impossible, upon that ground, there should have been so many little kingdoms but only one universal monarchy if men had not been at liberty to separate themselves from their families and their government, be it what it will that was set up in it, and go and make distinct commonwealths and other governments as they thought fit.

116. This has been the practice of the world from its first beginning to this day; nor is it now any more hindrance to the freedom of mankind, that they are born under constituted and ancient polities that have established laws and set forms of government, than if they were born in the woods amongst the unconfined inhabitants that run loose in them. For those who would persuade us that by being born under any government we are naturally subjects to it, and have no more any title or pretence to the freedom of the state of Nature, have no other reason (bating that of paternal power, which we have already answered) to produce for it, but only because our fathers or progenitors passed away their natural liberty, and thereby bound up themselves and their posterity to a perpetual subjection to the government which they themselves submitted to. It is true that whatever engagements or promises any one made for himself, he is under the obligation of them, but cannot by any compact whatsoever bind his children or posterity. For his son, when a man, being altogether as free as the father, any act of the father can no more give away the liberty of the son than it can of anybody else. He may, indeed, annex such conditions to the land he enjoyed, as a subject of any commonwealth, as may oblige his son to be of that community, if he will enjoy those possessions which were his father's, because that estate being his father's property, he may dispose or settle it as he pleases.

117. And this has generally given the occasion to the mistake in this matter; because commonwealths not permitting any part of their dominions to be dismembered, nor to be enjoyed by any but those of their community, the son cannot ordinarily enjoy the possessions of his father but under the same terms his father did, by becoming a member of the society, whereby he puts himself presently under the government he finds there established, as much as any other subject of that commonweal. And thus the consent of free men, born under government, which only makes them members of it, being given separately in their turns, as each comes to be of age, and not in a multitude together, people take no notice of it, and thinking it not done at all, or not necessary, conclude they are naturally subjects as they are men.

118. But it is plain governments themselves understand it otherwise; they claim no power over the son because of that they had over the father; nor look on children as being their subjects, by their fathers being so. If a subject of England have a child by an Englishwoman in France, whose subject is he? Not the King of England's; for he must have leave to be admitted to the privileges of it. Nor the King of France's, for how then has his father a liberty to bring him away, and breed him as he pleases; and whoever was judged as a traitor or deserter, if he left, or warred against a country, for being barely born in it of parents that were aliens there? It is plain, then, by the practice of governments themselves, as well as by the law of right reason, that a child is born a subject of no country nor government. He is under his father's tuition and authority till he come to age of discretion, and then he is a free man, at liberty what government he will put himself under, what body politic he will unite himself to. For if an Englishman's son born in France be at liberty, and may do so, it is evident there is no tie upon him by his father being a subject of that kingdom, nor is he bound up by any compact of his ancestors; and why then hath not his son, by the same reason, the same liberty, though he be born anywhere else? Since the power that a father hath naturally over his children is the same wherever they be born, and the ties of natural obligations are not bounded by the positive limits of kingdoms and commonwealths.

119. Every man being, as has been showed, naturally free, and nothing being able to put him into subjection to any earthly power, but only his own consent, it is to be considered what shall be understood to be a sufficient declaration of a man's consent to make him subject to the laws of any government. There is a common distinction of an express and a tacit consent, which will concern our present case. Nobody doubts but an express consent of any man, entering into any society, makes him a perfect member of that society, a subject of that government. The difficulty is, what ought to be looked upon as a tacit consent, and how far it binds—i.e., how far any one shall be looked on to have consented, and thereby submitted to any government, where he has made no expressions of it at all. And to this I say, that every man that hath any possession or enjoyment of any part of the dominions of any government doth hereby give his tacit consent, and is as far forth obliged to obedience to the laws of that government, during such enjoyment, as any one under it, whether this his possession be of land to him and his heirs for ever, or a lodging only for a week; or whether it be barely travelling freely on the highway; and, in effect, it reaches as far as the very being of any one within the territories of that government.

120. To understand this the better, it is fit to consider that every man when he at first incorporates himself into any commonwealth, he, by his uniting himself thereunto, annexes also, and submits to the community those possessions which he has, or shall acquire, that do not already belong to any other government. For it would be a direct contradiction for any one to enter into society with others for the securing and regulating of property, and yet to suppose his land, whose property is to be regulated by the laws of the society, should be exempt from the jurisdiction of that government to which he himself, and the property of the land, is a subject. By the same act, therefore, whereby any one unites his person, which was before free, to any commonwealth, by the same he unites his possessions, which were before free, to it also; and they become, both of them, person and possession, subject to the government and dominion of that commonwealth as long as it hath a being. Whoever therefore, from thenceforth, by inheritance, purchases permission, or otherwise enjoys any part of the land so annexed to, and under the government of that commonweal, must take it with the condition it is under—that is, of submitting to the government of the commonwealth, under whose jurisdiction it is, as far forth as any subject of it.

121. But since the government has a direct jurisdiction only over the land and reaches the possessor of it (before he has actually incorporated himself in the society) only as he dwells upon and enjoys that, the obligation any one is under by virtue of such enjoyment to submit to the government begins and ends with the enjoyment; so that whenever the owner, who has given nothing but such a tacit consent to the government will, by donation, sale or otherwise, quit the said possession, he is at liberty to go and incorporate himself into any other commonwealth, or agree with others to begin a new one in vacuis locis, in any part of the world they can find free and unpossessed; whereas he that has once, by actual agreement and any express declaration, given his consent to be of any commonweal, is perpetually and indispensably obliged to be, and remain unalterably a subject to it, and can never be again in the liberty of the state of Nature, unless by any calamity the government he was under comes to be dissolved.

122. But submitting to the laws of any country, living quietly and enjoying privileges and protection under them, makes not a man a member of that society; it is only a local protection and homage due to and from all those who, not being in a state of war, come within the territories belonging to any government, to all parts whereof the force of its law extends. But this no more makes a man a member of that society, a perpetual subject of that commonwealth, than it would make a man a subject to another in whose family he found it convenient to abide for some time, though, whilst he continued in it, he were obliged to comply with the laws and submit to the government he found there. And thus we see that foreigners, by living all their lives under another government, and enjoying the privileges and protection of it, though they are bound, even in conscience, to submit to its administration as far forth as any denizen, yet do not thereby come to be subjects or members of that commonwealth. Nothing can make any man so but his actually entering into it by positive engagement and express promise and compact. This is that which, I think, concerning the beginning of political societies, and that consent which makes any one a member of any commonwealth.

**Chapter IX, Of the Ends of Political Society and Government**

123. If man in the state of Nature be so free as has been said, if he be absolute lord of his own person and possessions, equal to the greatest and subject to nobody, why will he part with his freedom, this empire, and subject himself to the dominion and control of any other power? To which it is obvious to answer, that though in the state of Nature he hath such a right, yet the enjoyment of it is very uncertain and constantly exposed to the invasion of others; for all being kings as much as he, every man his equal, and the greater part no strict observers of equity and justice, the enjoyment of the property he has in this state is very unsafe, very insecure. This makes him willing to quit this condition which, however free, is full of fears and continual dangers; and it is not without reason that he seeks out and is willing to join in society with others who are already united, or have a mind to unite for the mutual preservation of their lives, liberties and estates, which I call by the general name—property.

124. The great and chief end, therefore, of men uniting into commonwealths, and putting themselves under government, is the preservation of their property; to which in the state of Nature there are many things wanting. Firstly, there wants an established, settled, known law, received and allowed by common consent to be the standard of right and wrong, and the common measure to decide all controversies between them. For though the law of Nature be plain and intelligible to all rational creatures, yet men, being biased by their interest, as well as ignorant for want of study of it, are not apt to allow of it as a law binding to them in the application of it to their particular cases.

125. Secondly, in the state of Nature there wants a known and indifferent judge, with authority to determine all differences according to the established law. For every one in that state being both judge and executioner of the law of Nature, men being partial to themselves, passion and revenge is very apt to carry them too far, and with too much heat in their own cases, as well as negligence and unconcernedness, make them too remiss in other men's.

126. Thirdly, in the state of Nature there often wants power to back and support the sentence when right, and to give it due execution. They who by any injustice offended will seldom fail where they are able by force to make good their injustice. Such resistance many times makes the punishment dangerous, and frequently destructive to those who attempt it.

127. Thus mankind, notwithstanding all the privileges of the state of Nature, being but in an ill condition while they remain in it are quickly driven into society. Hence it comes to pass, that we seldom find any number of men live any time together in this state. The inconveniencies that they are therein exposed to by the irregular and uncertain exercise of the power every man has of punishing the transgressions of others, make them take sanctuary under the established laws of government, and therein seek the preservation of their property. It is this that makes them so willingly give up every one his single power of punishing to be exercised by such alone as shall be appointed to it amongst them, and by such rules as the community, or those authorised by them to that purpose, shall agree on. And in this we have the original right and rise of both the legislative and executive power as well as of the governments and societies themselves.

128. For in the state of Nature to omit the liberty he has of innocent delights, a man has two powers. The first is to do whatsoever he thinks fit for the preservation of himself and others within the permission of the law of Nature; by which law, common to them all, he and all the rest of mankind are one community, make up one society distinct from all other creatures, and were it not for the corruption and viciousness of degenerate men, there would be no need of any other, no necessity that men should separate from this great and natural community, and associate into lesser combinations. The other power a man has in the state of Nature is the power to punish the crimes committed against that law. Both these he gives up when he joins in a private, if I may so call it, or particular political society, and incorporates into any commonwealth separate from the rest of mankind.

129. The first power—viz., of doing whatsoever he thought fit for the preservation of himself and the rest of mankind, he gives up to be regulated by laws made by the society, so far forth as the preservation of himself and the rest of that society shall require; which laws of the society in many things confine the liberty he had by the law of Nature.

130. Secondly, the power of punishing he wholly gives up, and engages his natural force, which he might before employ in the execution of the law of Nature, by his own single authority, as he thought fit, to assist the executive power of the society as the law thereof shall require. For being now in a new state, wherein he is to enjoy many conveniencies from the labour, assistance, and society of others in the same community, as well as protection from its whole strength, he is to part also with as much of his natural liberty, in providing for himself, as the good, prosperity, and safety of the society shall require, which is not only necessary but just, since the other members of the society do the like.

131. But though men when they enter into society give up the equality, liberty, and executive power they had in the state of Nature into the hands of the society, to be so far disposed of by the legislative as the good of the society shall require, yet it being only with an intention in every one the better to preserve himself, his liberty and property (for no rational creature can be supposed to change his condition with an intention to be worse), the power of the society or legislative constituted by them can never be supposed to extend farther than the common good, but is obliged to secure every one's property by providing against those three defects above mentioned that made the state of Nature so unsafe and uneasy. And so, whoever has the legislative or supreme power of any commonwealth, is bound to govern by established standing laws, promulgated and known to the people, and not by extemporary decrees, by indifferent and upright judges, who are to decide controversies by those laws; and to employ the force of the community at home only in the execution of such laws, or abroad to prevent or redress foreign injuries and secure the community from inroads and invasion. And all this to be directed to no other end but the peace, safety, and public good of the people.

## Chapter X, Of the Forms of a Commonwealth

132. The majority having, as has been showed, upon men's first uniting into society, the whole power of the community naturally in them, may employ all that power in making laws for the community from time to time, and executing those laws by officers of their own appointing, and then the form of the government is a perfect democracy; or else may put the power of making laws into the hands of a few select men, and their heirs or successors, and then it is an oligarchy; or else into the hands of one man, and then it is a monarchy; if to him and his heirs, it is a hereditary monarchy; if to him only for life, but upon his death the power only of nominating a successor, to return to them, an elective monarchy. And so accordingly of these make compounded and mixed forms of government, as they think good. And if the legislative power be at first given by the majority to one or more persons only for their lives, or any limited time, and then the supreme power to revert to them again, when it is so reverted the community may dispose of it again anew into what hands they please, and so constitute a new form of government; for the form of government depending upon the placing the supreme power, which is the legislative, it being impossible to conceive that an inferior power should prescribe to a superior, or any but the supreme make laws, according as the power of making laws is placed, such is the form of the commonwealth.

133. By "commonwealth" I must be understood all along to mean not a democracy, or any form of government, but any independent community which the Latins signified by the word civitas, to which the word which best answers in our language is "commonwealth," and most properly expresses such a society of men which "community" does not (for there may be subordinate communities in a government), and "city" much less. And therefore, to avoid ambiguity, I crave leave to use the word "commonwealth" in that sense, in which sense I find the word used by King James himself, which I think to be its genuine signification, which, if anybody dislike, I consent with him to change it for a better.

## Chapter XI, Of the Extent of the Legislative Power

134. The great end of men's entering into society being the enjoyment of their properties in peace and safety, and the great instrument and means of that being the laws established in that society, the first and fundamental positive law of all commonwealths is the establishing of the legislative power, as the first and fundamental natural law which is to govern even the legislative. Itself is the preservation of the society and (as far as will consist with the public good) of every person in it. This legislative is not only the supreme power of the commonwealth, but sacred and unalterable in the hands where the community have once placed it. Nor can any edict of anybody else, in what form soever conceived, or by what power soever backed, have the force and obligation of a law which has not its sanction from that legislative which the public has chosen and appointed; for without this the law could not have that which is absolutely necessary to its being a law, the consent of the society, over whom nobody can have a power to make laws7 but by their own consent and by authority received from them; and therefore all the obedience, which by the most solemn ties any one can be obliged to pay, ultimately terminates in this supreme power, and is directed by those laws which it enacts. Nor can any oaths to any foreign power whatsoever, or any domestic subordinate power, discharge any member of the society from his obedience to the legislative, acting pursuant to their trust, nor oblige him to any obedience contrary to the laws so enacted or farther than they do allow, it being ridiculous to imagine one can be tied ultimately to obey any power in the society which is not the supreme.

135. Though the legislative, whether placed in one or more, whether it be always in being or only by intervals, though it be the supreme power in every commonwealth, yet, first, it is not, nor can possibly be, absolutely arbitrary over the lives and fortunes of the people. For it being but the joint power of every member of the society given up to that person or assembly which is legislator, it can be no more than those persons had in a state of Nature before they entered into society, and gave it up to the community. For nobody can transfer to another more power than he has in himself, and nobody has an absolute arbitrary power over himself, or over any other, to destroy his own life, or take away the life or property of another. A man, as has been proved, cannot subject himself to the arbitrary power of another; and having, in the state of Nature, no arbitrary power over the life, liberty, or possession of another, but only so much as the law of Nature gave him for the preservation of himself and the rest of mankind, this is all he doth, or can give up to the commonwealth, and by it to the legislative power, so that the legislative can have no more than this. Their power in the utmost bounds of it is limited to the public good of the society.8 It is a power that hath no other end but preservation, and therefore can never have a right to destroy, enslave, or designedly to impoverish the subjects; the obligations of the law

of Nature cease not in society, but only in many cases are drawn closer, and have, by human laws, known penalties annexed to them to enforce their observation. Thus the law of Nature stands as an eternal rule to all men, legislators as well as others. The rules that they make for, other men's actions must, as well as their own and other men's actions, be conformable to the law of Nature— i.e., to the will of God, of which that is a declaration, and the fundamental law of Nature being the preservation of mankind, no human sanction can be good or valid against it.

136. Secondly, the legislative or supreme authority cannot assume to itself a power to rule by extemporary arbitrary decrees, but is bound to dispense justice and decide the rights of the subject by promulgated standing laws,9 and known authorised judges. For the law of Nature being unwritten, and so nowhere to be found but in the minds of men, they who, through passion or interest, shall miscite or misapply it, cannot so easily be convinced of their mistake where there is no established judge; and so it serves not as it aught, to determine the rights and fence the properties of those that live under it, especially where every one is judge, interpreter, and executioner of it too, and that in his own case; and he that has right on his side, having ordinarily but his own single strength, hath not force enough to defend himself from injuries or punish delinquents. To avoid these inconveniencies which disorder men's properties in the state of Nature, men unite into societies that they may have the united strength of the whole society to secure and defend their properties, and may have standing rules to bound it by which every one may know what is his. To this end it is that men give up all their natural power to the society they enter into, and the community put the legislative power into such hands as they think fit, with this trust, that they shall be governed by declared laws, or else their peace, quiet, and property will still be at the same uncertainty as it was in the state of Nature.

137. Absolute arbitrary power, or governing without settled standing laws, can neither of them consist with the ends of society and government, which men would not quit the freedom of the state of Nature for, and tie themselves up under, were it not to preserve their lives, liberties, and fortunes, and by stated rules of right and property to secure their peace and quiet. It cannot be supposed that they should intend, had they a power so to do, to give any one or more an absolute arbitrary power over their persons and estates, and put a force into the magistrate's hand to execute his unlimited will arbitrarily upon them; this were to put themselves into a worse condition than the state of Nature, wherein they had a liberty to defend their right against the injuries of others, and were upon equal terms of force to maintain it, whether invaded by a single man or many in combination. Whereas by supposing they have given up themselves to the absolute arbitrary power and will of a legislator, they have disarmed themselves, and armed him to make a prey of them when he pleases; he being in a much worse condition that is exposed to the arbitrary power of one man who has the command of a hundred thousand than he that is exposed to the arbitrary power of a hundred thousand single men, nobody being secure, that his will who has such a command is better than that of other men, though his force be a hundred thousand times stronger. And, therefore, whatever form the commonwealth is under, the ruling power ought to govern by declared and received laws, and not by extemporary dictates and undetermined resolutions, for then mankind will be in a far worse condition than in the state of Nature if they shall have armed one or a few men with the joint power of a multitude, to force them to obey at pleasure the exorbitant and unlimited decrees of their sudden thoughts, or unrestrained, and till that moment, unknown wills, without having any measures set down which may guide and justify their actions. For all the power the government has, being only for the good of the society, as it ought not to be arbitrary and at pleasure, so it ought to be exercised by established and promulgated laws, that both the people may know their duty, and be safe and secure within the limits of the law, and the rulers, too, kept within their due bounds, and not be tempted by the power they have in their hands to employ it to purposes, and by such measures as they would not have known, and own not willingly.

138. Thirdly, the supreme power cannot take from any man any part of his property without his own consent. For the preservation of property being the end of government, and that for which men enter into society, it necessarily supposes and requires that the people should have property, without which they must be supposed to lose that by entering into society which was the end for which they entered into it; too gross an absurdity for any man to own. Men, therefore, in society having property, they have such a right to the goods, which by the law of the community are theirs, that nobody hath a right to take them, or any part of them, from them without their own consent; without this they have no property at all. For I have truly no property in that which another can by right take from me when he pleases against my consent. Hence it is a mistake to think that the supreme or legislative power of any commonwealth can do what it will, and dispose of the estates of the subject arbitrarily, or take any part of them at pleasure. This is not much to be feared in governments where the legislative consists wholly or in part in assemblies which are variable, whose members upon the dissolution of the assembly are subjects under the common laws of their country, equally with the rest. But in governments where the legislative is in one lasting assembly, always in being, or in one man as in absolute monarchies, there is danger still, that they will think themselves to have a distinct interest from the rest of the community, and so will be apt to increase their own riches and power by taking what they think fit from the people. For a

man's property is not at all secure, though there be good and equitable laws to set the bounds of it between him and his fellow-subjects, if he who commands those subjects have power to take from any private man what part he pleases of his property, and use and dispose of it as he thinks good.

139. But government, into whosesoever hands it is put, being as I have before shown, entrusted with this condition, and for this end, that men might have and secure their properties, the prince or senate, however it may have power to make laws for the regulating of property between the subjects one amongst another, yet can never have a power to take to themselves the whole, or any part of the subjects' property, without their own consent; for this would be in effect to leave them no property at all. And to let us see that even absolute power, where it is necessary, is not arbitrary by being absolute, but is still limited by that reason and confined to those ends which required it in some cases to be absolute, we need look no farther than the common practice of martial discipline. For the preservation of the army, and in it of the whole commonwealth, requires an absolute obedience to the command of every superior officer, and it is justly death to disobey or dispute the most dangerous or unreasonable of them; but yet we see that neither the sergeant that could command a soldier to march up to the mouth of a cannon, or stand in a breach where he is almost sure to perish, can command that soldier to give him one penny of his money; nor the general that can condemn him to death for deserting his post, or not obeying the most desperate orders, cannot yet with all his absolute power of life and death dispose of one farthing of that soldier's estate, or seize one jot of his goods; whom yet he can command anything, and hang for the least disobedience. Because such a blind obedience is necessary to that end for which the commander has his power—viz., the preservation of the rest, but the disposing of his goods has nothing to do with it.

140. It is true governments cannot be supported without great charge, and it is fit every one who enjoys his share of the protection should pay out of his estate his proportion for the maintenance of it. But still it must be with his own consent—i.e., the consent of the majority, giving it either by themselves or their representatives chosen by them; for if any one shall claim a power to lay and levy taxes on the people by his own authority, and without such consent of the people, he thereby invades the fundamental law of property, and subverts the end of government. For what property have I in that which another may by right take when he pleases to himself?

141. Fourthly. The legislative cannot transfer the power of making laws to any other hands, for it being but a delegated power from the people, they who have it cannot pass it over to others. The people alone can appoint the form of the commonwealth, which is by constituting the legislative, and appointing in whose hands that shall be. And when the people have said, "We will submit, and be governed by laws made by such men, and in such forms," nobody else can say other men shall make laws for them; nor can they be bound by any laws but such as are enacted by those whom they have chosen and authorised to make laws for them.

142. These are the bounds which the trust that is put in them by the society and the law of God and Nature have set to the legislative power of every commonwealth, in all forms of government. First: They are to govern by promulgated established laws, not to be varied in particular cases, but to have one rule for rich and poor, for the favourite at Court, and the countryman at plough. Secondly: These laws also ought to be designed for no other end ultimately but the good of the people. Thirdly: They must not raise taxes on the property of the people without the consent of the people given by themselves or their deputies. And this properly concerns only such governments where the legislative is always in being, or at least where the people have not reserved any part of the legislative to deputies, to be from time to time chosen by themselves. Fourthly: Legislative neither must nor can transfer the power of making laws to anybody else, or place it anywhere but where the people have.

## Chapter XII, The Legislative, Executive, and Federative Power of the Commonwealth

143. The legislative power is that which has a right to direct how the force of the commonwealth shall be employed for preserving the community and the members of it. Because those laws which are constantly to be executed, and whose force is always to continue, may be made in a little time, therefore there is no need that the legislative should be always in being, not having always business to do. And because it may be too great temptation to human frailty, apt to grasp at power, for the same persons who have the power of making laws to have also in their hands the power to execute them, whereby they may exempt themselves from obedience to the laws they make, and suit the law, both in its making and execution, to their own private advantage, and thereby come to have a distinct interest from the rest of the community, contrary to the end of society and

government. Therefore in well-ordered commonwealths, where the good of the whole is so considered as it ought, the legislative power is put into the hands of divers persons who, duly assembled, have by themselves, or jointly with others, a power to make laws, which when they have done, being separated again, they are themselves subject to the laws they have made; which is a new and near tie upon them to take care that they make them for the public good.

144. But because the laws that are at once, and in a short time made, have a constant and lasting force, and need a perpetual execution, or an attendance thereunto, therefore it is necessary there should be a power always in being which should see to the execution of the laws that are made, and remain in force. And thus the legislative and executive power come often to be separated.

145. There is another power in every commonwealth which one may call natural, because it is that which answers to the power every man naturally had before he entered into society. For though in a commonwealth the members of it are distinct persons, still, in reference to one another, and, as such, are governed by the laws of the society, yet, in reference to the rest of mankind, they make one body, which is, as every member of it before was, still in the state of Nature with the rest of mankind, so that the controversies that happen between any man of the society with those that are out of it are managed by the public, and an injury done to a member of their body engages the whole in the reparation of it. So that under this consideration the whole community is one body in the state of Nature in respect of all other states or persons out of its community. 146. This, therefore, contains the power of war and peace, leagues and alliances, and all the transactions with all persons and communities without the commonwealth, and may be called federative if any one pleases. So the thing be understood, I am indifferent as to the name. 147. These two powers, executive and federative, though they be really distinct in themselves, yet one comprehending the execution of the municipal laws of the society within itself upon all that are parts of it, the other the management of the security and interest of the public without with all those that it may receive benefit or damage from, yet they are always almost united. And though this federative power in the well or ill management of it be of great moment to the commonwealth, yet it is much less capable to be directed by antecedent, standing, positive laws than the executive, and so must necessarily be left to the prudence and wisdom of those whose hands it is in, to be managed for the public good. For the laws that concern subjects one amongst another, being to direct their actions, may well enough precede them. But what is to be done in reference to foreigners depending much upon their actions, and the variation of designs and interests, must be left in great part to the prudence of those who have this power committed to them, to be managed by the best of their skill for the advantage of the commonwealth. 148. Though, as I said, the executive and federative power of every community be really distinct in themselves, yet they are hardly to be separated and placed at the same time in the hands of distinct persons. For both of them requiring the force of the society for their exercise, it is almost impracticable to place the force of the commonwealth in distinct and not subordinate hands, or that the executive and federative power should be placed in persons that might act separately, whereby the force of the public would be under different commands, which would be apt some time or other to cause disorder and ruin.

**Chapter XIII, Of the Subordination of the Powers of the Commonwealth**

149. Though in a constituted commonwealth standing upon its own basis and acting according to its own nature—that is, acting for the preservation of the community, there can be but one supreme power, which is the legislative, to which all the rest are and must be subordinate, yet the legislative being only a fiduciary power to act for certain ends, there remains still in the people a supreme power to remove or alter the legislative, when they find the legislative act contrary to the trust reposed in them. For all power given with trust for the attaining an end being limited by that end, whenever that end is manifestly neglected or opposed, the trust must necessarily be forfeited, and the power devolve into the hands of those that gave it, who may place it anew where they shall think best for their safety and security. And thus the community perpetually retains a supreme power of saving themselves from the attempts and designs of anybody, even of their legislators, whenever they shall be so foolish or so wicked as to lay and carry on designs against the liberties and properties of the subject. For no man or society of men having a power to deliver up their preservation, or consequently the means of it, to the absolute will and arbitrary dominion of another, whenever any one shall go about to bring them into such a slavish condition, they will always have a right to preserve what they have not a power to part with, and to rid themselves of those who invade this fundamental, sacred, and unalterable law of self-preservation for which they entered into society. And thus the community may be said in this respect to be always the supreme power, but not as considered under any form of government, because this power of the people can never take place till the government be dissolved.

150. In all cases whilst the government subsists, the legislative is the supreme power. For what can give laws to another must needs be superior to him, and since the legislative is no otherwise legislative of the society but by the right it has to make laws for all the parts, and every member of the society prescribing rules to their actions, they are transgressed, the legislative must needs be the supreme, and all other powers in any members or parts of the society derived from and subordinate to it.

151. In some commonwealths where the legislative is not always in being, and the executive is vested in a single person who has also a share in the legislative, there that single person, in a very tolerable sense, may also be called supreme; not that he has in himself all the supreme power, which is that of law-making, but because he has in him the supreme execution from whom all inferior magistrates derive all their several subordinate powers, or, at least, the greatest part of them; having also no legislative superior to him, there being no law to be made without his consent, which cannot be expected should ever subject him to the other part of the legislative, he is properly enough in this sense supreme. But yet it is to be observed that though oaths of allegiance and fealty are taken to him, it is not to him as supreme legislator, but as supreme executor of the law made by a joint power of him with others, allegiance being nothing but an obedience according to law, which, when he violates, he has no right to obedience, nor can claim it otherwise than as the public person vested with the power of the law, and so is to be considered as the image, phantom, or representative of the commonwealth, acted by the will of the society declared in its laws, and thus he has no will, no power, but that of the law. But when he quits this representation, this public will, and acts by his own private will, he degrades himself, and is but a single private person without power and without will; the members owing no obedience but to the public will of the society.

152. The executive power placed anywhere but in a person that has also a share in the legislative is visibly subordinate and accountable to it, and may be at pleasure changed and displaced; so that it is not the supreme executive power that is exempt from subordination, but the supreme executive power vested in one, who having a share in the legislative, has no distinct superior legislative to be subordinate and accountable to, farther than he himself shall join and consent, so that he is no more subordinate than he himself shall think fit, which one may certainly conclude will be but very little. Of other ministerial and subordinate powers in a commonwealth we need not speak, they being so multiplied with infinite variety in the different customs and constitutions of distinct commonwealths, that it is impossible to give a particular account of them all. Only thus much which is necessary to our present purpose we may take notice of concerning them, that they have no manner of authority, any of them, beyond what is by positive grant and commission delegated to them, and are all of them accountable to some other power in the commonwealth.

153. It is not necessary—no, nor so much as convenient—that the legislative should be always in being; but absolutely necessary that the executive power should, because there is not always need of new laws to be made, but always need of execution of the laws that are made. When the legislative hath put the execution of the laws they make into other hands, they have a power still to resume it out of those hands when they find cause, and to punish for any mal-administration against the laws. The same holds also in regard of the federative power, that and the executive being both ministerial and subordinate to the legislative, which, as has been shown, in a constituted commonwealth is the supreme, the legislative also in this case being supposed to consist of several persons; for if it be a single person it cannot but be always in being, and so will, as supreme, naturally have the supreme executive power, together with the legislative, may assemble and exercise their legislative at the times that either their original constitution or their own adjournment appoints, or when they please, if neither of these hath appointed any time, or there be no other way prescribed to convoke them. For the supreme power being placed in them by the people, it is always in them, and they may exercise it when they please, unless by their original constitution they are limited to certain seasons, or by an act of their supreme power they have adjourned to a certain time, and when that time comes they have a right to assemble and act again.

154. If the legislative, or any part of it, be of representatives, chosen for that time by the people, which afterwards return into the ordinary state of subjects, and have no share in the legislative but upon a new choice, this power of choosing must also be exercised by the people, either at certain appointed seasons, or else when they are summoned to it; and, in this latter case, the power of convoking the legislative is ordinarily placed in the executive, and has one of these two limitations in respect of time:—that either the original constitution requires their assembling and acting at certain intervals; and then the executive power does nothing but ministerially issue directions for their electing and assembling according to due forms; or else it is left to his prudence to call them by new elections when the occasions or exigencies of the public require the amendment of

old or making of new laws, or the redress or prevention of any inconveniencies that lie on or threaten the people.

155. It may be demanded here, what if the executive power, being possessed of the force of the commonwealth, shall make use of that force to hinder the meeting and acting of the legislative, when the original constitution or the public exigencies require it? I say, using force upon the people, without authority, and contrary to the trust put in him that does so, is a state of war with the people, who have a right to reinstate their legislative in the exercise of their power. For having erected a legislative with an intent they should exercise the power of making laws, either at certain set times, or when there is need of it, when they are hindered by any force from what is so necessary to the society, and wherein the safety and preservation of the people consists, the people have a right to remove it by force. In all states and conditions the true remedy of force without authority is to oppose force to it. The use of force without authority always puts him that uses it into a state of war as the aggressor, and renders him liable to be treated accordingly.

156. The power of assembling and dismissing the legislative, placed in the executive, gives not the executive a superiority over it, but is a fiduciary trust placed in him for the safety of the people in a case where the uncertainty and variableness of human affairs could not bear a steady fixed rule. For it not being possible that the first framers of the government should by any foresight be so much masters of future events as to be able to prefix so just periods of return and duration to the assemblies of the legislative, in all times to come, that might exactly answer all the exigencies of the commonwealth, the best remedy could be found for this defect was to trust this to the prudence of one who was always to be present, and whose business it was to watch over the public good. Constant, frequent meetings of the legislative, and long continuations of their assemblies, without necessary occasion, could not but be burdensome to the people, and must necessarily in time produce more dangerous inconveniencies, and yet the quick turn of affairs might be sometimes such as to need their present help; any delay of their convening might endanger the public; and sometimes, too, their business might be so great that the limited time of their sitting might be too short for their work, and rob the public of that benefit which could be had only from their mature deliberation. What, then, could be done in this case to prevent the community from being exposed some time or other to imminent hazard on one side or the other, by fixed intervals and periods set to the meeting and acting of the legislative, but to entrust it to the prudence of some who, being present and acquainted with the state of public affairs, might make use of this prerogative for the public good? And where else could this be so well placed as in his hands who was entrusted with the execution of the laws for the same end? Thus, supposing the regulation of times for the assembling and sitting of the legislative not settled by the original constitution, it naturally fell into the hands of the executive; not as an arbitrary power depending on his good pleasure, but with this trust always to have it exercised only for the public weal, as the occurrences of times and change of affairs might require. Whether settled periods of their convening, or a liberty left to the prince for convoking the legislative, or perhaps a mixture of both, hath the least inconvenience attending it, it is not my business here to inquire, but only to show that, though the executive power may have the prerogative of convoking and dissolving such conventions of the legislative, yet it is not thereby superior to it.

157. Things of this world are in so constant a flux that nothing remains long in the same state. Thus people, riches, trade, power, change their stations; flourishing mighty cities come to ruin, and prove in time neglected desolate corners, whilst other unfrequented places grow into populous countries filled with wealth and inhabitants. But things not always changing equally, and private interest often keeping up customs and privileges when the reasons of them are ceased, it often comes to pass that in governments where part of the legislative consists of representatives chosen by the people, that in tract of time this representation becomes very unequal and disproportionate to the reasons it was at first established upon. To what gross absurdities the following of custom when reason has left it may lead, we may be satisfied when we see the bare name of a town, of which there remains not so much as the ruins, where scarce so much housing as a sheepcote, or more inhabitants than a shepherd is to be found, send as many representatives to the grand assembly of law-makers as a whole county numerous in people and powerful in riches. This strangers stand amazed at, and every one must confess needs a remedy; though most think it hard to find one, because the constitution of the legislative being the original and supreme act of the society, antecedent to all positive laws in it, and depending wholly on the people, no inferior power can alter it. And, therefore, the people when the legislative is once constituted, having in such a government as we have been speaking of no power to act as long as the government stands, this inconvenience is thought incapable of a remedy.

158. Salus populi suprema lex is certainly so just and fundamental a rule, that he who sincerely follows it cannot dangerously err. If, therefore, the executive who has the power of convoking the legislative, observing rather the true proportion than fashion of representation, regulates not by old custom, but true reason, the

number of members in all places, that have a right to be distinctly represented, which no part of the people, however incorporated, can pretend to, but in proportion to the assistance which it affords to the public, it cannot be judged to have set up a new legislative, but to have restored the old and true one, and to have rectified the disorders which succession of time had insensibly as well as inevitably introduced; for it being the interest as well as intention of the people to have a fair and equal representative, whoever brings it nearest to that is an undoubted friend to and establisher of the government, and cannot miss the consent and approbation of the community; prerogative being nothing but a power in the hands of the prince to provide for the public good in such cases which, depending upon unforeseen and uncertain occurrences, certain and unalterable laws could not safely direct. Whatsoever shall be done manifestly for the good of the people, and establishing the government upon its true foundations is, and always will be, just prerogative. The power of erecting new corporations, and therewith new representatives, carries with it a supposition that in time the measures of representation might vary, and those have a just right to be represented which before had none; and by the same reason, those cease to have a right, and be too inconsiderable for such a privilege, which before had it. It is not a change from the present state which, perhaps, corruption or decay has introduced, that makes an inroad upon the government, but the tendency of it to injure or oppress the people, and to set up one part or party with a distinction from and an unequal subjection of the rest. Whatsoever cannot but be acknowledged to be of advantage to the society and people in general, upon just and lasting measures, will always, when done, justify itself; and whenever the people shall choose their representatives upon just and undeniably equal measures, suitable to the original frame of the government, it cannot be doubted to be the will and act of the society, whoever permitted or proposed to them so to do.

**Chapter XIV, Of Prerogative**

159. Where the legislative and executive power are in distinct hands, as they are in all moderated monarchies and well-framed governments, there the good of the society requires that several things should be left to the discretion of him that has the executive power. For the legislators not being able to foresee and provide by laws for all that may be useful to the community, the executor of the laws, having the power in his hands, has by the common law of Nature a right to make use of it for the good of the society, in many cases where the municipal law has given no direction, till the legislative can conveniently be assembled to provide for it; nay, many things there are which the law can by no means provide for, and those must necessarily be left to the discretion of him that has the executive power in his hands, to be ordered by him as the public good and advantage shall require; nay, it is fit that the laws themselves should in some cases give way to the executive power, or rather to this fundamental law of Nature and government—viz., that as much as may be all the members of the society are to be preserved. For since many accidents may happen wherein a strict and rigid observation of the laws may do harm, as not to pull down an innocent man's house to stop the fire when the next to it is burning; and a man may come sometimes within the reach of the law, which makes no distinction of persons, by an action that may deserve reward and pardon; it is fit the ruler should have a power in many cases to mitigate the severity of the law, and pardon some offenders, since the end of government being the preservation of all as much as may be, even the guilty are to be spared where it can prove no prejudice to the innocent.

160. This power to act according to discretion for the public good, without the prescription of the law and sometimes even against it, is that which is called prerogative; for since in some governments the lawmaking power is not always in being and is usually too numerous, and so too slow for the dispatch requisite to execution, and because, also, it is impossible to foresee and so by laws to provide for all accidents and necessities that may concern the public, or make such laws as will do no harm, if they are executed with an inflexible rigour on all occasions and upon all persons that may come in their way, therefore there is a latitude left to the executive power to do many things of choice which the laws do not prescribe.

161. This power, whilst employed for the benefit of the community and suitably to the trust and ends of the government, is undoubted prerogative, and never is questioned. For the people are very seldom or never scrupulous or nice in the point or questioning of prerogative whilst it is in any tolerable degree employed for the use it was meant—that is, the good of the people, and not manifestly against it. But if there comes to be a question between the executive power and the people about a thing claimed as a prerogative, the tendency of the exercise of such prerogative, to the good or hurt of the people, will easily decide that question.

162. It is easy to conceive that in the infancy of governments, when commonwealths differed little from families in number of people, they differed from them too but little in number of laws; and the governors being as

the fathers of them, watching over them for their good, the government was almost all prerogative. A few established laws served the turn, and the discretion and care of the ruler supplied the rest. But when mistake or flattery prevailed with weak princes, to make use of this power for private ends of their own and not for the public good, the people were fain, by express laws, to get prerogative determined in those points wherein they found disadvantage from it, and declared limitations of prerogative in those cases which they and their ancestors had left in the utmost latitude to the wisdom of those princes who made no other but a right use of it—that is, for the good of their people.

163. And therefore they have a very wrong notion of government who say that the people have encroached upon the prerogative when they have got any part of it to be defined by positive laws. For in so doing they have not pulled from the prince anything that of right belonged to him, but only declared that that power which they indefinitely left in his or his ancestors' hands, to be exercised for their good, was not a thing they intended him, when he used it otherwise. For the end of government being the good of the community, whatsoever alterations are made in it tending to that end cannot be an encroachment upon anybody; since nobody in government can have a right tending to any other end; and those only are encroachments which prejudice or hinder the public good. Those who say otherwise speak as if the prince had a distinct and separate interest from the good of the community, and was not made for it; the root and source from which spring almost all those evils and disorders which happen in kingly governments. And indeed, if that be so, the people under his government are not a society of rational creatures, entered into a community for their mutual good, such as have set rulers over themselves, to guard and promote that good; but are to be looked on as a herd of inferior creatures under the dominion of a master, who keeps them and works them for his own pleasure or profit. If men were so void of reason and brutish as to enter into society upon such terms, prerogative might indeed be, what some men would have it, an arbitrary power to do things hurtful to the people.

164. But since a rational creature cannot be supposed, when free, to put himself into subjection to another for his own harm (though where he finds a good and a wise ruler he may not, perhaps, think it either necessary or useful to set precise bounds to his power in all things), prerogative can be nothing but the people's permitting their rulers to do several things of their own free choice where the law was silent, and sometimes too against the direct letter of the law, for the public good and their acquiescing in it when so done. For as a good prince, who is mindful of the trust put into his hands and careful of the good of his people, cannot have too much prerogative- that is, power to do good, so a weak and ill prince, who would claim that power his predecessors exercised, without the direction of the law, as a prerogative belonging to him by right of his office, which he may exercise at his pleasure to make or promote an interest distinct from that of the public, gives the people an occasion to claim their right and limit that power, which, whilst it was exercised for their good, they were content should be tacitly allowed.

165. And therefore he that will look into the history of England will find that prerogative was always largest in the hands of our wisest and best princes, because the people observing the whole tendency of their actions to be the public good, or if any human frailty or mistake (for princes are but men, made as others) appeared in some small declinations from that end, yet it was visible the main of their conduct tended to nothing but the care of the public. The people, therefore, finding reason to be satisfied with these princes, whenever they acted without, or contrary to the letter of the law, acquiesced in what they did, and without the least complaint, let them enlarge their prerogative as they pleased, judging rightly that they did nothing herein to the prejudice of their laws, since they acted conformably to the foundation and end of all laws—the public good.

166. Such God-like princes, indeed, had some title to arbitrary power by that argument that would prove absolute monarchy the best government, as that which God Himself governs the universe by, because such kings partake of His wisdom and goodness. Upon this is founded that saying, "That the reigns of good princes have been always most dangerous to the liberties of their people." For when their successors, managing the government with different thoughts, would draw the actions of those good rulers into precedent and make them the standard of their prerogative—as if what had been done only for the good of the people was a right in them to do for the harm of the people, if they so pleased— it has often occasioned contest, and sometimes public disorders, before the people could recover their original right and get that to be declared not to be prerogative which truly was never so; since it is impossible anybody in the society should ever have a right to do the people harm, though it be very possible and reasonable that the people should not go about to set any bounds to the prerogative of those kings or rulers who themselves transgressed not the bounds of the public good. For "prerogative is nothing but the power of doing public good without a rule." 167. The power of calling parliaments in England, as to precise time, place, and duration, is certainly a prerogative of the king, but still with this trust, that it shall be made use of for the good of the nation as the exigencies of the times and variety of occasion shall require. For it being impossible to foresee which should always be the fittest place for them to

assemble in, and what the best season, the choice of these was left with the executive power, as might be best subservient to the public good and best suit the ends of parliament.

168. The old question will be asked in this matter of prerogative, "But who shall be judge when this power is made a right use of?" I answer: Between an executive power in being, with such a prerogative and a legislative that depends upon his will for their convening, there can be no judge on earth. As there can be none between the legislative and the people, should either the executive or the legislative, when they have got the power in their hands, design, or go about to enslave or destroy them, the people have no other remedy in this, as in all other cases where they have no judge on earth, but to appeal to Heaven; for the rulers in such attempts, exercising a power the people never put into their hands, who can never be supposed to consent that anybody should rule over them for their harm, do that which they have not a right to do. And where the body of the people, or any single man, are deprived of their right, or are under the exercise of a power without right, having no appeal on earth they have a liberty to appeal to Heaven whenever they judge the cause of sufficient moment. And therefore, though the people cannot be judge, so as to have, by the constitution of that society, any superior power to determine and give effective sentence in the case, yet they have reserved that ultimate determination to themselves which belongs to all mankind, where there lies no appeal on earth, by a law antecedent and paramount to all positive laws of men, whether they have just cause to make their appeal to Heaven. And this judgement they cannot part with, it being out of a man's power so to submit himself to another as to give him a liberty to destroy him; God and Nature never allowing a man so to abandon himself as to neglect his own preservation. And since he cannot take away his own life, neither can he give another power to take it. Nor let any one think this lays a perpetual foundation for disorder; for this operates not till the inconvenience is so great that the majority feel it, and are weary of it, and find a necessity to have it amended. And this the executive power, or wise princes, never need come in the danger of; and it is the thing of all others they have most need to avoid, as, of all others, the most perilous.

**Chapter XV, Of Paternal, Political and Despotical Power, Considered Together**

169. Though I have had occasion to speak of these separately before, yet the great mistakes of late about government having, as I suppose, arisen from confounding these distinct powers one with another, it may not perhaps be amiss to consider them here together.

170. First, then, paternal or parental power is nothing but that which parents have over their children to govern them, for the children's good, till they come to the use of reason, or a state of knowledge, wherein they may be supposed capable to understand that rule, whether it be the law of Nature or the municipal law of their country, they are to govern themselves by—capable, I say, to know it, as well as several others, who live as free men under that law. The affection and tenderness God hath planted in the breasts of parents towards their children makes it evident that this is not intended to be a severe arbitrary government, but only for the help, instruction, and preservation of their offspring. But happen as it will, there is, as I have proved, no reason why it should be thought to extend to life and death, at any time, over their children, more than over anybody else, or keep the child in subjection to the will of his parents when grown to a man and the perfect use of reason, any farther than as having received life and education from his parents obliges him to respect, honour, gratitude, assistance, and support, all his life, to both father and mother. And thus, it is true, the paternal is a natural government, but not at all extending itself to the ends and jurisdictions of that which is political. The power of the father doth not reach at all to the property of the child, which is only in his own disposing.

171. Secondly, political power is that power which every man having in the state of Nature has given up into the hands of the society, and therein to the governors whom the society hath set over itself, with this express or tacit trust, that it shall be employed for their good and the preservation of their property. Now this power, which every man has in the state of Nature, and which he parts with to the society in all such cases where the society can secure him, is to use such means for the preserving of his own property as he thinks good and Nature allows him; and to punish the breach of the law of Nature in others so as (according to the best of his reason) may most conduce to the preservation of himself and the rest of mankind; so that the end and measure of this power, when in every man's hands, in the state of Nature, being the preservation of all of his society—that is, all mankind in general—it can have no other end or measure, when in the hands of the magistrate, but to preserve the members of that society in their lives, liberties, and possessions, and so cannot be an absolute, arbitrary power over their lives and fortunes, which are as much as possible to be preserved; but a power to make laws, and annex such penalties to them as may tend to the preservation of the whole, by cutting off those parts, and those only, which are so corrupt that they threaten the sound and healthy, without which no

severity is lawful. And this power has its original only from compact and agreement and the mutual consent of those who make up the community.

172. Thirdly, despotical power is an absolute, arbitrary power one man has over another, to take away his life whenever he pleases; and this is a power which neither Nature gives, for it has made no such distinction between one man and another, nor compact can convey. For man, not having such an arbitrary power over his own life, cannot give another man such a power over it, but it is the effect only of forfeiture which the aggressor makes of his own life when he puts himself into the state of war with another. For having quitted reason, which God hath given to be the rule betwixt man and man, and the peaceable ways which that teaches, and made use of force to compass his unjust ends upon another where he has no right, he renders himself liable to be destroyed by his adversary whenever he can, as any other noxious and brutish creature that is destructive to his being. And thus captives, taken in a just and lawful war, and such only, are subject to a despotical power, which, as it arises not from compact, so neither is it capable of any, but is the state of war continued. For what compact can be made with a man that is not master of his own life? What condition can he perform? And if he be once allowed to be master of his own life, the despotical, arbitrary power of his master ceases. He that is master of himself and his own life has a right, too, to the means of preserving it; so that as soon as compact enters, slavery ceases, and he so far quits his absolute power and puts an end to the state of war who enters into conditions with his captive.

173. Nature gives the first of these—viz., paternal power to parents for the benefit of their children during their minority, to supply their want of ability and understanding how to manage their property. (By property I must be understood here, as in other places, to mean that property which men have in their persons as well as goods.) Voluntary agreement gives the second—viz., political power to governors, for the benefit of their subjects, to secure them in the possession and use of their properties. And forfeiture gives the third—despotical power to lords for their own benefit over those who are stripped of all property.

174. He that shall consider the distinct rise and extent, and the different ends of these several powers, will plainly see that paternal power comes as far short of that of the magistrate as despotical exceeds it; and that absolute dominion, however placed, is so far from being one kind of civil society that it is as inconsistent with it as slavery is with property. Paternal power is only where minority makes the child incapable to manage his property; political where men have property in their own disposal; and despotical over such as have no property at all.

**Chapter XVI, Of Conquest**

175. Though governments can originally have no other rise than that before mentioned, nor polities be founded on anything but the consent of the people, yet such have been the disorders ambition has filled the world with, that in the noise of war, which makes so great a part of the history of mankind, this consent is little taken notice of; and, therefore, many have mistaken the force of arms for the consent of the people, and reckon conquest as one of the originals of government. But conquest is as far from setting up any government as demolishing a house is from building a new one in the place. Indeed, it often makes way for a new frame of a commonwealth by destroying the former; but, without the consent of the people, can never erect a new one.

176. That the aggressor, who puts himself into the state of war with another, and unjustly invades another man's right, can, by such an unjust war, never come to have a right over the conquered, will be easily agreed by all men, who will not think that robbers and pirates have a right of empire over whomsoever they have force enough to master, or that men are bound by promises which unlawful force extorts from them. Should a robber break into my house, and, with a dagger at my throat, make me seal deeds to convey my estate to him, would this give him any title? Just such a title by his sword has an unjust conqueror who forces me into submission. The injury and the crime is equal, whether committed by the wearer of a crown or some petty villain. The title of the offender and the number of his followers make no difference in the offence, unless it be to aggravate it. The only difference is, great robbers punish little ones to keep them in their obedience; but the great ones are rewarded with laurels and triumphs, because they are too big for the weak hands of justice in this world, and have the power in their own possession which should punish offenders. What is my remedy against a robber that so broke into my house? Appeal to the law for justice. But perhaps justice is denied, or I am crippled and cannot stir; robbed, and have not the means to do it. If God has taken away all means of seeking remedy, there is nothing left but patience. But my son, when able, may seek the relief of the law, which I am denied; he or his son may renew his appeal till he recover his right. But the conquered, or their children,

have no court—no arbitrator on earth to appeal to. Then they may appeal, as Jephtha did, to Heaven, and repeat their appeal till they have recovered the native right of their ancestors, which was to have such a legislative over them as the majority should approve and freely acquiesce in. If it be objected this would cause endless trouble, I answer, no more than justice does, where she lies open to all that appeal to her. He that troubles his neighbour without a cause is punished for it by the justice of the court he appeals to. And he that appeals to Heaven must be sure he has right on his side, and a right, too, that is worth the trouble and cost of the appeal, as he will answer at a tribunal that cannot be deceived, and will be sure to retribute to every one according to the mischiefs he hath created to his fellow-subjects—that is, any part of mankind. From whence it is plain that he that conquers in an unjust war can thereby have no title to the subjection and obedience of the conquered.

177. But supposing victory favours the right side, let us consider a conqueror in a lawful war, and see what power he gets, and over whom. First, it is plain he gets no power by his conquest over those that conquered with him. They that fought on his side cannot suffer by the conquest, but must, at least, be as much free men as they were before. And most commonly they serve upon terms, and on condition to share with their leader, and enjoy a part of the spoil and other advantages that attend the conquering sword, or, at least, have a part of the subdued country bestowed upon them. And the conquering people are not, I hope, to be slaves by conquest, and wear their laurels only to show they are sacrifices to their leader's triumph. They that found absolute monarchy upon the title of the sword make their heroes, who are the founders of such monarchies, arrant "draw-can-sirs," and forget they had any officers and soldiers that fought on their side in the battles they won, or assisted them in the subduing, or shared in possessing the countries they mastered. We are told by some that the English monarchy is founded in the Norman Conquest, and that our princes have thereby a title to absolute dominion, which, if it were true (as by the history it appears otherwise), and that William had a right to make war on this island, yet his dominion by conquest could reach no farther than to the Saxons and Britons that were then inhabitants of this country. The Normans that came with him and helped to conquer, and all descended from them, are free men and no subjects by conquest, let that give what dominion it will. And if I or anybody else shall claim freedom as derived from them, it will be very hard to prove the contrary; and it is plain, the law that has made no distinction between the one and the other intends not there should be any difference in their freedom or privileges. 178. But supposing, which seldom happens, that the conquerors and conquered never incorporate into one people under the same laws and freedom; let us see next what power a lawful conqueror has over the subdued, and that I say is purely despotical. He has an absolute power over the lives of those who, by an unjust war, have forfeited them, but not over the lives or fortunes of those who engaged not in the war, nor over the possessions even of those who were actually engaged in it. 179. Secondly, I say, then, the conqueror gets no power but only over those who have actually assisted, concurred, or consented to that unjust force that is used against him. For the people having given to their governors no power to do an unjust thing, such as is to make an unjust war (for they never had such a power in themselves), they ought not to be charged as guilty of the violence and injustice that is committed in an unjust war any farther than they actually abet it, no more than they are to be thought guilty of any violence or oppression their governors should use upon the people themselves or any part of their fellowsubjects, they having empowered them no more to the one than to the other. Conquerors, it is true, seldom trouble themselves to make the distinction, but they willingly permit the confusion of war to sweep all together; but yet this alters not the right; for the conqueror's power over the lives of the conquered being only because they have used force to do or maintain an injustice, he can have that power only over those who have concurred in that force; all the rest are innocent, and he has no more title over the people of that country who have done him no injury, and so have made no forfeiture of their lives, than he has over any other who, without any injuries or provocations, have lived upon fair terms with him.

180. Thirdly, the power a conqueror gets over those he overcomes in a just war is perfectly despotical; he has an absolute power over the lives of those who, by putting themselves in a state of war, have forfeited them, but he has not thereby a right and title to their possessions. This I doubt not but at first sight will seem a strange doctrine, it being so quite contrary to the practice of the world; there being nothing more familiar in speaking of the dominion of countries than to say such an one conquered it, as if conquest, without any more ado, conveyed a right of possession. But when we consider that the practice of the strong and powerful, how universal soever it may be, is seldom the rule of right, however it be one part of the subjection of the conquered not to argue against the conditions cut out to them by the conquering swords.

181. Though in all war there be usually a complication of force and damage, and the aggressor seldom fails to harm the estate when he uses force against the persons of those he makes war upon, yet it is the use of force only that puts a man into the state of war. For whether by force he begins the injury, or else having quietly and by fraud done the injury, he refuses to make reparation, and by force maintains it, which is the same thing as at first to have done it by force; it is the unjust use of force that makes the war. For he that breaks open my

house and violently turns me out of doors, or having peaceably got in, by force keeps me out, does, in effect, the same thing; supposing we are in such a state that we have no common judge on earth whom I may appeal to, and to whom we are both obliged to submit, for of such I am now speaking. It is the unjust use of force, then, that puts a man into the state of war with another, and thereby he that is guilty of it makes a forfeiture of his life. For quitting reason, which is the rule given between man and man, and using force, the way of beasts, he becomes liable to be destroyed by him he uses force against, as any savage ravenous beast that is danger-ous to his being.

182. But because the miscarriages of the father are no faults of the children, who may be rational and peace-able, notwithstanding the brutishness and injustice of the father, the father, by his miscarriages and violence, can forfeit but his own life, and involves not his children in his guilt or destruction. His goods which Nature, that willeth the preservation of all mankind as much as is possible, hath made to belong to the children to keep them from perishing, do still continue to belong to his children. For supposing them not to have joined in the war either through infancy or choice, they have done nothing to forfeit them, nor has the conqueror any right to take them away by the bare right of having subdued him that by force attempted his destruction, though, perhaps, he may have some right to them to repair the damages he has sustained by the war, and the defence of his own right, which how far it reaches to the possessions of the conquered we shall see by-and-by; so that he that by conquest has a right over a man's person, to destroy him if he pleases, has not thereby a right over his estate to possess and enjoy it. For it is the brutal force the aggressor has used that gives his ad-versary a right to take away his life and destroy him, if he pleases, as a noxious creature; but it is damage sus-tained that alone gives him title to another man's goods; for though I may kill a thief that sets on me in the highway, yet I may not (which seems less) take away his money and let him go; this would be robbery on my side. His force, and the state of war he put himself in, made him forfeit his life, but gave me no title to his goods. The right, then, of conquest extends only to the lives of those who joined in the war, but not to their es-tates, but only in order to make reparation for the damages received and the charges of the war, and that, too, with reservation of the right of the innocent wife and children.

183. Let the conqueror have as much justice on his side as could be supposed, he has no right to seize more than the vanquished could forfeit; his life is at the victor's mercy, and his service and goods he may appropri-ate to make himself reparation; but he cannot take the goods of his wife and children, they too had a title to the goods he enjoyed, and their shares in the estate he possessed. For example, I in the state of Nature (and all commonwealths are in the state of Nature one with another) have injured another man, and refusing to give satisfaction, it is come to a state of war wherein my defending by force what I had gotten unjustly makes me the aggressor. I am conquered; my life, it is true, as forfeit, is at mercy, but not my wife's and children's. They made not the war, nor assisted in it. I could not forfeit their lives, they were not mine to forfeit. My wife had a share in my estate, that neither could I forfeit. And my children also, being born of me, had a right to be main-tained out of my labour or substance. Here then is the case: The conqueror has a title to reparation for dam-ages received, and the children have a title to their father's estate for their subsistence. For as to the wife's share, whether her own labour or compact gave her a title to it, it is plain her husband could not forfeit what was hers. What must be done in the case? I answer: The fundamental law of Nature being that all, as much as may be, should be preserved, it follows that if there be not enough fully to satisfy both—viz., for the con-queror's losses and children's maintenance, he that hath and to spare must remit something of his full satisfac-tion, and give way to the pressing and preferable title of those who are in danger to perish without it.

184. But supposing the charge and damages of the war are to be made up to the conqueror to the utmost far-thing, and that the children of the vanquished, spoiled of all their father's goods, are to be left to starve and perish, yet the satisfying of what shall, on this score, be due to the conqueror will scarce give him a title to any country he shall conquer. For the damages of war can scarce amount to the value of any considerable tract of land in any part of the world, where all the land is possessed, and none lies waste. And if I have not taken away the conqueror's land which, being vanquished, it is impossible I should, scarce any other spoil I have done him can amount to the value of mine, supposing it of an extent any way coming near what I had overrun of his, and equally cultivated too. The destruction of a year's product or two (for it seldom reaches four or five) is the utmost spoil that usually can be done. For as to money, and such riches and treasure taken away, these are none of Nature's goods, they have but a phantastical imaginary value; Nature has put no such upon them. They are of no more account by her standard than the Wampompeke of the Americans to an European prince, or the silver money of Europe would have been formerly to an American. And five years' product is not worth the perpetual inheritance of land, where all is possessed and none remains waste, to be taken up by him that is disseised, which will be easily granted, if one do but take away the imaginary value of money, the disproportion being more than between five and five thousand; though, at the same time, half a year's product is more worth than the inheritance where, there being more land than the inhabitants possess and make use of, any one has liberty to make use of the waste. But their conquerors take little care to possess themselves of the

lands of the vanquished. No damage therefore that men in the state of Nature (as all princes and governments are in reference to one another) suffer from one another can give a conqueror power to dispossess the posterity of the vanquished, and turn them out of that inheritance which ought to be the possession of them and their descendants to all generations. The conqueror indeed will be apt to think himself master; and it is the very condition of the subdued not to be able to dispute their right. But, if that be all, it gives no other title than what bare force gives to the stronger over the weaker; and, by this reason, he that is strongest will have a right to whatever he pleases to seize on.

185. Over those, then, that joined with him in the war, and over those of the subdued country that opposed him not, and the posterity even of those that did, the conqueror, even in a just war, hath, by his conquest, no right of dominion. They are free from any subjection to him, and if their former government be dissolved, they are at liberty to begin and erect another to themselves.

186. The conqueror, it is true, usually by the force he has over them, compels them, with a sword at their breasts, to stoop to his conditions, and submit to such a government as he pleases to afford them; but the inquiry is, what right he has to do so? If it be said they submit by their own consent, then this allows their own consent to be necessary to give the conqueror a title to rule over them. It remains only to be considered whether promises, extorted by force, without right, can be thought consent, and how far they bind. To which I shall say, they bind not at all; because whatsoever another gets from me by force, I still retain the right of, and he is obliged presently to restore. He that forces my horse from me ought presently to restore him, and I have still a right to retake him. By the same reason, he that forced a promise from me ought presently to restore it —i.e., quit me of the obligation of it; or I may resume it myself—i.e., choose whether I will perform it. For the law of Nature laying an obligation on me, only by the rules she prescribes, cannot oblige me by the violation of her rules; such is the extorting anything from me by force. Nor does it at all alter the case, to say I gave my promise, no more than it excuses the force, and passes the right, when I put my hand in my pocket and deliver my purse myself to a thief who demands it with a pistol at my breast.

187. From all which it follows that the government of a conqueror, imposed by force on the subdued, against whom he had no right of war, or who joined not in the war against him, where he had right, has no obligation upon them.

188. But let us suppose that all the men of that community being all members of the same body politic, may be taken to have joined in that unjust war, wherein they are subdued, and so their lives are at the mercy of the conqueror.

189. I say this concerns not their children who are in their minority. For since a father hath not, in himself, a power over the life or liberty of his child, no act of his can possibly forfeit it; so that the children, whatever may have happened to the fathers, are free men, and the absolute power of the conqueror reaches no farther than the persons of the men that were subdued by him, and dies with them; and should he govern them as slaves, subjected to his absolute, arbitrary power, he has no such right of dominion over their children. He can have no power over them but by their own consent, whatever he may drive them to say or do, and he has no lawful authority, whilst force, and not choice, compels them to submission.

190. Every man is born with a double right. First, a right of freedom to his person, which no other man has a power over, but the free disposal of it lies in himself. Secondly, a right before any other man, to inherit, with his brethren, his father's goods.

191. By the first of these, a man is naturally free from subjection to any government, though he be born in a place under its jurisdiction. But if he disclaim the lawful government of the country he was born in, he must also quit the right that belonged to him, by the laws of it, and the possessions there descending to him from his ancestors, if it were a government made by their consent.

192. By the second, the inhabitants of any country, who are descended and derive a title to their estates from those who are subdued, and had a government forced upon them, against their free consents, retain a right to the possession of their ancestors, though they consent not freely to the government, whose hard conditions were, by force, imposed on the possessors of that country. For the first conqueror never having had a title to the land of that country, the people, who are the descendants of, or claim under those who were forced to submit to the yoke of a government by constraint, have always a right to shake it off, and free themselves from the usurpation or tyranny the sword hath brought in upon them, till their rulers put them under such a frame of government as they willingly and of choice consent to (which they can never be supposed to do, till either

they are put in a full state of liberty to choose their government and governors, or at least till they have such standing laws to which they have, by themselves or their representatives, given their free consent, and also till they are allowed their due property, which is so to be proprietors of what they have that nobody can take away any part of it without their own consent, without which, men under any government are not in the state of free men, but are direct slaves under the force of war). And who doubts but the Grecian Christians, descendants of the ancient possessors of that country, may justly cast off the Turkish yoke they have so long groaned under, whenever they have a power to do it?

193. But granting that the conqueror, in a just war, has a right to the estates, as well as power over the persons of the conquered, which, it is plain, he hath not, nothing of absolute power will follow from hence in the continuance of the government. Because the descendants of these being all free men, if he grants them estates and possessions to inhabit his country, without which it would be worth nothing, whatsoever he grants them they have so far as it is granted property in; the nature whereof is, that, without a man's own consent, it cannot be taken from him.

194. Their persons are free by a native right, and their properties, be they more or less, are their own, and at their own dispose, and not at his; or else it is no property. Supposing the conqueror gives to one man a thousand acres, to him and his heirs for ever; to another he lets a thousand acres, for his life, under the rent of L50 or L500 per annum. Has not the one of these a right to his thousand acres for ever, and the other during his life, paying the said rent? And hath not the tenant for life a property in all that he gets over and above his rent, by his labour and industry, during the said term, supposing it be double the rent? Can any one say, the king, or conqueror, after his grant, may, by his power of conqueror, take away all, or part of the land, from the heirs of one, or from the other during his life, he paying the rent? Or, can he take away from either the goods or money they have got upon the said land at his pleasure? If he can, then all free and voluntary contracts cease, and are void in the world; there needs nothing but power enough to dissolve them at any time, and all the grants and promises of men in power are but mockery and collusion. For can there be anything more ridiculous than to say, I give you and yours this for ever, and that in the surest and most solemn way of conveyance can be devised, and yet it is to be understood that I have right, if I please, to take it away from you again tomorrow?

195. I will not dispute now whether princes are exempt from the laws of their country, but this I am sure, they owe subjection to the laws of God and Nature. Nobody, no power can exempt them from the obligations of that eternal law. Those are so great and so strong in the case of promises, that Omnipotency itself can be tied by them. Grants, promises, and oaths are bonds that hold the Almighty, whatever some flatterers say to princes of the world, who, all together, with all their people joined to them, are, in comparison of the great God, but as a drop of the bucket, or a dust on the balance- inconsiderable, nothing!

196. The short of the case in conquest, is this: The conqueror, if he have a just cause, has a despotical right over the persons of all that actually aided and concurred in the war against him, and a right to make up his damage and cost out of their labour and estates, so he injure not the right of any other. Over the rest of the people, if there were any that consented not to the war, and over the children of the captives themselves or the possessions of either he has no power, and so can have, by virtue of conquest, no lawful title himself to dominion over them, or derive it to his posterity; but is an aggressor, and puts himself in a state of war against them, and has no better a right of principality, he, nor any of his successors, than Hingar, or Hubba, the Danes, had here in England, or Spartacus, had be conquered Italy, which is to have their yoke cast off as soon as God shall give those under their subjection courage and opportunity to do it. Thus, notwithstanding whatever title the kings of Assyria had over Judah, by the sword, God assisted Hezekiah to throw off the dominion of that conquering empire. "And the Lord was with Hezekiah, and he prospered; wherefore he went forth, and he rebelled against the king of Assyria, and served him not" (II Kings 18. 7). Whence it is plain that shaking off a power which force, and not right, hath set over any one, though it hath the name of rebellion, yet is no offence before God, but that which He allows and countenances, though even promises and covenants, when obtained by force, have intervened. For it is very probable, to any one that reads the story of Ahaz and Hezekiah attentively, that the Assyrians subdued Ahaz, and deposed him, and made Hezekiah king in his father's lifetime, and that Hezekiah, by agreement, had done him homage, and paid him tribute till this time.

**Chapter XVII, Of Usurpation**

197. As conquest may be called a foreign usurpation, so usurpation is a kind of domestic conquest, with this difference—that an usurper can never have right on his side, it being no usurpation but where one is got into

the possession of what another has right to. This, so far as it is usurpation, is a change only of persons, but not of the forms and rules of the government; for if the usurper extend his power beyond what, of right, belonged to the lawful princes or governors of the commonwealth, it is tyranny added to usurpation.

198. In all lawful governments the designation of the persons who are to bear rule being as natural and necessary a part as the form of the government itself, and that which had its establishment originally from the people—the anarchy being much alike, to have no form of government at all, or to agree that it shall be monarchical, yet appoint no way to design the person that shall have the power and be the monarch—all commonwealths, therefore, with the form of government established, have rules also of appointing and conveying the right to those who are to have any share in the public authority; and whoever gets into the exercise of any part of the power by other ways than what the laws of the community have prescribed hath no right to be obeyed, though the form of the commonwealth be still preserved, since he is not the person the laws have appointed, and, consequently, not the person the people have consented to. Nor can such an usurper, or any deriving from him, ever have a title till the people are both at liberty to consent, and have actually consented, to allow and confirm in him the power he hath till then usurped.

**Chapter XVIII, Of Tyranny**

199. As usurpation is the exercise of power which another hath a right to, so tyranny is the exercise of power beyond right, which nobody can have a right to; and this is making use of the power any one has in his hands, not for the good of those who are under it, but for his own private, separate advantage. When the governor, however entitled, makes not the law, but his will, the rule, and his commands and actions are not directed to the preservation of the properties of his people, but the satisfaction of his own ambition, revenge, covetousness, or any other irregular passion.

200. If one can doubt this to be truth or reason because it comes from the obscure hand of a subject, I hope the authority of a king will make it pass with him. King James, in his speech to the Parliament, 1603, tells them thus: "I will ever prefer the weal of the public and of the whole commonwealth, in making of good laws and constitutions, to any particular and private ends of mine, thinking ever the wealth and weal of the commonwealth to be my greatest weal and worldly felicity—a point wherein a lawful king doth directly differ from a tyrant; for I do acknowledge that the special and greatest point of difference that is between a rightful king and an usurping tyrant is this—that whereas the proud and ambitious tyrant doth think his kingdom and people are only ordained for satisfaction of his desires and unreasonable appetites, the righteous and just king doth, by the contrary, acknowledge himself to be ordained for the procuring of the wealth and property of his people." And again, in his speech to the Parliament, 1609, he hath these words: "The king binds himself, by a double oath, to the observation of the fundamental laws of his kingdom—tacitly, as by being a king, and so bound to protect, as well the people as the laws of his kingdom; and expressly by his oath at his coronation; so as every just king, in a settled kingdom, is bound to observe that paction made to his people, by his laws, in framing his government agreeable thereunto, according to that paction which God made with Noah after the deluge: 'Hereafter, seedtime, and harvest, and cold, and heat, and summer, and winter, and day, and night, shall not cease while the earth remaineth.' And therefore a king, governing in a settled kingdom, leaves to be a king, and degenerates into a tyrant, as soon as he leaves off to rule according to his laws." And a little after: "Therefore, all kings that are not tyrants, or perjured, will be glad to bound themselves within the limits of their laws, and they that persuade them the contrary are vipers, pests, both against them and the commonwealth." Thus, that learned king, who well understood the notions of things, makes the difference betwixt a king and a tyrant to consist only in this: that one makes the laws the bounds of his power and the good of the public the end of his government; the other makes all give way to his own will and appetite.

201. It is a mistake to think this fault is proper only to monarchies. Other forms of government are liable to it as well as that; for wherever the power that is put in any hands for the government of the people and the preservation of their properties is applied to other ends, and made use of to impoverish, harass, or subdue them to the arbitrary and irregular commands of those that have it, there it presently becomes tyranny, whether those that thus use it are one or many. Thus we read of the thirty tyrants at Athens, as well as one at Syracuse; and the intolerable dominion of the Decemviri at Rome was nothing better.

202. Wherever law ends, tyranny begins, if the law be transgressed to another's harm; and whosoever in authority exceeds the power given him by the law, and makes use of the force he has under his command to compass that upon the subject which the law allows not, ceases in that to be a magistrate, and acting without

authority may be opposed, as any other man who by force invades the right of another. This is acknowledged in subordinate magistrates. He that hath authority to seize my person in the street may be opposed as a thief and a robber if he endeavours to break into my house to execute a writ, notwithstanding that I know he has such a warrant and such a legal authority as will empower him to arrest me abroad. And why this should not hold in the highest, as well as in the most inferior magistrate, I would gladly be informed. Is it reasonable that the eldest brother, because he has the greatest part of his father's estate, should thereby have a right to take away any of his younger brothers' portions? Or that a rich man, who possessed a whole country, should from thence have a right to seize, when he pleased, the cottage and garden of his poor neighbour? The being rightfully possessed of great power and riches, exceedingly beyond the greatest part of the sons of Adam, is so far from being an excuse, much less a reason for rapine and oppression, which the endamaging another without authority is, that it is a great aggravation of it. For exceeding the bounds of authority is no more a right in a great than a petty officer, no more justifiable in a king than a constable. But so much the worse in him as that he has more trust put in him, is supposed, from the advantage of education and counsellors, to have better knowledge and less reason to do it, having already a greater share than the rest of his brethren.

203. May the commands, then, of a prince be opposed? May he be resisted, as often as any one shall find himself aggrieved, and but imagine he has not right done him? This will unhinge and overturn all polities, and instead of government and order, leave nothing but anarchy and confusion.

204. To this I answer: That force is to be opposed to nothing but to unjust and unlawful force. Whoever makes any opposition in any other case draws on himself a just condemnation, both from God and man; and so no such danger or confusion will follow, as is often suggested.

205. First. As in some countries the person of the prince by the law is sacred, and so whatever he commands or does, his person is still free from all question or violence, not liable to force, or any judicial censure or condemnation. But yet opposition may be made to the illegal acts of any inferior officer or other commissioned by him, unless he will, by actually putting himself into a state of war with his people, dissolve the government, and leave them to that defence, which belongs to every one in the state of Nature. For of such things, who can tell what the end will be? And a neighbour kingdom has showed the world an odd example. In all other cases the sacredness of the person exempts him from all inconveniencies, whereby he is secure, whilst the government stands, from all violence and harm whatsoever, than which there cannot be a wiser constitution. For the harm he can do in his own person not being likely to happen often, nor to extend itself far, nor being able by his single strength to subvert the laws nor oppress the body of the people, should any prince have so much weakness and ill-nature as to be willing to do it. The inconveniency of some particular mischiefs that may happen sometimes when a heady prince comes to the throne are well recompensed by the peace of the public and security of the government in the person of the chief magistrate, thus set out of the reach of danger; it being safer for the body that some few private men should be sometimes in danger to suffer than that the head of the republic should be easily and upon slight occasions exposed.

206. Secondly. But this privilege, belonging only to the king's person, hinders not but they may be questioned, opposed, and resisted, who use unjust force, though they pretend a commission from him which the law authorises not; as is plain in the case of him that has the king's writ to arrest a man which is a full commission from the king, and yet he that has it cannot break open a man's house to do it, nor execute this command of the king upon certain days nor in certain places, though this commission have no such exception in it; but they are the limitations of the law, which, if any one transgress, the king's commission excuses him not. For the king's authority being given him only by the law, he cannot empower any one to act against the law, or justify him by his commission in so doing. The commission or command of any magistrate where he has no authority, being as void and insignificant as that of any private man, the difference between the one and the other being that the magistrate has some authority so far and to such ends, and the private man has none at all; for it is not the commission but the authority that gives the right of acting, and against the laws there can be no authority. But notwithstanding such resistance, the king's person and authority are still both secured, and so no danger to governor or government.

207. Thirdly. Supposing a government wherein the person of the chief magistrate is not thus sacred, yet this doctrine of the lawfulness of resisting all unlawful exercises of his power will not, upon every slight occasion, endanger him or embroil the government; for where the injured party may be relieved and his damages repaired by appeal to the law, there can be no pretence for force, which is only to be used where a man is intercepted from appealing to the law. For nothing is to be accounted hostile force but where it leaves not the remedy of such an appeal. and it is such force alone that puts him that uses it into a state of war, and makes it lawful to resist him. A man with a sword in his hand demands my purse on the highway, when perhaps I have not

12d. in my pocket. This man I may lawfully kill. To another I deliver £100 to hold only whilst I alight, which he refuses to restore me when I am got up again, but draws his sword to defend the possession of it by force. I endeavour to retake it. The mischief this man does me is a hundred, or possibly a thousand times more than the other perhaps intended me (whom I killed before he really did me any); and yet I might lawfully kill the one and cannot so much as hurt the other lawfully. The reason whereof is plain; because the one using force which threatened my life, I could not have time to appeal to the law to secure it, and when it was gone it was too late to appeal. The law could not restore life to my dead carcass. The loss was irreparable; which to prevent the law of Nature gave me a right to destroy him who had put himself into a state of war with me and threatened my destruction. But in the other case, my life not being in danger, I might have the benefit of appealing to the law, and have reparation for my £100 that way.

208. Fourthly. But if the unlawful acts done by the magistrate be maintained (by the power he has got), and the remedy, which is due by law, be by the same power obstructed, yet the right of resisting, even in such manifest acts of tyranny, will not suddenly, or on slight occasions, disturb the government. For if it reach no farther than some private men's cases, though they have a right to defend themselves, and to recover by force what by unlawful force is taken from them, yet the right to do so will not easily engage them in a contest wherein they are sure to perish; it being as impossible for one or a few oppressed men to disturb the government where the body of the people do not think themselves concerned in it, as for a raving madman or heady malcontent to overturn a well-settled state, the people being as little apt to follow the one as the other.

209. But if either these illegal acts have extended to the majority of the people, or if the mischief and oppression has light only on some few, but in such cases as the precedent and consequences seem to threaten all, and they are persuaded in their consciences that their laws, and with them, their estates, liberties, and lives are in danger, and perhaps their religion too, how they will be hindered from resisting illegal force used against them I cannot tell. This is an inconvenience, I confess, that attends all governments whatsoever, when the governors have brought it to this pass, to be generally suspected of their people, the most dangerous state they can possibly put themselves in; wherein they are the less to be pitied, because it is so easy to be avoided. It being as impossible for a governor, if he really means the good of his people, and the preservation of them and their laws together, not to make them see and feel it, as it is for the father of a family not to let his children see he loves and takes care of them.

210. But if all the world shall observe pretences of one kind, and actions of another, arts used to elude the law, and the trust of prerogative (which is an arbitrary power in some things left in the prince's hand to do good, not harm, to the people) employed contrary to the end for which it was given; if the people shall find the ministers and subordinate magistrates chosen, suitable to such ends, and favoured or laid by proportionably as they promote or oppose them; if they see several experiments made of arbitrary power, and that religion underhand favoured, though publicly proclaimed against, which is readiest to introduce it, and the operators in it supported as much as may be; and when that cannot be done, yet approved still, and liked the better, and a long train of acting show the counsels all tending that way, how can a man any more hinder himself from being persuaded in his own mind which way things are going; or, from casting about how to save himself, than he could from believing the captain of a ship he was in was carrying him and the rest of the company to Algiers, when he found him always steering that course, though cross winds, leaks in his ship, and want of men and provisions did often force him to turn his course another way for some time, which he steadily returned to again as soon as the wind, weather, and other circumstances would let him?

**Chapter XIX, Of the Dissolution of Government**

211. He that will, with any clearness, speak of the dissolution of government, ought in the first place to distinguish between the dissolution of the society and the dissolution of the government. That which makes the community, and brings men out of the loose state of Nature into one politic society, is the agreement which every one has with the rest to incorporate and act as one body, and so be one distinct commonwealth. The usual, and almost only way whereby this union is dissolved, is the inroad of foreign force making a conquest upon them. For in that case (not being able to maintain and support themselves as one entire and independent body) the union belonging to that body, which consisted therein, must necessarily cease, and so every one return to the state he was in before, with a liberty to shift for himself and provide for his own safety, as he thinks fit, in some other society. Whenever the society is dissolved, it is certain the government of that society cannot remain. Thus conquerors' swords often cut up governments by the roots, and mangle societies to pieces, separating the subdued or scattered multitude from the protection of and dependence on that society

which ought to have preserved them from violence. The world is too well instructed in, and too forward to allow of this way of dissolving of governments, to need any more to be said of it; and there wants not much argument to prove that where the society is dissolved, the government cannot remain; that being as impossible as for the frame of a house to subsist when the materials of it are scattered and displaced by a whirlwind, or jumbled into a confused heap by an earthquake.

212. Besides this overturning from without, governments are dissolved from within: First. When the legislative is altered, civil society being a state of peace amongst those who are of it, from whom the state of war is excluded by the umpirage which they have provided in their legislative for the ending all differences that may arise amongst any of them; it is in their legislative that the members of a commonwealth are united and combined together into one coherent living body. This is the soul that gives form, life, and unity to the commonwealth; from hence the several members have their mutual influence, sympathy, and connection; and therefore when the legislative is broken, or dissolved, dissolution and death follows. For the essence and union of the society consisting in having one will, the legislative, when once established by the majority, has the declaring and, as it were, keeping of that will. The constitution of the legislative is the first and fundamental act of society, whereby provision is made for the continuation of their union under the direction of persons and bonds of laws, made by persons authorised thereunto, by the consent and appointment of the people, without which no one man, or number of men, amongst them can have authority of making laws that shall be binding to the rest. When any one, or more, shall take upon them to make laws whom the people have not appointed so to do, they make laws without authority, which the people are not therefore bound to obey; by which means they come again to be out of subjection, and may constitute to themselves a new legislative, as they think best, being in full liberty to resist the force of those who, without authority, would impose anything upon them. Every one is at the disposure of his own will, when those who had, by the delegation of the society, the declaring of the public will, are excluded from it, and others usurp the place who have no such authority or delegation.

213. This being usually brought about by such in the commonwealth, who misuse the power they have, it is hard to consider it aright, and know at whose door to lay it, without knowing the form of government in which it happens. Let us suppose, then, the legislative placed in the concurrence of three distinct persons:- First, a single hereditary person having the constant, supreme, executive power, and with it the power of convoking and dissolving the other two within certain periods of time. Secondly, an assembly of hereditary nobility. Thirdly, an assembly of representatives chosen, pro tempore, by the people. Such a form of government supposed, it is evident:

214. First, that when such a single person or prince sets up his own arbitrary will in place of the laws which are the will of the society declared by the legislative, then the legislative is changed. For that being, in effect, the legislative whose rules and laws are put in execution, and required to be obeyed, when other laws are set up, and other rules pretended and enforced than what the legislative, constituted by the society, have enacted, it is plain that the legislative is changed. Whoever introduces new laws, not being thereunto authorised, by the fundamental appointment of the society, or subverts the old, disowns and overturns the power by which they were made, and so sets up a new legislative.

215. Secondly, when the prince hinders the legislative from assembling in its due time, or from acting freely, pursuant to those ends for which it was constituted, the legislative is altered. For it is not a certain number of men—no, nor their meeting, unless they have also freedom of debating and leisure of perfecting what is for the good of the society, wherein the legislative consists; when these are taken away, or altered, so as to deprive the society of the due exercise of their power, the legislative is truly altered. For it is not names that constitute governments, but the use and exercise of those powers that were intended to accompany them; so that he who takes away the freedom, or hinders the acting of the legislative in its due seasons, in effect takes away the legislative, and puts an end to the government.

216. Thirdly, when, by the arbitrary power of the prince, the electors or ways of election are altered without the consent and contrary to the common interest of the people, there also the legislative is altered. For if others than those whom the society hath authorised thereunto do choose, or in another way than what the society hath prescribed, those chosen are not the legislative appointed by the people.

217. Fourthly, the delivery also of the people into the subjection of a foreign power, either by the prince or by the legislative, is certainly a change of the legislative, and so a dissolution of the government. For the end why people entered into society being to be preserved one entire, free, independent society to be governed by its own laws, this is lost whenever they are given up into the power of another.

218. Why, in such a constitution as this, the dissolution of the government in these cases is to be imputed to the prince is evident, because he, having the force, treasure, and offices of the State to employ, and often persuading himself or being flattered by others, that, as supreme magistrate, he is incapable of control; he alone is in a condition to make great advances towards such changes under pretence of lawful authority, and has it in his hands to terrify or suppress opposers as factious, seditious, and enemies to the government; whereas no other part of the legislative, or people, is capable by themselves to attempt any alteration of the legislative without open and visible rebellion, apt enough to be taken notice of, which, when it prevails, produces effects very little different from foreign conquest. Besides, the prince, in such a form of government, having the power of dissolving the other parts of the legislative, and thereby rendering them private persons, they can never, in opposition to him, or without his concurrence, alter the legislative by a law, his consent being necessary to give any of their decrees that sanction. But yet so far as the other parts of the legislative any way contribute to any attempt upon the government, and do either promote, or not, what lies in them, hinder such designs, they are guilty, and partake in this, which is certainly the greatest crime men can be guilty of one towards another.

219. There is one way more whereby such a government may be dissolved, and that is: When he who has the supreme executive power neglects and abandons that charge, so that the laws already made can no longer be put in execution; this is demonstratively to reduce all to anarchy, and so effectively to dissolve the government. For laws not being made for themselves, but to be, by their execution, the bonds of the society to keep every part of the body politic in its due place and function. When that totally ceases, the government visibly ceases, and the people become a confused multitude without order or connection. Where there is no longer the administration of justice for the securing of men's rights, nor any remaining power within the community to direct the force, or provide for the necessities of the public, there certainly is no government left. Where the laws cannot be executed it is all one as if there were no laws, and a government without laws is, I suppose, a mystery in politics inconceivable to human capacity, and inconsistent with human society.

220. In these, and the like cases, when the government is dissolved, the people are at liberty to provide for themselves by erecting a new legislative differing from the other by the change of persons, or form, or both, as they shall find it most for their safety and good. For the society can never, by the fault of another, lose the native and original right it has to preserve itself, which can only be done by a settled legislative and a fair and impartial execution of the laws made by it. But the state of mankind is not so miserable that they are not capable of using this remedy till it be too late to look for any. To tell people they may provide for themselves by erecting a new legislative, when, by oppression, artifice, or being delivered over to a foreign power, their old one is gone, is only to tell them they may expect relief when it is too late, and the evil is past cure. This is, in effect, no more than to bid them first be slaves, and then to take care of their liberty, and, when their chains are on, tell them they may act like free men. This, if barely so, is rather mockery than relief, and men can never be secure from tyranny if there be no means to escape it till they are perfectly under it; and, therefore, it is that they have not only a right to get out of it, but to prevent it.

221. There is, therefore, secondly, another way whereby governments are dissolved, and that is, when the legislative, or the prince, either of them act contrary to their trust. For the legislative acts against the trust reposed in them when they endeavour to invade the property of the subject, and to make themselves, or any part of the community, masters or arbitrary disposers of the lives, liberties, or fortunes of the people.

222. The reason why men enter into society is the preservation of their property; and the end while they choose and authorise a legislative is that there may be laws made, and rules set, as guards and fences to the properties of all the society, to limit the power and moderate the dominion of every part and member of the society. For since it can never be supposed to be the will of the society that the legislative should have a power to destroy that which every one designs to secure by entering into society, and for which the people submitted themselves to legislators of their own making: whenever the legislators endeavour to take away and destroy the property of the people, or to reduce them to slavery under arbitrary power, they put themselves into a state of war with the people, who are thereupon absolved from any farther obedience, and are left to the common refuge which God hath provided for all men against force and violence. Whensoever, therefore, the legislative shall transgress this fundamental rule of society, and either by ambition, fear, folly, or corruption, endeavour to grasp themselves, or put into the hands of any other, an absolute power over the lives, liberties, and estates of the people, by this breach of trust they forfeit the power the people had put into their hands for quite contrary ends, and it devolves to the people, who have a right to resume their original liberty, and by the establishment of a new legislative (such as they shall think fit), provide for their own safety and security, which is the end for which they are in society. What I have said here concerning the legislative in general holds true also concerning the supreme executor, who having a double trust put in him, both to have a part in the legislative and the supreme execution of the law, acts against both, when he goes about to set up his own

arbitrary will as the law of the society. He acts also contrary to his trust when he employs the force, treasure, and offices of the society to corrupt the representatives and gain them to his purposes, when he openly pre-engages the electors, and prescribes, to their choice, such whom he has, by solicitation, threats, promises, or otherwise, won to his designs, and employs them to bring in such who have promised beforehand what to vote and what to enact. Thus to regulate candidates and electors, and new model the ways of election, what is it but to cut up the government by the roots, and poison the very fountain of public security? For the people having reserved to themselves the choice of their representatives as the fence to their properties, could do it for no other end but that they might always be freely chosen, and so chosen, freely act and advise as the necessity of the commonwealth and the public good should, upon examination and mature debate, be judged to require. This, those who give their votes before they hear the debate, and have weighed the reasons on all sides, are not capable of doing. To prepare such an assembly as this, and endeavour to set up the declared abettors of his own will, for the true representatives of the people, and the law-makers of the society, is certainly as great a breach of trust, and as perfect a declaration of a design to subvert the government, as is possible to be met with. To which, if one shall add rewards and punishments visibly employed to the same end, and all the arts of perverted law made use of to take off and destroy all that stand in the way of such a design, and will not comply and consent to betray the liberties of their country, it will be past doubt what is doing. What power they ought to have in the society who thus employ it contrary to the trust that along with it in its first institution, is easy to determine; and one cannot but see that he who has once attempted any such thing as this cannot any longer be trusted.

223. To this, perhaps, it will be said that the people being ignorant and always discontented, to lay the foundation of government in the unsteady opinion and uncertain humour of the people, is to expose it to certain ruin; and no government will be able long to subsist if the people may set up a new legislative whenever they take offence at the old one. To this I answer, quite the contrary. People are not so easily got out of their old forms as some are apt to suggest. They are hardly to be prevailed with to amend the acknowledged faults in the frame they have been accustomed to. And if there be any original defects, or adventitious ones introduced by time or corruption, it is not an easy thing to get them changed, even when all the world sees there is an opportunity for it. This slowness and aversion in the people to quit their old constitutions has in the many revolutions that have been seen in this kingdom, in this and former ages, still kept us to, or after some interval of fruitless attempts, still brought us back again to, our old legislative of king, lords and commons; and whatever provocations have made the crown be taken from some of our princes' heads, they never carried the people so far as to place it in another line.

224. But it will be said this hypothesis lays a ferment for frequent rebellion. To which I answer: First: no more than any other hypothesis. For when the people are made miserable, and find themselves exposed to the ill usage of arbitrary power, cry up their governors as much as you will for sons of Jupiter, let them be sacred and divine, descended or authorised from Heaven; give them out for whom or what you please, the same will happen. The people generally ill treated, and contrary to right, will be ready upon any occasion to ease themselves of a burden that sits heavy upon them. They will wish and seek for the opportunity, which in the change, weakness, and accidents of human affairs, seldom delays long to offer itself He must have lived but a little while in the world, who has not seen examples of this in his time; and he must have read very little who cannot produce examples of it in all sorts of governments in the world.

225. Secondly: I answer, such revolutions happen not upon every little mismanagement in public affairs. Great mistakes in the ruling part, many wrong and inconvenient laws, and all the slips of human frailty will be borne by the people without mutiny or murmur. But if a long train of abuses, prevarications, and artifices, all tending the same way, make the design visible to the people, and they cannot but feel what they lie under, and see whither they are going, it is not to be wondered that they should then rouse themselves, and endeavour to put the rule into such hands which may secure to them the ends for which government was at first erected, and without which, ancient names and specious forms are so far from being better, that they are much worse than the state of Nature or pure anarchy; the inconveniencies being all as great and as near, but the remedy farther off and more difficult.

226. Thirdly: I answer, that this power in the people of providing for their safety anew by a new legislative when their legislators have acted contrary to their trust by invading their property, is the best fence against rebellion, and the probable means to hinder it. For rebellion being an opposition, not to persons, but authority, which is founded only in the constitutions and laws of the government: those, whoever they be, who, by force, break through, and, by force, justify their violation of them, are truly and properly rebels. For when men, by entering into society and civil government, have excluded force, and introduced laws for the preservation of property, peace, and unity amongst themselves, those who set up force again in opposition to the laws, do re-

bellare—that is, bring back again the state of war, and are properly rebels, which they who are in power, by the pretence they have to authority, the temptation of force they have in their hands, and the flattery of those about them being likeliest to do, the proper way to prevent the evil is to show them the danger and injustice of it who are under the greatest temptation to run into it.

227. In both the forementioned cases, when either the legislative is changed, or the legislators act contrary to the end for which they were constituted, those who are guilty are guilty of rebellion. For if any one by force takes away the established legislative of any society, and the laws by them made, pursuant to their trust, he thereby takes away the umpirage which every one had consented to for a peaceable decision of all their controversies, and a bar to the state of war amongst them. They who remove or change the legislative take away this decisive power, which nobody can have but by the appointment and consent of the people, and so destroying the authority which the people did, and nobody else can, set up, and introducing a power which the people hath not authorised, actually introduce a state of war, which is that of force without authority; and thus by removing the legislative established by the society, in whose decisions the people acquiesced and united as to that of their own will, they untie the knot, and expose the people anew to the state of war. And if those, who by force take away the legislative, are rebels, the legislators themselves, as has been shown, can be no less esteemed so, when they who were set up for the protection and preservation of the people, their liberties and properties shall by force invade and endeavour to take them away; and so they putting themselves into a state of war with those who made them the protectors and guardians of their peace, are properly, and with the greatest aggravation, rebellantes, rebels.

228. But if they who say it lays a foundation for rebellion mean that it may occasion civil wars or intestine broils to tell the people they are absolved from obedience when illegal attempts are made upon their liberties or properties, and may oppose the unlawful violence of those who were their magistrates when they invade their properties, contrary to the trust put in them, and that, therefore, this doctrine is not to be allowed, being so destructive to the peace of the world; they may as well say, upon the same ground, that honest men may not oppose robbers or pirates, because this may occasion disorder or bloodshed. If any mischief come in such cases, it is not to be charged upon him who defends his own right, but on him that invades his neighbour's. If the innocent honest man must quietly quit all he has for peace sake to him who will lay violent hands upon it, I desire it may be considered what kind of a peace there will be in the world which consists only in violence and rapine, and which is to be maintained only for the benefit of robbers and oppressors. Who would not think it an admirable peace betwixt the mighty and the mean, when the lamb, without resistance, yielded his throat to be torn by the imperious wolf? Polyphemus's den gives us a perfect pattern of such a peace. Such a government wherein Ulysses and his companions had nothing to do but quietly to suffer themselves to be devoured. And no doubt Ulysses, who was a prudent man, preached up passive obedience, and exhorted them to a quiet submission by representing to them of what concernment peace was to mankind, and by showing what inconveniencies might happen if they should offer to resist Polyphemus, who had now the power over them.

229. The end of government is the good of mankind; and which is best for mankind, that the people should be always exposed to the boundless will of tyranny, or that the rulers should be sometimes liable to be opposed when they grow exorbitant in the use of their power, and employ it for the destruction, and not the preservation, of the properties of their people?

230. Nor let any one say that mischief can arise from hence as often as it shall please a busy head or turbulent spirit to desire the alteration of the government. It is true such men may stir whenever they please, but it will be only to their own just ruin and perdition. For till the mischief be grown general, and the ill designs of the rulers become visible, or their attempts sensible to the greater part, the people, who are more disposed to suffer than right themselves by resistance, are not apt to stir. The examples of particular injustice or oppression of here and there an unfortunate man moves them not. But if they universally have a persuasion grounded upon manifest evidence that designs are carrying on against their liberties, and the general course and tendency of things cannot but give them strong suspicions of the evil intention of their governors, who is to be blamed for it? Who can help it if they, who might avoid it, bring themselves into this suspicion? Are the people to be blamed if they have the sense of rational creatures, and can think of things no otherwise than as they find and feel them? And is it not rather their fault who put things in such a posture that they would not have them thought as they are? I grant that the pride, ambition, and turbulency of private men have sometimes caused great disorders in commonwealths, and factions have been fatal to states and kingdoms. But whether the mischief hath oftener begun in the people's wantonness, and a desire to cast off the lawful authority of their rulers, or in the rulers' insolence and endeavours to get and exercise an arbitrary power over their people, whether oppression or disobedience gave the first rise to the disorder, I leave it to impartial history to determine. This I am sure, whoever, either ruler or subject, by force goes about to invade the rights of either prince

or people, and lays the foundation for overturning the constitution and frame of any just government, he is guilty of the greatest crime I think a man is capable of, being to answer for all those mischiefs of blood, rapine, and desolation, which the breaking to pieces of governments bring on a country; and he who does it is justly to be esteemed the common enemy and pest of mankind, and is to be treated accordingly.

231. That subjects or foreigners attempting by force on the properties of any people may be resisted with force is agreed on all hands; but that magistrates doing the same thing may be resisted, hath of late been denied; as if those who had the greatest privileges and advantages by the law had thereby a power to break those laws by which alone they were set in a better place than their brethren; whereas their offence is thereby the greater, both as being ungrateful for the greater share they have by the law, and breaking also that trust which is put into their hands by their brethren.

232. Whosoever uses force without right—as every one does in society who does it without law—puts himself into a state of war with those against whom he so uses it, and in that state all former ties are cancelled, all other rights cease, and every one has a right to defend himself, and to resist the aggressor. This is so evident that Barclay himself—that great assertor of the power and sacredness of kings—is forced to confess that it is lawful for the people, in some cases, to resist their king, and that, too, in a chapter wherein he pretends to show that the Divine law shuts up the people from all manner of rebellion. Whereby it is evident, even by his own doctrine, that since they may, in some cases, resist, all resisting of princes is not rebellion.

His words are these:

"Quod siquis dicat, Ergone populus tyrannicae crudelitati et furori jugulum semper praebebit? Ergone multitudo civitates suas fame, ferro, et flamma vastari, seque, conjuges, et liberos fortunae ludibrio et tyranni libidini exponi, inque omnia vitae pericula omnesque miserias et molestias a rege deduci patientur? Num illis quod omni animantium generi est a natura tributum, denegari debet, ut sc. vim vi repellant, seseque ab injuria tueantur? Huic breviter responsum sit, populo universo negari defensionem, quae juris naturalis est, neque ultionem quae praeter naturam est adversus regem concedi debere. Quapropter si rex non in singulares tantum personas aliquot privatum odium exerceat, sed corpus etiam reipublicae, cujus ipse, caput est—i.e., totum populum, vel insignem aliquam ejus partem immani et intoleranda saevitia seu tyrannide divexet; populo, quidem hoc casu resistendi ac tuendi se ab injuria potestas competit, sed tuendi se tantum, non enim in principem invadendi: et restituendae injuriae illatae, non recedendi a debita reverentia propter acceptum injuriam. Praesentem denique impetum propulsandi non vim praeteritam ulciscendi jus habet. Horum enim alterum a natura est, ut vitani scilicet corpusque tueamur. Alterum vero contra naturam, ut inferior de superiori supplicium sumat. Quod itaque populus malum, antequam factum sit, impedire potest, ne fiat, id postquam factum est, in regem authorem sceleris vindicare non potest, populus igitur hoc amplius quam privatus quispiam habet: Quod huic vel ipsis adversariis judicibus, excepto Buchanano, nullum nisi in patientia remedium superest. Cum ille si intolerabilis tyrannis est (modicum enim ferre omnino debet) resistere cum reverentia possit."— Barclay, Contra Monarchomachos, iii. 8.

In English thus:

233. "But if any one should ask: Must the people, then, always lay themselves open to the cruelty and rage of tyranny—must they see their cities pillaged and laid in ashes, their wives and children exposed to the tyrant's lust and fury, and themselves and families reduced by their king to ruin and all the miseries of want and oppression, and yet sit still— must men alone be debarred the common privilege of opposing force with force, which Nature allows so freely to all other creatures for their preservation from injury? I answer: Self-defence is a part of the law of Nature; nor can it be denied the community, even against the king himself; but to revenge themselves upon him must, by no means, be allowed them, it being not agreeable to that law. Wherefore, if the king shall show an hatred, not only to some particular persons, but sets himself against the body of the commonwealth, whereof he is the head, and shall, with intolerable ill-usage, cruelly tyrannise over the whole, or a considerable part of the people; in this case the people have a right to resist and defend themselves from injury; but it must be with this caution, that they only defend themselves, but do not attack their prince. They may repair the damages received, but must not, for any provocation, exceed the bounds of due reverence and respect. They may repulse the present attempt, but must not revenge past violences. For it is natural for us to defend life and limb, but that an inferior should punish a superior is against nature. The mischief which is designed them the people may prevent before it be done, but, when it is done, they must not revenge it on the king, though author of the villany. This, therefore, is the privilege of the people in general above what any private person hath: That particular men are allowed, by our adversaries themselves (Buchanan only excepted),

to have no other remedy but patience; but the body of the people may, with respect, resist intolerable tyranny, for when it is but moderate they ought to endure it."

234. Thus far that great advocate of monarchical power allows of resistance.

235. It is true, he has annexed two limitations to it, to no purpose: First. He says it must be with reverence. Secondly. It must be without retribution or punishment; and the reason he gives is, "because an inferior cannot punish a superior." First. How to resist force without striking again, or how to strike with reverence, will need some skill to make intelligible. He that shall oppose an assault only with a shield to receive the blows, or in any more respectful posture, without a sword in his hand to abate the confidence and force of the assailant, will quickly be at an end of his resistance, and will find such a defence serve only to draw on himself the worse usage. This is as ridiculous a way of resisting as Juvenal thought it of fighting: Ubi tu pulsas, ego vapulo tantum. And the success of the combat will be unavoidably the same he there describes it: Libertas pauperis haec est; Pulsatus rogat, et pugnis concisus, adorat, Ut liceat paucis cum dentibus inde reverti. This will always be the event of such an imaginary resistance, where men may not strike again. He, therefore, who may resist must be allowed to strike. And then let our author, or anybody else, join a knock on the head or a cut on the face with as much reverence and respect as he thinks fit. He that can reconcile blows and reverence may, for aught I know, deserve for his pains a civil, respectful cudgelling wherever he can meet with it. Secondly. As to his second—"An inferior cannot punish a superior"—that is true, generally speaking, whilst he is his superior. But to resist force with force, being the state of war that levels the parties, cancels all former relation of reverence, respect, and superiority; and then the odds that remains is—that he who opposes the unjust aggressor has this superiority over him, that he has a right, when he prevails, to punish the offender, both for the breach of the peace and all the evils that followed upon it. Barclay, therefore, in another place, more coherently to himself, denies it to be lawful to resist a king in any case. But he there assigns two cases whereby a king may unking himself.

His words are:

"Quid ergo, nulline casus incidere possunt quibus populo sese erigere atque in regem impotentius dominantem arma capere et invadere jure suo suaque authoritate liceat? Nulli certe quamdiu rex manet. Semper enim ex divinis id obstat, Regem honorificato, et qui potestati resistit, Dei ordinationi resistit; non alias igitur in eum populo potestas est quam si id committat propter quod ipso jure rex esse desinat. Tunc enim se ipse principatu exuit atque in privatis constituit liber; hoc modo populus et superior efficitur, reverso ad eum scilicet jure illo quod ante regem inauguratum in interregno habuit. At sunt paucorum generum commissa ejusmodi quae hunc effectum pariunt. At ego cum plurima animo perlustrem, duo tantum invenio, duos, inquam, casus quibus rex ipso facto ex rege non regem se facit et omni honore et dignitate regali atque in subditos potestate destituit; quorum etiam meminit Winzerus. Horum unus est, si regnum disperdat, quemadmodum de Nerone fertur, quod is nempe senatum populumque Romanum atque adeo urbem ipsam ferro flammaque vastare, ac novas sibi sedes quaerere decrevisset. Et de Caligula, quod palam denunciarit se neque civem neque principem senatui amplius fore, inque animo habuerit, interempto utriusque ordinis electissimo, quoque Alexandriam commigrare, ac ut populum uno ictu interimeret, unam ei cervicem optavit. Talia cum rex aliquis meditatur et molitur serio, omnem regnandi curam et animum ilico abjicit, ac proinde imperium in subditos amittit, ut dominus servi pro derelicto habiti, dominium. 236. "Arlter casus est, si rex in alicujus clientelam se contulit, ac regnum quod liberum a majoribus et populo traditum accepit, alienae ditioni mancipavit. Nam tunc quamvis forte non ea mente id agit populo plane ut incommodet; tamen quia quod praecipuum est regiae dignitatis amisit, ut summus scilicet in regno secundum Deum sit, et solo Deo inferior, atque populum etiam totum ignorantem vel invitum, cujus libertatem sartam et tectam conservare debuit, in alterius gentis ditionem et potestatem dedidit; hac velut quadam rengi abalienatione effecit, ut nec quod ipse in regno imperium habuit retineat, nec in eum cui collatum voluit, juris quicquam transferat, atque ita eo facto liberum jam et suae potestatis populum relinquit, cujus rei exemplum unum annales Scotici suppeditant."—Barclay, Contra Monarchomachos, I. iii., c. 16.

Which may be thus Englished:

237. "What, then, can there no case happen wherein the people may of right, and by their own authority, help themselves, take arms, and set upon their king, imperiously domineering over them? None at all whilst he remains a king. 'Honour the king,' and 'he that resists the power, resists the ordinance of God,' are Divine oracles that will never permit it. The people, therefore, can never come by a power over him unless he does something that makes him cease to be a king; for then he divests himself of his crown and dignity, and returns to the state of a private man, and the people become free and superior; the power which they had in the inter-

regnum, before they crowned him king, devolving to them again. But there are but few miscarriages which bring the matter to this state. After considering it well on all sides, I can find but two. Two cases there are, I say, whereby a king, ipso facto, becomes no king, and loses all power and regal authority over his people, which are also taken notice of by Winzerus. The first is, if he endeavour to overturn the government—that is, if he have a purpose and design to ruin the kingdom and commonwealth, as it is recorded of Nero that he re-solved to cut off the senate and people of Rome, lay the city waste with fire and sword, and then remove to some other place; and of Caligula, that he openly declared that he would be no longer a head to the people or senate, and that he had it in his thoughts to cut off the worthiest men of both ranks, and then retire to Alexan-dria; and he wished that the people had but one neck that he might dispatch them all at a blow. Such designs as these, when any king harbours in his thoughts, and seriously promotes, he immediately gives up all care and thought of the commonwealth, and, consequently, forfeits the power of governing his subjects, as a mas-ter does the dominion over his slaves whom he hath abandoned.

238. "The other case is, when a king makes himself the dependent of another, and subjects his kingdom, which his ancestors left him, and the people put free into his hands, to the dominion of another. For however, perhaps, it may not be his intention to prejudice the people, yet because he has hereby lost the principal part of regal dignity—viz., to be next and immediately under God, supreme in his kingdom; and also because he betrayed or forced his people, whose liberty he ought to have carefully preserved, into the power and domin-ion of a foreign nation. By this, as it were, alienation of his kingdom, he himself loses the power he had in it before, without transferring any the least right to those on whom he would have bestowed it; and so by this act sets the people free, and leaves them at their own disposal. One example of this is to be found in the Scotch annals."

239. In these cases Barclay, the great champion of absolute monarchy, is forced to allow that a king may be resisted, and ceases to be a king. That is in short—not to multiply cases—in whatsoever he has no authority, there he is no king, and may be resisted: for wheresoever the authority ceases, the king ceases too, and be-comes like other men who have no authority. And these two cases that he instances differ little from those above mentioned, to be destructive to governments, only that he has omitted the principle from which his doc-trine flows, and that is the breach of trust in not preserving the form of government agreed on, and in not in-tending the end of government itself, which is the public good and preservation of property. When a king has dethroned himself, and put himself in a state of war with his people, what shall hinder them from prosecuting him who is no king, as they would any other man, who has put himself into a state of war with them, Barclay, and those of his opinion, would do well to tell us. Bilson, a bishop of our Church, and a great stickler for the power and prerogative of princes, does, if I mistake not, in his treatise of "Christian Subjection," acknowledge that princes may forfeit their power and their title to the obedience of their subjects; and if there needed au-thority in a case where reason is so plain, I could send my reader to Bracton, Fortescue, and the author of the "Mirror," and others, writers that cannot be suspected to be ignorant of our government, or enemies to it. But I thought Hooker alone might be enough to satisfy those men who, relying on him for their ecclesiastical polity, are by a strange fate carried to deny those principles upon which he builds it. Whether they are herein made the tools of cunninger workmen, to pull down their own fabric, they were best look. This I am sure, their civil policy is so new, so dangerous, and so destructive to both rulers and people, that as former ages never could bear the broaching of it, so it may be hoped those to come, redeemed from the impositions of these Egyptian under-taskmasters, will abhor the memory of such servile flatterers, who, whilst it seemed to serve their turn, resolved all government into absolute tyranny, and would have all men born to what their mean souls fitted them—slavery.

240. Here it is like the common question will be made: Who shall be judge whether the prince or legislative act contrary to their trust? This, perhaps, ill-affected and factious men may spread amongst the people, when the prince only makes use of his due prerogative. To this I reply, The people shall be judge; for who shall be judge whether his trustee or deputy acts well and according to the trust reposed in him, but he who deputes him and must, by having deputed him, have still a power to discard him when he fails in his trust? If this be reasonable in particular cases of private men, why should it be otherwise in that of the greatest moment, where the welfare of millions is concerned and also where the evil, if not prevented, is greater, and the redress very difficult, dear, and dangerous?

241. But, farther, this question, Who shall be judge? cannot mean that there is no judge at all. For where there is no judicature on earth to decide controversies amongst men, God in heaven is judge. He alone, it is true, is judge of the right. But every man is judge for himself, as in all other cases so in this, whether another hath put himself into a state of war with him, and whether he should appeal to the supreme judge, as Jephtha did.

242. If a controversy arise betwixt a prince and some of the people in a matter where the law is silent or doubtful, and the thing be of great consequence, I should think the proper umpire in such a case should be the body of the people. For in such cases where the prince hath a trust reposed in him, and is dispensed from the common, ordinary rules of the law, there, if any men find themselves aggrieved, and think the prince acts contrary to, or beyond that trust, who so proper to judge as the body of the people (who at first lodged that trust in him) how far they meant it should extend? But if the prince, or whoever they be in the administration, decline that way of determination, the appeal then lies nowhere but to Heaven. Force between either persons who have no known superior on earth or, which permits no appeal to a judge on earth, being properly a state of war, wherein the appeal lies only to heaven; and in that state the injured party must judge for himself when he will think fit to make use of that appeal and put himself upon it.

243. To conclude. The power that every individual gave the society when he entered into it can never revert to the individuals again, as long as the society lasts, but will always remain in the community; because without this there can be no community—no commonwealth, which is contrary to the original agreement; so also when the society hath placed the legislative in any assembly of men, to continue in them and their successors, with direction and authority for providing such successors, the legislative can never revert to the people whilst that government lasts: because, having provided a legislative with power to continue for ever, they have given up their political power to the legislative, and cannot resume it. But if they have set limits to the duration of their legislative, and made this supreme power in any person or assembly only temporary; or else when, by the miscarriages of those in authority, it is forfeited; upon the forfeiture of their rulers, or at the determination of the time set, it reverts to the society, and the people have a right to act as supreme, and continue the legislative in themselves or place it in a new form, or new hands, as they think good.

The End

**The Social Contract from 1762**


by Jean Jacques Rousseau


## BOOK I

I MEAN to inquire if, in the civil order, there can be any sure and legitimate rule of administration, men being taken as they are and laws as they might be. In this inquiry I shall endeavour always to unite what right sanctions with what is prescribed by interest, in order that justice and utility may in no case be divided.

I enter upon my task without proving the importance of the subject. I shall be asked if I am a prince or a legislator, to write on politics. I answer that I am neither, and that is why I do so. If I were a prince or a legislator, I should not waste time in saying what wants doing; I should do it, or hold my peace.

As I was born a citizen of a free State, and a member of the Sovereign, I feel that, however feeble the influence my voice can have on public affairs, the right of voting on them makes it my duty to study them: and I am happy, when I reflect upon governments, to find my inquiries always furnish me with new reasons for loving that of my own country.

## 1. SUBJECT OF THE FIRST BOOK

MAN is born free; and everywhere he is in chains. One thinks himself the master of others, and still remains a greater slave than they. How did this change come about? I do not know. What can make it legitimate? That question I think I can answer.

If I took into account only force, and the effects derived from it, I should say: "As long as a people is compelled to obey, and obeys, it does well; as soon as it can shake off the yoke, and shakes it off, it does still better; for, regaining its liberty by the same right as took it away, either it is justified in resuming it, or there was no justification for those who took it away." But the social order is a sacred right which is the basis of all other rights. Nevertheless, this right does not come from nature, and must therefore be founded on conventions. Before coming to that, I have to prove what I have just asserted.

## 2. THE FIRST SOCIETIES

THE most ancient of all societies, and the only one that is natural, is the family: and even so the children remain attached to the father only so long as they need him for their preservation. As soon as this need ceases, the natural bond is dissolved. The children, released from the obedience they owed to the father, and the father, released from the care he owed his children, return equally to independence. If they remain united, they continue so no longer naturally, but voluntarily; and the family itself is then maintained only by convention.

This common liberty results from the nature of man. His first law is to provide for his own preservation, his first cares are those which he owes to himself; and, as soon as he reaches years of discretion, he is the sole judge of the proper means of preserving himself, and consequently becomes his own master.

The family then may be called the first model of political societies: the ruler corresponds to the father, and the people to the children; and all, being born free and equal, alienate their liberty only for their own advantage. The whole difference is that, in the family, the love of the father for his children repays him for the care he takes of them, while, in the State, the pleasure of commanding takes the place of the love which the chief cannot have for the peoples under him.

Grotius denies that all human power is established in favour of the governed, and quotes slavery as an example. His usual method of reasoning is constantly to establish right by fact.[1] It would be possible to employ a more logical method, but none could be more favourable to tyrants.

It is then, according to Grotius, doubtful whether the human race belongs to a hundred men, or that hundred men to the human race: and, throughout his book, he seems to incline to the former alternative, which is also the view of Hobbes. On this showing, the human species is divided into so many herds of cattle, each with its ruler, who keeps guard over them for the purpose of devouring them.

As a shepherd is of a nature superior to that of his flock, the shepherds of men, i.e., their rulers, are of a nature superior to that of the peoples under them. Thus, Philo tells us, the Emperor Caligula reasoned, concluding equally well either that kings were gods, or that men were beasts.

The reasoning of Caligula agrees with that of Hobbes and Grotius. Aristotle, before any of them, had said that men are by no means equal naturally, but that some are born for slavery, and others for dominion.

Aristotle was right; but he took the effect for the cause. Nothing can be more certain than that every man born in slavery is born for slavery. Slaves lose everything in their chains, even the desire of escaping from them: they love their servitude, as the comrades of Ulysses loved their brutish condition.[2] If then there are slaves by nature, it is because there have been slaves against nature. Force made the first slaves, and their cowardice perpetuated the condition.

I have said nothing of King Adam, or Emperor Noah, father of the three great monarchs who shared out the universe, like the children of Saturn, whom some scholars have recognised in them. I trust to getting due thanks for my moderation; for, being a direct descendant of one of these princes, perhaps of the eldest branch, how do I know that a verification of titles might not leave me the legitimate king of the human race? In any case, there can be no doubt that Adam was sovereign of the world, as Robinson Crusoe was of his island, as long as he was its only inhabitant; and this empire had the advantage that the monarch, safe on his throne, had no rebellions, wars, or conspirators to fear.

## 3. THE RIGHT OF THE STRONGEST

THE strongest is never strong enough to be always the master, unless he transforms strength into right, and obedience into duty. Hence the right of the strongest, which, though to all seeming meant ironically, is really laid down as a fundamental principle. But are we never to have an explanation of this phrase? Force is a physical power, and I fail to see what moral effect it can have. To yield to force is an act of necessity, not of will — at the most, an act of prudence. In what sense can it be a duty?

Suppose for a moment that this so-called "right" exists. I maintain that the sole result is a mass of inexplicable nonsense. For, if force creates right, the effect changes with the cause: every force that is greater than the first succeeds to its right. As soon as it is possible to disobey with impunity, disobedience is legitimate; and, the strongest being always in the right, the only thing that matters is to act so as to become the strongest. But what kind of right is that which perishes when force fails? If we must obey perforce, there is no need to obey because we ought; and if we are not forced to obey, we are under no obligation to do so. Clearly, the word "right" adds nothing to force: in this connection, it means absolutely nothing.

Obey the powers that be. If this means yield to force, it is a good precept, but superfluous: I can answer for its never being violated. All power comes from God, I admit; but so does all sickness: does that mean that we are forbidden to call in the doctor? A brigand surprises me at the edge of a wood: must I not merely surrender my purse on compulsion; but, even if I could withhold it, am I in conscience bound to give it up? For certainly the pistol he holds is also a power.

Let us then admit that force does not create right, and that we are obliged to obey only legitimate powers. In that case, my original question recurs.

## 4. SLAVERY

SINCE no man has a natural authority over his fellow, and force creates no right, we must conclude that conventions form the basis of all legitimate authority among men.

If an individual, says Grotius, can alienate his liberty and make himself the slave of a master, why could not a whole people do the same and make itself subject to a king? There are in this passage plenty of ambiguous words which would need explaining; but let us confine ourselves to the word *alienate*. To alienate is to give or to sell. Now, a man who becomes the slave of another does not give himself; he sells himself, at the least for his subsistence: but for what does a people sell itself? A king is so far from furnishing his subjects with their subsistence that he gets his own only from them; and, according to Rabelais, kings do not live on nothing. Do subjects then give their persons on condition that the king takes their goods also? I fail to see what they have left to preserve.

It will be said that the despot assures his subjects civil tranquillity. Granted; but what do they gain, if the wars his ambition brings down upon them, his insatiable avidity, and the vexatious conduct of his ministers press harder on them than their own dissensions would have done? What do they gain, if the very tranquillity they enjoy is one of their miseries? Tranquillity is found also in dungeons; but is that enough to make them desirable places to live in? The Greeks imprisoned in the cave of the Cyclops lived there very tranquilly, while they were awaiting their turn to be devoured.

To say that a man gives himself gratuitously, is to say what is absurd and inconceivable; such an act is null and illegitimate, from the mere fact that he who does it is out of his mind. To say the same of a whole people is to suppose a people of madmen; and madness creates no right.

Even if each man could alienate himself, he could not alienate his children: they are born men and free; their liberty belongs to them, and no one but they has the right to dispose of it. Before they come to years of discretion, the father can, in their name, lay down conditions for their preservation and well-being, but he cannot give them irrevocably and without conditions: such a gift is contrary to the ends of nature, and exceeds the rights of paternity. It would therefore be necessary, in order to legitimise an arbitrary government, that in every generation the people should be in a position to accept or reject it; but, were this so, the government would be no longer arbitrary.

To renounce liberty is to renounce being a man, to surrender the rights of humanity and even its duties. For him who renounces everything no indemnity is possible. Such a renunciation is incompatible with man's nature; to remove all liberty from his will is to remove all morality from his acts. Finally, it is an empty and contradictory convention that sets up, on the one side, absolute authority, and, on the other, unlimited obedience. Is it not clear that we can be under no obligation to a person from whom we have the right to exact everything? Does not this condition alone, in the absence of equivalence or exchange, in itself involve the nullity of the act? For what right can my slave have against me, when all that he has belongs to me, and, his right being mine, this right of mine against myself is a phrase devoid of meaning?

Grotius and the rest find in war another origin for the so-called right of slavery. The victor having, as they hold, the right of killing the vanquished, the latter can buy back his life at the price of his liberty; and this convention is the more legitimate because it is to the advantage of both parties.

But it is clear that this supposed right to kill the conquered is by no means deducible from the state of war. Men, from the mere fact that, while they are living in their primitive independence, they have no mutual relations stable enough to constitute either the state of peace or the state of war, cannot be naturally enemies. War is constituted by a relation between things, and not between persons; and, as the state of war cannot arise out of simple personal relations, but only out of real relations, private war, or war of man with man, can exist neither in the state of nature, where there is no constant property, nor in the social state, where everything is under the authority of the laws.

Individual combats, duels and encounters, are acts which cannot constitute a state; while the private wars, authorised by the Establishments of Louis IX, King of France, and suspended by the Peace of God, are abuses of feudalism, in itself an absurd system if ever there was one, and contrary to the principles of natural right and to all good polity.

War then is a relation, not between man and man, but between State and State, and individuals are enemies only accidentally, not as men, nor even as citizens,[3] but as soldiers; not as members of their country, but as its defenders. Finally, each State can have for enemies only other States, and not men; for between things disparate in nature there can be no real relation.

Furthermore, this principle is in conformity with the established rules of all times and the constant practice of all civilised peoples. Declarations of war are intimations less to powers than to their subjects. The foreigner, whether king, individual, or people, who robs, kills or detains the subjects, without declaring war on the prince, is not an enemy, but a brigand. Even in real war, a just prince, while laying hands, in the enemy's country, on all that belongs to the public, respects the lives and goods of individuals: he respects rights on which his own are founded. The object of the war being the destruction of the hostile State, the other side has a right to kill its defenders, while they are bearing arms; but as soon as they lay them down and surrender, they cease to be enemies or instruments of the enemy, and become once more merely men, whose life no one has any right to take. Sometimes it is possible to kill the State without killing a single one of its members; and war gives no right which is not necessary to the gaining of its object. These principles are not those of Grotius: they are not based on the authority of poets, but derived from the nature of reality and based on reason.

The right of conquest has no foundation other than the right of the strongest. If war does not give the conqueror the right to massacre the conquered peoples, the right to enslave them cannot be based upon a right which does not exist. No one has a right to kill an enemy except when he cannot make him a slave, and the right to enslave him cannot therefore be derived from the right to kill him. It is accordingly an unfair exchange to make him buy at the price of his liberty his life, over which the victor holds no right. Is it not clear that there is a vicious circle in founding the right of life and death on the right of slavery, and the right of slavery on the right of life and death?

Even if we assume this terrible right to kill everybody, I maintain that a slave made in war, or a conquered people, is under no obligation to a master, except to obey him as far as he is compelled to do so. By taking an equivalent for his life, the victor has not done him a favour; instead of killing him without profit, he has killed him usefully. So far then is he from acquiring over him any authority in addition to that of force, that the state of war continues to subsist between them: their mutual relation is the effect of it, and the usage of the right of war does not imply a treaty of peace. A convention has indeed been made; but this convention, so far from destroying the state of war, presupposes its continuance.

So, from whatever aspect we regard the question, the right of slavery is null and void, not only as being illegitimate, but also because it is absurd and meaningless. The words *slave* and *right* contradict each other, and are mutually exclusive. It will always be equally foolish for a man to say to a man or to a people: "I make with you a convention wholly at your expense and wholly to my advantage; I shall keep it as long as I like, and you will keep it as long as I like."

## 5. THAT WE MUST ALWAYS GO BACK TO A FIRST CONVENTION

EVEN if I granted all that I have been refuting, the friends of despotism would be no better off. There will always be a great difference between subduing a multitude and ruling a society. Even if scattered individuals were successively enslaved by one man, however numerous they might be, I still see no more than a master and his slaves, and certainly not a people and its ruler; I see what may be termed an aggregation, but not an association; there is as yet neither public good nor body politic. The man in question, even if he has enslaved half the world, is still only an individual; his interest, apart from that of others, is still a purely private interest. If this same man comes to die, his empire, after him, remains scattered and without unity, as an oak falls and dissolves into a heap of ashes when the fire has consumed it.

A people, says Grotius, can give itself to a king. Then, according to Grotius, a people is a people before it gives itself. The gift is itself a civil act, and implies public deliberation. It would be better, before examining the act by which a people gives itself to a king, to examine that by which it has become a people; for this act, being necessarily prior to the other, is the true foundation of society.

Indeed, if there were no prior convention, where, unless the election were unanimous, would be the obligation on the minority to submit to the choice of the majority? How have a hundred men who wish for a master the right to vote on behalf of ten who do not? The law of majority voting is itself something established by convention, and presupposes unanimity, on one occasion at least.

## 6. THE SOCIAL COMPACT

I SUPPOSE men to have reached the point at which the obstacles in the way of their preservation in the state of nature show their power of resistance to be greater than the resources at the disposal of each individual for his maintenance in that state. That primitive condition can then subsist no longer; and the human race would perish unless it changed its manner of existence.

But, as men cannot engender new forces, but only unite and direct existing ones, they have no other means of preserving themselves than the formation, by aggregation, of a sum of forces great enough to overcome the resistance. These they have to bring into play by means of a single motive power, and cause to act in concert.

This sum of forces can arise only where several persons come together: but, as the force and liberty of each man are the chief instruments of his self-preservation, how can he pledge them without harming his own interests, and neglecting the care he owes to himself? This difficulty, in its bearing on my present subject, may be stated in the following terms:

*"The problem is to find a form of association which will defend and protect with the whole common force the person and goods of each associate, and in which each, while uniting himself with all, may still obey himself alone, and remain as free as before."*

This is the fundamental problem of which the *Social Contract* provides the solution.

The clauses of this contract are so determined by the nature of the act that the slightest modification would make them vain and ineffective; so that, although they have perhaps never been formally set forth, they are everywhere the same and everywhere tacitly admitted and recognised, until, on the violation of the social compact, each regains his original rights and resumes his natural liberty, while losing the conventional liberty in favour of which he renounced it.

These clauses, properly understood, may be reduced to one — the total alienation of each associate, together with all his rights, to the whole community; for, in the first place, as each gives himself absolutely, the conditions are the same for all; and, this being so, no one has any interest in making them burdensome to others.

Moreover, the alienation being without reserve, the union is as perfect as it can be, and no associate has anything more to demand: for, if the individuals retained certain rights, as there would be no common superior to decide between them and the public, each, being on one point his own judge, would ask to be so on all; the state of nature would thus continue, and the association would necessarily become inoperative or tyrannical.

Finally, each man, in giving himself to all, gives himself to nobody; and as there is no associate over whom he does not acquire the same right as he yields others over himself, he gains an equivalent for everything he loses, and an increase of force for the preservation of what he has.

If then we discard from the social compact what is not of its essence, we shall find that it reduces itself to the following terms:

*"Each of us puts his person and all his power in common under the supreme direction of the general will, and, in our corporate capacity, we receive each member as an indivisible part of the whole."*

At once, in place of the individual personality of each contracting party, this act of association creates a moral and collective body, composed of as many members as the assembly contains votes, and receiving from this act its unity, its common identity, its life and its will. This public person, so formed by the union of all other persons formerly took the name of *city*,[4] and now takes that of *Republic* or *body politic*; it is called by its members *State* when passive. *Sovereign* when active, and *Power* when compared with others like itself. Those who are associated in it take collectively the name of *people*, and severally are called *citizens*, as sharing in the sovereign power, and *subjects*, as being under the laws of the State. But these terms are often confused and taken one for another: it is enough to know how to distinguish them when they are being used with precision.

## 7. THE SOVEREIGN

THIS formula shows us that the act of association comprises a mutual undertaking between the public and the individuals, and that each individual, in making a contract, as we may say, with himself, is bound in a double capacity; as a member of the Sovereign he is bound to the individuals, and as a member of the State to the Sovereign. But the maxim of civil right, that no one is bound by undertakings made to himself, does not apply in this case; for there is a great difference between incurring an obligation to yourself and incurring one to a whole of which you form a part.

Attention must further be called to the fact that public deliberation, while competent to bind all the subjects to the Sovereign, because of the two different capacities in which each of them may be regarded, cannot, for the opposite reason, bind the Sovereign to itself; and that it is consequently against the nature of the body politic for the Sovereign to impose on itself a law which it cannot infringe. Being able to regard itself in only one capacity, it is in the position of an individual who makes a contract with himself; and this makes it clear that there neither is nor can be any kind of fundamental law binding on the body of the people — not even the social contract itself. This does not mean that the body politic cannot enter into undertakings with others, provided the contract is not infringed by them; for in relation to what is external to it, it becomes a simple being, an individual.

But the body politic or the Sovereign, drawing its being wholly from the sanctity of the contract, can never bind itself, even to an outsider, to do anything derogatory to the original act, for instance, to alienate any part of itself, or to submit to another Sovereign. Violation of the act by which it exists would be self-annihilation; and that which is itself nothing can create nothing.

As soon as this multitude is so united in one body, it is impossible to offend against one of the members without attacking the body, and still more to offend against the body without the members resenting it. Duty and interest therefore equally oblige the two contracting parties to give each other help; and the same men should seek to combine, in their double capacity, all the advantages dependent upon that capacity.

Again, the Sovereign, being formed wholly of the individuals who compose it, neither has nor can have any interest contrary to theirs; and consequently the sovereign power need give no guarantee to its subjects, because it is impossible for the body to wish to hurt all its members. We shall also see later on that it cannot hurt any in particular. The Sovereign, merely by virtue of what it is, is always what it should be.

This, however, is not the case with the relation of the subjects to the Sovereign, which, despite the common interest, would have no security that they would fulfil their undertakings, unless it found means to assure itself of their fidelity.

In fact, each individual, as a man, may have a particular will contrary or dissimilar to the general will which he has as a citizen. His particular interest may speak to him quite differently from the common interest: his absolute and naturally independent existence may make him look upon what he owes to the common cause as a gratuitous contribution, the loss of which will do less harm to others than the payment of it is burdensome to himself; and, regarding the moral person which constitutes the State as a *persona ficta*, because not a man, he may wish to enjoy the rights of citizenship without being ready to fulfil the duties of a subject. The continuance of such an injustice could not but prove the undoing of the body politic.

In order then that the social compact may not be an empty formula, it tacitly includes the undertaking, which alone can give force to the rest, that whoever refuses to obey the general will shall be compelled to do so by the whole body. This means nothing less than that he will be forced to be free; for this is the condition which, by giving each citizen to his country, secures him against all personal dependence. In this lies the key to the working of the political machine; this alone legitimises civil undertakings, which, without it, would be absurd, tyrannical, and liable to the most frightful abuses.

## 8. THE CIVIL STATE

THE passage from the state of nature to the civil state produces a very remarkable change in man, by substituting justice for instinct in his conduct, and giving his actions the morality they had formerly lacked. Then only, when the voice of duty takes the place of physical impulses and right of appetite, does man, who so far had considered only himself, find that he is forced to act on different principles, and to consult his reason before listening to his inclinations. Although, in this state, he deprives himself of some advantages which he got from nature, he gains in return others so great, his faculties are so stimulated and developed, his ideas so extended, his feelings so ennobled, and his whole soul so uplifted, that, did not the abuses of this new condition often degrade him below that which he left, he would be bound to bless continually the happy moment which took him from it for ever, and, instead of a stupid and unimaginative animal, made him an intelligent being and a man.

Let us draw up the whole account in terms easily commensurable. What man loses by the social contract is his natural liberty and an unlimited right to everything he tries to get and succeeds in getting; what he gains is civil liberty and the proprietorship of all he possesses. If we are to avoid mistake in weighing one against the other, we must clearly distinguish natural liberty, which is bounded only by the strength of the individual, from civil liberty, which is limited by the general will; and possession, which is merely the effect of force or the right of the first occupier, from property, which can be founded only on a positive title.

We might, over and above all this, add, to what man acquires in the civil state, moral liberty, which alone makes him truly master of himself; for the mere impulse of appetite is slavery, while obedience to a law which we prescribe to ourselves is liberty. But I have already said too much on this head, and the philosophical meaning of the word liberty does not now concern us.

## 9. REAL PROPERTY

EACH member of the community gives himself to it, at the moment of its foundation, just as he is, with all the resources at his command, including the goods he possesses. This act does not make possession, in changing hands, change its nature, and become property in the hands of the Sovereign; but, as the forces of the city are incomparably greater than those of an individual, public possession is also, in fact, stronger and more irrevocable, without being any more legitimate, at any rate from the point of view of foreigners. For the State, in relation to its members, is master of all their goods by the social contract, which, within the State, is the basis of all rights; but, in relation to other powers, it is so only by the right of the first occupier, which it holds from its members.

The right of the first occupier, though more real than the right of the strongest, becomes a real right only when the right of property has already been established. Every man has naturally a right to everything he needs; but the positive act which makes him proprietor of one thing excludes him from everything else. Having his share, he ought to keep to it, and can have no further right against the community. This is why the right of the first occupier, which in the state of nature is so weak, claims the respect of every man in civil society. In this right we are respecting not so much what belongs to another as what does not belong to ourselves.

In general, to establish the right of the first occupier over a plot of ground, the following conditions are necessary: first, the land must not yet be inhabited; secondly, a man must occupy only the amount he needs for his subsistence; and, in the third place, possession must be taken, not by an empty ceremony, but by labour and cultivation, the only sign of proprietorship that should be respected by others, in default of a legal title.

In granting the right of first occupancy to necessity and labour, are we not really stretching it as far as it can go? Is it possible to leave such a right unlimited? Is it to be enough to set foot on a plot of common ground, in order to be able to call yourself at once the master of it? Is it to be enough that a man has the strength to expel others for a moment, in order to establish his right to prevent them from ever returning? How can a man or a people seize an immense territory and keep it from the rest of the world except by a punishable usurpation, since all others are being robbed, by such an act, of the place of habitation and the means of subsistence which nature gave them in common? When Nunez Balboa, standing on the sea-shore, took possession of the South Seas and the whole of South America in the name of the crown of Castile, was that enough to dispossess all their actual inhabitants, and to shut out from them all the princes of the world? On such a showing, these ceremonies are idly multiplied, and the Catholic King need only take possession all at once, from his apartment, of the whole universe, merely making a subsequent reservation about what was already in the possession of other princes.

We can imagine how the lands of individuals, where they were contiguous and came to be united, became the public territory, and how the right of Sovereignty, extending from the subjects over the lands they held, became at once real and personal. The possessors were thus made more dependent, and the forces at their command used to guarantee their fidelity. The advantage of this does not seem to have been felt by ancient monarchs, who called themselves Kings of the Persians, Scythians, or Macedonians, and seemed to regard themselves more as rulers of men than as masters of a country. Those of the present day more cleverly call themselves Kings of France, Spain, England, etc.: thus holding the land, they are quite confident of holding the inhabitants.

The peculiar fact about this alienation is that, in taking over the goods of individuals, the community, so far from despoiling them, only assures them legitimate possession, and changes usurpation into a true right and enjoyment into proprietorship. Thus the possessors, being regarded as depositaries of the public good, and having their rights respected by all the members of the State and maintained against foreign aggression by all its forces, have, by a cession which benefits both the public and still more themselves, acquired, so to speak, all that they gave up. This paradox may easily be explained by the distinction between the rights which the Sovereign and the proprietor have over the same estate, as we shall see later on.

It may also happen that men begin to unite one with another before they possess anything, and that, subsequently occupying a tract of country which is enough for all, they enjoy it in common, or share it out among themselves, either equally or according to a scale fixed by the Sovereign. However the acquisition be made, the right which each individual has to his own estate is always subordinate to the right which the community has over all: without this, there would be neither stability in the social tie, nor real force in the exercise of Sovereignty.

I shall end this chapter and this book by remarking on a fact on which the whole social system should rest: i.e., that, instead of destroying natural inequality, the fundamental compact substitutes, for such physical inequality as nature may have set up between men, an equality that is moral and legitimate, and that men, who may be unequal in strength or intelligence, become every one equal by convention and legal right.[5]


1. "Learned inquiries into public right are often only the history of past abuses; and troubling to study them too deeply is a profitless infatuation" (*Essay on the Interests of France in Relation to its Neighbours*, by the Marquis d'Argenson). This is exactly what Grotius has done.

2. See a short treatise of Plutarch's entitled *That Animals Reason*.

3. The Romans, who understood and respected the right of war more than any other nation on earth, carried their scruples on this head so far that a citizen was not allowed to serve as a volunteer without engaging himself expressly against the enemy, and against such and such an enemy by name. A legion in which the younger Cato was seeing his first service under Popilius having been reconstructed, the elder Cato wrote to Popilius that, if he wished his son to continue serving under him, he must administer to him a new military oath, because, the first having been annulled, he was no longer able to bear arms against the enemy. The same Cato wrote to his son telling him to take great care not to go into battle before taking this new oath. I know that the siege of Clusium and other isolated events can be quoted against me; but I am citing laws and customs. The Romans are the people that least often transgressed its laws; and no other people has had such good ones.

4. The real meaning of this word has been almost wholly lost in modern times; most people mistake a town for a city, and a townsman for a citizen. They do not know that houses make a town, but citizens a city. The same mistake long ago cost the Carthaginians dear. I have never read of the title of citizens being given to the subjects of any prince, not even the ancient Macedonians or the English of to-day, though they are nearer liberty than any one else. The French alone everywhere familiarly adopt the name of citizens, because, as can be seen from their dictionaries, they have no idea of its meaning; otherwise they would be guilty in usurping it, of the crime of *lèse-majesté*: among them, the name expresses a virtue, and not a right. When Bodin spoke of our citizens and townsmen, he fell into a bad blunder in taking the one class for the other. M. d'Alembert has avoided the error, and, in his article on Geneva, has clearly distinguished the four orders of men (or even five,

counting mere foreigners) who dwell in our town, of which two only compose the Republic. No other French writer, to my knowledge, has understood the real meaning of the word citizen.

5. Under bad governments, this equality is only apparent and illusory: it serves only to keep the pauper in his poverty and the rich man in the position he has usurped. In fact, laws are always of use to those who possess and harmful to those who have nothing: from which it follows that the social state is advantageous to men only when all have something and none too much.

## BOOK II

### 1. THAT SOVEREIGNTY IS INALIENABLE

THE first and most important deduction from the principles we have so far laid down is that the general will alone can direct the State according to the object for which it was instituted, i.e., the common good: for if the clashing of particular interests made the establishment of societies necessary, the agreement of these very interests made it possible. The common element in these different interests is what forms the social tie; and, were there no point of agreement between them all, no society could exist. It is solely on the basis of this common interest that every society should be governed.

I hold then that Sovereignty, being nothing less than the exercise of the general will, can never be alienated, and that the Sovereign, who is no less than a collective being, cannot be represented except by himself: the power indeed may be transmitted, but not the will.

In reality, if it is not impossible for a particular will to agree on some point with the general will, it is at least impossible for the agreement to be lasting and constant; for the particular will tends, by its very nature, to partiality, while the general will tends to equality. It is even more impossible to have any guarantee of this agreement; for even if it should always exist, it would be the effect not of art, but of chance. The Sovereign may indeed say: "I now will actually what this man wills, or at least what he says he wills"; but it cannot say: "What he wills tomorrow, I too shall will" because it is absurd for the will to bind itself for the future, nor is it incumbent on any will to consent to anything that is not for the good of the being who wills. If then the people promises simply to obey, by that very act it dissolves itself and loses what makes it a people; the moment a master exists, there is no longer a Sovereign, and from that moment the body politic has ceased to exist.

This does not mean that the commands of the rulers cannot pass for general wills, so long as the Sovereign, being free to oppose them, offers no opposition. In such a case, universal silence is taken to imply the consent of the people. This will be explained later on.

### 2. THAT SOVEREIGNTY IS INDIVISIBLE

SOVEREIGNTY, for the same reason as makes it inalienable, is indivisible; for will either is, or is not, general;[6] it is the will either of the body of the people, or only of a part of it. In the first case, the will, when declared, is an act of Sovereignty and constitutes law: in the second, it is merely a particular will, or act of magistracy — at the most a decree.

But our political theorists, unable to divide Sovereignty in principle, divide it according to its object: into force and will; into legislative power and executive power; into rights of taxation, justice and war; into internal administration and power of foreign treaty. Sometimes they confuse all these sections, and sometimes they distinguish them; they turn the Sovereign into a fantastic being composed of several connected pieces: it is as if they were making man of several bodies, one with eyes, one with arms, another with feet, and each with nothing besides. We are told that the jugglers of Japan dismember a child before the eyes of the spectators; then they throw all the members into the air one after another, and the child falls down alive and whole. The conjuring tricks of our political theorists are very like that; they first dismember the Body politic by an illusion worthy of a fair, and then join it together again we know not how.

This error is due to a lack of exact notions concerning the Sovereign authority, and to taking for parts of it what are only emanations from it. Thus, for example, the acts of declaring war and making peace have been regarded as acts of Sovereignty; but this is not the case, as these acts do not constitute law, but merely the application of a law, a particular act which decides how the law applies, as we shall see clearly when the idea attached to the word *law* has been defined.

If we examined the other divisions in the same manner, we should find that, whenever Sovereignty seems to be divided, there is an illusion: the rights which are taken as being part of Sovereignty are really all subordinate, and always imply supreme wills of which they only sanction the execution.

It would be impossible to estimate the obscurity this lack of exactness has thrown over the decisions of writers who have dealt with political right, when they have used the principles laid down by them to pass judgment on the respective rights of kings and peoples. Every one can see, in Chapters III and IV of the First

Book of Grotius, how the learned man and his translator, Barbeyrac, entangle and tie themselves up in their own sophistries, for fear of saying too little or too much of what they think, and so offending the interests they have to conciliate. Grotius, a refugee in France, ill-content with his own country, and desirous of paying his court to Louis XIII, to whom his book is dedicated, spares no pains to rob the peoples of all their rights and invest kings with them by every conceivable artifice. This would also have been much to the taste of Barbeyrac, who dedicated his translation to George I of England. But unfortunately the expulsion of James II, which he called his "abdication," compelled him to use all reserve, to shuffle and to tergiversate, in order to avoid making William out a usurper. If these two writers had adopted the true principles, all difficulties would have been removed, and they would have been always consistent; but it would have been a sad truth for them to tell, and would have paid court for them to no one save the people. Moreover, truth is no road to fortune, and the people dispenses neither ambassadorships, nor professorships, nor pensions.

## 3. WHETHER THE GENERAL WILL IS FALLIBLE

IT follows from what has gone before that the general will is always right and tends to the public advantage; but it does not follow that the deliberations of the people are always equally correct. Our will is always for our own good, but we do not always see what that is; the people is never corrupted, but it is often deceived, and on such occasions only does it seem to will what is bad.

There is often a great deal of difference between the will of all and the general will; the latter considers only the common interest, while the former takes private interest into account, and is no more than a sum of particular wills: but take away from these same wills the pluses and minuses that cancel one another,[7] and the general will remains as the sum of the differences.

If, when the people, being furnished with adequate information, held its deliberations, the citizens had no communication one with another, the grand total of the small differences would always give the general will, and the decision would always be good. But when factions arise, and partial associations are formed at the expense of the great association, the will of each of these associations becomes general in relation to its members, while it remains particular in relation to the State: it may then be said that there are no longer as many votes as there are men, but only as many as there are associations. The differences become less numerous and give a less general result. Lastly, when one of these associations is so great as to prevail over all the rest, the result is no longer a sum of small differences, but a single difference; in this case there is no longer a general will, and the opinion which prevails is purely particular.

It is therefore essential, if the general will is to be able to express itself, that there should be no partial society within the State, and that each citizen should think only his own thoughts:[8] which was indeed the sublime and unique system established by the great Lycurgus. But if there are partial societies, it is best to have as many as possible and to prevent them from being unequal, as was done by Solon, Numa and Servius. These precautions are the only ones that can guarantee that the general will shall be always enlightened, and that the people shall in no way deceive itself.

## 4. THE LIMITS OF THE SOVEREIGN POWER

IF the State is a moral person whose life is in the union of its members, and if the most important of its cares is the care for its own preservation, it must have a universal and compelling force, in order to move and dispose each part as may be most advantageous to the whole. As nature gives each man absolute power over all his members, the social compact gives the body politic absolute power over all its members also; and it is this power which, under the direction of the general will, bears, as I have said, the name of Sovereignty.

But, besides the public person, we have to consider the private persons composing it, whose life and liberty are naturally independent of it. We are bound then to distinguish clearly between the respective rights of the citizens and the Sovereign,[2] and between the duties the former have to fulfil as subjects, and the natural rights they should enjoy as men.

Each man alienates, I admit, by the social compact, only such part of his powers, goods and liberty as it is important for the community to control; but it must also be granted that the Sovereign is sole judge of what is important.

Every service a citizen can render the State he ought to render as soon as the Sovereign demands it; but the Sovereign, for its part, cannot impose upon its subjects any fetters that are useless to the community, nor can it even wish to do so; for no more by the law of reason than by the law of nature can anything occur without a cause.

The undertakings which bind us to the social body are obligatory only because they are mutual; and their nature is such that in fulfilling them we cannot work for others without working for ourselves. Why is it that the general will is always in the right, and that all continually will the happiness of each one, unless it is because there is not a man who does not think of "each" as meaning him, and consider himself in voting for all? This proves that equality of rights and the idea of justice which such equality creates originate in the preference each man gives to himself, and accordingly in the very nature of man. It proves that the general will, to be really such, must be general in its object as well as its essence; that it must both come from all and apply to all; and that it loses its natural rectitude when it is directed to some particular and determinate object, because in such a case we are judging of something foreign to us, and have no true principle of equity to guide us.

Indeed, as soon as a question of particular fact or right arises on a point not previously regulated by a general convention, the matter becomes contentious. It is a case in which the individuals concerned are one party, and the public the other, but in which I can see neither the law that ought to be followed nor the judge who ought to give the decision. In such a case, it would be absurd to propose to refer the question to an express decision of the general will, which can be only the conclusion reached by one of the parties and in consequence will be, for the other party, merely an external and particular will, inclined on this occasion to injustice and subject to error. Thus, just as a particular will cannot stand for the general will, the general will, in turn, changes its nature, when its object is particular, and, as general, cannot pronounce on a man or a fact. When, for instance, the people of Athens nominated or displaced its rulers, decreed honours to one, and imposed penalties on another, and, by a multitude of particular decrees, exercised all the functions of government indiscriminately, it had in such cases no longer a general will in the strict sense; it was acting no longer as Sovereign, but as magistrate. This will seem contrary to current views; but I must be given time to expound my own.

It should be seen from the foregoing that what makes the will general is less the number of voters than the common interest uniting them; for, under this system, each necessarily submits to the conditions he imposes on others: and this admirable agreement between interest and justice gives to the common deliberations an equitable character which at once vanishes when any particular question is discussed, in the absence of a common interest to unite and identify the ruling of the judge with that of the party.

From whatever side we approach our principle, we reach the same conclusion, that the social compact sets up among the citizens an equality of such a kind, that they all bind themselves to observe the same conditions and should therefore all enjoy the same rights. Thus, from the very nature of the compact, every act of Sovereignty, i.e., every authentic act of the general will, binds or favours all the citizens equally; so that the Sovereign recognises only the body of the nation, and draws no distinctions between those of whom it is made up. What, then, strictly speaking, is an act of Sovereignty? It is not a convention between a superior and an inferior, but a convention between the body and each of its members. It is legitimate, because based on the social contract, and equitable, because common to all; useful, because it can have no other object than the general good, and stable, because guaranteed by the public force and the supreme power. So long as the subjects have to submit only to conventions of this sort, they obey no-one but their own will; and to ask how far the respective rights of the Sovereign and the citizens extend, is to ask up to what point the latter can enter into undertakings with themselves, each with all, and all with each.

We can see from this that the sovereign power, absolute, sacred and inviolable as it is, does not and cannot exceed the limits of general conventions, and that every man may dispose at will of such goods and liberty as these conventions leave him; so that the Sovereign never has a right to lay more charges on one subject than on another, because, in that case, the question becomes particular, and ceases to be within its competency.

When these distinctions have once been admitted, it is seen to be so untrue that there is, in the social contract, any real renunciation on the part of the individuals, that the position in which they find themselves as a result of the contract is really preferable to that in which they were before. Instead of a renunciation, they have made an advantageous exchange: instead of an uncertain and precarious way of living they have got one that is better and more secure; instead of natural independence they have got liberty, instead of the power to harm others security for themselves, and instead of their strength, which others might overcome, a right which social union makes invincible. Their very life, which they have devoted to the State, is by it constantly protected; and when they risk it in the State's defence, what more are they doing than giving back what they have received from it? What are they doing that they would not do more often and with greater danger in the state of nature, in which they would inevitably have to fight battles at the peril of their lives in defence of that which is the means of their preservation? All have indeed to fight when their country needs them; but then no one has ever to fight for himself. Do we not gain something by running, on behalf of what gives us our security, only some of the risks we should have to run for ourselves, as soon as we lost it?

## 5. THE RIGHT OF LIFE AND DEATH

THE question is often asked how individuals, having no right to dispose of their own lives, can transfer to the Sovereign a right which they do not possess. The difficulty of answering this question seems to me to lie in its being wrongly stated. Every man has a right to risk his own life in order to preserve it. Has it ever been said that a man who throws himself out of the window to escape from a fire is guilty of suicide? Has such a crime ever been laid to the charge of him who perishes in a storm because, when he went on board, he knew of the danger?

The social treaty has for its end the preservation of the contracting parties. He who wills the end wills the means also, and the means must involve some risks, and even some losses. He who wishes to preserve his life at others' expense should also, when it is necessary, be ready to give it up for their sake. Furthermore, the citizen is no longer the judge of the dangers to which the law-desires him to expose himself; and when the prince says to him: "It is expedient for the State that you should die," he ought to die, because it is only on that condition that he has been living in security up to the present, and because his life is no longer a mere bounty of nature, but a gift made conditionally by the State.

The death-penalty inflicted upon criminals may be looked on in much the same light: it is in order that we may not fall victims to an assassin that we consent to die if we ourselves turn assassins. In this treaty, so far from disposing of our own lives, we think only of securing them, and it is not to be assumed that any of the parties then expects to get hanged.

Again, every malefactor, by attacking social rights, becomes on forfeit a rebel and a traitor to his country; by violating its laws be ceases to be a member of it; he even makes war upon it. In such a case the preservation of the State is inconsistent with his own, and one or the other must perish; in putting the guilty to death, we slay not so much the citizen as an enemy. The trial and the judgment are the proofs that he has broken the social treaty, and is in consequence no longer a member of the State. Since, then, he has recognised himself to be such by living there, he must be removed by exile as a violator of the compact, or by death as a public enemy; for such an enemy is not a moral person, but merely a man; and in such a case the right of war is to kill the vanquished.

But, it will be said, the condemnation of a criminal is a particular act. I admit it: but such condemnation is not a function of the Sovereign; it is a right the Sovereign can confer without being able itself to exert it. All my ideas are consistent, but I cannot expound them all at once.

We may add that frequent punishments are always a sign of weakness or remissness on the part of the government. There is not a single ill-doer who could not be turned to some good. The State has no right to put to death, even for the sake of making an example, any one whom it can leave alive without danger.

The right of pardoning or exempting the guilty from a penalty imposed by the law and pronounced by the judge belongs only to the authority which is superior to both judge and law, i.e., the Sovereign; each its right in this matter is far from clear, and the cases for exercising it are extremely rare. In a well-governed State, there are few punishments, not because there are many pardons, but because criminals are rare; it is when a State is in decay that the multitude of crimes is a guarantee of impunity. Under the Roman Republic, neither the Senate nor the Consuls ever attempted to pardon; even the people never did so, though it sometimes revoked its own decision. Frequent pardons mean that crime will soon need them no longer, and no one can help seeing whither that leads. But I feel my heart protesting and restraining my pen; let us leave these questions to the just man who has never offended, and would himself stand in no need of pardon.

## 6. LAW

BY the social compact we have given the body politic existence and life; we have now by legislation to give it movement and will. For the original act by which the body is formed and united still in no respect determines what it ought to do for its preservation.

What is well and in conformity with order is so by the nature of things and independently of human conventions. All justice comes from God, who is its sole source; but if we knew how to receive so high an inspiration, we should need neither government nor laws. Doubtless, there is a universal justice emanating from reason alone; but this justice, to be admitted among us, must be mutual. Humanly speaking, in default of natural sanctions, the laws of justice are ineffective among men: they merely make for the good of the wicked and the undoing of the just, when the just man observes them towards everybody and nobody observes them towards him. Conventions and laws are therefore needed to join rights to duties and refer justice to its object. In the state of nature, where everything is common, I owe nothing to him whom I have promised nothing; I recognise as belonging to others only what is of no use to me. In the state of society all rights are fixed by law, and the case becomes different.

But what, after all, is a law? As long as we remain satisfied with attaching purely metaphysical ideas to the word, we shall go on arguing without arriving at an understanding; and when we have defined a law of nature, we shall be no nearer the definition of a law of the State.

I have already said that there can be no general will directed to a particular object. Such an object must be either within or outside the State. If outside, a will which is alien to it cannot be, in relation to it, general; if within, it is part of the State, and in that case there arises a relation between whole and part which makes them two separate beings, of which the part is one, and the whole minus the part the other. But the whole minus a part cannot be the whole; and while this relation persists, there can be no whole, but only two unequal parts; and it follows that the will of one is no longer in any respect general in relation to the other.

But when the whole people decrees for the whole people, it is considering only itself; and if a relation is then formed, it is between two aspects of the entire object, without there being any division of the whole. In that case the matter about which the decree is made is, like the decreeing will, general. This act is what I call a law.

When I say that the object of laws is always general, I mean that law considers subjects *en masse* and actions in the abstract, and never a particular person or action. Thus the law may indeed decree that there shall be privileges, but cannot confer them on anybody by name. It may set up several classes of citizens, and even lay down the qualifications for membership of these classes, but it cannot nominate such and such persons as belonging to them; it may establish a monarchical government and hereditary succession, but it cannot choose a king, or nominate a royal family. In a word, no function which has a particular object belongs to the legislative power.

On this view, we at once see that it can no longer be asked whose business it is to make laws, since they are acts of the general will; nor whether the prince is above the law, since he is a member of the State; nor whether the law can be unjust, since no one is unjust to himself; nor how we can be both free and subject to the laws, since they are but registers of our wills.

We see further that, as the law unites universality of will with universality of object, what a man, whoever he be, commands of his own motion cannot be a law; and even what the Sovereign commands with regard to a particular matter is no nearer being a law, but is a decree, an act, not of sovereignty, but of magistracy.

I therefore give the name "Republic" to every State that is governed by laws, no matter what the form of its administration may be: for only in such a case does the public interest govern, and the *res publica* rank as a *reality*. Every legitimate government is republican;[10] what government is I will explain later on.

Laws are, properly speaking, only the conditions of civil association. The people, being subject to the laws, ought to be their author: the conditions of the society ought to be regulated solely by those who come together to form it. But how are they to regulate them? Is it to be by common agreement, by a sudden inspiration? Has the body politic an organ to declare its will? Who can give it the foresight to formulate and announce its acts in advance? Or how is it to announce them in the hour of need? How can a blind multitude, which often does not know what it wills, because it rarely knows what is good for it, carry out for itself so great and difficult an enterprise as a system of legislation? Of itself the people wills always the good, but of itself it by no means always sees it. The general will is always in the right, but the judgment which guides it is not always enlightened. It must be got to see objects as they are, and sometimes as they ought to appear to it; it must be shown the good road it is in search of, secured from the seductive influences of individual wills, taught to see times and spaces as a series, and made to weigh the attractions of present and sensible advantages against the danger of distant and hidden evils. The individuals see the good they reject; the public wills the good it does not see. All stand equally in need of guidance. The former must be compelled to bring their wills into conformity with their reason; the latter must be taught to know what it wills. If that is done, public enlightenment leads to the union of understanding and will in the social body: the parts are made to work exactly together, and the whole is raised to its highest power. This makes a legislator necessary.

## 7. THE LEGISLATOR

IN order to discover the rules of society best suited to nations, a superior intelligence beholding all the passions of men without experiencing any of them would be needed. This intelligence would have to be wholly unrelated to our nature, while knowing it through and through; its happiness would have to be independent of us, and yet ready to occupy itself with ours; and lastly, it would have, in the march of time, to look forward to a distant glory, and, working in one century, to be able to enjoy in the next.[11] It would take gods to give men laws.

What Caligula argued from the facts, Plato, in the dialogue called the *Politicus*, argued in defining the civil or kingly man, on the basis of right. But if great princes are rare, how much more so are great legislators? The former have only to follow the pattern which the latter have to lay down. The legislator is the engineer who invents the machine, the prince merely the mechanic who sets it up and makes it go. "At the birth of societies," says Montesquieu, "the rulers of Republics establish institutions, and afterwards the institutions mould the rulers."[12]

He who dares to undertake the making of a people's institutions ought to feel himself capable, so to speak, of changing human nature, of transforming each individual, who is by himself a complete and solitary whole, into part of a greater whole from which he in a manner receives his life and being; of altering man's constitution for the purpose of strengthening it; and of substituting a partial and moral existence for the physical and independent existence nature has conferred on us all. He must, in a word, take away from man his own resources and give him instead new ones alien to him, and incapable of being made use of without the help of other men. The more completely these natural resources are annihilated, the greater and the more lasting are those which he acquires, and the more stable and perfect the new institutions; so that if each citizen is nothing and can do nothing without the rest, and the resources acquired by the whole are equal or superior to the ag-gregate of the resources of all the individuals, it may be said that legislation is at the highest possible point of perfection.

The legislator occupies in every respect an extraordinary position in the State. If he should do so by reason of his genius, he does so no less by reason of his office, which is neither magistracy, nor Sovereignty. This of-fice, which sets up the Republic, nowhere enters into its constitution; it is an individual and superior function, which has nothing in common with human empire; for if he who holds command over men ought not to have command over the laws, he who has command over the laws ought not any more to have it over men; or else his laws would be the ministers of his passions and would often merely serve to perpetuate his injustices: his private aims would inevitably mar the sanctity of his work.

When Lycurgus gave laws to his country, he began by resigning the throne. It was the custom of most Greek towns to entrust the establishment of their laws to foreigners. The Republics of modern Italy in many cases followed this example; Geneva did the same and profited by it.[13] Rome, when it was most prosperous, suf-fered a revival of all the crimes of tyranny, and was brought to the verge of destruction, because it put the leg-islative authority and the sovereign power into the same hands.

Nevertheless, the decemvirs themselves never claimed the right to pass any law merely on their own authori-ty. "Nothing we propose to you," they said to the people, "can pass into law without your consent. Romans, be yourselves the authors of the laws which are to make you happy."

He, therefore, who draws up the laws has, or should have, no right of legislation, and the people cannot, even if it wishes, deprive itself of this incommunicable right, because, according to the fundamental compact, only the general will can bind the individuals, and there can be no assurance that a particular will is in conformity with the general will, until it has been put to the free vote of the people. This I have said already; but it is worth while to repeat it.

Thus in the task of legislation we find together two things which appear to be incompatible: an enterprise too difficult for human powers, and, for its execution, an authority that is no authority.

There is a further difficulty that deserves attention. Wise men, if they try to speak their language to the com-mon herd instead of its own, cannot possibly make themselves understood. There are a thousand kinds of ideas which it is impossible to translate into popular language. Conceptions that are too general and objects that are too remote are equally out of its range: each individual, having no taste for any other plan of govern-ment than that which suits his particular interest, finds it difficult to realise the advantages he might hope to draw from the continual privations good laws impose. For a young people to be able to relish sound principles of political theory and follow the fundamental rules of statecraft, the effect would have to become the cause; the social spirit, which should be created by these institutions, would have to preside over their very founda-tion; and men would have to be before law what they should become by means of law. The legislator there-fore, being unable to appeal to either force or reason, must have recourse to an authority of a different order, capable of constraining without violence and persuading without convincing.

This is what has, in all ages, compelled the fathers of nations to have recourse to divine intervention and cred-it the gods with their own wisdom, in order that the peoples, submitting to the laws of the State as to those of nature, and recognising the same power in the formation of the city as in that of man, might obey freely, and bear with docility the yoke of the public happiness.

This sublime reason, far above the range of the common herd, is that whose decisions the legislator puts into the mouth of the immortals, in order to constrain by divine authority those whom human prudence could not move.[14] But it is not anybody who can make the gods speak, or get himself believed when he proclaims him-self their interpreter. The great soul of the legislator is the only miracle that can prove his mission. Any man may grave tablets of stone, or buy an oracle, or feign secret intercourse with some divinity, or train a bird to whisper in his ear, or find other vulgar ways of imposing on the people. He whose knowledge goes no further may perhaps gather round him a band of fools; but he will never found an empire, and his extravagances will quickly perish with him. Idle tricks form a passing tie; only wisdom can make it lasting. The Judaic law, which still subsists, and that of the child of Ishmael, which, for ten centuries, has ruled half the world, still proclaim the great men who laid them down; and, while the pride of philosophy or the blind spirit of faction sees in them no more than lucky impostures, the true political theorist admires, in the institutions they set up, the great and powerful genius which presides over things made to endure.

We should not, with Warburton, conclude from this that politics and religion have among us a common object, but that, in the first periods of nations, the one is used as an instrument for the other.

## 8. THE PEOPLE

AS, before putting up a large building, the architect surveys and sounds the site to see if it will bear the weight, the wise legislator does not begin by laying down laws good in themselves, but by investigating the fitness of the people, for which they are destined, to receive them. Plato refused to legislate for the Arcadians and the Cyrenæans, because he knew that both peoples were rich and could not put up with equality; and good laws and bad men were found together in Crete, because Minos had inflicted discipline on a people already burdened with vice.

A thousand nations have achieved earthly greatness, that could never have endured good laws; even such as could have endured them could have done so only for a very brief period of their long history. Most peoples, like most men, are docile only in youth; as they grow old they become incorrigible. When once customs have become established and prejudices inveterate, it is dangerous and useless to attempt their reformation; the people, like the foolish and cowardly patients who rave at sight of the doctor, can no longer bear that any one should lay hands on its faults to remedy them.

There are indeed times in the history of States when, just as some kinds of illness turn men's heads and make them forget the past, periods of violence and revolutions do to peoples what these crises do to individuals: horror of the past takes the place of forgetfulness, and the State, set on fire by civil wars, is born again, so to speak, from its ashes, and takes on anew, fresh from the jaws of death, the vigour of youth. Such were Sparta at the time of Lycurgus, Rome after the Tarquins, and, in modern times, Holland and Switzerland after the expulsion of the tyrants.

But such events are rare; they are exceptions, the cause of which is always to be found in the particular constitution of the State concerned. They cannot even happen twice to the same people, for it can make itself free as long as it remains barbarous, but not when the civic impulse has lost its vigour. Then disturbances may destroy it, but revolutions cannot mend it: it needs a master, and not a liberator. Free peoples, be mindful of this maxim: "Liberty may be gained, but can never be recovered."

Youth is not infancy. There is for nations, as for men, a period of youth, or, shall we say, maturity, before which they should not be made subject to laws; but the maturity of a people is not always easily recognisable, and, if it is anticipated, the work is spoilt. One people is amenable to discipline from the beginning; another, not after ten centuries. Russia will never be really civilised, because it was civilised too soon. Peter had a genius for imitation; but he lacked true genius, which is creative and makes all from nothing. He did some good things, but most of what he did was out of place. He saw that his people was barbarous, but did not see that it was not ripe for civilisation: he wanted to civilise it when it needed only hardening. His first wish was to make Germans or Englishmen, when he ought to have been making Russians; and he prevented his subjects from ever becoming what they might have been by persuading them that they were what they are not. In this fashion too a French teacher turns out his pupil to be an infant prodigy, and for the rest of his life to be nothing whatsoever. The empire of Russia will aspire to conquer Europe, and will itself be conquered. The Tartars, its subjects or neighbours, will become its masters and ours, by a revolution which I regard as inevitable. Indeed, all the kings of Europe are working in concert to hasten its coming.

## 9. THE PEOPLE (*continued*)

As nature has set bounds to the stature of a well-made man, and, outside those limits, makes nothing but giants or dwarfs, similarly, for the constitution of a State to be at its best, it is possible to fix limits that will make it neither too large for good government, nor too small for self-maintenance. In every body politic there is a *maximum* strength which it cannot exceed and which it only loses by increasing in size. Every extension of the social tie means its relaxation; and, generally speaking, a small State is stronger in proportion than a great one.

A thousand arguments could be advanced in favour of this principle. First, long distances make administration more difficult, just as a weight becomes heavier at the end of a longer lever. Administration therefore becomes more and more burdensome as the distance grows greater; for, in the first place, each city has its own, which is paid for by the people: each district its own, still paid for by the people: then comes each province, and then the great governments, satrapies, and vice-royalties, always costing more the higher you go, and always at the expense of the unfortunate people. Last of all comes the supreme administration, which eclipses all the rest. All these over charges are a continual drain upon the subjects; so far from being better governed by all these different orders, they are worse governed than if there were only a single authority over them. In the meantime, there scarce remain resources enough to meet emergencies; and, when recourse must be had to these, the State is always on the eve of destruction.

This is not all; not only has the government less vigour and promptitude for securing the observance of the laws, preventing nuisances, correcting abuses, and guarding against seditious undertakings begun in distant places; the people has less affection for its rulers, whom it never sees, for its country, which, to its eyes, seems like the world, and for its fellow-citizens, most of whom are unknown to it. The same laws cannot suit so many diverse provinces with different customs, situated in the most various climates, and incapable of enduring a uniform government. Different laws lead only to trouble and confusion among peoples which, living under the same rulers and in constant communication one with another, intermingle and intermarry, and, coming under the sway of new customs, never know if they can call their very patrimony their own. Talent is buried, virtue unknown and vice unpunished, among such a multitude of men who do not know one another, gathered together in one place at the seat of the central administration. The leaders, overwhelmed with business, see nothing for themselves; the State is governed by clerks. Finally, the measures which have to be taken to maintain the general authority, which all these distant officials wish to escape or to impose upon, absorb all the energy of the public, so that there is none left for the happiness of the people. There is hardly enough to defend it when need arises, and thus a body which is too big for its constitution gives way and falls crushed under its own weight.

Again, the State must assure itself a safe foundation, if it is to have stability, and to be able to resist the shocks it cannot help experiencing, as well as the efforts it will be forced to make for its maintenance; for all peoples have a kind of centrifugal force that makes them continually act one against another, and tend to aggrandise themselves at their neighbours' expense, like the vortices of Descartes. Thus the weak run the risk of being soon swallowed up; and it is almost impossible for any one to preserve itself except by putting itself in a state of equilibrium with all, so that the pressure is on all sides practically equal.

It may therefore be seen that there are reasons for expansion and reasons for contraction; and it is no small part of the statesman's skill to hit between them the mean that is most favourable to the preservation of the State. It may be said that the reason for expansion, being merely external and relative, ought to be subordinate to the reasons for contraction, which are internal and absolute. A strong and healthy constitution is the first thing to look for; and it is better to count on the vigour which comes of good government than on the resources a great territory furnishes.

It may be added that there have been known States so constituted that the necessity of making conquests entered into their very constitution, and that, in order to maintain themselves, they were forced to expand ceaselessly. It may be that they congratulated themselves greatly on this fortunate necessity, which none the less indicated to them, along with the limits of their greatness, the inevitable moment of their fall.

## 10. THE PEOPLE (*continued*)

A BODY politic may be measured in two ways — either by the extent of its territory, or by the number of its people; and there is, between these two measurements, a right relation which makes the State really great. The men make the State, and the territory sustains the men; the right relation therefore is that the land should suffice for the maintenance of the inhabitants, and that there should be as many inhabitants as the land can maintain. In this proportion lies the *maximum* strength of a given number of people; for, if there is too much land, it is troublesome to guard and inadequately cultivated, produces more than is needed, and soon gives rise to wars of defence; if there is not enough, the State depends on its neighbours for what it needs over and above, and this soon gives rise to wars of offence. Every people, to which its situation gives no choice save that between commerce and war, is weak in itself: it depends on its neighbours, and on circumstances; its existence can never be more than short and uncertain. It either conquers others, and changes its situation, or it is conquered and becomes nothing. Only insignificance or greatness can keep it free.

No fixed relation can be stated between the extent of territory and the population that are adequate one to the other, both because of the differences in the quality of land, in its fertility, in the nature of its products, and in the influence of climate, and because of the different tempers of those who inhabit it; for some in a fertile country consume little, and others on an ungrateful soil much. The greater or less fecundity of women, the conditions that are more or less favourable in each country to the growth of population, and the influence the legislator can hope to exercise by his institutions, must also be taken into account. The legislator therefore should not go by what he sees, but by what he foresees; he should stop not so much at the state in which he actually finds the population, as at that to which it ought naturally to attain. Lastly, there are countless cases in which the particular local circumstances demand or allow the acquisition of a greater territory than seems necessary. Thus, expansion will be great in a mountainous country, where the natural products, i.e., woods and pastures, need less labour, where we know from experience that women are more fertile than in the plains, and where a great expanse of slope affords only a small level tract that can be counted on for vegetation. On the other hand, contraction is possible on the coast, even in lands of rocks and nearly barren sands, because there fishing makes up to a great extent for the lack of land-produce, because the inhabitants have to congregate together more in order to repel pirates, and further because it is easier to unburden the country of its superfluous inhabitants by means of colonies.

To these conditions of law-giving must be added one other which, though it cannot take the place of the rest, renders them all useless when it is absent. This is the enjoyment of peace and plenty; for the moment at which a State sets its house in order is, like the moment when a battalion is forming up, that when its body is least capable of offering resistance and easiest to destroy. A better resistance could be made at a time of absolute disorganisation than at a moment of fermentation, when each is occupied with his own position and not with the danger. If war, famine, or sedition arises at this time of crisis, the State will inevitably be overthrown.

Not that many governments have not been set up during such storms; but in such cases these governments are themselves the State's destroyers. Usurpers always bring about or select troublous times to get passed, under cover of the public terror, destructive laws, which the people would never adopt in cold blood. The moment chosen is one of the surest means of distinguishing the work of the legislator from that of the tyrant.

What people, then, is a fit subject for legislation? One which, already bound by some unity of origin, interest, or convention, has never yet felt the real yoke of law; one that has neither customs nor superstitions deeply ingrained, one which stands in no fear of being overwhelmed by sudden invasion; one which, without entering into its neighbours' quarrels, can resist each of them single-handed, or get the help of one to repel another; one in which every member may be known by every other, and there is no need to lay on any man burdens too heavy for a man to bear; one which can do without other peoples, and without which all others can do;[15] one which is neither rich nor poor, but self-sufficient; and, lastly, one which unites the consistency of an ancient people with the docility of a new one. Legislation is made difficult less by what it is necessary to build up than by what has to be destroyed; and what makes success so rare is the impossibility of finding natural simplicity together with social requirements. All these conditions are indeed rarely found united, and therefore few States have good constitutions.

There is still in Europe one country capable of being given laws — Corsica. The valour and persistency with which that brave people has regained and defended its liberty well deserves that some wise man should teach it how to preserve what it has won. I have a feeling that some day that little island will astonish Europe.

## 11. THE VARIOUS SYSTEMS OF LEGISLATION

IF we ask in what precisely consists the greatest good of all, which should be the end of every system of legislation, we shall find it reduce itself to two main objects, liberty and equality — liberty, because all particular dependence means so much force taken from the body of the State and equality, because liberty cannot exist without it.

I have already defined civil liberty; by equality, we should understand, not that the degrees of power and riches are to be absolutely identical for everybody; but that power shall never be great enough for violence, and shall always be exercised by virtue of rank and law; and that, in respect of riches, no citizen shall ever be wealthy enough to buy another, and none poor enough to be forced to sell himself:[16] which implies, on the part of the great, moderation in goods and position, and, on the side of the common sort, moderation in avarice and covetousness.

Such equality, we are told, is an unpractical ideal that cannot actually exist. But if its abuse is inevitable, does it follow that we should not at least make regulations concerning it? It is precisely because the force of circumstances tends continually to destroy equality that the force of legislation should always tend to its maintenance.

But these general objects of every good legislative system need modifying in every country in accordance with the local situation and the temper of the inhabitants; and these circumstances should determine, in each case, the particular system of institutions which is best, not perhaps in itself, but for the State for which it is destined. If, for instance, the soil is barren and unproductive, or the land too crowded for its inhabitants, the people should turn to industry and the crafts, and exchange what they produce for the commodities they lack. If, on the other hand, a people dwells in rich plains and fertile slopes, or, in a good land, lacks inhabitants, it should give all its attention to agriculture, which causes men to multiply, and should drive out the crafts, which would only result in depopulation, by grouping in a few localities the few inhabitants there are.[17] If a nation dwells on an extensive and convenient coast-line, let it cover the sea with ships and foster commerce and navigation. It will have a life that will be short and glorious. If, on its coasts, the sea washes nothing but almost inaccessible rocks, let it remain barbarous and ichthyophagous: it will have a quieter, perhaps a better, and certainly a happier life. In a word, besides the principles that are common to all, every nation has in itself something that gives them a particular application, and makes its legislation peculiarly its own. Thus, among the Jews long ago and more recently among the Arabs, the chief object was religion, among the Athenians letters, at Carthage and Tyre commerce, at Rhodes shipping, at Sparta war, at Rome virtue. The author of *The Spirit of the Laws* has shown with many examples by what art the legislator directs the constitution towards each of these objects. What makes the constitution of a State really solid and lasting is the due observance of what is proper, so that the natural relations are always in agreement with the laws on every point, and law only serves, so to speak, to assure, accompany and rectify them. But if the legislator mistakes his object and adopts a principle other than circumstances naturally direct; if his principle makes for servitude while they make for liberty, or if it makes for riches, while they make for populousness, or if it makes for peace, while they make for conquest — the laws will insensibly lose their influence, the constitution will alter, and the State will have no rest from trouble till it is either destroyed or changed, and nature has resumed her invincible sway.

## 12. THE DIVISION OF THE LAWS

IF the whole is to be set in order, and the commonwealth put into the best possible shape, there are various relations to be considered. First, there is the action of the complete body upon itself, the relation of the whole to the whole, of the Sovereign to the State; and this relation, as we shall see, is made up of the relations of the intermediate terms.

The laws which regulate this relation bear the name of political laws, and are also called fundamental laws, not without reason if they are wise. For, if there is, in each State, only one good system, the people that is in possession of it should hold fast to this; but if the established order is bad, why should laws that prevent men from being good be regarded as fundamental? Besides, in any case, a people is always in a position to change its laws, however good; for, if it choose to do itself harm, who can have a right to stop it?

The second relation is that of the members one to another, or to the body as a whole; and this relation should be in the first respect as unimportant, and in the second as important, as possible. Each citizen would then be perfectly independent of all the rest, and at the same time very dependent on the city; which is brought about always by the same means, as the strength of the State can alone secure the liberty of its members. From this second relation arise civil laws.

We may consider also a third kind of relation between the individual and the law, a relation of disobedience to its penalty. This gives rise to the setting up of criminal laws, which, at bottom, are less a particular class of law than the sanction behind all the rest.

Along with these three kinds of law goes a fourth, most important of all, which is not graven on tablets of marble or brass, but on the hearts of the citizens. This forms the real constitution of the State, takes on every day new powers, when other laws decay or die out, restores them or takes their place, keeps a people in the ways in which it was meant to go, and insensibly replaces authority by the force of habit. I am speaking of morality, of custom, above all of public opinion; a power unknown to political thinkers, on which none the less success in everything else depends. With this the great legislator concerns himself in secret, though he seems to confine himself to particular regulations; for these are only the arc of the arch, while manners and morals, slower to arise, form in the end its immovable keystone.

Among the different classes of laws, the political, which determine the forms of the government, are alone relevant to my subject.

6. To be general, a will need not always be unanimous; but every vote must be counted: any exclusion is a breach of generality.

7. "Every interest," says the Marquis d'Argenson, "has different principles. The agreement of two particular interests is formed by opposition to a third." He might have added that the agreement of all interests is formed by opposition to that of each. If there were no different interests, the common interest would be barely felt, as it would encounter no obstacle; all would go on of its own accord, and politics would cease to be an art.

8. "In fact," says Machiavelli, "there are some divisions that are harmful to a Republic and some that are advantageous. Those which stir up sects and parties are harmful; those attended by neither are advantageous. Since, then, the founder of a Republic cannot help enmities arising, he ought at least to prevent them from growing into sects" (*History of Florence*, Book vii).

9. Attentive readers, do not, I pray, be in a hurry to charge me with contradicting myself. The terminology made it unavoidable, considering the poverty of the language; but wait and see.

10. I understand by this word, not merely an aristocracy or a democracy, but generally any government directed by the general will, which is the law. To be legitimate, the government must be, not one with the Sovereign, but its minister. In such a case even a monarchy is a Republic. This will be made clearer in the following book.

11. A people becomes famous only when its legislation begins to decline. We do not know for how many centuries the system of Lycurgus made the Spartans happy before the rest of Greece took any notice of it.

12. Montesquieu, *The Greatness and Decadence of the Romans*, ch. i.

13. Those who know Calvin only as a theologian much under-estimate the extent of his genius. The codification of our wise edicts, in which he played a large part, does him no less honour than his *Institute*. Whatever revolution time may bring in our religion, so long as the spirit of patriotism and liberty still lives among us, the memory of this great man will be for ever blessed.

14. "In truth," says Machiavelli, "there has never been, in any country, an extraordinary legislator who has not had recourse to God; for otherwise his laws would not have been accepted: there are, in fact, many useful truths of which a wise man may have knowledge without their having in themselves such clear reasons for their being so as to be able to convince others" (*Discourses on Livy*, Bk. v, ch. xi).

15. If there were two neighbouring peoples, one of which could not do without the other, it would be very hard on the former, and very dangerous for the latter. Every wise nation, in such a case, would make haste to

free the other from dependence. The Republic of Thiascala, enclosed by the Mexican Empire, preferred doing without salt to buying from the Mexicans, or even getting it from them as a gift. The Thiascalans were wise enough to see the snare hidden under such liberality. They kept their freedom, and that little State, shut up in that great Empire, was finally the instrument of its ruin.

16. If the object is to give the State consistency, bring the two extremes as near to each other as possible; allow neither rich men nor beggars. These two estates, which are naturally inseparable, are equally fatal to the common good; from the one come the friends of tyranny, and from the other tyrants. It is always between them that public liberty is put up to auction; the one buys, and the other sells.

17. "Any branch of foreign commerce," says M. d'Argenson, "creates on the whole only apparent advantage for the kingdom in general; it may enrich some individuals, or even some towns; but the nation as a whole gains nothing by it, and the people is no better off."


# BOOK III

BEFORE speaking of the different forms of government, let us try to fix the exact sense of the word, which has not yet been very clearly explained.

## 1. GOVERNMENT IN GENERAL

I WARN the reader that this chapter requires careful reading, and that I am unable to make myself clear to those who refuse to be attentive. Every free action is produced by the concurrence of two causes; one moral, i.e., the will which determines the act; the other physical, i.e., the power which executes it. When I walk towards an object, it is necessary first that I should will to go there, and, in the second place, that my feet should carry me. If a paralytic wills to run and an active man wills not to, they will both stay where they are. The body politic has the same motive powers; here too force and will are distinguished, will under the name of legislative power and force under that of executive power. Without their concurrence, nothing is, or should be, done.

We have seen that the legislative power belongs to the people, and can belong to it alone. It may, on the other hand, readily be seen, from the principles laid down above, that the executive power cannot belong to the generality as legislature or Sovereign, because it consists wholly of particular acts which fall outside the competency of the law, and consequently of the Sovereign, whose acts must always be laws.

The public force therefore needs an agent of its own to bind it together and set it to work under the direction of the general will, to serve as a means of communication between the State and the Sovereign, and to do for the collective person more or less what the union of soul and body does for man. Here we have what is, in the State, the basis of government, often wrongly confused with the Sovereign, whose minister it is.

What then is government? An intermediate body set up between the subjects and the Sovereign, to secure their mutual correspondence, charged with the execution of the laws and the maintenance of liberty, both civil and political.

The members of this body are called magistrates or *kings*, that is to say *governors*, and the whole body bears the name *prince*.[18] Thus those who hold that the act, by which a people puts itself under a prince, is not a contract, are certainly right. It is simply and solely a commission, an employment, in which the rulers, mere officials of the Sovereign, exercise in their own name the power of which it makes them depositaries. This power it can limit, modify or recover at pleasure; for the alienation of such a right is incompatible with the nature of the social body, and contrary to the end of association.

I call then *government*, or supreme administration, the legitimate exercise of the executive power, and prince or magistrate the man or the body entrusted with that administration.

In government reside the intermediate forces whose relations make up that of the whole to the whole, or of the Sovereign to the State. This last relation may be represented as that between the extreme terms of a continuous proportion, which has government as its mean proportional. The government gets from the Sovereign the orders it gives the people, and, for the State to be properly balanced, there must, when everything is reckoned in, be equality between the product or power of the government taken in itself, and the product or power of the citizens, who are on the one hand sovereign and on the other subject.

Furthermore, none of these three terms can be altered without the equality being instantly destroyed. If the Sovereign desires to govern, or the magistrate to give laws, or if the subjects refuse to obey, disorder takes the place of regularity, force and will no longer act together, and the State is dissolved and falls into despotism or anarchy. Lastly, as there is only one mean proportional between each relation, there is also only one good government possible for a State. But, as countless events may change the relations of a people, not only may different governments be good for different peoples, but also for the same people at different times.

In attempting to give some idea of the various relations that may hold between these two extreme terms, I shall take as an example the number of a people, which is the most easily expressible.

Suppose the State is composed of ten thousand citizens. The Sovereign can only be considered collectively and as a body; but each member, as being a subject, is regarded as an individual: thus the Sovereign is to the subject as ten thousand to one, i.e., each member of the State has as his share only a ten-thousandth part of the sovereign authority, although he is wholly under its control. If the people numbers a hundred thousand, the condition of the subject undergoes no change, and each equally is under the whole authority of the laws, while his vote, being reduced to a hundred-thousandth part, has ten times less influence in drawing them up. The subject therefore remaining always a unit, the relation between him and the Sovereign increases with the number of the citizens. From this it follows that, the larger the State, the less the liberty.

When I say the relation increases, I mean that it grows more unequal. Thus the greater it is in the geometrical sense, the less relation there is in the ordinary sense of the word. In the former sense, the relation, considered according to quantity, is expressed by the quotient; in the latter, considered according to identity, it is reckoned by similarity.

Now, the less relation the particular wills have to the general will, that is, morals and manners to laws, the more should the repressive force be increased. The government, then, to be good, should be proportionately stronger as the people is more numerous.

On the other hand, as the growth of the State gives the depositaries of the public authority more temptations and chances of abusing their power, the greater the force with which the government ought to be endowed for keeping the people in hand, the greater too should be the force at the disposal of the Sovereign for keeping the government in hand. I am speaking, not of absolute force, but of the relative force of the different parts of the State.

It follows from this double relation that the continuous proportion between the Sovereign, the prince and the people, is by no means an arbitrary idea, but a necessary consequence of the nature of the body politic. It follows further that, one of the extreme terms, viz., the people, as subject, being fixed and represented by unity, whenever the duplicate ratio increases or diminishes, the simple ratio does the same, and is changed accordingly. From this we see that there is not a single unique and absolute form of government, but as many governments differing in nature as there are States differing in size.

If, ridiculing this system, any one were to say that, in order to find the mean proportional and give form to the body of the government, it is only necessary, according to me, to find the square root of the number of the people, I should answer that I am here taking this number only as an instance; that the relations of which I am speaking are not measured by the number of men alone, but generally by the amount of action, which is a combination of a multitude of causes; and that, further, if, to save words, I borrow for a moment the terms of geometry, I am none the less well aware that moral quantities do not allow of geometrical accuracy.

The government is on a small scale what the body politic which includes it is on a great one. It is a moral person endowed with certain faculties, active like the Sovereign and passive like the State, and capable of being resolved into other similar relations. This accordingly gives rise to a new proportion, within which there is yet another, according to the arrangement of the magistracies, till an indivisible middle term is reached, i.e., a single ruler or supreme magistrate, who may be represented, in the midst of this progression, as the unity between the fractional and the ordinal series.

Without encumbering ourselves with this multiplication of terms, let us rest content with regarding government as a new body within the State, distinct from the people and the Sovereign, and intermediate between them.

There is between these two bodies this essential difference, that the State exists by itself, and the government only through the Sovereign. Thus the dominant will of the prince is, or should be, nothing but the general will or the law; his force is only the public force concentrated in his hands, and, as soon as he tries to base any absolute and independent act on his own authority, the tie that binds the whole together begins to be loosened. If finally the prince should come to have a particular will more active than the will of the Sovereign, and should employ the public force in his hands in obedience to this particular will, there would be, so to speak, two Sovereigns, one rightful and the other actual, the social union would evaporate instantly, and the body politic would be dissolved.

However, in order that the government may have a true existence and a real life distinguishing it from the body of the State, and in order that all its members may be able to act in concert and fulfil the end for which it was set up, it must have a particular personality, a sensibility common to its members, and a force and will of its own making for its preservation. This particular existence implies assemblies, councils, power and deliberation and decision, rights, titles, and privileges belonging exclusively to the prince and making the office of magistrate more honourable in proportion as it is more troublesome. The difficulties lie in the manner of so ordering this subordinate whole within the whole, that it in no way alters the general constitution by affirmation of its own, and always distinguishes the particular force it possesses, which is destined to aid in its preservation, from the public force, which is destined to the preservation of the State; and, in a word, is always ready to sacrifice the government to the people, and never to sacrifice the people to the government.

Furthermore, although the artificial body of the government is the work of another artificial body, and has, we may say, only a borrowed and subordinate life, this does not prevent it from being able to act with more or less vigour or promptitude, or from being, so to speak, in more or less robust health. Finally, without departing directly from the end for which it was instituted, it may deviate more or less from it, according to the manner of its constitution.

From all these differences arise the various relations which the government ought to bear to the body of the State, according to the accidental and particular relations by which the State itself is modified, for often the government that is best in itself will become the most pernicious, if the relations in which it stands have altered according to the defects of the body politic to which it belongs.

## 2. THE CONSTITUENT PRINCIPLE IN THE VARIOUS FORMS OF GOVERNMENT

TO set forth the general cause of the above differences, we must here distinguish between government and its principle, as we did before between the State and the Sovereign.

The body of the magistrate may be composed of a greater or a less number of members. We said that the relation of the Sovereign to the subjects was greater in proportion as the people was more numerous, and, by a clear analogy, we may say the same of the relation of the government to the magistrates.

But the total force of the government, being always that of the State, is invariable; so that, the more of this force it expends on its own members, the less it has left to employ on the whole people.

The more numerous the magistrates, therefore, the weaker the government. This principle being fundamental, we must do our best to make it clear.

In the person of the magistrate we can distinguish three essentially different wills: first, the private will of the individual, tending only to his personal advantage; secondly, the common will of the magistrates, which is relative solely to the advantage of the prince, and may be called corporate will, being general in relation to the government, and particular in relation to the State, of which the government forms part; and, in the third place, the will of the people or the sovereign will, which is general both in relation to the State regarded as the whole, and to the government regarded as a part of the whole.

In a perfect act of legislation, the individual or particular will should be at zero; the corporate will belonging to the government should occupy a very subordinate position; and, consequently, the general or sovereign will should always predominate and should be the sole guide of all the rest.

According to the natural order, on the other hand, these different wills become more active in proportion as they are concentrated. Thus, the general will is always the weakest, the corporate will second, and the individual will strongest of all: so that, in the government, each member is first of all himself, then a magistrate, and then a citizen — in an order exactly the reverse of what the social system requires.

This granted, if the whole government is in the hands of one man, the particular and the corporate will are wholly united, and consequently the latter is at its highest possible degree of intensity. But, as the use to which the force is put depends on the degree reached by the will, and as the absolute force of the government is invariable, it follows that the most active government is that of one man.

Suppose, on the other hand, we unite the government with the legislative authority, and make the Sovereign prince also, and all the citizens so many magistrates: then the corporate will, being confounded with the general will, can possess no greater activity than that will, and must leave the particular will as strong as it can possibly be. Thus, the government, having always the same absolute force, will be at the lowest point of its relative force or activity.

These relations are incontestable, and there are other considerations which still further confirm them. We can see, for instance, that each magistrate is more active in the body to which he belongs than each citizen in that to which he belongs, and that consequently the particular will has much more influence on the acts of the government than on those of the Sovereign; for each magistrate is almost always charged with some governmental function, while each citizen, taken singly, exercises no function of Sovereignty. Furthermore, the bigger the State grows, the more its real force increases, though not in direct proportion to its growth; but, the State remaining the same, the number of magistrates may increase to any extent, without the government gaining any greater real force; for its force is that of the State, the dimension of which remains equal. Thus the relative force or activity of the government decreases, while its absolute or real force cannot increase.

Moreover, it is a certainty that promptitude in execution diminishes as more people are put in charge of it: where prudence is made too much of, not enough is made of fortune; opportunity is let slip, and deliberation results in the loss of its object.

I have just proved that the government grows remiss in proportion as the number of the magistrates increases; and I previously proved that, the more numerous the people, the greater should be the repressive force. From this it follows that the relation of the magistrates to the government should vary inversely to the relation of the subjects to the Sovereign; that is to say, the larger the State, the more should the government be tightened, so that the number of the rulers diminish in proportion to the increase of that of the people.

It should be added that I am here speaking of the relative strength of the government, and not of its rectitude: for, on the other hand, the more numerous the magistracy, the nearer the corporate will comes to the general will; while, under a single magistrate, the corporate will is, as I said, merely a particular will. Thus, what may be gained on one side is lost on the other, and the art of the legislator is to know how to fix the point at which the force and the will of the government, which are always in inverse proportion, meet in the relation that is most to the advantage of the State.

## 3. THE DIVISION OF GOVERNMENTS

WE saw in the last chapter what causes the various kinds or forms of government to be distinguished according to the number of the members composing them: it remains in this to discover how the division is made.

In the first place, the Sovereign may commit the charge of the government to the whole people or to the majority of the people, so that more citizens are magistrates than are mere private individuals. This form of government is called *democracy*.

Or it may restrict the government to a small number, so that there are more private citizens than magistrates; and this is named *aristocracy*.

Lastly, it may concentrate the whole government in the hands of a single magistrate from whom all others hold their power. This third form is the most usual, and is called *monarchy*, or royal government.

It should be remarked that all these forms, or at least the first two, admit of degree, and even of very wide differences; for democracy may include the whole people, or may be restricted to half. Aristocracy, in its turn, may be restricted indefinitely from half the people down to the smallest possible number. Even royalty is susceptible of a measure of distribution. Sparta always had two kings, as its constitution provided; and the Roman Empire saw as many as eight emperors at once, without it being possible to say that the Empire was split up. Thus there is a point at which each form of government passes into the next, and it becomes clear that, under three comprehensive denominations, government is really susceptible of as many diverse forms as the State has citizens.

There are even more: for, as the government may also, in certain aspects, be subdivided into other parts, one administered in one fashion and one in another, the combination of the three forms may result in a multitude of mixed forms, each of which admits of multiplication by all the simple forms.

There has been at all times much dispute concerning the best form of government, without consideration of the fact that each is in some cases the best, and in others the worst.

If, in the different States, the number of supreme magistrates should be in inverse ratio to the number of citizens, it follows that, generally, democratic government suits small States, aristocratic government those of middle size, and monarchy great ones. This rule is immediately deducible from the principle laid down. But it is impossible to count the innumerable circumstances which may furnish exceptions.

## 4. DEMOCRACY

HE who makes the law knows better than any one else how it should be executed and interpreted. It seems then impossible to have a better constitution than that in which the executive and legislative powers are united; but this very fact renders the government in certain respects inadequate, because things which should be distinguished are confounded, and the prince and the Sovereign, being the same person, form, so to speak, no more than a government without government.

It is not good for him who makes the laws to execute them, or for the body of the people to turn its attention away from a general standpoint and devote it to particular objects. Nothing is more dangerous than the influence of private interests in public affairs, and the abuse of the laws by the government is a less evil than the corruption of the legislator, which is the inevitable sequel to a particular standpoint. In such a case, the State being altered in substance, all reformation becomes impossible, A people that would never misuse governmental powers would never misuse independence; a people that would always govern well would not need to be governed.

If we take the term in the strict sense, there never has been a real democracy, and there never will be. It is against the natural order for the many to govern and the few to be governed. It is unimaginable that the people should remain continually assembled to devote their time to public affairs, and it is clear that they cannot set up commissions for that purpose without the form of administration being changed.

In fact, I can confidently lay down as a principle that, when the functions of government are shared by several tribunals, the less numerous sooner or later acquire the greatest authority, if only because they are in a position to expedite affairs, and power thus naturally comes into their hands.

Besides, how many conditions that are difficult to unite does such a government presuppose! First, a very small State, where the people can readily be got together and where each citizen can with ease know all the rest; secondly, great simplicity of manners, to prevent business from multiplying and raising thorny problems; next, a large measure of equality in rank and fortune, without which equality of rights and authority cannot long subsist; lastly, little or no luxury — for luxury either comes of riches or makes them necessary; it corrupts at once rich and poor, the rich by possession and the poor by covetousness; it sells the country to softness and vanity, and takes away from the State all its citizens, to make them slaves one to another, and one and all to public opinion.

This is why a famous writer has made virtue the fundamental principle of Republics;[E1] for all these conditions could not exist without virtue. But, for want of the necessary distinctions, that great thinker was often inexact, and sometimes obscure, and did not see that, the sovereign authority being everywhere the same, the same principle should be found in every well-constituted State, in a greater or less degree, it is true, according to the form of the government.

It may be added that there is no government so subject to civil wars and intestine agitations as democratic or popular government, because there is none which has so strong and continual a tendency to change to another form, or which demands more vigilance and courage for its maintenance as it is. Under such a constitution above all, the citizen should arm himself with strength and constancy, and say, every day of his life, what a virtuous Count Palatine[19] said in the Diet of Poland: *Malo periculosam libertatem quam quietum servitium.*[20]

Were there a people of gods, their government would be democratic. So perfect a government is not for men.

## 5. ARISTOCRACY

WE have here two quite distinct moral persons, the government and the Sovereign, and in consequence two general wills, one general in relation to all the citizens, the other only for the members of the administration. Thus, although the government may regulate its internal policy as it pleases, it can never speak to the people save in the name of the Sovereign, that is, of the people itself, a fact which must not be forgotten.

The first societies governed themselves aristocratically. The heads of families took counsel together on public affairs. The young bowed without question to the authority of experience. Hence such names as *priests, elders, senate*, and *gerontes*. The savages of North America govern themselves in this way even now, and their government is admirable.

But, in proportion as artificial inequality produced by institutions became predominant over natural inequality, riches or power[21] were put before age, and aristocracy became elective. Finally, the transmission of the father's power along with his goods to his children, by creating patrician families, made government hereditary, and there came to be senators of twenty.

There are then three sorts of aristocracy — natural, elective and hereditary. The first is only for simple peoples; the third is the worst of all governments; the second is the best, and is aristocracy properly so called.

Besides the advantage that lies in the distinction between the two powers, it presents that of its members being chosen; for, in popular government, all the citizens are born magistrates; but here magistracy is confined to a few, who become such only by election.[22] By this means uprightness, understanding, experience and all other claims to pre-eminence and public esteem become so many further guarantees of wise government.

Moreover, assemblies are more easily held, affairs better discussed and carried out with more order and diligence, and the credit of the State is better sustained abroad by venerable senators than by a multitude that is unknown or despised.

In a word, it is the best and most natural arrangement that the wisest should govern the many, when it is assured that they will govern for its profit, and not for their own. There is no need to multiply instruments, or get twenty thousand men to do what a hundred picked men can do even better. But it must not be forgotten that corporate interest here begins to direct the public power less under the regulation of the general will, and that a further inevitable propensity takes away from the laws part of the executive power.

If we are to speak of what is individually desirable, neither should the State be so small, nor a people so simple and upright, that the execution of the laws follows immediately from the public will, as it does in a good democracy. Nor should the nation be so great that the rulers have to scatter in order to govern it and are able to play the Sovereign each in his own department, and, beginning by making themselves independent, end by becoming masters.

But if aristocracy does not demand all the virtues needed by popular government, it demands others which are peculiar to itself; for instance, moderation on the side of the rich and contentment on that of the poor; for it seems that thorough-going equality would be out of place, as it was not found even at Sparta.

Furthermore, if this form of government carries with it a certain inequality of fortune, this is justifiable in order that as a rule the administration of public affairs may be entrusted to those who are most able to give them their whole time, but not, as Aristotle maintains, in order that the rich may always be put first. On the contrary, it is of importance that an opposite choice should occasionally teach the people that the deserts of men offer claims to pre-eminence more important than those of riches.

## 6. MONARCHY

So far, we have considered the prince as a moral and collective person, unified by the force of the laws, and the depositary in the State of the executive power. We have now to consider this power when it is gathered together into the hands of a natural person, a real man, who alone has the right to dispose of it in accordance with the laws. Such a person is called a monarch or king.

In contrast with other forms of administration, in which a collective being stands for an individual, in this form an individual stands for a collective being; so that the moral unity that constitutes the prince is at the same time a physical unity, and all the qualities, which in the other case are only with difficulty brought together by the law, are found naturally united.

Thus the will of the people, the will of the prince, the public force of the State, and the particular force of the government, all answer to a single motive power; all the springs of the machine are in the same hands, the whole moves towards the same end; there are no conflicting movements to cancel one another, and no kind of constitution can be imagined in which a less amount of effort produces a more considerable amount of action. Archimedes, seated quietly on the bank and easily drawing a great vessel afloat, stands to my mind for a skilful monarch, governing vast states from his study, and moving everything while he seems himself unmoved.

But if no government is more vigorous than this, there is also none in which the particular will holds more sway and rules the rest more easily. Everything moves towards the same end indeed, but this end is by no means that of the public happiness, and even the force of the administration constantly shows itself prejudicial to the State.

Kings desire to be absolute, and men are always crying out to them from afar that the best means of being so is to get themselves loved by their people. This precept is all very well, and even in some respects very true. Unfortunately, it will always be derided at court. The power which comes of a people's love is no doubt the greatest; but it is precarious and conditional, and princes will never rest content with it. The best kings desire to be in a position to be wicked, if they please, without forfeiting their mastery: political sermonisers may tell them to their hearts' content that, the people's strength being their own, their first interest is that the people should be prosperous, numerous and formidable; they are well aware that this is untrue. Their first personal interest is that the people should be weak, wretched, and unable to resist them. I admit that, provided the subjects remained always in submission, the prince's interest would indeed be that it should be powerful, in order that its power, being his own, might make him formidable to his neighbours; but, this interest being merely secondary and subordinate, and strength being incompatible with submission, princes naturally give the preference always to the principle that is more to their immediate advantage. This is what Samuel put strongly before the Hebrews, and what Machiavelli has clearly shown. He professed to teach kings; but it was the people he really taught. His *Prince* is the book of Republicans.[23]

We found, on general grounds, that monarchy is suitable only for great States, and this is confirmed when we examine it in itself. The more numerous the public administration, the smaller becomes the relation between the prince and the subjects, and the nearer it comes to equality, so that in democracy the ratio is unity, or absolute equality. Again, as the government is restricted in numbers the ratio increases and reaches its *maximum* when the government is in the hands of a single person. There is then too great a distance between prince and people, and the State lacks a bond of union. To form such a bond, there must be intermediate orders, and princes, personages and nobility to compose them. But no such things suit a small State, to which all class differences mean ruin.

If, however, it is hard for a great State to be well governed, it is much harder for it to be so by a single man; and every one knows what happens when kings substitute others for themselves.

An essential and inevitable defect, which will always rank monarchical below the republican government, is that in a republic the public voice hardly ever raises to the highest positions men who are not enlightened and capable, and such as to fill them with honour; while in monarchies those who rise to the top are most often merely petty blunderers, petty swindlers, and petty intriguers, whose petty talents cause them to get into the highest positions at Court, but, as soon as they have got there, serve only to make their ineptitude clear to the public. The people is far less often mistaken in its choice than the prince; and a man of real worth among the king's ministers is almost as rare as a fool at the head of a republican government. Thus, when, by some fortunate chance, one of these born governors takes the helm of State in some monarchy that has been nearly overwhelmed by swarms of "gentlemanly" administrators, there is nothing but amazement at the resources he discovers, and his coming marks an era in his country's history.

For a monarchical State to have a chance of being well governed, its population and extent must be proportionate to the abilities of its governor. It is easier to conquer than to rule. With a long enough lever, the world could be moved with a single finger; to sustain it needs the shoulders of Hercules. However small a State may be, the prince is hardly ever big enough for it. When, on the other hand, it happens that the State is too small for its ruler, in these rare cases too it is ill governed, because the ruler, constantly pursuing his great designs, forgets the interests of the people, and makes it no less wretched by misusing the talents he has, than a ruler of less capacity would make it for want of those he had not. A kingdom should, so to speak, expand or contract with each reign, according to the prince's capabilities; but, the abilities of a senate being more constant in quantity, the State can then have permanent frontiers without the administration suffering.

The disadvantage that is most felt in monarchical government is the want of the continuous succession which, in both the other forms, provides an unbroken bond of union. When one king dies, another is needed; elections leave dangerous intervals and are full of storms; and unless the citizens are disinterested and upright to a degree which very seldom goes with this kind of government, intrigue and corruption abound. He to whom the State has sold itself can hardly help selling it in his turn and repaying himself, at the expense of the weak, the money the powerful have wrung from him. Under such an administration, venality sooner or later spreads through every part, and peace so enjoyed under a king is worse than the disorders of an interregnum.

What has been done to prevent these evils? Crowns have been made hereditary in certain families, and an order of succession has been set up, to prevent disputes from arising on the death of kings. That is to say, the disadvantages of regency have been put in place of those of election, apparent tranquillity has been preferred to wise administration, and men have chosen rather to risk having children, monstrosities, or imbeciles as rulers to having disputes over the choice of good kings. It has not been taken into account that, in so exposing ourselves to the risks this possibility entails, we are setting almost all the chances against us. There was sound sense in what the younger Dionysius said to his father, who reproached him for doing some shameful deed by asking, "Did I set you the example?" "No," answered his son, "but your father was not king."

Everything conspires to take away from a man who is set in authority over others the sense of justice and reason. Much trouble, we are told, is taken to teach young princes the art of reigning; but their education seems to do them no good. It would be better to begin by teaching them the art of obeying. The greatest kings whose praises history tells were not brought up to reign: reigning is a science we are never so far from possessing as when we have learnt too much of it, and one we acquire better by obeying than by commanding. *"Nam utilissimus idem ac brevissimus bonarum malarumque rerum delectus cogitare quid aut nolueris sub alio principe, aut volueris."*[24]

One result of this lack of coherence is the inconstancy of royal government, which, regulated now on one scheme and now on another, according to the character of the reigning prince or those who reign for him, cannot for long have a fixed object or a consistent policy — and this variability, not found in the other forms of government, where the prince is always the same, causes the State to be always shifting from principle to principle and from project to project. Thus we may say that generally, if a court is more subtle in intrigue, there is more wisdom in a senate, and Republics advance towards their ends by more consistent and better considered policies; while every revolution in a royal ministry creates a revolution in the State; for the principle common to all ministers and nearly all kings is to do in every respect the reverse of what was done by their predecessors.

This incoherence further clears up a sophism that is very familiar to royalist political writers; not only is civil government likened to domestic government, and the prince to the father of a family — this error has already been refuted — but the prince is also freely credited with all the virtues he ought to possess, and is supposed to be always what he should be. This supposition once made, royal government is clearly preferable to all others, because it is incontestably the strongest, and, to be the best also, wants only a corporate will more in conformity with the general will.

But if, according to Plato,[25] the "king by nature" is such a rarity, how often will nature and fortune conspire to give him a crown? And, if royal education necessarily corrupts those who receive it, what is to be hoped from a series of men brought up to reign? It is, then, wanton self-deception to confuse royal government with government by a good king. To see such government as it is in itself, we must consider it as it is under princes who are incompetent or wicked: for either they will come to the throne wicked or incompetent, or the throne will make them so.

These difficulties have not escaped our writers, who, all the same, are not troubled by them. The remedy, they say, is to obey without a murmur: God sends bad kings in His wrath, and they must be borne as the scourges of Heaven. Such talk is doubtless edifying; but it would be more in place in a pulpit than in a political book. What are we to think of a doctor who promises miracles, and whose whole art is to exhort the sufferer to patience? We know for ourselves that we must put up with a bad government when it is there; the question is how to find a good one.

## 7. MIXED GOVERNMENTS

STRICTLY speaking, there is no such thing as a simple government. An isolated ruler must have subordinate magistrates; a popular government must have a head. There is therefore, in the distribution of the executive power, always a gradation from the greater to the lesser number, with the difference that sometimes the greater number is dependent on the smaller, and sometimes the smaller on the greater.

Sometimes the distribution is equal, when either the constituent parts are in mutual dependence, as in the government of England, or the authority of each section is independent, but imperfect, as in Poland. This last form is bad; for it secures no unity in the government, and the State is left without a bond of union.

Is a simple or a mixed government the better? Political writers are always debating the question, which must be answered as we have already answered a question about all forms of government.

Simple government is better in itself, just because it is simple. But when the executive power is not sufficiently dependent upon the legislative power, i.e., when the prince is more closely related to the Sovereign than the people to the prince, this lack of proportion must be cured by the division of the government; for all the parts have then no less authority over the subjects, while their division makes them all together less strong against the Sovereign.

The same disadvantage is also prevented by the appointment of intermediate magistrates, who leave the government entire, and have the effect only of balancing the two powers and maintaining their respective rights. Government is then not mixed, but moderated.

The opposite disadvantages may be similarly cured, and, when the government is too lax, tribunals may be set up to concentrate it. This is done in all democracies. In the first case, the government is divided to make it weak; in the second, to make it strong: for the *maxima* of both strength and weakness are found in simple governments, while the mixed forms result in a mean strength.

## 8. THAT ALL FORMS OF GOVERNMENT DO NOT SUIT ALL COUNTRIES

LIBERTY, not being a fruit of all climates, is not within the reach of all peoples. The more this principle, laid down by Montesquieu[22] is considered, the more its truth is felt; the more it is combated, the more chance is given to confirm it by new proofs.

In all the governments that there are, the public person consumes without producing. Whence then does it get what it consumes? From the labour of its members. The necessities of the public are supplied out of the superfluities of individuals. It follows that the civil State can subsist only so long as men's labour brings them a return greater than their needs.

The amount of this excess is not the same in all countries. In some it is considerable, in others middling, in yet others nil, in some even negative. The relation of product to subsistence depends on the fertility of the climate, on the sort of labour the land demands, on the nature of its products, on the strength of its inhabitants, on the greater or less consumption they find necessary, and on several further considerations of which the whole relation is made up.

On the other side, all governments are not of the same nature: some are less voracious than others, and the differences between them are based on this second principle, that the further from their source the public contributions are removed, the more burdensome they become. The charge should be measured not by the amount of the impositions, but by the path they have to travel in order to get back to those from whom they came. When the circulation is prompt and well-established, it does not matter whether much or little is paid; the people is always rich and, financially speaking, all is well. On the contrary, however little the people gives, if that little does not return to it, it is soon exhausted by giving continually: the State is then never rich, and the people is always a people of beggars.

It follows that, the more the distance between people and government increases, the more burdensome tribute becomes: thus, in a democracy, the people bears the least charge; in an aristocracy, a greater charge; and, in monarchy, the weight becomes heaviest. Monarchy therefore suits only wealthy nations; aristocracy, States of middling size and wealth; and democracy, States that are small and poor.

In fact, the more we reflect, the more we find the difference between free and monarchical States to be this: in the former, everything is used for the public advantage; in the latter, the public forces and those of individuals are affected by each other, and either increases as the other grows weak; finally, instead of governing subjects to make them happy, despotism makes them wretched in order to govern them.

We find then, in every climate, natural causes according to which the form of government which it requires can be assigned, and we can even say what sort of inhabitants it should have.

Unfriendly and barren lands, where the product does not repay the labour, should remain desert and uncultivated, or peopled only by savages; lands where men's labour brings in no more than the exact *minimum* necessary to subsistence should be inhabited by barbarous peoples: in such places all polity is impossible. Lands where the surplus of product over labour is only middling are suitable for free peoples; those in which the soil is abundant and fertile and gives a great product for a little labour call for monarchical government, in order that the surplus of superfluities among the subjects may be consumed by the luxury of the prince: for it is better for this excess to be absorbed by the government than dissipated among the individuals. I am aware that there are exceptions; but these exceptions themselves confirm the rule, in that sooner or later they produce revolutions which restore things to the natural order.

General laws should always be distinguished from individual causes that may modify their effects. If all the South were covered with Republics and all the North with despotic States, it would be none the less true that, in point of climate, despotism is suitable to hot countries, barbarism to cold countries, and good polity to temperate regions. I see also that, the principle being granted, there may be disputes on its application; it may be said that there are cold countries that are very fertile, and tropical countries that are very unproductive. But this difficulty exists only for those who do not consider the question in all its aspects. We must, as I have already said, take labour, strength, consumption, etc., into account.

Take two tracts of equal extent, one of which brings in five and the other ten. If the inhabitants of the first consume four and those of the second nine, the surplus of the first product will be a fifth and that of the second a tenth. The ratio of these two surpluses will then be inverse to that of the products, and the tract which produces only five will give a surplus double that of the tract which produces ten.

But there is no question of a double product, and I think no one would put the fertility of cold countries, as a general rule, on an equality with that of hot ones. Let us, however, suppose this equality to exist: let us, if you will, regard England as on the same level as Sicily, and Poland as Egypt — further south, we shall have Africa and the Indies; further north, nothing at all. To get this equality of product, what a difference there must be in tillage: in Sicily, there is only need to scratch the ground; in England, how men must toil! But, where more hands are needed to get the same product, the superfluity must necessarily be less.

Consider, besides, that the same number of men consume much less in hot countries. The climate requires sobriety for the sake of health; and Europeans who try to live there as they would at home all perish of dysentery and indigestion. "We are," says Chardin, "carnivorous animals, wolves, in comparison with the Asiatics. Some attribute the sobriety of the Persians to the fact that their country is less cultivated; but it is my belief that their country abounds less in commodities because the inhabitants need less. If their frugality," he goes on, "were the effect of the nakedness of the land, only the poor would eat little; but everybody does so. Again, less or more would be eaten in various provinces, according to the land's fertility; but the same sobriety is found throughout the kingdom. They are very proud of their manner of life, saying that you have only to look at their hue to recognise how far it excels that of the Christians. In fact, the Persians are of an even hue; their skins are fair, fine and smooth; while the hue of their subjects, the Armenians, who live after the European fashion, is rough and blotchy, and their bodies are gross and unwieldy."

The nearer you get to the equator, the less people live on. Meat they hardly touch; rice, maize, curcur, millet and cassava are their ordinary food. There are in the Indies millions of men whose subsistence does not cost a halfpenny a day. Even in Europe we find considerable differences of appetite between Northern and Southern peoples. A Spaniard will live for a week on a German's dinner. In the countries in which men are more voracious, luxury therefore turns in the direction of consumption. In England, luxury appears in a well-filled table; in Italy, you feast on sugar and flowers.

Luxury in clothes shows similar differences. In climates in which the changes of season are prompt and violent, men have better and simpler clothes; where they clothe themselves only for adornment, what is striking is more thought of than what is useful; clothes themselves are then a luxury. At Naples, you may see daily walking in the Pausilippeum men in gold-embroidered upper garments and nothing else. It is the same with buildings; magnificence is the sole consideration where there is nothing to fear from the air. In Paris and London, you desire to be lodged warmly and comfortably; in Madrid, you have superb salons, but not a window that closes, and you go to bed in a mere hole.

In hot countries foods are much more substantial and succulent; and the third difference cannot but have an influence on the second. Why are so many vegetables eaten in Italy? Because there they are good, nutritious and excellent in taste. In France, where they are nourished only on water, they are far from nutritious and are thought nothing of at table. They take up all the same no less ground, and cost at least as much pains to cultivate. It is a proved fact that the wheat of Barbary, in other respects inferior to that of France, yields much more flour, and that the wheat of France in turn yields more than that of northern countries; from which it may be inferred that a like gradation in the same direction, from equator to pole, is found generally. But is it not an obvious disadvantage for an equal product to contain less nourishment?

To all these points may be added another, which at once depends on and strengthens them. Hot countries need inhabitants less than cold countries, and can support more of them. There is thus a double surplus, which is all to the advantage of despotism. The greater the territory occupied by a fixed number of inhabitants, the more difficult revolt becomes, because rapid or secret concerted action is impossible, and the government can easily unmask projects and cut communications; but the more a numerous people is gathered together, the less can the government usurp the Sovereign's place: the people's leaders can deliberate as safely in their houses as the prince in council, and the crowd gathers as rapidly in the squares as the prince's troops in their quarters. The advantage of tyrannical government therefore lies in acting at great distances. With the help of the rallying-points it establishes, its strength, like that of the lever,[26] grows with distance. The strength of the people, on the other hand, acts only when concentrated: when spread abroad, it evaporates and is lost, like powder scattered on the ground, which catches fire only grain by grain. The least populous countries are thus the fittest for tyranny: fierce animals reign only in deserts.

## 9. THE MARKS OF A GOOD GOVERNMENT

THE question "What absolutely is the best government?" is unanswerable as well as indeterminate; or rather, there are as many good answers as there are possible combinations in the absolute and relative situations of all nations.

But if it is asked by what sign we may know that a given people is well or ill governed, that is another matter, and the question, being one of fact, admits of an answer.

It is not, however, answered, because everyone wants to answer it in his own way. Subjects extol public tranquillity, citizens individual liberty; the one class prefers security of possessions, the other that of person; the one regards as the best government that which is most severe, the other maintains that the mildest is the best; the one wants crimes punished, the other wants them prevented; the one wants the State to be feared by its neighbours, the other prefers that it should be ignored; the one is content if money circulates, the other demands that the people shall have bread. Even if an agreement were come to on these and similar points, should we have got any further? As moral qualities do not admit of exact measurement, agreement about the mark does not mean agreement about the valuation.

For my part, I am continually astonished that a mark so simple is not recognised, or that men are of so bad faith as not to admit it. What is the end of political association? The preservation and prosperity of its members. And what is the surest mark of their preservation and prosperity? Their numbers and population. Seek then nowhere else this mark that is in dispute. The rest being equal, the government under which, without external aids, without naturalisation or colonies, the citizens increase and multiply most, is beyond question the best. The government under which a people wanes and diminishes is the worst. Calculators, it is left for you to count, to measure, to compare.[27]

## 10. THE ABUSE OF GOVERNMENT AND ITS TENDENCY TO DEGENERATE

AS the particular will acts constantly in opposition to the general will, the government continually exerts itself against the Sovereignty. The greater this exertion becomes, the more the constitution changes; and, as there is in this case no other corporate will to create an equilibrium by resisting the will of the prince, sooner or later the prince must inevitably suppress the Sovereign and break the social treaty. This is the unavoidable and inherent defect which, from the very birth of the body politic, tends ceaselessly to destroy it, as age and death end by destroying the human body.

There are two general courses by which government degenerates: i.e., when it undergoes contraction, or when the State is dissolved.

Government undergoes contraction when it passes from the many to the few, that is, from democracy to aristocracy, and from aristocracy to royalty. To do so is its natural propensity.[28] If it took the backward course from the few to the many, it could be said that it was relaxed; but this inverse sequence is impossible.

Indeed, governments never change their form except when their energy is exhausted and leaves them too weak to keep what they have. If a government at once extended its sphere and relaxed its stringency, its force would become absolutely nil, and it would persist still less. It is therefore necessary to wind up the spring and tighten the hold as it gives way: or else the State it sustains will come to grief.

The dissolution of the State may come about in either of two ways.

First, when the prince ceases to administer the State in accordance with the laws, and usurps the Sovereign power. A remarkable change then occurs: not the government, but the State, undergoes contraction; I mean that the great State is dissolved, and another is formed within it, composed solely of the members of the government, which becomes for the rest of the people merely master and tyrant. So that the moment the government usurps the Sovereignty, the social compact is broken, and all private citizens recover by right their natural liberty, and are forced, but not bound, to obey.

The same thing happens when the members of the government severally usurp the power they should exercise only as a body; this is as great an infraction of the laws, and results in even greater disorders. There are then, so to speak, as many princes as there are magistrates, and the State, no less divided than the government, either perishes or changes its form.

When the State is dissolved, the abuse of government, whatever it is, bears the common name of *anarchy*. To distinguish, democracy degenerates into *ochlocracy*, and aristocracy into *oligarchy;* and I would add that royalty degenerates into *tyranny;* but this last word is ambiguous and needs explanation.

In vulgar usage, a tyrant is a king who governs violently and without regard for justice and law. In the exact sense, a tyrant is an individual who arrogates to himself the royal authority without having a right to it. This is how the Greeks understood the word "tyrant": they applied it indifferently to good and bad princes whose authority was not legitimate.[29] *Tyrant* and *usurper* are thus perfectly synonymous terms.

In order that I may give different things different names, I call him who usurps the royal authority a *tyrant*, and him who usurps the sovereign power a *despot*. The tyrant is he who thrusts himself in contrary to the laws to govern in accordance with the laws; the despot is he who sets himself above the laws themselves. Thus the tyrant cannot be a despot, but the despot is always a tyrant.

## 11. THE DEATH OF THE BODY POLITIC

SUCH is the natural and inevitable tendency of the best constituted governments. If Sparta and Rome perished, what State can hope to endure for ever? If we would set up a long-lived form of government, let us not even dream of making it eternal. If we are to succeed, we must not attempt the impossible, or flatter ourselves that we are endowing the work of man with a stability of which human conditions do not permit.

The body politic, as well as the human body, begins to die as soon as it is born, and carries in itself the causes of its destruction. But both may have a constitution that is more or less robust and suited to preserve them a longer or a shorter time. The constitution of man is the work of nature; that of the State the work of art. It is not in men's power to prolong their own lives; but it is for them to prolong as much as possible the life of the State, by giving it the best possible constitution. The best constituted State will have an end; but it will end later than any other, unless some unforeseen accident brings about its untimely destruction.

The life-principle of the body politic lies in the sovereign authority. The legislative power is the heart of the State; the executive power is its brain, which causes the movement of all the parts. The brain may become paralysed and the individual still live. A man may remain an imbecile and live; but as soon as the heart ceases to perform its functions, the animal is dead.

The State subsists by means not of the laws, but of the legislative power. Yesterday's law is not binding to-day; but silence is taken for tacit consent, and the Sovereign is held to confirm incessantly the laws it does not abrogate as it might. All that it has once declared itself to will it wills always, unless it revokes its declaration.

Why then is so much respect paid to old laws? For this very reason. We must believe that nothing but the excellence of old acts of will can have preserved them so long: if the Sovereign had not recognised them as throughout salutary, it would have revoked them a thousand times. This is why, so far from growing weak, the laws continually gain new strength in any well constituted State; the precedent of antiquity makes them daily more venerable: while wherever the laws grow weak as they become old, this proves that there is no longer a legislative power, and that the State is dead.

## 12. HOW THE SOVEREIGN AUTHORITY MAINTAINS ITSELF

THE Sovereign, having no force other than the legislative power, acts only by means of the laws; and the laws being solely the authentic acts of the general will, the Sovereign cannot act save when the people is assembled. The people in assembly, I shall be told, is a mere chimera. It is so to-day, but two thousand years ago it was not so. Has man's nature changed?

The bounds of possibility, in moral matters, are less narrow than we imagine: it is our weaknesses, our vices and our prejudices that confine them. Base souls have no belief in great men; vile slaves smile in mockery at the name of liberty.

Let us judge of what can be done by what has been done. I shall say nothing of the Republics of ancient Greece; but the Roman Republic was, to my mind, a great State, and the town of Rome a great town. The last census showed that there were in Rome four hundred thousand citizens capable of bearing arms, and the last computation of the population of the Empire showed over four million citizens, excluding subjects, foreigners, women, children and slaves.

What difficulties might not be supposed to stand in the way of the frequent assemblage of the vast population of this capital and its neighbourhood. Yet few weeks passed without the Roman people being in assembly, and even being so several times. It exercised not only the rights of Sovereignty, but also a part of those of government. It dealt with certain matters, and judged certain cases, and this whole people was found in the public meeting-place hardly less often as magistrates than as citizens.

If we went back to the earliest history of nations, we should find that most ancient governments, even those of monarchical form, such as the Macedonian and the Frankish, had similar councils. In any case, the one incontestable fact I have given is an answer to all difficulties; it is good logic to reason from the actual to the possible.

## 13. THE SAME (*continued*)

IT is not enough for the assembled people to have once fixed the constitution of the State by giving its sanction to a body of law; it is not enough for it to have set up a perpetual government, or provided once for all for the election of magistrates. Besides the extraordinary assemblies unforeseen circumstances may demand, there must be fixed periodical assemblies which cannot be abrogated or prorogued, so that on the proper day the people is legitimately called together by law, without need of any formal summoning.

But, apart from these assemblies authorised by their date alone, every assembly of the people not summoned by the magistrates appointed for that purpose, and in accordance with the prescribed forms, should be regarded as unlawful, and all its acts as null and void, because the command to assemble should itself proceed from the law.

The greater or less frequency with which lawful assemblies should occur depends on so many considerations that no exact rules about them can be given. It can only be said generally that the stronger the government the more often should the Sovereign show itself.

This, I shall be told, may do for a single town; but what is to be done when the State includes several? Is the sovereign authority to be divided? Or is it to be concentrated in a single town to which all the rest are made subject?

Neither the one nor the other, I reply. First, the sovereign authority is one and simple, and cannot be divided without being destroyed. In the second place, one town cannot, any more than one nation, legitimately be made subject to another, because the essence of the body politic lies in the reconciliation of obedience and liberty, and the words subject and Sovereign are identical correlatives the idea of which meets in the single word "citizen."

I answer further that the union of several towns in a single city is always bad, and that, if we wish to make such a union, we should not expect to avoid its natural disadvantages. It is useless to bring up abuses that belong to great States against one who desires to see only small ones; but how can small States be given the strength to resist great ones, as formerly the Greek towns resisted the Great King, and more recently Holland and Switzerland have resisted the House of Austria?

Nevertheless, if the State cannot be reduced to the right limits, there remains still one resource; this is, to allow no capital, to make the seat of government move from town to town, and to assemble by turn in each the Provincial Estates of the country.

People the territory evenly, extend everywhere the same rights, bear to every place in it abundance and life: by these means will the State become at once as strong and as well governed as possible. Remember that the walls of towns are built of the ruins of the houses of the countryside. For every palace I see raised in the capital, my mind's eye sees a whole country made desolate.

## 14. THE SAME (*continued*)

THE moment the people is legitimately assembled as a sovereign body, the jurisdiction of the government wholly lapses, the executive power is suspended, and the person of the meanest citizen is as sacred and inviolable as that of the first magistrate; for in the presence of the person represented, representatives no longer exist. Most of the tumults that arose in the comitia at Rome were due to ignorance or neglect of this rule. The consuls were in them merely the presidents of the people; the tribunes were mere speakers;[30] the senate was nothing at all.

These intervals of suspension, during which the prince recognises or ought to recognise an actual superior, have always been viewed by him with alarm; and these assemblies of the people, which are the aegis of the body politic and the curb on the government, have at all times been the horror of rulers: who therefore never spare pains, objections, difficulties, and promises, to stop the citizens from having them. When the citizens are greedy, cowardly, and pusillanimous, and love ease more than liberty, they do not long hold out against the redoubled efforts of the government; and thus, as the resisting force incessantly grows, the sovereign authority ends by disappearing, and most cities fall and perish before their time.

But between the sovereign authority and arbitrary government there sometimes intervenes a mean power of which something must be said.

## 15. DEPUTIES OR REPRESENTATIVES

AS soon as public service ceases to be the chief business of the citizens, and they would rather serve with their money than with their persons, the State is not far from its fall. When it is necessary to march out to war, they pay troops and stay at home: when it is necessary to meet in council, they name deputies and stay at home. By reason of idleness and money, they end by having soldiers to enslave their country and representatives to sell it.

It is through the hustle of commerce and the arts, through the greedy self-interest of profit, and through softness and love of amenities that personal services are replaced by money payments. Men surrender a part of their profits in order to have time to increase them at leisure. Make gifts of money, and you will not be long without chains. The word *finance* is a slavish word, unknown in the city-state. In a country that is truly free, the citizens do everything with their own arms and nothing by means of money; so far from paying to be exempted from their duties, they would even pay for the privilege of fulfilling them themselves. I am far from taking the common view: I hold enforced labour to be less opposed to liberty than taxes.

The better the constitution of a State is, the more do public affairs encroach on private in the minds of the citizens. Private affairs are even of much less importance, because the aggregate of the common happiness furnishes a greater proportion of that of each individual, so that there is less for him to seek in particular cares. In a well-ordered city every man flies to the assemblies: under a bad government no one cares to stir a step to get to them, because no one is interested in what happens there, because it is foreseen that the general will will not prevail, and lastly because domestic cares are all-absorbing. Good laws lead to the making of better ones; bad ones bring about worse. As soon as any man says of the affairs of the State *What does it matter to me?* the State may be given up for lost.

The lukewarmness of patriotism, the activity of private interest, the vastness of States, conquest and the abuse of government suggested the method of having deputies or representatives of the people in the national assemblies. These are what, in some countries, men have presumed to call the Third Estate. Thus the individual interest of two orders is put first and second; the public interest occupies only the third place.

Sovereignty, for the same reason as makes it inalienable, cannot be represented; it lies essentially in the general will, and will does not admit of representation: it is either the same, or other; there is no intermediate possibility. The deputies of the people, therefore, are not and cannot be its representatives: they are merely its stewards, and can carry through no definitive acts. Every law the people has not ratified in person is null and void — is, in fact, not a law. The people of England regards itself as free; but it is grossly mistaken; it is free only during the election of members of parliament. As soon as they are elected, slavery overtakes it, and it is nothing. The use it makes of the short moments of liberty it enjoys shows indeed that it deserves to lose them.

The idea of representation is modern; it comes to us from feudal government, from that iniquitous and absurd system which degrades humanity and dishonours the name of man. In ancient republics and even in monarchies, the people never had representatives; the word itself was unknown. It is very singular that in Rome, where the tribunes were so sacrosanct, it was never even imagined that they could usurp the functions of the people, and that in the midst of so great a multitude they never attempted to pass on their own authority a single plebiscitum. We can, however, form an idea of the difficulties caused sometimes by the people being so numerous, from what happened in the time of the Gracchi, when some of the citizens had to cast their votes from the roofs of buildings.

Where right and liberty are everything, disadvantages count for nothing. Among this wise people everything was given its just value, its lictors were allowed to do what its tribunes would never have dared to attempt; for it had no fear that its lictors would try to represent it.

To explain, however, in what way the tribunes did sometimes represent it, it is enough to conceive how the government represents the Sovereign. Law being purely the declaration of the general will, it is clear that, in the exercise of the legislative power, the people cannot be represented; but in that of the executive power, which is only the force that is applied to give the law effect, it both can and should be represented. We thus see that if we looked closely into the matter we should find that very few nations have any laws. However that may be, it is certain that the tribunes, possessing no executive power, could never represent the Roman people by right of the powers entrusted to them, but only by usurping those of the senate.

In Greece, all that the people had to do, it did for itself; it was constantly assembled in the public square. The Greeks lived in a mild climate; they had no natural greed; slaves did their work for them; their great concern was with liberty. Lacking the same advantages, how can you preserve the same rights? Your severer climates add to your needs;[31] for half the year your public squares are uninhabitable; the flatness of your languages unfits them for being heard in the open air; you sacrifice more for profit than for liberty, and fear slavery less than poverty.

What then? Is liberty maintained only by the help of slavery? It may be so. Extremes meet. Everything that is not in the course of nature has its disadvantages, civil society most of all. There are some unhappy circumstances in which we can only keep our liberty at others' expense, and where the citizen can be perfectly free only when the slave is most a slave. Such was the case with Sparta. As for you, modern peoples, you have no slaves, but you are slaves yourselves; you pay for their liberty with your own. It is in vain that you boast of this preference; I find in it more cowardice than humanity.

I do not mean by all this that it is necessary to have slaves, or that the right of slavery is legitimate: I am merely giving the reasons why modern peoples, believing themselves to be free, have representatives, while ancient peoples had none. In any case, the moment a people allows itself to be represented, it is no long free: it no longer exists.

All things considered, I do not see that it is possible henceforth for the Sovereign to preserve among us the exercise of its rights, unless the city is very small. But if it is very small, it will be conquered? No. I will show later on how the external strength of a great people[32] may be combined with the convenient polity and good order of a small State.

## 16. THAT THE INSTITUTION OF GOVERNMENT IS NOT A CONTRACT

THE legislative power once well established, the next thing is to establish similarly the executive power; for this latter, which operates only by particular acts, not being of the essence of the former, is naturally separate from it. Were it possible for the Sovereign, as such, to possess the executive power, right and fact would be so confounded that no one could tell what was law and what was not; and the body politic, thus disfigured, would soon fall a prey to the violence it was instituted to prevent.

As the citizens, by the social contract, are all equal, all can prescribe what all should do, but no one has a right to demand that another shall do what he does not do himself. It is strictly this right, which is indispensable for giving the body politic life and movement, that the Sovereign, in instituting the government, confers upon the prince.

It has been held that this act of establishment was a contract between the people and the rulers it sets over it-self, — a contract in which conditions were laid down between the two parties binding the one to command and the other to obey. It will be admitted, I am sure, that this is an odd kind of contract to enter into. But let us see if this view can be upheld.

First, the supreme authority can no more be modified than it can be alienated; to limit it is to destroy it. It is absurd and contradictory for the Sovereign to set a superior over itself; to bind itself to obey a master would be to return to absolute liberty.

Moreover, it is clear that this contract between the people and such and such persons would be a particular act; and from this is follows that it can be neither a law nor an act of Sovereignty, and that consequently it would be illegitimate.

It is plain too that the contracting parties in relation to each other would be under the law of nature alone and wholly without guarantees of their mutual undertakings, a position wholly at variance with the civil state. He who has force at his command being always in a position to control execution, it would come to the same thing if the name "contract" were given to the act of one man who said to another: "I give you all my goods, on condition that you give me back as much of them as you please."

There is only one contract in the State, and that is the act of association, which in itself excludes the existence of a second. It is impossible to conceive of any public contract that would not be a violation of the first.

## 17. THE INSTITUTION OF GOVERNMENT

UNDER what general idea then should the act by which government is instituted be conceived as falling? I will begin by stating that the act is complex, as being composed of two others — the establishment of the law and its execution.

By the former, the Sovereign decrees that there shall be a governing body established in this or that form; this act is clearly a law.

By the latter, the people nominates the rulers who are to be entrusted with the government that has been estab-lished. This nomination, being a particular act, is clearly not a second law, but merely a consequence of the first and a function of government.

The difficulty is to understand how there can be a governmental act before government exists, and how the people, which is only Sovereign or subject, can, under certain circumstances, become a prince or magistrate.

It is at this point that there is revealed one of the astonishing properties of the body politic, by means of which it reconciles apparently contradictory operations; for this is accomplished by a sudden conversion of Sovereignty into democracy, so that, without sensible change, and merely by virtue of a new relation of all to all, the citizens become magistrates and pass from general to particular acts, from legislation to the execution of the law.

This changed relation is no speculative subtlety without instances in practice: it happens every day in the English Parliament, where, on certain occasions, the Lower House resolves itself into Grand Committee, for the better discussion of affairs, and thus, from being at one moment a sovereign court, becomes at the next a mere commission; so that subsequently it reports to itself, as House of Commons, the result of its proceedings in Grand Committee, and debates over again under one name what it has already settled under another.

It is, indeed, the peculiar advantage of democratic government that it can be established in actuality by a simple act of the general will. Subsequently, this provisional government remains in power, if this form is adopted, or else establishes in the name of the Sovereign the government that is prescribed by law; and thus the whole proceeding is regular. It is impossible to set up government in any other manner legitimately and in accordance with the principles so far laid down.

## 18. HOW TO CHECK THE USURPATIONS OF GOVERNMENT

WHAT we have just said confirms Chapter 16, and makes it clear that the institution of government is not a contract, but a law; that the depositaries of the executive power are not the people's masters, but its officers; that it can set them up and pull them down when it likes; that for them there is no question of contract, but of obedience and that in taking charge of the functions the State imposes on them they are doing no more than fulfilling their duty as citizens, without having the remotest right to argue about the conditions.

When therefore the people sets up an hereditary government, whether it be monarchical and confined to one family, or aristocratic and confined to a class, what it enters into is not an undertaking; the administration is given a provisional form, until the people chooses to order it otherwise.

It is true that such changes are always dangerous, and that the established government should never be touched except when it comes to be incompatible with the public good; but the circumspection this involves is a maxim of policy and not a rule of right, and the State is no more bound to leave civil authority in the hands of its rulers than military authority in the hands of its generals.

It is also true that it is impossible to be too careful to observe, in such cases, all the formalities necessary to distinguish a regular and legitimate act from a seditious tumult, and the will of a whole people from the clamour of a faction. Here above all no further concession should be made to the untoward possibility than cannot, in the strictest logic, be refused it. From this obligation the prince derives a great advantage in preserving his power despite the people, without it being possible to say he has usurped it; for, seeming to avail himself only of his rights, he finds it very easy to extend them, and to prevent, under the pretext of keeping the peace, assemblies that are destined to the re-establishment of order; with the result that he takes advantage of a silence he does not allow to be broken, or of irregularities he causes to be committed, to assume that he has the support of those whom fear prevents from speaking, and to punish those who dare to speak. Thus it was that the decemvirs, first elected for one year and then kept on in office for a second, tried to perpetuate their power by forbidding the comitia to assemble; and by this easy method every government in the world, once clothed with the public power, sooner or later usurps the sovereign authority.

The periodical assemblies of which I have already spoken are designed to prevent or postpone this calamity, above all when they need no formal summoning; for in that case, the prince cannot stop them without openly declaring himself a law-breaker and an enemy of the State.

The opening of these assemblies, whose sole object is the maintenance of the social treaty, should always take the form of putting two propositions that may not be suppressed, which should be voted on separately.

The first is: "Does it please the Sovereign to preserve the present form of government?"

The second is: "Does it please the people to leave its administration in the hands of those who are actually in charge of it?"

I am here assuming what I think I have shown; that there is in the State no fundamental law that cannot be revoked, not excluding the social compact itself; for if all the citizens assembled of one accord to break the compact, it is impossible to doubt that it would be very legitimately broken. Grotius even thinks that each man can renounce his membership of his own State, and recover his natural liberty and his goods on leaving the country.[33] It would be indeed absurd if all the citizens in assembly could not do what each can do by himself.

18. Thus at Venice the College, even in the absence of the Doge, is called "Most Serene Prince."
19. The Palatine of Posen, father of the King of Poland, Duke of Lorraine.
20. I prefer liberty with danger to peace with slavery.
21. It is clear that the word *optimales* meant, among the ancients, not the best, but the most powerful.

22. It is of great importance that the form of the election of magistrates should be regulated by law; for if it is left at the discretion of the prince, it is impossible to avoid falling into hereditary aristocracy, as the Republics of Venice and Berne actually did. The first of these has therefore long been a State dissolved; the second, however, is maintained by the extreme wisdom of the senate, and forms an honourable and highly dangerous exception.

23. Machiavelli was a proper man and a good citizen; but, being attached to the court of the Medici, he could not help veiling his love of liberty in the midst of his country's oppression. The choice of his detestable hero, Caesar Borgia, clearly enough shows his hidden aim; and the contradiction between the teaching of the *Prince* and that of the *Discourses on Livy* and the *History of Florence* shows that this profound political thinker has so far been studied only by superficial or corrupt readers. The Court of Rome sternly prohibited his book. I can well believe it; for it is that Court it most clearly portrays.

24. Tacitus, *Histories*, i. 16. "For the best, and also the shortest way of finding out what is good and what is bad is to consider what you would have wished to happen or not to happen, had another than you been Emperor."

25. In the *Statesman.*

26. This does not contradict what I said before (Book II, ch. 9) about the disadvantages of great States; for we were then dealing with the authority of the government over the members, while here we are dealing with its force against the subjects. Its scattered members serve it as rallying-points for action against the people at a distance, but it has no rallying-point for direct action on its members themselves. Thus the length of the lever is its weakness in the one case, and its strength in the other.

27. On the same principle it should be judged what centuries deserve the preference for human prosperity. Those in which letters and arts have flourished have been too much admired, because the hidden object of their culture has not been fathomed, and their fatal effects not taken into account. *"Idque apud imperitos humanitas vocabatur, cum pars servitutis esset."* (Fools called "humanity" what was a part of slavery, Tacitus, *Agricola*, 31.) Shall we never see in the maxims books lay down the vulgar interest that makes their writers speak? No, whatever they may say, when, despite its renown, a country is depopulated, it is not true that all is well, and it is not enough that a poet should have an income of 100,000 francs to make his age the best of all. Less attention should be paid to the apparent repose and tranquillity of the rulers than to the well-being of their nations as wholes, and above all of the most numerous States. A hail-storm lays several cantons waste, but it rarely makes a famine. Outbreaks and civil wars give rulers rude shocks, but they are not the real ills of peoples, who may even get a respite, while there is a dispute as to who shall tyrannise over them. Their true prosperity and calamities come from their permanent condition: it is when the whole remains crushed beneath the yoke, that decay sets in, and that the rulers destroy them at will, and *"ubi solitudinem faciunt, pacem appellant."* (Where they create solitude, they call it peace, Tacitus, *Agricola*, 31.) When the bickerings of the great disturbed the kingdom of France, and the Coadjutor of Paris took a dagger in his pocket to the Parliament, these things did not prevent the people of France from prospering and multiplying in dignity, ease and freedom. Long ago Greece flourished in the midst of the most savage wars; blood ran in torrents, and yet the whole country was covered with inhabitants. It appeared, says Machiavelli, that in the midst of murder, proscription and civil war, our republic only throve: the virtue, morality and independence of the citizens did more to strengthen it than all their dissensions had done to enfeeble it. A little disturbance gives the soul elasticity; what makes the race truly prosperous is not so much peace as liberty.

28. The slow formation and the progress of the Republic of Venice in its lagoons are a notable instance of this sequence; and it is most astonishing that, after more than twelve hundred years' existence, the Venetians seem to be still at the second stage, which they reached with the *Serrar di Consiglio* in 1198. As for the ancient Dukes who are brought up against them, it is proved, whatever the *Squittinio della libertà veneta* may say of them, that they were in no sense sovereigns.

A case certain to be cited against my view is that of the Roman Republic, which, it will be said, followed exactly the opposite course, and passed from monarchy to aristocracy and from aristocracy to democracy. I by no means take this view of it.

What Romulus first set up was a mixed government, which soon deteriorated into despotism. From special causes, the State died an untimely death, as new-born children sometimes perish without reaching manhood. The expulsion of the Tarquins was the real period of the birth of the Republic. But at first it took on no constant form, because, by not abolishing the patriciate, it left half its work undone. For, by this means, hereditary aristocracy, the worst of all legitimate forms of administration, remained in conflict with democracy, and the form of the government, as Machiavelli has proved, was only fixed on the establishment of the tribunate: only then was there a true government and a veritable democracy. In fact, the people was then not only Sovereign, but also magistrate and judge; the senate was only a subordinate tribunal, to temper and concentrate the government, and the consuls themselves, though they were patricians, first magistrates, and absolute generals in war, were in Rome itself no more than presidents of the people.

From that point, the government followed its natural tendency, and inclined strongly to aristocracy. The patriciate, we may say, abolished itself, and the aristocracy was found no longer in the body of patricians as at Venice and Genoa, but in the body of the senate, which was composed of patricians and plebeians, and even in the body of tribunes when they began to usurp an active function: for names do not affect facts, and, when the people has rulers who govern for it, whatever name they bear, the government is an aristocracy.

The abuse of aristocracy led to the civil wars and the triumvirate. Sulla, Julius Caesar and Augustus became in fact real monarchs; and finally, under the despotism of Tiberius, the State was dissolved. Roman history then confirms, instead of invalidating, the principle I have laid down.

29. *"Omnes enim et habentur et dicuntur tyranni, qui potestate utuntur perpetua in ea civitate quæ libertate usa est"* (Cornelius Nepos, *Life of Miltiades*). (For all those are called and considered tyrants, who hold perpetual power in a State that has known liberty.) It is true that Aristotle (*Ethics*, Book viii, chapter x) distinguishes the tyrant from the king by the fact that the former governs in his own interest, and the latter only for the good of his subjects; but not only did all Greek authors in general use the word *tyrant* in a different sense, as appears most clearly in Xenophon's *Hiero*, but also it would follow from Aristotle's distinction that, from the very beginning of the world, there has not yet been a single king.

30. In nearly the same sense as this word has in the English Parliament. The similarity of these functions would have brought the consuls and the tribunes into conflict, even had all jurisdiction been suspended.

31. To adopt in cold countries the luxury and effeminacy of the East is to desire to submit to its chains; it is indeed to bow to them far more inevitably in our case than in theirs.

32. I had intended to do this in the sequel to this work, when in dealing with external relations I came to the subject of confederations. The subject is quite new, and its principles have still to be laid down.

33. Provided, of course, he does not leave to escape his obligations and avoid having to serve his country in the hour of need. Flight in such a case would be criminal and punishable, and would be, not withdrawal, but desertion.


# BOOK IV


## 1. THAT THE GENERAL WILL IS INDESTRUCTIBLE


AS long as several men in assembly regard themselves as a single body, they have only a single will which is concerned with their common preservation and general well-being. In this case, all the springs of the State are vigorous and simple and its rules clear and luminous; there are no embroilments or conflicts of interests; the common good is everywhere clearly apparent, and only good sense is needed to perceive it. Peace, unity and equality are the enemies of political subtleties. Men who are upright and simple are difficult to deceive because of their simplicity; lures and ingenious pretexts fail to impose upon them, and they are not even subtle enough to be dupes. When, among the happiest people in the world, bands of peasants are seen regulating affairs of State under an oak, and always acting wisely, can we help scorning the ingenious methods of other nations, which make themselves illustrious and wretched with so much art and mystery?

A State so governed needs very few laws; and, as it becomes necessary to issue new ones, the necessity is universally seen. The first man to propose them merely says what all have already felt, and there is no question of factions or intrigues or eloquence in order to secure the passage into law of what every one has already decided to do, as soon as he is sure that the rest will act with him.

Theorists are led into error because, seeing only States that have been from the beginning wrongly constituted, they are struck by the impossibility of applying such a policy to them. They make great game of all the absurdities a clever rascal or an insinuating speaker might get the people of Paris or London to believe. They do not know that Cromwell would have been put to "the bells" by the people of Berne, and the Duc de Beaufort on the treadmill by the Genevese.

But when the social bond begins to be relaxed and the State to grow weak, when particular interests begin to make themselves felt and the smaller societies to exercise an influence over the larger, the common interest changes and finds opponents: opinion is no longer unanimous; the general will ceases to be the will of all; contradictory views and debates arise; and the best advice is not taken without question.

Finally, when the State, on the eve of ruin, maintains only a vain, illusory and formal existence, when in every heart the social bond is broken, and the meanest interest brazenly lays hold of the sacred name of "public good," the general will becomes mute: all men, guided by secret motives, no more give their views as citizens than if the State had never been; and iniquitous decrees directed solely to private interest get passed under the name of laws.

Does it follow from this that the general will is exterminated or corrupted? Not at all: it is always constant, unalterable and pure; but it is subordinated to other wills which encroach upon its sphere. Each man, in detaching his interest from the common interest, sees clearly that he cannot entirely separate them; but his share in the public mishaps seems to him negligible beside the exclusive good he aims at making his own. Apart from this particular good, he wills the general good in his own interest, as strongly as any one else. Even in selling his vote for money, he does not extinguish in himself the general will, but only eludes it. The fault he commits is that of changing the state of the question, and answering something different from what he is asked. Instead of saying, by his vote, "It is to the advantage of the State," he says, "It is of advantage to this or that man or party that this or that view should prevail." Thus the law of public order in assemblies is not so much to maintain in them the general will as to secure that the question be always put to it, and the answer always given by it.

I could here set down many reflections on the simple right of voting in every act of Sovereignty — a right which no one can take from the citizens — and also on the right of stating views, making proposals, dividing and discussing, which the government is always most careful to leave solely to its members, but this important subject would need a treatise to itself, and it is impossible to say everything in a single work.

## 2. VOTING

IT may be seen, from the last chapter, that the way in which general business is managed may give a clear enough indication of the actual state of morals and the health of the body politic. The more concert reigns in the assemblies, that is, the nearer opinion approaches unanimity, the greater is the dominance of the general will. On the other hand, long debates, dissensions and tumult proclaim the ascendancy of particular interests and the decline of the State.

This seems less clear when two or more orders enter into the constitution, as patricians and plebeians did at Rome; for quarrels between these two orders often disturbed the comitia, even in the best days of the Republic. But the exception is rather apparent than real; for then, through the defect that is inherent in the body politic, there were, so to speak, two States in one, and what is not true of the two together is true of either separately. Indeed, even in the most stormy times, the plebiscita of the people, when the Senate did not interfere with them, always went through quietly and by large majorities. The citizens having but one interest, the people had but a single will.

At the other extremity of the circle, unanimity recurs; this is the case when the citizens, having fallen into servitude, have lost both liberty and will. Fear and flattery then change votes into acclamation; deliberation ceases, and only worship or malediction is left. Such was the vile manner in which the senate expressed its views under the Emperors. It did so sometimes with absurd precautions. Tacitus observes that, under Otho, the senators, while they heaped curses on Vitellius, contrived at the same time to make a deafening noise, in order that, should he ever become their master, he might not know what each of them had said.

On these various considerations depend the rules by which the methods of counting votes and comparing opinions should be regulated, according as the general will is more or less easy to discover, and the State more or less in its decline.

There is but one law which, from its nature, needs unanimous consent. This is the social compact; for civil association is the most voluntary of all acts. Every man being born free and his own master, no one, under any pretext whatsoever, can make any man subject without his consent. To decide that the son of a slave is born a slave is to decide that he is not born a man.

If then there are opponents when the social compact is made, their opposition does not invalidate the contract, but merely prevents them from being included in it. They are foreigners among citizens. When the State is instituted, residence constitutes consent; to dwell within its territory is to submit to the Sovereign.[34]

Apart from this primitive contract, the vote of the majority always binds all the rest. This follows from the contract itself. But it is asked how a man can be both free and forced to conform to wills that are not his own. How are the opponents at once free and subject to laws they have not agreed to?

I retort that the question is wrongly put. The citizen gives his consent to all the laws, including those which are passed in spite of his opposition, and even those which punish him when he dares to break any of them. The constant will of all the members of the State is the general will; by virtue of it they are citizens and free.[35] When in the popular assembly a law is proposed, what the people is asked is not exactly whether it approves or rejects the proposal, but whether it is in conformity with the general will, which is their will. Each man, in giving his vote, states his opinion on that point; and the general will is found by counting votes. When therefore the opinion that is contrary to my own prevails, this proves neither more nor less than that I was mistaken, and that what I thought to be the general will was not so. If my particular opinion had carried the day I should have achieved the opposite of what was my will; and it is in that case that I should not have been free.

This presupposes, indeed, that all the qualities of the general will still reside in the majority: when they cease to do so, whatever side a man may take, liberty is no longer possible.

In my earlier demonstration of how particular wills are substituted for the general will in public deliberation, I have adequately pointed out the practicable methods of avoiding this abuse; and I shall have more to say of them later on. I have also given the principles for determining the proportional number of votes for declaring that will. A difference of one vote destroys equality; a single opponent destroys unanimity; but between equality and unanimity, there are several grades of unequal division, at each of which this proportion may be fixed in accordance with the condition and the needs of the body politic.

There are two general rules that may serve to regulate this relation. First, the more grave and important the questions discussed, the nearer should the opinion that is to prevail approach unanimity. Secondly, the more the matter in hand calls for speed, the smaller the prescribed difference in the numbers of votes may be allowed to become: where an instant decision has to be reached, a majority of one vote should be enough. The first of these two rules seems more in harmony with the laws, and the second with practical affairs. In any case, it is the combination of them that gives the best proportions for determining the majority necessary.

## 3. ELECTIONS

IN the elections of the prince and the magistrates, which are, as I have said, complex acts, there are two possible methods of procedure, choice and lot. Both have been employed in various republics, and a highly complicated mixture of the two still survives in the election of the Doge at Venice.

"Election by lot," says Montesquieu, "is democratic in nature."[E3] I agree that it is so; but in what sense? "The lot," he goes on, "is a way of making choice that is unfair to nobody; it leaves each citizen a reasonable hope of serving his country." These are not reasons.

If we bear in mind that the election of rulers is a function of government, and not of Sovereignty, we shall see why the lot is the method more natural to democracy, in which the administration is better in proportion as the number of its acts is small.

In every real democracy, magistracy is not an advantage, but a burdensome charge which cannot justly be imposed on one individual rather than another. The law alone can lay the charge on him on whom the lot falls. For, the conditions being then the same for all, and the choice not depending on any human will, there is no particular application to alter the universality of the law.

In an aristocracy, the prince chooses the prince, the government is preserved by itself, and voting is rightly ordered.

The instance of the election of the Doge of Venice confirms, instead of destroying, this distinction; the mixed form suits a mixed government. For it is an error to take the government of Venice for a real aristocracy. If the people has no share in the government, the nobility is itself the people. A host of poor Barnabotes never gets near any magistracy, and its nobility consists merely in the empty title of Excellency, and in the right to sit in the Great Council. As this Great Council is as numerous as our General Council at Geneva, its illustrious members have no more privileges than our plain citizens. It is indisputable that, apart from the extreme disparity between the two republics, the *bourgeoisie* of Geneva is exactly equivalent to the *patriciate* of Venice; our *natives* and *inhabitants* correspond to the *townsmen* and the *people* of Venice; our *peasants* correspond to the *subjects* on the mainland; and, however that republic be regarded, if its size be left out of account, its government is no more aristocratic than our own. The whole difference is that, having no life-ruler, we do not, like Venice, need to use the lot.

Election by lot would have few disadvantages in a real democracy, in which, as equality would everywhere exist in morals and talents as well as in principles and fortunes, it would become almost a matter of indifference who was chosen. But I have already said that a real democracy is only an ideal.

When choice and lot are combined, positions that require special talents, such as military posts, should be filled by the former; the latter does for cases, such as judicial offices, in which good sense, justice, and integrity are enough, because in a State that is well constituted, these qualities are common to all the citizens.

Neither lot nor vote has any place in monarchical government. The monarch being by right sole prince and only magistrate, the choice of his lieutenants belongs to none but him. When the Abbé de Saint-Pierre proposed that the Councils of the King of France should be multiplied, and their members elected by ballot, he did not see that he was proposing to change the form of government.

I should now speak of the methods of giving and counting opinions in the assembly of the people; but perhaps an account of this aspect of the Roman constitution will more forcibly illustrate all the rules I could lay down. It is worth the while of a judicious reader to follow in some detail the working of public and private affairs in a Council consisting of two hundred thousand men.

## 4. THE ROMAN COMITIA

WE are without well-certified records of the first period of Rome's existence; it even appears very probable that most of the stories told about it are fables; indeed, generally speaking, the most instructive part of the history of peoples, that which deals with their foundation, is what we have least of. Experience teaches us every day what causes lead to the revolutions of empires; but, as no new peoples are now formed, we have almost nothing beyond conjecture to go upon in explaining how they were created.

The customs we find established show at least that these customs had an origin. The traditions that go back to those origins, that have the greatest authorities behind them, and that are confirmed by the strongest proofs, should pass for the most certain. These are the rules I have tried to follow in inquiring how the freest and most powerful people on earth exercised its supreme power.

After the foundation of Rome, the new-born republic, that is, the army of its founder, composed of Albans, Sabines and foreigners, was divided into three classes, which, from this division, took the name of *tribes*. Each of these tribes was subdivided into ten *curiæ*, and each *curia* into *decuriæ*, headed by leaders called *curiones* and *decuriones*.

Besides this, out of each tribe was taken a body of one hundred *Equites* or Knights, called a *century*, which shows that these divisions, being unnecessary in a town, were at first merely military. But an instinct for greatness seems to have led the little township of Rome to provide itself in advance with a political system suitable for the capital of the world.

Out of this original division an awkward situation soon arose. The tribes of the Albans (Ramnenses) and the Sabines (Tatienses) remained always in the same condition, while that of the foreigners (Luceres) continually grew as more and more foreigners came to live at Rome, so that it soon surpassed the others in strength. Servius remedied this dangerous fault by changing the principle of cleavage, and substituting for the racial division, which he abolished, a new one based on the quarter of the town inhabited by each tribe. Instead of three tribes he created four, each occupying and named after one of the hills of Rome. Thus, while redressing the inequality of the moment, he also provided for the future; and in order that the division might be one of persons as well as localities, he forbade the inhabitants of one quarter to migrate to another, and so prevented the mingling of the races.

He also doubled the three old centuries of Knights and added twelve more, still keeping the old names, and by this simple and prudent method, succeeded in making a distinction between the body of Knights, and the people, without a murmur from the latter.

To the four urban tribes Servius added fifteen others called rural tribes, because they consisted of those who lived in the country, divided into fifteen cantons. Subsequently, fifteen more were created, and the Roman people finally found itself divided into thirty-five tribes, as it remained down to the end of the Republic.

The distinction between urban and rural tribes had one effect which is worth mention, both because it is without parallel elsewhere, and because to it Rome owed the preservation of her morality and the enlargement of her empire. We should have expected that the urban tribes would soon monopolise power and honours, and lose no time in bringing the rural tribes into disrepute; but what happened was exactly the reverse. The taste of the early Romans for country life is well known. This taste they owed to their wise founder, who made rural and military labours go along with liberty, and, so to speak, relegated to the town arts, crafts, intrigue, fortune and slavery.

Since therefore all Rome's most illustrious citizens lived in the fields and tilled the earth, men grew used to seeking there alone the mainstays of the republic. This condition, being that of the best patricians, was honoured by all men; the simple and laborious life of the villager was preferred to the slothful and idle life of the *bourgeoisie* of Rome; and he who, in the town, would have been but a wretched proletarian, became, as a labourer in the fields, a respected citizen. Not without reason, says Varro, did our great-souled ancestors establish in the village the nursery of the sturdy and valiant men who defended them in time of war and provided for their sustenance in time of peace. Pliny states positively that the country tribes were honoured because of the men of whom they were composed; while cowards men wished to dishonour were transferred, as a public disgrace, to the town tribes. The Sabine Appius Claudius, when he had come to settle in Rome, was loaded with honours and enrolled in a rural tribe, which subsequently took his family name. Lastly, freedmen always entered the urban, arid never the rural, tribes: nor is there a single example, throughout the Republic, of a freedman, though he had become a citizen, reaching any magistracy.

This was an excellent rule; but it was carried so far that in the end it led to a change and certainly to an abuse in the political system.

First the censors, after having for a long time claimed the right of transferring citizens arbitrarily from one tribe to another, allowed most persons to enrol themselves in whatever tribe they pleased. This permission certainly did no good, and further robbed the censorship of one of its greatest resources. Moreover, as the great and powerful all got themselves enrolled in the country tribes, while the freedmen who had become citizens remained with the populace in the town tribes, both soon ceased to have any local or territorial meaning, and all were so confused that the members of one could not be told from those of another except by the registers; so that the idea of the word *tribe* became personal instead of real, or rather came to be little more than a chimera.

It happened in addition that the town tribes, being more on the spot, were often the stronger in the comitia and sold the State to those who stooped to buy the votes of the rabble composing them.

As the founder had set up ten *curiæ* in each tribe, the whole Roman people, which was then contained within the walls, consisted of thirty *curiæ*, each with its temples, its gods, its officers, its priests and its festivals, which were called *compitalia* and corresponded to the *paganalia*, held in later times by the rural tribes.

When Servius made his new division, as the thirty *curiæ* could not be shared equally between his four tribes, and as he was unwilling to interfere with them, they became a further division of the inhabitants of Rome, quite independent of the tribes: but in the case of the rural tribes and their members there was no question of *curiæ*, as the tribes had then become a purely civil institution, and, a new system of levying troops having been introduced, the military divisions of Romulus were superfluous. Thus, although every citizen was enrolled in a tribe, there were very many who were not members of a *curia*.

Servius made yet a third division, quite distinct from the two we have mentioned, which became, in its effects, the most important of all. He distributed the whole Roman people into six classes, distinguished neither by place nor by person, but by wealth; the first classes included the rich, the last the poor, and those between persons of moderate means. These six classes were subdivided into one hundred and ninety-three other bodies, called centuries, which were so divided that the first class alone comprised more than half of them, while the last comprised only one. Thus the class that had the smallest number of members had the largest number of centuries, and the whole of the last class only counted as a single subdivision, although it alone included more than half the inhabitants of Rome.

In order that the people might have the less insight into the results of this arrangement, Servius tried to give it a military tone: in the second class he inserted two centuries of armourers, and in the fourth two of makers of instruments of war: in each class, except the last, he distinguished young and old, that is, those who were under an obligation to bear arms and those whose age gave them legal exemption. It was this distinction, rather than that of wealth, which required frequent repetition of the census or counting. Lastly, he ordered that the assembly should be held in the Campus Martius, and that all who were of age to serve should come there armed.

The reason for his not making in the last class also the division of young and old was that the populace, of whom it was composed, was not given the right to bear arms for its country: a man had to possess a hearth to acquire the right to defend it, and of all the troops of beggars who to-day lend lustre to the armies of kings, there is perhaps not one who would not have been driven with scorn out of a Roman cohort, at a time when soldiers were the defenders of liberty.

In this last class, however, *proletarians* were distinguished from *capite censi*. The former, not quite reduced to nothing, at least gave the State citizens, and sometimes, when the need was pressing, even soldiers. Those who had nothing at all, and could be numbered only by counting heads, were regarded as of absolutely no account, and Marius was the first who stooped to enrol them.

Without deciding now whether this third arrangement was good or bad in itself, I think I may assert that it could have been made practicable only by the simple morals, the disinterestedness, the liking for agriculture and the scorn for commerce and for love of gain which characterised the early Romans. Where is the modern people among whom consuming greed, unrest, intrigue, continual removals, and perpetual changes of fortune, could let such a system last for twenty years without turning the State upside down? We must indeed observe that morality and the censorship, being stronger than this institution, corrected its defects at Rome, and that the rich man found himself degraded to the class of the poor for making too much display of his riches.

From all this it is easy to understand why only five classes are almost always mentioned, though there were really six. The sixth, as it furnished neither soldiers to the army nor votes in the Campus Martius,[36] and was almost without function in the State, was seldom regarded as of any account.

These were the various ways in which the Roman people was divided. Let us now see the effect on the assemblies. When lawfully summoned, these were called *comitia:* they were usually held in the public square at Rome or in the Campus Martius, and were distinguished as *comitia curiata, comitia centuriata,* and *comitia tributa,* according to the form under which they were convoked. The *comitia curiata* were founded by Romulus; the *centuriata* by Servius; and the *tributa* by the tribunes of the people. No law received its sanction and no magistrate was elected, save in the comitia; and as every citizen was enrolled in a *curia,* a century, or a tribe, it follows that no citizen was excluded from the right of voting, and that the Roman people was truly sovereign both *de jure* and *de facto.*

For the comitia to be lawfully assembled, and for their acts to have the force of law, three conditions were necessary. First, the body or magistrate convoking them had to possess the necessary authority; secondly, the assembly had to be held on a day allowed by law; and thirdly, the auguries had to be favourable.

The reason for the first regulation needs no explanation; the second is a matter of policy. Thus, the comitia might not be held on festivals or market-days, when the country-folk, coming to Rome on business, had not time to spend the day in the public square. By means of the third, the senate held in check the proud and restive people, and meetly restrained the ardour of seditious tribunes, who, however, found more than one way of escaping this hindrance.

Laws and the election of rulers were not the only questions submitted to the judgment of the comitia: as the Roman people had taken on itself the most important functions of government, it may be said that the lot of Europe was regulated in its assemblies. The variety of their objects gave rise to the various forms these took, according to the matters on which they had to pronounce.

In order to judge of these various forms, it is enough to compare them. Romulus, when he set up *curia,* had in view the checking of the senate by the people, and of the people by the senate, while maintaining his ascendancy over both alike. He therefore gave the people, by means of this assembly, all the authority of numbers to balance that of power and riches, which he left to the patricians. But, after the spirit of monarchy, he left all the same a greater advantage to the patricians in the influence of their clients on the majority of votes. This excellent institution of patron and client was a masterpiece of statesmanship and humanity without which the patriciate, being flagrantly in contradiction to the republican spirit, could not have survived. Rome alone has the honour of having given to the world this great example, which never led to any abuse, and yet has never been followed.

As the assemblies by *curiæ* persisted under the kings till the time of Servius, and the reign of the later Tarquin was not regarded as legitimate, royal laws were called generally *leges curiatæ.*

Under the Republic, the *curiæ,* still confined to the four urban tribes, and including only the populace of Rome, suited neither the senate, which led the patricians, nor the tribunes, who, though plebeians, were at the head of the well-to-do citizens. They therefore fell into disrepute, and their degradation was such, that thirty lictors used to assemble and do what the *comitia curiata* should have done.

The division by centuries was so favourable to the aristocracy that it is hard to see at first how the senate ever failed to carry the day in the comitia bearing their name, by which the consuls, the censors and the other curule magistrates were elected. Indeed, of the hundred and ninety-three centuries into which the six classes of the whole Roman people were divided, the first class contained ninety-eight; and, as voting went solely by centuries, this class alone had a majority over all the rest. When all these centuries were in agreement, the rest of the votes were not even taken; the decision of the smallest number passed for that of the multitude, and it may be said that, in the *comitia centuriata,* decisions were regulated far more by depth of purses than by the number of votes.

But this extreme authority was modified in two ways. First, the tribunes as a rule, and always a great number of plebeians, belonged to the class of the rich, and so counterbalanced the influence of the patricians in the first class.

The second way was this. Instead of causing the centuries to vote throughout in order, which would have meant beginning always with the first, the Romans always chose one by lot which proceeded alone to the election; after this all the centuries were summoned another day according to their rank, and the same election was repeated, and as a rule confirmed. Thus the authority of example was taken away from rank, and given to the lot on a democratic principle.

From this custom resulted a further advantage. The citizens from the country had time, between the two elections, to inform themselves of the merits of the candidate who had been provisionally nominated, and did not have to vote without knowledge of the case. But, under the pretext of hastening matters, the abolition of this custom was achieved, and both elections were held on the same day.

The *comitia tributa* were properly the council of the Roman people. They were convoked by the tribunes alone; at them the tribunes were elected and passed their plebiscita. The senate not only had no standing in them, but even no right to be present; and the senators, being forced to obey laws on which they could not vote, were in this respect less free than the meanest citizens. This injustice was altogether ill-conceived, and was alone enough to invalidate the decrees of a body to which all its members were not admitted. Had all the patricians attended the comitia by virtue of the right they had as citizens, they would not, as mere private individuals, have had any considerable influence on a vote reckoned by counting heads, where the meanest proletarian was as good as the *princeps senatus.*

It may be seen, therefore, that besides the order which was achieved by these various ways of distributing so great a people and taking its votes, the various methods were not reducible to forms indifferent in themselves, but the results of each were relative to the objects which caused it to be preferred.

Without going here into further details, we may gather from what has been said above that the *comitia tributa* were the most favourable to popular government, and the *comitia centuriata* to aristocracy. The *comitia curiata*, in which the populace of Rome formed the majority, being fitted only to further tyranny and evil designs, naturally fell into disrepute, and even seditious persons abstained from using a method which too clearly revealed their projects. It is indisputable that the whole majesty of the Roman people lay solely in the *comitia centuriata*, which alone included all; for the *comitia curiata* excluded the rural tribes, and the *comitia tributa* the senate and the patricians.

As for the method of taking the vote, it was among the ancient Romans as simple as their morals, although not so simple as at Sparta. Each man declared his vote aloud, and a clerk duly wrote it down; the majority in each tribe determined the vote of the tribe, the majority of the tribes that of the people, and so with *curiæ* and centuries. This custom was good as long as honesty was triumphant among the citizens, and each man was ashamed to vote publicly in favour of an unjust proposal or an unworthy subject; but, when the people grew corrupt and votes were bought, it was fitting that voting should be secret in order that purchasers might be restrained by mistrust, and rogues be given the means of not being traitors.

I know that Cicero attacks this change, and attributes partly to it the ruin of the Republic. But though I feel the weight Cicero's authority must carry on such a point, I cannot agree with him; I hold, on the contrary, that, for want of enough such changes, the destruction of the State must be hastened. Just as the regimen of health does not suit the sick, we should not wish to govern a people that has been corrupted by the laws that a good people requires. There is no better proof of this rule than the long life of the Republic of Venice, of which the shadow still exists, solely because its laws are suitable only for men who are wicked.

The citizens were provided, therefore, with tablets by means of which each man could vote without any one knowing how he voted: new methods were also introduced for collecting the tablets, for counting voices, for comparing numbers, etc.; but all these precautions did not prevent the good faith of the officers charged with these functions[37] from being often suspect. Finally, to prevent intrigues and trafficking in votes, edicts were issued; but their very number proves how useless they were.

Towards the close of the Republic, it was often necessary to have recourse to extraordinary expedients in order to supplement the inadequacy of the laws. Sometimes miracles were supposed; but this method, while it might impose on the people, could not impose on those who governed. Sometimes an assembly was hastily called together, before the candidates had time to form their factions: sometimes a whole sitting was occupied with talk, when it was seen that the people had been won over and was on the point of taking up a wrong position. But in the end ambition eluded all attempts to check it; and the most incredible fact of all is that, in the midst of all these abuses, the vast people, thanks to its ancient regulations, never ceased to elect magistrates, to pass laws, to judge cases, and to carry through business both public and private, almost as easily as the senate itself could have done.

## 5. THE TRIBUNATE

WHEN an exact proportion cannot be established between the constituent parts of the State, or when causes that cannot be removed continually alter the relation of one part to another, recourse is had to the institution of a peculiar magistracy that enters into no corporate unity with the rest. This restores to each term its right relation to the others, and provides a link or middle term between either prince and people, or prince and Sovereign, or, if necessary, both at once.

This body, which I shall call the *tribunate*, is the preserver of the laws and of the legislative power. It serves sometimes to protect the Sovereign against the government, as the tribunes of the people did at Rome; sometimes to uphold the government against the people, as the Council of Ten now does at Venice; and sometimes to maintain the balance between the two, as the Ephors did at Sparta.

The tribunate is not a constituent part of the city, and should have no share in either legislative or executive power; but this very fact makes its own power the greater: for, while it can do nothing, it can prevent anything from being done. It is more sacred and more revered, as the defender of the laws, than the prince who executes them, or than the Sovereign which ordains them. This was seen very clearly at Rome, when the proud patricians, for all their scorn of the people, were forced to bow before one of its officers, who had neither auspices nor jurisdiction.

The tribunate, wisely tempered, is the strongest support a good constitution can have; but if its strength is ever so little excessive, it upsets the whole State. Weakness, on the other hand, is not natural to it: provided it is something, it is never less than it should be.

It degenerates into tyranny when it usurps the executive power, which it should confine itself to restraining, and when it tries to dispense with the laws, which it should confine itself to protecting. The immense power of the Ephors, harmless as long as Sparta preserved its morality, hastened corruption when once it had begun. The blood of Agis, slaughtered by these tyrants, was avenged by his successor; the crime and the punishment of the Ephors alike hastened the destruction of the republic, and after Cleomenes Sparta ceased to be of any account. Rome perished in the same way: the excessive power of the tribunes, which they had usurped by degrees, finally served, with the help of laws made to secure liberty, as a safeguard for the emperors who destroyed it. As for the Venetian Council of Ten, it is a tribunal of blood, an object of horror to patricians and people alike; and, so far from giving a lofty protection to the laws, it does nothing, now they have become degraded, but strike in the darkness blows of which no one dare take note.

The tribunate, like the government, grows weak as the number of its members increases. When the tribunes of the Roman people, who first numbered only two, and then five, wished to double that number, the senate let them do so, in the confidence that it could use one to check another, as indeed it afterwards freely did.

The best method of preventing usurpations by so formidable a body, though no government has yet made use of it, would be not to make it permanent, but to regulate the periods during which it should remain in abeyance. These intervals, which should not be long enough to give abuses time to grow strong, may be so fixed by law that they can easily be shortened at need by extraordinary commissions.

This method seems to me to have no disadvantages, because, as I have said, the tribunate, which forms no part of the constitution, can be removed without the constitution being affected. It seems to be also efficacious, because a newly restored magistrate starts not with the power his predecessor exercised, but with that which the law allows him.

## 6. THE DICTATORSHIP

THE inflexibility of the laws, which prevents them from adapting themselves to circumstances, may, in certain cases, render them disastrous, and make them bring about, at a time of crisis, the ruin of the State. The order and slowness of the forms they enjoin require a space of time which circumstances sometimes withhold. A thousand cases against which the legislator has made no provision may present themselves, and it is a highly necessary part of foresight to be conscious that everything cannot be foreseen.

It is wrong therefore to wish to make political institutions so strong as to render it impossible to suspend their operation. Even Sparta allowed its laws to lapse.

However, none but the greatest dangers can counterbalance that of changing the public order, and the sacred power of the laws should never be arrested save when the existence of the country is at stake. In these rare and obvious cases, provision is made for the public security by a particular act entrusting it to him who is most worthy. This commitment may be carried out in either of two ways, according to the nature of the danger.

If increasing the activity of the government is a sufficient remedy, power is concentrated in the hands of one or two of its members: in this case the change is not in the authority of the laws, but only in the form of administering them. If, on the other hand, the peril is of such a kind that the paraphernalia of the laws are an obstacle to their preservation, the method is to nominate a supreme ruler, who shall silence all the laws and suspend for a moment the sovereign authority. In such a case, there is no doubt about the general will, and it is clear that the people's first intention is that the State shall not perish. Thus the suspension of the legislative authority is in no sense its abolition; the magistrate who silences it cannot make it speak; he dominates it, but cannot represent it. He can do anything, except make laws.

The first method was used by the Roman senate when, in a consecrated formula, it charged the consuls to provide for the safety of the Republic. The second was employed when one of the two consuls nominated a dictator:[38] a custom Rome borrowed from Alba.

During the first period of the Republic, recourse was very often had to the dictatorship, because the State had not yet a firm enough basis to be able to maintain itself by the strength of its constitution alone. As the state of morality then made superfluous many of the precautions which would have been necessary at other times, there was no fear that a dictator would abuse his authority, or try to keep it beyond his term of office. On the contrary, so much power appeared to be burdensome to him who was clothed with it, and he made all speed to lay it down, as if taking the place of the laws had been too troublesome and too perilous a position to retain.

It is therefore the danger not of its abuse, but of its cheapening, that makes me attack the indiscreet use of this supreme magistracy in the earliest times. For as long as it was freely employed at elections, dedications and purely formal functions, there was danger of its becoming less formidable in time of need, and of men growing accustomed to regarding as empty a title that was used only on occasions of empty ceremonial.

Towards the end of the Republic, the Romans, having grown more circumspect, were as unreasonably sparing in the use of the dictatorship as they had formerly been lavish. It is easy to see that their fears were without foundation, that the weakness of the capital secured it against the magistrates who were in its midst; that a dictator might, in certain cases, defend the public liberty, but could never endanger it; and that the chains of Rome would be forged, not in Rome itself, but in her armies. The weak resistance offered by Marius to Sulla, and by Pompey to Cæsar, clearly showed what was to be expected from authority at home against force from abroad.

This misconception led the Romans to make great mistakes; such, for example, as the failure to nominate a dictator in the Catilinarian conspiracy. For, as only the city itself, with at most some province in Italy, was concerned, the unlimited authority the laws gave to the dictator would have enabled him to make short work of the conspiracy, which was, in fact, stifled only by a combination of lucky chances human prudence had no right to expect.

Instead, the senate contented itself with entrusting its whole power to the consuls, so that Cicero, in order to take effective action, was compelled on a capital point to exceed his powers; and if, in the first transports of joy, his conduct was approved, he was justly called, later on, to account for the blood of citizens spilt in violation of the laws. Such a reproach could never have been levelled at a dictator. But the consul's eloquence carried the day; and he himself, Roman though he was, loved his own glory better than his country, and sought, not so much the most lawful and secure means of saving the State, as to get for himself the whole honour of having done so.[39] He was therefore justly honoured as the liberator of Rome, and also justly punished as a law-breaker. However brilliant his recall may have been, it was undoubtedly an act of pardon.

However this important trust be conferred, it is important that its duration should be fixed at a very brief period, incapable of being ever prolonged. In the crises which lead to its adoption, the State is either soon lost, or soon saved; and, the present need passed, the dictatorship becomes either tyrannical or idle. At Rome, where dictators held office for six months only, most of them abdicated before their time was up. If their term had been longer, they might well have tried to prolong it still further, as the decemvirs did when chosen for a year. The dictator had only time to provide against the need that had caused him to be chosen; he had none to think of further projects.

## 7. THE CENSORSHIP

AS the law is the declaration of the general will, the censorship is the declaration of the public judgment: public opinion is the form of law which the censor administers, and, like the prince, only applies to particular cases.

The censorial tribunal, so far from being the arbiter of the people's opinion, only declares it, and, as soon as the two part company, its decisions are null and void.

It is useless to distinguish the morality of a nation from the objects of its esteem; both depend on the same principle and are necessarily indistinguishable. There is no people on earth the choice of whose pleasures is not decided by opinion rather than nature. Right men's opinions, and their morality will purge itself. Men always love what is good or what they find good; it is in judging what is good that they go wrong. This judgment, therefore, is what must be regulated. He who judges of morality judges of honour; and he who judges of honour finds his law in opinion.

The opinions of a people are derived from its constitution; although the law does not regulate morality, it is legislation that gives it birth. When legislation grows weak, morality degenerates; but in such cases the judgment of the censors will not do what the force of the laws has failed to effect.

From this it follows that the censorship may be useful for the preservation of morality, but can never be so for its restoration. Set up censors while the laws are vigorous; as soon as they have lost their vigour, all hope is gone; no legitimate power can retain force when the laws have lost it.

The censorship upholds morality by preventing opinion from growing corrupt, by preserving its rectitude by means of wise applications, and sometimes even by fixing it when it is still uncertain. The employment of seconds in duels, which had been carried to wild extremes in the kingdom of France, was done away with merely by these words in a royal edict: "As for those who are cowards enough to call upon seconds." This judgment, in anticipating that of the public, suddenly decided it. But when edicts from the same source tried to pronounce duelling itself an act of cowardice, as indeed it is, then, since common opinion does not regard it as such, the public took no notice of a decision on a point on which its mind was already made up.

I have stated elsewhere[40] that as public opinion is not subject to any constraint, there need be no trace of it in the tribunal set up to represent it. It is impossible to admire too much the art with which this resource, which we moderns have wholly lost, was employed by the Romans, and still more by the Lacedæmonians.

A man of bad morals having made a good proposal in the Spartan Council, the Ephors neglected it, and caused the same proposal to be made by a virtuous citizen. What an honour for the one, and what a disgrace for the other, without praise or blame of either! Certain drunkards from Samos[41] polluted the tribunal of the

Ephors: the next day, a public edict gave Samians permission to be filthy. An actual punishment would not have been so severe as such an impunity. When Sparta has pronounced on what is or is not right, Greece makes no appeal from her judgments.

## 8. CIVIL RELIGION

AT first men had no kings save the gods, and no government save theocracy. They reasoned like Caligula, and, at that period, reasoned aright. It takes a long time for feeling so to change that men can make up their minds to take their equals as masters, in the hope that they will profit by doing so.

From the mere fact that God was set over every political society, it followed that there were as many gods as peoples. Two peoples that were strangers the one to the other, and almost always enemies, could not long recognise the same master: two armies giving battle could not obey the same leader. National divisions thus led to polytheism, and this in turn gave rise to theological and civil intolerance, which, as we shall see hereafter, are by nature the same.

The fancy the Greeks had for rediscovering their gods among the barbarians arose from the way they had of regarding themselves as the natural Sovereigns of such peoples. But there is nothing so absurd as the erudition which in our days identifies and confuses gods of different nations. As if Moloch, Saturn, and Chronos could be the same god! As if the Phoenician Baal, the Greek Zeus, and the Latin Jupiter could be the same! As if there could still be anything common to imaginary beings with different names!

If it is asked how in pagan times, where each State had its cult and its gods, there were no wars of religion, I answer that it was precisely because each State, having its own cult as well as its own government, made no distinction between its gods and its laws. Political war was also theological; the provinces of the gods were, so to speak, fixed by the boundaries of nations. The god of one people had no right over another. The gods of the pagans were not jealous gods; they shared among themselves the empire of the world: even Moses and the Hebrews sometimes lent themselves to this view by speaking of the God of Israel. It is true, they regarded as powerless the gods of the Canaanites, a proscribed people condemned to destruction, whose place they were to take; but remember how they spoke of the divisions of the neighbouring peoples they were forbidden to attack! "Is not the possession of what belongs to your god Chamos lawfully your due?" said Jephthah to the Ammonites. "We have the same title to the lands our conquering God has made his own."[42] Here, I think, there is a recognition that the rights of Chamos and those of the God of Israel are of the same nature.

But when the Jews, being subject to the Kings of Babylon, and, subsequently, to those of Syria, still obstinately refused to recognise any god save their own, their refusal was regarded as rebellion against their conqueror, and drew down on them the persecutions we read of in their history, which are without parallel till the coming of Christianity.[43]

Every religion, therefore, being attached solely to the laws of the State which prescribed it, there was no way of converting a people except by enslaving it, and there could be no missionaries save conquerors. The obligation to change cults being the law to which the vanquished yielded, it was necessary to be victorious before suggesting such a change. So far from men fighting for the gods, the gods, as in Homer, fought for men; each asked his god for victory, and repaid him with new altars. The Romans, before taking a city, summoned its gods to quit it; and, in leaving the Tarentines their outraged gods, they regarded them as subject to their own and compelled to do them homage. They left the vanquished their gods as they left them their laws. A wreath to the Jupiter of the Capitol was often the only tribute they imposed.

Finally, when, along with their empire, the Romans had spread their cult and their gods, and had themselves often adopted those of the vanquished, by granting to both alike the rights of the city, the peoples of that vast empire insensibly found themselves with multitudes of gods and cults, everywhere almost the same; and thus paganism throughout the known world finally came to be one and the same religion.

It was in these circumstances that Jesus came to set up on earth a spiritual kingdom, which, by separating the theological from the political system, made the State no longer one, and brought about the internal divisions which have never ceased to trouble Christian peoples. As the new idea of a kingdom of the other world could never have occurred to pagans, they always looked on the Christians as really rebels, who, while feigning to submit, were only waiting for the chance to make themselves independent and their masters, and to usurp by guile the authority they pretended in their weakness to respect. This was the cause of the persecutions.

What the pagans had feared took place. Then everything changed its aspect: the humble Christians changed their language, and soon this so-called kingdom of the other world turned, under a visible leader, into the most violent of earthly despotisms.

However, as there have always been a prince and civil laws, this double power and conflict of jurisdiction have made all good polity impossible in Christian States; and men have never succeeded in finding out whether they were bound to obey the master or the priest.

Several peoples, however, even in Europe and its neighbourhood, have desired without success to preserve or restore the old system: but the spirit of Christianity has everywhere prevailed. The sacred cult has always remained or again become independent of the Sovereign, and there has been no necessary link between it and the body of the State. Mahomet held very sane views, and linked his political system well together; and, as long as the form of his government continued under the caliphs who succeeded him, that government was indeed one, and so far good. But the Arabs, having grown prosperous, lettered, civilised, slack and cowardly, were conquered by barbarians: the division between the two powers began again; and, although it is less apparent among the Mahometans than among the Christians, it none the less exists, especially in the sect of Ali, and there are States, such as Persia, where it is continually making itself felt.

Among us, the Kings of England have made themselves heads of the Church, and the Czars have done the same: but this title has made them less its masters than its ministers; they have gained not so much the right to change it, as the power to maintain it: they are not its legislators, but only its princes. Wherever the clergy is a corporate body,[44] it is master and legislator in its own country. There are thus two powers, two Sovereigns, in England and in Russia, as well as elsewhere.

Of all Christian writers, the philosopher Hobbes alone has seen the evil and how to remedy it, and has dared to propose the reunion of the two heads of the eagle, and the restoration throughout of political unity, without which no State or government will ever be rightly constituted. But he should have seen that the masterful spirit of Christianity is incompatible with his system, and that the priestly interest would always be stronger than that of the State. It is not so much what is false and terrible in his political theory, as what is just and true, that has drawn down hatred on it.[45]

I believe that if the study of history were developed from this point of view, it would be easy to refute the contrary opinions of Bayle and Warburton, one of whom holds that religion can be of no use to the body politic, while the other, on the contrary, maintains that Christianity is its strongest support. We should demonstrate to the former that no State has ever been founded without a religious basis, and to the latter, that the law of Christianity at bottom does more harm by weakening than good by strengthening the constitution of the State. To make myself understood, I have only to make a little more exact the too vague ideas of religion as relating to this subject.

Religion, considered in relation to society, which is either general or particular, may also be divided into two kinds: the religion of man, and that of the citizen. The first, which has neither temples, nor altars, nor rites, and is confined to the purely internal cult of the supreme God and the eternal obligations of morality, is the religion of the Gospel pure and simple, the true theism, what may be called natural divine right or law. The other, which is codified in a single country, gives it its gods, its own tutelary patrons; it has its dogmas, its rites, and its external cult prescribed by law; outside the single nation that follows it, all the world is in its sight infidel, foreign and barbarous; the duties and rights of man extend for it only as far as its own altars. Of this kind were all the religions of early peoples, which we may define as civil or positive divine right or law.

There is a third sort of religion of a more singular kind, which gives men two codes of legislation, two rulers, and two countries, renders them subject to contradictory duties, and makes it impossible for them to be faithful both to religion and to citizenship. Such are the religions of the Lamas and of the Japanese, and such is Roman Christianity, which may be called the religion of the priest. It leads to a sort of mixed and anti-social code which has no name.

In their political aspect, all these three kinds of religion have their defects. The third is so clearly bad, that it is waste of time to stop to prove it such. All that destroys social unity is worthless; all institutions that set man in contradiction to himself are worthless.

The second is good in that it unites the divine cult with love of the laws, and, making country the object of the citizens' adoration, teaches them that service done to the State is service done to its tutelary god. It is a form of theocracy, in which there can be no pontiff save the prince, and no priests save the magistrates. To die for one's country then becomes martyrdom; violation of its laws, impiety; and to subject one who is guilty to public execration is to condemn him to the anger of the gods: *Sacer estod*.

On the other hand, it is bad in that, being founded on lies and error, it deceives men, makes them credulous and superstitious, and drowns the true cult of the Divinity in empty ceremonial. It is bad, again, when it becomes tyrannous and exclusive, and makes a people bloodthirsty and intolerant, so that it breathes fire and slaughter, and regards as a sacred act the killing of every one who does not believe in its gods. The result is to place such a people in a natural state of war with all others, so that its security is deeply endangered.

There remains therefore the religion of man or Christianity — not the Christianity of to-day, but that of the Gospel, which is entirely different. By means of this holy, sublime, and real religion all men, being children of one God, recognise one another as brothers, and the society that unites them is not dissolved even at death.

But this religion, having no particular relation to the body politic, leaves the laws in possession of the force they have in themselves without making any addition to it; and thus one of the great bonds that unite society considered in severally fails to operate. Nay, more, so far from binding the hearts of the citizens to the State, it has the effect of taking them away from all earthly things. I know of nothing more contrary to the social spirit.

We are told that a people of true Christians would form the most perfect society imaginable. I see in this supposition only one great difficulty: that a society of true Christians would not be a society of men.

I say further that such a society, with all its perfection, would be neither the strongest nor the most lasting: the very fact that it was perfect would rob it of its bond of union; the flaw that would destroy it would lie in its very perfection.

Every one would do his duty; the people would be law-abiding, the rulers just and temperate; the magistrates upright and incorruptible; the soldiers would scorn death; there would be neither vanity nor luxury. So far, so good; but let us hear more.

Christianity as a religion is entirely spiritual, occupied solely with heavenly things; the country of the Christian is not of this world. He does his duty, indeed, but does it with profound indifference to the good or ill success of his cares. Provided he has nothing to reproach himself with, it matters little to him whether things go well or ill here on earth. If the State is prosperous, he hardly dares to share in the public happiness, for fear he may grow proud of his country's glory; if the State is languishing, he blesses the hand of God that is hard upon His people.

For the State to be peaceable and for harmony to be maintained, all the citizens without exception would have to be good Christians; if by ill hap there should be a single self-seeker or hypocrite, a Catiline or a Cromwell, for instance, he would certainly get the better of his pious compatriots. Christian charity does not readily allow a man to think hardly of his neighbours. As soon as, by some trick, he has discovered the art of imposing on them and getting hold of a share in the public authority, you have a man established in dignity; it is the will of God that he be respected: very soon you have a power; it is God's will that it be obeyed: and if the power is abused by him who wields it, it is the scourge wherewith God punishes His children. There would be scruples about driving out the usurper: public tranquillity would have to be disturbed, violence would have to be employed, and blood spilt; all this accords ill with Christian meekness; and after all, in this vale of sorrows, what does it matter whether we are free men or serfs? The essential thing is to get to heaven, and resignation is only an additional means of doing so.

If war breaks out with another State, the citizens march readily out to battle; not one of them thinks of flight; they do their duty, but they have no passion for victory; they know better how to die than how to conquer. What does it matter whether they win or lose? Does not Providence know better than they what is meet for them? Only think to what account a proud, impetuous and passionate enemy could turn their stoicism! Set over against them those generous peoples who were devoured by ardent love of glory and of their country, imagine your Christian republic face to face with Sparta or Rome: the pious Christians will be beaten, crushed and destroyed, before they know where they are, or will owe their safety only to the contempt their enemy will conceive for them. It was to my mind a fine oath that was taken by the soldiers of Fabius, who swore, not to conquer or die, but to come back victorious — and kept their oath. Christians would never have taken such an oath; they would have looked on it as tempting God.

But I am mistaken in speaking of a Christian republic; the terms are mutually exclusive. Christianity preaches only servitude and dependence. Its spirit is so favourable to tyranny that it always profits by such a *régime*. True Christians are made to be slaves, and they know it and do not much mind: this short life counts for too little in their eyes.

I shall be told that Christian troops are excellent. I deny it. Show me an instance. For my part, I know of no Christian troops. I shall be told of the Crusades. Without disputing the valour of the Crusaders, I answer that, so far from being Christians, they were the priests' soldiery, citizens of the Church. They fought for their spiritual country, which the Church had, somehow or other, made temporal. Well understood, this goes back to paganism: as the Gospel sets up no national religion, a holy war is impossible among Christians.

Under the pagan emperors, the Christian soldiers were brave; every Christian writer affirms it, and I believe it: it was a case of honourable emulation of the pagan troops. As soon as the emperors were Christian, this emulation no longer existed, and, when the Cross had driven out the eagle, Roman valour wholly disappeared.

But, setting aside political considerations, let us come back to what is right, and settle our principles on this important point. The right which the social compact gives the Sovereign over the subjects does not, we have seen, exceed the limits of public expediency.[46] The subjects then owe the Sovereign an account of their opinions only to such an extent as they matter to the community. Now, it matters very much to the community that each citizen should have a religion. That will make him love his duty; but the dogmas of that religion concern the State and its members only so far as they have reference to morality and to the duties which he who professes them is bound to do to others. Each man may have, over and above, what opinions he pleases, without it being the Sovereign's business to take cognisance of them; for, as the Sovereign has no authority in the other world, whatever the lot of its subjects may be in the life to come, that is not its business, provided they are good citizens in this life.

There is therefore a purely civil profession of faith of which the Sovereign should fix the articles, not exactly as religious dogmas, but as social sentiments without which a man cannot be a good citizen or a faithful subject.[47] While it can compel no one to believe them, it can banish from the State whoever does not believe them — it can banish him, not for impiety, but as an anti-social being, incapable of truly loving the laws and justice, and of sacrificing, at need, his life to his duty. If any one, after publicly recognising these dogmas, behaves as if he does not believe them, let him be punished by death: he has committed the worst of all crimes, that of lying before the law.

The dogmas of civil religion ought to be few, simple, and exactly worded, without explanation or commentary. The existence of a mighty, intelligent and beneficent Divinity, possessed of foresight and providence, the life to come, the happiness of the just, the punishment of the wicked, the sanctity of the social contract and the laws: these are its positive dogmas. Its negative dogmas I confine to one, intolerance, which is a part of the cults we have rejected.

Those who distinguish civil from theological intolerance are, to my mind, mistaken. The two forms are inseparable. It is impossible to live at peace with those we regard as damned; to love them would be to hate God who punishes them: we positively must either reclaim or torment them. Wherever theological intolerance is admitted, it must inevitably have some civil effect;[48] and as soon as it has such an effect, the Sovereign is no longer Sovereign even in the temporal sphere: thenceforce priests are the real masters, and kings only their ministers.

Now that there is and can be no longer an exclusive national religion, tolerance should be given to all religions that tolerate others, so long as their dogmas contain nothing contrary to the duties of citizenship. But whoever dares to say: *Outside the Church is no salvation*, ought to be driven from the State, unless the State is the Church, and the prince the pontiff. Such a dogma is good only in a theocratic government; in any other, it is fatal. The reason for which Henry IV is said to have embraced the Roman religion ought to make every honest man leave it, and still more any prince who knows how to reason.

## 9. CONCLUSION

Now that I have laid down the true principles of political right, and tried to give the State a basis of its own to rest on, I ought next to strengthen it by its external relations, which would include the law of nations, commerce, the right of war and conquest, public right, leagues, negotiations, treaties, etc. But all this forms a new subject that is far too vast for my narrow scope. I ought throughout to have kept to a more limited sphere.

34. This should of course be understood as applying to a free State; for elsewhere family, goods, lack of a refuge, necessity, or violence may detain a man in a country against his will; and then his dwelling there no longer by itself implies his consent to the contract or to its violation.

35. At Genoa, the word *Liberty* may be read over the front of the prisons and on the chains of the galley-slaves. This application of the device is good and just. It is indeed only malefactors of all estates who prevent the citizen from being free. In the country in which all such men were in the galleys, the most perfect liberty would be enjoyed.

36. I say "in the Campus Martius" because it was there that the *comitia* assembled by centuries; in its two other forms the people assembled in the *forum* or elsewhere; and then the *capite censi* had as much influence and authority as the foremost citizens.

37. *Custodes, diribitores, rogatores suffragiorum.*

38. The nomination was made secretly by night, as if there were something shameful in setting a man above the laws.

39. That is what he could not be sure of, if he proposed a dictator; for he dared not nominate himself, and could not be certain that his colleague would nominate him.

40. I merely call attention in this chapter to a subject with which I have dealt at greater length in my *Letter to M. d'Alembert*.

41. They were from another island, which the delicacy of our language forbids me to name on this occasion.

42. *Nonne ea quæ possidet Chamos deus tuus, tibi jure debentur?* (Judges, 11:24.) Such is the text in the Vulgate. Father de Carrières translates: "Do you not regard yourselves as having a right to what your god possesses?" I do not know the force of the Hebrew text: but I perceive that, in the Vulgate, Jephthah positively recognises the right of the god Chamos, and that the French translator weakened this admission by inserting an "according to you," which is not in the Latin.

43. It is quite clear that the Phocian War, which was called "the Sacred War," was not a war of religion. Its object was the punishment of acts of sacrilege, and not the conquest of unbelievers.

44. It should be noted that the clergy find their bond of union not so much in formal assemblies, as in the communion of Churches. Communion and excommunication are the social compact of the clergy, a compact which will always make them masters of peoples and kings. All priests who communicate together are fellow-citizens, even if they come from opposite ends of the earth. This invention is a masterpiece of statesmanship: there is nothing like it among pagan priests; who have therefore never formed a clerical corporate body.

45. See, for instance, in a letter from Grotius to his brother (April 11, 1643), what that learned man found to praise and to blame in the *De Cive*. It is true that, with a bent for indulgence, he seems to pardon the writer the good for the sake of the bad; but all men are not so forgiving.

46. "In the republic," says the Marquis d'Argenson, "each man is perfectly free in what does not harm others." This is the invariable limitation, which it is impossible to define more exactly. I have not been able to deny myself the pleasure of occasionally quoting from this manuscript, though it is unknown to the public, in order to do honour to the memory of a good and illustrious man, who had kept even in the Ministry the heart of a good citizen, and views on the government of his country that were sane and right.

47. Cæsar, pleading for Catiline, tried to establish the dogma that the soul is mortal: Cato and Cicero, in refutation, did not waste time in philosophising. They were content to show that Cæsar spoke like a bad citizen, and brought forward a doctrine that would have a bad effect on the State. This, in fact, and not a problem of theology, was what the Roman senate had to judge.

48. Marriage, for instance, being a civil contract, has civil effects without which society cannot even subsist. Suppose a body of clergy should claim the sole right of permitting this act, a right which every intolerant religion must of necessity claim, is it not clear that in establishing the authority of the Church in this respect, it will be destroying that of the prince, who will have thenceforth only as many subjects as the clergy choose to allow him? Being in a position to marry or not to marry people according to their acceptance of such and such a doctrine, their admission or rejection of such and such a formula, their greater or less piety, the Church alone, by the exercise of prudence and firmness, will dispose of all inheritances, offices and citizens, and even of the State itself, which could not subsist if it were composed entirely of bastards? But, I shall be told, there will be appeals on the ground of abuse, summonses and decrees; the temporalities will be seized. How sad! The clergy, however little, I will not say courage, but sense it has, will take no notice and go its way: it will quietly allow appeals, summonses, decrees and seizures, and, in the end, will remain the master. It is not, I think, a great sacrifice to give up a part, when one is sure of securing all.

**The Constitution of Pennsylvania from 1776**

By the Founding Fathers of the United States of America

WHEREAS all government ought to be instituted and supported for
the security and protection of the community as such, and to enable the individuals who compose it to
enjoy their natural rights, and the other blessings which the Author of existence has bestowed upon man;
and whenever these great ends of government are not obtained, the people have a right, by common
consent to change it, and take such measures as to them may appear necessary to promote their safety
and happiness. AND WHEREAS the inhabitants of this commonwealth have in consideration of
protection only, heretofore acknowledged allegiance to the king of Great Britain ; and the said king has
not only withdrawn that protection, but commenced, and still continues to carry on, with unabated
vengeance, a most cruel and unjust war against them, employing therein, not only the troops of Great
Britain, but foreign mercenaries, savages and slaves, for the avowed purpose of reducing them to a total
and abject submission to the despotic domination of the British parliament, with many other acts of
tyranny, (more fully set forth in the declaration of Congress) whereby all allegiance and fealty to the
said king and his successors, are dissolved and at an end, and all power and authority derived from him
ceased in these colonies. AND WHEREAS it is absolutely necessary for the welfare and safety of the
inhabitants of said colonies, that they be henceforth free and independent States, and that just,
permanent, and proper forms of government exist in every part of them, derived from and founded on
the authority of the people only, agreeable to the directions of the honourable American Congress. We,
the representatives of the freemen of Pennsylvania, in general convention met, for the express purpose of
framing such a government, confessing the goodness of the great Governor of the universe (who alone
knows to what degree of earthly happiness mankind may attain, by perfecting the arts of government) in
permitting the people of this State, by common consent, and without violence, deliberately to form for
themselves such just rules as they shall think best, for governing their future society; and being fully
convinced, that it is our indispensable duty to establish such original principles of government, as will
best promote the general happiness of the people of this State, and their posterity, and provide for future
improvements, without partiality for, or prejudice against any particular class, sect, or denomination of
men whatever, do, by virtue of the authority vested in us by our constituents, ordain, declare, and
establish, the following Declaration of Rights and Frame of Government, to be the CONSTITUTION of
this commonwealth, and to remain in force therein for ever, unaltered, except in such articles as shall
hereafter on experience be found to require improvement, and which shall by the same authority of the
people, fairly delegated as this frame of government directs, be amended or improved for the more
effectual obtaining and securing the great end and design of all government, herein before mentioned.

## A DECLARATION OF THE RIGHTS OF THE INHABITANTS OF THE COMMONWEALTH, OR STATE OF PENNSYLVANIA

I. That all men are born equally free and independent, and have certain natural, inherent and inalienable
rights, amongst which are, the enjoying and defending life and liberty, acquiring, possessing and
protecting property, and pursuing and obtaining happiness and safety.

II. That all men have a natural and unalienable right to worship Almighty God according to the dictates
of their own consciences and understanding: And that no man ought or of right can be compelled to
attend any religious worship, or erect or support any place of worship, or maintain any ministry, contrary
to, or against, his own free will and consent: Nor can any man, who acknowledges the being of a God,
be justly deprived or abridged of any civil right as a citizen, on account of his religious sentiments or
peculiar mode of religious worship : And that no authority can or ought to be vested in, or assumed by
any power whatever, that shall in any case interfere with, or in any manner controul, the right of
conscience in the free exercise of religious worship.

III. That the people of this State have the sole, exclusive and inherent right of governing and regulating the internal police of the same.

IV. That all power being originally inherent in, and consequently derived from, the people; therefore all officers of government, whether legislative or executive, are their trustees' and servants, and at all times accountable to them.

V. That government is, or ought to be, instituted for the common benefit, protection and security of the people, nation or community; and not for the particular emolument or advantage of any single man, family, or sett of men, who are a part only of that community ; And that the community hath an indubitable, unalienable and, indefeasible right to reform, alter, or abolish government in such manner as shall be by that community judged most conducive to the public weal.

VI. That those who are employed in the legislative and executive business of the State, may be restrained from oppression, the people have a right, at such periods as they may think proper, to reduce their public officers to a private station, and supply the vacancies by certain and regular elections.

VII. That all elections ought to be free; and that. all free men having a sufficient evident, common interest with, and attachment to the community, have a right to elect officers, or to be elected into one.

VIII. That every member of society hath a right to be protected in the enjoyment of life, liberty and property, and therefore is bound to contribute his proportion towards the expense of that protection, and yield his personal service when necessary, or an equivalent thereto: But no part of a man's property can be justly taken from him, or applied to public uses, without his own consent, or that of his legal representatives: Nor can any man who is conscientiously scrupulous of bearing arms, be justly compelled thereto, if he will pay such equivalent, nor are the people bound by any laws, but such as they have in like manner assented to, for their common good.

IX. That in all prosecutions for criminal offences, a man hath a right to be heard by himself and his council, to demand the cause and nature of his accusation, to be confronted with the witnesses, to call for evidence in his favour, and a speedy public trial, by an impartial jury-of the country, without the unanimous consent of which jury he cannot be found guilty ; nor can he be compelled to give evidence against himself ; nor can any man be justly deprived of his liberty except by the laws of the land, or the judgment of his peers.

X. That the people have a right to hold themselves, their houses, papers, and possessions free from search and seizure, and therefore warrants without oaths or affirmations first made, affording a sufficient foundation for them, and whereby any officer or messenger may be commanded or required to search suspected places, or to seize any person or persons, his or their property, not particularly described, are contrary to that right, and ought not to be granted.

XI. That in controversies respecting property, and in suits between man and man, the parties have a right to trial by jury, which ought to be held sacred.

XII: That the people have a right to freedom of speech, and of writing, and publishing their sentiments; therefore the freedom of the press ought not to be restrained.

XIII. That the people have a right to bear arms for the defence of themselves and the state ; and as standing armies in the time of peace are dangerous to liberty, they ought not to be kept up; And that the military should be kept under strict subordination to, and governed by, the civil power.

XIV. That a frequent recurrence to fundamental principles, and a firm adherence to justice, moderation, temperance, industry, and frugality are absolutely necessary to preserve the blessings of liberty, and keep a government free: The people ought therefore to pay particular attention to these points in. the choice of officers and representatives, and have a right to exact a due and constant regard to them, from their legislatures and magistrates, in the making and executing such laws as are necessary for the good government of the state.

XV. That all men have a natural inherent right to emigrate from one state to another that will receive them, or to form a new state in vacant countries, or in such countries as they can purchase, whenever they think that thereby they may promote their own happiness.

XVI. That the people have a right to assemble together, to consult for their common good, to instruct their representatives, and to apply to the legislature for redress of grievances, by address, petition, or remonstrance.

## PLAN OR FRAME OF GOVERNMENT FOR THE COMMONWEALTH OR STATE OF PENNSYL-VANIA

SECTION 1. The commonwealth or state of Pennsylvania shall be governed hereafter by an assembly of the representatives of the free- men of the same, and a president and council, in manner and form following-

SECT. 2. The supreme legislative power shall be vested in a house of representatives of the freemen of the commonwealth or state of Pennsylvania.

SECT. 3. The supreme executive power shall be vested in a president and council.

SECT. 4. Courts of justice shall be established in the city of Philadelphia, and in every county of this state.

SECT. 5. The freemen of this commonwealth and their sons shall
be trained and armed for its defence under such regulations, restrictions, and exceptions as the general assembly shall by law direct, preserving always to the people the right of choosing their colonels and all commissioned officers under that rank, in such manner and as often as by the said laws shall be directed.

SECT. 6. Every freemen of the full age of twenty-one years, having resided in this state for the space of one whole year next before the day of election for representatives, and paid public taxes during that time, shall enjoy the right of an elector: Provided always, that sons of freeholders of the age of twentyone years shall be intitled to vote although they have not paid taxes.

SECT. 7. The house of representatives of the freemen of this commonwealth shall consist of persons most noted for wisdom and virtue, to be chosen by the freemen of every city and county of this commonwealth respectively. And no person shall be elected unless he has resided in the city or county for which he shall be chosen two years immediately before the said election; nor shall any member, 'while he continues such, hold any other office, except in the militia.

SECT. 8. No person shall be capable of being elected a member to serve in the house of representatives of the freemen of this commonwealth more than four years in seven.

SECT. 9. The members of the house of representatives shall be chosen annually by ballot, by the freemen of the commonwealth, on the second Tuesday in October forever, (except this present year,) and shall meet on the fourth Monday of the same month, and shall be stiled, The general assembly of the representatives of the freemen of Pennsylvania, and shall have power to choose their speaker, the treasurer of the state, and their other officers; sit on their own adjournments ; prepare bills and enact them into laws; judge of the elections and qualifications of their own members ; they may expel a member, but not a second time for the same cause; they may administer oaths or affirmations on examination of witnesses; redress grievances.; impeach state criminals ; grant charters of incorporation; constitute towns, boroughs, cities, and counties ; and shall have all other powers necessary for the legislature of a free state or commonwealth: But they shall have no power to add to, alter, abolish, or infringe any part of this constitution.

SECT. 10. A quorum of the house of representatives shall consist of two-thirds of the whole number of members elected ; and having met and chosen their speaker, shall each of them before they proceed to business take and subscribe, as-well the oath or affirmation of fidelity and allegiance hereinafter directed, as the following oath or affirmation, viz: I _____ do swear (or affirm) that as a member of this assembly, I will not propose or assent to any bill, vote, or resolution, which shall appear to me injurious to the people;' nor do or consent to any act or thing whatever, that shall have a tendency to lessen or abridge their rights and privileges, as declared in the constitution of this state; but will in all things conduct myself as a faithful honest representative and guardian, of the people, according to the best of my judgment and abilities.
And each member, before he takes his seat, shall make and subscribe the following declaration, viz :
I do believe in one God, the creator and governor of the universe, the rewarder of the good and the punisher of the wicked. And I do acknowledge the Scriptures of the Old and New Testament to be given by Divine inspiration.
And no further or other religious test shall ever hereafter be required of any civil officer or magistrate in this State.

SECT. 11. Delegates to represent this state in congress shall be chosen by ballot by the future general assembly at their first meeting, and annually forever afterwards, as long as such representation shall be necessary. Any delegate may be superseded at any time, by the general assembly appointing another in his stead. No man shall sit in congress longer than two years successively, nor be capable of re-election for three years afterwards: and no person who holds any office in the gift of the congress shall hereafter be elected to represent this commonwealth in congress.

SECT. 12. If any city or cities, county or counties shall neglect or refuse to elect and send representatives to the general assembly, two-thirds of the members from the cities or counties that do elect and send representatives, provided they be a majority of the cities and counties of the whole state, when met, shall have all the powers of the general assembly, as fully and amply as if the whole were present.

SECT. 13. The doors of the house in which the representatives of the freemen of this state shall sit in general assembly, shall be, and remain open for the admission of all persons who behave decently, except only when the welfare of this state may require the doors to be shut.

SECT. 14. The votes and proceedings of the general assembly shall be printed weekly during their sitting, with the yeas and nays, on any question, vote or resolution, where any two members require it, except when the vote is taken by ballot; and when the yeas and nays are so taken every member shall have a right to insert the reasons of his vote upon the minutes, if he desires it.

SECT. 15. To the end that laws before they are enacted may be more maturely considered, and the inconvenience of hasty determinations as much as possible prevented, all bills of public nature shall be printed for the consideration of the people, before they are read in general assembly the last time for debate and amendment; and, except on occasions of sudden necessity, shall not be passed into laws until the next session of assembly; and for the more perfect satisfaction of the public, the reasons and motives for making such laws shall be fully and clearly expressed in the preambles.

SECT. 16. The stile of the laws of this commonwealth shall be, " Be it enacted, and it is hereby enacted by the representatives of the freemen of the commonwealth of Pennsylvania in general assembly met, and by the authority of the same." And the general assembly shall affix their seal to every bill, as soon as it is enacted into a law, which seal shall be kept by the assembly, and shall be called, The seal of the laws of Pennsylvania, and shall not be used for any other purpose.

SECT. 17. The city of Philadelphia and each county of this commonwealth respectively, shall on the first Tuesday of November in this present year, and on the second Tuesday of October annually for the two next succeeding years, viz. the year one thousand seven hundred and seventy-seven, and the year one thousand seven hundred and seventy-eight, choose six persons to represent them in general assembly. But as representation in proportion to the number of taxable inhabitants is the only principle which can at all times secure liberty, and make the voice of a majority of the people the law of the land; therefore the general assembly shall cause complete lists of the taxable inhabitants in the city and each county in the commonwealth respectively, to be taken and returned to them, on or before the last meeting. of the assembly elected in the year one thousand seven hundred and seventy-eight, who shall appoint a representation to each, in proportion to the number of taxables in such returns ; which representation shall continue for the next seven years afterwards at the end of which, a new return of the taxable inhabitants shall be made, and a representation agreeable thereto appointed by the said assembly, and so on septennially forever. The wages of the representatives in general assembly, and all other state charges shall be paid out of the state treasury.

SECT. 18. In order that the freemen of this commonwealth may enjoy the benefit of election as equally as may be until the representation shall commence, as directed in the foregoing section, each county at its own choice may be divided into districts, hold elections therein, and elect their representatives in the county, and their other elective officers, as shall be hereafter regulated by the general assembly of this state, And no inhabitant of this state shall have more than one annual vote at the general election for representatives in assembly.

SECT. 19. For the present the supreme executive council of this state shall consist of twelve persons chosen in the following manner: The freemen of the city of Philadelphia, and of the counties of Philadelphia, Chester, and Bucks, respectively, shall choose by ballot one person for the city, and one for each county aforesaid, to serve for three years and no longer, at the time and place for electing representatives in general assembly. The freemen of the counties of Lancaster, York, Cumberland, and Berks, shall, in like manner elect one person for each county respectively, to serve as counsellors for two years and no longer. And the counties of Northampton, Bedford,Northumberland and Westmoreland, respectively, shall, in like manner, elect one person for each county, to serve as counsellors for one year, and no longer. And at the expiration of the time for which each counsellor was chosen to serve, the freemen of the city of Philadelphia, and of the several counties in this state, respectively, shall elect one person to serve as counsellor for three years and no longer; and so on every third year forever. By this mode of election and continual rotation; more men will be trained to public business, there will in every subsequent year be found in the council a number of persons acquainted with the proceedings of the foregoing years, whereby the business will be more consistently conducted, and moreover the danger of establishing an inconvenient aristocracy will be effectually prevented. All vacancies in the council that may happen by death, resignation, or otherwise, shall be filled at the next general election for representatives in general assembly, unless a particular election for that purpose shall be sooner appointed by the president and council. No member of the general assembly or delegate in congress, shall be chosen a member of the council. The president and vice-president shall be chosen annually by the joint ballot of the general assembly and council, of the members of the council. Any person having served as a counsellor for three successive years; shall be incapable of holding that office for four years afterwards. Every member of the council shall be a justice of the peace for the whole commonwealth, by virtue of his office.
In case new additional counties shall hereafter be erected in this state, such county or counties shall elect a counsellor, and such county or counties shall be annexed to the next neighbouring counties, and shall take rotation with such counties.
The council shall meet annually, at the same time and place with the general assembly.
The treasurer of the state, trustees of the loan office, naval officers, collectors, of customs or excise, judge of the admirality, attornies general, sheriffs, and prothonotaries, shall not be capable of a seat in the general assembly, executive council, or continental congress.

SECT. 20. The president, and in his absence the vice-president, with the council, five of whom shall be a quorum, shall have power to appoint and commissionate judges, naval officers, judge of the admiralty, attorney general and all other officers, civil and military, except such as are chosen by the general assembly or the people, agreeable to this frame of government, and the laws that may be made hereafter ; and shall supply every vacancy in any office, occasioned by death, resignation, removal or disqualification, until the office can be filled in the time and manner directed by law or this constitution. They are to correspond with other states, and transact business with the officers of government, civil and military ; and to prepare such business as may appear to them necessary to lay before the general assembly. They shall sit as judges, to hear and determine on impeachments, taking to their assistance for advice only, the justices of the supreme court. And shall have power to grant pardons, and remit fines, in all cases whatsoever, except in cases of. impeachment; and in cases of treason and murder, shall have power to grant reprieves, but not to pardon, until the end of the next sessions of assembly ; but there shall be no remission or mitigation of punishments on impeachments, except by act of the legislature; they are also to take care that the laws be faithfully executed; they are to expedite the execution of such measures as may be resolved upon by the general assembly ; and they may draw upon the treasury for such sums as shall be appropriated by the house: They may also lay embargoes, or prohibit the exportation of any commodity, for any time, not exceeding thirty days, in the recess of the house only: They may grant such licences, as shall be directed by law, and shall have power to call together the general assembly when necessary, before the day to which they shall stand adjourned. The president shall be commander in chief of the forces of the state, but shall not command in person, except advised thereto by the council, and then only so long as they shall approve thereof. The president and council shall have a secretary, and keep fair books of their proceedings, wherein any counsellor may enter his dissent, with his reasons in support of it.

SECT. 21. All commissions shall be in the name, and by the authority of the freemen of the commonwealth of Pennsylvania, sealed with the state seal, signed by the president or vice-president, and attested by the secretary; which seal shall be kept by the council.

SECT. 22. Every officer of state, whether judicial or executive, shall be liable to be impeached by the general assembly, either when in office, or after his resignation or removal for mal-administration: All impeachments shall be before the president or vice-president and council, who shall hear and determine the same.

SECT. 23. The judges of the supreme court of judicature shall have fixed salaries, be commissioned for seven years only, though capable of re-appointment at the end of that term, but removable for misbehaviour at any time by the general assembly ; they shall not be allowed to sit as members in the continental congress, executive council, or general assembly, nor to hold any other office civil or military, nor to take or receive fees or perquisites of any kind.

SECT. 24. The supreme court, and the several courts of common pleas of this commonwealth, shall, besides the powers usually exercised by such courts, have the powers of a court of chancery, so far as relates to the perpetuating testimony, obtaining evidence from places not within this state, and the care of the persons and estates of those who are non compotes mentis, and such other powers as may be found necessary by future general assemblies, not inconsistent with this constitution.

SECT. 25. Trials shall be by jury as heretofore: And it is recommended to the legislature of this state, to provide by law against every corruption or partiality in the choice, return, or appointment of juries.

SECT. 26. Courts of sessions, common pleas, and orphans courts shall be held quarterly in each city and county; and the legislature shall have power to establish all such other courts as they may judge for the good of the inhabitants of the state. All courts shall be open, and justice shall be impartially administered without corruption or unnecessary delay: All their officers shall be paid an adequate but moderate compensation for their services: And if any officer shall take greater or other fees than the law allows him, either directly or indirectly, it shall ever after disqualify him from holding any office in this state.

SECT. 27. All prosecutions shall commence in the name and by the authority of the freemen of the commonwealth of Pennsylvania; and all indictments shall conclude with these words, "Against the peace and dignity of the same." The style of all process hereafter in this state shall be, The commonwealth of Pennsylvania.

SECT. 28. The person of a debtor, where there is not a strong presumption, of fraud, shall not be continued in prison, after delivering up, bona fide, all his estate real and personal, for the use of his creditors, in such manner as shall be hereafter regulated by law. All prisoners shall be bailable by sufficient sureties, unless for capital offences, when the proof is evident, or presumption great.

SECT. 29. Excessive bail shall not be exacted for bailable offences: And all fines shall be moderate.

SECT. 30. Justices of the peace shall be elected by the freeholders of each city and county respectively, that is to say, two or more persons may be chosen for each ward, township, or district, as the law shall hereafter direct : And their names shall be returned to the president in council, who shall commissionate one or more of them for each ward, township, or district so returning, for seven years, removable for misconduct by the general assembly. But, if any city or county, ward, township, or district in this commonwealth, shall hereafter incline to change the manner of appointing their justices of the peace as settled in this article, the general assembly may make laws to regulate the same, agreeable to the desire of a majority of the freeholders of the city or county, ward, township; or district so applying. No justice of the peace shall sit in the general assembly unless he first resigns his commission ; nor shall he be allowed to take any fees, nor any salary or allowance, except such as the future legislature may grant.

SECT. 31. Sheriffs and coroners shall be elected annually in each city and county, by the freemen; that is to say, two persons for each office, one of whom for each, is to be commissioned by the president in council. No person shall continue in the office of sheriff more than three successive years, or be capable of being again elected during four years afterwards. The election shall be held at the same time and place appointed for the election of representatives: And the commissioners and assessors, and other officers chosen by the people, shall also be then and there elected, as has been usual heretofore, until altered or otherwise regulated by the future legislature of this state.

SECT. 32. All elections, whether by the people or in general assembly, shall be by ballot, free and voluntary: And any elector; who shall receive any gift or reward for his vote, in meat, drink, monies, or otherwise, shall forfeit his right to elect for that time, and suffer such other penalties as future laws shall direct: And any person who shall directly or indirectly give, promise, or bestow any such rewards to be elected, shall be thereby rendered incapable to serve for the ensuing year.

SECT. 33. All fees, licence money, fines and forfeitures heretofore granted, or paid to the governor, or his deputies for the support of government, shall hereafter be paid into the public treasury, unless altered or abolished by the future legislature.

SECT. 34. A register's office for the probate of wills and granting letters of administration, and an office for the recording of deeds, shall be kept in each city and county: The officers to be appointed by the general assembly, removable at their pleasure, and to be commissioned by the president in council.

SECT. 35. The printing presses shall be free to every person who undertakes to examine the proceedings of the legislature, or any part of government.

SECT. 36. As every freeman to preserve his independence, (if without a sufficient estate) ought to have some profession, calling, trade or farm, whereby he may honestly subsist, there can be no necessity for, nor use in establishing offices of profit, the usual effects of which are dependence and servility unbecoming freemen, in the possessors and expectants ; faction, contention, corruption, and disorder among the people. But if any man is called into public service, to the prejudice of his private affairs, he has a right to a reasonable compensation: And whenever an office, through increase of fees or otherwise becomes so profitable as to occasion many to apply for it, the profits ought to be lessened by the legislature.

SECT. 37. The future legislature of this state, shall regulate intails in such a manner as to prevent perpetuities.

SECT. 38. The penal laws as heretofore used shall be reformed by the legislature of this state, as soon as may be, and punishments made in some cases less sanguinary, and in general more proportionate to the crimes.

SECT. 39. To deter more effectually from the commission of crimes, by continued visible punishments of long duration, and to make sanguinary punishments less necessary ; houses ought to be provided for punishing by hard labour, those who shall be convicted of crimes not capital; wherein the criminals shall be imployed for the benefit of the public, or for reparation of injuries done to private persons: And all persons at proper times shall be admitted to see the prisoners at their labour.

SECT. 40. Every officer, whether judicial, executive or military, in authority under this commonwealth, shall take the following oath or affirmation of allegiance, and general oath of office before he enters on the execution of his office.

## THE OATH OR AFFIRMATION OF ALLEGIANCE

I_____ do swear (or affirm) that I will be true and faithful to the commonwealth of Pennsylvania.: And that I will not directly or indirectly do any act or thing prejudicial or injurious to the constitution or government thereof, as established by the convention,.

## THE OATH OR AFFIRMATION OF OFFICE

I _____do swear (or affirm) that I will faithfully execute the office of _____ for the _____of ____ and will do equal right and justice to all men, to the best of my judgment and abilities, according to law.

SECT. 41. No public tax, custom or contribution shall be imposed upon, or paid by the people of this state, except by a law for that purpose: And before any law be made for raising it, the purpose for which any tax is to be raised ought to appear clearly to the legislature to be of more service to the community than the money would be, if not collected; which being well observed, taxes can never be burthens.

SECT. 42. Every foreigner of good character who comes to settle in this state, having first taken an oath or affirmation of allegiance to the same, may purchase, or by other just means acquire, hold, and transfer land or other real estate; and after one year's residence, shall be deemed a free denizen thereof, and entitled to all the rights of a natural born subject of this state, except that he shall not be capable of being elected a representative until after two years residence.

SECT. 43. The inhabitants of this state shall have liberty to fowl and hunt in seasonable times on the lands they hold, and on all other lands therein not inclosed ; and in like manner to fish in all boatable waters, and others not private property.

SECT. 44. A school or schools shall be established in each county by the legislature, for the convenient instruction of youth, with such salaries to the masters paid by the public, as may enable them to instruct youth at low prices: And all useful learning shall be duly encouraged and promoted in one or more universities.

SECT. 45. Laws for the encouragement of virtue, and prevention of vice and immorality, shall be made and constantly kept in force, and provision shall be made for their due execution : And all religious societies or bodies of men heretofore united or incorporated for the advancement of religion or learning, or for other pious and charitable purposes, shall be encouraged and protected in the enjoyment of the privileges, immunities and estates which they were accustomed to enjoy, or could of right have enjoyed, under the laws and former constitution of this state.

SECT. 46. The declaration of rights is hereby declared to be a part of the constitution of this commonwealth, and ought never to be violated on any pretence whatever.

SECT. 47. In order that the freedom of the commonwealth may be preserved inviolate forever, there shall be chosen by ballot by the freemen in each city and county respectively, on the second- Tuesday in October, in the year one thousand seven hundred and eighty-three, and on the second Tuesday in October, in every seventh year thereafter, two persons in each city and county of this state, to be called the COUNCIL OF CENSORS; who shall meet together on the second Monday of November next ensuing their election ; the majority of whom shall be a quorum in every case, except as to calling a convention, in which two-thirds of the whole number elected shall agree: And whose duty it shall be to enquire whether the constitution has been preserved inviolate in every part; and whether the legislative and executive branches of government have performed their duty as guardians of the people, or assumed to themselves, or exercised other or greater powers than they are intitled to by the constitution: They are also to enquire whether the public taxes have been justly laid and collected in all parts of this commonwealth, in what manner the public monies have been disposed of, and whether the laws have been duly executed. For these purposes they shall have power to send for persons, papers, and records; they shall-have authority to pass public censures, to order impeachments, and to recommend to the legislature the repealing such laws as appear to them to have been enacted contrary to the principles of the constitution. These powers they shall continue to have, for and during the space of one year from the day of their election and no longer: The said council of censors shall also have power to call a convention, to meet within two years after their sitting, if there appear to them an absolute necessity of amending any article of the constitution which may be defective, explaining such as may be thought not clearly expressed, and of adding such as are necessary for the preservation of the rights and happiness of the people: But the articles to be amended, and the amendments proposed, and such articles as are proposed to be added or abolished, shall be promulgated at least six months before the day appointed for the election of such convention, for the previous consideration of the people, that they may have an Opportunit.y of instructing their delegates on the subject.


Passed in Convention the 28th day of September, 1776, and signed by their order.

The Prince (1532), The Leviathan (1651), The Two Treatises of Government (1689), The Social Contract (1762), The Constitution of Pennsylvania (1776) - The Original Texts from Machiavelli, Hobbes, Locke, Rousseau and The Founding Fathers of the United States of America

Niccolo Machiavelli
William K. Marriott
Thomas Hobbes
John Locke
Jean Jaques Rousseau
G. D. H. Cole
Peter Kanzler

© 2020 Peter Kanzler

Peter Kanzler
Adolf-Kolping-Str. 44
31139 Hildesheim